QUANTITATIVE RESEARCH METHODS FOR COMMUNICATION

Jason S. Wrench
State University of New York at New Paltz

Candice Thomas-Maddox
Ohio University Lancaster

Virginia Peck Richmond
University of Alabama at Birmingham

James C. McCroskey
University of Alabama at Birmingham

QUANTITATIVE RESEARCH METHODS FOR COMMUNICATION

A Hands-On Approach

New York   Oxford
OXFORD UNIVERSITY PRESS
2008

Oxford University Press, Inc., publishes works that further Oxford University's
objective of excellence in research, scholarship, and education.

Oxford   New York
Auckland   Cape Town   Dar es Salaam   Hong Kong   Karachi
Kuala Lumpur   Madrid   Melbourne   Mexico City   Nairobi
New Delhi   Shanghai   Taipei   Toronto

With offices in
Argentina   Austria   Brazil   Chile   Czech Republic   France   Greece
Guatemala   Hungary   Italy   Japan   Poland   Portugal   Singapore
South Korea   Switzerland   Thailand   Turkey   Ukraine   Vietnam

Published by Oxford University Press, Inc.
198 Madison Avenue, New York, New York 10016
http://www.oup.com

Oxford is a registered trademark of Oxford University Press

Library of Congress Cataloging-in-Publication Data

Quantitative research methods for communication : a hands-on approach /
Jason S. Wrench...[et al.].
       p. cm.
   Includes bibliographical references.
   ISBN 978-0-19-533747-1 (alk. paper)
   1. Communication—Research—Methodology.   I. Wrench, Jason S.
      p91.3.Q36 2008
      302.207´2—dc22   2007015837

Printing number: 9 8 7 6 5

Printed in the United States of America
on acid-free paper.

CONTENTS

PREFACE

Statistical thinking will one day be as necessary a qualification for efficient citizenship as the ability to read and write.

H. G. Wells

This quotation from H. G. Wells is probably one of the most commonly used quotations when discussing the world of quantitative research. H. G. Wells (1866–1946) realized that understanding how statistics function within our world was no longer a luxury of scientists and mathematicians but a necessary endeavor for all citizens. Sadly, in the twenty-first century increasing numbers of people are functionally numerically illiterate. John Allen Paulos (1988) first tackled the notion of numerical illiteracy or innumeracy by defining innumeracy as "an inability to deal comfortably with the fundamental notions of number and chance" (p. 3). Unfortunately, most people simply do not understand enough about the world of statistics and scientific research to make much sense of the statistics in their daily lives. People are constantly bombarded with statistics, and most are simply unable to accurately process the information to any usable degree. Milroy (2001) argued that with the proliferation of science and pseudo-science today, people need to be able to engage in strategic junk science judo.

While this book does not attempt to correct all of the problems associated with innumeracy, it is intended to engage communication students on two levels. On the first level, this textbook hopes to teach readers the basics of the scientific process necessary in quantitative communication research. While college students typically learned the scientific method in elementary school, most simply cannot accurately translate this understanding outside the physical sciences. In this text we promote a strategic use of the scientific method when conducting quantitative research examining communication topics. Along the way we hope that students begin to understand the steps necessary for conducting research in a manner that is transferable to other parts of their lives. Scientific and statistical processes are the same whether they are utilized by communication researchers or medical researchers. Therefore, one of our goals for this text is simply to educate readers about the scientific method and the most commonly used statistical tools. While the examples used throughout this textbook are focused on communication-related phenomena, we believe that students can learn to transfer this knowledge into other areas of science and statistics when faced with them.

On a second level, we hope to help students engage in real quantitative research projects of real importance. The four authors of this textbook have a history of working with both undergraduate and graduate students to develop, write, present, and publish quantitative research projects. We all believe that the only way for students to truly learn and grasp quantitative research methods is through real examples and hands-on work. In our vast experience teaching quantitative research methods, we have learned that students cannot transfer theoretical knowledge of research methods and statistics to actual projects and data sets unless they have actively engaged the research process when learning. In other words, it's one thing to read about what a correlation is and how correlations work, and quite a different thing to find significant relationships in real datasets. For this reason, we have incorporated five unique factors within this text:

1. Actual Data Sample

One unique component to this text is an actual data set that was collected by the authors of the project with its expressed purpose for use in this textbook. A series of research scales written by the authors of this book were used in the creation of a survey instrument:

Nominal Variables (biological sex, political affiliation, and year in school)
Ordinal Variable (time spent each week online)
Interval Variables (communication apprehension, willingness to communicate, ethnocentrism, humor assessment, nonverbal immediacy, sociocommunicative orientation—assertiveness and responsiveness, attitude about college, and belief that everyone should be required to take public speaking in college)
Ratio Variable (age)

This dataset will be made available to book users in three different formats: SPSS, SAS, or text. By having three options available, a teacher can easily choose the format he or she prefers. Furthermore, because data were collected from 325 actual people, students can actually experience what it is like to manipulate data to receive real answers to research questions and hypotheses. Furthermore, the CD-ROM will also contain the example statistics discussed in the textbook in all three formats as well.

In essence, students will be able to conduct statistical tests on actual data and double check that the findings we report in the textbook match the findings they are able to find using a statistical software package.

2. Actual Data Sample

The authors of this text made an agreement to republish a series of 10 articles published in either *Communication Research Reports* or *Communication Quarterly*, two journals published by the Eastern Communication Association, for inclusion on the CD-ROM that accompanies this textbook. The articles were chosen because they tend to be exemplars on how to conduct specific aspects of the research methods process. When selecting the articles for inclusion on the CD-ROM, we included articles from a wide array of communication contexts (communication traits, instructional, listening, mediated, organizational, public relations, etc.). The articles chosen for this book are:

SCALE DEVELOPMENT

McCroskey, J. C., Richmond, V. P., Johnson, A. D., & Smith, H. T. (2004). Organizational orientations theory and measurement: Development of measures and preliminary investigations. *Communication Quarterly, 52,* 1–14.

Thomas, C. E, Richmond, V. P., & McCroskey, J. C. (1994). The association between immediacy and socio-communicative style. *Communication Research Reports, 11,* 107–115.

Wrench, J. S., & Richmond, V. P. (2004). Understanding the psychometric properties of the Humor Assessment instrument through an analysis of the relationships between teacher humor assessment and instructional communication variables in the college classroom. *Communication Research Reports, 21,* 92–103.

Chi-Square

Brummans, B. H. J. M., & Miller, K. (2004). The effect of ambiguity on the implementation of a social change initiative. *Communication Research Reports, 21*, 1–10.

t-Tests

Weber, K., Fornash, B., Corrigan, M, & Neupauer, N. C. (2003). The effect of interest on recall: An experiment. *Communication Research Reports, 20*, 116–123.

One-Way Analysis of Variance (ANOVA)

Boiarsky, G., Long, M., Thayer, G. (1999). Formal features in children's science television: Sound effects, visual pace, and topic shifts. *Communication Research Reports, 16*, 185–192.

Correlation

Cheseboro, J. (1999). The relationship between listening styles and conversational sensitivity. *Communication Research Reports, 16*, 233–238.

Punyanunt, N. M. (2000). The effects of humor on perceptions of compliance-gaining in the college classroom. *Communication Research Reports, 176*, 30–38.

Regression

Rocca, K. A., & Vogl-Bauer, S. (1999). Trait verbal aggression, sports fan identification, and perceptions of appropriate sports fan communication. *Communication Research Reports, 16*, 239–248.

Wrench, J. S., & Booth-Butterfield, M. (2003). Increasing patient satisfaction and compliance: An examination of physician humor orientation, compliance-gaining strategies, and perceived credibility. *Communication Quarterly, 51*, 482–503.

3. **Hand Calculations and Statistical Package Summaries**

This book takes students step by step through the statistical computation process. While many books attempt to teach students the mathematical process for computing statistical tests, this book clearly spells out each step in the necessary sequence to come to an end result. In fact, in the classroom, this process has consistently been used, and students find the mathematical computations to be one of the easiest parts of learning quantitative research methods. We believe that students need to learn how to calculate the problems by hand because the physical process of calculating helps to solidify the understanding of how the mathematical process works.

In addition to providing the hand computations, we also provide information on how to conduct statistical tests using the two most commonly used statistical packages: Statistical Package for the Social Sciences (SPSS) and Statistical Analysis Software (SAS). We understand that most researchers do not calculate lengthy tests by hand, so demonstrating how the various statistical processes can be calculated using both programs helps the students conduct their own statistical analyses using the software packages. In addition to the instruction for both SPSS and SAS, we also provide printouts of statistical results utilizing both software packages. We understand that knowing how to correctly use the software packages is one thing and being able to accurately read and interpret the statistical output is something completely different.

4. Glossary

The book contains an extensive glossary with commonly confused terms. We always tell our students that learning quantitative research methods is akin to learning a foreign language. For this reason, we have provided the students with a "language guide" to help them remember definitions.

5. Qualitative Research Chapter

Finally, we asked two prominent scholars in the field of qualitative and critical research, James W. Chesebro and Deborah J. Borisoff, to write a chapter for this book on qualitative research. While the purpose of this text is to focus on quantitative research methods in communication, we strongly believe that students should at least be exposed to qualitative research methods so that they can more clearly differentiate between the two epistemological approaches. We believe that this chapter (located in Appendix A) is a very balanced and helpful introduction to the differences in epistemology and the tools utilized to draw research conclusions.

Students are often intimidated on the first day of a research methods class. This textbook is based on years of in-classroom teaching experience and was written expressly to help alleviate the fear students may have by structuring a learning environment that clearly helps students succeed. Students who have learned quantitative research methods using the methods discussed in this textbook have gone on to have careers that utilize quantitative research both in the private sector and in academia. While the bulk of this text is based on our own experiences as both students and as teachers of quantitative research methods, we want to thank the editorial teams at Roxbury Publishers and Oxford University Press for shepherding this project through its various phases. Furthermore, we also want to thank the reviewers who gave us such great insight along the way as we have written this text: Jonathan Bowman, John Courtright, Douglas Ferguson, Marian L. Houser, Kumi Ishii, Canchu Lin, L. David Schuelke, and Celeste Walls.

Finally, each of the authors has a number of individuals that must be thanked for their help along the way.

Jason Wrench

I wish to dedicate this book to the people who helped guide me along the way in my formal training in quantitative research methods: Mrs. Neoka Perez, Dr. Krista Blevins Cohlmia, Dr. K. David Roach, Dr. Steven Hines, Dr. Carol S. Parke, Dr. Stan Cohen, and the West Virginia University communication studies faculty. Furthermore, I thank James C. McCroskey and Virginia Peck Richmond for their mentoring when I was a graduate student, and their continued mentoring and friendship as I have become an academic and researcher as well.

Candice Thomas-Maddox

I wish to express my sincere gratitude to the faculty at West Virginia University whose patience and guidance instilled in me an appreciation for quantitative methods. To Virginia Richmond and Jim McCroskey—your dedication to helping your students navigate the world of research is unsurpassed. Thank you for serving as mentors and friends. I dedicate this book to Rick, Greyson, and Parker—I could not have completed this project without your patience and support—thank you for understanding when I needed to be at the computer.

Virginia Peck Richmond and James C. McCroskey

We want to thank our colleagues at the University of Alabama at Birmingham and West Virginia University. We would like to acknowledge the work of the editors at both Roxbury Press and Oxford University Press for their guidance and support in the publication of this book.

REFERENCES

Milroy, S. J. (2001). *Junk science judo: Self-defense against health scares and scams.* Washington, DC: Cato Institute.

Paulos, J. A. (1988). *Innumeracy: Mathematical illiteracy and its consequences.* New York: Hill & Wang.

QUANTITATIVE RESEARCH METHODS
FOR COMMUNICATION

An Introduction to Communication Research

Every day people around the globe participate in an activity that helps shape our understanding of the world. This activity is research. Ever since you were a child in elementary school you've been taught all kinds of facts. What most students don't stop to think about is where these "facts" come from in the first place. Whether it was learning that Newton created his theory of gravity after having an apple fall on his head or memorizing all of the elements in the periodic table, most of your academic endeavors have been built around knowledge that has not always existed. At some point in history, a scientist has actually had to conduct a research study to determine what we today often take for granted as common knowledge.

While most people are familiar with many basic facts about the physical sciences, or the study of the objective aspects of nature (biology, chemistry, physics, astronomy, etc.), as a result of K–12 schooling, people don't tend to be as aware of the research in the area called the social sciences. The social sciences consist of a group of fields that set out to study how humans live and interact. These include many different disciplines: anthropology, communication, cultural studies, economics, education, geography, history, linguistics, political sciences, psychology, sociology, social work, and so on. All of these fields have at their core a desire to understand how humans live and interact. Although each social scientific field may approach the study of human life and interaction differently, they all have the same basic origin in history. This chapter will first present a brief history of the development of social science and then talk specifically about how the field of communication has become what it is today.

The History of the Social Sciences

The earliest recorded scientists would be very shocked to see the division that exists today between the physical sciences and social sciences. In ancient Greece the physical sciences and philosophy were perceived as handmaidens as one informed the other. Most of the ancient Greek philosophers wrote not only about science but also about rhetoric, poetry, drama, and other intrinsically human-oriented topics. For example, Hippocrates of Cos (460–466 B.C.) is most noted for the oath that all physicians take that states that physicians should first do no harm. Hippocrates was also the first researcher in history to start classifying his patients by various temperaments, which is now seen as the general origin of personality theory that modern social scientists study today. To Hippocrates, science was an extremely important part of understanding the world in both the physical sense and the humanistic sense; he wrote, "There are in fact, two things: science, and opinion; the former begets knowledge, the latter ignorance." Even later Greek thinkers like Plato and Aristotle often wrote on both physical and social scientific topics and sometimes combined the two together. Plato used geometrical proofs (physical science tool) to demonstrate his perspective on the intrinsic state of knowledge (social scientific concept). Aristotle studied planetary motion with the same rigor and scientific processes that he studied poetry and rhetoric. To the ancient Greeks, both physical nature and human social processes were avenues of research to be done scientifically.

This lack of division between physical and social sciences stayed fairly intact until the publication of the three volumes of Sir Isaac Newton's *Philosophiae Naturalis Principia Mathematica* (Mathematical Principles of Natural Philosophy) in 1687. In essence, Newton sets forth in the three volumes the foundation of classical mechanics and his law of gravity. Newton's publication revolutionized scientific thought because he argued that the underlying rule of all physical nature was mathematics. While physical scientists quickly latched onto and successfully applied Newton's writings, eventually many scientists studying the social aspects of humans tried to make their research more mathematically oriented as well. This trend of physical sciences creating revolutions that remake how we understand science continued with the publication of Charles Darwin's theory of natural selection. While mathematics clearly impacted physics and chemistry, natural selection revolutionized how biologists understood biology. Yet again, the physical sciences were light years ahead of social scientists in their understanding of nature, but eventually the social scientists came to understand how Darwin's theory actually applied to the social sciences. In fact, Sigmund Freud (in Austria) and William James (in the United States) were the first social scientists to examine how natural selection could be applied in the social sciences.

During the late 1800s and early 1900s, the rise of quantitative or mathematical measurement in the physical sciences quickly became the norm. Ernest Rutherford, the father of nuclear physics, once wrote that any knowledge that cannot be measured numerically is a poor sort of knowledge. Ultimately, during the early 1900s a rift emerged between humanists, who believed in universal human qualities (rationality, common history, experience, and belief), and social scientists, who saw the necessity to objectively quantify human experience. In the field of communication, we also saw this debate occurring within our own ranks.

At the turn of the twentieth century, James A. Winans (1915) and Everett Lee Hunt (1915) led an interdisciplinary debate over the need for research in public speaking. Winans wanted scientific research conducted on three levels: speech pathology, speech psychology, and rhetorical history. Hunt, on the other hand, believed that the scientific approach was antithetical to the enthusiasm and inspiration that was needed for good public speakers. This divergence of ideology created what is commonly referred to as the social science versus humanist debate in the field of communication studies, which has continued for the greater part of the twentieth and now into the twenty-first century.

Social scientific research really started finding its own way after World War I as research in a variety of new avenues began to flourish. In 1918, William Isaac Thomas and Florian Znaniecki defined social psychology as "the study of attitudes." Along with the development of attitudinal research, Jowett and O'Donnell (1992) note:

> Other social sciences such as sociology and psychology were also stimulated by the need to pursue questions about human survival in an age in which social strain grew heavy with concerns about warfare, genocide, economic depression, and human relationships. These questions were about influence, leadership, decision making, and changes in people, institutions, and nations. Such questions were also related to the phenomena of propaganda, public opinion, attitude change, and communication. (p. 123)

Overall, the period after World War I saw a quick rate of research in the social sciences. By the 1920s, marketing agencies were surveying consumer behavior while politicians and media outlets realized that the new techniques being created by social scientists to research humans could be used to examine political preferences. With the burgeoning need for social scientific research, Likert (1932), Guttman (1944), and Osgood (1952) developed three measures of attitudes that are still used by researchers today (these will be discussed in greater detail in Chapters 6 and 9).

When World War II broke out in Europe, the U.S. government turned to social scientists to understand propaganda, attitudes, and persuasion (Albarraćin, Johnson, & Zanna, 2006). Quickly the U.S. government realized that to maintain morale during wartime the media was going to be extremely important. The creation of the U.S. Office of War Information was one step in this effort (Lazarsfeld & Stanton, 1944). By 1941, Lazarsfeld published the first review of the discipline of communication based on his and others' research at the Bureau of Applied Social Research. Ultimately, Lazarsfeld determined that communication could be broken into four categories: (1) who, (2) said what, (3) to whom, and (4) with what effect. Obviously, the U.S. government was most interested in the last category as a way to fuel the war effort at home.

At the conclusion of World War II, the shift in social scientific communication research took its next major step as a result of a group of 30 researchers at Yale University led by Carl Hovland. The primary purpose of the research conducted by the Yale group was to analyze how attitude change occurred. Overall, the Yale group examined a wide range of differing variables all shown to influence persuasion: source credibility, personality traits, argument ordering, explicit versus implicit conclusions, and fear appeals (Hovland, Janis, & Kelly, 1953). The legacy of the research conducted by Hovland and his colleagues ultimately led future researchers to examine other communication contexts.

Today the contexts for research in the field of communication are numerous. In fact, in 2004 Wickersham, Sherblom, and Richmond published a 20-year retrospective (1984–2004) of the types of empirical articles published in *Communication Research Reports* (*CRR*). Since its first publication, *CRR* has been solely devoted to short, concise quantitative research articles. As a result of the nature of *CRR*, analyzing the concepts published in the journal allows researchers to see the overarching scope of the field of empirical communication research.

Communication concept explored	No. of articles	% of total
General Communication	229	9.8
Relationships	116	4.9
Perception	90	3.8
Apprehension	68	2.9
Students	53	2.3
Self	45	1.9
Television	44	1.9
Behavior	37	1.6
Satisfaction	35	1.5
Culture	35	1.5
Social	34	1.5
Interpersonal	33	1.4
Organizations	32	1.4
Style	31	1.3
Teacher	31	1.3
Public	31	1.3
Gender	28	1.2
Development	28	1.2
Verbal	27	1.2
Anxiety	27	1.2
Roles	27	1.2
Aggression	26	1.1
Competence	26	1.1
Classroom	26	1.1
Motivation	26	1.1
Interaction	25	1.1
Influence	23	1.0
American	23	1.0
Immediacy	22	0.9
Sex	21	0.9
Messages	21	0.9
Group	20	0.9
Japan	20	0.9
Nonverbal	20	0.9

Figure 1.1 Articles Published in *Communication Research Reports*

Figure 1.1 contains the results of the Wickersham, Sherblom, and Richmond (2004) study. Overall, the top four concepts explored in *CRR* are general communication, relationships, perception, and apprehension, which have been directly influenced by research in both attitudes and persuasion initiated during the early and mid-1900s. Along with an expansion in the type of research that qualifies as "communication research," our understanding of communication has also changed. For this reason, the next part of this chapter is devoted to an explanation of the authors of this text's view of communication.

The Nature of Communication

The word "communication" has many different definitions, but the one we will use in this textbook states that communication is "the process by which one person stimulates meaning in the mind(s) of another person (or persons) through verbal and nonverbal messages" (McCroskey, 2006, pp. 20–21). While other definitions may view communication from a different perspective, we see communication as primarily meaning focused. In order for us to comprehend this definition fully, a few of its parts need some clarification. The word "process" suggests that human communication is dynamic and changing, or the notion that communication does not start, stop, or break. Berlo (1960) suggested that communication is like the river described by the Greek philosopher Heraclitus, who believed that it was impossible to step in the same river twice because the moment you take your foot out of the water the river changes so much that it really isn't the same river. In life, humans are constantly changing as we go through various events, and our communication with other people also naturally evolves over time. Therefore, humans never communicate in the same way twice. Even professional actors who recite the same lines over and over again never recite those lines in the same way twice.

The second part of the definition of "communication" involves the phrase "stimulating meaning in the mind(s) of another person (or persons)." The basic goal of communication is to take some thought that you have inside your head and determine the appropriate method for getting the thought in your head into another person's or group people's head(s). Through the processes of stimulating meaning, we develop, cultivate, share, expand, and reshape ideas. Rare is the occasion where we develop an idea completely on our own. The very thoughts that lead to an idea occur as a result of our experiences of talking with others, reading various literatures, and simply observing and interacting with the world around us. Such ideas or combinations of ideas are the meaning stimulated through the verbal and nonverbal messages that are exchanged. But before we can discuss verbal and nonverbal messages, we need to explain the basic model of communication.

Claude Shannon and Warren Weaver (1949) developed a model for describing the process of communication for the Bell Telephone Company. The Shannon and Weaver model was very simple because it was designed to explain how people use telephones. The telephone is designed with two basic parts: a source you talk into and a receiver where you hear people on the other end. The full Shannon–Weaver model is often referred to as the source–message–channel–receiver (SMCR) model. The source is the person(s) who originates a message. This person(s) goes through a process called encoding to create a message. McCroskey and Wheeless (1976) defined encoding as "the process of creating messages that we believe represent the meaning to be communicated and are likely to stimulate similar meaning in the mind of a receiver" (p. 24). In other words, encoding involves translating ideas and information inside your head into messages that can be sent to a receiver(s). Encoding requires some degree of accuracy and precision in order for effective communication to take place because if your receiver cannot understand what you are saying, then communication will be ineffective. Inaccurate and imprecise encoding often leads to confusion. Therefore, it is very important to select messages that have similar meanings for us and our receiver(s).

Of course, where the source sends messages, a receiver receives messages. As receivers of messages, we must receive messages and assign meaning to them. The process we go through as receivers to assign meaning to messages is called decoding. The meaning we assign a given message depends to a great degree on previous messages we have received from either the source and/or our previous experiences. Often the meaning(s) we assign specific messages may not be close to the meaning intended by the source. Remember when you first started analyzing poetry in school and your teacher would tell you about the hidden meanings within a poem that you simply didn't see at all? Verbal and nonverbal communication and meaning can function the same way; people often completely miss the meaning of a message or assign a meaning to the message that was never intended. For communication to be effective, it is necessary for us, as receivers, to consider our background and experience compared with the background and experience of the source, which may require that we put ourselves in the other person's shoes. The converse of this is also true. As sources of messages, we need to know who our receivers are. If I were going to talk about media to a group of college freshman, using references to Lawrence Welk and Ed Sullivan might not be very useful (if you don't know who either of those men is, you just proved our point).

The next part of the SMCR model is the message. A message is any verbal or nonverbal stimulus that stimulates meaning in a receiver. So just like our definition of "communication" in this textbook is meaning focused, so is the basic model of communication. The message is simply what you want your receiver(s) to know, feel, and/or do when you are done communicating.

The last part of the SMCR model of communication is the channel. A channel is *the means by which a message is carried from one person to another*. In communication, we typically talk about two primary channels: verbal and nonverbal. By "verbal messages" we mean language. Language *is a system of symbols or codes that represent certain ideas or meanings*. The use of symbols and codes is regulated by a set of formal rules, which we call grammar and syntax. We transmit these messages either in spoken or in written form. Today, approximately 5000 oral languages exist, but no single language is spoken or understood by a majority of humans, although Mandarin is spoken by more people in the world than any other language. Thus, even today, when people travel to various parts of the world they often resort to communicating messages through nonverbal channels. "Nonverbal messages" refer to *any messages other than verbal*. These messages include such things as tone of voice, eye movements, hand gestures, and facial expressions. All in all, nonverbal messages are extremely important. Nonverbal researchers have estimated that between 65 and 93% of our understanding of a source's message is a result of how we decode the source's nonverbal communication. In essence, humans tend to look more to how a source communicates instead of the language choices he or she uses to communicate, which doesn't mean that language is unimportant, only that meaning is a combination of both verbal and nonverbal messages.

As for communication channels, both verbal and nonverbal channels can be utilized when communicating messages. However, verbal and nonverbal channels are not the only channels available to communicators. A mediated channel is *any channel that uses some kind of mediating device to help transmit information*. For example, telephones, e-mail, newspapers, television, radio, and text messaging are all examples of technologies that help mediate communication between people. Whether two people are on opposite sides of the world using mediated channels to communicate or sitting side-by-side text-messaging each other to avoid eavesdroppers, people in today's world are constantly communicating via mediated messages. The first medium used to communicate messages was cave drawings, but cave drawings were neither efficient nor particularly effective channels for communicating anything but the most primitive of thoughts. In fact, some people try to make a case for prehistoric extraterrestrial contact based on the drawings found in caves. In essence, people can see pretty much anything they want in a cave drawing, so as a historical tool the cave drawings are not very reliable. Such drawings slowly evolved into more complex picture systems as they took on more substantial forms where specific pictures were intended to mean things, which ultimately evolved into written language. If the history of human communication were represented by a typical 12-inch ruler, the history of writing would be included in less than the last ¼ of an inch.

The most rapid improvement in mediated channels has occurred in the last 150 years. Ever since the first message was sent by Morse code in 1844, mediated technology has constantly been improving. From Morse code to radios, to televisions, to cable televisions, to the Internet, to whatever comes next, mediated technology is constantly evolving. For this reason, many people in the field of communication devote themselves to the study of mediated communications. In the field of communication, the letter "s" at the end of the word "communication" is used to signify mediated technologies. The field of mass communications studies how mediated technologies communicate messages to large numbers of people. However, most of the research within the field of communication does not examine mediated technologies, so the letter "s" must not be added to the word "communication" unless one is specifically talking about communication occurring through mediated technologies.

Now that we have discussed both the history of social science research and the nature of communication, the rest of the chapter will briefly explain the organization of this volume.

Understanding the Book's Format

The authors of this book have more then 100 years combined experience conducting empirical research in the field of communication. Historically, West Virginia University's (WVU) department of communication studies has mentored many of the top quantitative researchers in the field, even though the department did not technically have its own doctorate program until the fall of 2006. Historically, individuals who graduated from WVU with a doctorate actually received their doctorate in education (either curriculum and instruction or educational psychology), so all WVU graduates have extensive training in both communication and educational theory and practice. Overall, the approach that WVU has historically taken to teach research methods has been successful because in 2003 WVU was listed as one of the top doctorate programs for graduates publishing research in the field (Hickson, Turner, & Bodon, 2003). Furthermore, WVU was the number one program for faculty research publications. For this reason, this book is going to take the approach used at WVU to train many of the most prolific quantitative researchers in the field. All four of the authors of this text have WVU roots: two as faculty (James C. McCroskey and Virginia P. Richmond) and two as program graduates (Candice Thomas-Maddox and Jason S. Wrench). In various analyses of the field, WVU graduates and faculty have consistently made very important contributions to the field of communication. Over a 30-year period, the instruction in quantitative research methods at WVU has been fine-tuned to enable both undergraduate and graduate researchers to quickly understand the research process. This book is the culmination of years of teaching instruction in research methods by all of the authors.

Chapters 2 and 3 are designed to introduce you to the basic aspects of communication research. In Chapter 2 we explore the meaning of empirical research and the scientific method, which is what this book is designed to teach you. If you are interested in non-quantitative research methods, we have included in Appendix A a chapter written by James Chesebro and Deborah Borisoff that discusses qualitative and critical research methods. In Chapter 3 we discuss the ethical standards that modern researchers are required to follow both philosophically and legally.

Chapters 4 and 5 take you through the basic process necessary for conducting research. In Chapter 4 we examine how to use libraries and other sources for finding research previously conducted on a given topic. In addition to basic library skill discussions, Chapter 4 will clearly lay out how to format papers and cite sources using the 5th Edition of the *American Psychological Association's Style Manual*. Chapter 5 will then break down each section of a research study and give tips and examples for writing these sections for your own research projects.

Chapters 6, 7, and 8 examine the smallest units of a research project, variables. In Chapter 6 we explain what variables are and discuss the different types of variables that exist in empirical sciences. In Chapter 7 we examine various communication variables. The communication variables discussed in Chapter 7 will help you understand the majority of the examples discussed in this text. Furthermore, an actual research dataset was collected on the variables discussed in this chapter; you can find this data set on the CD-ROM that accompanies this textbook. In Chapter 8 we discuss some basic mathematical concepts that help researchers describe specific variables.

Chapters 9 and 10 explain how social scientists measure human behavior and perceptions and how to make sure these measurements are reliable and valid. In Chapter 9 we discuss how researchers measure communicative behaviors and perceptions. In Chapter 10 we discuss two extremely important characteristics involved in the measurement process that must be clearly followed for research to be meaningful (reliability and validity).

In Chapters 11, 12, and 13 we explore three common techniques for conducting communication research: survey, content analysis, and experiment. In Chapter 11 we examine survey research. The methods discussed in this chapter date back to the techniques created during the 1930s and 1940s by the social scientists studying human attitudes. In Chapter 12 we explore the research method called content analysis. Chapter 13 will present the nature of experiments and various methods researchers can employ to ensure that experiments are successful.

Chapters 14 and 15 explore some basic concepts related to research methods: sampling and hypothesis testing. Chapter 14 explains how to go about finding the appropriate research participants to ensure your research projects are successful and meaningful. Chapter 15 provides the basic explanation for how the statistical process is actually conducted. While this chapter is the densest chapter to read, the information contained in it is extremely important to understanding the next six chapters.

Each of Chapters 16 through 20 will examine a different statistical tool that can help you in answering actual questions about communication phenomena. The first segment in these chapters will walk you through the step-by-step process necessary to compute by hand statistical formulas. This is the part of quantitative research methods that many students are very nervous about when first learning. Trust us, if you follow our step-by-step instructions, you will have no problems whatsoever learning how to calculate these mathematical formulas. In the first part of every chapter you will be presented with a scenario for the type of statistical test each chapter represents. These scenarios are designed to help you compute the statistical tests by hand. For this reason, the data used in these examples are fabricated to make the math as easy as possible. Although the first examples in each chapter may be interesting, they are not based on actual empirical data. In addition to calculating the problems by hand, you will also be provided with statistical output using the Windows version of the Statistical Package for the Social Sciences (SPSS) version 15.0 and statistical output using the Windows version of the Statistical Analysis Software (SAS) version 9.0. Both SPSS and SAS are considered the top tools used by quantitative communication researchers.

The second segment in Chapters 16 through 20 will consist of real data–driven research questions from the data set that was collected for this textbook. In these examples you will be presented first with a research scenario and then with the SPSS and SAS results, similarly to the examples in the first part. The biggest difference between these examples and the examples in the first part of the chapters is that these examples are based on actual collected data, so these are real research findings. We could have used the examples in the second half of each chapter to compute the statistics by hand, but that process would have been much more complicated and not beneficial to your understanding of the mathematical processes needed to compute these statistics.

The third, and final, segment in Chapters 16 through 20 will examine the articles on the CD-ROM that came with this book. In order to see how each of these statistical tests can actually be used by researchers to answer actual hypotheses and research questions, we recommend that you read the first two sections of every chapter first, then read the corresponding article on the CD-ROM, and then finally examine the analysis of the article we have provided for you in the chapter. By completing the readings in the way we recommend, you will be able to determine if you truly understand the statistical concept and how it can be employed in research.

In Chapter 21 we further your understanding of statistical devices by introducing you to eight advanced statistical tools that are commonly seen in communication literature. While we will not show you how the computations are performed by hand or how to perform the analyses on the computer software packages, we will provide you with the theory behind the statistical tool, a real example, and an American Psychological Association (APA) write-up for each device. The goal of this chapter is not to enable you to conduct these statistical procedures, but to provide you with enough information to understand what these procedures are when you run into them in journal articles.

The final chapter in this book, Chapter 22, is designed to discuss the processes that researchers go through to present their findings to other people. This chapter will examine how to design effective research posters for presentation at conferences and conventions, how to deliver papers at conferences and conventions, and how to submit your original research for possible publication.

Conclusion

The authors of this textbook have a passion for conducting unique and interesting communication research. We sincerely hope that you will learn to share our passion for research as you take this journey with us through this text. In the next chapter, we will explain the process researchers go through when conducting scientific research in communication.

KEY TERMS

Channel
Communication
Communications
Decoding
Encoding

Feedback
Language
Message
Nonverbal Messages
Physical Science

Receiver
Social Science
Source
Theory of Natural Selection
Verbal Messages

REFERENCES

Albarracín, D., Johnson, B. T., & Zanna, M. P. (Eds.). (2006). *The handbook of attitudes.* Mahwah, NJ: Lawrence Erlbaum.

Berlo, D. K. (1960). *The process of communication.* New York: Holt, Rinehart & Winston.

Guttman, L. (1944). A basis for scaling qualitative data. *American Sociological Review, 9,* 139–150.

Hickson, M., III., Turner, J., & Bodon, J. (2003). Research productivity in communication: An analysis, 1996–2001. *Communication Research Reports, 20,* 308–319.

Hovland, C. I., Janis, I. L., & Kelly, H. H. (1953). *Communication and persuasion: Psychological studies of opinion change.* New Haven, CT: Yale University Press.

Hunt, E. L. (1915). The scientific spirit in public speaking. *The Quarterly Journal of Public Speaking, 1,* 185–193.

Jowett, G. S., & O'Donnell, V. (1992). *Propaganda and Persuasion* (2nd ed.). Newbury Park, CA: Sage.

Lazarsfeld, P. (1941). Remarks on administrative and critical communications research. *Studies in Philosophy and Social Science, 9,* 2–16.

Lazarsfeld, P., & Stanton, F. N. (1944). *Radio research, 1942–43*. New York: Duell, Sloan, & Pearce.

Likert, R. (1932). A technique for the measurement of attitudes. *Archives of Psychology, 140*, 1–55.

McCroskey, J. C. (2006). *An introduction to rhetorical communication: A western rhetorical perspective* (9th ed.). Boston: Allyn & Bacon.

McCroskey, J. C., & Wheeless, L. R. (1976). *An Introduction to Human Communication*, Boston: Allyn and Bacon.

Osgood, C. E (1952). The nature and measurement of meaning. *Psychological Bulletin, 49*, 197–262.

Shannon, C. E., & Weaver, W. (1949). *The mathematical theory of communication*. Urbana, IL: The University of Illinois Press.

Thomas, W. I., & Znaniecki, F. (1918). *The Polish peasant in Europe and America: Primary-group organization*. Chicago: University of Chicago Press.

Wickersham, J. A., Sherblom, J. C., & Richmond, V. P. (2004). A twenty year retrospective on a research community: An analysis of scholarship published in *Communication Research Reports* (1984 to 2004). *Communication Research Reports, 21*, 437–444.

Winans, J. A. (1915). The need for research. *The Quarterly Journal of Public Speaking, 1*, 17–23.

Empirical Research

Have you ever read a textbook in a communication course and wondered where all the information came from? Have you ever wondered how your university professors became so smart? Well, the simple and complicated answer to both these questions is research. Now for many readers, when we say "research" you may be thinking of the type of research you did in an English class where you looked at various books, articles, and Internet websites and tried to write a paper incorporating the information from those sources into your paper. While this type of research is extremely important, it's not what we're referring to when we say "research." This textbook's definition of the word "research" can best be understood by looking at one of the definitions provided by Merriam-Webster's Dictionary (n.d.): "studious inquiry or examination; especially: investigation or experimentation aimed at the discovery and interpretation of facts, revision of accepted theories or laws in the light of new facts, or practical application of such new or revised theories or laws." This definition implies that "research" is the use of the scientific method to answer questions. We will further explain the idea of the "scientific method" later in this chapter, but before we explain the scientific approach to conducting research, a quick discussion of the major epistemological approaches to research will be presented.

Epistemological Approaches to Scholarship

There are many epistemological approaches to scholarship. An epistemology is a way of knowing. In the field of human communication, researchers have many different tools available to go about attempting to "know" something. No one option has been accepted by all scholars. In fact, epistemological approaches preferred by some scholars are totally rejected by others.

The two most prominent epistemological approaches in this discipline are scientific (also known as quantitative) and humanism (also known as qualitative and/or critical). While many scholars have chosen one of these and won't have anything to do with the other, which they consider a less scholarly approach and/or one that is inappropriate for their study, some scholars attempt to employ both epistemological approaches when they search for answers. Very few researchers, however, are able to use both approaches with a high level of success because often the processes fundamental to them are not compatible. Furthermore, mastering either of these scholarly approaches is extremely difficult. As a result, the most successful scholars typically devote the great majority of their efforts to one approach or the other.

In all but the smallest communication departments, you will find at least one researcher devoted to each epistemological approach. However, some departments that seek to have greater depth (greater emphasis in one approach) rather than breadth (trying to cover both approaches) in their program will choose to pick one or the other. Departments that choose to hire only faculty who utilize a specific epistemological approach often are recognized in the field for the epistemology they have chosen. Typically, only a few of the larger departments in the United States are recognized for their excellence in both approaches. Unfortunately, universities with both epistemological approaches represented by their faculty end up being recognized for excellence in neither.

While we generally refer to the work conducted by most qualitative researchers as humanistic, we should note that there are many qualitative researchers who are scientific. For a qualitative researcher to be considered scientific, he or she must follow the scientific method as we will describe in great detail in this chapter. However, much qualitative research is subjective (knowledge arises out of the researcher's own opinions and perceptions) and based on very small samples that cannot be used to explain larger groups of people. Conversely, quantitative research attempts to be very objective, or to create knowledge by examining facts through the scientific method without distorting the findings by personal feelings, prejudices, and interpretations. Furthermore, quantitative research generally relies on large samples of people that can help us understand what is occurring within a larger group.

This book focuses on quantitative/scientific epistemology for research. However, it is important that beginners, which this book presumes you are, to be exposed to both epistemological approaches to communication scholarship. After you have completed your initial study of quantitative research you probably will want to stay with that approach. However, if you decide that the qualitative/critical approach may fit you better, it is certainly not too late to opt to take a course in that approach to scholarship. Many communication programs will even require you to take courses in quantitative, qualitative, and critical research methods to ensure that you have a breadth of knowledge about how knowledge is arrived at within the field. Many scholars, including the authors of this book, believe that all scholars (undergraduate students, graduate students, and academic professionals) should be exposed to the three main approaches to communication scholarship, because the only way to engage in academic discourse is to have a strong foundation in all three methodological approaches to research. Appendix A introduces you to the humanist epistemology (qualitative and critical research methods), but the remainder of this chapter will explain the basic underlying processes and assumptions of the scientific approach to communication research.

The Scientific Approach to Communication Research

The idea of a method for determining things scientifically is as old as the notion of science itself. The ancient Egyptians and Greeks both created systems for determining knowledge through a process that is loosely related to what we now know as the scientific method. Furthermore, advances were made in the scientific method as a result of Muslim philosophers who believed that experiments should be used to test opposing theories. Our current understanding of the scientific method was first theorized by Sir Francis Bacon and René Descartes, later crystallized by Charles Sanders Pierce in 1878 in his article "How to Make Our Ideas Clear." Overall, the notion of there being a method for discovering scientific laws has been around for millennia. Whether you are a physical scientist (biologist, chemist, physicist, etc.) or a social scientist (psychologist, sociologist, communication researcher, etc.), the basic processes for conducting research stem out of the scientific method. When you were in elementary school, you were probably introduced to the scientific method in much the same way we were. So, before we can go further talking about the scientific approach to communication research, we need to revisit the scientific method.

SCIENTIFIC METHOD

The scientific method actually relates to the definition provided earlier from Webster's Dictionary for the word "research." In essence, as Figure 2.1 illustrates, there are four primary steps to the scientific process as it is commonly discussed by all scientists. Where one starts in the process is slightly arbitrary, but it is usually most helpful if we start with the "theories" step and explain from that point forward in the process.

Theories

A theory is a proposed explanation for how a set of natural phenomena will occur, capable of making predictions about the phenomena for the future, and capable of being falsified through empirical observation (West & Turner, 2006). Let's break this definition down and examine the major components of the definition. First, a theory should be able to either explain or describe a natural phenomenon (observable event). According to sociologist Gwynn Nettler (1970), an explanation is an attempt to satisfy one's curiosity about an observable event. In one of our favorite movies, *The Gods Must Be Crazy*, a Bushman named Xi who lives in Botswana is presented a gift from "the gods." In reality, the so-called "gift" is actually a Coke bottle accidentally dropped by a pilot flying above the tribe. Ultimately, the Bushmen become very jealous of each other because there is only one Coke bottle, which causes the tribe to rename the bottle "the evil thing." The majority of the movie then is the story of Xi attempting to take the bottle to the end of the world and return "the evil thing" to the gods. In essence, the Bushmen were faced with a new and unexplainable event, the appearance of the bottle, and were forced to create an explanation for how the bottle appeared in their tribe after falling from the sky. The Bushmen's explanation for the observable event was that the gods had given them the bottle. This example is actually

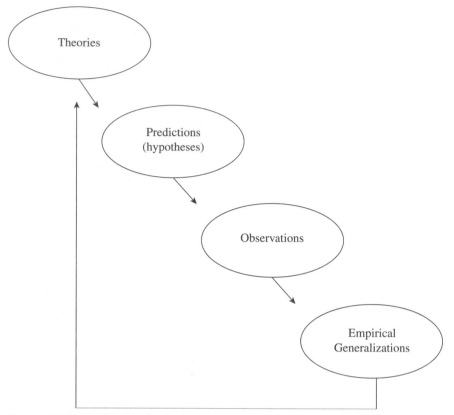

Figure 2.1 Scientific Method

only one type of explanation that people give to observable events and is called "appealing to authority," because the explanation centers around the gods as being wise in their decision to give the Bushmen the bottle. The second way of explaining phenomena is to label the phenomena. Humans use labeling constantly with children to help explain why their parents do things. A child might ask, "Why do we wash our hands?," in response to which the parent explains the concept of bacteria and disease in a very basic way the child can understand. This is also seen in the Bushmen when the "gift from the gods" causes jealousy among the tribe members and gets labeled "the evil thing." The third way to explain phenomena is to evoke empathy, or show how a phenomenon had good, just, or moral reasons. For example, when explaining his reasoning to the American public for invading Iraq, President George W. Bush appealed to the American people, explaining that Iraq had weapons of mass destruction and it was the just and moral thing to invade Iraq to prevent Saddam Hussein from being able to use those weapons. The fourth way to explain a phenomenon is to define terms or give examples. For example, university professors often forget how large their vocabularies are and occasionally make the mistake of using a word on an examination that many students do not know. To explain what the word means, we'll try to think of other words (synonyms) that a student may be more familiar with to help her or him understand what the question is actually asking. The last way people can go about explaining phenomena is to appeal to general empirical rules. For example, when people experience stage fright, they often will have sweaty palms. Sweaty palms occur during anxious periods because our body goes into a fight-or-flight mode, so blood is actually being pumped to our extremities (arms and legs) at a fast rate, which causes the internal temperature to rise in our extremities in case we have to fight what is causing us anxiety or run really fast. While this physiological response to fear is useful when you come face to face with a man-eating bear in the wilderness, it's not very useful when you have to give a public speech. In this example, we explained why sweaty palms occur by relating the physiological response to what we empirically know about how the body reacts to fear. Ultimately, appealing to general empirical rules as a method for explaining phenomena is extremely important because it's the only way to explain the past and present and help us predict what could happen in the future, which is the second part of the definition of theory provided earlier.

Our explanation of the behavior (fight-or-flight leads to sweaty palms) helps us to formulate predictions (when fearful, people's hands are more likely to sweat). When we talk about theories, our ultimate goal is to be able to predict, explain, and control a phenomenon. If a theory is of any use, the theory for why a behavior occurs should help direct us to ways to control the phenomenon. For example, recent research has shown that certain psychiatric medications can actually decrease an individual's level of anxiety even in situations where he or she has to give public speeches (Stein, Stein, Goodwin, Kumar, & Hunter, 2001; Van Ameringen, Lane, Walker, Bowen, Chokka, Goldner, et al., 2001; Van Ameringen, Mancini, Oakman, & Farvolden, 1999). Overall, we can predict that people who experience high levels of anxiety while giving a speech will have sweaty palms. We can explain why this occurs through the research that has been conducted by scientists in the area of physiological responses to fear that result in a fight-or-flight state. Finally, based on new research conducted in the area of psychopharmacology, we can now better control the physiological tendency to experience anxiety, thus preventing sweaty palms while giving a speech.

The last part of the definition of "theory" is often the hardest part for nonscientists to completely understand. Karl Popper first argued in the 1930s that a theory must be falsifiable through empirical research (Popper, 1968). In essence, for a theory to truly be a theory, there must be a way to test it empirically. The word "empiricism" was originally coined by the Roman skeptic Sextus Empiricus in reference to Greek physicians, who rejected beliefs in the divine nature of illness (i.e., you're sick because you made Zeus mad); instead the physicians relied on the observation of phenomena as perceived in experience through the five senses (touch, smell, hear, see, taste). In other words, empiricism is the belief that science is only acceptable insofar as the phenomenon in question can be "sensed" by average people. For example, people may not be able to see atoms with their naked eyes, but they can use powerful microscopes to observe atoms. However, there are no microscopes or telescopes powerful enough to observe little green men living on Mars or any other known planet beyond Earth. For this reason, we can create scientific theories about atoms, but we cannot create scientific theories about extraterrestrial life forms.

Predictions/Hypotheses

The second step in the scientific method is the development of predictions about the relationship between phenomena that come in the form of hypotheses. A hypothesis is the conclusion that occurs at the end of a series of propositions. A proposition is a statement that either confirms something or denies something. While there are many types of propositions, the most important to researchers are conditional or hypothetical propositions, which consist of two primary parts: antecedent and consequent. An antecedent is an "if" statement, and a consequent is a "then" statement. For example, "If I was born in the United States (antecedent), then I am an American (consequent)." Or "If this month is June (antecedent), then next month is July (consequent)." In the world of propositions, the antecedent causes the consequent to be true if the antecedent is true. In both of the examples we used here, the consequent is true if the antecedent is true. If someone is born in the United States, then he or she is an American. If the current month is June, the next month on the calendar is going to have to be July because we do not randomly shuffle the months just for the fun of it every year.

From hypothetical propositions we can make the next step to forming arguments. An argument is a set of propositions in which one follows logically as a conclusion from the others. In the world of logic, logicians illustrate arguments through the syllogism. A basic syllogism has three propositions (two premises and one conclusion). The most famous syllogism was given by the philosopher Aristotle more than 2000 years ago:

Major Premise:	All men are mortal.
Minor Premise:	Socrates is a man.
Conclusion:	Therefore, Socrates is mortal.

However, one of the problems with syllogisms is that that for the syllogism to be accurate, we have to trust that the premises are true. If our syllogism starts with false premises, then the conclusion can never be true. For example:

Major Premise:	All extraterrestrials are rich.
Minor Premise:	I am an extraterrestrial.
Conclusion:	Therefore, I am rich.

This syllogism, while correct in form, clearly is not true, and the conclusion cannot be trusted to tell us anything meaningful about the world around us. You can also have the flip side of this problem—a completely invalid syllogism that is based on true statements. For example:

Major Premise:	All mammals are living.
Minor Premise:	All lizards are reptiles.
Conclusion:	Therefore, all lizards are living.

While all three statements are true, the major premise and the minor premise do not go together at all. In essence, you're dealing with apples and oranges in the major and minor premises. Therefore, the conclusion that one would draw based on the major and minor premises may be true, but the syllogism is considered invalid because of the breakdown in the logical process. Ultimately, then, a hypothesis is a valid conclusion that is arrived at by a series of hypothetical propositions.

The following is an example from a student research paper attempting to determine the major premise, the minor premise, and the conclusion. See if you think this argument is logical.

Major Premise:	Lack of conflict discussion leads to insecurity in the workplace.
Minor Premise:	Cooperation among employees minimizes conflict.
Conclusion:	Cooperation aids individuals in the management of conflict, and conflict discussion leads to solution-oriented conflict-management strategies.

Let's examine this argument to see where the problem actually lies. The major premise clearly says that the less people talk about conflict, the more insecure they are. The minor premise goes on to state that employees who cooperate have less conflict. The conclusion then says two different things: (1) if employees cooperate with each other, then somehow the cooperation will aid in the management of conflict, and (2) talking about conflicts helps people find a solution. The first conclusion simply doesn't make sense because it is not very specific and we have no idea what "aids individuals in the management of conflict" actually means. This could indicate that people will have more conflict or less conflict—we simply cannot tell based on the information provided in the syllogism. The second conclusion introduces a new term that was not seen in either the major or minor premise (solution-oriented conflict management strategies). If the term is not mentioned in any of the earlier propositions, it cannot magically appear in the conclusion of a logical argument. Finally, the major and minor premises really have nothing to do with one another. The major premise discusses the lack of conflict while the minor premise talks about minimizing conflict. While the two ideas may sound similar, they really are not the same, so you cannot put them together to form a logical argument.

Let's now examine an example from a student paper of an argument that actually has true major and minor premises and true conclusion:

Major Premise:	Passengers on airplanes like flight attendants who use humor.
Minor Premise:	There is a positive relationship between liking someone and trusting them.
Conclusion:	Therefore, flight attendants who use humor will be more trusted by passengers.

In this example we have a major premise (funny flight attendants are liked) that clearly relates to the minor premise (liking and trust are related), which leads to the conclusion that funny flight attendants will be trusted. In essence, we can now hypothesize that flight attendants who are perceived as humorous will be more trusted than flight attendants who are not perceived as humorous. Note that both propositions are true because previous research in the area of flight attendant communication has generated empirical evidence to make those statements possible. In essence, when examining the major and minor premises that are used to create arguments in research, the propositions are based on actual empirical findings from previously conducted research. In other words, the premises are not simply made up because they help someone form an argument. If you do not have previous empirical research to help support your argument's propositions, then the propositions cannot be used to form any kind of conclusion.

Observations

The next step in the scientific method is referred to as observations. The observations part of the scientific method is where a researcher attempts to test the hypotheses created in the previous step. The most rigorous way to test a theory is to employ an experiment of some kind that directly allows a researcher to control a variable and then see the ramifications of this variable. For physical scientists, controlling a variable is very easy—when one adds baking soda to vinegar we will always get the "volcanic" reaction we saw as a child in our earth sciences classes. You could perform this experiment hundreds of times with varying brands of baking soda and vinegar, and you will always have the same reaction. Unfortunately, the social sciences are not as neat and easy because people do not always react the same. You cannot always take one funny flight attendant and expect everyone to react to that flight attendant in the same way, because many other characteristics of that flight attendant could influence passengers' perceptions of her or him (e.g., biological sex, hair color, uniform, ethnicity, sexual attractiveness, etc.). For this reason, a certain amount of error is inherent in social scientific research simply because humans provide social scientists with too many possibilities. However, there are certain processes that social scientists can use to make sure that when they are testing theories they weed out as much uncertainty as possible. These issues will be discussed in much greater detail in Chapters 13 and 14; for now, let's test the hypothesis discussed above: "Flight attendants who use humor will be more trusted by passengers."

This hypothesis was actually created by a couple of undergraduate students who wanted to conduct research on the airline industry. There are a number of ways a researcher could go about observing this hypothesis. First, a researcher could fly hundreds of airlines seeking out funny and not-so-funny flight attendants. Obviously, clear criteria would have to be used to determine whether or not a flight attendant was funny. The researcher could then ask passengers if they trust the flight attendants and keep a record of responses. Unfortunately, flying many different airlines and getting people's responses could be very costly, so maybe a researcher will opt to conduct an experiment instead. The researcher could have a video or audio tape of a flight attendant being funny or not-so-funny, and then get participants' reactions to the flight attendant. In this case, the researcher manipulates whether or not the participants see the funny flight attendant or the not-so-funny flight attendant videos. After viewing one video or the other, the researcher could have the participants fill out a scale that measures the participants' perceptions of the video flight attendant's trustworthiness. While obviously watching video tapes is not the most accurate way of observing this phenomenon, it's clearly the one that is the most cost efficient.

However, when observing a phenomenon, researchers must take great care that their observations are empirical, objective, and controlled. We've already discussed the nature of empiricism earlier in this chapter, so we will not go into great detail here other than to say that empiricism with regard to observations basically means that scientists must make sure that what they are observing can be observed. If scientists cannot determine a way to make observations of some kind about a specific phenomenon, then they cannot study the phenomenon, so the phenomenon is beyond the domain of science. Along with this notion is the idea that research must be able to empirically test a phenomenon. You may be wondering how social scientists observe what's going on inside people's heads, and you would be right to question this because social scientists cannot read brain waves and translate them to actual thoughts. For this reason, social scientists have created very specific ways to indirectly observe phenomena that cannot be easily observed through one of the five senses. I'm sure at some point in your undergraduate career you have been asked to fill out a research scale or questionnaire of some kind. These scales and questionnaires are examples of indirect ways that social scientists have created to observe what is going on inside of someone's head.

As previously stated, scientists must be both empirical and objective when they are observing phenomena during research. By objective, we mean that a scientist needs to make sure that her or his personal emotions, predictions, and biases do not get in the way of the observation. For example, imagine a scientist interviewing students about their tendency to drink alcohol right before giving a speech in class. The more the student talks about her or his drinking behavior, the more the interviewer starts to scowl and give the student dirty looks. Do you think the student will be forthright and honest about her or his drinking behavior? Probably not. For this reason, scientists have to make sure that they are as objective as humanly possible when conducting research. Another aspect of objectivity is reporting exactly what one finds in research, not just what one wants to find. Often when researchers pose hypotheses and test them, the hypotheses will not be supported. While there can be hundreds of reasons for why a hypothesis does not turn out the way a researcher expects it to, the researcher has an obligation to the scientific community to report those results and make them available for critique.

Finally, when observing a phenomenon, a researcher needs to make sure that he or she takes every step possible to control the research process. By "control" researchers refer to the process where an individual both prevents personal biases from interfering with the research study and makes sure there are no other explanations for what is seen in the study. We've already discussed the importance of preventing personal biases and will go into greater detail about how to do this in Chapters 13 and 14, so let's focus on how to prevent other explanations for observations. A story that is often repeated as a warning when discussing explanations of observations is the story of Clever Hans. Clever Hans was an Arabian stallion purchased in 1888 by Wilhelm Von Osten. Von Osten theorized that animals were intelligent beings, and Von Osten believed that with the proper education he could teach a horse to do simple arithmetic. By the end of Hans' education, he could answer many arithmetic questions from simple square roots to telling the time. The answers given by Hans came in the form of him pounding the number with his hoof the correct number of times on the ground. The horse could even answer mathematical questions when Von Osten wasn't present. Many researchers observed Hans and believed that Von Osten had educated the horse. Even the esteemed director of the Berlin Psychological Insitute, Carl Stumpf, declared that Von Osten had educated Hans in 1904.

One researcher, Oskar Pfungst, decided to empirically test Hans through a simple, controlled experiment. First, Pfungst would have Von Osten look at a flash card and see the answer and then test Hans. When Von Osten knew the answer to the question, Hans' answers were always correct. Then Pfungst had Von Osten show Hans the card without Von Osten knowing the answer, and Hans' answers became very random. Pfungst concluded that somehow Von Osten was giving Hans the answers without even knowing that he was. At this point Pfungst turned his attention to Von Osten as the teacher and observed his behavior. Pfungst started noticing that the teacher, whether Von Osten or another person, actually started changing her or his posture by standing up straighter as the horse neared the correct answer. When the teacher would stand fully erect, Hans knew he could stop pounding his hoof. Pfungst published his findings in 1907 in a book entitled Clever Hans: The Horse of Mr. Von Osten. In the Clever Hans example, we see both what happens when a scientist isn't objective in observing a phenomenon (how Von Osten actually nonverbally cued the horse's responses) and how another scientist, Pfungst, came into the situation and determined how to control for other possible explanations and got to the bottom of what was really going on with Clever Hans.

Empirical Generalizations

The final stage in the process of the scientific method is the creation of empirical generalizations. An empirical generalization is an attempt to describe a phenomenon based on what we know about the phenomenon at this time. Of course, our empirical generalizations are based on what we observed in the previous step of the scientific method. For example, in an initial study looking at flight attendant humor, the students conducting the research had participants read flight attendant preflight briefings (this is where the flight attendants show you all the doors, explain what to do with the yellow mask when it falls from the ceiling, and what to do in case you crash). One preflight safety briefing was very standard and covered all of the basics required by the Federal Aviation Administration, and in the second briefing the students added a lot of humor. Overall, the results of the study indicated that people did not trust the flight attendant in the humorous script (Wrench, Millhouse, & Sharp, in press). In fact, participants trusted the bland flight attendant more than the funny flight attendant. In essence, the hypothesis was not supported. Unethical researchers may just pretend this finding didn't happen and not present the results because this finding is contrary to previous research in humor. However, even results that go against common opinions on the subject are important for a number of reasons. First, this result could indicate that in situations where people feel their safety is involved, humor isn't appreciated. In essence, the airline industry could be a context where previous research in humor isn't applicable. Second, the finding could be a result of the method used in the experiment. The student researchers relied on written scripts where they manipulated humor (one plain script versus one funny script). The written humor may be interpreted differently if the participants in the study had viewed an actor or actress performing the script instead of the participants reading the script themselves. Overall, there are limitations to this study, and any good study will be up front about those limitations. If we do not know the limitations to a study, people may attempt to overgeneralize the study and start campaigns to pass laws banning flight-attendant humor.

Overall, when we attempt to generalize what we have learned in a study to the real world, we must be very honest about how we are applying our research findings. Preventing a "hasty generalization," or generalizing to something when not enough evidence is available to make the generalization, is often a problem that scientists have to avoid in their own writing and in how others use their research. In the world of communication, media scholars often investigate how the effects of violence in the media relate to violence in the real world. While the media scholars will correctly attribute limits to their results, often politicians will inaccurately attempt to use media research in their attempts to get various media banned. However, scientists should not investigate a phenomenon thinking of the political ramifications of their findings. One area in which there are ramifications to communication research is biological sex differences and communication. Empirical research generally shows that about 1% of a person's communicative behavior can be attributed to her or his biological sex (Canary & Hause, 1993); however, this finding contradicts what many people believe, which has largely been supported by pop psychologists like John Gray, who wrote the book *Men Are from Mars, Women Are from Venus* (1992). Sadly, scientists who conflict with conventional wisdom often have problems in society, and those who buy into conventional wisdom see those scientists who try to thwart convention as "having an axe to grind." Remember, Pope John Paul II fully conceded in 1992 that the Catholic Church's teaching that the sun was stationary was wrong and that Galileo's assertion during the 1600s was correct—the earth traveled around the sun. Overall, scientists typically do not think about how their research will be used by nonscientists or how people who disagree with research will react. Unfortunately, research is often used in ways that was never intended, and people who disagree with research can be very vocal.

Ultimately, the empirical generalizations made should lead to refinements in one's theory. As we learn more about theory, we need to change our theory to take into account what we have learned about our theory through the empirical process. For example, while a general theory of humor shows that humor is very positive in most communicative contexts, we may need to limit the scope of a general theory of humor as a result of the initial findings in the use of flight attendant humor. Maybe our theory needs to have a new clause that says humor is positive in communicative interactions except in situations where people feel their safety is involved. However, once you make adjustments to the theory, you need to empirically test those adjustments, and thus the cycle of research continues.

Conclusion

Scientists typically begin a program of research with little more than a few questions and speculations. Scientists may also speculate that something causes something else, or something is just related to something else. As the research program generates more data and results, these speculations may move toward becoming real theory. If one does not have solid quantitative research results to support one's theory, all that is left is speculation.

Nevertheless, the line dividing speculation and theory is less than perfect. Generally, when researchers are just guessing about what is going on in the real world, they are using speculation and more frequently use research questions to guide their efforts. When a body of data and results allows a scientist to begin building a formal description of what is going on, he or she is developing theory. Depending on the results obtained, the theory may be strongly supported, but it may not. The theory may get partial support and need to be modified to be consistent with the results obtained, or the theory may fail to receive meaningful support from the research outcomes.

Many scientists work on both describing what goes on and explaining why these things occur. Some scientists focus primarily on the descriptive phase of scholarship. They often are described as employing inductive methods. Other scientists focus primarily on the explanation phase of scholarship. They are described as employing deductive methods. While some people may want to argue which is more important, inductive or deductive research, this is a pretty much a "Which comes first, the chicken or the egg?" situation. Both are critical to the advance of science.

The term "theory" is used for many purposes and in many ways. There are theories that are meaningless (chicken or egg?) and there are theories that are important (the theory that a certain medication will kill cancer). You can check yourself as to how valuable your theory is in your own mind. Would you bet real money that, if properly tested, your theory would be proven correct? How much? Five cents? Fifty dollars? Fifty thousand dollars? Five hundred thousand dollars? Five million dollars? While this may seem like a silly game, it isn't. Many scientists must get grant support to conduct their research. They have to convince granting agencies to provide the resources to do their research. Not only does the scientist have to believe her or his theory is worth the financial risk, he or she must be able to get others to believe it as well. People typically are not highly committed to their speculations or guesses. However, people are likely to be very committed to theories that they and others believe to be strong, solid theories supported by empirical research (anyone want to jump off a skyscraper and test the theory of gravity?).

Everybody is entitled to an opinion, and as noted by the number of bloggers on the Internet, in most circumstances most people have an opinion. However, not everyone's opinion is equal in value to everyone else's opinion. The value of a scientist's opinion depends on the scientific support he or she has available. What are the data? What are the research results? How many replications are available? How much variance can the theory predict in realistic studies? Are there solid research results reported by credible scholars that suggest the theory is not right? Quantitative researchers depend on the results of data analyses for determining the validity of a theory, not someone's opinion. Science makes a maximum effort to keep the emotions and beliefs of a researcher separate from the evaluation of a theory. In contrast, the emotions and values of the researcher are a critical part of the decision making in much of the qualitative research (Appendix A). The researcher's thoughts contribute directly to the results of the research. While it often is not possible to keep the scientific researcher's thinking and/or believing 100% out of decisions about results in quantitative research, at least there is an extreme effort to do so.

Now that we have introduced you to the basic concepts involved in the scientific process of research, we can focus on the necessity of conducting research in an ethical and responsible manner in the next chapter.

KEY TERMS

Antecedent
Appeal to Authority
Appeal to General
Argument
Consequent
Empirical Generalization
Empirical Rules
Empiricism
Epistemology

Evoke Empathy
Explanation
Hasty Generalization
Humanism
Hypothesis
Label the Phenomena
Major Premise
Minor Premise
Objective

Proposition
Research
Science
Scientific Method
Subjective
Syllogism
Theory

REFERENCES

Canary, D. J., & Hause, K. S. (1993). Is there any reason to research sex differences in communication? *Communication Quarterly, 41*, 129–144.

Gray, J. (1992). *Men are from Mars, women are from Venus: A practical guide for improving communication and getting what you want in your relationships.* New York: HarperCollins.

Merriam-Webster (n.d.). Research. Retrieved December 16, 2006, from http://www.m-w.com/dictionary/research

Nettler, G. (1970). *Explanations.* New York: McGraw-Hill.

Peirce, C. S. (1878). How to make our ideas clear. *Popular Science Monthly, 12*, 286–302.

Pfungst, O. (1911). *Clever Hans (the horse of Mr. Von Osten): A contribution to experimental animal and human psychology* (Trans. C. L. Rahn). New York: Henry Holt. (Originally published in German, 1907).

Popper, K. R. (1968). *The logic of scientific discovery.* New York: Harper & Row.

Stein, D. J., Stein, M. B., Goodwin, W., Kumar, R., & Hunter, B. (2001). The selective serotonin reuptake inhibitor paroxetine is effective in more generalized and in less generalized social anxiety disorder. *Psychopharmacology, 158*, 267–272.

Van Ameringen, M. A., Lane, R. M., Walker, J. R., Bowen, R. C., Chokka, P. R., Goldner, E. M., et al. (2001). Sertraline treatment of generalized social phobia: A 20-week, double-blind, placebo-controlled study. *American Journal of Psychiatry, 158*, 275–281.

Van Ameringen, M., Mancini, C., Oakman, J. M., & Farvolden, P. (1999). Selective serotonin reuptake inhibitors in the treatment of social phobia: The emerging gold standard. *CNS Drugs, 11*, 307–315.

West, R., & Turner, L. H. (2006). *Introducing communication theory: Analysis and application* (3rd ed.). Boston, MA: McGraw-Hill.

Wrench, J. S., Millhouse, B., & Sharp, D. (in press). Laughing before takeoff: Humor, sex, and the preflight safety briefing. *Human Communication.*

Research Ethics

The word "ethics" evokes many images in different people. Typically, determining what is "ethical" falls along two tracks of thinking: theological or philosophical. Theologians will determine the rightness or wrongness of a behavior by searching specific religious texts, oral teachings, or traditions. Philosophers, on the other hand, concern themselves primarily with the question, "What should a person do?" Whether a person uses a theological or philosophical stance for determining the ethicality of behavior, understanding ethics is important to almost any endeavor. For example, what do you think of the ethicality of the following eight research scenarios:

1. Researchers use rural African American men to study the course of an untreated disease. During the course of the study, the men receive free examinations and medical care. However, the men did not receive information about the disease, were not informed that they

were participating in research, and were not told that the research would not benefit them directly. Even after a known treatment for the disease was discovered, the participants were not informed of the new treatment and the research continued for decades, which led to the death of many study participants.

2. Researchers wanting to study whether or not people would intervene when someone was about to experience harm decide to stage a crime. The researchers, with the consent of the shop owner, staged a burglary at a liquor store and then watched how bystanders reacted to the experiment.

3. A researcher wanting to understand the psychological processes involved in men who have sex with other men in public toilets poses as a voyeur or "watchqueen," an individual whose job it is to warn individuals who are engaging in public sex acts if someone is coming. After performing the job of "watchqueen," the researcher would then write down the license plate numbers of the men. The researcher would then trace the men's identities through the Department of Motor Vehicles under the guise of a market researcher. Once the researcher knew who the men were, he would approach them at their residences and interview them a year later to learn more about them.

4. Researchers are interested in understanding how juries decide verdicts. To examine jury deliberations, the researchers get permission from a judge to record the deliberations (using audio means only) of six actual juries.

5. Researchers interested in watching how the roles of "guard" and "prisoner" influence subject reactions create a mock prison in the basement of a university building. Participants were assigned to either the category of "guard" or "prisoner," which they would then live as for a 2-week period in the mock prison.

6. A researcher interested in understanding the how obedience to authority figures works devises an experiment under the guise of a teacher–learner scenario. In the experiment, participants are told that they are going to deliver electrical shocks at increasing levels to a learner in another room when the learner does not correctly answer a question. The learner is actually a member of the research project and no shocking actually occurs during the course of the research project. The goal of the project is to determine how long a participant will keep shocking the learner, even after the learner starts protesting, if the participant is encouraged by the researcher to continue with the shocks.

7. A researcher wants to determine if media campaigns can discourage adolescents from drinking alcohol. To provide baseline measures of actual consumption of alcohol, area adolescents were surveyed with the promise of confidentiality. Unknown to the adolescents, one of the strategies the researchers planned on using was the publication of the data in the local newspaper. The strategy proved very effective, with many parents clamping down on their adolescents' drinking behavior.

8. A researcher interested in understanding what it is like to be an undergraduate at a university in the twenty-first century decides to enroll. The researcher enrolls in her university as an entering first year student and lives in the dorm after getting permission from her institutional research board. During the researcher's year as an undergraduate, she takes classes, makes friends, participants in intercollegiate sports, and joins various student organizations. The researcher also interviews undergraduate students living in her dorm or taking classes with her. She has her interview participants fill out a consent form, explaining that the researcher is conducting a study on perceptions of undergraduates that may be published. For the most part, the participants do not know that the researcher is actually a university professor and researcher.

You may be thinking to yourself that these research projects are completely ridiculous and no one would ever actually think of completing any projects like these. However, you would be wrong. All of the above examples are actual research projects that were conducted during the 1900s and early 2000s.

The first research scenario is commonly referred to as the Tuskegee Syphilis Study and lasted from 1932 to 1972. In 1972, when it became apparent that the U.S. Public Health Services was involved in violating the basic human rights of the research participants, the U.S. public was outraged, especially since penicillin, a good treatment option for syphilis, had been around and available since World War II. In essence, the researchers kept their research project going despite the fact that adequate treatment options were available for the study participants. Ultimately, the U.S. Senate held hearings on this study and other alleged health care abuses and passed the National Research Act of 1974, which created a policy for protecting human subjects in federal regulations, and created the National Commission for the Protection of Human Subjects of Biomedical and Behavioral Research. The National Commission for the Protection of Human Subjects of Biomedical and Behavioral Research would then go on to produce the Belmont Report or the *Ethical Principles and Guidelines for the Protection of Human Subjects of Research.*

The second example, staging of a liquor store burglary, was conducted by Bibb Latané and John Darley (1970). In this study, the two researchers conducted a staged burglary to watch bystanders' reactions. One bystander responded by calling the police. The police showed up to the scene of the "crime," guns drawn and ready to arrest the researchers. Needless to say, this research experiment could have ended very badly for both the researchers and the bystanders alike.

The third research example was conducted by Laud Humphreys (1975) to examine what types of men engage in anonymous sex in public restrooms with other men. Humphreys' study was seen as both positive and negative by most researchers. Scholars believed that Humphreys' ability to carefully guard the actual identities of his research participants was to be applauded; however, his failure to obtain consent from his participants, his lying to the Department of Motor Vehicles to obtain his participants' home addresses, and his approaching the participants a year later in their home environments is indefensible. In Humphreys' defense, at the time when he was conducting his research, homosexuality was still illegal in most states with the penalty of jail time. Scholars look at Humphreys' research today and believe that it could have caused his participants undue psychological, financial, and legal harm.

The fourth study mentioned above is commonly referred to as the Wichita Jury Study of 1954. The researchers were allowed to tape record six jury deliberations in Wichita, Kansas, without the jurors' knowledge of their participation in the research study. When this project came to light, the research was widely criticized by reporters and politicians around the country. This research project was seen as undermining the judicial system because, as Vaughan (1967) said, surveillance "threatens impartiality to the extent that it introduces any question of possible embarrassment, coercion, or other such considerations into the minds of actual jurors" (p. 72). Ultimately, the U.S. Senate passed a law prohibiting the recording of jury deliberations.

The fifth study, the prison simulation study, was conducted by Zimbardo, Haney, Banks, and Jaffe (1973) in a basement at Stanford University. On the surface, this study may not seem too bad. However, the problems with this study lay not in what was being studied as much as the problems that arose out of the methods used to study the phenomenon. When people were labeled as "prisoners" or "guards," a cognitive shift occurred and they started to confuse who they were in real life with their new personas. Guards started to physically and psychologically abuse the prisoners. Prisoners either became rebellious and fought back against the guards or they broke down and did the guard's wishes even if those wishes were inhumane. Ultimately, the 2-week experiment was closed after 6 days. Critics of this study believe that the researchers did not do enough upfront to guarantee the safety (both psychological and physical) of all the participants—guards and prisoners.

The sixth study mentioned above is commonly referred to as the Milgram Study. The project leader was Stanley Milgram (1974), who wanted to understand how authority figures impacted people's decisions to comply with requests or mandates. After World War II, many researchers started studying how Hitler had gotten many regular people to blindly follow orders and commit atrocities associated with the Holocaust. While Milgram's study did not involve killing people, it did involve inflicting pain on another person. Participation in Milgram's study caused many people severe psychological discomfort because the participants actually believed they were inflicting pain on the learner in the other room. Of the 40 members of the general public paid to take part in the study, all complied with the order to administer shocks up to 300 V (marked intense shock). As many as 26 responded obediently to the experimenter's urging to apply the maximum 450 V. Video tapes of the Milgram study actually show adult males crying while continuing to shock the learner in the other room. One participant was so overcome by stress that he had a convulsive seizure. Furthermore, Milgram and his colleagues had not thought about the long-term effects of the study on their participants' psyche.

The seventh study mentioned above, the adolescent alcohol consumption project, was a study conducted by Charles Atkin and reported by Garramone and Kennamer (1989). In this case, the question of ethics came in the form of the adolescents who felt deceived by the researcher. The adolescents had been open with the researcher about their alcohol consumption. When the researcher then published the results in the newspaper, many parents quickly clamped down on their children's behavior, and the adolescents felt their confidentiality had been violated. Atkins argued that the individual participant's confidentiality had not been violated, but the confidentiality of the group as a whole had been. However, the adolescents were participating in illegal underage drinking, so the question could also be posed, as Atkin did, "Does one have a *right* to do something illegal?" In essence, the publication of the research findings in the local paper enabled parents to prevent illegal adolescent behavior.

The final study mentioned above was written under the pseudonym Rebekah Nathan and was published in 2005. The book was published under a pseudonym in order to protect the student participants who volunteered to be interviewed or who lived in the dorm or attended classes with the researcher. However, the researcher's real name, Cathy Small, was discovered long before her book ever hit the shelf. While many researchers applaud Dr. Small's use of her anthropological background to study modern college students in their natural environment in a way reminiscent of how Jane Goodall studied chimpanzees in their natural habitat, Small's methods have caused quite a stir in the academic community. Is it ethical to enter a college dorm under false pretenses and watch the students in their natural environment? Is it ethical to have students sign informed consent forms for participating in a research project when the participants do not know who the researcher really is? The participants would naturally assume that Small was a fellow undergraduate and the chances of her research ever reaching print unlikely, so were Small's participants really informed?

All eight of the above studies are important to the history of ethics in research because each one has forced researchers to reevaluate how research ought to be done. This chapter will explain the current state of ethics in research and how it applies to the field of communication. To examine ethics in communication research, we will first explore the meaning of the term "ethics" in more detail, examine the three-prong test for ethics established by the 1979 Belmont Report (persons, beneficence, and justice), explain the purpose and place of institutional review boards (IRBs) in research, and pose some basic ethical questions for communication researchers.

Defining Ethics

While the study of ethical considerations dates back thousands of years, the modern analysis of ethics resides primarily in the understanding of two basic concepts: means and ends (McCroskey, Wrench, & Richmond, 2003). Means are the tools or behaviors that one employs to achieve a desired outcome. Means can be either good or bad. Ends are those outcomes that one desires to achieve. Just like means, ends can be either good or bad. Figure 3.1 demonstrates the four combinations of good and bad means and ends.

GOOD MEANS–GOOD END: ETHICAL BEHAVIOR

The first quadrant of the ethical diagram depicts what happens when someone has good means and a good end. For example, a researcher wants to conduct a research study to examine the influence that health campaign television advertisements have on positively changing health behaviors. The researcher brings in a group of participants and informs them of the project, obtains their consent, does not lie to them, and conducts the study in a very ethical manner. The result of the study ultimately helps public health officials design appropriate mediated campaigns. Ultimately, in this example the means and the ends are both positive. This would be considered ethical behavior or communication.

BAD MEANS–BAD END: UNETHICAL BEHAVIOR

The second quadrant of the ethical diagram depicts the exact opposite of the first quadrant, or what happens when someone has bad means and a bad end. Some of the results seen in the Milgram study clearly would fall into this category. Researchers deceived their participants and then one of the participants had a seizure because of the stress he was under during the experiment. Who knows how many of the participants had severe psychological trauma after the fact?

BAD MEANS–GOOD END: MACHIAVELLIAN ETHIC

While the first two quadrants are fairly straightforward in their ethical understanding, the other two quadrants in the ethical diagram are not as clear-cut. The third quadrant is an example of what happens when a person employs bad means to achieve a good end. This concept is referred to as the Machiavellian ethic because Niccolò Machiavelli believed that the ends justify the means. Machiavelli's greatest work, *The Prince*, written in 1513, created much controversy because he wrote that princes should retain absolute control of their lands

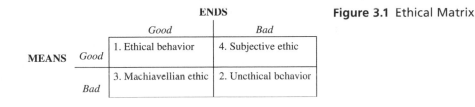

Figure 3.1 Ethical Matrix

		ENDS	
		Good	Bad
MEANS	Good	1. Ethical behavior	4. Subjective ethic
	Bad	3. Machiavellian ethic	2. Unethical behavior

and should use any means necessary to accomplish this end, including deceit. This notion was so outlandish that Pope Clement VIII described it as heretical.

This ethical perspective still is seen as outlandish and unethical by many today. The following is an example of how the Machiavelli ethic can be seen in a research situation. If a researcher overstates her or his findings (bad means) about the harmful nature of a drug in order to get people to stop doing it (good ends), is this researcher ethical? Some would consider it perfectly ethical behavior if it causes people to stop using a harmful substance, but others would say it is not ethical because the researcher had to lie to get the behavioral change.

GOOD MEANS-BAD END: SUBJECTIVE ETHIC

The fourth quadrant of the ethical diagram (Figure 3.1) examines what happens when a person employs good means that result in a bad end. For example, a media researcher conducts research on how to appropriately deliver communicated messages during a political campaign. A political candidate gets hold of the research and sees how he can use the study's findings to create manipulative messages that will get him elected. In essence, the researcher conducted the research in an ethical manner (the mean), which led to the manipulation of the populace by a political candidate (the end). Is research ethical if it can later be used for harm? Many researchers who worked on the Manhattan Project, which resulted in the creation of the atomic bomb, did not think about the loss of life and devastation their research would ultimately bring on the world.

Hopefully by this point you are starting to see that the world of research ethics is not completely clear-cut. For the most part, research is not innately ethical or unethical. Research can be methodologically sound or methodologically problematic, but determining whether or not a researcher is being ethical is quite complicated, and there are a number of opinions as to what constitutes ethical versus unethical research behavior. The U.S. federal government has stepped in and provided a number of guidelines that researchers must follow by law.

The Belmont Report's Effect on Research Ethics

In 1979, The National Commission for the Protection of Human Subjects of Biomedical and Behavioral Research completed the report entitled *Ethical Principles and Guidelines for the Protection of Human Subjects of Research*, which is commonly referred to as the Belmont Report. The Belmont Report devised three basic principles that all researchers using human subjects, regardless of research area, should be accountable for in their research. First, *researchers should respect all possible research participants as autonomous individuals who have the capability of making decisions about their participation in a research project.* In essence, a researcher must make sure that her or his research participants are informed about their participation in the research process without coercion. Furthermore, researchers should also make sure that possible participants are adequately informed about the purpose of the research, the voluntary nature of research, and the risks that may be associated with participation. This first part of the Belmont Report is commonly referred to as the ethical standard of "informed consent." This ethical standard also has a second component that researchers must be aware of because not all possible participants have the ability to intellectually discern for themselves whether participation in a research endeavor is ok, so possible participants with "diminished autonomy" may need additional protections. You may be wondering what types of people fall into the category of "diminished autonomy." In essence, the Belmont Report realized that children and adults, who mentally cannot make informed decisions, should not be allowed to volunteer for the research process. Under current standards prisoners, fetuses, pregnant women, terminally ill individuals, students, employees, comatose patients, and persons under the age of 18 or who are legally given to the care of an adult because of severe developmental disorders or dementias fall into the diminished autonomy category as well. These populations are highly studied groups, so it's not that they cannot be studied, only that you must get informed consent from a legal guardian.

The second ethical principle spelled out in the Belmont Report is the need for researchers to *guarantee beneficence*. The "principle of beneficence" obligates researchers to make sure that during the research process they maximize possible benefits and minimize possible harms to the research participants themselves. For this reason, one question that is often asked of researchers when designing a research study is, "How will this study benefit the participants?" As a general response, the authors of this book think this question is extremely important not only because ethically we should be attempting to enhance our participants' lives while minimizing possible harms, but because good research ought to make people's lives better. Too often researchers study small aspects of human communication that have no direct impact or bearing on real people's lives. For example, if research in the area of interpersonal relationships does not ultimately help people understand the interpersonal communication process better and lead to more successful interpersonal communication relationships, then what's the point of the research itself? You can peruse any discipline's journals and see many studies that make you wonder, "Why did they do that?!" In fact, there's an association dedicated to ridiculous research that gives out the yearly Ig Nobels and publishes the interdisciplinary journal the *Annals of Improbable Research*. Some of the past Ig Nobel winners have fed Prozac to clams, watched brain activity of locusts while watching *Star Wars*, noted the effect of country music on suicide, noted that when people concentrate they may miss the woman in the gorilla suit, and studied and classified belly button lint. To view the entire list of Ig Nobel winners dating back to 1991, you can visit the *Annals of Improbable Research* website at http://www.improb.com/. In other words, please do not end up on the Ig Nobel list as a researcher. For all the humor this list actually provides, these research projects started as legitimate projects. To avoid creating a research project that is absurd, always ask yourself how your research could actually better the lives of your research participants.

The third, and final, Belmont Report ethical standard is that of *justice*. By justice, the authors of the report believed that those who take the risks of research should also receive the benefits from that research. As was seen in the Tuskegee case, lower income African American men were basically used as guinea pigs who received none of the benefits of the findings. For this reason, researchers today must make sure that risks and benefits are fairly distributed within society without bias. This is not to say that you cannot single out specific groups that you want to research, only that there needs to be a clear justification for this singling out and that the benefits would ultimately help that group. For example, maybe you want to examine differences in communication phenomena between patients and physicians when the patients and physicians are of different races. You may decide to examine Hispanic patients' perceptions of Anglo/Caucasian (White) physicians. While the risk of harm as a result of this study would probably be very minimal, every study contains some element of risk (either physical or psychological). The basic reasoning behind the notion of justice is that historically a lot of medical research was conducted on ethnically diverse groups or people on the lower rungs of the social hierarchy, but the benefits of the research only impacted those people at the top of the social hierarchy (primarily White males). Ultimately, researchers must ask themselves if some classes of people are overrepresented in their samples because of their availability, their compromised position, or their vulnerability. If the answer to these questions is "yes," is there a clear justification for their inclusion, or were they selected inappropriately and will thus bear the brunt of the possible risks of the study? For the most part, this is not generally a problem communication researchers have faced. Communication researchers have generally not conducted studies that have serious risks beyond psychological discomfort. And while psychological discomfort can be serious, very few studies in communication would violate the justice principle of ethicality.

Institutional Review Boards

By 1981, the Department of Health and Human Services and the Food and Drug Administration approved a series of federal guidelines, Title 45, *Code of Federal Regulations*, Part 46 (45 CFR 46), which established the "Common Rule." The Common Rule established a set of guidelines for the rights, welfare, and protection of research participants. One of the most important aspects of the Common Rule was the requirement that any institution that received federal funding and federal agencies themselves must establish an IRB to review all research proposals for possible risks to research participants and to make sure that all research participants are informed of their rights as research participants. To further understand the nature of IRBs, this section will examine IRB basics, informed consent, and the IRB process.

INSTITUTIONAL REVIEW BOARD BASICS

The IRB was established by 45 CFR 46 to ensure that past research atrocities like the Tuskegee experiment did not happen again on U.S. soil. Ultimately, IRBs are charged with the task of ensuring that researchers take appropriate steps in protecting and informing research participants. According to the National Institutes of Health (NIH) (2002), a research participant is "a living individual about whom a researcher obtains either: (1) data through intervention or interaction with the individual; or (2) identifiable private information" (p. 16). Data through intervention is data that would occur in biomedical research situations. For example, one common type of medical publication is the case study. A medical case study is when a physician sees an interesting medical case and then writes an article for a medical journal detailing the case. In this research instance, the information was obtained about the patient during a routine medical intervention, so for a physician to publish this information, he or she would need to obtain consent from either the patient or her or his legal guardian. Even if the physician does not use the person's name or photograph in the article, he or she is still obligated to obtain consent (more on this in the next section). The second type of data can be acquired through interaction with the participant. If a communication researcher runs focus groups, investigates a culture, or hands out surveys, he or she is obtaining information about an individual through interaction, so the individual with whom the researcher is acting is a research participant. Finally, a research participant is someone who could be identified through identifiable private information. For example, maybe you want to determine if females and males differ in their likelihood of taking communication courses in high school, so you request to see high school transcripts for all incoming first year students at your university. While you may not think this is a big deal, when high school students apply for college and forward their transcripts to colleges, they are sending them to the college under the notion that the transcripts would be used to determine applicants' eligibility for entrance to the university, not for a communication research project. For this reason, high school transcripts would be considered private information and a researcher would have to obtain every first year student's permission to use the transcripts for research purposes.

Another basic ethical dilemma that IRBs tackle is whether or not a participant should be paid for her or his participation. Researchers often offer some form of payment for an individual's participation in a research study. Whether the payment comes in the form of money or extra credit, payment is payment. Unfortunately, there are no standard rules for how payments should work other than the notion that coercion of participants is wrong. For this reason, undergraduate students who are asked to participate in a research project are often offered extra credit for their participation. Since the extra credit points are above and beyond the points within the course itself, the "payment" is not coercion. Some IRBs will take "payment" a step further and require alternative extra credit opportunities for individuals who do not want to participate in the study itself. One common form of alternative activity is to have students read and abstract an article related to the study itself. However, if your IRB asks for an alternative exercise for individuals who do not want to participate, make sure the alternatives are equitable. For example, if it takes 10 minutes to fill out a survey, it should take 10 minutes to complete the alternative extra credit opportunity as well. Furthermore, some ethicists take it a step further and actually argue that extra credit sways students to participate in a study, which theoretically will alter the results within a study because without the extra credit the students wouldn't participate.

The last basic aspect of IRBs is the determination and understanding of anonymity, privacy, and confidentiality. Many researchers when they are first starting research often mistake the terms "anonymity," "privacy," and "confidentiality." However, as far as an IRB is concerned, there are very important distinctions between three concepts. First, anonymity occurs when a researcher does not know who participated in a study or which results belong to which participants in a study. For example, one of the authors of this text has done considerable work with online surveying. He sends out e-mails to various target groups requesting participation. While this method of data gathering is problematic, it does allow him to target groups that would otherwise be out of his reach. Participants who then decide to participate fill out a survey on a website. Ultimately, the researcher has no way of knowing who filled out his survey, so the process is completely anonymous. The second term, privacy, according to the NIH (2002), is "defined in terms of having control over the extent, timing, and circumstances of sharing oneself (physically, behaviorally, or intellectually) with others" (p. 23). Research participants willingly give information about themselves to researchers under the understanding that the researcher will only share this information when it is necessary. For this process to work, all researchers must make sure they keep the information learned from a research participant private. Under the 1996 Health Insurance Portability and Accountability Act (HIPPA), privacy has entered a new stage of understanding. Under HIPPA, there are new classifications for what is deemed protected health information (PHI). PHI is any individually identifiable health information (e.g., demographic data and biological specimens) that is transmitted or maintained by a covered entity (Wrench, 2002). While most communication researchers are not going to be investigating any PHI, it is possible that people involved in health communication research may research PHI, so they should make sure they investigate HIPPA's effect on researchers in biomedical research to make sure they are in compliance with HIPPA statutes regarding research. For more on HIPPA responsibilities, talk to your campus' IRB.

Along with privacy we must explore the third term, "confidentiality," because the two terms are interrelated. Confidentiality "pertains to the treatment of information an individual has disclosed in a relationship of trust and with the expectation that it will not, without permission, be divulged to others in ways that are inconsistent with the understanding of the original disclosure" (NIH, 2002, p. 24). Confidentiality is making sure that you do not divulge any information about a participant that could lead to her or his identification. Some common ways of keeping confidentiality include removing signed consent forms from surveys, substituting codes for identifiers (instead of male, it becomes "1" on a code sheet), properly disposing of computer data and other paper (generally with a shredder), limiting access to identifiable data (typically only to immediate investigators), and storing files in a secure space. Furthermore, it is also important to educate any research assistants on the necessity of confidentiality. While most communication projects warrant little risk and confidentiality isn't a huge problem, there are studies in communication that have examined more sensitive areas like illegal, drug, and sexual behaviors that warrant a closer scrutiny of the IRB on a researcher's protection of her or his participants' confidentiality.

One side note should be explained at this point involving confidentiality. The August 2005 issue of the *Journal of Applied Communication* focused on the process of communication researchers interacting with IRBs. While there were many horror stories in the mix, most criticisms were met with positive experiences as well. One interesting narrative (pp. 228–230) tells an experience of being subpoenaed by a district attorney. The researcher was investigating what types of evidence jurors used to render decisions. The researcher had conducted interviews with various jurors after the conclusion of a number of trials. After the interviews were conducted, the researcher received a subpoena in which the defense attorney wanted to ask the researcher whether "the jurors had said anything to me about their verdict in the case that did not pertain to the facts presented at the trial" (p. 229). The researcher immediately called the university IRB because the researcher didn't know what to do because the participants had filled out a consent form guaranteeing confidentiality. Ultimately, one of the arguments the university attorney made on behalf of the researcher was that the researcher "had a moral and contractual duty to not answer questions about what the jurors told me. The jurors would be put in jeopardy if I was forced to disclose the confidential information they provided" (p. 229). While the judge in this case agreed with the defendant (the researcher), this is not always the case. Unfortunately, researchers are not granted a privileged status like patient–physician, lawyer–client, or spouses when it comes to information. In essence, researchers can be compelled to disclose what was learned or be incarcerated for contempt of court. However, federal provisions under the Public Health Act can allow you to petition the Secretary of Health and Human Services for a Certificate of Confidentiality. A Certificate of Confidentiality enables a researcher to engaged in "biomedical, behavioral, clinical, or other research (including research on mental health and on the use of and effect of alcohol and other psychoactive drugs) to protect the privacy of individuals who are the subjects of such research" (NIH, 2002, p. 25). If you are ever researching a highly sensitive topic that involves illegal activity, you will want to work closely with your IRB to see if it is possible for you to receive a Certificate of Confidentiality.

INFORMED CONSENT

Throughout this chapter we have mentioned the need to inform participants about the nature of research and any possible risks associated with research. This section will go into further detail about the nature of informed consent and how to prepare a consent document for distribution during a research study. Informed consent is a "person's voluntary agreement, based upon adequate knowledge and understanding of relevant information, to participate in research" (NIH, 2002, p. 64). In essence, a researcher must provide any potential participants with adequate information about the purpose of the study, how long the study will last, experimental procedures, alternatives, the known risks, and any known benefits. The researcher must also explain to participants how they can ask questions about the research project and about their rights as research participants. Figure 3.2 is an example of an informed consent document used by one of the authors of this text in a project examining how personalized coaching impacted weight loss.

The consent document in Figure 3.2 contains a great deal of information in a very brief format. Let's examine the various parts of the document itself. The first paragraph explains who the researcher is and what the purpose of the project is. The first sentence of the next paragraph explains how long an individual's participation will last (15–20 minutes). We then learn that the researcher has determined that there are no foreseeable risks involved in the study. The participant is then informed that her or his participation is voluntary and that he or she may quit at any time during the study. This sentence is important because many participants believe that once they start they cannot stop, which simply is not the case. Legally, a person has the right to opt out of research at any point during a research project. Admittedly, researchers prefer for research participants to stay through the entire project, but researchers must respect an individual participant's wishes to stop participating in the study. The next sentence explains that participation or lack of participation will not affect an individual's standing with the organization that the researcher was using to conduct the research. This line is also very common in research involving students, but would read something like

---

Hello!

My name is *Name of Researcher* and I am a professor in the School of Communication Studies at *Name of University*. I am conducting research to examine the impact that your wellness coach has had on weight loss and weight loss motivation. As a health communication researcher, I am interested in what you have to say about your wellness coach. I am specifically interested in the interpersonal relationship you have developed and continue to develop with your coach.

Completing this questionnaire should take approximately 15–20 minutes. There are no known risks to participation in this study. Your participation is completely voluntary and you may end your participation at any time. Whether you choose to participate in this study or not will in no way affect your relationship with your wellness coach or your relationship with *Organization's Name*. Your responses will be kept confidential and no one directly involved with the *Organization's Name* will have access to your completed questionnaire. The completed questionnaires will only be accessible to me. After I analyze the results, all questionnaires will be destroyed.

After reading this letter, if you choose to participate in this study, please sign the form at the bottom indicating your willingness to do so. Next, please complete the attached questionnaire. Please be honest and as complete as possible with your answers. Once you have completed the survey, please return it to the questionnaire collection box provided.

Thank you for your time. I greatly appreciate your willingness to complete this questionnaire. If you have any questions or concerns about this research study, please feel free to phone me at *Phone #* or via e-mail at *e-mail address*. If you have any questions regarding your rights as a research participant, please contact *Director's Name*, Director of Research Compliance, *University's Name*, *Director's Phone Number*.

Thank you again for your help.

I certify that I have read and understand this consent form and agree to participate as a subject in the research described. I agree that known risks to me have been explained to my satisfaction and I understand that no compensation is available from *University's Name* and its employees for any injury resulting from my participation in this research. I certify that I am 18 years of age or older. My participation in this research is given voluntarily. I understand that I may discontinue participation at any time without penalty or loss of any benefits to which I may otherwise be entitled. I certify that I have been given a copy of this consent form to take with me.

| Printed Name | Signature | Date |

Figure 3.2 Informed Consent Document—Signature Required

"Your participation in this study is completely voluntary, and will in no way affect your grade or athletic standing." This clause basically informs a participant that whether he or she decides to participate in a research project, the participation will not negatively affect her or his grade or prevent her or him from participating in athletics. The next sentence on the consent form explains to the participant that the organization will not have access to the responses of the questionnaires and that the participants' responses will be kept confidential, accessible only to the researcher, and will be destroyed when the project is completed. The next paragraph explains that if the participant decides to participate then he or she needs to sign the consent statement at the bottom of the page, fill out the questionnaire, and return the whole packet to the collection box. The next paragraph simply explains how to get a hold of the researcher if the participant has any questions, and how to get a hold of the director of research compliance at the researcher's university if the participant has questions about her or his rights as a participant in a research project. You'll notice that the actual consent box that a participant signs is very loaded with legal terminology, basically making sure the participant understands the nature of the research, is volunteering to be a participant, understands that the university is not liable for injury, is over 18 (or not a child), has the right to stop participating, and has been given the option of taking a consent form.

While the above is the most standard kind of consent form one will see in research, there is another form that is often used that does not require an individual to sign something for consent. Researchers can generally request an IRB for permission to not have a signed consent for one of two possible reasons:

1. A signed consent form would be the only record linking the participant and the research, which could result in potential harm resulting from breach of confidentiality. In this case, each participant will be asked whether he or she wants documentation linking her or himself with research, and the participant's wishes will govern.

2. The research presents no more than minimal risk of harm to the participants and involves no procedures for which written consent is normally required outside of the research context.

In these cases, the following text is added as a paragraph to the consent form seen in Figure 3.2 instead of a signed statement:

> Returning this questionnaire certifies that you have read and understand this consent form and agree to be a participant in the research described. Additionally, you agree that known risks for your participation have been explained to your satisfaction and you understand that no compensation is available from [your university's name] and its employees for any injury resulting from your participation in this research. Participation in this study also certifies that you are 18 years of age or older. Please understand that you may discontinue participation at any time without penalty or loss of any benefits to which you may otherwise be entitled.

You'll notice that the same basic information that was in the signed consent form is available in the above statement. In this version, however, the participant is not required to sign off on her or his understanding of the consent. Instead, active participation in the research endeavor is a sign of informed consent.

There is one very tricky ethical dilemma that must come under scrutiny in the informed consent process—deception. What if telling the participants about the nature of the research will skew their responses? For example, in the study conducted by Stanley Milgram discussed at the beginning of this chapter, he clearly did not inform his research participants that he was studying the effects of how authority figures impact people's decisions to comply with requests or mandates. Instead he told his participants that they were taking part in a study designed to examine negative feedback (electrical shocks) on the learning process. Should deception be allowed? In essence, lying about the purpose of the study to receive a good study result is a clear example of the Machiavellian ethic discussed earlier in this chapter. IRBs unfortunately do not handle deception in a uniform manner at every university. For this reason, if you are planning on using deception within your study, you will want to make sure you talk to your IRB prior to developing your IRB proposal (more on this in the next section) to learn what they will and will not allow. One thing can be guaranteed, however; if you are planning on deceiving during your informed consent, you will need to debrief your participants at the conclusion of their participation. In the debrief, you will need to explain to your participants that they were deceived, what the purpose of your deception was, and what the nature of the project really is. You may be thinking to yourself, *well I won't actually lie to my participants; I just may not be as complete as I should be in explaining the nature of the project itself.* Under typical IRB guidelines, if your disclosure is incomplete, as a researcher you will need to debrief your participants as well.

INSTITUTIONAL REVIEW BOARD PROCESSES

This section will briefly explain the IRB process to which all researchers who use human subjects must adhere. As mentioned earlier, the development of the IRB was set forth in 45 CFR 46 in 1981 as a ramification of the Belmont Report. Every university will have an Office of Research Compliance, Office of Funded Projects, Office of Institutional Research, or some other name where the university's IRB will be housed (we will be using the word university in this section, but it also applies to IRBs in other locations like foundations, research firms, or governmental agencies). Federal regulations mandate that the IRB must have at least five members from various backgrounds. Membership on the IRB should be diverse and often will include both university personnel and members of the community (at least one non-university member). If IRBs are going to be overseeing research involving protected groups (children, pregnant women, prisoners, or physically/mentally disabled persons), then at least one member of the IRB must have a specialization in working with these populations.

Each IRB is also given the job of overseeing all of the research that is conducted at that university. At the most basic level, IRBs ensure that human rights are protected and that informed consent occurs in all research. To do this, IRBs have several jobs they must complete. First, IRBs must review the full protocols for every planned research study and then determine whether or not the research plans do not expose participants to unreasonable risks. Second, the IRB must periodically review all research projects currently underway to ensure that human protections are still in place. Third, IRBs should examine adverse events (unexpected harms that result from a study), interim findings, and any recent literature in the project area that could force a change in the IRB protocol. Unfortunately, many types of research are dangerous and could cause unforeseen harm to an individual. If and when this happens during a study, a researcher is obligated to report the adverse event to the IRB, which will then investigate the research protocol to see if changes need to be made or the project shut down completely. Some IRBs will also want to see your findings along the way. In short-term studies (lasting less than 5 years), IRBs may just want to see the demographic makeup of your participants on a yearly basis. For longer studies (greater than 5 years), IRBs may want more detailed updates along the way. IRBs should also be up to date on current trends in research that could force a change in an IRB protocol. Again, while not common in communication research, changes made as a result of new research is more common in biomedical research. The last responsibility of the IRB is to investigate suspected or alleged protocol violations, complaints expressed by research participants, or violations of institutional policies. In essence, an IRB must make sure that the researcher is doing what he or she said he or she was going to do.

Beyond the basic responsibilities of the IRB, IRBs have the authority to engage in four different behaviors. First, university IRBs have the ability to approve, disapprove, or terminate all research activities at the university. Second, IRBs have the ability to require modifications to research protocols (both new and previously approved protocols). Third, IRBs have the ability to require researchers to divulge more information than the information mandated in 45 CFR 46 if the IRB believes additional information will add to the protections of participants' rights and safety. And finally, IRBs have the ability to require or waive informed consent.

Before you get to the IRB stage of a research project, you will be required by your university to fill out an IRB protocol. Every university has the ability to create its own unique IRB protocol, which is adjusted to its specific needs. Some IRB protocols are one page in length, and others could be up to 30–50 pages in length, depending on the nature of your project and the specific documentation your IRB wants to see. Once your IRB protocol is completed, you will generally be asked what kind of review your project should receive. There are three levels of review that IRBs have at their disposal: exempt, expedited, and full-board.

EXEMPT REVIEW

Exempt review technically means that you are exempted from undergoing an IRB review. Having an exempt review does not mean that you do not have to submit your IRB protocol. However, some institutions will have different sets of IRB protocol documents for this level of review. Other institutions will only have one set of IRB protocol documents for all three levels of review. Again, make sure you check with your individual institution about the IRB process. This chapter is designed to introduce you to the generalities of ethics in research and the IRB process, not to be a definitive answer on how your university's IRB ought to run.

The exempt review can be granted to a research protocol if the project contains low-risk research and is exempted from federal regulations concerning IRB review and approval. In 45 CFR 46, six categories for research exemptions were created, as seen in Figure 3.3.

A lot of the research that is conducted by communication researchers will fall under this type of IRB review. Specifically, a lot of communication research will fall under Category 2 exemption since communication research relies heavily on survey procedures, interview procedures, and/or observation of public behavior. However, just because you think your research will fall under Category 2 for exempt research does not mean that your IRB will agree with you. Many researchers will think their research is exempt, only to have their research bumped up to the next level of review, the expedited review.

EXPEDITED REVIEW

The expedited review is designed for research projects that still have minimal risk; if minor changes are needed in previously approved research, an IRB may want to examine your documents more closely. Do not think that just because you are collecting surveys that your project is automatically exempt. Surveys that ask people highly sensitive information (illegal behavior, substance use, or sexual behavior) are often reviewed at this level. Typically, the chair of the IRB will review research protocols at this level or review. If he or she is not confident in her or his understanding of the research protocol, the IRB chair may send it to an IRB member or small group of members who specialize in that type of research. If the research is highly controversial, beyond a minimal risk, or involves confidentiality problems, the IRB chair will require that a research protocol be examined by the full IRB.

FULL-BOARD REVIEW

A full-board review occurs when the chair of the IRB believes that a research protocol is beyond a minimal risk and that the complete IRB should make a decision as to whether or

1. Research conducted in established or commonly accepted educational settings, involving normal educational practices (e.g., research on regular and special education instructional strategies or research on the effectiveness of or the comparison among instructional techniques, curricula, or classroom management methods).

2. Research involving the use of educational tests (cognitive, diagnostic, aptitude, achievement), survey procedures, interview procedures, or observation of public behavior, unless:
   (a) Information obtained is recorded in such a manner that human participants can be identified, directly or through identifiers linked to the participants.
   (b) Any disclosure of the human participants' responses outside the research could reasonably place the participants at risk of criminal or civil liability or be damaging to the participants' financial standing, employability, or reputation.

3. Research involving the use of educational tests (cognitive, diagnostic, aptitude, achievement), survey procedures, interview procedures, or observation of public behavior that is not exempt under the previous paragraph, if:
   (a) The human participants are elected or appointed public officials or candidates for public office.
   (b) Federal statute(s) require(s) without exception that the confidentiality of the personally identifiable information will be maintained throughout the research and thereafter.

4. Research involving the collection or study of existing data, documents, records, pathological specimens, or diagnostic specimens, if these sources are publicly available or if the information is recorded by the investigator in such a manner that participants cannot be identified, directly or through identifiers linked to the participants.

5. Research and demonstration projects which are conducted by or subject to the approval of federal department or agency heads, and designed to study, evaluate, or otherwise examine:
   (a) Public benefit or service programs.
   (b) Procedures for obtaining benefits or services under those programs.
   (c) Possible changes in or alternatives to those programs or procedures.
   (d) Possible changes in methods or levels of payment for benefits or services under those programs.

6. Taste and food quality evaluation and consumer acceptance studies.

Figure 3.3 Exempt Categories

not a research protocol should be allowed. Pretty much anything that falls outside the exemptions seen in Figure 3.3 can be cause for a full-board review, depending on the university. Typically, IRBs meet once a month at large universities and quarterly at small ones. Some IRBs only meet as needed, so they do not have a specific time frame for reviewing research protocols. If you suspect that your research study will not be exempt, it is often best to plan on a full-board review. If you get lucky and the IRB chair does not think your need a full-board review but rather an expedited review, you will have already completed the work for that level of review.

Specific Ethical Issues for Research

Up to this point this chapter has primarily examined research ethics from an institutional perspective. However, a number of major ethical issues affect the research situation: data accuracy, data sharing, duplicate data publication, post hoc hypothesis revision, participant identity protection, authorship credit, and plagiarism.

Data Accuracy

The first ethical issue relates to the accuracy of your data. Historically, a number of researchers have been found falsifying data in the sciences. Data falsification occurs any time one manipulates or alters the data to achieve the results wanted by the researcher. For example, perhaps a researcher predicted that men who view magazine advertisements of scantily clad women will have more negative views of women. To examine this research question, the researcher conducts a study and finds out that the hypothesis just isn't true. If the researcher then decides to change some participants' scores to slant the study in the direction her or she wants, then the researcher would be falsifying data, which is highly unethical. One of the hardest things for researchers is when a hypothesis just doesn't pan out. However, as scientists we cannot have an agenda for our research. For example, maybe the researcher in our example wanted the data to help further a feminist agenda against advertising. If the data does not support the hypothesis, then the data does not support the hypothesis and should be reported as such. Unfortunately, people both inside and outside of academia will often attach political agendas to scientific research. While it is very tempting to slant our research results in a specific political direction, as researchers we must be honest and forthcoming with all of our results, not just the ones we like.

Data Sharing

Another reason to avoid falsifying data is because researchers are expected to openly share their data with other researchers if asked to do so. Since social scientists are expected to further our understanding of the human process, the only way future scientists can build upon our work is to have access to both the published analysis of our work and the actual data used for publication. There are several reasons why other researchers might be interested in seeing your actual data. First, other researchers may want to reexamine your results if a finding does not make sense. Let's face it, we all make mistakes, and often researchers will make mistakes when reporting results. While the review process a research study goes through before publication should catch any glaring errors, this is not always the case. Second, there is an advanced statistical process called meta-analysis, which attempts to pool the results from numerous studies that examine a specific phenomenon to achieve a greater understanding. While people conducting a meta-analysis can use published results much of the time, meta-analytic research is often much more useful when the original data are used. We must also mention that there is one giant exception to sharing data—if releasing data will violate the participants' rights to anonymity and confidentiality because there is no way to de-identify the data (i.e., unlinkable to the participants), then the researcher has an ethical obligation to protect her or his participants.

Duplicate Data Publication

The next ethical issue that researchers must be aware of is the concept of duplicate data publication, or publishing the same set of data in two different research publications. In academia, publication is considered one of the three pillars of an academic's job (along with teaching and service). While different colleges and universities will have varying degrees of publication requirements for untenured professors, most colleges and universities today expect faculty to publish. For this reason, meeting a college or university's publication requirements is extremely important and extremely competitive. However, some unethical researchers have published the same manuscript or the same data in more than one publication. In essence, these unethical researchers have double-dipped their chip in the salsa, and we all know that is just plain wrong. Along the same lines, other unethical researchers have presented the same paper at numerous conferences. Colleges and universities typically give researchers money to present research at academic conferences, so presenting the same paper at numerous conferences is basically seen as a way to cheat the college or university. Furthermore, if you are presenting the same paper at multiple conferences or publishing identical research in more than one journal, you are also preventing other researchers from presenting and publishing. Conferences and journals have finite space available, so if you double-dip, you prevent someone else from either presenting or publishing.

POST HOC HYPOTHESIS REVISION

The second major ethical area for communication researchers is related to the first because this ethical dilemma involves the treatment of data in relation to proposed hypotheses. This ethical issue involves the revising of hypotheses once an individual receives her or his results. Imagine a researcher predicts, based on previous research, that there will be a relationship between an organization's culture and the organization's web page content. If the researcher then finds that the organization's web page has nothing to do with the organization's culture, her or his proposed hypothesis would be wrong. Most people do not like being wrong, so it is very tempting to just alter the hypothesis (or say that an organization's culture and content on the organization's web page would not be related to each other). When a researcher alters her or his hypotheses to fit the data, the scientific method is weakened, which leads to inaccurate research that cannot help foster future intellectual thought.

PARTICIPANT IDENTITY DISCLOSURES

The third ethical consideration for communication researchers relates to information previously discussed in this chapter—protecting our participants' identities. Often communication researchers will examine sensitive information from participants that could embarrass or harm them (either personally or professionally) if the information was made public. For this reason, communication researchers must make sure that the information obtained from participants is protected. In large-scale quantitative projects, individual participant identity is easier to protect because it is impossible to ascertain one person's responses in a data set that contains 200 participants. However, qualitative researchers often examine data from only a handful of people, so altering demographic information and changing participant names is often necessary to maintain confidentiality.

AUTHORSHIP CREDIT

Authorship credit is basically the notion that ethical researchers give credit where credit is due. According to an article written by the ethics committee of the American Psychological Association (1992), there are three basic aspects to the ethical standard for authorship credit. First, authors should only take credit for research they have actually conducted or to which they have contributed. Historically, there have been cases where researchers have stolen another person's data and published that data as their own. At the same time, one should also note that there is an ethical obligation to make sure that all parties who have actually contributed to the research get credit for their participation, which also relates to the second standard. The second standard for authorship credit is to accurately give credit to all parties involved in the research process. While this may seem to be common sense, there have been a few unethical researchers who would not give students credit for their contribution to research. Whether a contributor is an undergraduate, masters, or doctoral student does not matter—all authors should get credit for their participation in research. Also involved in this ethical standard is the order in which researchers are listed. When listing all of the researchers for an article, authors should be listed in the order of their contribution, not alphabetically or by some other contrived listing format. You may be wondering why the order of authors matters. Well, academia (especially tenure and promotion committees) views the listing of authors very seriously. Often researchers will only get credit from their college or university if they are the principal author or the first author on an article. Ultimately, the order in which authors are listed is somewhat arbitrary, but researchers should be as objective as possible when listing authors to indicate the level of contribution of each one. The final standard for determining authorship credit has to do with a specific type of article, one that stems from a student's master's thesis or doctoral dissertation. According to the ethics committee, if an article contains multiple authors and is based on a thesis or dissertation, then the student should be listed as the first author.

PLAGIARISM

The last ethical area for communication researchers relates to the commonly discussed academic problem of plagiarism. Any time a writer does not properly cite or give credit to any source of information, he or she is plagiarizing. Communication scholars do not claim the "words and ideas of another as their own; they give credit where credit is due" (APA, 2001, p. 349). While the cited sentence in the previous sentence was taken from the American Psychological Association's *Publication Manual*, the sentence is equally applicable for communication scholars. Notice that while the sentence could equally apply to both psychologists and communication researchers, the authors of this text still have cited the American Psychological Association for the information because we did not write it originally ourselves. When people plagiarize, they steal other people's intellectual property and quite possibly infringe upon copyright laws. In the next two chapters we will discuss how to research and how to write research articles. We will emphasize how to correctly cite information using the style format created by the American Psychological Association. For more on how to avoid plagiarism, we recommend Stern (2007).

Conclusion

In this chapter we have examined the ethics of conducting research in today's academic environment. We started the chapter by exploring some of the more controversial research that has been conducted. Then we discussed the nature of ethics and what this meant for communication researchers. Next, we examined the legacy of the Tuskegee experiment and how it ushered in a new era of responsibility and oversight in research involving human subjects. Finally, we discussed four ethical dilemmas that communication researchers often face. While the IRB process is not perfect, it is designed to prevent atrocities that have been seen in previous research. One of the biggest problems that critics have of the IRB process is that it is highly controlled by a biomedical model of research that does not apply well to social scientists (Dougherty & Kramer, 2005; Hamilton, 2005; Koerner, 2005). Maybe one day there will be separate evaluation processes for social scientific and biomedical research endeavors; however, until that happens, we must learn how to present our research protocols in as clear a way as possible for a variety of different audiences.

KEY TERMS

Anonymity
Authorship Credit
Belmont Report
Confidentiality
Data Falsification
Data Sharing
Define Terms or Give
  Examples
Diminished Autonomy
Duplicate Data Publishing

Ends
Ethics
Ethical Behavior
Informed Consent
Institutional Review Board
Justice
Machiavellian Ethic
Means
Plagiarism

Post Hoc Hypothesis
  Revision
Principle of Beneficence
Privacy
Protected Health
  Information (PHI)
Research Participant
Subjective Ethic
Unethical Behavior

REFERENCES

Dougherty, D. S., & Kramer, M. W. (2005). A rationale for scholarly examination of Institutional Review Boards: A case study. *Journal of Applied Communication Research, 33*, 183–188.

Ethics Committee. (1992). Ethical principles of psychologists and Code of Conduct. *American Psychologist, 47*, 1612–1628.

Garramone, G. M., & Kennamer, J. D. (1989). Ethical considerations in mass communications research. *Journal of Mass Media Ethics, 4*, 174–185.

Hamilton, A. (2005). The development and operation of IRBs: Medical regulations and social science. *Journal of Applied Communication Research, 33*, 189–203.

Humphreys, L. (1975). *Tearoom trade: Impersonal sex in public places.* Chicago: Aldine.

Koerner, A. F. (2005). Communication scholars' communication and relationship with their IRBs. *Journal of Applied Communication Research, 33*, 231–241.

Latané, B., & Darley, J. M. (1970). *The unresponsive bystander: Why doesn't he help?* Englewood Cliffs, NJ: Prentice-Hall.

McCroskey, J. C., Wrench, J. S., & Richmond, V. P., (2003). *Principles of public speaking.* Indianapolis, IN: The College Network.

Milgram, S. (1974). *Obedience to authority: An experimental view.* New York: Harper & Row.

Natham, R. (2005). *My freshman year: What a professor learned by becoming a student.* Ithaca, NY: Cornell University Press.

National Institutes of Health. (2002). *Human participant protections education for research teams.* Washington, DC: US Department of Health and Human Services National Institutes of Health.

Publication Manual of the American Psychological Association (5th ed.). (2001). Washington, DC: American Psychological Association.

Stern, L. (2007). *What every student should know about…avoiding plagiarism.* Boston: Allyn & Bacon.

Vaughan, T. R. (1967). Governmental intervention in social research: Political and ethical dimensions in the Wichita jury recordings. In G. Sjoberg (Ed.), *Ethics, politics, and social research* (pp. 50–77). Cambridge, MA: Schenkman.

Wrench, J. S. (2002). *HIPPA for research: Understanding how the Health Insurance Portability & Accountability Act of 1996 affects clinical research.* Lewisburg, WV: West Virginia School of Osteopathic Medicine.

Zimbardo, P. G., Haney, C., Banks, W. C., & Jaffe, D. (1973, April 8). The mind is a formidable jailer: A pirandellian prison. *New York Times Magazine, 122*, 38–60.

Searching for Previous Research and APA Style

Formulating an idea for a research project can be intriguing, or it can be frustrating. If the researcher already has a question or idea in mind, the process can be relatively easy, in fact it could almost be considered a "mystery" to be solved. However, there are aspects of the process that can be frustrating if the researcher lacks the knowledge or tools for finding answers.

Chapter 1 focused on the role of theory in social scientific research and provided a model of communication. While the topics we discuss in this chapter can be applied to any social scientific field, as communication researchers we must always keep communication in our minds when thinking about research. This chapter provides an overview of the research process and will assist in creating a road map for conducting a communication research project. After all, before starting out on a journey it's a good idea to have a game plan for getting there! At the conclusion of this chapter, you will be able to identify a communication topic to research, understand the options available for examining and summarizing the communication research that already exists on your topic, and organize and cite sources of information to report your research.

Research takes time and should be approached in much the same way that a mystery would be analyzed on your favorite TV crime drama. Before beginning the investigation, the "detective" (researcher) must establish a game plan. The investigator should have a fairly good idea of the question to be answered, or he or she will spend many hours working to solve nothing at all. In order to understand the background of the question or mystery, evidence in the form of information and facts must be gathered. All of the evidence must be synthesized or organized in order to help you, the researcher/detective, establish a logical answer to the research/mystery.

In research, there are five preliminary steps to beginning a research project that will be discussed in this chapter: (1) identifying the question or topic to investigate; (2) clarifying the research question and generating a list of key terms and concepts; (3) locating potential sources of background information on the topic; (4) organizing and evaluating information; and (5) citing sources of information using a standard format.

Step One: Identifying the Topic

The first step in beginning the communication research project involves choosing a topic or question about communication to investigate. For some people, picking a communication topic can be one of the most daunting tasks. After all, the research project will consume a considerable amount of time, so researchers often put pressure on themselves to find the "perfect" communication topic. Some researchers have indicated that choosing a topic has been the easiest part of their research process because they draw on events that have happened in their own lives and seek answers. For example, maybe you'll be reading a research article and some question will pop into your head, or maybe you'll just be taking a shower one morning and go *Hmmm, I wonder if anyone has researched that before!?* Every researcher has a different process he or she goes through when creating a research project. However, there are some tips that can assist you in finding a research topic to start your research journey.

First and foremost, be sure that you understand why you are doing the research. Are you doing the research to get published or because you have to take a research methods class and are given an assignment to complete? Even before you begin thinking about a topic, you need to clarify why you are conducting the research in the first place. Some questions to consider if conducting research for a college class may include:

- Is the focus on a specific communication context or phenomenon? For example, is the goal of the project to select a topic that focuses on communication in the health care setting? Or is the goal of the project to examine a personality variable as it relates to communication?
- What types of sources are required? Should the search for sources focus exclusively on scholarly journals, or can sources from popular magazines and newspapers be included? Can websites be included as sources?

- Is there a particular number of resources that should be cited?
- What style format should be used? Is American Psychological Association (APA) format acceptable, or should the project adhere to Modern Language Association (MLA) guidelines or another format (Chicago Style, International Medical Journal Style, etc.)?

If you are not conducting research for a specific class, there are other questions you need to consider as well:

- Are you conducting the research for an organization or for your own personal use?
- What do you plan to do with the research when it's been conducted? (publish it, present it somewhere, etc.)
- Will other people be interested in the research you are conducting?

The second step to ensuring a successful research experience involves selecting a topic that interests you personally. You will experience greater motivation to spend time exploring sources and collecting data if the topic is one that you have an interest in studying. Since this book assumes that you plan on focusing your research to examine a communication phenomenon, keep reminding yourself to concentrate on messages and meaning when identifying the research topic.

Research ideas can come from a variety of sources or experiences. Ideas can result from a conversation, other research articles, media examples, current events, or even a professor! If you experience difficulty in identifying a research topic, consider brainstorming. Get together with a group of friends or family members and generate a list of ideas. Browse through current magazines and newspapers to see if there is a "hot" topic that has been the subject of attention. Examine a textbook or browse a subject-specific online database on a library website (for example, Communication and Mass Media Complete—CMCC in EBSCO Host) for ideas. Conduct a word or subject search using key terms that describe your interests.

As stated earlier, an idea for research can result from a casual conversation. For example, the idea for a study conducted by Thomas, Booth-Butterfield, and Booth-Butterfield (1995) resulted from a lunch conversation between friends. During the conversation, the friends discussed what had happened during the previous weekend. One of the women (Stacey) mentioned that she had visited her sister and her niece. During dinner Stacey had casually asked her sister, "So when is Joe [your husband] moving out?" The shocked expression on her niece's face followed by the question, "Why is Daddy moving out?" led her to the realization that she had just disclosed to her niece that her parents were divorcing before they had an opportunity to discuss it with her. Her niece became upset and angry, and accused her mother of lying to her. Stacey felt horrible! Would Stacey's niece continue to blame her sister for the divorce? As a result of hearing this story, Thomas, Booth-Butterfield, and Booth-Butterfield (1995) decided to investigate the impact of disclosure of the decision to divorce on a child's level of communication satisfaction with her or his parents. More specifically, the researchers wanted to see if children reported more communication satisfaction with the parent who told them about the decision to divorce. Would the child of a divorce perceive the parent who revealed the decision to divorce as being more honest and the other parent as being more deceptive?

To exhaust all options for identifying the topic for a project, consider a variety of sources for potential topics. Three possible sources include reflecting on personal experiences, reviewing literature, and developing questions from existing theories. Let's build on the earlier example regarding the use of personal experiences. We discussed how the idea for a research study on divorce disclosures evolved from a personal conversation. In research methods classes we have taught, students often use their own experiences to come up with ideas for research projects. One student decided to research the verbal aggressiveness of hockey parents as a result of watching parents yelling and screaming at the teams, players, and officials during his son's hockey games. Another student decided to research the use of interpersonal deception after watching several episodes of a reality television show *Big Brother*. Both of these topics were the result of personal experiences. Yet another student focused on communication strategies used to inform employees of impending downsizing in a local organization after reading an article in her local newspaper. Potential research topics are everywhere!

Yet another major way that researchers often find topics is by reading the literature within a specific communication context. For example, maybe you're reading an article on computer-mediated communication. While reading the article you realize that a lot of research has examined the use of chat rooms and instant messaging, but no one has really looked at how cell phone text messaging affects communication. Most research studies conducted probably stem from this type of initial noticing of "gaps" in research. These gaps come in a variety of different forms:

1. Some researchers realize that there is information missing in a specific context, like our example comparing computer instant messaging to cell phone text messaging. While research on computer instant messaging has been around for a decade, cell phone text messaging is still a fairly recent phenomenon, so it is clearly a new context to revisit older research findings.

2. A second type of gap you may notice deals with samples. For example, maybe when looking at research on the use of e-mail you notice that little research has been conducted on retired individuals. Obviously, retired people and college students may have very different uses for e-mail, so examining a communication phenomenon in different samples is extremely important.

3. A third type of research occurs when you notice that information simply needs to be updated. Research in the area of computer-mediated communication dates back to the late 1980s and early 1990s. While the research results of the late 1980s were interesting, do those results still hold true in the twenty-first century? As computer and Internet technology have rapidly advanced, do people still respond to computer-mediated communication in the same way as they did in the late 1990s? Since people change with time, revisiting older studies in an updated fashion can be extremely important.

4. The fourth type of research gap comes in the form of conceptual gaps, i.e., simply no one has studied a specific concept. While talking with other researchers or reading research literature, we often have "aha" moments where we realize that some aspect of human communication hasn't been studied at all. Of course, it's always important to doublecheck the literature to make sure that your "new" concept is actually something someone hasn't studied under a different term.

5. The last gap that researchers attempt to answer is theoretically driven. If you remember our discussion of theories in Chapter 2, we discussed the notion that theories must be able to be proven false. For this reason, scientists will often examine a theory to make sure the theory stays true across a wide range of communication circumstances. Since theoretically driven research is extremely common in communication, let's look at this area in more detail.

Berger and Calabrese (1975) created one of the most important theories of interpersonal communication called uncertainty reduction theory (URT). At its very basic level, URT posits that people will attempt to reduce uncertainty through our interactions with others in initial interactions. The goal of these initial interactions is to increase our ability to make *predictions* about another person in order to *explain* the outcomes of the interaction. One of the reasons why URT has had the longevity that is has had in communication is because it is built on eight axioms (generally accepted principles or rules). While we cannot go into detail here about the eight axioms of URT, we do recommend that you read either Berger and Calabrese (1975) or the summary of URT research by West and Turner (2006). For our example, we will examine the eighth axiom from Berger and Calabrese: shared communication networks reduce uncertainty, while lack of shared networks increases uncertainty. In essence, this axiom posits the idea that the more people have shared communication networks (they find out they have friends in common, coworkers in common, etc.), the less uncertainty they will experience while interacting. However, the more different their communication networks are (they know none of the same people), the more uncertainty they will have while interacting. When completing theoretically driven research, researchers will look at a part of a theory and think, "How can I test the theory?" Maybe you want to examine parental uncertainty while interacting with their children's teachers. So you set out to determine if parents who have more communication network ties with teachers (e.g., they go to the same church, have friends in common, belong to the same social group) experience less uncertainty while interacting with their children's teachers than parents who share no common communication networks with their children's teachers. In essence, we have chosen to examine part of a theory, determined how to use the theory in a specific communication context, and can now set out to either provide more support for the theory or possibly provide information that contradicts the theory.

Overall, this section has introduced you to a variety of different methods researchers can use to go about creating research studies. Whether a researcher simply has an "a-ha" moment at 3 AM or sets out to purposely test a theory, the next step in the research process is to further clarify the research question and generate a list of key terms to help you find previously conducted research.

Step Two: Clarifying the Research Question and Generating Key Terms

Once a general topic has been identified, the next step is to develop and refine the topic to begin the search for existing information. There are three primary steps involved in this process: (1) state your topic in the form of a question (realize that this may result in more than one question depending on your topic); (2) identify key terms and concepts from the question(s); and (3) generate a list of key term synonyms that can be used to search for background information.

STATING THE TOPIC IN THE FORM OF A RESEARCH QUESTION

The first step in refining your topic involves stating your research topic in the form of a question. We've included a worksheet (Figure 4.1) that can assist you in working through the process of clarifying the research question and identifying potential sources. Note that the first step asks for the *initial* research question. We use the term "initial" because the research question may undergo multiple revisions as you examine existing sources of information. You may discover that the initial question is too broad or too narrow. Or once you begin the search for information, you might find out that your initial question has already been answered through previous research.

Suppose you've recently experienced the end of a romantic relationship. Based on your own experience, you decide that the topic of your research project will be terminating relationships. Since this topic is extremely broad, we need to narrow the focus to help formulate

1. **What is your initial research question(s)?**

2. **What do you already know about this topic?** List any information you currently have about your topic

3. **What keywords can you use to assist you in conducting a library search?** Be sure to include synonyms for all terms identified!

4. **What resources should you examine to begin your review of literature?**

Electronic databases	Websites	Encyclopedias/ Handbooks

5. **Begin your search for information.** Be sure to complete a summary sheet for each source you think will be useful for your study!

6. **Review and evaluate the information.** What did you discover from your research?

What questions have been answered?

What questions remain unanswered?

Should any studies be replicated?

7. **Evaluate your sources.** Now that the initial research process is complete, revise your initial research question.

Figure 4.1 Research Planning Worksheet

a specific research question. Some things you might want to consider in refining your topic and writing the initial research questions might include:

- What type of relationship should be examined? Friendships, romantic relationships, or family relationships?
- Is there a particular relational role that should be the focus of the study? The person who initiates the termination? Or the recipient?
- How is communication related to the topic? Should the focus be on strategies used to terminate relationships?

As you can see, there are several "mini-questions" that need to be addressed before creating the initial research question. Let's suppose you decided that the focus of your study will be on the messages used by partners to communicate the end of a romantic relationship. The initial research question could be phrased as, "What communication strategies are used to terminate romantic relationships?" That's simple enough! But keep in mind that this research question may need to be revised as we continue through the remaining steps indicated on the Research Planning Worksheet (Figure 4.1).

Step 2 on the worksheet asks the researcher to identify what information is already known about the topic. Think about your own experiences and what you've studied in communication, psychology, family studies, history, biology, or any other class that you've taken. People in a wide variety of fields help communication scholars more fully understand communication phenomenon. What do you already know about communication strategies that are used to end romantic relationships? Probably the most obvious thing that you already know is that relational partners might avoid engaging in communication behaviors. You might even recall studying relationship dissolution in an interpersonal communication class. Maybe your own experience involved the use of deception. Brainstorm and think of anything that you already know about the topic. This information will be useful as you begin generating key concepts to describe your research topic.

IDENTIFYING KEY TERMS AND SYNONYMOUS TERMS

Once the initial research question has been developed, the next step involves identifying key words and concepts that can be used to describe the ideas included in your question.

Let's take a closer look at how Wrench and Booth-Butterfield (2003) generated the topic and research questions for their study examining physicians' use of humor and patient compliance and satisfaction. This project evolved as a result of their interest in humor, health communication, and compliance. Following are some initial questions that created the foundation for the study:

- Are patients more likely to listen to the advice of doctors who are humorous?
- Are patients more satisfied if their doctor uses humor?
- Do patients perceive doctors who use humor as being more credible?

By examining the questions more closely, key concepts and terms emerge to guide the search for information that has already been published on the topic. Create a list of the key terms included in your questions, but realize that these terms alone might not be sufficient to conduct your review of existing literature. Additional terms that are synonymous with the key terms should be included in the list of words that will be used to conduct the library search. Don't be afraid to list any and all words that could be used to describe your topic. Be sure to include both broad and narrow terms to describe each concept. Figure 4.2 includes sample questions and key terms that could be used to find sources for Wrench and

Questions	Key terms from questions	Related terms
Are patients more likely to listen to the directions of doctors who are humorous?	patient listen doctor	obey compliance requests message physician health
Are patients more satisfied if their doctor uses humor?	patient satisfaction doctor humor	physician message health
Do patients perceive doctors who use humor as being more credible?	patient doctor humor credibility	physician expertise

Figure 4.2 Key and Related Search Terms

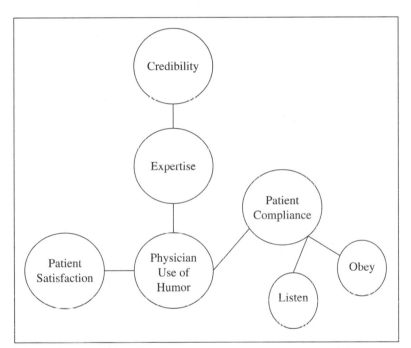

Figure 4.3 Brainstorming Map

Booth-Butterfield's study. The column on the far right lists synonyms for the key terms that were taken directly from potential research questions.

As you generate lists of key terms to represent the research question, it may be useful to visually represent and organize your ideas by creating a concept map (also known as a web diagram). Doing so will create a picture of concepts that fit together and can assist in organizing ideas as you begin writing your review of literature (see Chapter 5). Think of the concept map as a "tree" for organizing ideas. The central concept of the research project serves as the tree trunk or the foundation for the project. The branches of the tree represent the concepts or ideas that the researcher wants to examine in relation to the central concept. Finally, the twigs are used to represent the terms that are synonymous with those represented by the branches. A concept map of Wrench and Booth-Butterfield's (2003) study might look like Figure 4.3. Since the concept of physician humor is central to the study, it is placed at the center of the diagram. Next, patient compliance, patient satisfaction, and expertise are included in the surrounding circles since the goal is to see how these concepts are linked to a doctor's use of humor. It is important to continue generating terms that are synonymous with these key concepts and to include additional terms on the diagram. Suppose when searching for information in the library you discover that the words used in the search returns only a few examples of books or articles that have examined the topic. At that point it is helpful to have the list of related terms to aid in broadening the search. If a search for physician humor and credibility results in only three articles, the terms "doctor" and "expertise" could be included in a subsequent search to see if more articles can be found. Remember to include communication, messages, and meaning as the central focus of your research.

Step Three: Locating Sources of Information

Once you've identified the initial research question and key concepts, the next task involves searching for information that has already been published on the topic. In Chapter 1 we stated that a primary goal of research is to produce new knowledge that explains the "how" and "why" of communication. In order to build new knowledge, it is important to search for the information that already exists on a topic. After all, how useful would it be to keep answering the same research question over and over? As you review existing articles on your topic, you will notice "gaps" or unanswered questions to help you refine your initial research question.

We also need to note that you are likely to come across two basic types of sources while looking for previous literature: primary and secondary. Hairston and Ruszkiewicz (1996) define primary sources as "materials on a topic upon which subsequent interpretations or studies are based, anything from firsthand documents such as poems, diaries, court records, and interviews to research results generated by experiments, surveys, ethnographies, and so on" (p. 547). While the first part of this definition is not useful for our discussion, the second part specifically relates to research results generated by experiments and surveys. In other words, primary research reports the results of a study actually conducted by the author(s). Secondary sources, on the other hand, are restatements or analyses of the primary research. For example, when you read an academic article, the first section is the review of literature. Within this review, the new article's author(s) summarizes pre-existing research on a subject. This summarization of pre-existing research is secondary because the new article's author did not conduct the research found in the literature review. Conversely, when the new article then explains what the author actually did in the study, the author is generating primary research because he or she is describing what was done in the current project. We want to make this distinction very clear here because many students fall into the trap of citing secondary sources from an author's literature review within the student's literature review without ever reading the original source. We always recommend going back to the original source whenever possible because you may find something in the primary source that is more helpful to your research than what is discussed by the secondary source. Avoiding the use of secondary sources within your own writing does not mean that secondary sources are not useful. Often if we read a secondary source written on a given topic at the beginning of the research process, we can cut the amount of time we have to spend looking for literature greatly because the secondary source can help us get an understanding of the breadth of information on a given topic. In essence, secondary sources are very useful when starting the research process because they help you quickly grasp the general research subject area before you delve into the primary research. There is one notable exception to the above-mentioned qualifications for use of secondary sources. If the primary source exists in a language you do not read, then citing the secondary source's translation of the primary source is appropriate. Now that we've explained the differences between primary and secondary sources, we can look at the types of primary sources that exist.

TYPES OF INFORMATION SOURCES

While it may be easy to turn on the computer and use a popular search engine such as Google or Yahoo! to compile a list of resources, scholarly research involves searching a variety of sources for relevant information. Obviously, the best place to begin a quest for information is your campus library. Remember—librarians are our friends, so treat them well. Librarians enjoy being asked to assist students in locating sources of information if you do it nicely! Think of the librarian as a tour guide. There are literally thousands of sources and strategies that can be used to search for existing literature. In fact, some of our former students have said that they avoid the library because they suffer from "information overload." There are so many sources of information that they aren't sure where to begin the search. A librarian can help navigate the options available to make your search more efficient and effective. Information about your research topic can come from a variety of sources. Of course, the sources you select for information will depend on the question you are trying to answer. The most common sources of information are books, magazines, scholarly journals, magazines, newspapers, encyclopedias, handbooks, and the World Wide Web.

A summary of the different types of information sources is included in Figure 4.4. The type of information needed will dictate the selection of the information source. Remember—research projects require you to conduct a review of existing scholarly literature on your topic. Students often flock to popular magazines and websites for information on a topic. After all, they are familiar with various magazines and they are fairly easy to locate. Students express reluctance about reviewing scholarly sources. The language used in journal articles is sometimes foreign to beginning researchers. But there are shortcuts that can help you sift through scholarly articles to locate information you can understand. We recommend reviewing the abstract first, which will provide an overview of the article. Next, skim the review of literature to see what key concepts the researchers examined in the project. Finally, take a look at the discussion section. What were the conclusions that the researcher made as a result of the study? As you progress through this book, we will provide you with more tools for interpreting and writing scholarly research, but for the time being it is important to note the differences between magazines and scholarly journal articles so you can understand what each has to offer when conducting your review of literature. A summary of their differences is provided in Figure 4.5.

Scholarly journals are fairly easy to identify based on the title alone. Many of them contain the word "journal" in the title, or they may contain a reference to the frequency of publication (e.g., "Quarterly" "Annual"). Another clue can be found by flipping through the pages of the publication. While popular magazines are designed to grab the reader's attention with their glossy pages and use of color and photographs, the appearance of scholarly magazines tends to be very plain. Rarely will you find photographs in these publications, rather you will notice the use of graphs, tables, and charts depicting the results of data analysis. Scholarly journals should always be at the top of your list of information sources to consult when conducting a research study. Figure 4.6 contains a list of many of the major journals in which communication research is published. While this list is long, it is in no way exhaustive. In fact, communication-related work is often published in a wide range of journals, so do not think that the list provided is exhaustive.

Source type	When to use	Examples
Books	• To search for comprehensive coverage of a topic. • To locate historical information on the topic. • To find summaries of research conducted on the topic.	• McGhee, P.E. (1999). *Health, healing and the amuse system: Humor as survival training*. Dubuque, IA: Kendall Hunt. • Robinson, V. (1991). *Humor and health professions* (2nd ed.). Thorofare, NJ: Slack.
Magazines	• To examine information or opinions on topics related to popular culture. • To locate current, up-to-date information on a topic. • To review articles written in general "layman" terms.	• Patients pleased; doctors surprised. (1998, June). *Physician's Management, 38*(6), 12. • Laugh it off. (2005, June). *Prevention, 58*(6), 55.
Scholarly journals	• To search for scholarly research articles. • To identify what research has already been conducted on a topic. • To review reference lists of existing research to assist in locating other potential sources.	• Wanzer, M., Booth-Butterfield, M., & Booth-Butterfield, S. (1995). The funny people: A source orientation to the communication of humor. *Communication Quarterly, 43,* 142–154. • Wolf, M.H., Putnam, S.M., James, S.A., & Stiles, W.B. (1978). The medical interview satisfaction scale: Development of a scale to measure patient perceptions of physician behavior. *Journal of Behavioral Medicine, 1,* 391–401.
Newspapers	• To identify the most current information on topic of interest. • To review editorial and commentaries on a topic of interest.	• Howlett, D. (2003, March 4). It hurts not to laugh. *USA Today,* p. D9.
Encyclopedias and handbooks	• To locate comprehensive summaries or background information on a topic. • To identify key concepts, authors, or dates.	• *Nature Encyclopedia of Life Sciences* • *Encyclopedia of Rhetoric* • *Handbook of Interpersonal Communication*
World Wide Web	• To locate statistics and quick facts. • To identify opinions of others on a topic. • To connect to library resources.	• http://www.thehumorcollection.org/health_articles.html. Retrieved July 25, 2005. • http://www.doaj.org—Directory of Open Access Journals

Figure 4.4 Types of Information Sources

	Scholarly	Popular
Author	Written by experts in a specific field. Institutional affiliation is typically included.	Written by staff members, freelance writers, or anonymous sources.
Audience	Readers familiar with discipline's terminology and research history. Typically professors, researchers, and students.	General audience
Documentation	Extensive citations to reference other research studies. Typically include a reference page.	Includes little or no documentation outside of quotes by "witnesses."
Writing style	Scholarly and formal	Informal, casual language designed to inform or entertain.
Review process	Peer-reviewed	Not peer-reviewed
Publication	Published less frequently (quarterly, annually)	Published frequently (weekly, monthly)
Appearance	Plain. Graphics typically include charts, tables, and graphs.	Appealing to the eye. Colorful with several pictures and advertisements.
Examples	*Communication Quarterly* *Journal of Applied Communication*	*Time* *Sports Illustrated* *US News and World Report*

Figure 4.5 Distinctions Between Scholarly Journals and Popular Magazines

Academy of Management Journal
American Anthropologist
American Behavioral Scientist
American Journal of Psychology
American Journal of Sociology
American Political Science Review
American Psychologist
American Sociological Review
Archives of Psychology
Argumentation and Advocacy
Asian Journal of Communication
Audio-Visual Communication Review
Australian Journal of Communication
Basic and Applied Social Psychology
Behavioral Science
Behavior
British Journal of Psychology
British Journal of Social and Clinical Psychology
British Journal of Sociology
Canadian Journal of Behavioral Science
Canadian Journal of Communication
Central States Speech Journal
Child Development
Columbia Journalism Review
Communication and Cognition
Communication and Critical/Cultural Studies
Communication and Research
Communication Book Notes Quarterly
Communication Education[2]
Communication Law and Policy
Communication Monographs[2]
Communication Quarterly[4]
Communication Reports[6]
Communication Research
Communication Research Reports[4]
Communication Studies[3]
Communication Teacher[2]
Communication Theory[1]
Communication Yearbook
Critical Studies in Mass Communication[2]
Current Directions in Psychological Science
Editor and Publisher
ETC: A Review of General Semantics
European Journal of Communication
European Journal of Social Psychology
Family Process
Family Relations
Gender and Communication
Group and Organization Management
Health Communication
Howard Journal of Communication
Human Communication Research[1]
Human Organization
Human Relationships
HUMOR
Intermedia

Journal of General Psychology
Journal of Health Communication
Journal of Homosexuality
Journal of Intercultural Communication
  Research
Journal of Intergroup Relations
Journal of International Communication
Journal of Marketing Research
Journal of Marriage and the Family
Journal of Media and Religion
Journal of Nonverbal Behavior
Journal of Personality and Social Psychology
Journal of Popular Culture
Journal of Popular Film and Television
Journal of Psychology
Journal of Social and Personal Relationships
Journal of Social Issues
Journal of Social Psychology
Journal of Speech and Hearing Research
Journal of Verbal Learning and Verbal
  Behavior
Journal of Written Communication
Journal of Public Relations Research
Journalism Educator
Journalism Monographs
Journalism & Mass Communications
  Quarterly
Language and Speech
Language and Society
Learning and Motivation
Management Communication Quarterly
Management Science
Mass Communication Review
Media, Culture, and Society
Memory and Cognition
New Jersey Journal of Communication
Newspaper Research Journal
Ohio Journal of Communication
Organizational Behavior and Human
Performance
Personality and Social Psychology Bulletin
Personal Relationships
Personnel Psychology
Philosophy and Rhetoric
Political Behavior
Political Communication
Political Communication Review
Political Science Quarterly
Politics and Society
Progress in Communication Science
Psychological Bulletin
Psychological Record
Psychological Reports
Psychological Review
Psychological Science
Psychological Science in the Public Interest

Figure 4.6 Partial List of Communication Journals

Continued

Continued

International Journal of Listening	*Public Relations Journal*
International Journal of Psychology	*Public Relations Quarterly*
International Organization	*Public Relations Review*
International Political Science Review	*Quarterly Journal of Speech*[2]
International Social Science Journal	*Qualitative Research Reports in*
Journal of Abnormal and Social Psychology	* Communication*[4]
Journal of Advertising	*Risk Analysis: An International Journal*
Journal of Advertising Research	*Science Communication*
Journal of Anthropological Research	*Semiotica*
Journal of Applied Behavior Analysis	*Sex Roles: A Journal of Research*
Journal of Applied Communication Research[2]	*Signs: Journal of Women in Culture and*
Journal of Applied Psychology	*Society*
Journal of Asian Pacific Communication	*Small Group Research*
Journal of Black Studies	*Social Forces*
Journal of Broadcasting and Electronic Media	*Social Science Research*
Journal of Business	*Sociological Inquiry*
Journal of Business Communication	*Sociological Methods and Research*
Journal of Business and Technical Communication	*Sociological Quarterly*
Journal of Business Research	*Sociology: Journal of the British Sociological*
Journal of Clinical Psychology	* Association*
Journal of Communication[1]	*Sociometry: Social Psychology Quarterly*
Journal of Communication and Religion	*Southern Communication Journal*[5]
Journal of Computer Mediated Communication	*Studies in Communication*
Journal of Conflict Resolution	*Television Quarterly*
Journal of Consumer Research	*Text and Performance Quarterly*[2]
Journal of Cross-Cultural Psychology	*The Review of Communication*[2]
Journal of Educational Psychology	*Vital Speeches of the Day*
Journal of Experimental Psychology	*Washington Journalism Review*
Journal of Experimental Social Psychology	*Western Journal of Communication*[6]
Journal of Family Communication	*Women's Studies*
Psychology of Women Quarterly	*Women's Studies in Communication*
Public Administration Review	*Women's Studies International Quarterly*
Public Opinion Quarterly	*World Communication*

[1] *Journal Sponsored by the International Communication Association.*
[2] *Journal Sponsored by the National Communication Association.*
[3] *Central States Communication Association.*
[4] *Eastern Communication Association.*
[5] *Southern States Communication Association.*
[6] *Western States Communication Association.*

LOCATING INFORMATION SOURCES

Just as a variety of information sources exist to assist you in conducting a review of existing literature on a topic, a variety of search tools exists to assist you in locating the specific sources of information. Often students comment that "I searched for books on the library home page and there are no sources on my topic." While this could be due to the fact that the topic is unique or recent and there may not be any books dedicated to the specific topic, as a researcher you shouldn't stop the quest for existing literature! Just as it is important to know which tools are most beneficial for fixing or building something, understanding which sources are the best "tools" to use in your search for sources is essential to a successful research project. A common mistake made by beginning researchers is that they experience "tunnel vision" when searching for sources. Remember the earlier example where we expanded the list of key terms to include in our search for information on physician use of humor? Just as we broadened our scope of concepts to explore, we need to broaden our scope of resources or tools to use in the search for literature. Three excellent tools for beginning the search include handbooks and subject encyclopedias, electronic databases, and the World Wide Web. The fourth item on your Research Planning Worksheet (Figure 4.1) asks you to identify examples of each of these tools to assist you in beginning your search for information.

Handbooks and Subject Encyclopedias

The first step in any research project should involve examining printed resources that provide comprehensive coverage of topics in a given subject area. Two excellent resources for locating general sources of information are handbooks and subject encyclopedias. Using your key concepts, a search of general reference resources can direct you to bibliographies and summaries of research that has been conducted on your topic. As you search these sources, be sure to take careful notes about any additional key terms and concepts used to describe your topic.

Handbooks provide a comprehensive summary of past research and often include commentaries or recommendations for future research directions. The handbook is an excellent starting point for identifying the themes that have been used to examine a topic. While they provide a broad look at communication, the fact that many handbooks focus on specific contexts make them useful for examining the historical foundations of a specific topic area. Examples of handbooks include the following:

- Handbook of Attitudes
- Handbook of Closeness and Intimacy
- Handbook of Communication and Social Interaction Skills
- Handbook of Communication Science
- Handbook of Conflict Communication
- Handbook of Family Communication
- Handbook of Gender and Communication
- Handbook of Group Communication Theory and Research
- Handbook of Health Communication
- Handbook of Instructional Communication: Rhetorical and Relational Perspectives
- Handbook of International and Intercultural Communication
- Handbook of Interpersonal Communication
- Handbook of Language and Social Interaction
- Handbook of Media Studies
- Handbook of Nonverbal Communication
- Handbook of Organizational Communication
- Handbook of Organizational Justice
- Handbook of Personality Development
- Handbook of Political Communication
- Handbook of Public Relations
- Handbook of Sexuality in Close Relationships
- Handbook of Visual Communication

- Media Handbook, The
- Work and Family Handbook, The

Subject encyclopedias are a bit different from the *Encyclopedia Britannica*, with which most of us are familiar. The *International Encyclopedia of Communication* was published in 1989 and most recently in 2007 and is the first communication subject encyclopedia of its kind. Bibliographies and articles covering a variety of communication contexts are included. The index of this source is particularly useful for building your list of key terms and concepts.

Electronic Databases

Considering the prevalence of computers in our lives, it should come as no surprise that the most efficient and comprehensive searches for sources are conducted using electronic databases. Your professors have probably shared stories of the "good old days" when they had to search for sources using tools called "card catalogs" and "periodical indexes." Listen to their stories (trust us, they're telling the truth!), hug your computer, and be thankful that search strategies have come a long way! A task that used to take researchers many hours can now be accomplished in a fraction of the time. With the list of key concepts identified in Step 2 in hand, it's time to begin the journey.

Electronic databases (also referred to as "computerized" or "online" databases) can be thought of as a virtual library index where you can search for articles and books. Have you ever looked in the index of a book to find a specific topic or concept? It's much easier to find the term "paralanguage" in a 300-page textbook with the assistance of the index. Electronic databases serve as an enormous index. They search through literally thousands of records in seconds to help you find books and articles containing the keywords you use to search. There are literally hundreds of databases to choose from, so the most difficult task may be selecting the one that best suits your research needs. Most libraries list databases both alphabetically and according to subject or content area for ease of searching. Figure 4.7 includes a sample list of electronic databases useful for locating resources specific to communication and related areas. Included in the right-hand column is information about the format of information in the database as well as a general description of the types of articles included. An excellent starting point to search for articles on any communication topics is the Communication and Mass Media Complete database (also known as CMMC) located in EBSCO Host. It contains abstracts, citations, and some full-text articles. It's important to note that libraries may not be able to provide access to all the databases included on this list. Many electronic databases require a subscription to allow access, so your ability to search particular databases is dependent on whether your library subscribes to them. Suppose your research topic is on teacher use of humor in the classroom. While CMMC is an excellent starting point for locating articles that have focused specifically on communication, be sure to search the ERIC database, which includes articles that have been published by scholars in the field of education. Figure 4.7 contains a list of a wide variety of databases that your college or university may have access to online. If you do not know if your library has access, ask your friendly research librarian for help.

Once you have identified the database that best suits your research needs, the next step involves selecting the type of search you wish to conduct. There are a variety of fields or criteria that can be used to search for articles. These include:

- Subject search—searches for key terms that the author has submitted to the subject field to describe the article or book
- Title search—searches the title field for words included in the title of an article or book
- Author search—searches for the author's name in the author field

Database	Type of information
Academic Search Premier	• Full text articles and abstracts • Social sciences, humanities, education, language/linguistics, and ethnic studies
Business Source Premiere	• Full text articles and abstracts • Management, economics, finance, and international business
Communication Abstracts	• Full text articles and abstracts • Interpersonal, mass, organizational, and small group communication; journalism; and public relations
Communications and Mass Media Complete	• Full text articles and abstracts • Access to bibliographic references, reviews, encyclopedias, and handbooks • Communication studies and media studies
ComAbstracts (CIOS)	• Citations, abstracts, and some full-text articles • Covers 60 primary communication journals
CQ Researcher (Congressional Quarterly)	• Full-text articles; complete summaries and information on all sides of the issue covered • Focus on current or controversial issues
ERIC	• Citations from journals and reports • Field of education and related areas • Sponsored by the U.S. Department of Education
Findarticles.com	• Full-text archive of published articles • Covers more than 500 magazines and journals • Topics include business, health, technology, entertainment, sports, and more
LexisNexis Academic	• Full text and abstracts • Popular, scholarly, trade, and professional periodicals.
Newspaper Source	• Selected full text articles, indexes, and abstracts • Over 180 regional U.S. newspapers, international newspapers, newswires, newspaper columns and other sources • Full-text television and radio news transcripts are provided from CBS News, FOX News, NPR, etc.
PsycINFO	• Abstracts, citations, and some full-text articles • Includes books, book chapters, and dissertations • Psychology and related disciplines
Papers First	• Full-text and abstracts • Papers presented at conferences worldwide, covering every congress, symposium, exposition, workshop, and meeting
Proceedings First	• Tables of contents of papers • Papers presented at conferences worldwide.
Social Science Citation Index	• Abstracts and citations • Coverage from nearly 50 social science disciplines

Figure 4.7 Types of Databases

We recommend conducting a subject search first. For example, the key terms "humor" and "physician" could be used to conduct a subject search. But suppose only a few results are returned from this search. Remember that the subject search only includes the key terms provided by the author to be entered into the subject field, and the terms you entered must match those that the author supplied exactly. Suppose the author described an article using the term "doctor" instead of "physician." It's likely your initial subject search would not retrieve this article.

Attempt the search again by entering the same phrase into a "keyword" or "word" search. A keyword search looks for a term anywhere in the library record. Essentially, a keyword search tells the computer to look for any instances where the words appear in the title or abstract rather than limiting the search to only those words that the author has supplied as subject descriptors.

What if your search of key terms results in only one or two articles? Or worse yet, suppose the results include more than 500 articles. Two tools—Boolean operators and truncation symbols—are available to help you expand or narrow your search. Using these tools will increase your search flexibility and maximize your research effectiveness.

First, Boolean operators can be used in situations such as these to help narrow or expand the search. Three of the most commonly used operator terms are "AND," "OR," and "NOT." When searching for articles that focus specifically on the use of humor in health contexts, it is beneficial to use the Boolean operator AND to narrow the focus. Doing so will return only a list of articles that include both terms. An example of the AND Boolean operator can be seen in the first example in Figure 4.8. In this example, we are looking for instances that involve the words "Humor" and "Health" at the same time.

The Boolean operator "NOT" can also be used to limit a search. This operator will exclude search terms from your search that might otherwise be included. When searching for articles about communication apprehension you might want to exclude any articles that include the term "shyness." Using NOT will help limit the results to those that focus specifically on apprehension. An example of the NOT Boolean operator can be seen in the second example in Figure 4.8. In this example, we are looking for instances that where the term "communication apprehension" exists but the word "shyness" is not also present.

In some cases, a researcher might discover that the topic needs to be expanded. To do so, the Boolean operator "OR" can be used to conduct a search of all articles that include either one of the search terms or the other. Suppose you were conducting a search for information about biased broadcast news coverage of the 2004 U.S. presidential election and want to include all media types that people use as sources of information. The Boolean operator OR could be used to tell the computer to search for any articles that contain at least one of the key terms included. An example of the OR Boolean operator can be seen in the last example in Figure 4.8. In this example, we are looking for instances where either the word "television" or the word "radio" is present.

The second flexibility aspect available in key work searches involves truncation symbols. Have you ever searched for something only to discover that you forgot to explore some of your options or look in some places? Truncation symbols are used to ensure that your search looks for every possible version of a word. While the symbol used to truncate a word will differ from library to library, the one most commonly used is the asterisk (*). Suppose you are searching for articles on the topic of children and divorce. In your list of key terms, you have identified "child" as a concept to explore. However, a search for the term "child" would overlook other versions of the word that might be used in subject fields. This search would not pick up articles that use the word "children" or "child's." To ensure that your search grabs all versions of a word, include a truncation symbol with your key term. Entering "child*" would return a list of articles with any versions of the word "child."

The World Wide Web

While electronic databases are the best tool for locating scholarly articles on a topic, the World Wide Web (WWW) can also assist in finding source of information. In instances where the topic has generated recent attention, it is essential that the researcher conduct a web search to obtain the most current information. After all, it can take anywhere from

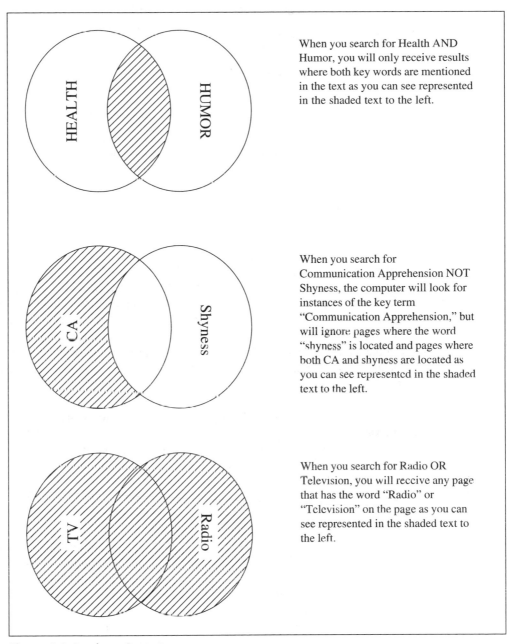

When you search for Health AND Humor, you will only receive results where both key words are mentioned in the text as you can see represented in the shaded text to the left.

When you search for Communication Apprehension NOT Shyness, the computer will look for instances of the key term "Communication Apprehension," but will ignore pages where the word "shyness" is located and pages where both CA and shyness are located as you can see represented in the shaded text to the left.

When you search for Radio OR Television, you will receive any page that has the word "Radio" or "Television" on the page as you can see represented in the shaded text to the left.

Figure 4.8 Boolean Operators

6 months to 2 years for scholarly articles to be published. That means that a significant period of time has elapsed prior to the article being listed on an electronic database. If you need to search for more current information, the WWW is the best tool for the job. The web offers a multitude of research benefits. In addition to searching for current information, it can be used to locate scholarly articles that are housed in databases that your campus library does not have available. Some of the most commonly used search engines are listed in Figure 4.9.

Search engine	URL
All the Web	www.alltheweb.com
Alta Vista	www.altavista.com
Ask Jeeves	www.ask.com
FirstGov	www.firstgov.gov
Google	www.google.com
HotBot	www.hotbot.com
MSN Search	www.search.msn.com
Yahoo	www.yahoo.com

Figure 4.9 Popular Web Search Engines

Some professors may advise students against using the web to search for information for a project. However, it is important to obtain clarification as to how they define "using the web." Most often, instructors prefer that students refrain from citing only information from websites as sources for a research paper. However, that doesn't mean that you shouldn't use the WWW to assist you in locating research articles. After all, searches of electronic databases are conducted using the computer, and the articles are often retrieved in electronic format rather than going to the printed version of the journal or newspaper. We'll discuss special methods for citing sources that are retrieved electronically later in this chapter. You wouldn't want to write a research paper on the topic of organizational culture and only cite information that you found through a Yahoo! search. However, you can locate scholarly articles on a topic using popular search engines if you take a few moments and search in the correct locations. For example, did you know that Google has a section dedicated to searching for scholarly articles? When conducting a search in Google, locate the "more" button on the right hand side of the list. Once you click on the "more" button, you will be taken to a page that lists a variety of different Google Databases that can be searched. The one we are most interested in is a database called "scholar," which searches for academic articles online. To visit the Google Scholar page, just click on the hyperlink. On the next screen, you'll notice an option titled "Scholar." All you have to do to conduct a search is to type in a key word or key term in to the search bar and click "OK." For example, type in the key term "communication apprehension" and you'll find nearly 2,500 web sources. You'll notice that many of the initial results have James McCroskey's name listed, which is a good sign since he is the originator of the term "communication apprehension." Conducting a search in this section will return lists of articles and books that have been included in scholarly publications. Many of these articles can be downloaded in full-text format, while others will include online access.

Beyond various Internet search engines that can help you find scholarly information on the Internet, a number of research organizations online are also helping to catalogue available scholarly journals that have full text access online. One such open access database is the Directory of Open Access Journals (DOAJ) (http://www.doaj.org). The DOAJ's goal is to provide scholarly information to both scholars and the general public at no cost. The DOAJ catalogued more than 2,000 full-text journals at the time this textbook was published, including a number of publications on the list in Figure 4.6, including the *American Communication Journal*, *Journal of Computer-Mediated Communication*, and *Journal of Intercultural Communication*.

For information pertaining specifically to communication, the Communication Institute for Online Scholarship (CIOS) is a not-for-profit service that has a searchable database of communication abstracts. While some of the functions of CIOS are free to the public, many functions do require a small annual fee. If you are going to be completing a lot of research, joining CIOS can be very cost-effective. Furthermore, CIOS also features open access books and journals on the website.

EVALUATING WEB SOURCES

Let's revisit our earlier statement about professors discouraging students from using web sources for research projects. It's not because they fear a conspiracy against libraries. Typically, instructors will discourage the use of web sources because of the difficulty in evaluating the quality of information located on sites. There is no peer review process for publishing information on the WWW. Anyone can post information on the web. A 14-year-old can create a website for a class project on media coverage of the recent election and include a personal commentary. If you fail to evaluate the credibility of the source, you could end up quoting a 14-year-old as an expert source for your persuasion research project. Four criteria should be used to examine the credibility and quality of web sources. These include accuracy, authority, currency, and objectivity.

Accuracy of a site can be evaluated by taking a closer look at its content. Is the information free of errors? If you notice spelling and writing errors on the site, this should be a signal that the author of the information hasn't taken care to proofread the material prior to publishing it on the web. Look to see if an editor for the site is listed. Unlike printed publications, web sources rarely go through any type of editorial process to check for errors.

In order to assess the authority of web sources, you should first look to see if the page is "signed." Who is the author? What credentials are listed on the site? If the site is sponsored by a credible organization, this lends credibility to the source of information. Suppose the site does not include any information about the author or sponsoring organization. Clues about the authority of the source can sometimes be identified by examining the web address (or URL) for the site. For example, suppose you are conducting a research project on the topic of assessing the credibility of web resources. During your search you locate a link to the following site: http://lib.nmsu.edu/instruction/eval.html. By examining the web address more closely, you notice that the article is published by someone at New Mexico State University, as identified by the ".edu" extension in the URL. Since the information is from an academic institution you can be fairly confident that it is a credible source. Other extensions that could signal credible sources include ".gov" (which are government sites) and ".org" (which are organization sites). One thing to be very careful of is information found on ".com" sites because often these websites are used for advertising, not to provide unbiased information to the public.

Currency of web resources can be determined by looking for dates that indicate when the site was created and when it was last updated. Dates will ensure that the information cited in a research paper is current. The dates of websites are typically included at the bottom of the page. Always be sure to check whether links to sites are still active. Don't include links to sites in your paper that are no longer in existence. Doing so indicates that you have not checked the currency of information you are citing.

Last, but certainly not least, the objectivity of the site should be assessed. Look for links on the site to sections titled "About," "Philosophy," or "Background" to provide information about the goal or mission of the site. As you browse the site, be sure to ask yourself if there is a hidden bias or purpose to including information on the page. If it does appear that there is a bias, ask yourself how this biased information could be useful to your project if you decide to include the information, or at least mention in your paper that the information may be biased because of the biases of the source.

At this point we believe we should also mention the problems that the Wikiworld poses for researchers. By this point in your academic career, you have undoubtedly come into contact with information from Wikipedia. Wikipedia is an open-source online encyclopedia that allows anyone to edit its entries. In essence, anyone can add information to Wikipedia that may or may not be actually factual. When we look at the four criteria for evaluating websites, Wikipedia only excels at one—currency. Yes, Wikipedia is great for current information and allows for new information to be added constantly. However, it does have three huge problems: (1) entries in Wikipedia consistently contain inaccurate information, (2) there is a lack of clear authority of the authors of the entries, (3) and there is no way to ascertain the author(s)' objectivity. In other words, Wikipedia may be a good launching point for getting a basic grasp on information, but it should never be considered a useable source for academic research. In essence, Wikipedia is a highly problematic secondary source of information. As we discussed earlier in this chapter, researchers should primarily use primary sources unless there is clear justification to use a secondary source. In an article by Read (2006), he recalls an interview he had with Jimmy Wales one of the cofounders of Wikipedia:

> I get an e-mail every week from some college student who says, "Help me; I cited you and I got an F on my paper." I always say the same thing: "For God's sake, you're in college now!" People really need to be educated not just about whatever topic they're looking for, but about the meta-question of, "How do you decide what to trust?" (p. A36)

In other words, even one of the cofounders of Wikipedia realizes that it should not be used for academic research purposes.

Step Four: Organizing and Evaluating Information

At this point in the research process, we need to emphasize the importance of maintaining a working bibliography. After all, why spend hours conducting research on a topic if you don't have a game plan for organizing the sources and information you locate? The bibliography is simply a list of sources that you have located and reviewed in conducting the review of literature. Trust us—eventually you will need this information as you cite sources of information in your "Review of Literature" and "References." It's much easier to record the information now rather than to recreate the list later. Nothing is more frustrating than beginning to put together a reference list only to discover missing information such as the year the source was published or the page numbers of an article.

SOURCE:	Book	Journal	Text Journal	Webpage	Magazine

Newspaper
Title:_____
Article Title (for journal, magazine or newspaper)

_____
Author(s) _____
Copyright Date OR if web site, date you used website_____
Publisher of book OR Sponsor of website_____
Place of Publication OR Web URL _____

NOTES:

_____
_____
_____
_____
_____

Figure 4.10 Source Record Card

Source	Citation elements needed
Book	• Author's name (may be more than one) • Date of publication/copyright • Title • Publisher • City/State where published
Print journal article	• Author's name (may be more than one) • Publication date • Title of article • Title of journal • Volume number • Issue number • Page numbers of article
Electronic full-text version of a print journal article	• Same info as for print journals • Database name or access path • Date the article was accessed • NOTE: Some electronic versions of articles may not include page numbers
Webpage	• Author's name • Title or description of the page • URL • Date the page was accessed
Magazine article	• Author's name • Publication date • Title of article • Title of magazine • Volume number • Issue number • Page numbers of article
Newspaper article	• Author's name (if available) • Publication date (month/day/year) • Title of article • Title of newspaper • Page number
Interviews with people	• Interviewee's name • Date of interview

Figure 4.11 APA Information

Effective library searches and organization strategies include the following steps:

- Step One: Using your list of key terms, begin searching general reference materials. Review handbooks, subject encyclopedias, electronic databases, websites, or other reference sources.

- Step Two: As you locate potential sources of information, complete a Source Record Card (see Figure 4.10) for each source. Be sure to include all required information—this will save the work of going back and looking for it later. The type of source will dictate the information that needs to be included in citations and references. Figure 4.11 provides a summary of the pieces of information needed to correctly cite sources.

- Step Three: Review the abstract as you locate each source. Next, review the discussion section if the article comes from a scholarly journal. If the source is a book, glance at the table of contents and index. This will be useful in determining if the source contains information that is relevant to your study.

• Step Four: Read through the bibliographies of sources that you locate. You might discover that the author has cited articles that would be useful for your study!

Step Five: Citing Sources of Information Using the APA Format

Given the wide variety of communication contexts (e.g., rhetoric, interpersonal, media studies, etc.), scholars may adopt diverse writing styles when reporting on the research in their particular area. Consider the fact that each student in this class has a unique writing style. If your professor didn't provide any guidelines for how the paper should be written, sources that should be included, or page length, chances are each paper written in your class would be vastly different in terms of format. The same is true for research that is published in academic journals. Guidelines exist to provide standards for how sources and references should be cited and how papers should be formatted.

Any researcher who is writing an article for publication is required to adhere to publication guidelines. While a host of different style manuals exist (e.g., MLA, The Chicago Manual of Style), the preferred format for most communication journals is APA. APA is a style of writing that was developed and is revised by the American Psychological Association (APA). Every detail of the format required for research papers is described in the *Publication Manual of the American Psychological Association* (5th ed., 2001). Most libraries keep a copy of the manual at the reference desk, and numerous online sites provide summaries for quick reference (http://www.apastyle.org/). In order to correctly adhere to format guidelines, it is important to understand what information needs to be referenced in a research paper and how sources of information should be cited. Figure 4.12 shows a checklist of format guidelines to refer to when preparing a research paper for submission to a conference or journal. Information about general formatting issues (such as margins, font size, and spacing) as well as details about the layout of subsequent pages and sections in the paper is included. It is important to note that this list is by no means comprehensive. Rather it is designed to provide a quick check to avoid falling into the APA style traps.

WHAT INFORMATION NEEDS TO BE REFERENCED?

As a general rule, all work done by other researchers that you wish to include in your own study must be referenced and cited. Any instance in which you include the exact words of another author must be quoted. Not giving proper credit to their work is considered to be plagiarism. Typically, any information you do not reference will be interpreted to be general knowledge or your own work. Information that is considered to be general knowledge does not need to be referenced. For example, we all know that George H. W. Bush was the president of the United States, so it is unnecessary to cite a source for that particular fact.

A good strategy to use when writing your paper is to build your reference list as you work on the text of the paper. As you include a source in the paper, scroll down to a reference page and list the source using APA format. This is where the information included on your Source Reference Cards (Figure 4.10) will come in handy. As a general rule, the reference page should begin on a separate page. The title "References" should be centered on the first line below the running head. All sources included in the references should be alphabetized by the first author's last name. Each reference includes four primary elements: the author(s) name, year of publication, title of book and or article, and retrieval information. An example of a reference for a journal article would look like the citation in Figure 4.13.

Section of Paper	Guidelines
General format	• 1-inch margins top, bottom, left, and right • 12 point font (Times Roman or Courier) • Double space throughout paper • Align along left margin • Paragraph indent five spaces • Page number located 1 inch from right edge of paper on first line of every page (including title page) • Running head on every page located five spaces to the left of the page number on every page • Use active voice
Page order	• Title • Abstract • Body of paper • References • Appendices • Footnotes • Tables • Figures
Title page	• This is always page 1 • Include running head, paper title, author, and institutional affiliation • All text is double-spaced
Abstract	• One paragraph summary of highlights of paper • Begins on page 2 • 120 words or less • Heading "Abstract" centered on first line below header • Body of abstract in block format
Body	• Begins on page 3 • Tile of paper centered on first line below header • Main headings (i.e., Methods, Results, Discussion) are centered using cap/lowercase letters • Subheadings are italicized and left justified using cap/lowercase letters
Reference page	• Begins on a separate page • Heading "References" is centered on first line after header • Names in alphabetical order of last name
Appendices	• Begins on a separate page • Heading "Appendix" is centered on first line below header • For more than one appendix use "Appendix A," "Appendix B," and so forth
Tables	• Begins on a separate page • Heading "Table 1" (or Table 2, etc.) is left justified on the fist line below the header. • Double space after the title "Table x" and type the table title left justified

Figure 4.12 APA Style Checklist

Figure 4.14 includes information for citing a variety of sources. If you have a source that is not included on this list, please consult your librarian, the APA Style Manual, or an online APA style guide.

CITING SOURCES OF INFORMATION

There are four general guidelines to consider when including citations. First, citations should be included for all sources of information that you have directly quoted in the paper. Second, citations should be included when summarizing or paraphrasing information from another source. Even though you aren't directly quoting the source, it is still important to let your

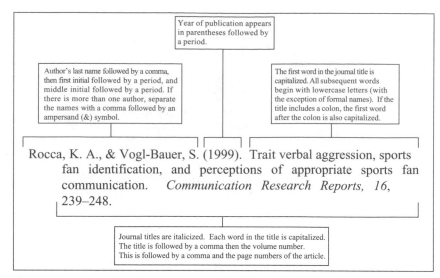

Figure 4.13 APA Citation

Source	Reference citation	Parenthetical citation
Entire book (one author)	McCroskey, J. C. (1998). *An introduction to communication in the classroom* (2nd ed). Acton, MA: Tapestry Press.	(McCroskey, 1998)
Entire book (two authors)	McCroskey, J. C., & Daly, J. A. (1987). *Personality and interpersonal communication.* Newbury Park, CA: Sage.	(McCroskey & Daly, 1987)
Entire book (multiple authors)	Richmond, V. P., Wrench, J. S., & Gorham, J. (2001). *Communication, affect, and learning in the classroom.* Acton, MA: Tapestry.	*First Citation* (Richmond, Wrench, & Gorham, 2001) *Subsequent Citations* (Richmond et al., 2001)
Chapter in an edited book	Spitzberg, B. H. (1994). The dark side of (in)competence. In W. R. Cupach & B. H. Spitzberg (Eds.), *The dark side of interpersonal communication* (pp. 25–49). Hillsdale, NJ: Lawrence Erlbaum.	(Spitzberg, 1994)
Journal article (one author)	Chesebro, J. (1999). The relationship between listening styles and conversational sensitivity. *Communication Research Reports, 16,* 233–238.	(Chesebro, 1999)
Journal article (multiple authors)	Infante, D. A., Myers, S. A., & Buerkel, R. A. (1994). Argument and verbal aggression in constructive and destructive family and organizational disagreements. *Western Journal of Communication, 58,* 73–84.	*First Citation* (Infante, Myers, & Buerkel, 1994) *Subsequent Citations* (Infante et al., 1994)
Magazine article	Farber, M. (1996, May 27). The old heave-ho: Fans' tossing things, be they confections or critters, has lost whatever charm it once had. *Sports Illustrated, 84,* 88.	(Farber, 1996)
Newspaper article	Sandberg, J. (2005, July 20). These ICU nurses use carpooling to prepare for work, decompress. *Wall Street Journal,* pp. B1–B5.	(Sandberg, 2005)
Newspaper article (no author)	Sports briefing. (2004, October 28). *New York Times,* p. D8.	("Sports Briefing," 2004)
Unpublished conference paper	Rocca, K. A., & Martin, M. M. (1998, April). *Verbal aggression and team identification: A sports fan's perspective.* Paper presented at the annual conference of the Eastern Communication Association, Saratoga Springs, NY.	(Rocca & Martin, 1998)
Internet site	McNamara, C. (1999). *Organizational culture.* Retrieved July 25, 2005 from http://www.mapnp.org/library/org_thry/culture/culture.htm	(McNamara, 1999)
Personal interview	Do not include in reference list since information is not considered to be recoverable data.	Charles Giardina (personal communication, July 25, 2005).

Figure 4.14 APA Citations

reader know where you located the original information. Third, citations should be used when you want to direct your reader's attention to relevant research or important facts or information. Finally, citations are not required for information that is common knowledge. We will discuss each of these in the sections that follow.

Parenthetical Citations

Parenthetical citations (also referred to as internal citations) are used when you are including information taken directly from another source. This enables the reader to identify where information was obtained, and it lends credibility and authority to your research. Citing sources of information is often one of the most difficult aspects of research writing for some students because they are reluctant to use the words of others. We've all received information from our instructors warning us about the penalties for plagiarizing the work of others. But don't forget that the very nature of scholarly research *requires* you to use the work of others to build a rationale for your own work. After all, the foundation for research is built on the unanswered questions or weaknesses of previous studies.

Parenthetical citations include three primary elements of information. These include the author's last name, the date of publication, and page number if a direct quote from the source is included in the text of the literature review. The format used to cite sources depends on the goal of the reference. If your goal is to highlight a specific concept or idea, typically the parenthetical citation information would be included at the end of the sentence. Suppose your goal is to highlight the scholarship of a particular researcher. The parenthetical citation should begin with the researcher's last name followed by the year of the article you are citing in parentheses. When the goal is to follow a chronological order when citing information, the year of the source should appear first, followed by the author's name. Examples of how to cite information for these three goals are included in Figure 4.15.

Quotations and Paraphrases

Quotations involve the use of another author's exact words in your study. It is important to give credit where credit is due. After all, not citing a source is considered to be plagiarism. As a general rule, use direct quotations only if you have a good reason for doing so. Including numerous quotations from sources causes the author's own voice and ideas to become "lost" in the project. Ensure proper credit is given to sources by using the author's exact words, including the quotations in quotation marks (unless you are citing a long source in which case it should be included in an indented block), and indicating the page number where the quotations is published.

Paraphrasing refers to including another author's ideas in your own words, and involves summarizing or highlighting one or two important points from the author. Consider the following example:

ORIGINAL

"It is important to recognize that no single artifact, value, or assumption is, or can create, an organization's culture" (Keyton, 2005, p. 28).

Focus of citation	Sample citation
Conceptual/Idea	Physicians and other medical professionals personally use humor as a means of coping with the uncertainty that surrounds the medical profession (Bosk, 1996; Wanzer, Booth-Butterfield, & Booth-Butterfield, 1997).
Researcher	Fitzpatrick (1993) described patient satisfaction as an "emotional link to healthcare."
Chronology	In 1991, Booth-Butterfield and Booth-Butterfield identified the concept of humor orientation, otherwise referred to as HO.

Figure 4.15 Internal Citations

PARAPHRASE

Keyton (2005) emphasizes that one cannot simply examine only one dimension of an organization and understand the creation or current culture. Rather, a researcher must be willing to examine multiple facets of the organization to gain a comprehensive understanding of the history and factors that have led to the existing culture.

Remember that paraphrases should always include the author's name and the year of the publication from which the information was retrieved. Typically paraphrases are not enclosed within quotation marks or indented. After all, these words represent your interpretation of the source's work and are not words taken directly from the article. Some find paraphrasing to be difficult at first. We recommend reviewing several examples of published work to increase your familiarity and comfort with the style used to cite information from other sources.

APA Paper Formatting

The last part of this chapter will discuss how to format your paper using APA style. While the next chapter will discuss what goes in each section of a paper, there are a few formatting issues we need to discuss first. In this section we will look at formatting issues related to the title page, abstract, first page, and reference page.

CREATING A TITLE PAGE

The title page is the page that goes on top of your actual document when you are getting ready to either turn in your paper to a professor or send your paper off to a conference or journal for possible publication. There are a number of unique parts of an APA title page that may be tricky if you are not used to working with APA style. Figure 4.16 shows what a title page should look like.

The first thing you may notice about an APA cover page is that it has something called a "running head." A running head is a series of words that is placed on every page followed by a page number so a reader knows that all of the pages with that running head on it belong to the same document. Often people who review manuscripts for conferences or publications will read 20–50 manuscripts at a time, so the running head prevents pages from getting misplaced or attached to the wrong document. A good running head should be distinct and relate to the overarching topic of your paper. A running head can be no longer than 50 characters counting letters, characters, and spacing between words. You'll notice that on the very first line of the cover page you type the words "Running head" followed by your actual running head in all capital letters. By doing this, you enable your reader to quickly see what your running head is. You'll also notice that your cover page also contains your running head in the upper right hand corner down ½ of an inch from the top of the page. Your running head is then followed by five spaces and then the page number. Most computer programs have header programs built in to enable you to place your running head and page numbers automatically rather than attempting to do it by hand.

Next on a cover page, you'll find the paper's title. A title should sell a reader on what the overarching topic of your paper is going to be about, so your reader can see if he or she wants to read further. APA recommends that your title be approximately 10–12 words, but this is only a guideline. Some titles are considerably longer, and some are shorter—it all depends on what you need so your intended audience will realize that your paper relates to a topic they are interested in reading. Titles should also avoid using abbreviations, opting instead for spelling out technical acronyms. Titles are often used for cataloging research articles and papers, so making sure that your title contains all of the appropriate key terms and words will make for a much more efficient title.

The last part of the title page consists of the author's name and university/professional affiliation or the authors' names and university/professional affiliations. Authors in academia are not listed alphabetically on a paper. Generally speaking, author names are listed according to who contributed the most to a specific project. While many articles have one author,

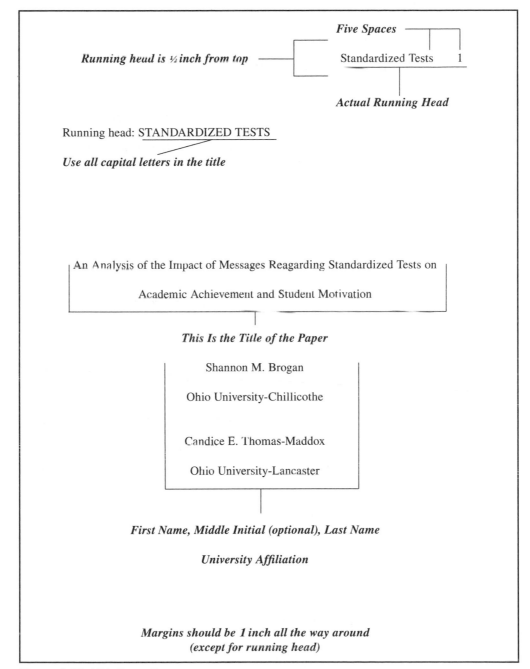

Figure 4.16 APA Cover Page

other projects have listed as many as 900 authors. Admittedly, most papers rarely have more than five authors, but some projects will have more people who have actually contributed to the success of the research project. Ultimately, the lead author on a project is the person who has contributed the most to the conceptualization and enactment of the research project itself and is listed as the first author. Often the first author then makes the determination of who shall be the second author, third author, and so on, on the cover page. In addition to listing the authors' names on a project, each author's university/organizational affiliation is also listed below her or his name.

CREATING AN ABSTRACT

The second page in an APA styled paper is an abstract. While what goes into an abstract will be discussed in the next chapter, we do want to discuss the basic formatting of an abstract at this point. Figure 4.17 contains an example abstract.

Abstracts should have 1-inch margins all the way around (except for the running head, which is still ½ inch from the top of the page). The word "Abstract" is centered on the first line, which should be one inch from the top of the page. The abstract should be double spaced and left-justified. "Left-justified" means that there is not an indention or tab on the first line of written text.

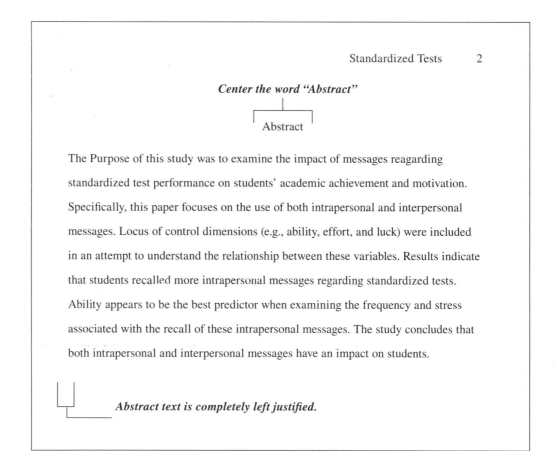

Figure 4.17 APA Abstract Formatting

CREATING THE FIRST PAGE

The third page of your paper is your first page of actual text and contains the text related to the actual paper you plan on writing. However, there are still a few important formatting issues that you should be aware of when creating your first page.

Figure 4.18 shows the first page of the paper by Brogan and Thomas-Maddox that we have been examining in the past few figures. You'll notice that the first few lines of the paper

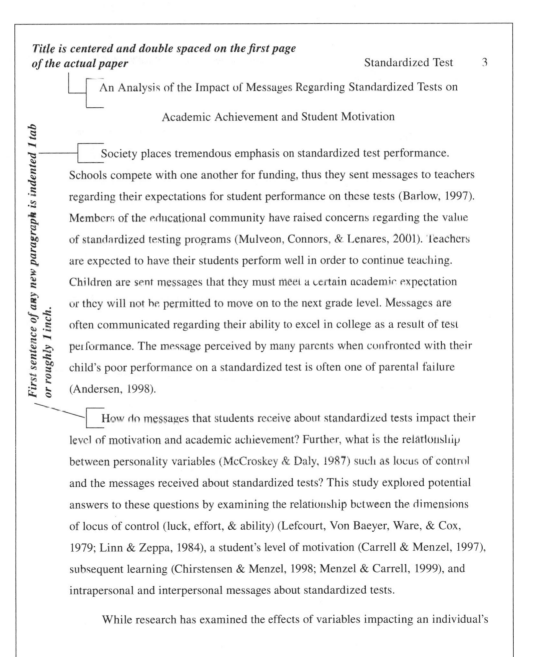

Title is centered and double spaced on the first page
of the actual paper   Standardized Test   3

An Analysis of the Impact of Messages Regarding Standardized Tests on

Academic Achievement and Student Motivation

First sentence of any new paragraph is indented 1 tab
or roughly 1 inch.

Society places tremendous emphasis on standardized test performance. Schools compete with one another for funding, thus they sent messages to teachers regarding their expectations for student performance on these tests (Barlow, 1997). Members of the educational community have raised concerns regarding the value of standardized testing programs (Mulveon, Connors, & Lenares, 2001). Teachers are expected to have their students perform well in order to continue teaching. Children are sent messages that they must meet a certain academic expectation or they will not be permitted to move on to the next grade level. Messages are often communicated regarding their ability to excel in college as a result of test performance. The message perceived by many parents when confronted with their child's poor performance on a standardized test is often one of parental failure (Andersen, 1998).

How do messages that students receive about standardized tests impact their level of motivation and academic achievement? Further, what is the relationship between personality variables (McCroskey & Daly, 1987) such as locus of control and the messages received about standardized tests? This study explored potential answers to these questions by examining the relationship between the dimensions of locus of control (luck, effort, & ability) (Lefcourt, Von Baeyer, Ware, & Cox, 1979; Linn & Zeppa, 1984), a student's level of motivation (Carrell & Menzel, 1997), subsequent learning (Chirstensen & Menzel, 1998; Menzel & Carrell, 1999), and intrapersonal and interpersonal messages about standardized tests.

While research has examined the effects of variables impacting an individual's

Figure 4.18 APA Style First Page

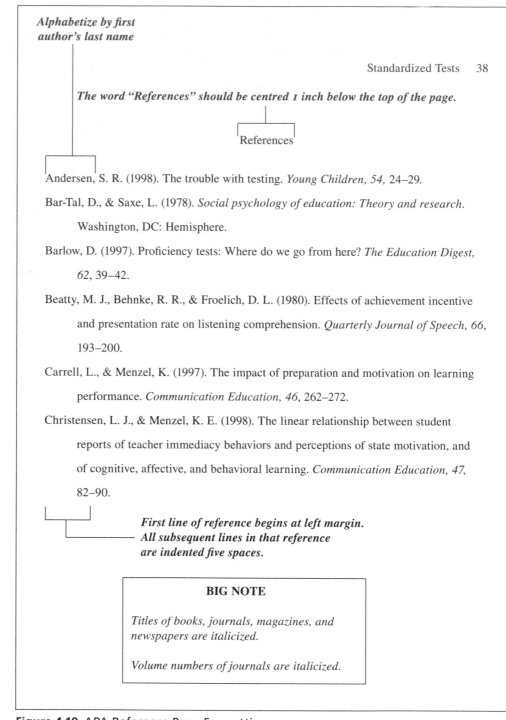

Figure 4.19 APA Reference Page Formatting

contain the same title that you have listed on the cover page. The reason your title is listed here as well as on your cover page is that often editors and conference reviewers do not ever see your cover page because academics use what is called "blind review." Blind review is the process where an editor or conference program planner sends out papers anonymously to other scholars and has them evaluate the scholarly quality of the paper. Since editors and conference program planners want honest feedback about the quality of the paper, papers should have no identifying marks on them that would let a reviewer know who the author is. For this reason, cover pages are taken off papers when they are sent out to reviewers, so it is important to have the title of your paper on the first page of the actual manuscript.

After the title on the first page of your written manuscript, you always indent new paragraphs using the tab function on your word processor. If you do not have a fancy word processor, one tab is approximately 10 spaces on your average keyboard. While this section gives you some basic information on how to format a paper, you should really buy a copy of the most recent version of the APA Style Manual because there are so many other formatting issues that we cannot go into in this textbook. Everything from politically correct language to formatting tables is covered in the APA Style Manual, so make sure you buy a copy if you have not already done so.

CREATING THE REFERENCE PAGE

The aspect of APA formatting we will discuss in this section is how to format a reference page using APA style. While you may have formatted work cited pages, a reference page is distinctly different. Figure 4.19 shows a brief reference page.

The first thing you will see on a reference page is the running head in the upper right hand corner, like it has been on every page of your manuscript. Next, you will have the word "References" centered 1 inch from the top of the page. From here, you place all of your references for every source that is cited within your manuscript alphabetically by the first author on the source. You'll notice that the first line of the citation is left justified, but the rest of the citation is aligned to the right 1 tab (or 10 spaces). Also, notice that the reference page is double spaced.

There are a lot of different problems that you can run into when creating a reference page, so we strongly urge you to buy a copy of the APA Style Manual because our brief help section here is simply not adequate to explain every citation you may face.

Conclusion

In this chapter we have examined how to pick a topic, how to find research materials using a variety of different tools, and how to use basic APA style. In the next chapter we will examine the various parts of a research paper with special attention paid to how to write literature reviews, how to write a rationale section (research questions and hypotheses), and writing method sections.

KEY TERMS

Abstract	Electronic Database	Secondary Source
APA Style	Paraphrase	Subject Search
Author Search	Parenthetical Citations	Title Search
Axiom	Primary Source	Truncation Symbols
Boolean Logic	Quotation	
Citation	Reference Page	

REFERENCES

Berger, C., & Calabrese, R. (1975). Some explorations in initial interaction and beyond: Toward a developmental theory of interpersonal communication. *Human Communication Research, 1,* 99–112.

Keyton, J. (2005). *Communication and organizational culture: A key to understanding work experiences.* Thousand Oaks, CA: Sage.

Publication manual of the American Psychological Association (5th ed.). (2001). Washington, DC: American Psychological Association.

Read, B. (2006, October 27). Students flock to an easy-to-use reference, but professors warn that it's no sure thing. *Chronicle of Higher Education, 53* (10), A36.

Rocca, K. A., & Vogl-Bauer, S. (1999). Trait verbal aggression, sports fan identification, and perceptions of appropriate sports fan communication. *Communication Research Reports, 16,* 239–248.

Thomas, C., Booth-Butterfield, M., & Booth-Butterfield, S. (1995). Perceptions of deception, divorce disclosures, and communication satisfaction with parents. *Western Journal of Communication, 59,* 228–245.

West, R., & Turner, L. H. (2006). *Introducing communication theory: Analysis and application.* (3rd ed.). Boston: McGraw-Hill.

Wrench, J. S., & Booth-Butterfield, M. (2003). Increasing patient satisfaction and compliance: An examination of physician humor orientation, compliance-gaining strategies, and perceived credibility. *Communication Quarterly, 51,* 482–503.

FURTHER READING

Anderson, C. E., Carrell, A. T., & Widdifield, J. L., Jr. (2007). *What every student should know about citing sources with APA documentation.* Boston: Allyn & Bacon.

Concise rules of APA style. (2005). Washington, DC: American Psychological Association.

Frey, L., Botan, C., & Kreps, G. (2000). *Investigating communication: An introduction to research methods* (2nd ed.). Englewood Cliffs, NJ: Prentice Hall.

Hairston, M., & Ruszkiewicz, J. J. (1996) *The Scott, Foresman handbook for writers* (4th ed.). New York: HarperCollins.

Hocking, J. E., Stacks, D. W., & McDermott, S. T. (2003). *Communication research* (3rd ed.). Boston: Allyn & Bacon.

Salkind, N. J. (2004). *Statistics for people who (think they) hate statistics* (2nd ed.). Thousand Oaks, CA: Sage.

Singleton, R. A., Jr., & Straits, B. C. (1999). *Approaches to social research* (3rd ed.). New York: Oxford University Press.

Research Structure and Literature Reviews

Organization is one of the most important processes in any endeavor we undertake in life. Many people try to jump right into the writing process without making sure all of the necessary tools, safeguards, and supplies are readily at hand. Have you ever tried to build something, only to realize halfway through your project that you do not have a tool that you need? Have you ever known someone who bought a do-it-yourself building project only to finish the project and realize that they have a number of leftover parts? The fact is, being organized helps people to see deficiencies and prepare for future success. Whether you are building a bridge or writing an article for a communication journal, you have to be organized in your thinking and layout to achieve success.

Many authors do not organize their research articles in an effective manner, only to realize halfway through the writing process that they are missing a key point. Other people finish writing a paper and realize that the paper has serious gaps in logic. Being an organized writer means selecting and arranging the appropriate ideas and materials for the paper into a logical and discernible pattern. In other words, an organized writer has thought out her or his paper and created a clear pattern that readers can follow. Additionally, if a reader can understand a paper, the reader will recall the information more easily.

Although most of the information in this chapter is similar to the information that students receive in basic public speaking courses every year, there are some specific aspects to organizing a research paper that are unique. This chapter will focus on how to organize an article into a format that will ultimately help readers retain information. To examine organization, this chapter will discuss the major parts of a research paper (abstract, literature review, methods, results, and discussion) in separate sections. Furthermore, this chapter will dissect portions of an article by Jason S. Wrench and Melanie Booth-Butterfield (2003) to aid in your understanding of the concepts discussed here. To read the entire article by Wrench and Booth-Butterfield, see the CD-ROM that came with this textbook.

The Abstract

You may have heard the old adage, "You never get a second chance to make a good first impression." This statement is undeniably true. No matter how hard we try, people will always remember the first time they met us. While writing a research paper is not exactly like meeting someone, the paper abstract is just as important as an introduction is when meeting a person. For example, if you bore someone the first time you meet them, the chances that the two of you will become friends is not very likely. Similarly, if you bore someone in your abstract, you will turn that person off to your paper immediately and possibly turn that person off to your topic in general. If you are an interesting person to talk to when you first meet someone, people will be drawn to you as a person. Likewise, if your paper has a good abstract, people will be drawn to you as an author and ultimately to your topic. An abstract, simply defined, is a short paragraph at the beginning of a scholarly paper that concisely and comprehensively explains the contents of the paper. In other words, an abstract is a snapshot of the overall paper.

According to the *Publication Manual of the American Psychological Association* (2001), an abstract should be accurate, self-contained, and concise/specific. First, an abstract should be accurate, or an abstract should correctly reflect what occurs in the paper itself. If your paper is about public speaking and your abstract discusses football, your abstract is clearly not reflecting what actually occurs in the paper itself. Second, an abstract should be self-contained; it should not need any specialized information for the reader to understand what it is communicating. To be self-contained, an abstract should clearly define any abbreviations and acronyms, spell out names of tests and/or drugs, define any unique terms, and accurately cite any relevant research in the abstract without directly quoting the source. Finally, a good abstract should be concise and specific. An abstract is not a complete retelling of your entire paper, but should give as much information as needed to help a potential reader understand what your paper is discussing. According to the American Psychological Association (APA) manual, an abstract should not be more than 120 words in length. Although that may sound like a lot of words, it really isn't. An abstract should explain to your readers your basic purpose for writing the paper and any relevant results and conclusions. However, many research projects can have upwards of 10–20 results or major conclusions, so it is usually best to limit your number of conclusions in the abstract to the five most important findings.

One note should be made about the abstract. While we are presenting the abstract at this point in this text in order to present the parts of a paper according to APA style in order, an abstract is written after everything else is complete. You cannot write a meaningful abstract until you have completed a study. Your abstract is like a quick snapshot of everything you did in your study.

This study examined the impact that patients' perceptions of a physician's humor orientation, credibility, and compliance gaining strategies had on their satisfaction and compliance. Perceived physician humor orientation positively related to perceived physician credibility, physician compliance-gaining strategies, and patient satisfaction. Other positive relationships among perceived physician credibility, physician compliance gaining strategies, and patient satisfaction emerged. Compliance did not relate significantly to physician humor orientation and perceived credibility. Aspects of patient satisfaction and physician use of compliance-gaining strategies affected compliance. Additionally, this study revealed minimal differences among data collection methods (undergraduate ($N = 44$), graduate ($N - 48$), general public ($N = 66$), and online participation ($N = 26$)).	General sentence explaining the overall purpose of the study. Goes into specific detail related to the various findings in this study. Lastly, the abstract mentions a secondary analysis examining the different data collection methods employed in this study.

Analysis	
Accurate	If you read the actual article completely, you will notice that the basic purpose discussed at the beginning of the abstract correctly explains what occurs throughout the study.
Self-contained	Although the abstract may be confusing if you do not know what the terminology means (e.g., perceived credibility, physician humor orientation, etc.), notice that no acronyms are used and tests were not specifically referred to by name. For example, instead of referring to a Physician's HO the authors specifically call it a physician's humor orientation.
Concise and specific	If you compare the results section with the results described above, you will notice that the results discussed above are the major results discussed in the article itself.

Figure 5.1 Article Abstract

Look at the abstract in Figure 5.1. Notice how the abstract explains in a brief manner what is actually discussed in the rest of the paper. Often when researchers are conducting literature searches, they will read only the abstract to see if the article may have useful information. In essence, understanding the purpose of an abstract can actual greatly reduce the time it takes to complete a full literature search.

The Introduction

Now that we have discussed the first part of a paper, we can focus on the "traditional" introduction of a research paper. A good introduction should have six basic components: an attention-getter, a link to the topic, a statement of the topic's significance, an espousal of credibility, a thesis statement, and a preview (McCroskey, Wrench, & Richmond, 2003).

ATTENTION-GETTER

The first part of an introduction is referred to as an attention-getter because this portion of an introduction should be able to grab your reader's attention. After the abstract, the first words in your paper are probably the most important words in your document. If you are able to grab your reader's attention in a unique or captivating way, your reader will continue to read what you have to say. There are a number of specific attention-getters that writers can use to successfully capture the reader's attention.

Using Statistics or Claims

One way to get the reader's attention is to alarm her or him with the use of a startling statistic or claim. People have a tendency to respond to information that has a statistical assessment attached. Although statistics can be very useful to demonstrate the extent to which there is a problem or the occurrence of a phenomenon, statistics can be misleading and come back to haunt a writer. When using statistical information, knowing how the statistic was generated can add credence to your message. Consider the following statement: "According to a new study, 50 percent of the people exposed to a new drug will develop liver cancer" (Hause & Botner, 2000). If in this drug trial only two people had been exposed to the drug, repeating the results from this study as an attention getter would be very misleading.

Likewise, startling claims can be made to grab a reader's attention. "You have a greater chance of dying in your car on the way to the airport than you do once you have entered the terminal" (Smith, 2000) could be a startling claim to begin a paper on air safety. The same concerns that apply to startling statistics apply to startling claims; you must know the validity of the claim you are making.

When deciding if a startling statistic or claim is a useful attention-getting device for a research paper, ask yourself three very important questions. (1) Will this statistic or claim cause some are to become interested in my research topic? Clearly, if you start your research paper with a dull statistic or claim, someone is not likely to read beyond the introduction. (2) Is the statistic or claim so outrageous that it could prevent someone from believing what I have to say? You have to be careful to avoid offending the reader's logic with a statistic or claim. If an author wrote that "100% of Americans who travel in trains die," people would laugh at the author and think he or she was nuts. If an author actually used this outlandish statement, it would not matter if the author had a citation for her or his statistic, people would be highly skeptical and simply dismiss the paper based on this one simple fact. (3) Is there a better way of grabbing the audience's attention? Always ask yourself this question when deciding uopon an attention-getting device. Often our first idea for an attention-getting device is not ultimately the best device we can use.

Posing a Rhetorical Question

A rhetorical question asks the reader to simply ponder the question internally without audibly responding to the question. Many research papers will start with stating right off the bat what the overall theme will be in the study by posing a rhetorical question. For example, if an author was planning on studying communication apprehension across the life cycle (children, teenagers, young adults, and retirement age), he or she might ask, "Although the importance of communication apprehension to communication scholars is clear, how does communication apprehension affect people across the life cycle?" From this question, the author could discuss various articles that have examined communication apprehension in various populations or various age groups.

Using an Acknowledged Fact

The next way to grab an audience's attention is to start with a widely acknowledged fact and build on that fact. To use an acknowledged fact as an introduction, the fact needs to be fairly universal so that anyone who reads the fact will have the ability to quickly understand and agree with what has been written. For example, in the article by Chesebro (1999) he started his article by saying:

> Most people have encountered different types of listeners. Some people seem quite responsive and notice even the slightest of our nonverbal cues. Others carefully scrutinize and analyze our messages. Some people can't wait until we just get to the point. Others look at their watches with

the hope that we will recognize that they would rather be somewhere else. The way in which our interaction partners listen is important to us when we are the ones doing the talking. (p. 234)

In this attention-getter, Chesebro has clearly identified common problems that everyone experiences and notices when communicating with other people.

Using a Story or Illustration

The next way that an author can grab a reader's attention is to tell a story that relates to her or his topic. For example, if you are writing a paper about how test anxiety affects student performance in the classroom, you could start your paper off by explaining how once there was a student who missed every test day because of her or his apprehension, which ultimately caused the student to fail. Another possible way to grab your audience's attention is to use an illustration.

Whereas stories are the telling of real or pseudo-real events that relate to your topic, illustrations are more general stories that can be applied to a variety of different contexts. For example, one famous illustration is the story of the frog that agrees to transport a scorpion on its back across the river on the condition that the scorpion will not sting him. During the trip, the scorpion stings the frog. While the scorpion and frog are drowning, the frog asks why the scorpion broke his promise, to which the scorpion responds, "I'm a scorpion; I sting things." This short illustration can be applied to a number of contexts. You could use this illustration to begin a paper on how humans have innate personalities that cannot be changed, on the problems of being too trusting, or on how organizations change. Ultimately, the usefulness of an illustration lies in an author's clear connection from the illustration to the topic at hand.

Quoting or Acknowledging a Source

The last, and most common, way of introducing a paper is to directly quote or acknowledge another source. As discussed in the previous chapter, directly quoting a source is when author A copies the exact text of author B's document and places it verbatim into author A's new work. For example, in the article by Brummans and Miller (2004) the authors started their article by quoting a chunk of text from Schumacher that read:

Ortega y Gasset once remarked that "life is fired at us point-blank." We cannot say: "Hold it! I am not quite ready. Wait until I have sorted things out." Decisions have to be taken that we are not ready for; aims have to be chosen that we cannot see clearly. (Schumacher, 1995, p. 15)

From this quotation, Brummans and Miller then discuss how in the information age life moves very quickly and our lives are earmarked by constant change.

The second way to grab an audience's attention is simply by acknowledging a source. As discussed in the previous chapter, acknowledging a source is when an author paraphrases specific information and then gives credit for that information to the scholars who are actually responsible for that information. For example, in the article by Weber, Fornash, Corrigan, and Neupauer (2003), the authors started their article with, "Much of the research conducted in the instructional realm has dealt with the effect of affective variables on cognitive learning" (Wanzer & Frymier, 1999). In this attention-getter, the authors did not directly quote from Wanzer and Frymier, they paraphrased what Wanzer and Frymier wrote in their study.

LINK TO TOPIC

The next major part of the introduction is the link from the attention-getter to the actual topic of your paper. Some attention-getters are very easy to link directly to your topic. For example, the attention-getter used by Chesebro (2003) discussed previously spends an entire paragraph explaining in common terms how he perceives the link between an individual's listening style and conversational sensitivity, which is the goal of his overall study. However, other attention-getters take a little more creativity to make a clear link to the topic. Of the examples listed in the previous section on attention-getting devices, the hardest one to directly link to a topic is usually an illustration (e.g., the scorpion and the frog), because an illustration is a metaphor for the topic itself, and not all metaphors are clearly seen by people reading them.

SIGNIFICANCE OF TOPIC

The third major step in the introduction of a paper is demonstrating why the topic is significant enough for your reader to care. If you are writing a paper about a communication phenomenon only seen by tribesman in a remote tribe in South America, you are going to have a hard time demonstrating why academics in the United States should care about your topic. However, if you can demonstrate that this communication phenomenon is similar to something we do in the United States or contradicts something we think is communication fact, then you can help others see why your topic is significant. One of the hardest facts to get new researchers to understand is that research for research's sake is not significant. Every researcher should be able to clearly answer the "Why should we care?" or "So what?" question in a couple of sentences.

ESPOUSAL OF CREDIBILITY

The fourth major component of the introduction of a paper is the espousal of one's credibility to write a paper on the subject. While in public speaking, we talk about espousing one's credibility in terms of your personal qualifications for speaking on a subject, in writing papers credibility is less self-drawn than through demonstration of complete and accurate research. If you have not completely researched a concept, a trained reader will clearly see gaps in your literature that are extremely important. Within your introduction, you need to start integrating literature appropriately to help build your case for both significance and to demonstrate that you have examined previous research and are not just stating your opinions. Even the number one researcher in the field of communication must demonstrate that a paper is thoroughly researched and is supported by the literature. For example, look at the article by McCroskey, Richmond, Johnson, and Smith (2004) to see how McCroskey and his colleagues thoroughly cite a lot of previous research before starting the literature review.

THESIS AND PREVIEW

The fifth component of a good introduction is the thesis statement. A thesis is a short, declarative sentence that explains to a reader the purpose of the paper itself. If you are writing a paper on how cults use thought reform (brainwashing) to influence their victims, for example, your thesis may be, "The process of thought reform, though often misunderstood, is not difficult when a person is unknowingly vulnerable to outside influences." After the thesis, an author generally transitions into a brief preview of what will be examined in the literature review.

In a preview, the author lists the specific sections that he or she is planning on covering in the literature review of the paper. For example, to preview the thought reform paper, one could say, "To understand how thought reform occurs, an analysis of the history of thought reform research, common thought reform tactics, and how cults use these tactics will be examined in this literature review followed by a series of hypotheses and research questions for the current study." In this case, each of the phrases mentioned in the preview would be a single distinct subsection written in the literature review.

Overall, the introduction portion of a paper is extremely important and truly focuses a reader's attention and helps a reader understand the scope and focus of a paper. This section has used a number of the articles from the CD-ROM that accompanied this textbook to illustrate various aspects of an introduction; an introduction by Wrench and Booth-Butterfield (2003) is shown in Figure 5.2.

At the end of visits to a personal physician, the physician generally will prescribe some sort of medication, treatment, or lifestyle change to help patients recover from, or cope with, medical problems. Since physicians reportedly have high credibility as healers in our society, one might assume that patients would follow their physician's directions. Yet, nearly 50% of all patients do not follow the prescribed treatment from their physicians (Stone, 1979). This statistic has not changed much in the last twenty years (Bullman, 1996). Such data link to a number of negative outcomes, not only for noncompliant patients, but others in the community as well. People who do not comply may contribute to higher medical costs and insurance rates because they are often subject to re-treatment as a result of therapeutic failures, recurring, or lingering infections, which can ultimately lead to surgical interventions and hospitalizations that initially are not necessary (Baskin, 1998). Surprisingly, noncompliance rates are as high for individuals suffering from severe chronic pain as they are for those having symptomless diseases (Tamaroff, Festa, Adesman, & Waco, 1992; Turk & Rudy, 1991). One possible way to rectify this lack of compliance is through better patient–physician interactions (Fitzpatrick, 1991). Therefore, it is useful to examine variables that may indicate whether one will follow a physician's directions.	Notice in the first two sentences how the purpose of this article is foreshadowed.

An introductory discussion of the problem of patient noncompliance is initiated here. |
| | Transition to thesis statement. |
| Our study concerned how a physician's perceived humor orientation, credibility, and communication competence relate to patients' levels of satisfaction and their compliance. We begin this report by examining scholarly literature concerning patient compliance, patient satisfaction, and medical humor. | Thesis statement.

Preview. |

Analysis

Attention-getter	This attention-getter was a statement of fact. Most people expect to be told about a medication, treatment, or lifestyle change at the conclusion of a medical interview.
Transition to topic	"Since physicians reportedly have high credibility as healers in our society, one might assume that patients would follow their physician's directions."
Significance of topic	Discussion of how noncompliance affects cost of medical care for everyone.
Espousal of credibility	Consistent citation of both primary and secondary sources throughout the introduction paragraph.
Thesis	"Our study concerned how a physician's perceived humor orientation, credibility, and communication competence relate to patients' levels of satisfaction and their compliance."
Preview	"We begin this report by examining scholarly literature concerning patient compliance, patient satisfaction, and medical humor."

Figure 5.2 Article Introduction

Literature Review

One of the most important parts of a research paper, and often the largest, is the literature review section. A literature review is the selection of available documents (published and unpublished) on a given topic that contain information, opinions, data, and evidence written from a particular point of view that aid in a reader's understanding of pertinent review prior to examining the results in a new study. For most people, the literature review is the easiest section to write and the one they are most familiar writing. In many ways, a literature review is like a series of brief research papers about various related topics.

In an article by Rocca and Vogl-Bauer (1999) looking at sports fans' perceptions of appropriate fan communication, the researchers looked at three major areas of literature in their article. First, the authors discussed some background on the popularity and known behavior of sports enthusiasts, then discussed verbal aggression, and finally discussed how individuals identify with various teams. By clearly explaining the research previously completed in the three subcategories, Rocca and Vogl-Bauer were able to help the reader gain a full understanding of the current state of research in each area and how the three separate research areas could be studied together in the "Rationale for Research Questions" section of their article.

Ultimately, there are five basic reasons for the literature review in scientific papers. First, a literature review provides and explains necessary vocabulary for readers. One of the fundamental aspects of a literature review is that it is educational and definitional. A literature review must clearly explain all technical terms related to that research paper. In academia, we often create terms that mean things slightly different than when used by the general public. For example, to communibiologists the term "psychoticism" refers to the degree to which an individual believes that society's rules pertain to her or him. If you ask people in the general public what psychoticism means, you'll probably get definitions related to psychological disturbances like antisocial personality disorder, schizophrenia, borderline personality disorder, and many other disorders. Even scholars in different subfields of the same discipline can examine the same term in slightly different ways, so it is always important to clearly specify what you mean by various terms in a literature review to make sure everyone is on the same page. Also, having clear definitions helps a researcher to "operationalize" her or his variables. Operationalizing variables is when a researcher determines how to measure a specific variable, which will be discussed in great detail in Chapter 9.

The second reason we have literature reviews in academic research papers is because literature reviews place our current research into a historical context, which help readers synthesize existing research in a concise manner. One of the basic goals of the literature review is to provide enough historical and conceptual information about a research topic so readers of the research will be able to adequately judge the merits and usefulness of a new research study. For example, if you were to write a literature review section about the variable *communication apprehension* and only mentioned articles written in the past year, you limit the type of information your readers will receive, and they will not have enough information to adequately judge your new study. This does not mean that you must include every article that has ever been written on the subject. In fact, in the National Communication Association's journals at the time this chapter was written, *communication apprehension* appeared in 47 different titles and was mentioned in 227 different articles. There is no way you can attempt to talk about each of these different articles in a literature review. In fact, there are actually around 10 different books that take on the concept of communication apprehension alone. Ultimately, when creating the historical context for a new study, it is important to find the most important pieces of research directly related to your study. Ultimately, if you find the best research sources, your reader should be able to understand where your new study fits into the history of research within a specific research area.

The third reason academics write literature reviews is because they aid in the explanation and rationalization for why specific variables have been chosen as an object of study in a research project. In quantitative research, scholars are never just studying one variable like communication apprehension. Instead, scholars examine a variety of variables together to gain an understanding of how those variables relate to or differ from each other. For example, the articles that accompany this text examine a wide array of different variables: Boiarsky, Long, and Thayer (1999)—children's television shows, content pacing, sound effects, and visual pacing; Brummans and Miller (2004)—organizational ambiguity and organizational effects; Chesebro (1999)—listening style and conversational sensitivity); Punyanunt (2000)—behavior alteration techniques, humor orientation, and humor effectiveness; McCroskey, Richmond, Johnson, and Smith (2004)—organizational orientations, job satisfaction, communication apprehension, nonverbal immediacy, sociocommunicative orientation, credibility, and human temperament; Rocca and Vogl-Bauer (1999)—verbal aggression, fan identification, and appropriate fan communicative messages; Thomas, Richmond, and McCroskey (1994)—nonverbal immediacy, sociocommunicative style; Weber, Fornash, Corrigan, and Neupauer (2003)—cognitive learning, learner empowerment, and nonverbal immediacy); Wrench and Booth-Butterfield (2003)—humor orientation, credibility, compliance-gaining strategies, patient satisfaction, and patient compliance. As you can see from the short list of articles we present along with this text, a large variety of communication variables are studied in these 10 articles. More importantly, no one article utilizes the same combination of variables. As you can see, some studies will only have a couple of variables being studied like Brummans and Miller (2004), who only study two variables in their article. And other studies will study a large number of variables; for instance, McCroskey et al. (2004) studied seven different variables. Ultimately, it is the job of a literature review to demonstrate why a researcher is studying only two variables or studying seven variables in a specific project.

The fourth major reason for writing a literature review is to help demonstrate what has been done in research and what still needs to be accomplished. We will never get to the point where there is no more research that needs to be accomplished in the field of communication. A literature review should demonstrate that you have examined the literature closely enough to know that there are still avenues that need to be explored. Although there are some studies that replicate or reconduct previously completed studies, most research completed is new. Whether you are researching previously studied variables in a new context (political, educational, romantic relationships, physician–patient relationships, etc.) or researching variables that have never been examined together at all, literature reviews aid in explaining what has not been studied yet and why it should be studied at all.

The last reason scholars write literature reviews is to help establish the argument being tested in the study. In every study there is some argument being made. Just like giving a persuasive speech, a literature review ends with a persuasive argument for either a hypothesis or a research question. While these hypotheses and research questions will be discussed in more detail below, let's go ahead and introduce the two concepts here. First, a hypothesis is defined as a statement about the relationship between independent and dependent variables, whereas a research question is an explicit question researchers ask about variables of interest. Ultimately, whether one is able to form a hypothesis or research question is dependent upon whether a researcher has the literature to support making a clear argument or hypothesis.

Now that we have examined the five main reasons academics write literature reviews, we can examine the two main sections of a literature review: previous research and study rationale.

PREVIOUS RESEARCH

The first major part of a literature review consists of an examination of pertinent previous research about the variables in your study. The previous research section of a literature review is what most people generally think of when they think about a literature review. This is the section where authors actually discuss previous research about the variables to be studied in the current paper or article. First and foremost, if you have completed your literature search in the way we discussed in the previous chapter, this section will be very easy to write. Writing the previous research section is the part of the research process with which most people are familiar. In fact, you've probably been writing traditional "research papers" since you were in junior high or middle school. After you've done your literature search, you simply need to determine how to organize the primary and secondary sources into a cohesive new product that clearly defines all key concepts, demonstrates the history of those concepts, and links those concepts together in your new research study to form your argument.

When organizing the previous research section in a literature review, there are two aspects to be considered (McCroskey, Wrench, & Richmond, 2003). The first aspect to organizing the previous research section relates to the overall organization and style. Many people, when writing the previous research section of a literature review, will have one organizational pattern they start with and keep throughout the entire previous literature section. In essence, an author can pick one organizational pattern and then use that pattern to tell a story within the literature review. However, other people will break their previous research section of the literature review into different subsections or groupings and then use similar or different organizational patterns for each subsection within the literature review.

Chronological

The first pattern for arranging main ideas is what is referred to as the chronological pattern. The chronological pattern places the main ideas in the order in which they appear in history—whether backwards or forwards. For example, if you were writing a literature review section that contains both communication apprehension and humor assessment, you would start off writing about communication apprehension, which has been around since the 1970s. You would start by only writing about communication apprehension until 2001, which was when the Humor Assessment was first published, and then you would continue writing the literature review from 2001 to the most current research incorporating information about both communication apprehension and humor assessment. In essence, you would cover 30 years of communication apprehension in your literature review before you integrated information about humor assessment. In this first instance of the chronological organizational pattern, the author would have used one organizational pattern to create one constant story throughout the previous research section of the literature review. Let's now see how the chronological organizational pattern can be used if a literature review is broken into subsections.

If an author decided to chunk pieces of information within a previous research section of a literature review, he or she could also easily use the chronological organizational pattern. Using the same example of communication apprehension and humor assessment as the variables being studied in a research project, the author would in one section explain the history of communication apprehension starting in the 1970s and continuing through the most recent research about communication apprehension. This historical perspective on communication apprehension would then be followed by a historical telling of the origins of humor assessment. While the history of humor assessment only dates back to 2001, a variety of research projects, both published and unpublished, have been written about the variable humor assessment, so a clear history of the concept does exist—even if it is much shorter.

Cause and Effect

The cause-and-effect organizational pattern is used to explain what causes a specific situation and what the effect of that situation is. For example, if you are writing a study about the use of a new miracle drug that can be used to help individuals with high levels of communication apprehension, you could start your previous research section of your literature review by explaining how neurochemical processes may be a strong root cause of communication apprehension. After explaining the cause of communication apprehension, you could then explain the various effects of having elevated levels of communication apprehension (lower self-esteem, less likely to be called on by a teacher, more likely to be fired, fewer friends, lower grades in school, etc.). Ultimately, this organizational pattern helps you establish why your study should take place. In other words, you demonstrated what researchers think causes communication apprehension and what happens if you have high levels of communication apprehension, so a new drug that can help lower people's levels of communication apprehension (or your new study) would be beneficial to highly communicative apprehensive people.

If you were studying multiple variables within a study, the cause-and-effect organizational format can also be very useful. If a researcher were examining racism and sexism, he or she may decide to write two separate sections on the causes and effects of both racism and sexism separately. If both the causes and the effects of racism and sexism are very similar, the researcher can then assert that the two concepts should be highly related to one another, which could be the purpose of the study.

Compare and Contrast

Another method for creating main points is the compare-and-contrast method. Comparing (showing how information is similar) and contrasting (showing how information is different) is a tool all of us have used on a number of occasions to help us analyze chunks of information. If you want to arrange the whole previous research section of your literature review using a compare-and-contrast organizational pattern, you could compare and contrast two similar but different variables using existing literature. For example, in communication, researchers try to differentiate between argumentativeness (discussing ideas and issues in a debate) and aggressiveness (attacking the other person). However, these two terms are often confused with one another by both scholars and lay-people. A literature review containing both communication variables could first show how the two variables are similar (compare), and then show how the variables are different (contrast). While this organizational pattern often consists of two main points (one section on comparing and one section on contrasting), an author can easily create an introduction point where basic information about the two variables is initially discussed. For example, you could spend a subsection of the previous research section of your literature review discussing what argumentativeness is and what aggression is. This subsection would be followed by a subsequent subsection where you talk about the similarities of argumentativeness and aggression, and finally a subsection where you examine how these two communication variables are different.

An author can also use the compare-and-contrast organizational pattern as an independent subsection by itself. Maybe one of the major research variables you are studying in a project is sociocommunicative orientation. To discuss sociocommunicative orientation using compare and contrast, you could discuss Richmond and McCroskey's (1990) concepts of sociocommunicative orientation (assertiveness and responsiveness) and compare and contrast them with Sandra Bem's (1974) concepts of masculinity and femininity. In essence, by the time this subsection of your literature is written, your audience would have a general understanding of sociocommunicative orientation and how it is functionally different from Bem's concepts of masculinity and femininity.

Problem–Cause–Solution

Another format for creating distinct main points is the problem–cause–solution format. In this specific format, you discuss what a problem is, what is causing the problem, and finally what the solution could be to correct the problem. Maybe a researcher wants to study whether or not a new training program helps people communicate better on a first date. The researcher can start her or his previous research section of the literature review by discussing the problems that many people face when dating (shyness, anxiety, not knowing what to say, etc.). The problems with first dates could be followed by a discussion of what causes these problems with first dates to occur (lack of dating experience, bad previous dating experiences, poor communication skills, etc.). Finally, the researcher could explain how to solve the problems that occur with first dates. Ultimately, the researcher could run a study to see if her or his "solution" to the first date problem actually works.

Psychological

The next way to organize your main ideas within a previous research section of a literature review is through a psychological organizational pattern, or "a" leads to "b" and "b" leads to "c." In most behavioral genetics research, researchers start with the premise that our genetics causes humans to have specific temperaments, and these temperaments cause humans to behave in specific ways. In other words, genetics (a) leads to temperament (b) and temperament (b) leads to human behavior (c), or "a" leads to "b" and "b" leads to "c." When using the psychological organizational pattern, a researcher needs to clearly show how previous literature has established causal relationships. However, if a researcher does not need to explain causal relationships, this organizational pattern is probably not very useful.

Categorical/Topical

The last organizational pattern for arranging the previous research subsection of the literature review is by using various categories or topics to lay out your main points. The categorical/topical pattern is the organizational pattern used most often by researchers. To use this organizational pattern, a researcher simply separates her or his main concepts or variables being explored in a study into separate subsections within the literature review. For example, if you are conducting a study and want to examine organizational orientations (upward mobile, ambivalent, and indifferent), sociocommunicative orientation (assertiveness and responsiveness), and workplace satisfaction, you could organize your previous research section into three main sections one for each variable.

You can also use this organizational pattern for your subsections if you have a section that has clearly delineated parts to it. In other words, you could organize your section on organizational orientations into three subsections or one for each orientation (upward mobile, ambivalent, and indifferent). You could organize sociocommunicative orientation into two subsections (assertiveness and responsiveness). While the first two variables can easily be sectioned off into their respective parts, workplace satisfaction would probably need to be organized using a different organizational pattern than discussed above. For this reason, there are three specific organizational patterns that can be used specifically when organizing a subsection: general to specific, specific to general, and known to unknown.

General to Specific

The first subsection organizational pattern is general to specific. Think of this organizational pattern as a funnel. The brim is very wide at the top (very general) and then gets very narrow at the bottom (very specific). This type of organizational pattern is useful when an author wants to start off writing about anything and everything about a topic and then narrow her or his way down to an aspect of that topic that relates to the current study. For example, if you are writing a subsection on communication apprehension for an article about workplace communication apprehension, you could start off by explaining what communication apprehension is, followed by some specific studies related to communication apprehension in general, and end with a discussion of any studies that have examined communication apprehension in the workplace.

Specific to General

The second subsection organizational pattern is specific to general. You can also think of this organizational pattern in terms of a funnel, but you have to turn that funnel upside down to get the effect. The brim is very narrow at top (very specific) and then gets very wide at the bottom (very general). Use this organizational pattern if you are trying to extrapolate some general ideas from specific information. Although it seems backward (and often is), this organizational pattern can be very useful if you are trying to see the large picture instead of a more narrowed one. If you were to use this organizational pattern, you could start your subsection on communication apprehension by talking about communication apprehension in the workplace, followed by a discussion of some specific studies related to communication apprehension in general, and end with a general discussion of communication apprehension.

Known to Unknown

The last organizational pattern specifically for subsections of your previous research is known to unknown. In this organizational pattern, an author discusses what we know about a specific topic or variable and then leads the reader to what we do not know about a topic or variable. What we know is based on what has been studied in the previous research, and what we don't know is based on what seems to be a big hole in the literature. For example, maybe you're studying talkaholism and you notice when doing your literature search that talkaholism has never been studied in intimate relationships. When you organize your subsection of talkaholism, you would start off with all the information that researchers have found about talkaholism and then finally lead into a discussion of the fact that research has never examined how talkaholism affects intimate relationships.

Now that we have examined a number of different ways that researchers can organize previous research when writing a literature review, let's switch our attention to the Wrench and Booth-Butterfield (2003) article to see how these researchers laid out their literature review. Figure 5.3 shows a subsection from their literature review examining "Humor in the Medical Context"—take a minute to read this subsection now. You'll notice that this subsection of the literature review is very categorical in what is discussed in each paragraph. To see how this subsection fits into the overall scheme of the article, read the previous literature section from the article on the accompanying CD-ROM that came with this textbook.

Study Rationale

After you have developed the background information for your study in the previous research section of the literature review, you are ready to explain to your readers why you have decided to perform the current study. The rationale section of the literature review is the subsection where you explain why and how you are going to perform your analysis of the variables you have described in your literature review. More importantly, the study rationale section of a literature review is where a researcher introduces her or his specific hypotheses and research questions. In Chapter 2 we discussed in great detail how researchers go about

Humor in the Medical Context

   In a recent study in the *Journal of American Medical Association*, Levinson, Roter, Mullooly, Dull, and Frankel (1997) reported that physicians who used humor and laughed more during patient–physician interactions were less likely to engender malpractice suits. The use of humor as a variable in medical research has proved to be positive for both patients and their caregivers. Patients exposed to humorous messages have lower levels of stress-related hormones (Berk, 1989); increased immunoglobulin rates (Lambert & Lambert, 1995; McClelland & Cheriff, 1997); increased helper T-cells (Berk, 1993); lower levels of pain (Adams & McGuire, 1986; Cohen, 1990; Pasquali, 1991); lower blood pressure (Fry & Savin, 1982); and faster recovery rates from illnesses (McClelland & Cheriff, 1997). A patient's sense of humor and the degree to which he or she actively seeks humorous messages are predictive of her or his perceived health and morale (Simon, 1990). In a study conducted by Gaberson (1991), patients exposed to humorous messages had lower levels of anxiety before operations and higher post operation recovery rates. The inclusion of humorous messages in the patient–physician relationship can reduce fear while promoting trust (Robinson, 1991). Overall, humor in the medical environment appears to have an overwhelmingly positive effect and seems likely to increase positive perceptions of caregivers and subsequently compliance with their directions (James, 1995).

   Physicians and other medical professionals personally use humor as a means of coping with the uncertainty that surrounds the medical profession (Bosk, 1996; Wanzer, Booth-Butterfield, & Booth-Butterfield, 1997). The use of humor appears to allow doctors and other medical personnel to ease tension (Ditlow, 1993). Medically speaking, the enactment of humor causes us to laugh, which physiologically increases endorphin levels, which, in turn, are associated with decreased anxiety levels (McGhee, 1996).

   Despite the benefits of integrating humor into the medical office, humor should not be unskillfully used. Mulkay (1988) mentions that humor has the potential to create a language of domination and opposition rather than collaboration. Misinterpretation of humorous language could force the individuals interacting to see each other as foes instead of collaborators (Witkin, 1999). Hence communicators must be aware of potential negative effects of poorly enacted or misperceived humor, as well as the potential of positive outcomes. It may be diagnostic that highly humor-oriented individuals spend more time rehearsing jokes when compared to minimally humor-oriented individuals (Honeycutt & Brown, 1998). Hopefully, a portion of this rehersal time involves considering the possible positive and negative implications of enacted humor. Honeycutt and Brown (1998) suggest that people who use humor well probably have a contingency plan if the first one fails to have the desired impact or leads to a negative outcome.

Right off the bat you should notice that this is clearly categorical. The other major categories in this literature review are patient compliance, patient satisfaction, perceived credibility, and compliance gaining strategies.

The first part of this subsection explains the biological benefits of humor.

The second part of this subsection examines the psychological benefits of humor in the medical environment.

Here we have a discussion of physician use of humor in the medical environment.

This section discusses problems and suggestions for using humor in the medical environment.

Figure 5.3 Literature Review Segment

creating arguments utilizing the findings of previous research. In empirical research, we must be able to form clear arguments before we can pose a hypothesis. As mentioned in Chapter 2, a hypothesis is a *tentative statement about the relationship between two or more variables.* This tentative statement occurs at the end of a logical argument. Unfortunately, researchers often will have questions they want to ask in research, but a logical argument simply cannot be created to offer support for a hypothesis. When a researcher cannot create a hypothesis, he or she may ask a research question. The difference between a hypothesis and a research question is the ability to form an argument for the proposed relationship or difference. In a hypothesis, we use the previous research to make a prediction that is logical, whereas in a research question the previous research cannot help us make a prediction, so we must simply ask a question. To aid in the clarification of the purpose of a study rationale, we will examine both hypotheses and research questions separately.

HYPOTHESES

A hypothesis is the backbone of modern scientific study, whether it be in the physical or social sciences. As defined previously, a hypothesis is a statement about the relationship between independent and dependent variables. Good hypotheses need to be testable, compatible with current knowledge, logically consistent, and simple. First, a useful hypothesis is a statement about the relationship or difference between two or more variables that can be tested. A person can say that after watching all science fiction movies he or she believes that all extraterrestrials will speak English, but unless he or she has the ability to sample all extraterrestrials then the statement is not a useful hypothesis because the statement cannot be tested. The key word when examining a hypothesis is "testable." A scientist must be able to perform a test of how two variables or phenomena might be related or differ.

A useful hypothesis also needs to be compatible with current knowledge about a specific topic. For example, in the study by Weber, Fornash, Corrigan, and Neupauer (2003), the authors examined the effect that student interest has on the college classroom. Previous research had found that if a college student was interested in the examples in a textbook, that student was able to remember more about the material longer than a college student who was not interested in the examples used in a textbook. While the authors had seen issues of interest in textbooks, no one had really examined how interesting examples affect cognitive recall after a lecture. Based on this previous research, the authors hypothesized that if college instructors used examples that were interesting to the students, the students would perform better on a test after a lecture. Notice how Weber et al. (2003) used what was previously seen in research to make an argument about what they would expect to see in a new, but related, context.

The Weber et al. (2003) hypothesis contains the words "if" and "then," which are necessary in a formalized hypothesis. But not all if–then statements are hypotheses. For example, "If I gamble, then I will get rich," is not really a hypothesis—it is a simple prediction. In a formalized hypothesis, a relationship or difference is stated. For example, to turn the gambling case into a formalized hypothesis, one could test if the frequency of winning is related to the amount of time spent playing slot machines. In this case the statement would read something like, "If a person spends more time playing slot machines, then her or his odds of winning goes up." If you always ask yourself if one thing is related to another, then you should be able to test it.

Many hypotheses are also multilayered and have a number of "if" statements before the "then" statement in the hypothesis. For example, in the Weber et al. (2003) study, you could have a the following if statements: (1) If student interest is important to cognitive recall with books and (2) if student interest functions the same way with lecturing and cognitive recall, then (3) student interest should relate to cognitive recall after a lecture. Notice that without all three statements together, a clear argument could not be made. An author cannot make a leap in logic without clearly attempting to explain what he or she is thinking when writing a hypothesis.

A third factor of good hypotheses is that they are logically consistent. In other words, a hypothesis cannot contradict itself and actually be a hypothesis. If while examining the literature you find that studies consistently disagree as to whether men or women are more ambivalent in the workplace, you will have problems generating a good hypothesis because your literature is inconsistent. If at any point you find yourself writing a justification for a hypothesis that says "it could be this or it could be that," then you really do not have a strong hypothesis and that hypothesis should probably be rewritten as a research question instead of as a hypothesis.

Finally, good hypotheses are simple. Before each hypothesis is stated in a research study, a short explanation of the relationship between research studies in the literature is given to explain why the hypothesis can be justified. If this explanation becomes too long or too confusing, it's not simple and is more likely to be logically faulty. In the Weber et al. (2003) article, the authors wrote, "Based on what is known about the relationship between affective variables and cognitive learning [citations given in original] coupled with the literature on text-based interest [citations given in original] we could expect that interest would be positively related to recall of lecture material" (p. 118). This short declarative statement clearly outlines the if–then statements and provides the basis for the actual hypothesis, which is "Lectures utilizing interest-based examples should result in participants with higher scores on subsequent tests of cognitive recall" (p. 118). While this section has introduced what a hypothesis is, we need to explain that there are two different types of hypotheses that a person can make when writing a research study.

One-Tailed Hypotheses

The first type of hypothesis is called a one-tail hypothesis or a hypothesis that predicts the specific nature of the relationship or difference. In the example above from Weber et al. (2003), the authors clearly indicated that lectures with interest-based examples would result in participants having higher scores on tests. This hypothesis predicted that students in classrooms where they heard interesting examples during lectures would score statistically significantly higher on cognitive recall (multiple choice tests) than students in classrooms that did not have interesting examples. Researchers can also write hypotheses to examine the relationship between two variables like Chesebro (1999) did when he wrote, "A positive relationship exists between the People listening style and conversational sensitivity" (p. 235). In this hypothesis, Chesebro is expecting to see a positive relationship between two variables (People listening style and conversational sensitivity).

Two-Tailed Hypotheses

The second type of hypothesis is called a two-tailed hypothesis, or a hypothesis that predicts that there is a significant difference or relationship, but does not indicate the specific nature of the difference (which group would have a higher score) or relationship (positive or negative). For example, if we wanted to write the Weber et al. (2003) hypothesis as a two-way hypothesis, it would read "lectures utilizing interest-based examples should result in different participant scores on subsequent tests of cognitive recall when compared to participant scores who did not hear interest-based examples during lectures." In this case, all we did is take out the direction of the hypothesis and make it more general. To rewrite Chesebro's (1999) hypothesis and make it two-way, we could write, "There will be a relationship between the People listening style and conversational sensitivity." In this case, we are no longer saying that we expect the relationship to be positive, but rather we are saying that we expect to see a relationship that could be either positive or negative.

So how does one choose between one- and two-tailed hypotheses? Ideally, if you have a strong enough argument for the direction of the relationship (positive or negative) or which nominal group will exhibit a variable to a greater degree (males or females; short or tall people; lower Social Economic Status (SES), middle SES, or upper SES; etc.), you should. However, if you write a hypothesis with a specific direction in mind, it alters the parameters of the statistical tests you will use. For this reason, many scholars argue that you should always be conservative and not write one-tailed hypotheses. When we examine Chapter 15, we will go into further detail about how one- or two-tailed hypotheses change the actual statistics.

The Null Hypothesis

Finally, when talking about hypotheses, it is extremely important to understand that in statistics researchers never test an actual alternative hypothesis (or the one listed in a research article as H_1). Instead, researchers always test the null hypothesis or the Null Monster!!! The null hypothesis is almost always expressed as the "nil" hypothesis—there are zero differences or zero relationships (Cohen, 1994). According to traditional scientific standards, we must assume that the null hypothesis is true until a researcher can provide support to the contrary (or that her or his alternative hypothesis is true). Let's imagine that your hypothesis is the following:

H_1: There **is** a relationship between eating pizza and public speaking anxiety.
In this case, you are predicting that eating pizza will relate to someone's level of public speaking anxiety. If this is your hypothesis (H_1), then your null hypothesis (H_0) must be the following:

H_0: There **is** **no** relationship between eating pizza and public speaking anxiety.
Again, the null hypothesis states that there is no difference or no relationship.

So, why then do we test the null hypothesis in statistics? Fisher (1935) posed the first argument for why we test the null hypothesis: we can never really prove anything as true using statistics; however, we can use statistics to prove that something is false. Based on this reasoning, we cannot prove a hypothesis, but we can prove that a null hypothesis is false. Imagine we observed 100 people who all had blue eyes and then made the statement, "everyone has blue eyes." All we would need to do is find one person with brown eyes to disprove the statement "everyone has blue eyes." More practically, the null hypothesis provides researchers a more general base to make predictions. If researchers were going to test the hypothesis that females and males differ in their attitudes about the usefulness of public speaking, do you test the hypothesis that females and males differ by a small amount, a medium amount, or a large amount. By testing the null hypothesis, researchers do not have to have a specific magnitude of difference in mind, they just have to test the null hypothesis that there is no difference at all.

In shorthand notation, a null hypothesis is always written as H_0 and a regular hypothesis is written as $H_{1, 2, \ldots x,}$ with x being an infinite number of study hypotheses. So, for the Weber et al. (2003) study, H_1 is "Lectures utilizing interest-based examples **should** result in participants with higher scores on subsequent tests of cognitive recall" and H_0 is "Lectures utilizing interest-based examples **will not** result in participants with higher scores on subsequent tests of cognitive recall." Furthermore, for the Chesebro's (1999) study, H_1 is "A **positive** relationship exists between the People listening style and conversational sensitivity" and H_0 is "**No** relationship exists between the People listening style and conversational sensitivity." Note that the words in bold make it either a hypothesis or the null hypothesis. The null version of Chesebro's hypothesis is not that there will be a negative relationship, but rather that no relationship will exist at all. If you rewrote the Chesebro hypothesis to read that there would be a negative relationship, you're just creating another hypothesis and not the null hypothesis. Remember, the null hypothesis is just the opposite of the actual hypothesis.

RESEARCH QUESTIONS

As mentioned earlier, a research question is an explicit question researchers ask about variables of interest. In other words, researchers often want to see if there are differences or relationships between variables, so they ask a question about the possibility of that difference or relationship in the rationale section of the literature review. For example, maybe you want to know if there is a difference between the overall scores of males and females and on the Personal Report of Communication Apprehension IV (PRCA IV). Although you could write your question like we just did, in formal research there are traditional ways of doing so. When preparing to ask a research question, a researcher needs to thoroughly explain why he or she believes a question should be asked. More importantly, a researcher needs to demonstrate that there is not enough evidence based on previous research to form a clear hypothesis. Just like a researcher has to explain the rationale for proposing a hypothesis, a researcher needs to explain her or his rationale for a research question as well. However, this rationale is not a formal argument establishing the possibility of a difference or relationship that is expected, but rather the rationale explains why there could be a difference or relationship between two or more variables. Just like hypotheses, there are two different types of research questions as well: directional and nondirectional.

Directional Research Questions

Directional research questions occur when a researcher asks if there is either a specific significant difference between two or more variables or a positive or negative relationship between two or more variables. To test for a difference, you could run a study to see if females or males consumed more alcohol in social settings by asking this research question: "Do males drink significantly more than females in social situations?" And if you wanted to test for a relationship, you could conduct a study to determine if there is a relationship between the amount of alcohol consumed and an individual's perceptions of opposite sex attractiveness. For this study you could propose a research question that reads: "Is there a positive relationship between drinking alcohol and individual perceptions of attractiveness?" Most importantly, both of these statements are questions and not hypothesis statements.

Nondirectional Research Questions

The second type of research question is the nondirectional research question—when a researcher asks if there is a difference or relationship between two or more variables. Most researchers who use research questions in a study will use a nondirectional research question. For example, you can write nondirectional research question to test for differences in alcohol consumption by males and females: "Is there a difference between consumption of alcohol by females and males during social events?" In this research question, the question was written to determine if there was a difference between men and women and alcohol consumption during social events. Again, this question does not predict a direction of the difference or that a difference will occur, only that there could be a difference. An example of a nondirectional research question for a relationship can be seen in Rocca and Vogl-Bauer's (1999) study. They asked, "What is the nature of the relationship between trait verbal aggression and sports fans' perceptions of appropriate communicative messages at sporting events?" In essence, this question wants to see how a fan's verbal aggression does or does not relate to her or his perceptions of appropriate communication at a sporting event. Notice that no indication of the nature of this relationship is discussed in this research question.

Overall, when determining whether to use hypotheses or research questions, you must first determine whether you have the quality and quantity of previously conducted research to support a hypothesis. If you do not have the literature to form a clear argument for a hypothesis, then create a research question to examine the possible difference or relationship between two or more variables. Figure 5.4 is a portion of the rationale in the study by Wrench and Booth-Butterfield (2003). To see the rest of the hypotheses and research questions from this study, examine the full text of this article on the accompanying CD-ROM.

The rest of this chapter will quickly discuss the other major sections in a research study because more information will be covered about each section in later chapters.

Method Section

The method section helps readers understand who the participants were in a study and how the study was conducted. The purpose of the method section is twofold. First, it enables readers to see exactly what you did and either agree with or question your research strategies when your readers are attempting to determine the overall significance of your research. Second, the method section allows future researchers to replicate what you have done in a consistent manner. According to the American Psychological Association (2001), the method section can be broken down into four basic areas: participants, apparatus, procedure, and instrumentation.

Recently, communication researchers have begun examining humor from an enactment perspective to see how individuals differ in the production of humorous messages (Booth-Butterfield & Booth-Butterfield, 1991; Punyanunt, 1997, 2000; Wanzer, Booth-Butterfield, & Booth-Butterfield, 1995, 1996a, 1996b, in press; Wanzer & Frymier, 1999). Booth-Butterfield and Booth-Butterfield (1991) identified the concept of humor orientation (HO), or an individual's predisposition to enact humorous messages in interpersonal situations. Research has shown humor orientation to be a positive trait among nurses (Wanzer et al., 1996b, 1997), in supervisor–subordinate relationships (Rizzo, Wanzer, & Booth-Butterfield, 1999), and in teacher–student relationships (Punyanunt, 1997, 2000; Wanzer & Frymier, 1999). Although no research has directly examined the effects of humor orientation in physician–patient interactions, the link is readily made to satisfaction and compliance.	This paragraph functions as the quick version of a study rationale. You'll notice that the beginning part explains that humor has been studied in a variety of different types of interpersonal situations, but it has not been studied in physician–patient interactions.
Fitzpatrick (1993) described patient satisfaction as an "emotional link to healthcare." And since humor creates a positive emotional state (Wrench & McCroskey, 2000), those patients who find their physicians humorous presumably would also be more satisfied than those patients who do not find their physicians humorous. Hence:	Starting here the authors make the link between emotion, humor, and satisfaction to generate a clear hypothesis.

H1:   Physicians with higher levels of perceived humor orientation will also have higher levels of patient satisfaction.

Analysis

This hypothesis is a very clear series of two If statements followed by a Then statement:

If (a):   Patient satisfaction is an emotional link to healthcare.
If (b):   Physician humor creates a positive emotional state in their patients.
Then: Physician humor will cause patients to be satisfied.

Figure 5.4 Rationale

PARTICIPANTS

First, when writing a method section you want to give as much detail about your participants as needed. While there are countless demographic questions you can ask participants, not everything is actually necessary when writing a literature review. The two most common demographic questions asked are sex and age. When reporting sex, it is best to do a simple frequency report followed by a percentile for the total population, e.g., 50 females (50%), 48 males (48%), and 2 (2%) participants who did not indicate their biological sex. Notice that we did report missing data in this answer. Often when people are filling out surveys they will accidentally miss one of the questions or opt to not answer a specific question, so you should go ahead and report these as missing data. When you are reporting a sample's mean age, it's important to also report the standard deviation. When writing articles using the APA style, report the sample age using the notation M (mean) and SD (standard deviation), both of which will be discussed in greater detail in Chapter 8. For example, when reporting the mean you could write, "Overall, the sample consisted of 245 participants with a mean age of 23.45 ($SD = 5.25$)," or "The 245 participants represented a typical college age sample ($M = 23.45$, $SD = 5.25$)." Whether you choose the first or the second way does not matter; it's ultimately a matter of personal writing style.

Whether you need to report other demographic characteristics such as ethnicity, sexual orientation, hair color, social economic status, etc. will depend on the overall purpose of your study. If you are running a study on the impact that hair color has on perceived physical attractiveness, then identifying your participants' hair colors could be extremely important. However, if you're running a study on the impact of verbal aggression on political campaigns, hair color is clearly not a useful demographic characteristic. Look at Figure 5.5 to see how Wrench and Booth-Butterfield (2003) described their participants. Notice that the researchers actually had four different subsamples about which they reported demographic characteristics.

APPARATUS

The second part of the method section is the apparatus subsection. In this subsection, researchers briefly describe any special equipment (apparatuses) or materials they used in the course of a specific study. According to the American Psychological Association (2001), standard laboratory equipment furniture, stopwatches, screens, pencils, paper, scantrons, etc., do not need to be mentioned. However, if you are running a study and use a magnetic resonance imaging or computed tomography scan, then you would need to elaborate on the equipment. Some researchers go so far as to add ordering instructions in an appendix if the equipment is very specialized. Also, if you build or have equipment built for you, it is often necessary to provide schematics or at least technical drawings of the equipment for your readers.

PROCEDURE

In the procedure section, you describe the exact procedures that were used in your study in a step-by-step fashion. In Figure 5.5, the very last paragraph is the procedure paragraph. This paragraph explains to the reader that participants were asked to fill out a questionnaire while thinking about their primary care physician. Notice that the paragraph is very short and not overly technical. In some studies, this paragraph could be expanded to three or four pages, depending on how technical your procedures are. In the article by Boiarsky, Long, and Thayer (1999), the researchers go into great detail describing how the children's shows

Participants

To maximize external validity, participants for this study represented four groups. Some participants were diverse undergraduates enrolled in communication courses at a large Middle Atlantic public university. This portion included 25 (56.8%) males and 19 (43.2%) females and constituted 16.9% of the total sample. The second segment of participants consisted of graduate students in an applied master's degree program. Individuals in this program are all adult students who primarily focus on their occupations while taking courses throughout the year in educational cohorts. This portion of the sample consisted of 7 (14.6%) males and 41 (85.4%) females and was 18.4% of the total sample. The third group included individuals from the general public, shopping at a mid-Atlantic mall. Trained student interviewers conducted surveys in the mall. The mall was attractive because its patrons represent a diverse community, not just people associated with the university. This portion of the sample consisted of 76 (53%) males and 66 (46%) females and constituted 54.8% of the total sample.

The final portion of the sample was the product of fifty Internet postings in AOL chat rooms asking for volunteers. The postings occurred over a two-day period in order to reach a wide range of individuals. Individuals in the chat rooms were also asked to forward the call for participants to any friends and family members. Those who decided to participate in the study received information concerning the World Wide Web site where they could participate. This portion of the sample consisted of 6 (23%) males and 20 (77%) females, or 10% of the total sample.

The overall sample included 146 females (55.5%) and 114 (43.3%) males. Mean ages were: undergraduate students, $M = 22$; master's students, $M = 38.6$; general public, $M = 38.7$; and Online, $M = 37.3$. The overall mean age of 35.7. The ethnic breakdown was: 46 (17.5%) African Americans, 189 (71.9%) Anglos/Caucasian, 9 (3.4%) Middle Eastern, 15 (5.7%) Asian, 6 (2.3%) Hispanic/Latino, 10 (3.8%) Native American, and 1 (.4%) other. A final demographic category, highest level of education, showed the following statistics: 46 (17.5%) high school/ GED, 70 (26.6%) some college, 12 (4.6%) associate's degree, 79 (30%) college degree, 40 (15.2%) graduate/professional degree, and 15 (5.7%) postgraduate. Thus, the sample was quite diverse in background representing a wide variety of perspectives.

Procedure

Participants completed the Humor Orientation Scale, Compliance-Gaining Questionnaire, Perceived Credibility Scale, and Patient Satisfaction Scale, with their personal physician as the object of focus. If they did not have a personal physician, they were instructed to think of the most recent physician with whom they had interacted. Participants then indicated on a 0–100 scale the extent to which they had followed their physician's prescriptions and/or treatments after their last visit.

The first part of the method section clearly explains where the sample came from in this study. This study had four different population groups.

Here the number and percentages of females and males for each subsample is given.

The overall sample is discussed here including demographic characteristics (biological sex, age, ethnicity, and education level). Notice that the Standard Deviations for the mean ages were not given. Generally speaking, it is always best to report Standard Deviations with means.

The procedure section explains what the study participants actually did during their participation.

Figure 5.5 Method Section

were selected for inclusion in the study; how the sample of episodes from each show was selected, and how the selected episodes were then coded for the study. Needless to say, a lot of very technical information was necessary to share in case any future researchers decided to replicate this specific study.

INSTRUMENTATION

The last part of the method section is the instrumentation or measurement section. The instrumentation or measurement section is where a researcher explains which research measures were used to measure the specific study variables. For example, if you were running a study examining the time it takes a talkaholic's heart rate to slow down after giving a public speech, you would need to explain how you measured talkaholism and her or his heart rate. Did you randomly observe people in public and then choose people to participate in your study who you thought talked a lot, or did you give them a scale that measures a person's trait talkaholism and then select your sample? Did you use an electrocardiogram to measure heart rate, or did you just use fingers on the wrist or neck to measure heart rate? Ultimately, how we go about measuring things is extremely important. In fact, Chapter 9 will go into detail regarding how we measure variables. For now, we can explain the basic components of what you need to write down in this specific section by examining how to write up the measurement part for a scale. First, an author needs to explain what the scale is attempting to measure and who wrote the scale. For example, in the article by Rocca and Vogl-Bauer (1999), they wrote a measurement section for verbal aggression:

> The Verbal Aggression Scale (VAS) has been found to be both valid and reliable in assessing verbal aggression (Infante & Wigley, 1986; Rubin, Palmgreen, & Sypher, 1994). The VAS is a 20-item Likert-type scale with response categories ranging from (1) *almost never true* to (5) *almost always true*. This measure includes 10 positive worded and 10 negatively worded items. The reliability has been .80 or above in several studies (Infante & Wigley, 1986; Rubin et al., 1994). Obtained reliability for the verbal aggression scale in this study was .81. The mean for the VAS was 50.73 out of a possible 100 (*SD* = 9.93).

Notice that the first sentence explains that the VAS is a research measure that has been used in previous research and has been shown to be both reliable and valid. After reading the next two sentences, a reader can tell that the VAS has 20 items (10 positively worded and 10 negatively word) and uses a 5-point Likert scale ranging from "*almost never true*" to "*almost always true*." The next two sentences examine the scale's reliability (reliability will be discussed in greater detail in Chapter 10). The first of the two reliability sentences explains the level of reliability that is typically seen by the VAS, and the second sentence reports the obtained reliability for the VAS in the researcher's study. In the last sentence, the researchers report the mean and standard deviation for the VAS as seen in the study. This paragraph is a quick way of reporting the necessary information a reader needs about any scale to be used in research. For another example of how to write up a scale in the measurement section, take a look at Figure 5.6. Notice that Wrench and Booth-Butterfield (2003) included a section on the scale's validity, which will be discussed in greater detail in Chapter 10. While it is always important to explain the validity of a scale, some journals and editors will require more information about a scale's validity than others. It is our recommendation to attempt to add as much validity information about a scale as possible up front and then take it out at a later time if it is deemed unnecessary or extraneous to your research project. It is always faster to take material out than to try to add material at a later point.

Results Section

At this point we will mention the results section only briefly because most of the last part of this book is devoted to running statistics and writing up results sections. The results section is the part of a research article that untrained individuals just pass over completely because

Measurement	This sentence is a very general introduction to the measurement section listing the scales used in the entire study.
This study incorporated three measures of patient perceptions of their physician's communicative behavior (Humor Orientation, Physician Credibility, and Physician Compliance Gaining) and two others relating to perceptions of themselves (Satisfaction and Compliance).	
Humor Orientation Scale. The Humor Orientation (HO) Scale is a 17-item, self-report measure that uses a 5-point Likert format ranging from "strongly disagree" to "strongly agree." Booth-Butterfield and Booth-Butterfield (1991) developed the HO to permit an encompassing look at an individual's overall propensity to use humorous communicative messages in interpersonal situations. An adapted version of this instrument permitted examination of the perceived humor orientation of a physician in a format similar to that in studies by Wanzer and Frymier (1999) and Rizzo, Wanzer, and Booth-Butterfield (1999) involving teachers and supervisors. Previous research examining humorous communication in the classroom has shown that perceived humor enactment enhances teacher evaluations (Bryant, Cominsky, Crane, & Zillmann, 1980; Javidi, Downs, & Nussbaum, 1988); student learning (Gorham & Christophel, 1990); perceptions of teacher nonverbal immediacy (Gorham & Crhistophel, 1990); and affect in the classroom (Wanzer & Frymier, 1999), suggesting criterion validity for HO.	Notice that the scale is named, format explained (Likert), author identified, and what the scale purports to measure is explained.

The authors then explain that the scale is used in a variety of contexts and relate some of the previous findings associated with the scale.

Authors explain validity of the scale. |
| The Humor Orientation scale demonstrates predictive validity in that it has specifically been related to enhanced perceptions of social attractiveness (Wanzer et al., 1996a), greater skill in humorous presentation of information (Wanzer et al., 1995), and heightened perceptions of liking for supervisors (Rizzo et al., 1999), all of which would be expected outcomes for someone who enacts humor effectively. Scores for the HO can range from 17 to 85. For this sample, the HO had a Cronbach's alpha of .91 ($M = 52.74$; $SD = 10.47$). | Authors explain overall scoring and then the scale's reliability. |

Figure 5.6 Instrumentation or Measurement

it is the section that contains the bulk of the statistical information in the article. A general idea for a results section is that you will have one to two paragraphs for each hypothesis or research question unless one statistical device is able to analyze multiple hypotheses or research questions simultaneously. Either way, onw should always explain in the first line of a paragraph what results are analyzed in that paragraph. It is often very helpful to say up front, "In this paragraph, hypothesis three will be analyzed, which stated . . ." Being up front about what is in a paragraph keeps you focused while writing and makes it easier for others to read. Overall, the results section is not a place to write fancy treatises on life or research. The results section is simply that—a place to present the statistical results from the study you have conducted. In Figure 5.7, an example of a portion of a results section from the Wrench and Booth-Butterfield (2003) article is presented.

Discussion Section

The discussion section of a research study is broken into three major parts: the results discussion, the limitations, and future research. The first part of a discussion section provides a researcher space to explain her or his interpretation of the basic results found within a study, which is sometimes referred to as the discussion of the results. The purpose of the results

The first hypothesis was that a physician's perceived humor orientation would relate to her or his patient's level of satisfaction. Testing this hypothesis occurred by means of a series of bivariate linear regression analyses involving three dimensions of the patient satisfaction variable (cognitive, affective, and behavioral), with physician's humor orientation as the dependent variable. The regression equation for the first analysis was as follows: *Cognitive Satisfaction = .26 Humor Orientation +* 21.22, $F (1, 260) = 36.66, p < .0001$. As hypothesized, the stronger the physicians' humor orientation, the more likely their patients were to report cognitive satisfaction. This equation suggests that accuracy in predicting the overall cognitive satisfaction would be moderate. The correlation between physician humor orientation and patient cognitive satisfaction was .35. Approximately 12% of the variance of cognitive satisfaction was accounted for by its linear relationship with physician humor orientation.

The resulting regression equation for the second analysis was as follows: *Affective Satisfaction = .30 Humor Orientation + 18.19,* $F (1, 261) = 57.52, p < .0001$. As hypothesized, physicians with a more pronounced humor orientation tended to have patients who were more affectively satisfied. With this equation, accuracy in predicting affective satisfaction would be moderate. The correlation between physician humor orientation and patient affective satisfaction was .43. Approximately 18% of the variance of affective satisfaction was accounted for by its linear relationship with physician humor orientation.

The regression equation for the last analysis relating to Hypothesis 1 was as follows: *Behavioral Satisfaction = .19 Humor Orientation +* 19.53, $F (1, 261) = 31.38, p < .0001$. As physicians' humor orientation increased, patients were more behaviorally satisfied. The predictive accuracy of humor orientation for the behavioral satisfaction measure was moderate. The correlation between physician humor orientation and patient behavioral satisfaction was .33, which accounts for 11% of the variance of behavioral satisfaction from its linear relationship with physician humor orientation.

Notice how the first line of the results section explains what the first hypothesis was.

To avoid making you more confused at this point, just trust us when we say that the rest of this section explains the statistical processes that were used to examine the first hypothesis in the Wrench and Booth-Butterfield (2003) study.

Figure 5.7 Results

discussion is to interpret results in light of the study outcomes and explain how readers can understand the study variables differently than they could at the onset of the study. The discussion section should be connected to the literature review by way of the hypotheses and research questions posed and the literature cited. However, a discussion section should not be a retelling of the arguments made when forming hypotheses in the rationale. Instead, a results discussion explains how a study has moved knowledge of the study variables forward from where the arguments were made during the rationale.

One of the primary reasons for having a discussion section is for an author to provide her or his reasoning for the why the results turned out the way they have. Specifically, an author needs to give reasons for why hypotheses were either supported or not supported and for why research questions were able to detect relationships and differences. One very important note that needs to be made is that your results did not prove or disprove anything at all. In academic writing, when discussing one's results, it's important to avoid language that makes it sound like you discovered or proved anything; instead you can support or not support hypotheses based on your research. At the same time, make sure you always tackle the results that are directly related to your hypotheses and research questions first and then discuss any interesting features in the results that are worthy of explanation. Furthermore, the discussion section is not the place to attempt to introduce new findings and results. Although you might occasionally include in the discussion section tables and figures that help explain a result you are discussing, the tables and figures must not contain new results.

While interpreting your results, you should also find yourself comparing your results with those found in the past literature. It is extremely important to integrate sources from your literature review to help in your explanation of your results. Your literature will help you determine if your results are in line with previous research or if your results are breaking new ground. If your results are consistent with previous research, you may feel your task is complete. However, the ultimate challenge is not reiterating research, but demonstrating how your findings actually add to the ever-growing body of research on your subject. In Figure 5.8, Wrench and Booth-Butterfield (2003) analyze one part of their results. Notice how in the first paragraph the authors establish how the whole section will be laid out followed by a quick preview. Writing your discussion section in this manner is primarily about organization and making it easy for your reader to follow where you are going with your findings.

The second part of the discussion section is the limitations subsection. When organizing a limitations subsection it's important to include discussions of both design flaw and procedural problems. A design flaw is an oversight that does not come to the surface until the data have been collected. In cases where a flaw in the design of the experiment is the cause or possible cause of a peculiar data pattern, the design flaw needs to be brought to the attention of your readers. One of the most common design flaws is that a lot of research, ours included, often relies on college student samples, which may or may not be representative of the general public. While a college student sample may not change a lot of results in research

The primary goal of this study was to determine how physicians' humor orientation, credibility, and use of compliance-gaining strategies relate to patient satisfaction and compliance. The findings revealed significant relationships suggesting that better physician communication skills were associated with improved patient perceptions of physician credibility and patient satisfaction. The following paragraphs focus on the relationship that a physician's humor orientation has on patient satisfaction and physician credibility, the relationship between patient satisfaction and physician credibility, the relationship of compliance-gaining strategies with physician–patient interactions, and the post hoc analysis of the data sources used.	The first sentence re-explains the basic reason for this study.

This sentence explains how the discussion section will be laid out (it's basically an easy-to-follow preview). |
| The first major area of emphasis was patients' perceptions of physician humor orientation and how these perceptions related to patient satisfaction and physician credibility. Results for the first hypothesis indicated that a physician's humor orientation accounted for a moderate portion of the variance in each of Wolf et al.'s (1978) three dimensions of patient satisfaction (cognitive, affective, and behavioral). These results indicate that a physician's enactment of humor as an interpersonal communication tool, in general, positively relates to a patient's level of satisfaction. Although a physician's humor orientation accounts for some of the variation in a patient's satisfaction, the low coefficients of determination indicate that it is not the primary variable determining what ultimately causes patient satisfaction. This finding is similar to the one that Fitzpatrick (1991) reported in looking at patient satisfaction and physician friendliness and previous research that has also linked humor orientation with friendliness (Wanzer, Booth-Butterfield, & Booth-Butterfield, 1996a). | This part explains actual findings that occurred in the results section related to physician humor orientation, patient satisfaction, and physician credibility.

Notice how the result is explained and previous research is integrated to aid in the reasoning for why this finding actually occurred in this study. |

Figure 5.8 Discussion

studies, it is also possible that college students could be systematically different from the general public. For example, if you are conducting a study on the amount of alcohol being consumed in a given week, it's possible that college students could consume more or less alcohol than the general public. If you do not attempt to correct this problem, you could end up with skewed results. Ultimately, when writing a discussion section it is very important to admit when you have an actual or potential design flaw.

The second type of problem that you will want to discuss in your limitations is a procedural problem. A procedural problem is usually a mistake made by an experimenter (or experimenters), either through carelessness or ignorance, which resulted in the data being collected in a way not intended by the design of the experiment. For example, maybe you are conducting a study examining heart rates during impromptu speeches. If immediately prior to the study you are offering your participants cookies and coffee while they are waiting (sugar and caffeine are stimulants), your results may be altered because of the stimulants and not the impromptu speeches. Again, if this kind of problem occurs, it is best to be forthright about the problem in your discussion section. In Figure 5.9, Wrench and Booth-Butterfield examine two possible limitations to their study.

The last part of the discussion section is the future directions of research subsection. The directions for research section is a paragraph or series of paragraphs explaining your ideas for where future research should go as a result of your study. The goal of all new research is to gain knowledge. However, when we gain knowledge, new questions will always surface, so good research should lead to both an increase in knowledge and new questions that can be posed for future research. When creating your future research subsection, make sure you are specific about future developments and do not write statements like "this needs more research" or "in the future, more research should be done." The purpose of this section is for you as a researcher to explain how you see future research in this area being conducted. Provide constructive and specific instructions to your readers about how they can further your study and answer some of the questions still left unanswered. For example, maybe your research found an odd relationship or difference that should be replicated. Or maybe someone should examine your variables in a different communication context to see if the same

Limitations. No matter how rigorously a study is conducted, there are always limitations. Measurement issues are of concern. First, using a single perception-oriented answer to determine whether or not a patient would comply with her or his doctor's medication/treatment may not be the best way to measure compliance. Although this was the method devised by Dillard and Burgoon (1985) and also used by Burgoon et al. (1987), the results could be enhanced by taking into account more situational variables that conceivably affect compliance.	This limitation is a form of a design flaw.
The second major limitation in this study is the online sample used. Although individuals on AOL and in the general public samples were randomly selected to participate in the study, the completed sample was still admittedly self-selected. In addition, the small number of individuals who did participate in the online version was somewhat unsettling. New and more accurate attempts at getting online participants should be developed. At the same time, contrary to Sheehan and Hoy's (1999) fear that online samples are not generalizable to a larger and more diverse population, the lack of a meaningful significant difference between the online sample and those involving the other means of data collection does show the promise of online samples. As use of the Internet becomes more prevalent, concerns about skewed online samples should recede.	This limitation is a form of a procedural problem.

Figure 5.9 Limitations

Conclusion. This study clearly linked communication variables (humor orientation, credibility, and compliance gaining) to patient satisfaction and compliance. It also demonstrated why physicians need to think consciously about how they are using communication during patient–physician interactions. Although the results may seem to be intuitively obvious to communication researchers, further explanation of communication concepts in unique professional and social contexts helps to validate our theoretical conceptualizations of human communication in applied settings. Additionally, information concerning patient–physician communication has the potential for improving patient compliance, minimizing malpractice claims, and improving patient satisfaction.	Notice that the first sentence clearly summarizes the major results. The rest of this paragraph is explaining the benefits of research in the area of patient–physician communication.

Figure 5.10 Conclusion

results appear. Anything possible future avenues of research that came about as a result of your study should be discussed.

The Conclusion

The last part of a research project is the concluding section. When reading a research article, it is very common to find that the concluding section doesn't exist. Just like when giving a speech, a research paper needs to have a very solid concluding device. The concluding section should briefly summarize the main finding(s) from your study and demonstrate that the main arguments made in your study are all clearly explained. Think of the concluding section as the dinner mint after eating a five-course meal. Itshould be brief, contain no new information, and neatly wrap up the paper. It is often helpful to end your paper by re-examining the attention-getter you used in the introduction of your paper if appropriate. In Figure 5.10, Wrench and Booth-Butterfield (2003) demonstrate how a conclusion can be easily written.

Conclusion

This chapter has focused on the basic parts of a research paper: abstract, introduction, literature review, method section, results, discussion, and conclusion. Although this style of writing is clearly not a writing format that most people learn in their formative school years, the tricks and tools you have learned for writing will greatly benefit you as you attempt to write your own research papers. The best piece of advice we can give you from our years of writing research articles is to write, edit, rewrite, edit again, and keep on writing. Most research articles barely resemble their first drafts by the time they are published in a scholarly journal. While the writing process is arduous and complex, the impact that you can have on the academic world and the rewards you get when you see your name in print are worth the process.

KEY TERMS

Abstract	Directional Research	Illustration
Apparatus	Questions	Instrumentation
Chronological Order	Discussion Section	Introduction
Comparison-and-Contrast	General-to-Specific Order	Known-to-Unknown Order
Order	Hypothesis	Literature Review

Method Section
Nondirectional Research
  Question
Null Hypothesis Research
  Question
One-Tailed Hypothesis
Preview

Problem–Cause–Solution
  Order
Procedures
Rationale
Research Participant
Research Question
Results Section

Rhetorical Question
Specific-to-General Order
Thesis
Topical Order
Two-Tailed Hypothesis

REFERENCES

American Psychological Association. (2001). *Publication manual of the American Psychological Association* (5th ed.). Washington, DC: American Psychological Association.

Bem, S. L. (1974). The measurement of psychological androgyny. *Journal of Consulting and Clinical Psychology, 47,* 155–162.

Boiarsky, G., Long, M., Thayer, G. (1999). Formal features in children's science television: Sound effects, visual pace, and topic shifts. *Communication Research Reports, 16,* 185–192.

Brummans, B. H. J. M., & Miller, K. (2004). The effect of ambiguity on the implementation of a social change initiative. *Communication Research Reports, 21,* 1–10.

Chesebro, J. (1999). The relationship between listening styles and conversational sensitivity. *Communication Research Reports, 16,* 233–238.

Cohen, J. (1994). The earth is round ($p < .05$). *American Psychologist, 49,* 997–1003.

Fisher, R. A. (1935). *The design of experiments.* Edinburgh, Oliver & Boyd.

McCroskey, J. C., Richmond, V. P., Johnson, A. D., & Smith, H. T. (2004). Organizational orientations theory and measurement: Development of measures and preliminary investigations. *Communication Quarterly, 52,* 1–14.

McCroskey, J. C., Wrench, J. S., & Richmond, V. P., (2003). *Principles of public speaking.* Indianapolis, IN: The College Network.

Punyanunt, N. M. (2000). The effects of humor on perceptions of compliance-gaining in the college classroom. *Communication Research Reports, 176,* 30–38.

Richmond, V. P., & McCroskey, J. C. (1990). Reliability and separation of factors on the assertiveness-responsiveness measure. *Psychological Reports, 67,* 449–450.

Rocca, K. A., & Vogl-Bauer, S. (1999). Trait verbal aggression, sports fan identification, and perceptions of appropriate sports fan communication. *Communication Research Reports, 16,* 239–248.

Thomas, C. E, Richmond, V. P., & McCroskey, J. C. (1994). The association between immediacy and sociocommunicative style. *Communication Research Reports, 11,* 107–115.

Weber, K., Fornash, B., Corrigan, M, & Neupauer, N. C. (2003). The effect of interest on recall: An experiment. *Communication Research Reports, 20,* 116–123.

Wrench, J. S., & Booth-Butterfield, M. (2003). Increasing patient satisfaction and compliance: An examination of physician humor orientation, compliance-gaining strategies, and perceived credibility. *Communication Quarterly, 51,* 482–503.

FURTHER READING

Cooper, H. (1998). *Synthesizing research: A guide for literature reviews* (3rd ed.). Thousand Oaks, CA: Sage.

Fink, A. (1998). Conducting research literature reviews: From paper to the Internet. Thousand Oaks, CA: Sage.

Hart, C. (1998). *Doing a literature review: Releasing the social science research imagination.* Thousand Oaks, CA: Sage

Variables

1. Define what a variable is.
2. Distinguish between abstract and concrete variables.
3. Understand the four units of analysis (individuals, dyads, groups, and organizations).
4. Know what variable aspects (attributes and values) are and how to determine them.
5. Know the three types of relationships (positive, negative, and neutral).
6. Know the two types of differences (kind and degree).
7. Distinguish between independent and dependent variables.
8. Be able to differentiate between the four levels of variables (nominal, ordinal, interval, and ratio).
9. Know the three basic types of interval scales (Likert, semantic differential/bipolar, and scalagram).
10. Be able to use a chart to determine which statistical test is the most appropriate to conduct.

Ask a researcher how a particular research project was developed and you will likely hear a fascinating story. Sometimes the stories about how projects were conceptualized are almost as intriguing as the research itself. Recall our discussion in Chapter 4 of the methods for conceptualizing a research topic—some topics evolve out of personal experiences and others may be the result of current events or unanswered questions from previous studies. Once the idea for a study has been identified, the real task is in creating a "recipe" for the research project. Just as a chef is responsible for identifying the food ingredients necessary for a gourmet dish, a researcher creates a list of research "ingredients" (more commonly referred to as "variables") that will be used to conduct a study. In this chapter we identify the research variables necessary for a successful project and discuss various methods of analysis.

How Are Research Projects Developed?

Recall the methods discussed in Chapter 4 for coming up with a research topic. Ideas for a project can come from a variety of sources—a conversation, other research articles, or media examples. Once the conceptual idea has been identified, the next task involves writing a specific research question and identifying key terms or concepts. Remember the list of key concepts that we discussed in Chapter 4 to assist you in conducting library research on the topic? The same list can be used to help you identify potential variables to include in your study and to narrow your research topic. Specific questions that may be beneficial to ask when determining the overarching research question could include:

• How is communication related to the topic?
• What specific communication behaviors are involved?
• Are there other factors that could potentially influence the behavior?

Answers to these and other questions involve identifying the specific "things" that should be examined in a study. Returning to our earlier analogy of the recipe, the answers to the questions often require a researcher to identify the research "ingredients" that will be included in the study to find answers.

Variables: Units of Analysis

Variables are the ingredients of research projects. A variable can be defined as *any entity that can take on a variety of different values*. The manipulation, measurement, and control of variables is the primary mission of research. In essence, it is a concept or construct that varies. Examples of variables include age, sex, or level of public speaking anxiety (or fear of public speaking). Each of these variables will take on a different value for different people at a given time. One participant in a study could be a 32-year-old female with low public speaking anxiety and another could be a 19-year-old male with moderate public speaking anxiety. Variables can be stable or variable as a result of the context or situation. Concrete variables are stable or consistent. Examples might include characteristics such as biological sex or birth order (e.g., first born, middle child, or the baby). Abstract variables are those that change or differ over time or across situations or contexts. Examples of abstract variables could include communication satisfaction or self-disclosure.

Researchers identify the specific variables or elements to compare differences between individual and groups. For example, we might compare the level of parent–child communication satisfaction for first-born, middle-born, and last-born children. In this instance, birth order is a concrete variable that remains constant. Communication satisfaction is classified as an abstract variable. Differences could emerge when asking a participant to report on the level of communication satisfaction with one's mother versus one's father. Let's take a look at another example. Suppose you wanted to compare the self-disclosure of men and women. In this study, biological sex would be considered a concrete variable—it does not change. Self-disclosure would be classified as an abstract variable. An individual may engage in different patterns of disclosure with friends compared to family members. As you can see from these examples, the next task is determining the research question to guide the project involves identifying the types of units that will serve as the focus of the study.

Types of Units

Once a researcher has determined the specific communication behaviors to include in a study, the next step involves determining the unit of analysis for the project. Most communication research examines communication in one of four units of analysis: individuals, dyads, groups, and organizations.

Communication studies examining individuals as the unit of analysis may focus on an individual's temperament, personality, or communication traits, or the research could focus on specific communication strategies or behaviors selected by a person. In their study of sports fans (located on the CD-ROM that accompanies this textbook), Rocca and Vogl-Bauer (1999) selected the individual as the unit of analysis. Data were collected to identify an individual's level of verbal aggressiveness (attacking the self-concepts of people instead of attacking the positions they espouse, e.g., "only an idiot would think that," "what kind of moron are you," etc.) and its relationship to perceptions of the appropriate communication at sporting events. Verbal aggressiveness and perceptions of appropriate behavior use the individual as the unit of analysis.

Research on dyads focuses on collecting information about two people involved in an interpersonal relationship. Barbato et al.'s (2003) study asked 202 parent–child pairs to complete questionnaires assessing perceptions of the family communication climate and interpersonal communication motives for interacting with one another. Results indicated that the communication climate had a significant influence on the motives selected for communicating in the dyad.

Sometimes the communication dynamics change when individuals are placed together in groups to accomplish a goal. Tim Kuhn and Marshall Scott Poole (2000) focused on 11 groups in two major corporations as the unit of analysis in their examination of the effects of group conflict management styles on decision making. They found that groups that were more integrated in their conflict styles and addressed conflict openly were more effective in decision making than groups that engaged in conflict avoidance or confrontational styles.

If a researcher is interested in identifying the ways in which organizational members interact with one another and the resulting impact on task completion, efficiency, satisfaction, or a host of other variables, the organization becomes the unit of analysis. Coombs and Holladay (2004) designed the Workplace Aggression Tolerance Questionnaire (WATC) to identify perceptions of appropriateness of workplace verbal aggression. While at first glance it may appear that the unit of analysis is an individual's perceptions, the core of the research focuses on appropriateness of behavior in the organizational context.

Identifying the unit of analysis is essential to maintain focus during the research project and to enable researchers to generalize results to similar units. However, it is important to resist the temptation to make inferences about individuals based on their group membership. The ecological fallacy is a concept similar to stereotyping and occurs when researchers assume that because a participant is a member of a specific group (such as a culture) he or she possesses all the same communication characteristics as the group. Similarly, assuming that one organization is similar to all others would lead to erroneous conclusions. It is important to keep in mind that units of analysis possess unique characteristics—after all, this is what makes communication research an exciting venture!

Aspects of Variables

Once the researcher has identified the unit of analysis for a particular study, the next step involves revisiting the list of variables that will be examined to identify the specific aspects associated with each variable. Let's examine two aspects of variables—attributes and values—in more detail.

Attributes refer to the specific categories of a variable. For example, the variable "biological sex" includes the attributes of male or female, while the variable "sociocommunicative orientation" has the attributes of assertiveness, responsiveness, and versatility. To ensure that you have included all relevant information for your own research study, be sure to consider the various categories or attributes for each variable you will be examining.

While attributes identify the categories for variables, values refer to the numerical designation assigned to each variable to allow for statistical analysis. Some variables, such as age, possess a numerical value on their own because the value of the variable already exists. Other variables may require a researcher to assign a number to represent each attribute of the variable. If biological sex of the respondent is a variable being examined, numerical values need to be assigned to designate male and female respondents. In this instance, values are arbitrarily assigned by the researcher. The number "1" can be used to represent males, and the number "2" can be used to represent females, or vice versa. As you assign values to each variable, it is important to write down this information because it will be important in the data-analysis phase.

Beyond attributes and values, all variables in statistical research enable researchers to generally understand two basic phenomena: relationships and differences. Just as the concept of interpersonal relationships refers to the connection between two people, "relationship" as a research concept refers to the correspondence or connection between two variables. The vast majority of communication studies are designed with the goal of identifying connections or relationships between variables. Michael Beatty (1988) set out to examine the relationship between an individual's level of public speaking anxiety and one's level of conspicuousness (feeling like you're in a giant spotlight and everyone is watching) and one's level of perceived similarity with one's audience. Relationships between variables typically fall into one of three categories: positive, negative, or neutral. Positive relationships exist when an increase in one variable produces an increase in the other variable, or a decrease in a variable corresponds with a decrease in the other variable. Beatty found that an individual's level of public speaking anxiety was positively related to an individual's level of conspicuousness. Increases in one variable (an individual's level of conspicuousness) correspond to increases in the other (level of public speaking anxiety). In other words, the more conspicuous a person feels, the more anxious he or she will be while engaging in public speaking. The opposite is also true—the less conspicuous a person feels, the less anxious he or she will be while engaging in public speaking. This relationship is visually represented in Figure 6.1.

A negative relationship exists when a decrease in one variable corresponds to an increase in the other variable, or vice versa. Beatty (1988) also found a negative relationship between public speaking anxiety and perceived similarity with one's audience. Increases in one variable (perceived similarity) correspond to decreases in the other variable (level of public speaking anxiety). In other words, the more a speaker perceives an audience as being similar to her or him, the less anxious he or she will be while engaging in public speaking. However, the converse is also true. The more dissimilar a speaker perceives her or his audience, the more anxious he or she will be. Figure 6.2 depicts a negative relationship.

In some instances, a researcher may discover that the variables selected for a study are not related to one another. Neutral relationship is another term use to refer to this lack of relationship, or when the change of one variable does not correspond with a change in another variable. Figure 6.3 provides a visual representation of two variables that have no relationship to one another. As you can see, no pattern in the data is evident when the points are plotted on the diagram. Hence, changes in one variable do not produce consistent changes in the other variable being studied. Examining the relationship between the amount of pizza one

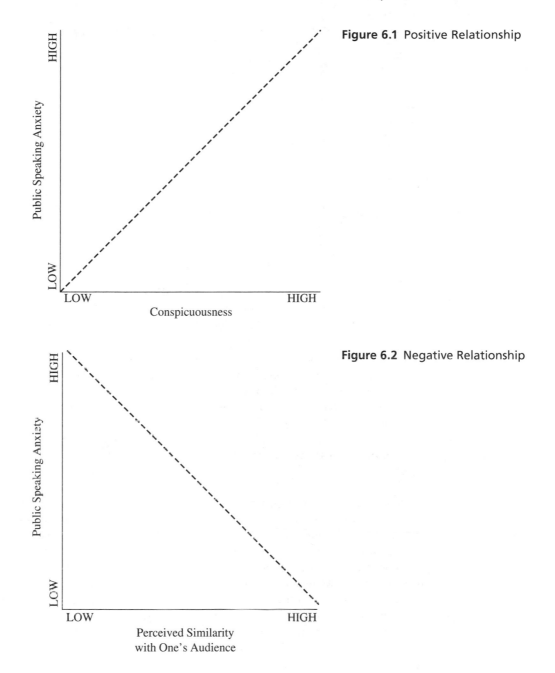

Figure 6.1 Positive Relationship

Figure 6.2 Negative Relationship

consumes and an individual's level of public speaking anxiety would likely result in a neutral relationship.

In addition to looking at differences, statistics enables researchers to examine differences. In research, differences fall into one of two categories: differences in kind and differences in degree. Differences in kind occur when two or more groups do different things associated with their groups. For example, football players play football and cheerleaders lead the crowd in cheers. The two groups (football players and cheerleaders) are fundamentally different and exhibit different behaviors. While it may be entertaining to some, we really do not want to see a 90-lb cheerleader being tackled by a 350-lb defensive lineman, nor would we want to see the

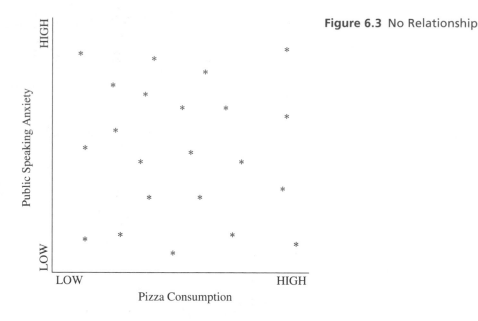

Figure 6.3 No Relationship

350-lb lineman trying to do a flip or toe touch. While differences in kind are interesting, they really do not relate to statistics except in that differences in kind create grouping variables (or nominal variables, which will be discussed shortly). Instead, quantitative researchers are often interested in differences of degree, or when two groups have differing degrees of a variable that they both display. For example, perhaps we wanted to determine if females and males differed in their levels of verbal aggression. We may give each group a survey to fill out and then look at the averages of the two groups. Statistical difference tests would then allow a research to determine whether the two groups have different averages on verbal aggression. In Figure 6.4 we have two curves representing theoretical scores on a test of verbal aggression. The curve to the left represents female verbal aggression scores and the curve to the right represents male verbal aggression scores. While eyeballing the two curves may make it appear that males have higher verbal aggression scores, researchers cannot use the eyeballing technique, which is why we use difference tests to determine if the two groups are really different.

However, difference tests only tell us half of the story. Let's pretend that the two curves seen in Figure 6.4 represent a difference between the male and female levels of verbal aggression. The curves can be "statistically different," but the difference between the female and male average could only be a matter of 4 or 5 points. For this reason, researchers are also interested in the magnitude of the difference (effect size), not just the fact that a difference exists. For example, look at the two curves in Figure 6.5. In the two curves, the difference between the male and female verbal aggression averages is much greater than the two curves seen in Figure 6.4.

This section introduced you to the basic concepts of relationships and differences; much of the rest of this book will examine these two concepts in much greater detail.

Types of Variables

To answer the research question or hypothesis, the next step in the process involves identifying the two types of variables identified as the focal points of the study. Variables can be classified as being independent or dependent. *Independent variables* are the part of the research

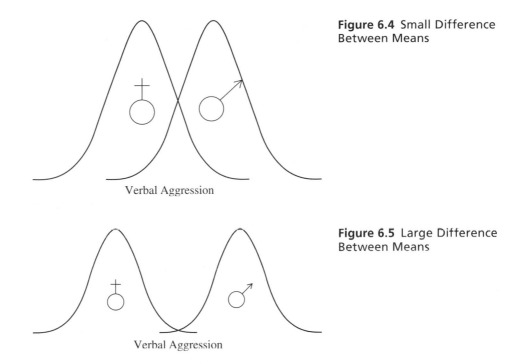

Figure 6.4 Small Difference Between Means

Verbal Aggression

Figure 6.5 Large Difference Between Means

Verbal Aggression

environment that are manipulated or changed. More specifically, the independent variable is what we are studying with respect to how it impacts a dependent variable.

Dependent variables, on the other hand, are not manipulated. They are recorded or measured, but they are not exposed to any type of alteration. Researchers look for any change in the dependent variable as a result of the manipulation of the independent variable. In essence, the goal of the research is to find out whether there is a change in the variable in response to the change or manipulation of the independent variable. While the distinction between dependent and independent is fairly easy when variables are used in an experimental situation, identifying the variables can be confusing in nonexperimental situations. Because of this, the term "criterion" variable is sometimes used to refer to the dependent variable.

So how can you determine which variable is the independent variable and which is the dependent variable in a study? Consider the following hypothesis from Weber et al.'s (2003) study on the effect of student interest in a topic on recall of information:

H: Lectures utilizing interest-based examples should result in participants with higher scores on subsequent tests of cognitive recall.

The independent variable in this hypothesis is lecture examples. Lectures were manipulated by showing students two different versions of videotapes: (1) lectures that incorporated current examples and (2) lectures using standard examples. Cognitive recall of information serves as the dependent variable. The researchers are trying to explain the difference in information recall as a result of the types of examples used in lectures.

Some studies examine variables that the researcher does not manipulate. Rather, the differences in a variable may be naturally occurring. Consider the following research question from a 1995 study examining communication satisfaction of children from divorced families (Thomas, Booth-Butterfield, & Booth-Butterfield, 1995):

H: Communication satisfaction with parents will be lower among children from divorced families than children from intact families.

At first glance it may be difficult to distinguish between the dependent and independent variables in this hypothesis, but take a moment and recall the definitions for both concepts. The study wanted to examine the level of communication satisfaction of children from divorced and intact families. Thus, family status (divorced or intact) is the independent variable for the hypothesis. The goal is to determine whether differences in family status affect the dependent variable or communication satisfaction.

Our third example is a little more difficult. Consider the following research question:

RQ: What is the relationship between parents who engage in verbally aggressive behavior at sporting events and a child's verbal aggressiveness?

According to this research question we simply want to ascertain a possible relationship between the two variables. In other words, there really isn't a dependent variable and an independent variable in this example. However, if we proposed that a parent's level of verbally aggressive behavior at sporting events caused her or his child's level of verbal aggression, then we could say that the parents' level of verbal aggression is the independent variable attempting to predict the child's level of verbal aggression.

If we were only dealing with independent and dependent variables in research, our task would be fairly simple. But we know that nothing in life can ever be as easy as it looks. Sometimes there are additional variables whose presence may impact the relationship between the dependent and independent variables. *Intervening variables* are often included in a study to determine if the effects of a change in the independent variable in turn cause a change in the dependent variable. If you wanted to examine the effect of teacher feedback on student motivation, it might be beneficial to consider the variable of self-esteem as a potential intervening variable. Positive feedback from a teacher may boost a student's level of self-esteem, which in turn may impact the level of motivation.

Antecedent variables also have the potential to affect the relationship found between the independent and dependent variable. These variables answer the question, "What happened prior to the time data were collected?" and shed light as to some of the differences that could emerge between the independent and dependent variables. A study examining the impact of conflict (independent variable) on marital satisfaction (dependent variable) should take into consideration possible antecedent variables that could potentially impact the results. For example, if both partners had incompatible personalities prior to marriage, this could lead them to experience or view conflict in their relationship differently than those who are deemed to be compatible. Similarly, if a person comes from a family where parents frequently engaged in conflict, the impact of conflict on marital satisfaction may be impacted as a result of the predetermined expectations for conflict.

Variable Levels

Another integral part of the research design process involves selecting variables to examine which will answer the proposed research question or hypothesis. Each variable selected for a study will be directly associated with identifying the particular statistical method appropriate for answering the research question. Variables can possess qualitative or quantitative characteristics. Variables with qualitative characteristics involve assigning items to group or categories to describe the population. No quantitative value is implied with these variables. On the other hand, quantitative variables are easily identified because they represent differences in quantity or amount. A research variable can be classified into one of four levels. These levels, listed in order of precision in measuring variables, are nominal, ordinal, interval, and ratio.

Nominal Variables

Nominal level data make up the variable level that is identified by its qualitative characteristics. To categorize nominal level data, simply name each characteristic by using categories that are mutually exclusive. It is important to remember that a characteristic can only be represented by one category of a variable. No logical order is followed for creating the categorization, and values can not be assigned quantitative values or rank ordered.

There are three primary rules for categorizing nominal level data. First, the categories used to classify the attributes must be mutually exclusive. Second, all categories used to represent the data must be equivalent. Remember the old adage, "Don't compare apples to oranges!" The same principle applies in developing nominal categories. Finally, all categories used to classify nominal level data must be exhaustive. Examples of nominal level data include political affiliation (a person can be a Democrat, Republican, other, or not registered) and sex (a participant is either a male or a female). As you can see from the categories created to describe each characteristic, a participant can only "fit" into one category. Thus, the categories established meet the first criteria of being mutually exclusive. Further, the categories used to represent the participants are exhaustive. A person can only be male or female, and the categories of "other" and "not registered" are included to capture all participants who are not registered Republicans or Democrats.

Descriptive statistics and frequency distributions are the primary method of data analysis for nominal level data from the data disk included with your text. The nominal variable "sex" can be described in terms of percentages of males (56.8%) and females (43.2%) or in terms of frequencies representing the number of participants that fall into each category (males = 183, females = 139). While a researcher would typically assign values to the categories of "male" and "female" for data entry purposes (perhaps a "1" to represent males and a "2" to represent females), it is important to note that these numbers have no relationship to the categories they represent. It would make no sense to try and compute a mean score for sex. Since the categories are mutually exclusive (a participant is either a male or a female), calculating a mean of 1.3 for sex would have no meaning. Instead, the mode is the typical statistic employed to describe nominal level data. It is meaningful to say that most participants were males. In instances where a researcher wants to examine the differences between two nominal level variables, a chi-square test is the most appropriate method of statistical analysis. This statistic will be discussed in more detail in Chapter 16.

Ordinal Variables

Ordinal variables allow us to rank order attributes with regard to which has less versus which has more of a characteristic. Ordinal variables have both qualitative and quantitative characteristics. Ordinal variables are qualitative because people are placed into categories that are used to represent characteristics; however, these categories have real numerical associations, so the variables are also quantitative. While there is a logical order to the creation of categories used to represent characteristics, it is important to note that the researcher is not able to make comparisons with regard to the magnitude of difference between categories. Examples of ordinal level data include socioeconomic status (lower, middle, or upper class), education level (elementary, junior high, high school, or college), or letter grades (A, B, C, D, or F). It is evident that there is a distinct difference between each of the levels, and there are quantitative differences between them, but we are unable to specify an amount or quantify the differences that exist. Suppose we know that the category of "middle class" is used to represent individuals with an income between $30,000 and $50,000. "Upper class" is the category used to represent those earning more than $50,000 per year. The difference between middle and upper class could be one penny (or the difference between $50,000 and $50,000.01) or millions of dollars.

There are three primary properties for categorizing ordinal variables. First, the categories must be mutually exclusive. That is, a participant can only "fit" into one of the categories. Second, the researcher must follow a logical ordering of the categories. Consider the ordinal variable of military rank. As a participant achieves status within the organization, a higher level of rank is awarded. Finally, each category must be balanced to represent the amount of a characteristic possessed by a participant.

To quantify ordinal level data for statistical analysis, numerical values are assigned to represent each category. However, the numbers used to represent each quality of the variable must increase such that higher numbers are used to represent high values. For example, a "1" could be assigned to represent lower class, "2" for middle class, and "3" for upper class. It is important to remember that the intervals between the numbers used to represent each category are not necessarily representative of equal distances or quantities, nor does a zero point exist.

Interval Variables

Interval level variables are quantitative and are classified in a logical order that represents equal distances between levels within each category. Examples of interval variables include levels of people's public speaking anxiety, levels of perceived similarity, and levels of perceived conspicuousness (to use the earlier example in this chapter when we discussed relationships). Interval variables enable a researcher to rank order items and to compare the magnitude of differences between each category. For example, McCroskey (1970) created the Personal Report of Public Speaking Anxiety (PRPSA) to measure an individual's level of public speaking anxiety, and scores on the scale range from 34 to 170, with higher scores indicating higher levels of anxiety while delivering a speech. We can say that a PRPSA score of 160 is higher than a PRPSA score of 80. However, we cannot state that an individual with a PRPSA score of 160 is twice as anxious as someone who has a PRPSA score of 80. This is because PRPSA does not have a zero as the scale's absolute starting point.

Three types of scales are used to measure interval level variables: Likert, semantic differential, and scalagram scales. In a Likert scale participants are presented with a number of statements and then asked to respond to those statements based on a preexisting scale. Figure 6.6 shows an example of a short Likert scale called the Homonegativity Short Form, created by Wrench (2005). You'll notice that this scale has 10 scale items, all generally measuring an individual's perception of gay and lesbian people. The scale is measured using a five-step system ranging from 1 (*Strongly Disagree*) to 5 (*Strongly Agree*). Each participant who fills out this scale only has five possible choices for each item on the scale: 1, 2, 3, 4, or 5. The scores for each individual item can be added together to achieve a composite score, which can then be used in various statistical analyses. McCroskey's (1970) PRPSA is another example of a Likert scale.

The second type of research scale commonly used to examine interval level measurements is the semantic differential or bipolar oppositely worded scale. The semantic differential scale consists of a series of adjectives that are oppositely worded (good/bad, happy/sad, eventful/uneventful, positive/negative, etc.). There then exists a continuum of possible choices between the adjectives, and participants are asked to select the number that most

Homonegativity Short Form

Instructions: Below are several descriptions of how you may feel. Please use the scale below to rate the degree to which each statement applies to you. Remember, we want you to be completely honest and we appreciate your cooperation.

Strongly Disagree	Disagree	Neutral	Agree	Strongly Agree
1	2	3	4	5

_____ 1. Gay and lesbian people make me nervous.
_____ 2. Homosexuality is perfectly normal.
_____ 3. I wouldn't want to have gay or lesbian friends.
_____ 4. I would trust a gay or lesbian person.
_____ 5. I fear homosexual persons will make sexual advances towards me.
_____ 6. I would have no problem living with someone who is gay or lesbian.
_____ 7. Homosexual behavior should be perfectly legal.
_____ 8. I would have a serious problem if I saw two men or women kissing in public.
_____ 9. I think that gay and lesbian people need civil rights protection.
_____ 10. When I see a gay or lesbian person I think, "What a waste."

SCORING: To compute your scores follow the instructions below:

1. How to Score:
   Step One: Add scores for items 1, 3, 5, 8, & 10.
   Step Two: Add scores for items 2, 4 6, 7, & 9.
   Step Three: Add 30 to Step One.
   Step Four: Subtract the score for Step Two from the score for Step Three.

Source:

Wrench, J. S. (2005). Development and validity testing of the homonegativity short form. *Journal of Intercultural Communication Research, 34,* 152–165.

Figure 6.6 Likert Scale

represents their perception between two the two adjectives. For example, we may ask participants to rate the movie *Charlie and the Chocolate Factory* using the adjectives "good" and "bad," with a choice of 1 to 7 between the two words. Numbers 1 and 7 indicate a very strong feeling. Numbers 2 and 6 indicate a strong feeling. Numbers 3 and 5 indicate a fairly weak feeling. Number 4 indicates you are undecided. If you thought the movie was pretty good but not just amazing, maybe you'd give the movie a rating of 2 or 3 because these are closest to the word "good," whereas if you thought it was the worst movie you had ever seen, then you might rate the movie as a 7 since it is closest to the word "bad." Figure 6.7 has another example of a bipolar scale. In this example, we see the job motivation, scale which is a retooling of Virginia Richmond's student motivation scale. The scale asks people to respond how they feel about work using five adjective pairs. When you add up the responses from all five adjective pairs, you can then use this number in a variety of statistical tests.

The last scale that is used to create an interval variable is called the Guttman or scalogram scale. While scalogram scales are interesting, they are rarely actually employed in communication research. The goal of a scalogram scale is to ascertain an individual's belief about a given topic. A perfect Guttman scale would consist of a set of unidimensional items that respondents rank in order from the least extreme to the most extreme position

Work Motivation Scale

Instructions: The following scale is designed to examine how you currently feel about work. Only think about this one class when filling out the following scale. Numbers 1 and 7 indicate a very strong feeling. Numbers 2 and 6 indicate a strong feeling. Numbers 3 and 5 indicate a fairly weak feeling. Number 4 indicates you are undecided.

Unmotivated	1	2	3	4	5	6	7	Motivated
Excited	7	6	5	4	3	2	1	Bored
Interested	7	6	5	4	3	2	1	Uninterested
Involved	7	6	5	4	3	2	1	Uninvolved
Dreading it	1	2	3	4	5	6	7	Looking forward to it

Scoring:

To determine your level of work motivation, add your scores for each question together.

Source:

Richmond, V. P. (1990). Communication in the classroom: Power and motivation. *Communication Education, 39,* 181–184.

Figure 6.7 Semantic Differential/Bi-Polar Scale

(Guttman, 1944). For example, maybe you wanted to determine how much homework is too much for high school students. You give them a list of 10 possible time frames ranging from zero to 10 hours of homework. You then have your participants answer Yes or No next to each time frame: "No Homework to 1 Hour" up to "10 Hours or More of Homework." The goal of a scalogram scale is that at some point along the way you will hit a cut-off point beyond which people will not go. For example, maybe someone believes that "4 to 5 Hours of Homework" is legitimate, but thinks "5 to 6 Hours of Homework" is unreasonable. If someone marks that "5 to 6 Hours of Homework" is unreasonable, we would not expect her or him two questions later to state that "7 to 9 Hours of Homework" is perfectly OK. In essence, a scalogram scale attempts to determine where people cut themselves off in relation to a specific belief. Figure 6.8 contains an example of a scalogram scale created to examine environmentalism.

You'll notice that as this scale progresses, each statement becomes slightly more radicalized with regards to an individual's perception of environmentalism.

Ratio Variables

Ratio variables are similar to interval variables with one notable exception—ratio variables have an absolute zero starting point to represent the absence of the characteristic. Examples of ratio variables include income, exam scores, temperature (when measured by the Kelvin scale, which has an absolute 0), and speed. Whereas we could not make statements regarding the magnitude of difference between categories of interval level data, we can make statements such as "An exam score of 50 is two times more than an exam score of 25." Since most

Environmentalism Scale		
Instructions: For each phrase circle whether you agree with that statement by circling YES or disagree with the statement by circling NO.		
1. I never throw trash on the ground because it hurts our environment	YES (1)	NO
2. I think recycling is a noble endeavor.	YES (2)	NO
3. I always participate in recycling in my city.	YES (3)	NO
4. My friends and family know my commitment to the environment.	YES (4)	NO
5. I would send a letter to a company that willfully hurts the environment.	YES (5)	NO
6. I vote for politicians based on their environmental policies and voting behaviors.	YES (6)	NO
7. I would picket a company that is hurting the environment.	YES (7)	NO
8. I would organize a campaign against a corporation that is polluting the environment.	YES (8)	NO
9. I would participate in tree spiking to prevent companies from destroying our environment.	YES (9)	NO
10. Bombing a company that hurts the environment is completely justifiable.	YES (10)	NO
Scoring: To score this measure, add the numbers under each YES answer selected. Scores can run from 0 to 57. Higher scores indicate a more radical environmental stance.		

Figure 6.8 Scalogram Scale

statistical analysis procedures view interval and ratio characteristics in the same way, the same statistical tests are used to describe and compare both types of variables.

A variety of statistical tests can be used to analyze interval and ratio level variables. The *t*-test (comparing two groups) and one-way ANOVA (comparing two or more groups) are the appropriate difference tests when analyzing interval/ratio variables. We will discuss *t*-tests in Chapter 17 and one-way ANOVAs in Chapter 18. To describe linear relationships between two or more interval variables, correlations (Chapter 19) or regression analyses (Chapter 20) are most appropriate.

Conclusion

Figure 6.9 summarizes the appropriate statistical tests to be used when analyzing each type of variable. For example, if a researcher wanted to test for differences on public speaking anxiety (an interval scale) between females and males (two groups), the researcher would need to conduct a *t*-test. In this example we started off with our interval scale, realized we had two groups we were testing (female and male), so the only choice for a statistical test was the *t*-test. If we had two or more ordinal variables and wanted to test for a relationship, what test

Interval/Ratio	Differences	Two groups	*t*-Test
		More than two groups	ANOVA
	Relationships	Two variables	Correlation
		More than two variables	Regression
Ordinal	Differences	Two groups	Mann-Whitney or *t*-Test
		More than two groups	ANOVA
	Relationships		Correlation
Nominal	Differences		Chi-square
	Relationships		Percentage differences

Figure 6.9 Summary of Appropriate Statistical Tests for Variable Levels

would we use? Well, according to our chart if we have two ordinal variables, the only test available for examining relationships is a correlation (specifically a Spearman's Rho correlation). Figure 6.9 will become *very* important later on this book.

Throughout this chapter we have discussed the steps involved in the process of creating your own recipe for a research project. Methods for selecting and classifying appropriate variables have been discussed, keeping in mind that variables must be selected to answer the proposed research question or hypothesis. Guidelines for choosing the appropriate statistical analyses for each type of variable were provided to ensure that the development of a solid design for your research study.

Key Terms

Abstract Variable
Antecedent Variable
Concrete Variable
Dependent Variable
Differences
Differences of Degree
Differences of Kind
Independent Variable
Interval Variable

Intervening Variable
Likert Scale
Negative Relationship
Neutral Relationship
Nominal Variable
Ordinal Variable
Parameter
Positive Relationship
Ratio Variable

Relationships
Scalogram
Semantic Differential/
Bipolar Scale
Suppressor Variables
Variable
Variable Attributes
Variable Values

References

Barbato, C. A., Graham, E. E., & Perse, E. M. (2003). Communicating in the family: An examination of the relationship of family communication climate and interpersonal communication motives. *Journal of Family Communication, 3*, 123–148.

Beatty, M. J. (1988). Situational and predispositional correlates of public speaking anxiety. *Communication Education, 37*, 28–39.

Coombs, W. T. & Holladay, S. J. (2004). Understanding the aggressive workplace: Development of the workplace aggression tolerance questionnaire. *Communication Studies, 55*, 481–497.

Guttman, L. (1944). A basis for scaling qualitative data. *American Sociological Review, 9,* 139–150.

Kuhn, T., & Poole, M. S. (2000). Do conflict management styles affect group decision making? *Human Communication Research, 26,* 558–591.

McCroskey, J. C. (1970). Measures of communication-bound anxiety. *Speech Monographs, 37,* 269–277.

Rocca, K. A., & Vogl-Bauer, S. (1999). Trait verbal aggression, sports fan identification, and perceptions of appropriate sports fan communication. *Communication Research Reports, 16,* 239–248.

Thomas, C., Booth-Butterfield, M., & Booth-Butterfield, S. (1995). Perceptions of deception, divorce disclosure, and communication satisfaction with parents. *Western Journal of Communication, 59,* 228–245.

Weber, K., Fornash, B., Corrigan, M., & Neupauer, N. (2003). The effect of interest on recall: An experiment. *Communication Research Reports, 20,* 116–123.

Wrench, J. S. (2005). Development and validity testing of the homonegativity short form. *Journal of Intercultural Communication Research, 34,* 152–165.

Wrench, J. S., & Booth-Butterfield, M. (2003). Increasing patient satisfaction and compliance: An examination of physician humor orientation, compliance-gaining strategies, and perceived credibility. *Communication Quarterly, 51,* 482–503.

Communication Variables

1 Understand the purpose of the book's dataset and how the data were collected.
2 Know which variables are nominal variables in the book's dataset.
3 Know which variables are ordinal variables in the book's dataset.
4 Know which variables are interval variables in the book's dataset.
5 Know which variables are ratio variables in the book's dataset.
6 Understand how personality traits influence human communication.
7 Explain the two levels of personality traits (internal and external).
8 Explain the dynamic and consistent aspects of personality traits.
9 Be able to differentiate between trait, context, audience, and situational behavior.
10 Be able to use the information learned in this chapter to write an APA method section.

In the previous chapter we introduced the major levels of variables that social science researchers are concerned with: nominal, ordinal, interval, and ratio. The authors of this book believe that the best way to really learn how to conduct quantitative research is to actually conduct quantitative research on real variables. For this reason, we decided to put together a study using some very common communication variables and then supply you, the reader, with the actual data gathered from real research participants.

In the spring of 2005, the authors of this book recruited 325 undergraduate students to participate in a research study, the data from which would be made available to the readers of this book. The goal of this data collection was to provide the readers of this text an actual data set that can be used to ask real research questions. The undergraduate students were offered extra credit for participating in this project. The questionnaire distributed can be seen in Appendix B exactly as we distributed it to the participants. Since the goal of this data set is to enable you to use real participant data to ask real research questions, we made sure that we had variables from each level (nominal, ordinal, interval, and ratio) in the dataset. This chapter will explain what each of the variables are that we collected for the dataset. While this chapter may seem somewhat out of place because it explores communication concepts and not methodological concepts, understanding the different variables discussed, how these variables are measured, and how they function will help you understand the real-world examples we will use throughout the entire book. We will look at the variables in the book data set not in the order in which they appear in Appendix B, but in groupings that represent the levels of measurement: nominal, ordinal, interval, and ratio.

Nominal Variables

As mentioned in the previous chapter, nominal variables are variables that are categorical in nature. In essence, placing people in one category should be fairly easy. In the case of the study created for this textbook, people should be able to place themselves in the category fairly easily. For the purposes of this book, we decided to include two nominal variables. The first variable was a very common nominal variable included in most research studies, biological sex. Biological sex, as a variable, has only two possible attributes (female and male). For a variable to be nominal, the categories must be equivalent (the categories of female and male are equivalent), the categories must be mutually exclusive (you cannot be both female and male), and the categories must be exhaustive (there is not a third or fourth biological sex).

The second nominal variable we included in this study was political affiliation. The concept of political affiliation is a fairly tricky one, so ultimately how participants will respond when asked "What is your political affiliation?" will ultimately depend on the categories a researcher provides her or his participants. We could have listed different political parties like Communist Party, Democratic Party, Green Party, Independent, Libertarian Party, Natural Law Party, Republic Party, and so on until we had listed every known political party in the United States, which would be a very long list. Instead, we opted to use the two prominent parties (Democratic and Republican) as two categories and then add a category for "Other" parties for anyone who belonged to one of those political parties outside the mainstream political process. However, upon further contemplation, we realized that those three categories really were not completely exhaustive. Not everyone in this country belongs to a political party or sees her- or himself as an independent voter. In fact, many people are simply not registered to vote at all. For this reason, we decided that our fourth category should be "Not Registered to Vote." Everyone who filled out the survey should fall into one of categories provided (Democrat, Republican, Other, or Not Registered to Vote). Not only are the categories exhaustive, someone who is not registered to vote is not someone who belongs to the Democratic Party, since registering to vote is how people join political parties in our country. Furthermore, someone who is a Republican cannot also be an Other, so our categories are mutually exclusive as well. And all of the categories relate to political affiliation (even Not Registered to Vote), so our categories are equivalent as well.

Ordinal Variables

In addition to the two nominal variables included in the study conducted for this book, we also included two ordinal variables. If you remember the discussion from the previous chapter on ordinal variables, ordinal variables are variables that can be ordered. We do not know the magnitude of the difference between the categories people are placed into, we just know that there is a difference between the categories in magnitude. For the purposes of the study conducted for this textbook, we created two ordinal variables for analysis: University Classification and Time Spent on the Internet. The first ordinal variable we used in this study was University Classification. We created a variable with five levels (Freshman, Sophomore, Junior, Senior, and Graduate Student). You may be wondering why these are ordinal and not nominal; the reason they are ordinal is the same reason someone is labeled as Upper Class as opposed to Middle Class—there's no true indication of magnitude. In college, these categories are based on the numbers of hours taken and passed, not on the number of years someone has been in school. For example, one of the authors of this textbook was 1 hour shy of being a sophomore at the beginning of his second year in college, but he was still classified as a freshman according to the university. On the flip side, how many of us have known people who are 8- or 9-year seniors?! In essence, the labels associated with University Classifications represent a difference between the classification levels, but we do not get any indication of the magnitude of this difference.

The second ordinal variable that we selected for inclusion in this book's data set was the amount of time someone spent online. Specifically, we asked the study participants to disclose how much time they spend online during a given week. We then provided the participants a series of categorical answers: 0–½ hour, ½–1 hour, 1–2 hours, 2–5 hours, 5–10 hours, 10–15 hours, 15–20 hours, and 20+ hours. With each categorical level we increase the magnitude of the difference, but the exact magnitude is not known. Someone who spends 80 hours a week online would fall into the 20+ hour group, as would someone who spends 21 hours a week online. In the same vein as University Classification, the difference in how one classifies her- or himself can be a matter of minutes. Maybe someone spends 9 hours and 45 minutes online on average, so he classifies himself as spending 5–10 hours online. However, another participant spends 10 hours and 15 minutes online on average, so she classifies herself as spending 10–15 hours online. All in all, this gradient of 30 minutes cannot be taken into account when dealing with the categorical nature in this ordinal variable.

Interval Variables

Most interval variables studied by communication researchers measure traits, behaviors, beliefs, and attitudes. Luckily, the study that we compiled for this measured all of those, so let's look at each category separately.

PERSONALITY TRAITS AND COMMUNICATION

Personality is the total psychological makeup of an individual, which is a reflection of her or his experiences, motivations, attitudes, beliefs, values, and behaviors, derived from the interaction of these elements with the environment external to the individual. Thus, personality can be defined as the sum of an individual's characteristics that make him or her unique (Hollander, 1976). If everyone had the same personality, we would all communicate the same way all the time in every situation. Thankfully, we do not all communicate the same way, and these differences in our communicative behaviors can be observed.

Ultimately, Hollander (1976) noted that personality consists of two basic dimensions that are important to communication researchers. The first dimension of personality distinguishes the external level (observable characteristics of an individual) of personality from the internal level (individual's attitudes, values, and beliefs, interests and aspirations, and motivations). We often use an individual's external personality to determine an individual's internal personality during interpersonal interactions. We may watch someone shake and turn red while giving a speech and surmise that the individual is experiencing a great deal of anxiety while giving the speech. Realistically, the person could just be very ill, which could cause the shaking and red flushing during the speech.

The second feature of personality distinguishes its dynamic aspects (degree to which a personality trait can change over time or during certain contexts or situations) from its consistent aspects (degree to which a personality trait does not change over time or during certain contexts or situations). In essence, we have a continuum of personality traits ranging from consistent to dynamic. Many external and internal factors can cause personality traits to change. For example, getting married, moving to another country, experiencing a crisis, losing a job, etc., can change how a person looks at life (internal level) and how he or she behaves (external level). There are, however, many aspects of our individual personalities that do not alter over time. Elements of the internal level of personality that are least likely to undergo change are those that compromise the consistent aspect of personality (e.g., values). Another reason why some personality traits are resistant to change is human genetics. There is an increasing body of research examining how our genetic code affects various personality traits. While this textbook is outside the purview of examining how genetics affects human behavior, we recommend reading Dean Hamer and Peter Copeland's (1998) *Living with Our Genes: Why They Matter More Than You Think* to examine how genetics influence various personality traits and Michael Beatty, James McCroskey, and Kristin Valencic's (2001) *The Biology of Communication: A Communibiological Perspective* to examine how genetics influence human communication specifically.

As humans we expect people to behave according to the way they think and feel. In other words, we expect the external behavior to be a window into the internal reality. So when we see someone shaking and turning red during a speech, we reach the conclusion that he or she is experiencing anxiety brought on by the speech itself. In reality, however, the internal and external personalities are not always in synch with each other at all. We may feel that someone who is shaking and flushing during a speech has anxiety, but there could be many other reasons that that specific behavior is being exhibited.

The perceptions we have about people based on their exhibited behaviors also affects how we view that person. In our daily interactions with others, we constantly assume that because an individual is exhibiting a particular behavior, he or she is "that kind of person." We make these assumptions because we expect internal and external personality traits to be consistent. Imagine you watch that same flustered speaker over an entire semester. And every time he or she speaks, you see the same shaking and turning red. After watching an individual shake and turn red every time he or she spoke, we would begin to see this anxiety as characteristic of her or his personality. As Hollander (1976) notes, it's only a short time until you begin to view this characteristic in others as a *trait*, or the way he or she "typically" behaves. In reality, there are four different ways that personality characteristics can be exhibited by specific individuals: traits, contexts, audience, and situational.

Trait

In the psychology of personality, "traits" refer to individual characteristics that are not found in all people, but only in relatively few. Traits are an individual's predispositions for responding in a certain way to various situations. A given trait will exhibit itself in almost any situation responded to by the individual. For example, if our anxious speaker from above was later seen talking in a meeting and was turning red in that communicative situation as well, we might conclude that this individual's communicative anxiety is clearly trait based because it is seen across multiple contexts.

CONTEXT

The second way that personality characteristics can be demonstrated by individuals is within specific contexts. The basic contexts that communication scholars examine are interpersonal, group, meeting, public, and mediated. Contexts are specific modes where behavior can be different. For example, maybe our anxious speaker only gets anxious when having to give a public speech (public context), but experiences no anxiety while communicating interpersonally, in groups, in a meeting, or when talking online. In this case, we can say that her or his speech anxiety is context based.

AUDIENCE

The third way that personality characteristics surface is dependent upon the audience with whom an individual is communicating. Different audiences have differing perspectives of how interactions should occur, so we tend to act differently based on the type of audience we are interacting with. Maybe our anxious speaker is perfectly fine while giving a speech to her or his Rotary Club, but gets anxious in front of someone who is giving her or him a grade. In this case, a teacher grading the student could cause the student to experience audience based speech anxiety.

SITUATIONAL

The final way in which personality characteristics surface depends on the situation. There are times when because of the situation we start communicating in a manner that is not normal for us. We refer to this behavior as situational because it is not generally replicated. In the case of our nervous speaker, it is possible that this person has never before in her or his life experienced any kind of anxiety while giving a speech, but during this one speech was overcome with anxiety. Sometimes, out of nowhere, we alter our normal communication patterns as a result of the situation, or our "odd" communicative behavior happens only within a specific situation.

Overall, personality differences manifest themselves in variations in communicative behavior. To take this concept one step further, we can examine the notion of a specific type of personality trait—a communication trait. A communication trait is a hypothetical construct that accounts for certain kinds of communication behaviors. Researchers in the field of communication have examined numerous communicative patterns that are trait-like because in some people they are not alterable; whereas in other people they can be situationally based. For the remainder of this chapter it is useful to think of all of the communication traits we are going to examine as existing along a four-point continuum (see Figure 7.1). Starting at one extreme end of the continuum and moving to the other extreme, the four points are communication behavior: (1) as a trait, (2) in a generalized context, (3) with a specific audience, and (4) within a specific situation.

Now that we have examined what personality and communication traits are, we can look at the various communication traits measured in this book using an interval scale. The interval variables that were selected for inclusion in this chapter are communication apprehension, ethnocentrism, humor assessment, nonverbal immediacy, sociocommunicative orientation, willingness to communicate, generalized belief, and generalized attitude.

COMMUNICATION APPREHENSION

Before we discuss the nature of this first communicative trait, please take a second and fill out the Personal Report of Communication Apprehension–24 (PRCA-24) in Figure 7.2.

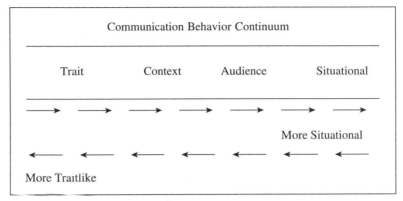

Figure 7.1 Communication Trait Continuum

Communication apprehension (CA) is defined as the fear or anxiety associated with either real or anticipated communication with another person or persons. Let's break this definition down into its various parts. First, CA is about fear and anxiety. Everyone exhibits fear and anxiety differently. Some people are generally fearful and anxious about almost everything, while other people are more focused in their fear and anxiety. People that are said to be High CA (scores between 80 and 120 on the PRCA-24) will experience fear and anxiety in every context when having to communicate (actual or real communication). However, people who are High CA do not stop having anxiety just because they do not have to engage in communication at this moment. In fact, people who are High CA experience apprehension and anxiety even when they *think* about having to communicate with another person (anticipate communication). High CA people often experience severe anxiety while practicing a public speech alone in their house, thinking about having to interact with someone interpersonally, or thinking about having to talk in group or meeting the next day. Research has shown that approximately one in five people or 20% of the general population suffers from High CA.

Scores on the PRCA-24 should be between 24 and 120. If your score is between 24 and 50, you are among those in our society who experience the least communication apprehension, to whom we refer as Low CA individuals. You are apt to be a higher talker and may actively seek out opportunities to interact with others. Very few, if any, communication situations cause you to be fearful or anxious. If your score is somewhere between 50 and 60, you experience less communication apprehension than most people. However, you are likely to feel some fear or anxiety about a few situations. If your score falls between 60 and 70, your level of communication apprehension is similar to that of most people. There are some communication situations that may cause you to feel anxious or tense; in others you will feel quite comfortable. If your score is between 70 and 80, you experience more communication apprehension than most people. Probably many communication situations cause you to be fearful and tense, but some do not bother you. If your score falls between 80 and 120, you are among those who experience the most communication apprehension. You are likely a low talker, one who actively avoids many communication situations because you feel much anxiety and tension in those situations.

While having high levels of CA (trait CA) is clearly going to impact a person's social life, having high levels of CA has also been shown to impact other areas of a person's life. Research has shown that High CA individuals tend to have low self-esteem and are more

DIRECTIONS: This instrument is composed of 24 statements concerning feelings about communicating with other people. Please indicate the degree to which each statement applies to you by marking whether you (1) strongly agree, (2) agree, (3) are undecided, (4) disagree, or (5) strongly disagree. Work quickly; record your first impression.

_____ 1. I dislike participating in group discussions.
_____ 2. Generally, I am comfortable while participating in group discussions.
_____ 3. I am tense and nervous while participating in group discussions.
_____ 4. I like to get involved in group discussions.
_____ 5. Engaging in a group discussion with new people makes me tense and nervous.
_____ 6. I am calm and relaxed while participating in group discussions.
_____ 7. Generally, I am nervous when I have to participate in a meeting.
_____ 8. Usually I am comfortable when I have to participate in a meeting.
_____ 9. I am very calm and relaxed when I am called upon to express an opinion at a meeting.
_____ 10. I am afraid to express myself at meetings.
_____ 11. Communicating at meetings usually makes me uncomfortable.
_____ 12. I am very relaxed when answering questions at a meeting.
_____ 13. While participating in a conversation with a new acquaintance, I feel very nervous.
_____ 14. I have no fear of speaking up in conversations.
_____ 15. Ordinarily I am very tense and nervous in conversations.
_____ 16. While conversing with a new acquaintance, I feel very relaxed.
_____ 17. Ordinarily I am very calm and relaxed in conversations.
_____ 18. I'm afraid to speak up in conversations.
_____ 19. I have no fear of giving a speech.
_____ 20. Certain parts of my body feel very tense and rigid while I am giving a speech.
_____ 21. I feel relaxed while giving a speech.
_____ 22. My thoughts become confused and jumbled when I am giving a speech.
_____ 23. I face the prospect of giving a speech with confidence.
_____ 24. While giving a speech, I get so nervous I forget facts I really know.

SCORING: To compute context subscores begin with a score of 18 for each context and follow the instructions below.

1. Group discussion—add scores for items 2, 4, & 6. Subtract scores for items 1, 3, & 5. Scores can range from 6 to 30.
2. Meetings—add scores for items 8, 9, & 12. Subtract scores for items 7, 10, & 11. Scores can range from 6 to 30.
3. Interpersonal—add scores for items 14, 16, & 17. Subtract scores for items 13, 15, & 18. Scores can range from 6 to 30.
4. Public speaking—add scores for items 19, 21, & 23. Subtract scores for items 20, 22, & 24. Scores can range from 6 to 30.

To compute the total score for the PRCA-24, add the four subscores. Total scores can range from 24 to 120. Scores above 80 = high CA; below 50 = low CA.

Source:

McCroskey, J. C. (1982). *An introduction to rhetorical communication* (4th ed). Englewood Cliffs, NJ: Prentice-Hall.

Figure 7.2 Personal Report of Communication Apprehension–24

prone to depression than Low CA individuals. High CA individuals are perceived as low intelligence by peers, teachers, and supervisors despite the fact that there is no re to support any difference in IQ levels based on an individual's CA. Research has show people with high levels of CA are less likely to visit their physicians, and when they d go to their physicians, they are less likely to ask questions about medical treatment and medication. Overall, CA impacts an individual in every aspect of her or his life. People who have high levels of CA can be truly crippled in our society.

Other people are likely to have contextually based CA, or they experience apprehension in one of the communicative contexts (interpersonal, meeting, group, or public). For example, an individual may experience CA while interacting with someone on a one-on-one basis but have no problem standing up before an audience of 1000 people and giving a speech. Yet other people experience CA more based on the audience with whom they must communicate. Almost everyone experiences CA at some point with a specific audience. Whether you're giving a presentation in front of your peers or your boss can impact the degree of anxiety that you may feel

The last type of CA that can occur is referred to as situationally based communication apprehension. Sometimes the uniqueness of a specific situation may cause you to experience anxiety. One of the authors of this text has given countless numbers of public speeches. During one particular speech, our colleague looked down and noticed that his hand was visibly shaking. He had never before in his life had a shaking hand while giving a speech. His outward nervousness made him even more anxious, and before he knew it he had no idea what he was saying because he was focusing on his own anxiety.

ETHNOCENTRISM

We all know that people around the world believe that "The United States is the best country on the face of the planet. Without the United States, the world would be less artistic, less moral, and less intelligent. In fact, if everyone would be more like the United States, this world would be much better off." Yep, people from around the world say this exact sentence—they just plug in their own country of origin in the place of "The United States." The Russians, Chinese, Australians, South Africans, Finns, Brazilians, Egyptians, Singaporeans, Puerto Ricans, and Japanese all feel their country is the best, and that if everyone would just behave like people in their country, the world would be much better off. Few things have been found to be truly "pancultural" (the same across all cultures), but this view that an individual's own culture is superior to all the rest is pancultural. The view that the customs and practices of one's own culture are superior to those of other cultures is known as ethnocentrism. People in all cultures are ethnocentric in varying degrees. McCroskey and Neulip (1997) created an ethnocentrism scale to measure this phenomenon. Before we start discussing the nature of ethnocentrism, please take a second and fill out the ethnocentrism scale in Figure 7.3.

The term "ethnocentrism" comes from the combination of two Greek words: *ethnos* (nation) and *kentron* (center). In combination, *ethnos* and *kentron* suggest that an individual's nation is the center of the universe. When one holds ethnocentric views, as virtually everyone does, an individual's culture is used as the standard by which all other cultures are evaluated. In fact, any deviation from an individual's culture is most likely (but not always) seen as negative, which indicates the inferiority of the *other* culture and the people from that culture. While ethnocentrism may sound innately bad, it is not inherently bad to have some level of ethnocentrism. In fact, ethnocentrism can be very positive.

One way in which ethnocentrism is positive is that it gives the people in a culture an identity and helps make them more cohesive, which helps promote positive and effective

Instructions: Below are items that relate to the cultures of different parts of the world. Work quickly and record your first reaction to each item. There are no right or wrong answers. Please indicate the degree to which you agree or disagree with each item using the following five-point scale:

Strongly Disagree	Disagree	Neutral	Agree	Strongly Agree
1	2	3	4	5

_____ 1. Most other cultures are backward compared to my culture.
_____ 2. My culture should be the role model for other cultures.
_____ 3. People from other cultures act strange when they come to my culture.
_____ 4. Lifestyles in other cultures are just as valid as those in my culture.
_____ 5. Other cultures should try to be more like my culture.
_____ 6. I am not interested in the values and customs of other cultures.
_____ 7. People in my culture could learn a lot from people in other cultures.
_____ 8. Most people from other cultures just don't know what's good for them.
_____ 9. I respect the values and customs of other cultures.
_____ 10. Other cultures are smart to look up to our culture.
_____ 11. Most people would be happier if they lived like people in my culture.
_____ 12. I have many friends from different cultures.
_____ 13. People in my culture have just about the best lifestyles of anywhere.
_____ 14. Lifestyles in other cultures are not as valid as those in my culture.
_____ 15. I am very interested in the values and customs of other cultures.
_____ 16. I apply my values when judging people who are different.
_____ 17. I see people who are similar to me as virtuous.
_____ 18. I do not cooperate with people who are different.
_____ 19. Most people in my culture just don't know what is good for them.
_____ 20. I do not trust people who are different.
_____ 21. I dislike interacting with people from different cultures.
_____ 22. I have little respect for the values and customs of other cultures.

SCORING: To compute your scores follow the instructions below:

1.   Drop questions 3, 6, 12, 15, 16, 17, 19

   Step One: Add scores for items 1, 2, 5, 8, 10, 11, 13, 14, 18, 20, 21 & 22.
   Step Two: Add scores for items 1, 2, 5, 8, 10, 11, 13, 14, 18, 20, 21 & 22.
   Step Three: Add 18 to Step One.
   Step Four: Subtract the score for Step Two from the score for Step Three.

The result is your Ethnocentrism score. Higher scores = higher levels of ethnocentrism.

Source:

Neuliep, J. W., & McCroskey, J. C. (1997). The development of a U.S. and generalized ethnocentrism scale. *Communication Research Reports, 14,* 385–398.

Interpretation:

Scores should be between 15 and 75. Most people score between 20 and 40. Scores over 32 are considered high.

Figure 7.3 Ethnocentrism Scale

communication among members of the culture. For a short period after September 11, 2001, people in the United States truly functioned as Americans. During this time period, Americans were very welcoming of all Americans, but very wary of anyone who was not an American citizen. At the same time, in New York on 9/11 people saw everyone around them as New Yorkers despite the amazing cultural diversity that exists in New York City. You may be thinking to yourself that these are just examples of patriotism, and you're right. Patriotism is innately ethnocentric. Wars are often fought in cultures because one culture views their way of life as something ultimately moral and worth fighting for.

Ethnocentrism, then, is the first line of defense for a culture. Without ethnocentric views, a culture is open to rapid and extreme changes that will result in the loss of cultural identity all together. Cultural groups are often afraid of being absorbed into another cultural group, so they often react very harshly and violently towards any encroaching culture. For example, many Middle Easterners are apprehensive about what they see as the "western influence" in their culture. As western culture (for the most part the United States) releases its media to a worldwide audience, there is great fear among Middle Easterners that their culture will be subsumed and authentic Muslim life will no longer be possible. For a group of people who have had a cultural presence for thousands of years, the thought of an outside influence destroying their culture is very scary, and ultimately some people react very angrily and violently towards this change. However, while ethnocentrism definitely serves as a positive protection against outside cultures attempting to destroy your culture, there are negative aspects to ethnocentrism as well: culture shock, stereotyping, and prejudice.

Culture shock occurs when an individual enters into a new culture that is different from her or his culture. When you first enter into a new culture, all kinds of things become new and frightening. Even moving from one part of the United States to another can bring on culture shock. If you've lived in the same place your entire life, shock may seem like a really strong word, but if you've ever moved to a different country, shock is not strong enough to explain how you feel. Everything is new, different, and worse for a while. At first, things are just new and different, which is what you experience when you vacation somewhere. Vacations are wonderful because they keep us in the new and different stage. However, if you've moved some where for an extended period of time, things go from new and different to worse. For example, imagine you move from Texas where everything is beef, fried, and smothered in gravy to Asia where food is mostly fish and other aquatic animals, rice, and vegetables. While eating sushi may be fun on vacation, when it becomes the only thing you can eat, you may start to get very disgruntled and long for a thick piece of beef, fried, and slathered in gravy. This point where you are disgruntled and frustrated is the culture shock stage. While most people are eventually able to adjust to the new culture, some people never do.

The second problem with ethnocentrism is that it leads to stereotyping. Stereotyping occurs when we view a group of people from a culture or co-culture (a culture that exists within a larger culture) as sharing one or several common characteristics. Many people in other parts of the world believe the stereotype that all Americans are rude, pushy, and bigoted because a handful of American tourists have behaved that way when visiting their country. You may be thinking that not all Americans are rude, pushy, and bigoted, which is correct. However, how many times have you thought that someone from another cultural group was going to be a specific way because of her or his membership within that cultural group? Such generalizations are a means of organizing our experiences and interactions with others. They help us make sense out of the differences we observe among individuals and groups. We need these kinds of generalizations so that we may better predict how people around us are likely to behave in response to our communicative efforts or everyday behavior. Stereotypes are a way of making sense out of the variations in people and behavior in our environment. When we stereotype, we tend to make three kinds of errors—we overestimate differences, underestimate differences, and see what we expect to see. Overestimating differences occurs when two people from differing cultural groups are very similar, but one or both of the people perceives them to be drastically different from each other. Underestimating differences occurs when two people from differing cultural groups perceive that they are very similar even though large differences actually exist between them. People who underestimate differences often behave like they would in their own culture and have no idea how rude they are being in a host culture because they don't think there is a difference. The last problem with stereotyping is that it leads people to see what they expect to see. If you believe that all purple people are thieves, and you hear a story on the news about a purple person being arrested for embezzlement, you'll think: *See, I was right, all purple people are thieves.* However, we filter out any information that is contrary to what we want to see. If we hear that a purple person gave back the extra change she received while shopping at the grocery store, we think this is the rare exception or think there was a more sinister motive to her giving back the change. In essence, people create these narrow perspectives of how "other people" should behave based on their stereotypes, and then pigeonp hole all people who belong to a cultural group as behaving according to the stereotype, which leads to the third negative aspect of stereotyping—prejudice.

Prejudice refers to making a priori (before the fact) judgments based on stereotypes. In other words, we may form the judgment today but not have cause to use it for days or months into the future. When we say the judgment is based on stereotypes, we indicate that the judgments are not based of the best of information. While the judgment may be applied to a person we have never even met or a behavior we have never observed, it is determined on the basis of limited information about a group of people about whom we may know very little and whose behavioral tendencies may only be the subject of conjecture. In short, prejudice means prejudging a person or a person's behavior on the basis of limited information about the culture or co-culture of which that person is a member. Prejudice leads to all sorts of antisocial behaviors, from discrimination (actively preventing another person from receiving equal treatment) to violence. We often refer to high levels of prejudice as the "isms:" racism (negative views of people from different ethnic and racial groups), sexism (believing that one biological sex is superior to the other), ageism (believing that people of a certain age are inferior), heterosexism (believing that everyone should be and should behave in a heterosexual manner), and lookism (believing that people with specific physical attributes—hair color, eye color, weight, height, etc.—are inferior to people with other physical attributes). Most of these prejudices are negative and view people in those groups in a very negative light.

HUMOR ASSESSMENT

Have you ever noticed that people who are able to get everyone around them laughing tend to have more friends and are invited to more parties? The ability to effectively use humor is a trait that many people wish they could have, but only some people seem to have that extra spark that makes their humor usage appear flawless. In an attempt to measure the extent to which an individual uses humor during interpersonal interactions, Wrench and Richmond (2004) created the Humor Assessment (HA) instrument. Before we start discussing the nature of an individual's humor assessment, please take a second and fill out the HA instrument in Figure 7.4.

Humor is an absolutely fascinating variable to study because of the rather dramatic effects that humor can have on people's every day lives. The ability to use humor as a tool for interpersonal communication has consistently been shown to be useful whether you are in the health care setting, classroom, or boardroom. In research that has examined humor in health

Directions: The following statements apply to how people communicate humor when relating to others. Indicate the degree to which each of these statements applies to you by filling in the number of your response in the blank before each item:

Strongly Disagree	Disagree	Neutral	Agree	Strongly Agree
1	2	3	4	5

_____ 1. I regularly communicate with others by joking with them.
_____ 2. People usually laugh when I makes a humorous remark.
_____ 3. I am not funny or humorous.
_____ 4. I can be amusing or humorous without having to tell a joke.
_____ 5. Being humorous is a natural communication orientation for me.
_____ 6. I cannot relate an amusing idea well.
_____ 7. My friends would say that I am a humorous or funny person.
_____ 8. People don't seem to pay close attention when I am being funny.
_____ 9. Even funny ideas and stories seem dull when I tell them.
_____ 10. I can easily relate funny or humorous ideas to the class.
_____ 11. I would say that I am not a humorous person.
_____ 12. I cannot be funny, even when asked to do so.
_____ 13. I relate amusing stories, jokes, and funny things very well to others.
_____ 14. Of all the people I know, I am one of the "least" amusing or funny persons.
_____ 15. I use humor to communicate in a variety of situations.
_____ 16. On a regular basis, I do not communicate with others by being humorous or entertaining.

SCORING: To compute your scores follow the instructions below:

1. How to Score:
    Step One: Add scores for items 1, 2, 4, 5, 7, 10, 13, & 15.
    Step Two: Add scores for items 3, 6, 8, 9, 11, 12, 14 & 16.
    Step Three: Add 48 to Step One.
    Step Four: Subtract the score for Step Two from the score for Step Three.

Scores should be between 16 and 80. Scores over 63 are considered high.

Source:

Wrench, J. S., & Richmond, V. P. (2004). Understanding the psychometric properties of the Humor Assessment instrument through an analysis of the relationships between teacher humor assessment and instructional communication variables in the college classroom. *Communication Research Reports, 21,* 92–103.

Figure 7.4 Humor Assessment Instrument (HA)

care settings (Wrench and Booth-Butterfield, 2003) (see the CD-ROM that accompanies this book for this article), physicians who are more humorous are perceived by patients as being more credible. Patients are also more satisfied with physicians who are funny and are actually less likely to sue a physician who uses moderate levels of humor during a medical interview. In the area of educational research, teachers who are more humorous are also perceived as more trustworthy and credible by their students when compared to teachers who are not perceived as humorous by their students. Students also like humorous teachers more than nonhumorous teachers, and even like the content more from humorous teachers than from nonhumorous teachers. In fact, teachers who are humorous in the classroom actually have students who learn more in the class. In the organizational setting, many businesses actually hire humor consultants to come in and "liven things up" around the office because a humorous work environment has been shown to increase productivity levels. Furthermore, employees who perceive their superiors as being humorous experience higher levels of job satisfaction and are less likely to quit their job, which ultimately saves an organization lots of money.

When you examine the results from research on humor in different contexts, it points in one direction—humor is a good thing. While what people find humorous is very culturally based, the ability to enact it appears to be more biologically based. When we talk about a cultural basis for what we find humorous, think about the types of stand-up comedians you like versus the type of comedians your parents or grandparents would like. What people within a different culture or co-culture enjoy as humorous is very dependent on what they are taught is funny. If you're taught that farting in public is rude and obnoxious, you will not find a "fart joke" funny, while other people will think the joke is hysterical.

NONVERBAL IMMEDIACY

Have you ever noticed that you are drawn to some people and not to others? One reason for this is an individual's level of nonverbal immediacy. Immediacy, as a general concept, refers to the degree of perceived physical or psychological distance between people in a relationship. An immediate relationship is one in which the people in the relationship see themselves as close (both physically and mentally) to one another. When we talk about physical closeness, we are not talking about intimacy—just a perception that the other person is physically near you. Have you ever noticed how some people can make themselves look unapproachable just by the way they hold their bodies and look at you? While these people may be in the same physical environment as you are, you probably will not perceive yourself to be close to these people. On the flip side, many people experience a certain feeling of closeness with a public speaker even though thay are 100 yards away from them during the speech. All of us communicate a certain presence to other people. How we hold our bodies and look at people will determine whether or not we start, continue, or terminate interactions with other people. Whom we desire to communicate with is communicated to that other person through both our verbal and our nonverbal messages. Thus, the verbal and nonverbal messages we send and receive in a relationship will define the level of immediacy that develops in that relationship. Figure 7.5 shows the Self-Report of Nonverbal Immediacy (SRNI-26).

As mentioned above, immediacy is created through both verbal and nonverbal messages. Such comments as "I see what you mean," "Tell me more," "That is a good point," and "I think so too" will create increased immediacy. Contrast these comments with the following: "Oh, shut up," "I do believe a village lost its idiot," "I thought of that years ago," and "Frankly, I don't care what you think." The first series of phrases helps to increase the perceived physical and psychological closeness between two people, while the second series of phrases only increases the perception of distance. Nonverbal immediacy, on the other hand, consists of communicative behaviors like leaning in toward the person while talking to her or him, maintaining eye contact, smiling, nodding your head, not folding your arms in front of you while talking, and many other behaviors. Nonimmediate nonverbal behaviors would be the opposite of the immediate ones, leaning away from the person while talking, avoiding eye contact, frowning or scowling, not moving your head at all (looking rigid), folding your arms in front of you, and many other behaviors. The Nonverbal Immediacy scale (Figure 7.5) was designed to examine an individual's tendency to employ different nonverbally immediate behaviors while avoiding communicative behaviors that are not nonverbally immediate. To see a wide variety of other nonverbally immediate behaviors, look at the 26 different items on the scale because each item represents a nonverbally immediate behavior if you scored it in step 1 or a non-nonverbally immediate behavior if you scored it in step 2.

DIRECTIONS: The following statements describe the ways some people behave while talking with or to others. Please indicate in the space at the left of each item the degree to which you believe the statement applies to **(fill in the target person's name or description)**. Please use the following 5-point scale:

1 = Never; 2 = Rarely; 3 = Occasionally; 4 = Often; 5 = Very Often

_____ 1. I use my hands and arms to gesture while talking to people.
_____ 2. I touch others on the shoulder or arm while talking to them.
_____ 3. I use a monotone or dull voice while talking to people.
_____ 4. I look over or away from others while talking to them.
_____ 5. I move away from others when they touch me while talking.
_____ 6. I have a relaxed body position when talking to people.
_____ 7. I frown while talking to people.
_____ 8. I avoid eye contact while talking to people.
_____ 9. I have a tense body position while talking to people.
_____ 10. I sit close or stand close to people while talking with them.
_____ 11. My voice is monotonous or dull when talking to people.
_____ 12. I use a variety of vocal expressions when talking to people.
_____ 13. I gesture when talking to people.
_____ 14. I am animated when talking to people.
_____ 15. I have a bland facial expression when talking to people.
_____ 16. I move closer to people when talking to them.
_____ 17. I look directly at people while talking to them.
_____ 18. I am stiff when talking to people.
_____ 19. I have a lot of vocal variety when talking to people.
_____ 20. I avoid gesturing while talking to people.
_____ 21. I lean toward people when talking to them.
_____ 22. I maintain eye contact with people when talking to them.
_____ 23. I try not to sit or stand close to people when talking with them.
_____ 24. I lean away from people when talking to them.
_____ 25. I smile when talking to people.
_____ 26. I avoid touching people when talking to them.

SCORING: To compute your scores follow the instructions below:

Step One: Add scores for items 1, 2, 6, 10, 12, 13, 14, 16, 17, 19, 21, 22, & 25.
Step Two: Add scores for items 3, 4, 5, 7, 8, 9, 11, 15, 18, 20, 23, 24, & 26.
Step Three: Add 78 to Step One.
Step Four: Subtract the score for Step Two from the score for Step Three.

Scores should be between 26 and 30. Scores over 112 for females and over 104 for males are considered high.

Figure 7.5 Nonverbal Immediacy Scale–Self-Report (NIS-S)

At this point you may be wondering why nonverbal immediacy is so important that we need to research it as a variable. Well, nonverbal immediacy has been linked to a number of important communication outcomes. First, immediacy will usually lead to an increase in communication between participants and interactants. When someone feels that another person is either physically or psychologically close to her or him, he or she becomes more relaxed and open to communication. Second, immediacy will lead to increased attentiveness by the receiver. If we perceive someone is immediate, we naturally focus attention on that person. So if you want someone to listen to what you are saying, employing nonverbally and verbally immediate behavior is a trick that can be used to get and maintain that person's attention. Third, immediacy will increase the likelihood that listening will improve between the interactants. People are more open to listening to what another person is saying to them when they perceive that the person is immediate. Fourth, immediacy leads to increased liking between interactants. If you perceive that someone is physically and psychologically close to you, you are simply going to like that person more. Overall, these four outcomes lead to more effective communication.

SOCIOCOMMUNICATIVE ORIENTATION

Psychologist Sandra Bem (1974) started researching the concepts of masculinity and femininity and created a scale she called the Bem Sex-Role Inventory (BSRI). The BSRI was originally constructed by having different groups of participants read a list of adjectives and determine which characteristics on the list were seen as more desirable in the United States for one biological sex or the other. After participants rated these lists, Bem determine that 20 items were ranked by females and males to be more desirable for a man (masculine scale) and 20 items were ranked by females and males to be more desirable for a woman (feminine scale). A number of researchers examined the BSRI and realized that what Bem thought she was measuring really wasn't a scale of maleness and femaleness, but rather a scale of how people interact with each other. For this reason, Richmond and McCroskey (1985) created a scale to measure how people communicate either assertively (Bem's masculinity) or responsively (Bem's femininity), and called the scale the Sociocommunicative Orientation scale. Figure 7.6 contains the Sociocommunicative Orientation scale, so please take a second and fill out the scale.

In the Sociocommunicative Orientation scale, two factors are measured: assertiveness and responsiveness. Assertiveness is the capacity to make requests, actively disagree, express positive or negative personal rights and feelings, initiate, maintain, or disengage from conversations, and stand up for oneself without attacking another. Bem's research originally suggested that these communicative behaviors were only enacted by males, but we all know many women who are equally adept at all of the assertive behaviors. While many women employ assertive communication behaviors, many societies stereotype appropriate male communication behavior as being closely associated with these behaviors. Conversely, responsiveness is the capacity to be sensitive to the communication of others, to be a good listener, to make others comfortable in communicating, and to recognize the needs and desires of others. Terms commonly used to describe a person who engages in responsive communication behaviors include helpful, sympathetic, compassionate, sensitive to needs of others, sincere, gentle, warm, tender, friendly, understanding, and (of course) responsive to others. Although such terms do describe the stereotypical perception of how females communicate in the United States, in a broader sense these terms describe any person who is open to the communication of others and empathetic with those others.

At this point we should note that sociocommunicative orientation, which is a self-report scale, is only half of the puzzle when examining this variable. The scale seen in Figure 7.6 can easily be retooled to examine someone else's behavior in what is called the Sociocommunicative Style scale using the following instructions: "Please indicate the degree to which you believe each of these characteristics applies to the [place name here] by marking whether you (5) strongly agree that it applies, (4) agree that it applies, (3) are undecided, (2) disagree that it applies, or (1) strongly disagree that it applies." A lot of research has examined how an individual's sociocommunicative style impacts people's perceptions of other behaviors. For example, research in instructional communication has found that highly assertive and

DIRECTIONS: The questionnaire below lists 20 personality characteristics. Please indicate the degree to which you believe each of these characteristics applies to YOU, as you normally communicate with others, by marking whether you (5) strongly agree that it applies, (4) agree that it applies, (3) are undecided, (2) disagree that it applies, or (1) strongly disagree that it applies. There are no right or wrong answers. Work quickly; record your first impression.

_____ 1. Helpful
_____ 2. Defends own beliefs
_____ 3. Independent
_____ 4. Responsive to others
_____ 5. Forceful
_____ 6. Has strong personality
_____ 7. Sympathetic
_____ 8. Compassionate
_____ 9. Assertive
_____ 10. Sensitive to the needs of others
_____ 11. Dominant
_____ 12. Sincere
_____ 13. Gentle
_____ 14. Willing to take a stand
_____ 15. Warm
_____ 16. Tender
_____ 17. Friendly
_____ 18. Acts as a leader
_____ 19. Aggressive
_____ 20. Competitive

Items 2, 3, 5, 6, 9, 11, 14, 18, 19, & 20 measure assertiveness. Add the scores on these items to get your assertiveness score. Items 1, 4, 7, 8, 10, 12, 13, 15, 16, & 17 measure responsiveness. Add the scores on these items to get your responsiveness score.

Source:

Richmond, V. P., & McCroskey, J. C. (1990). Reliability and separation of factors on the assertiveness-responsiveness scale. *Psychological Reports, 67,* 449–450.

Figure 7.6 Sociocommunicative Orientation Scale

responsive teachers are perceived as more nonverbally immediate, more trustworthy, and more humorous. In fact, teachers that are highly responsive have been shown to have students who learn more, are more satisfied with their teacher, and are more likely to talk to their teacher outside of class. Sociocommunicative style has also been examined in the health care setting examining a patient's perception of her or his physician's sociocommunicative style. In the health care setting, physician assertiveness and responsiveness were both shown to relate to patient perceptions of her or his physician's credibility. Furthermore, patients who perceived their physicians as responsive were more satisfied and believed they received good medical care cpm[ared to patients who did not perceive their physicians as responsive. These results were also seen in subordinate supervisor relationships in organizations. Subordinates who perceived their supervisors as assertive and responsive also perceived their supervisors as credible. And subordinates who perceived their supervisors as assertive and responsive also reported higher levels of job satisfaction and motivation. Overall, sociocommunicative orientation/style has been shown to be an extremely important communication variable.

WILLINGNESS TO COMMUNICATE

The next interval variable is the variable Willingness to Communicate (WTC). Communication research has found that some people are more likely to initiate communicative interactions than others. Judee Burgoon (1976) initiated this line of research by examining the construct she labeled as "unwillingness to communicate," which she described as a "chronic tendency to avoid and/or devalue oral communication" (p. 60). McCroskey and Richmond (1987) retooled the concept to examine an individual's general attitude toward communicating with other people. McCroskey (1992) wrote that "the construct is that of an orientation toward communication which we have referred to previously as a predisposition to avoid communication . . . a behavioral tendency regarding talking frequency" (p. 21). In essence, willingness to communicate can be defined as the tendency of an individual to engage in communication with other people. Please complete the Willingness to Communicate scale in Figure 7.7. Carefully read the directions on this scale because it is not a Likert-type scale and can throw off some participants because it asks for percentages.

Willingness to communicate, as previous mentioned, examines the extent to which an individual initiates or avoids communication. Look at your scores for WTC. Do you have any areas in which you exhibit a low willingness to communicate? Maybe you have a high WTC in public speaking situations but a low WTC in meetings? You may have a high WTC score in every context, but a very low WTC with strangers. Your individual WTC is very deeply rooted and has been shown to a large genetic basis.

Research has shown that an individual's level of communication apprehension (CA) is probably the best predictor of a person's level of WTC. If someone is high CA, then he or she is probably low WTC, and vice versa. WTC is generally thought of as a trait-based predisposition that determines the degree to which people communicate in a variety of contexts (interpersonal, meeting, group, and public). Whether a person is willing to communicate with another in a given interpersonal example (e.g., student–teacher, parent–child, subordinate–supervisor, etc.) is often affected by situational constraints within the encounter such as the nature of the relationship of the interactants. Someone may be very willing to talk to a teacher, but less willing to talk to her or his supervisor. While WTC is dependent upon the situation, people usually exhibit regular WTC tendencies across situations, contexts, and audiences.

When people talk about WTC, they often mistake it for the term shyness, which is not the same thing. Shyness is the behavioral tendency to not initiate communication and/or respond

---

DIRECTIONS: Below are 20 situations in which a person might choose to communicate or not to communicate. Presume you have *completely free choice*. Determine the percentage of times you would *choose to initiate communication* in each type of situation. Indicate in the space at the left what percent of the time you would choose to communicate. Choose any numbers between 0 and 100.

_____ 1. Talk with a service station attendant.
_____ 2. Talk with a physician.
_____ 3. Present a talk to a group of strangers.
_____ 4. Talk with an acquaintance while standing in line.
_____ 5. Talk with a salesperson in a store.
_____ 6. Talk in a large meeting of friends.
_____ 7. Talk with a police officer.
_____ 8. Talk in a small group of strangers.

Figure 7.7 Willingness to Communicate

_____ 9. Talk with a friend while standing in line.
_____ 10. Talk with a waiter/waitress in a restaurant.
_____ 11. Talk in a large meeting of acquaintances.
_____ 12. Talk with a stranger while standing in line.
_____ 13. Talk with a secretary.
_____ 14. Present a talk to a group of friends.
_____ 15. Talk in a small group of acquaintances.
_____ 16. Talk with a garbage collector.
_____ 17. Talk in a large meeting of strangers.
_____ 18. Talk with a spouse (or girl/boyfriend).
_____ 19. Talk in a small group of friends.
_____ 20. Present a talk to a group of acquaintances.

SCORING: The WTC permits computation of one total score and seven subscores. The range for all scores is 0–100. Follow the procedures outlined below.

1. Group discussion—add scores for items 8, 15, & 19; divide sum by 3. Scores above 89 = high WTC, scores below 57 = low WTC in this context.
2. Meetings—add scores for items 6, 11, & 17; divide sum by 3. Scores above 80 = high WTC, scores below 39 = low WTC in this context.
3. Interpersonal—add scores for items 4, 9, & 12; divide sum by 3. Scores above 94 = high WTC, scores below 64 = low WTC in this context.
4. Public speaking—add scores for items 3, 14, & 20; divide sum by 3. Scores above 78 = high WTC, scores below 33 = low WTC in this context.
5. Stranger—add scores for items 3, 8, 12, & 17; divide sum by 4. Scores above 63 = high WTC, scores below 18 = low WTC with these receivers.
6. Acquaintance—add scores for items 4, 11, 15, & 20; divide sum by 4. Scores above 92 = high WTC, scores below 57 = low WTC with these receivers.
7. Friends—add scores for items 6, 9, 14, & 19; divide sum by 4. Scores above 99 = high WTC, scores below 71 = low WTC with these receivers.

To compute the total score for the WTC, add the totals for stranger, friend, and acquaintance; then divide by 3.

Group discussion	> 89 High WTC, < 57 Low WTC
Meetings	> 80 High WTC, < 39 Low WTC
Interpersonal conversations	> 94 High WTC, < 64 Low WTC
Public speaking	> 78 High WTC, < 33 Low WTC
Stranger	> 63 High WTC, < 18 Low WTC
Acquaintance	> 92 High WTC, < 57 Low WTC
Friend	> 99 High WTC, < 71 Low WTC
Total WTC	> 82 High Overall WTC < 52 Low Overall WTC

Source:

McCroskey, J. C. (1992). Reliability and validity of the willingness to communicate scale. _Communication Quarterly, 40,_ 16–25.

to the initiatives of others. Shyness stems from a preference for noncommunication by the individual—a reduced willingness to communicate. WTC may be considered an attitude toward initiating communication or, as some prefer, the person's intent or disposition toward the behavior of initiating communication. This notion of shyness is very similar to communication apprehension, previous defined in this chapter as the fear or anxiety associated with either real or anticipated communication with another person or persons.

Ultimately, when one examines the interrelationships between CA, WTC, and shyness, the three constructs can appear very similar. However, as far as how communication researchers utilize the terms, they do not overlap in definition: CA is what a person feels (they feel fear or anxiety); shyness is the degree to which one refrains from actual communication; and WTC is one's inclination to talk.

While research has shown that there are a number of possible causes (both nature and nurture) for an individual's WTC level, WTC as a variable is interesting in how it relates to other communication variables in research. Previous research in WTC has primarily occurred in classrooms and health care and organizational settings. First, research has found that students with low WTC levels participated less in the classroom than students with high scores. Students who have high WTC scores have also been shown to be perceived as more communicatively competent by others than students with low WTC scores.

In essence, not every person you run into who is quiet has the same reasons for being quiet; however, the consequences of being perceived as quiet are similar. As we discussed earlier in this chapter, people who are quiet are generally perceived as less intelligent, lazy, and unfriendly, so quiet people have a number of stereotypes they must battle simply based on their degree of wilingness to talk.

BELIEFS AND ATTITUDES

Generalized Belief Scale

Unlike the previous interval variables discussed in this section, the next two variables are a little different because they are designed to be utilized in a wide variety of contexts. The Generalized Belief Scale was created by McCroskey (1966) as a tool for examining the strength of an individual's belief on a given topic. Beliefs concern our perception of reality about whether something is true or false. The scale that you can see in Figure 7.8 is designed to be a very general scale that can be utilized in a number of different situations. In essence, the scale in Figure 7.8 could be used to measure a person's belief about abortion, euthanasia, capital punishment, or, as we have in this case, the belief that "everyone should be required to take public speaking in college."

Generalized Attitude Measure

The second scale in this section that has the ability to measure different things every time it is employed is the Generalized Attitude Measure. Like the Generalized Belief Scale, it is designed to measure a range of different attitudes depending on what needs to be analyzed by a researcher. An attitude is defined as a predisposition to respond to people, ideas, or objects in an evaluative way. When we define an attitude as a predisposition, we define an attitude as an individual's tendency to do something. Here it is a tendency to *evaluate* people, ideas, or objects. The word "evaluative" in this definition means making judgments of good or bad, desirable or undesirable, likable or unlikable, etc. In essence, there are countless numbers of attitudes that an individual could measure using the Generalized Attitude Scale. For example, you could use it to measure an individual's attitude about sex, broccoli, public speaking, or, as we have in this book, higher education. Figure 7.9 contains

Instructions: On the scales below, please indicate the degree to which you believe the following statement **"Everyone Should Be Required to Take Public Speaking in College."** Numbers "1" and "7" indicate a very strong feeling. Numbers "2" and "6" indicate a strong feeling. Numbers "3" and "5" indicate a fairly week feeling. Number "4" indicates you are undecided or do not understand the adjective pairs themselves. There are no right or wrong answers. *Only circle one number per line.*

1.	Agree	7	6	5	4	3	2	1	Disagree
2.	False	1	2	3	4	5	6	7	True
3.	Incorrect	1	2	3	4	5	6	7	Correct
4.	Right	7	6	5	4	3	2	1	Wrong
5.	Yes	7	6	5	4	3	2	1	No

* To compute your score, simply add up the numbers you circled.

Sources:

McCroskey, J. C. (1966). *Experimental studies of the effects of ethos and evidence in persuasive communication.* Unpublished doctoral dissertation. Pennsylvania State University.

McCroskey, J. C., & Richmond, V. P. (1989). Bipolar scales. In P. Emmert & L. L. Barker (Eds.), *Measurement of Communication Behavior* (pp. 154–167). New York: Longman.

Figure 7.8 Generalized Belief Scale

Instructions: On the scales below, please indicate your feelings about **"Higher Education."** Numbers "1" and "7" indicate a very strong feeling. Numbers "2" and "6" indicate a strong feeling. Numbers "3" and "5" indicate a fairly week feeling. Number "4" indicates you are undecided or do not understand the adjective pairs themselves. There are no right or wrong answers. *Only circle one number per line.*

1.	Good	7	6	5	4	3	2	1	Bad
2.	Wrong	1	2	3	4	5	6	7	Right
3.	Harmful	1	2	3	4	5	6	7	Beneficial
4.	Fair	7	6	5	4	3	2	1	Unfair
5.	Wise	7	6	5	4	3	2	1	Foolish
6.	Negative	1	2	3	4	5	6	7	Positive

* To compute your score, simply add up the numbers you circled.

Sources:

McCroskey, J. C. (1966). *Experimental studies of the effects of ethos and evidence in persuasive communication.* Unpublished doctoral dissertation. Pennsylvania State University.

McCroskey, J. C., & Richmond, V. P. (1989). Bipolar scales. In P. Emmert & L. L. Barker (Eds.), *Measurement of Communication Behavior* (pp. 154–167). New York: Longman.

Figure 7.9 Generalized Attitude Measure

the Generalized Attitude Measure retooled to measure an individual's attitude about higher education.

We believe that studying beliefs and attitudes is extremely important for communication researchers. By using the word "believe," we imply that for us (not necessarily for everyone else) the study of beliefs and attitudes is a true, correct, appropriate set of variables to study. We "believe" in the studying of beliefs and attitudes by communication researchers. We also think that studying beliefs and attitudes is good, so we have a positive attitude toward it. Belief has to do with our perceptions of reality; whereas attitude has to do with our evaluation of that reality.

In this section we have examined six interval variables using a Likert scale (communication apprehension, ethnocentrism, humor assessment, nonverbal immediacy, sociocommunicative orientation, and willingness to communicate) and two variables using a bipolar scale (belief that everyone should take public speaking in college and attitude toward higher education). In the next section we will examine the ratio variable we collected data on in this study.

Ratio Variables

For the dataset collected for this book, we decided to include one ratio variable. For a variable to be seen as ratio, the distance between attributes has real quantitative meaning and has an absolute zero. Age is the only variable that has a scale with attributes that have real quantitative meaning and an absolute zero. I know for a fact that someone who is 12 years old is exactly twice as old as someone who is 6 years old. You cannot say the same thing with interval variables. I could not say that someone with a CA score of 80 is twice as apprehensive as someone with a CA score of 40 because the ranges do not have real quantitative meaning. Furthermore, age does have an absolute zero. Of course, with humans the absolute zero for age is birth. In fact, in the study we had a range of ages from 18 to 48 years of age with an average age of 21.68.

Writing Up Scales Using APA

Up to this point, we've discussed the variables collected for this text's real-world dataset. Being able to identify the different variables and the different measurement levels is only part of the picture when conducting a research project. Once a researcher has determined which variables should be examined in a research study, he or she needs to clearly explain the variables in the method section of the research paper in a very clear and concise fashion. For this reason, this section will walk you through how to more clearly write a method section than originally discussed in Chapter 4.

PARTICIPANTS

According to Chapter 4, the first part of a method section should report who the participants were. You need to report basic demographic characteristics (sex and age) of the participants along with how you were able to attract them. All of the numbers we are going need for this section will be calculated in the next chapter, so for now trust us that these numbers do come from somewhere and have a legitimate purpose. Here is an example of how this might appear in APA:

> Participants for this study were undergraduate students taking both lower and upper division courses at a large mid-Atlantic university. In spring of 2005, 325 undergraduate students agreed to participate in this project. In the study sample, there were 139 (42.8%) females, 183 (563 %) males, and 3 (0.9%) who did not respond to the biological sex question. The age of this sample ranged from 18 to 48 with a mean of 21.68 ($SD = 3.69$).

> Further demographic variables were also collected to examine school classification and political affiliation. Our sample contained 1 (0.3%) freshman, 39 (12%) sophomores, 141 (43.4%) juniors, 137 (42.2%) seniors, 4 (1.2%) graduate students, and 3 (0.9%) who did not respond to the question. The recorded political affiliations of the study participants are as follows: 117 (36%) Democrats, 144 (44.3%) Republicans, 39 (12%) others, 21 (6.5%) participants who are not registered to vote, and 4 (1.2%) who did not respond to the question.

PROCEDURES

Once you have explained who your sample was you need to explain the apparatus used in the research if you used one discussed in Chapter 5. Because this study did not use an apparatus, we can move on and discuss the procedures used in this study. When discussing the procedures, you should be as brief as possible while giving all of the appropriate and necessary information about what you did. For example, here is how you could describe the procedures for this project:

> The study participants were approached during their communication class and asked to participate in the study. All participants were handed a copy of the survey instrument that contained a cover letter explaining the purpose of the study. Participants were asked to sign and detach the cover page if they consented to filling out the questionnaire. All students who participated received extra credit for their participation. An alternative extra credit assignment was available to students who did not opt to participate in the study.

In this example, we start by explaining that all students were approached during class and asked to participate in the study. We then specified that we obtained consent, which is required by law (see Chapter 3), from the participants indicating their desire for their participation. We also informed our potential readers that all students who participated in the project were given extra credit, but we did not coerce anyone into filling out the survey because we had an alternative extra credit assignment that participants could choose to complete if they were uncomfortable with the study.

INSTRUMENTATION

Once you have finished with the first three parts of a Method section, you need to explain all of the measurement tools employed in your study. In this study, we had all eight interval scales plus one ordinal scale that needs to be explained. To explain a scale, you start by telling your audience who the creator of the scale was and what the scale is supposed to be measuring. You then explain how the scale is formatted including a discussion of type of scale (Likert, bipolar, or scalogram), numerical scale used (5 steps, 7 steps, or 10 steps), range possible on the scale, range received on the scale, and how to interpret scale results. For example:

> The Personal Report of Communication Apprehension-24 (PRCA-24) was created by McCroskey (1982) to measure an individual's level of fear or anxiety associated with either real or anticipated

PRCA-24. The Personal Report of Communication Apprehension–24 was created by McCroskey (1982) to measure an individual's level of fear or anxiety associated with either real or anticipated communication with another person or persons. The scale consists of 24 Likert items ranging from (1) *strongly agree* to (5) *strongly disagree* with a range of scores from 24 to 120, which was seen in this study. Higher scores are designed to indicate higher levels of communication apprehension.

Ethnocentrism. The Ethnocentrism Scale was created by Neuliep and McCroskey (1997) to measure an individual's tendency to feel that her or his culture is the center of the universe. The revised version of the scale employed here (Neuliep & McCroskey, 2000; McCroskey, 2001) consists of 22 Likert items ranging from (1) *strongly disagree* to (5) *strongly agree*. Fifteen of the items are scored; the remaining items are used as distracters. This scale has a possible range of 15–75; however, the range seen in this study was 16–61. Higher scores are designed to indicate higher levels of ethnocentrism.

Humor Assessment. The Humor Assessment (HA) was created by Wrench and Richmond (2004) to measure an individual's use of humor as a communicative device in interpersonal relationships. The scale was originally published in Richmond, Wrench, and Gorham (2001) as a tool for teachers to assess their own use of humor in the classroom. The HA was then validated by Wrench and McCroskey (2001), who found that it functioned distinctly different from M. Booth-Butterfield and S. Booth-Butterfield's (1991) Humor Orientation scale. The HA consists of 16 Likert type items range from 1 *strongly disagree* to 5 *strongly agree* with a range of scores from 16 to 80, which was seen in this study. Higher scores on the HA indicate a higher extent to which an individual uses humor while communicating interpersonally.

Nonverbal Immediacy Scale. The Nonverbal Immediacy Scale was created by Richmond, McCroskey, and Johnson (2003) to measure a receiver's perceived nonverbal immediacy between her- or himself and a source. The scale consists of 26 Likert-type items ranging from (1) *strongly disagree* to (5) *strongly agree*. This scale has a possible range of 26–130; however, the range seen in this study was 63–130. Higher scores are designed to indicate higher levels of nonverbally immediate behavior.

Sociocommunicative Orientation. The Sociocommunicative Orientation scale was created by Richmond and McCroskey (1985) as an instructional tool to examine the extent to which individuals use assertive or responsive communication. The instrument was first utilized in research by Thompson, Ishii, and Klopf (1990) and Ishii, Thompson, and Klopf (1990) to examine cultural differences in assertive and responsive communication. After the publication of these two articles, Richmond and McCroskey (1990) demonstrated the reliability and dimensionality of the measure itself. The sociocommunicative orientation scale consists of 10 items on each factor for a total of 20 items. Participants are asked to respond to short descriptive phrases that range from one to five words in length that indicate ways in which they may communicate. The measure asks a participant to respond in terms of how well the item applies to her or him using a Likert scale from (1) *strongly disagree that it applies* to (5) *strongly agree that it applies*. Each factor can range from 10 to 50. In the current study, assertiveness had a range from 19 to 50 and responsiveness had a range from 20 to 50. Higher scores on each factor are designed to represent either higher assertive or responsive communicative behaviors.

Willingness to Communicate. The Willingness to Communicate (WTC) scale was devised by McCroskey (1992) to measures a person's willingness to initiate communication with another person or persons. The scale consists of 20 items. Each of the items is designed to measure whether an individual would initiate communication in a specific situation or with a specific individual. Eight of the items are fillers and 12 are scored as part of the scale. Using a 101-point range from 0 (never) to 100 (always), participants are asked to indicate the percentage of time they would choose to communicate in each type of situation. Ultimately, the scores on the 12 items are added together to create a composite score, with higher scores indicating a higher willingness to communicate. Scores on the WTC scale can range from 0 to 100; however, scores

Figure 7.10 APA Write-Ups for Scales

in the current study ranged from 18.25 to 100. Higher scores on the WTC scale are designed to indicate stronger likelihoods to initiate communicative interactions.

Generalized Belief Scale. The Generalized Belief Scale was created by McCroskey (1966) and validated by McCroskey and Richmond (1996). The Generalized Belief Measure was created by McCroskey (1966) as a way to measure beliefs about specific concepts. By attaining an individual's general belief about a given topic, the researcher can measure the degree to which an individual believes in a given statement. The statement measured in this study was "Everyone Should Be Required to Take Public Speaking in College." The belief statement is then measured using a five-item semantic differential scale with seven steps. The Generalized Belief Scale has a range of 5 to 35, which was seen in this study. Higher scores on the Generalized Belief Scale indicate stronger beliefs.

Generalized Attitude Measure. The Generalized Attitude Measure was a scale originally created by McCroskey (1966) and later validated by McCroskey and Richmond (1989) as a tool for determining someone's overall attitude about a specific subject. The Generalized Attitude Measure is measured using a six-item semantic differential scale with seven steps. For the purposes of this study, the Generalized Attitude Measure was utilized to determine the attitude of participants about higher education. The Generalized Attitude Measure has a range of 6–42; however, a range of 19–42 was seen in this study. Higher scores on the Generalized Attitude Measure indicate more positive attitudes.

Time on the Internet. In addition to the above interval variables, one ordinal variable was also collected in this study to examine the amount of time an individual spends communicating using the Internet. In response to the question how much time they spend online during a given week, participants were given the following categories to select from: 0–½ hour, ½–1 hour, 1–2 hours, 2–5 hours, 5–10 hours, 10–15 hours, 15–20 hours, and 20+ hours. This is similar to the method used by Wrench, Fiore, and McCroskey (2005) to examine the same construct.

communication with another person or persons. The scale consists of 24 Likert-type items ranging from 1 (*strongly agree*) to 5 (*strongly disagree*) with a range of scores from 24 to 120, which was seen in this study. Higher scores are designed to indicate higher levels of communication apprehension.

In this example, we wrote about the PRCA-24. The first sentence explains that McCroskey (1982) write the PRCA-24 to measure CA. The second sentence explains that the scale consists of 24 scale items that were written in a Likert-type format with five steps (1 [*strongly agree*], 2 [*agree*], 3 [*neutral*], 4 [*disagree*], and 5 [*strongly disagree*]). Notice that you only have to give the first step and the last step because researchers who see those two will immediately understand how to interpret the scores. The second sentence also contains the range of possible scores available on the PRCA-24 and mentions that the range was found in the study. The last sentence then explains how the scores can be interpreted. Specifically, the higher someone's PRCA-24 score is, the higher her or his level of CA is. Figure 7.10 shows the complete list of variable write-ups using APA style.

Conclusion

In this chapter we have examined a wide variety of communication variables that were collected for inclusion in this book's accompanying data set. The variables discussed in this chapter will be used numerous times throughout the rest of this book, so make sure you understand the variables: how they function in the world, how they are measured, and what they mean to communication researchers. In the next chapter we will go further into how each of the above scales was made by talking about the scale-development process.

KEY TERMS

Assertiveness
Attitudes
Audience Specific Behavior
Beliefs
Communication
　Apprehension
Contextual Behavior
Culture Shock

Ethnocentrism
Humor Assessment
Nonverbal Immediacy
Pancultural
Personality
Prejudice
Responsiveness
Situational Behavior

Sociocommunicative
　Orientation
Sociocommunicative Style
Stereotypes
Trait Behavior
Verbal Immediacy
Willingness to
　Communicate

REFERENCES

Beatty, M. J., McCroskey, J. C., & Valencic, K. M. (2001). *The biology of communication: A communibiological perspective*. Cresskill, NJ: Hampton Press.

Bem, S. L. (1974). The measurement of psychological androgyny. *Journal of Consulting and Clinical Psychology, 47,* 155–162.

Booth-Butterfield, M., & Booth-Butterfield, S. (1991). Individual differences in the communication of humorous messages. *Southern Communication Journal, 56,* 43–40.

Burgoon, J. K. (1976). The unwillingness-to-communicate scale: Development and validation. *Communication Monographs, 43,* 60–69.

Hammer, D. H., & Copeland, P. (1998). *Living with our genes: Why they matter more than you think*. New York: Doubleday.

Hollander, E. P. (1976). *Principles and methods of social psychology* (3rd ed.). New York: Oxford University Press.

Ishii, S., Thompson, C. A., & Klopf, D. W. (1990). A comparison of assertiveness/responsiveness construct between Japanese and Americans. *Otsuma Review, 23,* 63–71.

McCroskey, J. C. (1966). *Experimental studies of the effects of ethos and evidence in persuasive communication*. Unpublished doctoral dissertation. Pennsylvania State University.

McCroskey, J. C. (1982). *An introduction to rhetorical communication* (4th ed). Englewood Cliffs, NJ: Prentice-Hall.

McCroskey, J. C. (1992). Reliability and validity of the willingness to communicate scale. *Communication Quarterly, 40,* 16–25.

McCroskey, J. C. (2001). *An introduction to rhetorical communication* (8th ed.). Needham Hills, MA: Allyn & Bacon.

McCroskey, J. C., & Richmond, V. P. (1987). Willingness to communicate. In J. C. McCroskey & J. A. Daly (Eds.), *Personality and interpersonal communication* (pp. 119–131). Newbury Park, CA: Sage.

McCroskey, J. C., & Richmond, V. P. (1989). Bipolar scales. In P. Emmert & L. L. Barker (Eds.), *Measurement of communication behavior* (pp. 154–167). New York: Longman.

McCroskey, J. C., & Richmond, V. P. (1996). *Fundamentals of human communication: An interpersonal perspective*. Prospect Heights, IL: Waveland Press.

Neulip, J. W., & McCroskey, J. C. (1997). Development of a US and generalized ethnocentrism scale. *Communication Research Reports, 14,* 385–398.

Neuliep, J. W., & McCroskey, J. S. (2000, April). *Ethnocentrism*. Paper presented at the meeting of the Eastern Communication Association. Pittsburgh, PA.

Richmond, V. P., & McCroskey, J. C. (1985). *Communication: Apprehension, avoidance, and effectiveness.* Scottsdale, AZ: Gorsuch Scarisbrick.

Richmond, V. P., & McCroskey, J. C. (1990). Reliability and separation of factors on the assertiveness-responsiveness measure. *Psychological Reports, 67,* 449–450.

Richmond, V. P., McCroskey, J. C., & Johnson, A. D. (2003). Development of the nonverbal immediacy scale (NIS): Measures of self- and other-perceived nonverbal immediacy. *Communication Quarterly, 51,* 504–517.

Richmond, V. P., Wrench, J. S., & Gorham, J. (2001). *Communication, affect, and learning in the classroom.* Acton, MA: Tapestry Press.

Thompson, C. A., Ishii, S., & Klopf, D. W. (1990). Japanese and Americans compared on assertiveness/responsiveness. *Psychological Reports, 66,* 829–830.

Wrench, J. S., Fiore, A. M., & McCroskey, J. C. (2005). The relationship between human temperament, communication apprehension, willingness to communicate, and computer-mediated communication competence and behaviors. Manuscript submitted for publication.

Wrench, J. S., & McCroskey, J. C. (2001). A temperamental understanding of humor communication and exhilaratability. *Communication Quarterly, 49,* 142–159.

Wrench, J. S., & Richmond, V. P. (2004). Understanding the psychometric properties of the Humor Assessment instrument through an analysis of the relationships between teacher humor assessment and instructional communication variables in the college classroom. *Communication Research Reports, 21,* 92–103.

Descriptive Statistics

Statistics is a term that conjures up many different meanings in the minds of students. Of course, the majority of students we have worked with express a high level of anxiety and apprehension about taking a course in research methods due to a fear of statistics. Be honest—were you excited at the prospect of taking this class? Our guess is that if given the choice, the majority of you would have preferred to take a different course. In fact, this is a good example of a statistic—the "majority."

Imagine we had the ability to have everyone in the world fill out the Personal Report of Communication Apprehension-24 (PRCA-24) scale. The average we would get for the entire world population on the PRCA-24 would be called a parameter because the average would refer to the entire population. However, it is almost impossible to achieve parameters because having an entire population fill out a scale is almost impossible unless the target population is very small. Instead, we often use smaller groups from within the entire population called samples. While we will discuss how we get samples in greater detail in Chapter 14, at this point just understand that a sample is a subset from within the whole population that allows researchers to make generalizations about the whole population. When we calculate information from a sample of data (for example, the sample data's PRCA-24 scores collected for this book), the calculation is referred to as a statistic. In essence, the parameter is the real average of communication apprehension in a population, and a statistic is the average of communication apprehension within a sample. In a perfect world, the two numbers would be identical, but there is always a certain amount of error that will exist between parameters and statistics. We will discuss this concept in greater detail in Chapter 15.

The goal of this chapter is to introduce you to the "not-so-scary" side of statistics. We've all seen commercials that say something like this: "Four out of five dentists recommend Chewing Gum Brand X for their patients who chew gum." The advertisement uses a statistic to illustrate that 80% of dentists would recommend Chewing Gum Brand X. It's much more effective than simply stating that "most dentists prefer Chewing Gum Brand X." When information is presented using terms like "most," "many," and "substantial," consumers are often skeptical and want to know the exact amount. Generally, we seek proof for claims that are made, and statistics serve as a source that lends credibility. Consider the grades that you earn in your classes. Suppose you take an exam and the instructor simply indicates that you "passed." Typically, the first question asked is "What percentage did I earn?" Students think statistics are scary, but when you stop to think about it, we encounter them every day of our lives.

THE BENEFITS OF STATISTICS

When considering the usefulness of statistics for communication researchers, three primary benefits are identified. Statistics can be thought of as tools used to describe, organize, and interpret information. First, statistics allow us to summarize or describe data. Statistics enable researchers to make predictions and make sense of the world around us. The ability of statistics to help us summarize data is incredible! For example, the U.S. Census conducted in 2000 collected information from more than 281 million people (http://factfinder.census.gov) Statistics are used to summarize massive amounts of information and enables researchers to describe the general U.S. population. For example, we know that 34,991,753 residents who participated in the census were over the age of 65. That represents 12.4% of the total U.S. population in 2000. Statistics help paint a picture of our nation's population by summarizing data from millions of participants and describing that data in a way that makes sense.

Statistics also enable us to organize information in a meaningful way in order to make predictions. If information about a sample group is known, that data can be organized and used to make predictions about the general population. For example, in her study of teachers' use of humor to gain student compliance, Punyanunt (2000) found that students were more likely to comply with requests that were humorous (this article is on the CD-ROM accompanying this book). By organizing these data, we can predict that if other teachers want to be effective in their compliance-gaining attempts, they should employ a humorous tone. Referring back to the earlier example for Chewing Gum Brand X you could predict that your dentist will likely recommend Chewing Gum Brand X if you were to ask what brand of gum you should chew.

Finally, statistics assist us in understanding and interpreting the world around us. We doubt that you could go through one day without encountering or using statistics in some way. Sports fans depend on statistics to understand where their favorite team is ranked, and consumers interpret the nutritional values on packages to assist them in making product choices in supermarkets. If you are a frequent reader of *USA Today*, you've probably noticed the "Snapshots" boxes located in the bottom corner on the cover page of each section. Topics explored in these quantitative surveys include everything from favorite food duos (e.g., macaroni and cheese vs. cereal and milk) to sources that influence decisions to purchase products (e.g., word-of-mouth vs. in-store promotions). Daily weather forecasts usually include statistical predictions, such as, "There is a 60% chance of scattered thundershowers for the region today." Your existence as a college student revolves around a statistic known as your grade point average (GPA). When you stop to think about it, you really know more about statistics than you thought.

Descriptive Versus Inferential Statistics

As stated earlier, one of the benefits of statistics is that they allow us to describe or summarize information. Descriptive statistics are used to organize and summarize information or data. Essentially, descriptive statistics allow a researcher to provide a description of what actually "exists" in the data. Data can be defined as *any record or observation*. Examples of data include the number of years employed, grade point average, annual income, gender, or the number of hours spent watching television each day. Researchers use descriptive statistics to help us reduce large amounts of data to a more manageable size. Perhaps one of the most commonly used descriptive statistics is percentages. Consider the following example—one way a university could use descriptive statistics is to summarize students in a particular class. For example, the class could be described as being comprised of 52% males and 48% females; 4% freshmen, 19% sophomores, 52% juniors, and 25% seniors; or 42% traditional students and 58% nontraditional students. A variety of data can be collected to describe different characteristics of the group. With the individual pieces of information (or data) collected from each student, a summary of the entire class can be calculated. The goal of this chapter is to provide you with statistical tools to assist you in describing groups of data.

Whereas descriptive statistics describe or summarize data, inferential statistics are often the next stage in data analysis. Once the researcher has summarized and described the data in terms of percentages or averages, the data can be further analyzed to make inferences from the smaller group of data (also known as the sample) to a larger group of data (also referred to as the population). Inferential statistics are used when a researcher wants to make predictions. In order to make predictions, researchers often (but not always) take the process of statistical analyses to the next level and use inferential statistics to draw conclusions and make predictions about a larger group based on a smaller group of data. It is important to reiterate the distinction between these two groups—the smaller group of participants that were selected for the study is referred to as the sample. A sample is defined as a subset of the larger population, or all the possible persons who could fall into a particular category. Since it is usually improbable that a researcher would be able to access all possible participants in the population, samples of participants are selected to best represent the entire group. Students in a communication research methods class at a university could be considered a sample of the population of all communication majors currently enrolled at that campus. In Chapter 14, methods for selecting samples will be discussed in more detail.

Suppose your university requires all students to complete a public speaking class prior to graduation. To determine whether this requirement is beneficial in preparing students for their careers, they decide to survey a sample of communication alumni from your school. Depending on the size of the school, surveying every single graduate might be a difficult and time-consuming task. Instead, a sample of alumni might be used to determine their perceptions of the usefulness of the public speaking requirement. Various statistics could be calculated for this sample of alumni. Suppose you asked alumni the following question: "On a scale of 1 to 10 (1 being lowest and 10 being highest) please indicate how valuable you perceive your public speaking class to be in preparing for your current career." Descriptive statistics could be used to provide an average rating for the perceived value of public speaking as reported by alumni in the sample.

What if you wanted to take your analyses to the next level and compare the results of those graduates who are frequently required to make presentations in their careers with those who do little or no public speaking? Inferential statistics could be used to make comparisons between these two groups and identify whether they differ in their perceptions of the value of the public speaking requirement. The concept of inferential statistics will be discussed in more depth in later chapters. For now, let's focus our attention on using statistics to describe data.

Measures of Central Tendency

One of the first questions typically asked when analyzing data from a group is, "What is the average score?" Recall the last time you received an exam back from an instructor. If you scored a 72% on the exam, your initial reaction might be to feel disappointed. However, suppose the instructor announces that the class average on the exam was a 63% so she is going to add points to the grades. Your disappointment turns to elation simply as the result of a statistic that is mentioned. No longer is your score considered to be "slightly below the average grade" (in this case 75%, which typically represents a grade of "C"). Rather, you learn that your grade is now considered well above the average for the class.

In order to measure the "center" or "middle" score in a group of data, researchers use what are commonly referred to as measures of central tendency. Three measures of central tendency that can be examined on a frequency distribution are the mean, median, and mode.

Mean

The mean, or average, is typically defined as the value that represents an entire group of scores. To calculate the mean, add all of the scores in the category you wish to summarize and divide the total by the number of scores. Researchers use two different types of means to describe data. If data have been collected from the entire population, the population mean is the best descriptor of the average score. The formula for calculating the population mean can be seen in Figure 8.1.

Since it is rare that a researcher is able to get data from all possible members of a population, the sample is used to best represent the entire group. Suppose a researcher wants to gauge student satisfaction with campus activities. It is highly unlikely that data could be collected from every student. Instead, a sample of students could be collected by visiting a sample of classes across different majors. The formula used to compute the sample mean is seen in Figure 8.2.

While the mean is a solid measure of central tendency for data sets that have a relatively normal distribution curve, it can be deceiving for data that are not symmetrically distributed due to extreme scores. Suppose you want to assess the average level of apprehension of five

$$\mu = \Sigma X \div N$$

μ = Population mean

ΣX = Sum of all scores within a population

N = Number of scores within a population

Figure 8.1 Population Mean

$$\bar{x} = \Sigma x \div n$$ **Figure 8.2** Sample Mean

$\bar{x}$ = Sample mean

Σx = Sum of all scores within a sample

n = Number of scores within a sample

students who completed the PRCA-24 scale whose scores were 98, 56, 49, 42, and 39. Simply by looking at the list of scores, it is evident that 98 is very different from the other four scores—thus, it is often referred to as an "extreme" score or outlier. Let's calculate the mean for the sample of PRCA-24 scores:

Step One: The first step to computing a sample mean is to add all of the numbers of a sample together. In our example, we simply add the five numbers (Σx) together and receive a summed total of 284:

$$98 + 56 + 49 + 42 + 39 = 284$$

Step Two: The second step in computing a sample mean is to take the summed total (Σx) in Step One and divide the sum (Σx) by the number of scores in the group (n). In our example, we received a Σx of 284 in Step One and we have five participants ($n = 5$), so we divide 284 by 5, or:

$$284/5 = 56.8$$

The mean of the five scores is 56.8, which turns out to be higher than the scores reported for four of the five team members. In this instance the mean is not very representative of the distribution. In cases where the mean score is biased or skewed by extreme scores, other measures of central tendency may offer a better summary of the data. One statistic that could be used in this instance is the median.

MEDIAN

The median is defined as the middle value in a list of data. In order to calculate the median, first list the data in order from smallest to largest. After you have sorted data in ascending order, identify the number that lies at the exact midpoint of the list. If the list has an odd number of items, the median is the middle entry in the list. If the list has an even number of items, add the two middle numbers and divide by two.

One way of thinking about the median is to consider it as a representation of percentile. A score that falls at the 75th percentile will lie at or above 75% of all the other scores in the distribution. The median is known as the true "50th percentile" score, or the point at which half of the scores fall above and the remaining half of the scores fall below.

Recall our earlier example, which examined a series of communication apprehension scores. In a set of scores where one or more score falls at an extreme end of the distribution, the median is perhaps the best choice for representing the middle value of the data set. Let's calculate the median for the sample of PRCA-24 scores:

Step One: The first step in finding a median in a set of data is to list all the scores in order from smallest to largest:

39   42   49   56   98

Step Two (if odd number of scores): The first step in finding a median in a set of data is to identify whether the data consist of an even or odd number of scores. If there is an odd number of scores (3 scores, 5 scores, 7 scores, etc.), simply find the midpoint of all the scores, which is your median. In our example, we have five scores, which is an odd number, so when we look at the third number in the set of five we have the number "49." So in this case, our median is 49.

Step Two (if even number of scores): Often sets of data will have an even number of scores (2 scores, 4 scores, 6 scores, 8 scores, etc.), so a different technique is needed for determining the median. If there is an even number of scores, add the two middle scores and divide them by the number "2" to find the median score. For example, suppose the data set from the earlier example looked like this after you rearranged the numbers from least to greatest:

$$39 \quad 42 \quad 49 \quad 51 \quad 56 \quad 98$$

To calculate the median, you would first find the scores in the middle of the data. In this case, we have six data points, so the two middle numbers would be the third and fourth numbers, or 49 and 51. To find the median, we first need to add the two middle numbers:

$$49 + 51 = 100$$

Once we have the summed total, we divide the number by two (since there are two numbers in involved in the sum total):

$$100/2 = 50$$

In this case the median for this example would be 50.

As mentioned earlier, the median is a better descriptive statistic to use when reporting on the average for data with extreme scores. Often the median will be stated as, "The median income of the average American family is . . ." The median allows for a more accurate representation of the data in situations like this.

MODE

Perhaps the least frequently cited descriptive statistic is the mode. The mode is defined as the value that occurs most frequently in a data set. An easy way to remember the definition for mode is to recall the phrase "mode is the most." It is the most general and least precise of all descriptive statistics. To calculate the mode, we're going to use the data from the even median example discussed above

Step One: The first step in finding a mode is to create a list of the values that occur in a data set. Be sure to list each value only once!

$$39 \quad 42 \quad 42 \quad 49 \quad 51 \quad 56 \quad 98$$

Step Two: Create a tally of the number of times that each score appears. The number "39" appears once, the number "42" appears twice, the number "49" appears once, the number "51" appears once, the number "56" appears once, and the number "98" appears once.

Step Three: The score or value that appears most often is the mode. In our example, the numbers "39," "49," "51," "56," and "98" appear only one time. However, the number "42" appears twice, so we would consider the number "42" as our mode because it is the number seen most often within our data.

Suppose we wanted to examine the data set included with this text. After calculating the frequency of political affiliations, the following data would be reported:

Republicans	144
Democrats	117
Other	39
Not Registered	21

What would the mode be for this data set? Be careful—your first instinct might be to indicate that "144" is the mode, but this is incorrect. "Republican" is the mode for the variable of political affiliation because it is the most frequently occurring value.

As mentioned earlier, a data set can have more than one mode. In instances where two values occur with equal frequency, the data set is defined as being bimodal. When a data set has more than two values that occur with the same frequency, the data are defined as being multimodal. Figure 8.3 provides you with one more look at how the mean, median, and mode compare for a set of scores measuring the level of communication apprehension.

So which statistic should you use to represent the data set? Let's use the example of reporting annual salaries for an organization. Suppose an organization employs 10 people who each earn an annual salary of $25,000. The production manager earns $50,000, while the supervisor earns $100,000. The mode ($25,000) would be the most accurate statistic to represent the salary that most people in the organization earn. However, if your goal is to make a strong impression on potential employees, you might decide that it's to your advantage to use the mean of $33,333 to attract more applicants. The decision is yours!

Often the decision of which measure of central tendency to use depends on the available data set. The mode is the best statistic for representing qualitative data such as political affiliation, sex, or class rank. Calculating an average for these types of data would be inaccurate. After all, it would not make sense to say that the average score for biological sex is 1.2—a participant is either female or male. It does make sense to report that "out of 325 respondents, most (144) indicated that they are Republican." Unfortunately, SPSS and SAS will not tell if you are running an incorrect statistical test, so you must be smarter than the computer program or you will end up running statistical tests that mean absolutely nothing. Without fail, at least one student every time we teach research methods will fall into this trap. They will think that because the computer will let them run a mean for biological sex that this mean is somehow meaningful, but it's not. Numbers can be computed for almost anything, but not all of these numbers are meaningful. Quantitative data require a researcher

Variable	CA	Represented as X
	39	
	42	
	42	Mode (occurs most frequently)
	49	Median (midpoint of data)
	51	
	56	
	98	
n	7	Number of cases
ΣX_i	377	Total or sum of all scores (ages)
$\overline{X}$	53.86	Mean or average score (age)

Figure 8.3 Mean, Median, and Mode for a Sample of PRCA Scores

to use either the mean or the median to report the measure of central tendency. As stated earlier, the median is best in situations where extreme scores exist so the average score is not misrepresented. The mean is the appropriate statistic for data sets where there are not extreme scores.

FREQUENCY DISTRIBUTIONS

Measures of central tendency are often visually depicted by constructing a frequency distribution. These frequency charts allow researchers to summarize and organize a set of data and enable them to identify trends. To create a frequency distribution, simply record the number of occurrences for each value in the data set. While the statistics could be computed by hand like we did above, it isn't very time efficient to do so. For this reason a variety of computer programs have been created to aid in this process. The two most commonly used statistical software packages used by communication researchers are SPSS and SAS. The following section expects that you (1) have a statistical software package you prefer to use and (2) know how to find and open files on a CD-ROM. If you look on the CD-ROM that came with this book, you will find a folder marked "Book Data Sets." In this folder you will find folders for SPSS data sets, SAS data sets, and Note Pad Data sets. The SPSS and SAS data sets can be used only by SPSS and SAS software packages. If you do not have SPSS or SAS but have a different statistical software package, you can use the Note Pad Data sets to import the data into whatever program you prefer to use following that program's specific instructions for importing a text file. However, we will only be discussing how to read and interpret results from SPSS and SAS in this book.

SPSS and Frequency Distributions

When using SPSS to calculate frequency distributions, you use the "cross tabs" function. For this example, open the SPSS data set called "Recoded Data Set" on the CD-ROM that accompanied this book. Once you open the data set, you need to create a frequency table. To get to the "Frequencies" function, go to the menu bar at the top of your screen and click on "Analyze." When you click on "Analyze," a dropdown menu will appear. Go to the second category on this menu, "Descriptive Statistics," and scroll over the arrow and another menu will appear to the right. In this menu, search for the "Frequencies" option and right click on it. As previously discussed, a Frequency table is a table that lists the numbers and percentages of given answers. For example, maybe you want to find out how many females and males there are in a given sample. To find this out, you would create a frequency table. To create a frequency table in SPSS, first you need to select the variable that you want create the table for by highlighting it (click on it once). Go ahead and scroll through the list of variables in the "Recoded Data Set" and right click on "Biological Sex [sex]." When you right click on "Biological Sex [sex]," the variable is highlighted in blue. You now want to click the click the arrow button to move "Biological Sex [sex]" to the "Variable(s)" list, which is the list of variables to be analyzed. When you click on the arrow button, the variable "Biological Sex [sex]" will be transferred from the left column (variables in the data set) to the right column (variables you want frequency tables for). At this point, all you need to do to achieve a frequency window is to click the "OK" button on the right-hand side of the screen. When you do this, the data in Figure 8.4 will appear.

You'll notice that we have provided all of the frequency information for four of the variables in the "Recoded Data Set" in Figure 8.4 (Biological Sex, Political Affiliation, Year in School, and Time Spent Online). We will discuss how to calculate means, medians, and modes using SPSS in the next section.

Frequencies

Stastics

Biological Sex

N	Valid	322
	Missing	3

Biological Sex

		Frequency	Percent	Valid Percent	Cumulative Percent
Valid	Male	183	56.3	56.8	56.8
	Female	139	42.8	43.2	100.0
	Total	322	99.1	100.0	
Missing	System	3	.9		
Total		325	100.0		

Figure 8.4 Frequency Table for Biological Sex

SAS and Frequency Distributions

At this point we will examine how to calculate a Frequency Chart using SAS as well. The variables we want to use in the Frequency Procedure are the same variables seen in Figure 8.4 for SPSS: biological sex (SEX), political affiliation (POLITICS), year in school (CLASSIFICATION), and time spent online (OL). The Frequency Procedure Command in SAS is PROC FREQ, which would look like this when entered into SAS:

PROC FREQ;

TABLES SEX POLITICS CLASSIFICATION OL;

The variable "POLITICS" is the political affiliation variable we examined in SPSS. You'll notice in the results in Figure 8.5 that the categories themselves are not actually labeled. Instead, the numerical values are shown. SPSS creates the Frequency Tables using the numbers, but allows a user to attach value names to values within a variable that are then printed on the SPSS output. SAS does not have this function, so you will want to make sure that you keep track of what you label as "1," "2," "3," and "4," or you will have no idea how to interpret your data printouts.

Once a frequency distribution has been constructed, the data can be also be graphically represented by creating a histogram. A histogram is a bar chart that represents the frequency with which each value for a variable occurs. Suppose we wanted to create a histogram for the following scores obtained on a statistics exam. A frequency distribution for the data would look like Figure 8.6. Using this information, a histogram (or bar graph) can be constructed to assist the researcher in identifying the shape of the data, the symmetry, and the presence of outliers (extreme scores). Each test score is included along the x-axis in ascending order, and the frequency with which each score occurs is plotted on the y-axis (Figure 8.7).

By glancing at the histogram, the researcher can determine if the set of data is normally distributed. The score with the highest frequency (in this case 70) falls at the middle of the normal distribution. Scores with lower frequencies are on either side of the mean. If the scores are distributed normally, the curve forms a bell shape. A closer look at the information

The FREQ Procedure

SEX	Frequency	Percent	Cumulative Frequency	Cumulative Percent
1	183	56.83	183	56.83
2	139	43.17	322	100.00

Frequency Missing = 3

1 = Male

2 = Female

The FREQ Procedure

POLITICS	Frequency	Percent	Cumulative Frequency	Cumulative Percent
1	117	36.45	117	36.45
2	144	44.86	261	81.31
3	39	12.15	300	93.46
4	21	6.54	321	100.00

Frequency Missing = 4

1 = Democrats

2 = Republicans

3 = Other

4 = Not Registered to Vote

CLASSIFICATION	Frequency	Percent	Frequency	Percent
1	1	0.31	1	0.31
2	39	12.11	40	12.42
3	141	43.79	181	56.21
4	137	42.55	318	98.76
5	4	1.24	322	100.00

Frequency Missing = 3

1 = First Year Student

2 = Sophomore

3 = Junior

4 = Senior

5 = Other

OL	Frequency	Percent	Cumulative Frequency	Cumulative Percent
1	11	3.41	11	3.41
2	14	4.33	25	7.74
3	41	12.69	66	20.43
4	109	33.75	175	54.18
5	76	23.53	251	77.71
6	37	11.46	288	89.16
7	13	4.02	301	93.19
8	22	6.81	323	100.00

Frequency Missing = 2

1 = 0-0.5 hours

2 = 0.5-1 hour

3 = 1-2 hours

4 = 2-5 hours

5 = 5-10 hours

6 = 10-15 hours

7 = 15-20 hours

8 = 20+ hours

Figure 8.5 PROC FREQ in SAS

Letter Grade	Score	Frequency
A	90	1
B	80	2
C	70	4
D	60	2
F	50	1

Figure 8.6 Frequency distribution of exam scores

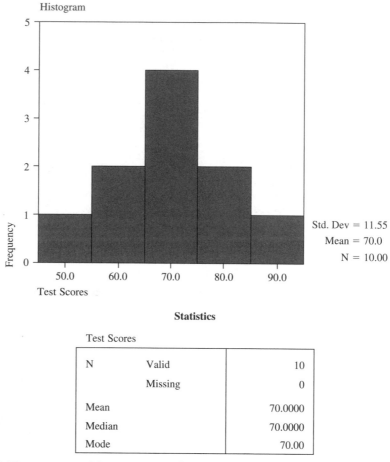

Std. Dev = 11.55
Mean = 70.0
N = 10.00

Statistics

Test Scores

N	Valid	10
	Missing	0
Mean		70.0000
Median		70.0000
Mode		70.00

Figure 8.7 Histogram and SPSS Statistics for a Normal Distribution of Exam Scores

provided in the SPSS output figure shows that the mean, median, and mode are all the same for this data set. In fact, statisticians refer to any distribution where the mean, median, and mode are the same as a bell curve.

So why should a researcher be concerned with the shape of the histogram? Normality of data is a condition for certain statistical analyses associated with hypothesis testing, which will be discussed in more detail in Chapter 15. While formal statistical tests can be used to test whether a distribution for a data set is normal, a simple glance at the histogram can speak volumes. It is important to note, however, that not all distribution curves are normal or bell shaped. Earlier we mentioned that a data set can have more than one mode. Remember—the mode is the value that occurs most often. If the midpoint in the curve is represented by the mode score, a data set that is bimodal would produce a shape that resembles an inverted bell curve. Consider the following hypothetical exam scores:

50, 50, 50, 60, 60, 70, 80. 80, 90, 90, 90

Notice that the scores of "50" and "90" occur with the same frequency—each appears three times in the list. Thus, the data set is bimodal. A histogram for this set of scores would look like Figure 8.8.

A closer look at the information provided in the SPSS output figure shows that the mean and median scores are the same for this data set, but multiple modes exist. (Note: SPSS only reports the smallest value for the mode.) You'll also note that SPSS will report multimodal distributions by placing a superscript letter "[a]" next to the mode on the SPSS printout.

SKEWNESS & KURTOSIS

More often than not, the data set you are analyzing will produce a curve that is asymmetrical, or skewed. A curve can be either positively skewed or negatively skewed. A positively skewed

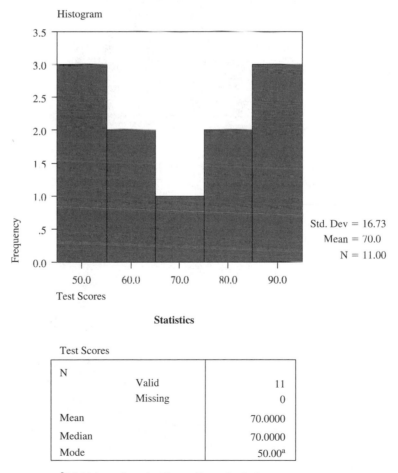

Histogram

Std. Dev = 16.73
Mean = 70.0
N = 11.00

Statistics

Test Scores

N		
	Valid	11
	Missing	0
Mean		70.0000
Median		70.0000
Mode		50.00[a]

[a] Multiple modes exist. The smallest value is shown

Figure 8.8 Histogram and SPSS Statistics for a Bimodal Distribution of Exam Scores

curve is one in which the tail of the curve is longer on the right side of the distribution. The majority of scores are low, causing the curve to be asymmetrical, with a long tail in the positive direction on a number line. The mean for a sample whose scores are positively skewed will be greater than the median or mode (Figure 8.9).

The opposite is true for a data set with negatively skewed scores. In this instance, the tail of the distribution curve is longer on the left side. The majority of the scores are high, creating a long tail in the negative direction on a number line. A mean for a sample that is negatively skewed will be less than the median or mode (Figure 8.10).

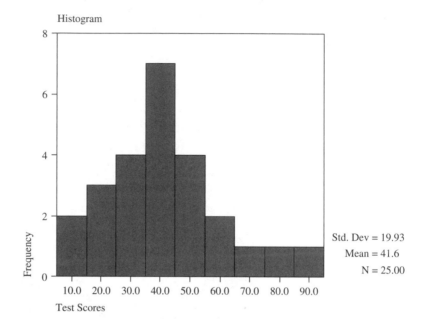

Figure 8.9 Positively Skewed Distribution of Exam Scores

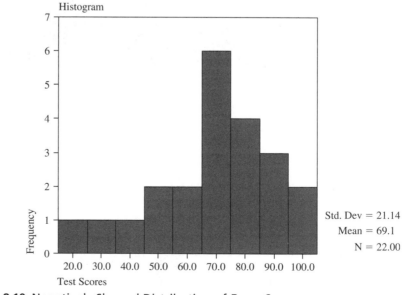

Figure 8.10 Negatively Skewed Distribution of Exam Scores

Statistics

Test Scores

N	Valid	21
	Missing	0
Mean		67.6190
Median		70.0000
Mode		70.00
Std. Deviation		20.4707
Skewness		–.766
Std. Error of Skewness		.501
Kurtosis		.289
Std. Error of Kurtosis		.972
Range		80.00
Minimum		20.00
Maximum		100.00

Figure 8.11 SPSS Frequency Distribution with Skewness and Kurtosis Scores

SPSS can also provide a statistical score regarding the skewness of a distribution. When computing frequencies for a variable, select the "Statistics" button and click on "Skewness." If the sample has a normal distribution, the skewness score will be equal to "0." A positively skewed sample will result in a positive score for skewness, and a negatively skewed score will result in a negative score.

SPSS can also calculate the kurtosis of the distribution curve. Kurtosis refers to the degree of peakedness of a distribution of scores. A kurtosis score greater than zero indicates a high, peaked curve with thin tails where the majority of values are in the peak of the curve and very few located in the tails of the distribution. A negative kurtosis score signals that the distribution curve is flat with several cases of scores located in the tails.

If you look at the results in Figure 8.11, you'll find a distribution where the mean is 67.62, the median is 70, the mode is 70, the skewness is –0.766, and the kurtosis is 0.289. With reference to skewness and kurtosis, the sample is negatively skewed (skewness is a negative number) and minimally peaked (kurtosis <greater than> 0).

If you want to find out the same information using SAS, you simply use the following PROC statement:

PROC MEANS SKEWNESS KURTOSIS;

VAR *Put in Desired Variable Here;*

Measures of Variability

As previously stated, measures of central tendency are the most commonly used statistics by consumers. However, averages only provide us with half of the information needed to describe the scores in a sample—the other half involves measures of variability. Variability reflects how scores differ from one another. Also referred to as "measures of dispersion," variability refers to how different each score is from the mean score. Four measures of variability can be used to assess the differences in scores: range, sum of squares, variance, and standard deviation.

RANGE

The most general measure of variability is the range. Simply stated, the range represents how far apart scores are from another, or the distance between the largest value and the smallest value in the data set. The range is calculated by subtracting the lowest score in the distribution from the highest score:

$$\text{Range} = X_{max} - X_{min}$$

Suppose the highest score obtained on an exam was 96 and the lowest score was 53. To find the range, you subtract X_{min} from X_{max} or the smallest score from the largest score. In our example, 53 is the smallest score and 96 is the largest score, so to find the range you subtract 53 from 96 or:

$$96 - 53 = 43$$

In this example, our range is 43. While this score tells us the gap between the high and low score, it does not provide any insight into how each score in the distribution differs from the mean or average score.

SUM OF SQUARES

The sum of squares is a concept seen quite often in both descriptive statistics (statistical tools used to describe a dataset—what we are examining in this chapter) and inferential statistics (statistical tools that allow researchers to make inferences about some unknown aspect of a population from a sample—Chapters 16–21 will examine inferential statistics). In social scientific research, people differ from one another, which makes it impossible for social scientists to make universal statements about all people. These individual differences, however, make up the bulk of what social scientists study. In fact, Thompson (2006) defines the sum of squares as the "information about both the amount and the origins of individual differences" (p. 60). Ultimately, the larger individual scores in a dataset differ from one another, the greater the sum of squares will become. Overall, the sum of squares is used in the calculating of many statistical tests, so understanding how it is computed is extremely important. Figure 8.12 contains the formula for the sum of squares.

The formula for the sum of squares is fairly easy to compute when you understand what the various parts in the formula mean. The first symbol (Σ) should be fairly familiar to you by this point in the chapter because it stands for the "sum of" something, or all of the numbers added together. The second symbol (X^2) is the squaring of an individual number. Do not confuse this symbol with the next symbol [$(\Sigma X)^2$], which is the sum of all of the numbers added together first and then the sum squared. The last symbol in the equation (N) is the number of people in the population. Since the calculating of the sum of squares is complicated, we will use a very small sample in this example. Let's say we ask four people how many hours they spend watching TV daily and we get the following responses: 1 hour, 0 hours, 6 hours, and 1 hour.

Step One: The first step in computing the sum of squares is to find the numbers that correspond to all of the parts of the equation. First, we want to find what is referred to as the

$$SS = \Sigma X^2 - \frac{(\Sigma X)^2}{N}$$

Figure 8.12 Sum of Squares Equation

sum of all of the X numbers squared (ΣX^2). To find ΣX^2 we first need to find each score's squared value. The first person in our sample indicated that he watched only 1 hour of TV daily, and the squared value for 1 is 1 (1*1 = 1). The second person in our sample indicated that she watched 0 hours of TV daily, and the squared value for 0 is 0 (0*0 = 0). The third person in our sample indicated that he watched 6 hours of TV daily, and the squared value for 6 is 36 (6*6 = 36). And the final person in our sample indicated that she watched 1 hour of TV daily, and the squared value for 1 is 1 (1*1 = 1). We now have the squared values for each X. To solve for ΣX^2, we simply need to add the four X^2 values together:

$$\Sigma X^2 = 1 + 0 + 36 + 1$$

$$\Sigma X^2 = 38$$

Step Two: The second step to computing the sum of squares is to determine the sum of all of the X numbers squared [$(\Sigma X)^2$]. To find $(\Sigma X)^2$, we first need to find out the value for the sum of X (ΣX), which is just a mathematical way of saying we need to add the individual scores together (1 + 0 + 6 + 1 = 8), so $\Sigma X = 8$. Once we know what the ΣX is, we simply need to square this value to find $(\Sigma X)^2$, so 8*8 = 64.

Step Three: At this point, the complicated math is complete, so we just need to plug the numbers into the equation in Figure 8.12 and compute the formula. We've already determined that that $\Sigma X^2 = 38$, $(\Sigma X)^2$ is 64, and N is 4. Let's complete the part of the formula to the right of the minus sign in the equation, or $(\Sigma X)^2/N$:

$$(\Sigma X)^2/N$$

$$64/4$$

$$16$$

$$\text{So, } (\Sigma X)^2/N = 16$$

We can then perform the subtraction part of the formula, $\Sigma X^2 - [(\Sigma X)^2/N]$. In this case we know that $\Sigma X^2 = 38$ and $[(\Sigma X)^2/N] = 16$, so we just subtract 16 from 38 or 38 − 16 = 22. At this point we have calculated the sum of square, and the answer is 22.

VARIANCE

Variance measures how wide or spread out a distribution is, or the average distance of the scores for an interval or ratio scale from the mean in squared units. Since our variance is dependent upon the sum of squares, we know that as our scores become more different the variance will increase. The opposite is also true—as the scores become more similar the variance will decrease. The formula in Figure 8.13 is used to compute the variance of a sample of scores.

When you look at this formula, you'll notice that in order to calculate variance you need to know two basic pieces of information: the sum of squares (SS) and the number of participants (N). Using the data used in the previous example (1, 0, 6, 1), we have already determined that

$$S^2 = \frac{SS}{N - 1}$$ **Figure 8.13** Variance Equation

the sum of squares was 22 and the number of participants was 4, so to calculate the variance we just need to plug the numbers into the appropriate places and solve for s^2:

$$s^2 = SS/(N-1)$$

$$s^2 = 22/(4-1)$$

$$s^2 = 22/3$$

$$s^2 = 7.3333$$

The variance for the sample (1, 0, 6, 1) is 7.3333.

STANDARD DEVIATION

The standard deviation of a sample is directly related to the variance of a sample. When we report variance, we are dealing with what is called a "squared metric" because the variance stems from the sum of squares. However, most people are not very good at understanding squared metrics by looking at them, so the standard deviation is simply the square root of the variance, which forms the descriptive statistic in a number that can be more easily applied to our sample scores. Ultimately, the standard deviation tells us on average how far each score differs from the average score. A standard deviation score of 3.12 indicates that, on average, each score in the distribution deviates plus or minus 3.12 points from the mean score. The larger the standard deviation score, the greater the distance between each score and the mean, and the more different the scores are from one another. The formula for calculating a standard deviation can be seen in Figure 8.14.

If the formula for the standard deviation looks familiar, it is; it can be calculated simply by taking the square root of the variance. In the previous step we determined that the variance for the sample (1, 0, 6, 1) was 7.3333. To determine the standard deviation, we simply take the square root of 7.3333, which is 2.708, or 2.71 after rounding.

Recall our earlier discussion of the normal distribution of scores. If a researcher is able to calculate the mean and standard deviation for a sample that has a normal distribution, a percentile score can be reported for the sample. In a normal distribution, approximately 68% of the scores are within one standard deviation of the mean score (Figure 8.15). Overall, nearly 95% of the scores fall within two standard deviations from the mean. So in a normal distribution most scores are relatively close to the mean score.

In the majority of research studies, the sample size is too large to calculate many of the statistics described in this chapter by hand. For this reason, we depend on statistical packages like SPSS and SAS to calculate the variance and standard deviations for us. To calculate the variance and standard deviation using SPSS for the variable communication apprehension, follow the steps discussed earlier for calculating the mean, only this time when you're looking at the Frequencies: Statistics Window, instead of clicking mean, median, and mode in the Central Tendency Box, you want to click on "Std. deviation," "Variance," "Minimum," and "Maximum" in the Dispersion Box. Then you can click OK and you will receive the printout seen in Figure 8.16.

$$SD = \sqrt{\frac{SS}{N-1}}$$ **Figure 8.14** Standard Deviation Equation

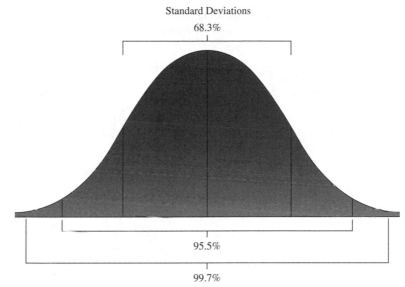

Figure 8.15 Standard Deviations and Percentiles

Statistics   **Figure 8.16** SPSS Results for Variability

Communication Apprehension Total

N	Valid	317
	Missing	8
Std. Deviation		17.1692
Variance		294.7811
Minimum		24.00
Maximum		120.00

The MEANS Procedure

Variable	N	Std Dev	Var	Minimum	Maximum

BIGCA	317	17.1691909	294.7776823	24.0000000	120.0000000

Figure 8.17 SAS Variability Output

If you want to find out the same information using SAS, you simply use the following PROC statement:

PROC MEANS STD VAR MIN MAX;

VAR CA;

The results for the SAS output can be found in Figure 8.17.

Frequencies for Nominal and Ordinal Variables

Biological Sex

		Frequency	Percent	Valid Percent	Cumulative Percent
Valid	Male	183	56.3	56.8	56.8
	Female	139	42.8	43.2	100.0
	Total	322	99.1	100.0	
Missing	System	3	.9		
Total		325	100.0		

Political Affiliation

		Frequency	Percent	Valid Percent	Cumulative Percent
Valid	Democrat	117	36.0	36.4	36.4
	Republican	144	44.3	44.9	81.3
	Other	39	12.0	12.1	93.5
	Not Registered to Vote	21	6.5	6.5	100.0
	Total	321	98.8	100.0	
Missing	System	4	1.2		
Total		325	100.0		

School Classification

		Frequency	Percent	Valid Percent	Cumulative Percent
Valid	First Year Student	1	.3	.3	.3
	Sophomore	39	12.0	12.1	12.4
	Junior	141	43.4	43.8	56.2
	Senior	137	42.2	42.5	98.8
	Other	4	1.2	1.2	100.0
	Total	322	99.1	100.0	
Missing	System	3	.9		
Total		325	100.0		

Figure 8.18 SPSS Dataset Information

Time Spent Online

		Frequency	Percent	Valid Percent	Cumulative Percent
Valid	0-.5 hour	11	3.4	3.4	3.4
	.5-1 hour	14	4.3	4.3	7.7
	1-2 hours	41	12.6	12.7	20.4
	2-5 hours	109	33.5	33.7	54.2
	5-10 hours	76	23.4	23.5	77.7
	10-15 hours	37	11.4	11.5	89.2
	15-20 hours	13	4.0	4.0	93.2
	25 + hours	22	6.8	6.8	100.0
	Total	323	99.4	100.0	
Missing	System	2	.6		
Total		325	100.0		

Measures of Variability for Interval and Ratio Variables

Statistics

		groupca	meetca	interca	publicca	bigca	bigethno	bigha	bigniss	assert	respon
N	Valid	317	317	317	317	317	324	319	319	322	322
	Missing	8	8	8	8	8	1	6	6	3	3
Mean		15.4069	15.7066	14.9779	18.4448	64.5363	37.5370	62.0627	95.2257	36.2857	39.3944
Median		15.0000	16.0000	15.0000	18.0000	66.0000	38.0000	163.0000	94.0000	37.0000	40.0000
Std. Deviation		5.07616	5.05843	4.46323	5.67536	17.16919	8.76677	9.82084	13.19016	5.95249	6.19941
Minimum		6.00	6.00	6.00	6.00	24.00	16.00	34.00	63.00	19.00	20.00
Maximum		30.00	30.00	30.00	30.00	120.00	61.00	80.00	130.00	50.00	50.00

Statistics

		groupwtc	meetwtc	interwtc	publiwtc	swtc	awtc	fwtc	bigwtc	belief	attitude
N	Valid	307	306	307	307	307	307	306	306	312	314
	Missing	18	19	18	18	18	18	19	19	13	11
Mean		74.8545	68.7386	74.6819	67.2595	48.2858	77.4283	88.4469	71.3633	20.4423	36.4013
Median		76.6667	68.3333	76.6667	70.0000	47.5000	81.2500	92.5000	72.5000	21.0000	38.0000
Std. Deviation		16.24242	19.16788	16.59207	19.72105	25.65960	18.61645	13.55947	15.65637	10.00883	6.10019
Minimum		5.00	9.00	26.67	.00	.00	6.25	32.50	18.25	5.00	19.00
Maximum		100.00	100.00	100.00	100.00	100.00	100.00	100.00	100.00	35.00	42.00

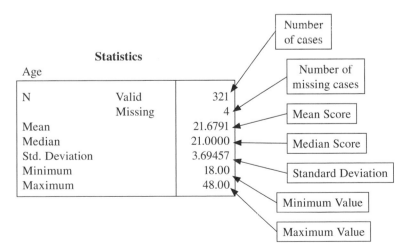

Statistics

Age

N	Valid	321
	Missing	4
Mean		21.6791
Median		21.0000
Std. Deviation		3.69457
Minimum		18.00
Maximum		48.00

Number of cases

Number of missing cases

Mean Score

Median Score

Standard Deviation

Minimum Value

Maximum Value

Dataset Variability

In the previous chapter we introduced you to the variables available in the data set that accompanies this book. In Figure 8.18 you will find the SPSS frequency lists for the nominal and ordinal variables in the dataset and the measures of variability for the interval and ratio variables. The same information computed by SAS can be found in Figure 8.19.

Frequencies for Nominal and Ordinal Variables

The FREQ Procedure

SEX	Frequency	Percent	Cumulative Frequency	Cumulative Percent
1	183	56.83	183	56.83
2	139	43.17	322	100.00

Frequency Missing = 3

POLITICS	Frequency	Percent	Cumulative Frequency	Cumulative Percent
1	117	36.45	117	36.45
2	144	44.86	261	81.31
3	39	12.15	300	93.46
4	21	6.54	321	100.00

Frequency Missing = 4

CLASSIFICATION	Frequency	Percent	Cumulative Frequency	Cumulative Percent
1	1	0.31	1	0.31
2	39	12.11	40	12.42
3	141	43.79	181	56.21
4	137	42.55	318	98.76
5	4	1.24	322	100.00

Frequency Missing = 3

OL	Frequency	Percent	Cumulative Frequency	Cumulative Percent
1	11	3.41	11	3.41
2	14	4.33	25	7.74
3	41	12.69	66	20.43
4	109	33.75	175	54.18
5	76	23.53	251	77.71
6	37	11.46	288	89.16
7	13	4.02	301	93.19
8	22	6.81	323	100.00

Frequency Missing = 2

Figure 8.19 SAS Dataset Information

Measures of Variability for Interval and Ratio Variables

The MEANS Procedure

Variable	N	Mean	Std Dev	Minimum	Maximum
GROUPCA	317	15.4069401	5.0761619	6.0000000	30.0000000
MEETCA	317	15.7066246	5.0584295	6.0000000	30.0000000
INTERCA	317	14.9779180	4.4632272	6.0000000	30.0000000
PUBLICCA	317	18.4447950	5.6753642	6.0000000	30.0000000
BIGCA	317	64.5362776	17.1691909	24.0000000	120.0000000
BIGETHNO	324	37.5370370	8.7667673	16.0000000	61.0000000
DICHA	319	62.0626959	9.8208394	34.0000000	80.0000000
BIGIMM	319	95.2257053	13.1901609	63.0000000	130.0000000
ASSERT	322	36.2857143	5.9524895	19.0000000	50.0000000
RESPON	322	39.3944099	6.1994146	20.0000000	50.0000000
GROUPWTC	307	74.8545060	16.2424164	5.0000000	100.0000000
MEETWTC	306	68.7385621	19.1678785	9.0000000	100.0000000
INTERWTC	307	74.6818675	16.5920701	26.6666667	100.0000000
PUBLICWTC	307	67.2595005	19.7210479	0	100.0000000
STANGER	307	48.2858306	25.6595980	0	100.0000000
ACQUAINTANCE	307	77.4283388	18.6164458	6.2500000	100.0000000
FRIEND	306	88.4468954	13.5594713	32.5000000	100.0000000
BIGWTC	306	71.3632898	15.6563683	18.2500000	100.0000000
BELIEF	312	20.4423077	10.0088324	5.0000000	35.0000000
ATTITUDE	314	36.4012739	6.1001858	19.0000000	42.0000000
AGE	321	21.6791277	3.6945696	18.0000000	48.0000000

Conclusion

For most of you, the initial thought of calculating statistics for a sample was probably overwhelming. Throughout this chapter we have presented information providing a description of the sample as well as identifying how diverse or spread out those scores are from the average. Statistics such as those discussed in this chapter are often referenced in everyday life. Now you can understand and interpret these statistics with confidence.

KEY TERMS

Bimodal
Data
Descriptive Statistics
Inferential Statistics
Kurtosis
Mean

Measures of Central
Tendency
Median
Mode
Outlier
Population
Range

Sample
Skewness
Standard Deviation
Statistic
Sum of Squares
Variance

REFERENCES

Punyanunt, N. M. (2000). The effects of humor on perceptions of compliance-gaining in the college classroom. *Communication Research Reports, 176,* 30–38.

Thompson, B. (2006). *Foundations of behavioral statistics: An insight-based approach.* New York: Guilford.

Further Reading

Abramson, J. H., & Abramson, Z. H. (2001). *Making sense of data: A self-instruction manual on the interpretation of epidemiological data* (3rd ed.). New York: Oxford.

Bruning, J. L., & Kintz, B. L. (1997). *Computational handbook of statistics* (4th ed.). New York: Longman.

Delwiche, L. D., & Slaughter, S. J. (2003). *The little SAS book: A primer* (3rd ed.). Cary, NC: SAS Press.

Gravetter, F. J., & Wallnau, L. B. (2000). *Statistics for the behavioral sciences* (5th ed.). Belmont, CA: Wadsworth/Thomson Learning.

Green, S. B., & Salkind, N. J. (2004). *Using SPSS for Windows and Macintosh: Analyzing and understanding data* (4th ed.). Upper Saddle River, NJ: Prentice Hall.

Hocking, J. E., Stacks, D. W., & McDermott, S. T. (2003). *Communication research* (3rd ed.). Boston: Allyn and Bacon.

Howell, D. C. (1997). *Statistical methods for psychology* (4th ed.). Belmont, CA: Duxbury Press.

Huff, D. (1954). *How to lie with statistics.* New York: W. W. Norton & Company.

Keller, D. K. (2006). *The Tao of statistics: A path to understanding (with no math).* Thousand Oaks, CA: Sage.

Pyrczak, F. (1999). *Statistics with a sense of humor: A humorous workbook and guide to study skills* (2nd ed.). Los Angeles: Pyrczak.

Salkind, N. J. (2004). *Statistics for people who (think they) hate statistics* (2nd ed.). Thousand Oaks, CA: Sage.

SAS Institute. (2004). *SAS 9.1 Companion for Windows.* Cary, NC: SAS Press.

Singleton, R. A., Jr., & Straits, B. C. (1999). *Approach to social research* (3rd ed.). New York: Oxford University Press.

Trochim, W. M. K. (2000). *The research methods knowledge base* (2nd ed.). Cincinnati, OH: Atomic Dog. Online available at: http://www.socialresearchmethods.net/

Measurement

When you hear the word "measurement," what comes to mind? Maybe you think of pulling out a ruler and seeing how long a line is, or pulling out a tape measure to measure the inseam of a pair of pants. In many ways, communication researchers define measurement in the same way as using a ruler or a tape measure. Measurement is *the process of systematic observation and assignment of numbers to phenomena according to rules*. The first part of this definition suggests that measurement is a process. The word process can be defined as a set of progressive, interdependent steps. In other words, when we measure something, there is a series of steps that we must go through. According to the definition, this series of steps helps us systematically observe a phenomenon and then assign numbers to a phenomenon. Let's look at what we mean by "observe" first. Obviously, for us to examine a phenomenon we must have the ability to see or perceive that phenomenon. If we cannot see or perceive a phenomenon, there is no way for us as researchers to measure it. Once a researcher has a general idea of what the phenomenon is, he or she can then assign numbers to it based on some set of established rules. In essence, when we know what the phenomenon is, we can then determine a way to quantify it, but we must be systematic in our quantification, so we must have some form of established rules.

Let's take the process of measuring a line as an example to walk us through this definition. First, we need to define what the phenomenon is that we are attempting to measure. In the case of a line, we are attempting to measure the length of something or in mathematics speak we are attempting to measure the greatest dimension of a plane or solid figure. In essence, length must have a beginning and it must have an end. Once we know what the phenomenon is, we can attempt to determine how we are going to assign numbers to that phenomenon. In the case of length, many different numerical categorizing systems have been created. In ancient Greece, one may have measured the line in daktylos, which was roughly equivalent to 1.8–2 centimeters. Centimeters are part of a measurement system for distance called the metric system, which is the international system of units created by French scientists at the request of Louis XVI in the late eighteenth century. In fact, in most countries around the world, the metric system is the measure of choice for measuring distance. However, in the United States we have our own system for measuring length called the U.S. customary units or English units. Whereas the metric system is based on millimeters, centimeters, meters, and kilometers; the U.S. customary units are based on the inch, foot, yard, and mile. This is not to say that the metric system and U.S. customary units are not related to each other, because 1 centimeter is equivalent to 0.3937 inches; however, each has its own specific rules for how measurement works. When we measure phenomena like distance, we do not combine the two systems of measurement because they have separate measurement rules. For example, we wouldn't tell someone to drive 6 kilometers and 5 miles because your average driver would need a calculator to figure out how far that actually is.

The two important considerations in all measurement are the procedures employed in observation and the rules employed in assignment of numbers. Suppose we wanted to know how many cars passed a certain intersection on any given day. We might ask several people who we know are frequently near that intersection how many cars they think pass the intersection in a given day. Person A might tell us he thinks about 300 or 400. Person B might say he figures between 100 and 200 and person C might suggest there are between 700 and 800 cars that pass in a given day. We cannot say, however, that we have engaged in measurement. We have not "systematically" observed the passing cars at the intersection. Rather our observation has been chaotic. A better way to determine how many cars pass an intersection would be to station a person at the intersection with a pencil and paper and each time a car drove by, he or she would mark down a "1." If we followed this procedure, we would be engaged in the two essential activities involved in measurement: systematic observation and assignment of numbers to objects according to rules. For some purposes, such low-level measurement might be adequate—if, for example, we were interested in determining the probability that we would be able to "hitch a ride" at that intersection. For many other purposes such low-level measurement would be inadequate. If we happen to be employed by the state highway department and wanted to estimate how long it would take for the road surface to wear out at that intersection, we would need to know how heavy the cars were.

Numbers and Things

In measurements, numbers are assigned to represent "things." It is important if our measurement is to be of any value that the numbers and the things are *isomorphic*. Isomorphism means identity or similarity of form. The question we are asking when we are concerned with whether or not our measurement is isomorphic with the thing being measured is, "Are our rules for numerical assignment tied to reality?" Let us presume, for example, that we wish to estimate the level of anxiety felt by a public speaker. As the speaker is speaking before us, we may rate her on a scale from 1 to 5 (low anxiety to high anxiety) on the basis of the distracting mannerisms she evidences in speaking. Such ratings would be isomorphic with anxiety if distracting mannerisms are positively related to anxiety, but if, as is actually the case, distracting mannerisms are more a product of habit and lack of experience in public speaking than they are a product of an internal state of anxiety, then our ratings are nonisomorphic. As such, the ratings are useless and we have "measured" nothing.

In many cases we are forced to assume that our assignment of numbers is isomorphic with reality. The reason this problem is so important is the fact that it is not legitimate to do anything with numbers that could not be done (if it were physically possible) with the thing that the number represents. Numbers don't know what we can do with them. We know that we can add them, subtract them, multiply them, or divide them. Sometimes we are justified in engaging in all of these operations, and sometimes we are not.

Review of Measurement Levels

The mathematical operations that are legitimate for a given set of participant scores depend on the level of measurement that has been achieved. There are four levels of measurement, as previously discussed in Chapter 6: nominal, ordinal, interval, and ratio. Before we discuss different methods for creating scales, let's reexamine these four levels just to reinforce how important it is for you to understand them.

NOMINAL

Nominal measurement is a simple classification. When we assign a person a number because he is a member of a certain classroom, we are engaged in nominal measurement. The numbers are arbitrarily selected and meaningless in themselves. For example, if we wish to measure the sex of the students in a class, we may choose to classify men as "1" and women as "2." Therefore, each male in the class is labeled a "1" and each female in the class a "2." The selection of "1" and "2" is very arbitrary. We could just as easily employ "469" and "932." None of the normal mathematical operations may be applied to the numbers assigned at this level of measurement. All that is permissible is to extend our measurement slightly and count up the number of people who were assigned "1" or "2." Thus we could determine that in our classroom there were 48 men and 40 women.

This is the lowest level of measurement and is seldom desired by the social scientist. In some cases it is the only level of measurement that would be isomorphic. In the example above, to think of measuring sex more precisely than "female" or "male" is somewhat ludicrous. If we wish to talk about something such as the "degree of maleness" or "degree of femaleness," we are talking about something more than sex, so we would measure something other than biological sex. Sex in human beings is only measurable at the nominal level, and a more "precise" measure would be nonisomorphic and meaningless.

ORDINAL

Ordinal or rank-order measurement assigns numbers to things in such a way as to reflect relationships among the things. While nominal measurement merely indicates the things that are different from one another, ordinal measurement indicates the direction of the difference in some meaningful way. Typical relationships among things are more favorable, more difficult, more preferred, higher, etc. In ordinal measurement, we may assign something at the lowest level "1," the thing that is just above it we may assign "2," and so on. For example, in most institutions of higher education seniors receive the nominal categorization of "4," juniors "3," sophomores "2," and freshmen "1." The way these numbers are customarily assigned is arbitrary. We could assign seniors "940," juniors "623," sophomores "212," and freshmen "5." Ordinal measurement only indicates the direction of the relationship between two things. If a sergeant wears three stripes, a corporal two stripes, and a private one stripe, this merely establishes a hierarchical relationship among the three military personnel. The sergeant could just as well wear seven stripes, the corporal two, and the private one. The relationship, as measured at the ordinal level, would still be exactly the same. Ordinal measurement, then, can tell us that the sergeant is more important (presuming that the number of stripes indicates importance) than the corporal and that the corporal is more important than the private. Ordinal measurement does not tell us how much more important the sergeant is than the corporal or the corporal is than the private. Even on the day a private is being promoted to corporal, he or she would still be classified as a private. People do not say that someone in the military is an almost corporal or has 1.9 stripes; he or she either has the rank of corporal or the rank of private—there is no in-between. In other words, ordinal measures allow us to see the hierarchical level between groups, but ordinal measures do not allow us to determine the degree to which people belong within these groups.

INTERVAL

Interval measurement has all of the characteristics of ordinal measurement and one crucial addition. Interval measurement identifies the distance between any two things that are measured. In interval measurement, we assign numbers to things in such ways that the distance between any two things is measured. In interval measurement, we assign numbers to things in such ways that the distance between things assigned "1" and "2" is equivalent to the distance between two things assigned "4" and "5." This assignment on the basis of equal intervals is essential to establish an isomorphic relationship between our use of numbers in measurement and the mathematical operations of many statistical tests.

The numbers that we use to indicate the distance of an interval are arbitrary. If the interval of distance is, for example, 36 inches, we may measure that the interval by employing the numbers, 36, 72, 108, etc., or we may use the numbers 1 (36), 2 (36 + 36), 3 (72 + 36), etc. The important consideration is that the difference between levels be consistently noted in our numerical scheme. The same degree of difference may be alluded to as "1" unit, "2" units, or "200" units. The numbers, in themselves, have no meaning, but the relationships between the numbers do. The most common example of interval measurement is the way we measure temperature (excluding the Kelvin scale). Typically, nonphysical scientists discuss temperature using both a Centigrade and a Fahrenheit system. Both measure exactly the same thing—temperature—but the scaling systems they employ are quite different. For example, on the Centigrade thermometer water freezes at 0 degrees, but on the Fahrenheit thermometer water freezes at 32 degrees. The important thing on interval scales, such as measurement of temperature, is that they are internally consistent in their assignment of numbers. The difference between 80 degrees and 78 degrees is exactly equivalent to the difference between 20 degrees and 18 degrees. The two degrees of difference must mean the same thing at any point on the scale.

Interval measures (Likert, semantic differential/bipolar, and scalogram scales) are probably the most common measures taken by social scientists because most scales created for examining various variables are interval oriented.

RATIO

A ratio scale has all of the characteristics of an interval scale, but in addition it has a true zero point as its origin. As we noted in the measurement of temperatures, zero could mean different things on the two different measures. In ratio measures, zero has an absolute value of its own. One deviation from the discussion above examining temperature is the Kelvin scale, which emphasizes that there is a point where atomic movement stops completely and is called absolute zero, so the Kelvin temperature scale would be a ratio scale because it has an absolute zero. Two common ratio measures are the measures employed for distance. We may use the metric system or the common system of inches, feet, and yards. In each case, zero means no distance. Zero meters and zero inches are exactly equivalent; they indicate the absence of distance. On interval scales it is not meaningful to compare the absolute numbers assigned in terms of their geometric relationships with each other. Such comparisons are possible with ratio scales. For example, a person who scores 60 on an intelligence measure is not necessarily precisely half as intelligent as a person who scores 120, but a city 500 miles away is precisely twice as far away as a city that is 250 miles away.

By this point you may be wondering, *I know how to measure distance, but what does this have to do with measuring communication?* This is a very good question. To help us answer that question we need to first look at the history of measurement with regard to human behavior.

A History of Measurement

As discussed in Chapter 1, the history of the social sciences is dependent on the scientific community's understanding of quantitative methods. Darwin, in his book *Origin of Species*, published in 1859, was the first to truly draw attention variation, or the idea that certain traits and attributes are selected to be passed from one generation to the next while others are not. Ultimately, some traits and attributes thrive while others die out. Darwin's work on genetic variation spurred the drive to measure individual differences. The first person to really set out to accomplish this task was Darwin's half cousin Francis Galton in 1892 in his text *Hereditary Genius*. The psychologist James McKeen Cattell was one of many people influenced by Galton's work. In fact, Cattell ultimately traveled to England to work with Galton and see how he was using statistics to understand humans. In 1890, Cattell was the first social scientist to develop measurements for nonphysical attributes. Cattell began to measure simple mental processes like the time it took subjects to perform simple mental acts like naming objects in a sequence or colors (Baldwin, Cattell, & Jastrow, 1889; Cattell, 1890, 1895). While at the University of Pennsylvania Cattell began to administer newly developed measures to students, which he ultimately labeled "mental tests." Ultimately "mental tests" became labeled mental measures or any tool used for the measurement of mental functions like attitudes, beliefs, cognitive knowledge, perceived knowledge, and personality/behavioral traits. Basically, any achievement test, personality test, aptitude test, intelligence test, or career choice test qualifies as a mental measure (Salkind, 2006). By the time the twentieth century rolled around, mental measurement began to pick up steam both in the United States and around the world.

In 1905, Alfred Binet, a French psychologist, was commissioned to create the first test to determine if children were functioning at lower than normal levels. Binet, along with his doctoral student Theodore Simon, ultimately created the Binet-Simon scale, which measured a child's adeptness at completing various age appropriate tasks (Binet, 1905). In essence, this became the first known intelligence test of its kind. Binet's research was then furthered by a Stanford University professor named Lewis Terman (1916). Of course, intelligence testing quickly turned to academic achievement testing when in 1937 the Stanford Achievement Test (SAT) became required for entry into Ivy League schools. As more and more high school students took the SAT and other entrance examinations were created, the Educational Testing Service (ETS) was ultimately created in 1947, which still oversees numerous tests including the SATs, GREs, TOFELs, and PRAXIS tests, just to name a few.

In addition to achievement tests, a new breed of measurements were also on the horizon as the United States went into World War I. While the notion of personality had been around since the time of Hippocrates, measuring personality really wasn't feasible until the early 1900s. The first modern personality test was created in 1920 by Robert Woodworth. Woodworth had been commissioned by the American Psychological Association on behalf of the U.S. military to create a measure of emotional stability that could be used to test new recruits. Woodworth eventually created the Woodworth Personal Data Sheet, which contained a series of 116 "yes" or "no" questions. Unfortunately, the test was developed too late in World War I to be used in the screening of new recruits, but the test did become the forerunner of future personality tests (Segal & Coolidge, 2003). Another test developed around the same time was Pressey and Pressey's (1919) Cross-Out Test. The Cross-Out Test had respondents cross out any words on a list that the respondent considered wrong, inappropriate, unpleasant, or worrisome. Pressey and Pressey believed that the resulting pattern of crossed out and un–crossed out words could be used to help categorize respondents' emotional states.

Beyond traditional personality testing, further methods for measuring attitudes became increasing important during the early 1900s. One of the most important figures in early measurement was Emory S. Bogardus, who was a prominent figure in sociology. He created a scale called the Bogardus Social Distance Scale, which was the first scale to attempt to measure people's willingness to interact with different types of people. The Social Distance Scale attempts to measure degrees of tolerance or prejudice between social groups (Bogardus, 1925). The Bogardus Social Distance Scale is considered the oldest attitudinal research scale still in use today. Beyond Bogardus's research, modern social scientific research has been transformed by the development of two specific measurement devices: Likert scales and semantic differential scales.

LIKERT SCALES

Another researcher interested in understanding attitudes named Rensis Likert was interested in developing a measure for attitudes. In 1932, Likert published a monograph based on his dissertation in which he developed a new attitude-scaling technique. The basic premise of the Likert scale was quite simplistic, but it revolutionized social scientific research. Likert started off with the idea of presenting respondents with a declarative statement of some kind (e.g., "Cold pizza is a good breakfast), and then he offered them a range of possible choices: *strongly disagree, disagree, neither agree nor disagree, agree,* or *strongly agree.* Respondents only have five choices, so people must select one of the categories. Since these categories have weighted distances, the answer on a single Likert item is considered ordinal because researchers cannot assume that respondents perceive the difference between the different levels evenly. However, if multiple Likert items are summed together, the summed total may be treated as interval data that actually measure a latent variable.

A *latent variable* or *hypothetical variable* is a variable that a researcher cannot directly observe, but is inferred from other variables that are observable and measured directly. For example, the statement "I dislike participating in group discussions" when measured using Likert's five steps (*strong disagree, disagree, neither agree nor disagree, agree,* or *strong agree*) is an ordinal variable. However, when we combine this statement with the other 23 statements on the Personal Report of Communication Apprehension–24, we end up with an interval variable that measures the latent variable "communication apprehension."

The first real discussion of the use of Likert scales in communication research was in 1967 by Arnold, McCroskey, and Prichard, who wrote a short introductory essay to the use and creation of Likert scales in *Today's Speech*. Likert scales have become very common in communication research. We will discuss creating Likert scales in much more detail later in this chapter. Now that we've discussed the history and purpose of the Likert scale, we can discuss the next major development in research measurement: semantic differential scaling.

SEMANTIC DIFFERENTIAL

The next major breakthrough in the area of attitudinal measurement came from Osgood (1952) and Osgood, Tannnenbaum, and Suci (1957). A semantic differential scale asks respondents to rate their opinions on a linear scale between two endpoints that have opposite meanings (e.g., Good/Bad, Dirty/Clean, Slow/Fast, Weak/Strong, Light/Heavy, Moral/Immoral, etc.). Between these two oppositely worded adjectives, there exists a series of steps. The most common number of steps in a semantic differential scale is seven, so instructions for a semantic differential test read like this: "Circle the number between the adjectives which best represents your beliefs. Numbers 1 and 7 indicate a very strong feeling. Numbers 2 and 6 indicate a strong feeling. Numbers 3 and 5 indicate a fairly weak feeling. Number 4 indicates you are undecided or do not understand the adjectives themselves." For example, maybe we want respondents to tell us whether they believe capital punishment is good or bad. We would place the adjectives "good" and "bad" on opposite sides of a continuum with seven steps like this:

Good   1   2   3   4   5   6   7   Bad

or

Good   __   __   __   __   __   __   __   Bad

Whether or not we actually have the physical numbers present in a semantic differential really isn't important as long as we, as the researchers, know that we have direct quantifiable distances between each step. Since these steps are weighted distances, the answer on a single semantic differential item is considered ordinal because researchers cannot assume that respondents perceive the difference between the steps evenly. However, if multiple semantic differential items are summed together, the summed total may be treated as interval data that actually measure a latent variable.

As discussed above, a *latent variable* is a variable that a researcher cannot directly observe, but can infer from other variables that are measured directly. For example, respondents can be asked to rate their supervisor using the following bipolar adjectives:

Intelligent   7   6   5   4   3   2   1   Unintelligent

This single semantic differential item is ordinal; however, when we combine this item with the 17 other semantic differential items on McCroskey and Teven's (1999) Source

Credibility Scale, we end up with an interval variable that measures the latent variable source credibility, which is broken down into three other latent variables: competence, trustworthiness, and caring/goodwill. Heis (1970) did have one major warning when constructing semantic differential scales: the adjectives must be relevant and understandable for respondents. For example, if you want to have respondents rate their interaction with someone, using the adjectives sweet/sour would not be as useful as the adjectives helpful/unhelpful. You should also avoid using jargon-loaded language that may be too specialized for nonscientists, like extraverted/introverted; you should opt to use more common adjectives like talkative/quiet.

The first real discussion of the use of semantic differential scales in communication research was in 1966 by Arnold, McCroskey, and Prichard, who wrote a short introductory essay about the use and creation of semantic differential scales in *Today's Speech*. Since then semantic differential scales have become very common in communication research. We should note that many researchers use the two terms semantic differential scales or bipolar adjective scales interchangeably.

Measuring Communication

In 2004, James McCroskey, Virginia Richmond, Aaron Johnson, and Heather Smith wanted to create research instruments to help measure the concept of organizational orientations theory, which stated that different people view their relationships with their jobs in very different ways (this article can be found on the CD-ROM accompanying this book). Some people see work as a central focus of their life, while other people see work as a means to an end—their social life. Ultimately, organizational orientations theory proposes that how people see their relationships with their jobs will impact various job-related outcomes. While this theory sounds very reasonable and some early research seemed to support the theory, the question that McCroskey et al. found problematic was how one goes about determining one's organizational orientation.

Also in 2004, Jason Wrench and Virginia Richmond were talking about yet another measurement-oriented problem. They noticed that a scale that had been previously developed by Melanie Booth-Butterfield and Steven Booth-Butterfield (1990) had a problem. This scale was called the humor orientation scale and allegedly measured the degree to which an individual used humor as a communicative tool in interpersonal relationships. However, when one looks at the humor orientation scale, all of the questions were centered around an individual's ability to tell jokes or funny stories. Is humor only about jokes and funny stories? If this were the case, comic legends like Mr. Bean and Charlie Chaplin would not even be considered humorous because they relied greatly on nonverbal forms of humor.

In both of the above examples, researchers were faced with a problem in measurement. McCroskey et al. (2004) needed to determine how to measure an individual's organizational orientation, and Wrench and Richmond (2004) needed to determine how to measure a person's use of humor in interpersonal interactions without relying on joke and story telling as the only form of humor. While both groups of authors could have outside observers watch people over an extended period of time to determine either their organizational orientation or tendency to use humor in communicative interactions, this process would take a long time and many hours of observation, which is unrealistic in most research circumstances. For this reason, research scales are often created to enable a researcher to ask participants about their personality traits/states, beliefs and attitudes, and knowledge. Let's look at each of these three categories separately.

PERSONALITY TRAITS/STATES

We first visited the concepts of traits and states back in Chapter 7 when we introduced the variables in the data set that accompanied this textbook. Just to refresh your memory let's discuss these two concepts again briefly. Trait behavior is behavior that that is assumed to be consistent across contexts and specific situations within particular constructs. For example, an individual's level of communication apprehension (CA) is fairly trait oriented. People with high levels of CA tend to be anxious about communication in any situation, in any communicative context, or with any audience. State behavior, on the other hand, is behavior that varies from one situation to another within the same context. Some people tend to be more state oriented in their communication apprehension. People that are not high CA, but rather more moderate in their CA, may only experience apprehension in one of the four major contexts (group, meeting, interpersonal, or public), or they may experience CA differently depending on the audience they are in front of at a given moment. While the first case is clearly more trait CA and the second case is state CA, we are able to measure this personality trait using the PRCA-24 scale. In essence, when researchers discuss personality traits or communication traits they are discussing the measurement of hypothetical constructs that accounts for certain behaviors. In the case of CA, the hypothetical construct is anxiety associated with either real or perceived communication. The hypothetical construct must be very clear, and if your hypothetical construct is not clear it can lead to serious measurement issues (see Chapter 10). Research has shown that the hypothetical construct CA can help account for a wide variety of communicative behaviors, ranging from the tendency to sweat while giving a speech to the likelihood of being hired for a job or promoted within one's current employment situation.

Personality traits/states can also be classified in terms of psychological and behavioral traits/states. Behaviorally oriented trait/state research scales involve both perceptions of one's own behavior and other individual's perceptions of one's behavior. For example, it would be very difficult to answer the PRCA-24 for another person because the questions are designed to measure an individual's internal psychological state while communicating with other people. However, we could ask people to look for observable signs of anxiety while giving a speech (lack of eye contact, discoloration of the skin, fidgeting, hand shaking, voice quivers, etc.). For example, the Nonverbal Immediacy Scale–Self Report is designed to measure an individual's perception of her or his own tendency to exhibit nonverbal behaviors that increase the feelings of immediacy in other people (I use my hands and arms to gesture while talking to people). However, the scale can be retooled to be Other Report, and then an individual can report the tendency of another person's use of nonverbal behaviors that increase feelings of immediacy (My teacher uses her or his hands and arms to gesture while talking to people). In both cases, the intent of the scale is not changed; the object of measurement is shifted from either the first person (my behavior) to another person (someone else's behavior).

Beliefs and Attitudes

The second classification of things that can be measured by a research scale are beliefs. As we discussed in Chapter 7, a belief is our perception of reality about whether something is true or false, whereas an attitude is a predisposition to respond to people, ideas, or objects in an evaluative way. In Chapter 7 we introduced two scales that can be employed to measure beliefs (generalized belief scale) and attitudes (generalized attitude scale). While these two scales are easy to employ to measure any belief or attitude, other scales can also be created to measure a belief.

One type of scale designed to measure a set of beliefs is called a scalogram scale. The purpose of a scalogram scale is to create a series of beliefs about a single topic starting very weak (I never throw trash on the ground because it hurts our environment) and moving to very strong (Bombing a company that hurts the environment is completely justifiable). The environmentalism scale discussed in Chapter 6 measured different beliefs that can people can have about environmentalism. With each new belief statement, a person answers either "Yes" or "No." If the scalogram scale is accurate, if a person says "No" to the first question, then he or she will say "No" to every item on the scale. If the person says "Yes" to the first three questions and then says "No" to the fourth question, then questions 5 through 10 should also be answered "No." In essence, a scalogram scale is designed to measure a series of beliefs and how strong a person holds those beliefs. While the authors of this book all think recycling is a noble endeavor, not all of us actually recycle regularly.

KNOWLEDGE

The last major type of variable that can be measured by a scale is real and/or perceived knowledge. All of us are very familiar with scales that attempt to measure perceived knowledge. A multiple choice or true–false test is a simple example of a scale that is designed to measure knowledge. Maybe you want to measure the effect that a teacher's choice of clothing has on retention of a lecture. The easiest way to determine retention of a lecture is to test participants about information that was in the lecture after the fact. In education, we constantly survey students' acquisition of cognitive knowledge in a class. A good teacher will understand that a test basically lets us know two different things: (1) how well every student understands the material and (2) how well our teaching methods are working for student understanding as a whole. There are some in education who actually believe that if all students fail a test, then the teacher has done a good job weeding out the bad students. However, what is more likely the case is that the testing mechanism was not appropriate or the teaching strategies are not working. While outside the purview of the current text, we should mention that there is an entire field of educational psychometrics or the creation and analysis of cognitive tests. While many of us hate standardized tests, a lot of time and politics goes into the creation of a standardized test. After students have taken a standardized test, psychometricians spend a lot of time analyzing the statistical properties of the standardized test to make sure the test is effective and appropriate.

The second type of knowledge that can be measured is perceived knowledge. While understanding what a person knows is important, it is also important to be able to measure what a person thinks he or she knows as well. Figure 9.1 shows the Risk Knowledge Index.

The Risk Knowledge Index was originally created by Wrench (2007) as a way to measure the degree to which an individual believed he or she understood the risk associated with a specific hazard (something that called cause loss of life or limb). In Figure 9.1, the scale is designed to measure an individual's perception of her or his knowledge of the risks associated with bungee jumping. We could have determined a person's perception of her or his perceived knowing by asking the question "How much do you know about the risks of bungee jumping from the range of 0 (I know nothing about the risks) to 9 (I know about all of the risks involved)?" However, a one-shot question can be problematic because it does not allow for a statistical way to determine if your sample's response to this question was random or consistent.

In this section we have examined the three primary variable types that can be analyzed through research scales (personality traits/states, beliefs and attitudes, and perceived and real knowledge). However, before one can measure anything at all, he or she must have a very clear idea of what the variable is that he or she is attempting to measure.

Instructions: Below are several descriptions dealing with the extent to which you are aware of the risks involved in bungee jumping. Please use the scale below to rate the degree to which each statement applies to your perceptions about your knowledge of the risk(s):

Strongly Disagree	**Disagree**	**Neutral**	**Agree**	**Strongly Agree**
1	2	3	4	5

_____ 1. I know the risks involved.
_____ 2. I do not feel knowledgeable about the risks involved.
_____ 3. The risks involved are very clear to me.
_____ 4. I do not know the risks involved.
_____ 5. I do not comprehend the risks involved.
_____ 6. My knowledge of the risks involved is limited.
_____ 7. I completely understand the risks involved.
_____ 8. I feel knowledgeable about the risks involved.
_____ 9. I comprehend the risks involved.
_____ 10. The risks involved are not clear to me.

SCORING: To compute your scores follow the instructions below:

Step One: Add scores for items 1, 3, 7, 8, & 9.
Step Two: Add scores for items 2, 4, 5, 6, & 10.
Step Three: Add 30 to Step One.
Step Four: Subtract the score for Step Two from the score for Step Three.

Interpreting Your Score:

Scores on the Risk Knowledge Index should be between 10 and 50. Individuals with scores above 40 are considered to have a high perceived understanding of a risk, and individuals with scores below 40 are considered to have a low perceived understanding a risk.

NOTE: The mean for risk knowledge tends to be fairly high.

Source:

Wrench, J. S. (2007). The influence of perceived risk knowledge on risk communication. *Communication Research Reports, 24,* 63–70.

Figure 9.1 Risk Knowledge Index

Developing Your Operationalization

In the two scale examples discussed in this section (organizational orientations and humor assessment), both scales started with what we call a germinal idea. A "germinal idea" is a term for that spark that causes an individual to realize that something new can be measured. We often get the ideas for new scales because we face real events in our lives that cause us to wonder about some communication phenomena, or maybe when reading a book you'll read what an author says and wonder *"Has anyone ever really studied this concept?"* Recently, two of our authors were having a late night discussion about organizational communication that led to the realization that there was a huge gap in the organizational communication measurement literature, which led to the creation of nine new scales. While a germinal idea can help you get the initial push to create a scale, it's the conceptualization of that germinal idea that allows you to start the measurement process.

Conceptualization is defined as *the development and clarification of concepts or your germinal idea*. Conceptualization is basically when you take a germinal idea and determine what it is that you want to measure and whether or not you can realistically measure something. One of the biggest problems that many researchers have when creating research scales is that they attempt to measure too much. For example, maybe you wanted to create a scale to measure an individual's perception of health communication. Well, what part of health communication are you interested in? Are you looking at communication between patients and physicians, patients and nurses, clients and therapists, clients and pharmacists, what!? In essence, a scale should be designed to measure a single concept or a set of concepts that are closely related to each other. For example, Richmond and McCroskey's (1990) sociocommunicative orientation scale measures the two related constructs of assertiveness and responsiveness. Realistically, each of those concepts could be measured separately by a single scale, but since the two concepts work together so closely, it makes sense to develop a single scale where both concepts could be analyzed together. However, you would not want to create a scale that attempts to measure assertiveness and conflict management because these are two separate concepts. While you could examine both of these concepts in a single research study, you would need to create two different scales: one for assertiveness and one for conflict management strategies.

Once you have determined the basic concept you are actually planning on measuring, you need to operationalize your concept. Operationalization is the *detailed description of the research operations or procedures necessary to assign units of analysis to the categories of a variable in order to represent conceptual properties*. The concept of operationalization applies to all forms of measurement, not just working with scales. For example, if you want to create a study where you are going to analyze the types of clothing people have on and their likelihood of spending money in a department store, you would need to create an a priori (before the fact) coding scheme for how you will classify clothing choices. So, if a woman comes in wearing a Gucci business suit and carries a Prada handbag, she would not be classified into the same category as a male wearing cut-off shorts and a tank top. This first form of operationalization is referred to as manipulation into categories. In essence, you operationalize that dress is some sort of nominal/categorical variable, and you purposefully classify people into different groups based on what they are wearing when they enter the store.

The second way we can operationalize a concept is to estimate the category either by observing existing records or by asking people. The observation of existing records is how Boiarsky, Long, and Thayer (1999) operationalized their concept in their article about children's science television (included on the CD-ROM included with this book). Boiarsky, Long, and Thayer examined a variety of mediated characteristics (sound effects per minute, cuts per minute, fades/dissolves per minute, wipes per minute, and topic shifts per minute) in a series of children's television shows (*Beakman's World, Bill Nye the Science Guy, Magic School Bus*, and *Newton's Apple*). Each of these shows was preexisting, so the researchers had to determine what it was they wanted to examine in the show and then operationalize how they would go about analyzing these mediated characteristics. By clearly spelling out the operationalization of coding procedures future researchers can (1) more accurately understand the findings of the study and (2) replicate the research in the future in either this genre or a different genre of television. Using preexisting sources of information for the collection of data can be very beneficial when doing research. However, as we discussed in the previous paragraph, you must have a clear idea of what you are looking for before you can truly operationalize your measurement process.

The last form of operationalization is asking for verbal/nonverbal reports of a phenomenon either through interviews or traditional surveys techniques. For example, maybe you want to determine the effect of a new political attack advertisement on the public. What kinds of questions would you want to know to determine "the effect"? Maybe you'd want to ask questions about the target of the attack ad's credibility, or ask questions about the attractiveness of the target of the attack ad after viewing it. While this first part is clearly more in line with the conceptualization part of the measurement process, the development of questions is part of the operationalization process. Operationalization is in essence the procedures we go through to place someone in a variable category. When Wrench and Richmond (2004) were first writing a new scale for measuring interpersonal humor, the two fell into the same trap that the Booth-Butterfields had fallen into when developing the humor orientation scale. It wasn't until a colleague read the initial version of the scale and noted that they had also included a number of items about jokes and humorous story telling that the two researchers realized that the scale needed to avoid such language altogether if it was to truly be a general humor measure. This process where you narrow the focus of the scale and really try to get at the basic concept being measured is the operationalization of the concept.

Now that we have discussed the initial steps necessary when creating a germinal idea for a scale, conceptualizing the scale, and then operationalizing the scale, we can turn our attention to the actual construction of research scales.

Constructing Questions

Writing research measures that will stand the test of time is not a task to underestimate at all. Too many people who are not familiar with the psychometric process of creating reliable and valid research measures think that creating a new scale is simply writing down a series of questions. Writing scale questions can be very problematic because even the slightest conjecture or ambiguity in an item can cause people to inaccurately respond to the item, which makes your scale's purpose and meaning to be highly suspect. Once you have determined what you really want to measure (through the conceptualization and operationalization processes), you can then begin to actually write a research scale. The following discussion is focused primarily on the creation of Likert-type scales because they are most often used by communication researchers. While some of the concepts may not directly apply to semantic differential/bipolar or scalogram scales, most of this discussion can be cross-applied to those scales as well. We will now examine 15 extremely important guidelines creating reliable and valid Likert-type research scales.

1. Start with twice as many items as you will need. When you are first developing a scale, you need to begin with nearly twice as many items as you think you will need in the long run. For example, if you want to have a 15-item scale to measure sibling communication satisfaction, you would need to start off with 30 items because some of your items will be problematic and will eventually be discarded from your scale either because they do not help the reliability of your scale or do not measure the actual construct you are attempting to measure (these will be discussed in Chapter 10). Since you need to write a considerable number of items for each scale you create, you will often find redundancy a necessity. One easy way to do this is to oppositely word each item you create later in the scale. For example, if you have a scale that you are writing 20 items for, you may want to have item #1 as "I like potatoes" and number 11 as "I do not like potatoes." In the long run, this will provide you with a healthy balance between positively worded and negatively worded items in your scale. The reason we have positively and negatively worded items in a scale is to make sure that a person is not randomly answering the questions without reading the questions. In other words, if we have both of those questions being answered by a Likert scale ranging from 1 (*strongly dis-agree*) to 5 (*strongly agree*), we would expect that if someone answers "5" to question one, he or she should also answer "1" to question #11 since the two questions are oppositely worded. This concept will be discussed in much greater detail in the next chapter.

2. Every item should reflect the construct. As a scale writer, make sure that every item that you write on a scale clearly (at least in your mind) reflects the construct you are attempting to measure. Again, you want to make sure that you don't have items on a scale that's supposed to be measuring physician use of story telling to contain items about patient apprehension while talking to her or his physician. While both scales could be important, the concepts should be operationalized separately into two different scales.

3. Use concise, clearly worded, unambiguous items. One of the problems that people have early on when creating scales is that they write survey items that are complex. Unfortunately, when working with the general public, the more simplistic a question is the more likely you will get an accurate response from your survey participants. You also want to make sure that the language you use in a scale item is simplistic enough for a wide audience. To avoid the pitfall of complicated language, always try to pilot test your scale with a group of people prior to mass distributing the scale to determine if there are any problem areas in the wording itself. If you know the test pilot group well, you may even ask them why they responded to specific questions in ways that you feel are opposite to how they should have scored based on their other answers. This will enable you to determine if any ambiguity has creped into your scale by accident.

4. Construct relatively short items (e.g., 20 words or less). As an extension of the last con-cept, not only do you want to avoid ambiguity, you really want to have items that are fairly short on a scale. The more text an individual has to read on a scale item, the more likely he or she will become confused and end up responding in a manner that is disjointed, which will skew your results. While we suggest that a single item on any given Likert scale should not exceed 20 words, the shorter you can make a scale item, the easier your scale will be to read and respond to by participants.

5. Pay attention to terminology in the item. Another extremely important problem to look out for when writing a scale is any jargon or discipline-specific terminology in the scale. Recently, some of the authors of this book were writing a scale to measure an individual's perception of an interactant's verbal and nonverbal communication during a specific type of romantic interaction. Upon further thinking about some of the scale items, we realized that not everyone may completely understand what is meant by verbal and nonverbal communica-tion since communication researchers have very specific meanings associated with the two terms. Ultimately, the researchers opted to provide a concise definition of the two terms prior to the scale to aid in the understanding of the two concepts by participants.

6. Avoid emotionally loaded items. Unless you are attempting to measure an individual's emotional state, emotionally loaded items should be avoided. What do we mean by emotion-ally loaded items? An emotionally loaded item is a scale item designed to assess an individ-ual's emotional response instead of her or his belief, attitude, or behavior. Suppose you want to create a scale for assessing a subordinate's perception of her or his supervisor's coaching and teaching on the job. You may have items like, "My supervisor makes sure I understand what I'm doing" or "My supervisor makes sure I understand what I did wrong when I make a mistake." In this scale, you would not want to have an item like "I hate it when my supervisor corrects my mistakes." Having items that cause people to respond to emotions in otherwise nonemotional scales can result in participants responding to the whole scale in an emotional state skewing your results.

7. Avoid leading items. Another trap you want to avoid when writing scale items involves leading items. A leading item is an item on a scale that clearly informs a person about the answer you are hoping to receive. For example, if you are creating a scale to measure the extent to which a teacher uses humor in a classroom, an item like "Good students always think their teachers use humor in the classroom" would be extremely inappropriate. Instead, you would want general items (e.g., "My teacher uses humor in the classroom") that avoid leading anyone to believe that they should answer the scale item in a specific socially desirable way.

8. Avoid loaded items. A loaded item is very similar to a leading item, just generally in the opposite direction. For example, if you are creating a scale about verbal aggression, you would not want an item to say something like "only an idiot cannot tell the difference between aggression and debate." Basically, if a person agrees with the statement, he or she is saying that there are lots of people that are idiots in the world, and if he or she disagrees with the statement then he or she is setting her or himself up to being labeled as an idiot for not seeing the difference between aggression and debate for her/himself.

9. Avoid double questions. One common problem that is often seen in scale items occurs when an individual attempts to write a scale item with two actual questions involved. For example, "I believe that all students should go to college, and I believe that all students should get a masters degree." While these two statements may both be true for some, they are not necessarily true for everyone. The best thing to do in this case would be to separate both statements out and ask them separately as two different items on the scale. When reading items on a scale, always double-check to see if a scale item is asking only one question.

10. Avoid questions with false premises. Often people will attempt to write scale items based on premises that simply are not factual. For example, if you are attempting to measure the degree to which one believes in the current president, you may ask a question like "Since people generally support the president, I believe the president is doing a good job." The premise of this item can be hotly contested, since many people do not support the president (any president). So if a question starts with a statement that is not factual, then the rest of the question will be ambiguous at best or unanswerable at worst.

11. Avoid using always, never. Using the words "always" and "never" often confuses people and can cause some participants to avoid answering an item at the extremes (like strongly agree/disagree on a 5-step Likert scale). If you had the item "I always communicate competently" on a scale, you could have problems because no one can honestly say they *always* communicate competently. On the flip side, if you substituted the word always for never, you would run into the same problem because no one can honestly say that they *never* communicate competently either.

12. Avoid double negatives/positives. As a whole, people find double negatives and double positives to be very confusing. You would not want to have items like, "Religious groups should not not have to pay taxes." In this case, streamlining the question and simply making it "Religious groups should have to pay taxes" makes the statement more direct and easier to understand.

13. Avoid hypothetical questions. If you ask people to respond to a hypothetical question, then you are going to get a hypothetical (i.e., made-up) answer. For example, if you create a scale on people's perceived interaction with extraterrestrial life forms, you're going to have people just randomly answering your scale because interaction with extraterrestrials can only be speculated upon, so no real answers can be given (except by a few people in New Mexico). As a researcher, it is best to keep scales and what you are measuring as concrete as humanly possible.

14. Avoid ambiguous pronoun references. When writing scales, you do not want to include pronouns that make the participant unsure of what you are asking in a scale item. For example, if you included the item "I would rather it not happen to me" on a scale about euthanasia, people would be highly suspect of what "it" actually is in this scale item. Instead, you would want to be as concrete as possible and reword the scale to read "I would rather not be euthanized" to avoid the ambiguous pronoun.

15. Consider recall issues for certain types of items. The last major concept that you want to keep in mind when writing a scale is the concept of recall. In essence, when we ask people to recall information about an attitude, belief, or behavior, we need to know whether what we are asking someone to remember can be remembered. We would not want to ask someone to recall the color of the tie a male physician was wearing 3 months earlier. We also need to think about whether the items on the scales we are creating force people to recall information that is unrealistic to be recalled at a later point. For example, if you are creating a scale on the posture one uses while standing, the scale may be difficult for people to accurately fill out if the target of the participants' observations hasn't been seen in a while.

Overall, we hope that you now understand that scale creation isn't simply about writing a series of sentences and attaching a bunch of Likert scales to those sentences. The art and science of research measurement is complex and takes a lot of time and effort to scientifically perform. Now that we have discussed how to create scales, we can examine how to put together a survey-based study.

Finding Mental Measures

Survey-based research is very prevalent in communication research. Thankfully, we do not have to spend all of our time creating new scales to conduct survey-based research. In fact, most studies do not attempt to reinvent the measurement wheel at all, and instead rely on combining previously existing scales in new ways that have not been explored. Literally thousands of research scales already exist, so there are millions of variable combinations that have yet to be explored. The more time you spend conducting survey research, the larger your collection of interval scales will ultimately become. If you're just starting out in research, you may not know where to turn to find scales, here are three books that may be useful for finding communication scales:

Manusov, V. (Ed.). (2005). *The sourcebook of nonverbal measures: Going beyond words.* Mahwah, NJ: Lawrence Erlbaum.

Rubin, R. B., Palmgreen, P., & Sypher, H. E. (Eds.). (2004). *Communication research measures: A sourcebook.* Mahwah, NJ: Lawrence Erlbaum.

Wrench, J. S., McCroskey, J. C., & Richmond, V. P. (2007). *Human communication in everyday life: Explanations and applications.* Boston: Allyn & Bacon.

These next five books may be useful for finding variables outside of the field of communication relating to communication phenomena:

Davis, C. M., Yarber, W. L., Bauserman, R., Schreer, G., & Davis, S. L. (Eds.). *Handbook of sexuality-related measures.* Thousand Oaks, CA: Sage.

Fields, D. L. (2002). *Taking measure of work: A guide to validated scales for organizational research and diagnosis.* Thousand Oaks, CA: Sage.

Goldman, B. A., & Mitchell, D. F. (2003). *Directory of unpublished experimental mental measures* (Vol. 8). Washington, DC: American Psychological Association. (see also Vol.1-7)

Hill, P. C., & Hood, R. W., Jr. (Eds.). (1999). *Measures of religiosity.* Birmingham, AL: Religious Education Press.

Robinson, J. P., Shaver, P. R., & Wrightsman, L. S. (Eds.). (1991). *Measures of personality and social psychological attitudes.* San Diego: Academic Press.

Robinson, J. P., Shaver, P. R., & Wrightsman, L. S. (Eds.). (1993). *Measures of political attitudes.* San Diego: Academic Press.

All in all, between these eight books there are more than 1000 research scales that could be utilized in human communication research. These books are generally laid out in the same way. First, a scale is introduced, previous findings related to the scale are discussed, the scale's reliability and validity are explored, and the scale items are presented. Since these scales are published in these collections, you do not have to get additional permission to use them for research purposes. However, just because the scale designers allow their scales to be freely used for research does not mean they will allow someone to use the scales for nonscholarly purposes without paying a fee.

There are also two online databases that can be useful when searching for mental measures. By 1938 so many new mental measures were being developed that Oscar K. Buros decided to publish the first volume of the *Mental Measures Yearbook*. The *Mental Measures Yearbook* attempts to locate and provide descriptions of the test, one or two reviews of the test, and references for how to find the test. The Buros Center for Testing (http://www.unl .edu/buros/) is still an active research center for mental measures, and the 16th volume of the *Mental Measures Yearbook* came out in 2005 (Spies & Plake). Your local library may have access to the *Mental Measures Yearbook* database through EBSCOhost. If you do not have access, cost for a single copy is $15, but this is just the cost for the measure review and does not include a copy of the measure itself. The Educational Testing Service (http://www.ets.org/) also has started compiling mental measures. If you are on ETS's website, click on the link that says "Find a Test." You will be taken to the Test Directory homepage. You will need to scroll down until you find the link to "Test Link," which is a database of over 25,000 mental measures. In fact, in a simple name search there are over 160 mental measures with the word "communication" in the title alone.

Measurement and Statistical Analysis

Because of the other chapters in this book, we will neither assume sophisticated knowledge of statistics nor attempt to explain statistical matters in any detail. However, it is important that a student studying measurement have very elementary knowledge of statistics so that he or she may be better able to evaluate the measuring instruments he or she chooses or develops.

There are essentially two types of statistical tests: parametric and nonparametric. A parameter is a value of a population. For example, if we administered an intelligence test to all of the people in the world, we might then add all of their scores together and divide by the number of people and obtain the "mean" or average score for all people on this measure of intelligence. This "mean" would be a parameter of the population. Since in most cases we are unable to apply any measure to all of the people to whom it might be applied, we are forced to employ samples from a population. All statistical tests make certain assumptions, but nonparametric statistical tests make no assumptions about parameters of the population from which the research sample was drawn, while parametric tests do make such assumptions. The important distinction between parametric and nonparametric statistical tests, for our purposes here, is that parametric tests assume that the level of measurement employed in obtaining the data was at least the interval level. Nonparametric tests make no such assumption. Parametric tests are normally considered to be more powerful, i.e., they are precise and less subject to error than nonparametric tests. Thus social scientists normally wish to employ parametric statistical procedures.

If we rigidly adhere to the characteristics required for the achievement of interval scales, we would be forced in many instances to employ nonparametric statistical tests even though we might prefer to employ parametric ones. In some cases, this is a particularly difficult problem because some parametric analyses have no equivalent nonparametric approach, e.g., factor analysis (see Chapter 21 for a brief explanation of factor analysis). Within the nominal, ordinal, interval, and ratio scaling category systems, most attitude measures fall in the ordinal or interval categories. It is highly unlikely to affect general results whether one treats the data as ordinal or interval, but a much wider range of techniques is available with interval measures.

Conclusion

In this chapter we have discussed a number of extremely important factors involved in measurement. We started by reviewing the purpose of measurement and the different levels of measurement (nominal, ordinal, interval, and ratio) and then examined the history of social scientific measurement that led to the creation of Likert scales and semantic differential/bipolar adjective scales. Next we talked about how we measure phenomena in communication, concluding with a discussion of how to write Likert-type items effectively. Finlly, we discussed where one can find mental measures and how mental measures are used in statistical research. However, our discussion of measurement isn't quite over yet. In the next chapter we will discuss two extremely important concepts related to measurement: reliability and validity.

KEY TERMS

Attitudes
Beliefs
Conceptualization
Cognitive Knowledge
Communication Trait
Germinal Idea
Isomorphism

Likert Scale
Lurker/Hypothetical
  Variable
Measurement
Mental Measure
Nonparametric
Operationalization

Parametric
Perceived Knowledge
Personality Traits
Semantic Differential/
  Bipolar Scale

REFERENCES

Arnold, W. E., McCroskey, J. C., & Prichard, S. (1966). The semantic differential. *Today's Speech, 14(4)*, 29–30.

Arnold, W. E., McCroskey, J. C., & Prichard, S. V. O. (1967). The Likert-type scale. *Today's Speech, 15*, 31–33.

Baldwin, J. M., Cattell, J. M., & Jastrow, J. (1889). Physical and mental tests. *Psychological Review, 5*, 172–179.

Benit, A. (1905). New methods for the diagnosis of the intellectual level of subnormals. *L'Année Psychologique, 12*, 191–244.

Bogardus, E. S. (1925). Measuring social distance. *Journal of Applied Sociology, 9*, 299–308.

Boiarsky, G., Long, M., & Thayer, G. (1999). Formal features in children's science television: Sound effects, visual pace, and topic shifts. *Communication Research Reports, 16*, 185–192.

Buros, O. K. (Ed.). (1938). *The 1938 mental measurements yearbook*. Lincoln, NB: University of Nebraska Press.

Cattell, J. M. (1895). Measurements of the accuracy of recollection. *Science, 2*, 761–766.

Cattell, J. M. (1890). Mental tests and measurements. *Mind, 15*, 373–381.

Darwin, C. (1859). *On the origin of species by means of natural selection*. London: Murray.

Galton, F. (1869). *Heredity genius: An inquiry into its laws and consequences*. New York: Macmillan. Online Available at: http://galton.org/books/hereditary-genius/

Heise, D. R. (1970). The semantic differential and attitude research. In G. F. Summers (Ed.), *Attitude measurement* (pp. 235–253). Chicago: Rand McNally.

Likert, R. (1932). A technique for the measurement of attitudes. *Archives of Psychology, 140*, 1–55.

McCroskey, J. C., Richmond, V. P., Johnson, A. D., & Smith, H. T. (2004). Organizational orientations theory and measurement: Development of measures and preliminary investigations. *Communication Quarterly, 52*, 1–14.

McCroskey, J. C., & Teven, J. J. (1999). Goodwill: A reexamination of the construct and its measurement. *Communication Monographs, 66*, 90–103.

Osgood, C. E. (1952). The nature and measurement of meaning. *Psychological Bulletin, 49*, 197–237.

Osgood, C. E., Tannenbaum, P. H., & Suci, G. J. (1957). *The measurement of meaning*. Urbana, IL: University of Illinois Press.

Pressey, S. L., & Pressey, L. W. (1919). Cross-out test, with suggestions as to a group scale of the emotions. *Journal of Applied Psychology, 3*, 138–150.

Richmond, V. P., & McCroskey, J. C. (1990). Reliability and separation of factors on the assertiveness-responsiveness measure. *Psychological Reports, 67*, 449–450.

Rocca, K. A., & Vogl-Bauer, S. (1999). Trait verbal aggression, sports fan identification, and perceptions of appropriate sports fan communication. *Communication Research Reports, 16*, 239–248.

Salkind, N. J. (2006). *Tests & measurement for people who (think they) hate tests & measurement*. Thousand Oaks, CA: Sage.

Salkind, N. J. (Ed.). (2006). *Encyclopedia of measurement and statistics*. Thousand Oaks, CA: Sage.

Segal, D. L., & Coolidge, F. L. (2003). Objective assessment of personality and psychopathology: An overview. In M. J. Hilsenroth, D. L. Segal, & M. Hersen (Eds.), *Comprehensive handbook of psychological assessment: Volume 2: Personality assessment* (pp. 3–13). New York: Wiley.

Spies, R. A., & Plake, B. S. (Eds.). (1938). *The sixteenth mental measurements yearbook*. Lincoln, NB: University of Nebraska Press.

Terman, L. M. (1916). *The measurement of intelligence*. Boston: Houghton Mifflin.

Woodworth, R. S. (1920). *Personal data sheet*. Chicago: Stoelting.

Wrench, J. S. (2007). The influence of perceived risk knowledge on risk communication. *Communication Research Reports, 24*, 1–8.

Wrench, J. S., & Richmond, V. P. (2004). Understanding the psychometric properties of the Humor Assessment instrument through an analysis of the relationships between teacher humor assessment and instructional communication variables in the college classroom. *Communication Research Reports, 21*, 92–103.

FURTHER READING

DeVellis, R. F. (1991). *Scale development: Theory and applications* (Applied Social Research Methods Series, volume 26). Newbury Park, CA: Sage.

Dillman, D. A. (2000). *Mail and internet surveys: The tailored design method* (2nd ed.). New York: Wiley.

Fowler, F. J., Jr. (1993). *Survey research methods* (2nd ed.). Newbury Park, CA: Sage.

Linn, R. L., & Grolund, N. E. (2000). *Measurement and assessment in teaching* (8th ed.). Upper Saddle, NJ: Merrill.

Singleton, R. A., Jr., & Straits, B. C. (1999). *Approach to social research* (3rd ed.). New York: Oxford University Press.

CHAPTER **10**

Reliability and Validity

CHAPTER OBJECTIVES

1   Understand what is meant by *reliability*.
2   Understand what reliable and unreliable patterns look like when people respond to scales.
3   Understand the different types of reliability discussed in this chapter (test–retest, alternate forms, split-half, Hoyt ANOVA, and Cronbach's alpha).
4   Know how to run both split-half and Chronbach's alpha reliabilities using SPSS and SAS.
5   Understand how to interpret alpha reliability output.
6   Be able to write up reliabilities using correct APA style.
7   Explain the three ways a researcher can improve her or his reliability.
8   Understand what is meant by *validity*.
9   Explain the three types of criterion validity (predictive, concurrent, and retrospective).
10   Understand the three methods to test a measure's construct or factorial validity.
11   Know the seven threats to validity.
12   Be able to explain the five basic problems with measurement that affect validity.
13   Examine a real case study related to measurement, reliability, and validity.

The purpose of this chapter is to explore two very important characteristics in measurement: reliability and validity. Let's begin by discussing reliability.

Reliability

When people think about the word *reliability*, numerous synonyms come to mind: dependable, accurate, honest, trustworthy, consistent, etc. While the word *reliability* is used in a very specific manner by quantitative researchers, those adjectives still hold true. Reliability for this text is defined as *the accuracy that a measure has in producing stable, consistent measurements.* The first part of this definition relates to the information we talked about in the previous chapter examining measurement, so ultimately reliability is about making sure our tools for measuring a phenomena are accurate. And we are dealing with whether or not the measurement has the ability to find consistent results. One of the authors of this book has a very unreliable cell phone—the clock on the cell phone is constantly changing. At one point in time you'll look down and the cell phone will say that it's 6:45, and you'll look down 5 minutes later and the cell phone will say that it's 10:15. Obviously, this particular cell phone is not a reliable tool for telling the time because a clock should not indicate that 3½ hours have passed in 5 minutes. Admittedly, social scientists do not generally sit around watching clocks and watches to ascertain their reliability as tools for measuring time, so we need to determine whether or not our tools for measurement are as reliable as a good clock.

In the social sciences, we quite often use research scales to conduct studies. Since research scales are a very common form of measurement, social scientists must make sure that these scales are reliable measurements of the constructs they claim to measure. One of the first things a researcher needs to determine when he or she has collected data is whether or not people have consistently filled out a research scale or completed the scale haphazardly. Imagine you just handed out the Generalized Attitude Scale about Higher Education to 300 people. How can you tell if people randomly filled out the scale or whether the participants put in the time and effort into their participation in a research project?

As stated above, reliability of a measuring instrument *is the accuracy that a measure has in producing stable, consistent measurements.* In other words, if I give you the same measure under the same conditions multiple times, your score should not change significantly. A perfectly reliable instrument would produce the same score every time it is administered even if it were administered an infinite number of times. Obviously, in measuring human beings it is impossible to measure an infinite number of times. Thus, we never know the precise reliability of our measures. Rather, we must estimate that reliability.

SCALAR RELIABILITY

Scalar reliability (the reliability of individual research scales) is the most common form of reliability assessed in quantitative research in communication. Almost every quantitative research study will employ at least one research scale, and we need to have a way to determine if people are consistently filling out the scale. In Figure 10.1 we have a copy of the Generalized Attitude Measure used in this book.

You'll notice that in this scale some of the adjective pairings are positively worded and some are negatively worded. For example, in the first pairing (Good/Bad) the word "Good" to the left receives a lower score (1) and the word "Bad" to the right receives a higher score (7), whereas, in the second pairing (Wrong/Right), the word "Wrong" to the left receives the lower score (1) and the word "Right" to the right receives the higher score (7). In this scale, is "Good" an equivalent to "Wrong"? Not at all! When researchers create scales, we often do so with items that are oppositely worded to determine whether or not people are just randomly answering the scale.

Imagine you had a participant in your study who filled out the scale like you see in Figure 10.2. You'll notice that in this case someone just went through and circled almost all 7s on the scale. In essence, this person perceives higher dducation to be bad, right, beneficial, unfair, foolish, and positive. Does this make sense to you? Well, don't worry—it doesn't make sense to us either. If a person consistently filled out the Generalized Attitude Measure it might look like Figure 10.3.

Instructions: On the scales below, please indicate your feelings about "**Higher Education**." Numbers "1" and "7" indicate a very strong feeling. Numbers "2" and "6" indicate a strong feeling. Numbers "3" and "5" indicate a fairly week feeling. Number "4" indicates you are undecided or do not understand the adjective pairs themselves. There are no right or wrong answers. *Only circle one number per line.*

1.	Good	1	2	3	4	5	6	7	Bad
2.	Wrong	1	2	3	4	5	6	7	Right
3.	Harmful	1	2	3	4	5	6	7	Beneficial
4.	Fair	1	2	3	4	5	6	7	Unfair
5.	Wise	1	2	3	4	5	6	7	Foolish
6.	Negative	1	2	3	4	5	6	7	Positive

To compute your score:
Step One: Add the scores from items 2, 3, & 6.
Step Two: Add the scores from items 1, 4, & 5.
Step Three: Add 24 to Step One.
Step Four: Subtract Step Two from Step Three.

Scores should be between 6 and 42.

Sources:

McCroskey, J. C. (1966). *Experimental studies of the effects of ethos and evidence in persuasive communication.* Unpublished doctoral dissertation. Pennsylvania State University.

McCroskey, J. C., & Richmond, V. P. (1989). Bipolar scales. In P. Emmert & L. L. Barker (Eds.), *Measurement of Communication Behavior* (pp. 154–167). New York: Longman.

Figure 10.1 Generalized Attitude Measure

1.	Good	1	2	3	4	(5)	6	7	Bad
2.	Wrong	1	2	3	4	5	6	(7)	Right
3.	Harmful	1	2	3	4	5	6	(7)	Beneficial
4.	Fair	1	2	3	4	5	6	(7)	Unfair
5.	Wise	1	2	3	4	5	6	(7)	Foolish
6.	Negative	1	2	3	4	5	6	(7)	Positive

Figure 10.2 Generalized Attitude Measure Scored Inconsistently

In the first case in Figure 10.3, you have someone who has a very strong, positive attitude toward higher education with a score of 42. In the second case, you have someone who has a moderately negative attitude with a score of 36. While this example was completed looking only at a bipolar adjective scale, the same principle holds true for a Likert scale as well.

1.	Good ① 2 3 4 5 6 7 Bad
2.	Wrong 1 2 3 4 5 6 ⑦ Right
3.	Harmful 1 2 3 4 5 6 ⑦ Beneficial
4.	Fair ① 2 3 4 5 6 7 Unfair
5.	Wise ① 2 3 4 5 6 7 Foolish
6.	Negative 1 2 3 4 5 6 ⑦ Positive

OR

1.	Good 1 2 3 4 5 ⑥ 7 Bad
2.	Wrong 1 ② 3 4 5 6 7 Right
3.	Harmful 1 ② 3 4 5 6 7 Beneficial
4.	Fair 1 2 3 4 5 ⑥ 7 Unfair
5.	Wise 1 2 3 4 5 ⑥ 7 Foolish
6.	Negative 1 ② 3 4 5 6 7 Positive

Figure 10.3 Generalized Attitude Measure Scored Consistently

If you have two questions ("I like public speaking" and "I dislike public speaking") on a Likert scale with five steps running from 1 (*strongly disagree*) to 5 (*strongly agree*), a consistent participant may score the first question with 5 and the second question with 1. However, if a participant scored the first question as a 1 and the second question as a 1, we have a problem with the participant's consistency. While we've talked about how an individual responds to a scale in this section, when looking at the overall picture of reliability in a study we look at a sample's responses to a scale collectively, not individual scores.

Now that we've looked at some of the basic principles behind the concept of reliability, we will turn our attention to a number of statistical tests that can be used to examine reliability. Specifically, we will discuss the test–retest, alternate forms, split-half, Hoyt, and Cronbach's forms of reliability.

Test–Retest Reliability

One of the most obvious methods for testing the reliability of an instrument is to measure the same thing on more than one occasion and see if you get the same score. This is the essence of the test–retest approach to reliability. If we presume that the thing we are measuring does not change, our measure should produce the exact same score the second time we use it as it did the first time. Test–retest reliability for attitude measures is estimated by administering the instrument to the same group of people on two occasions, separated by some given amount of time. The subjects' scores at "time 1" and "time 2" are then subjected to statistical analysis to obtain a correlation coefficient. This correlation coefficient is referred to as a reliability coefficient, or an estimate of the degree of association between the scores at time 1 and time 2. Reliability coefficients may vary to the same degree that correlation coefficients signify consistent measurement. Good attitude-measuring instruments normally produce test–retest reliability coefficients of 0.70 or above, and many coefficients are 0.90 or above. If a researcher finds a test–retest reliability below 0.70, then her or his participants are not responding to the scale in a consistent manner. Conversely, test–retest reliability coefficients of about 0.90 indicate that people are filling out the scale at time 1 and time 2 in almost identical fashions.

Alternate Forms Reliability

The logic and procedure for alternate forms reliability estimation are essentially the same as that for test–retest reliability. In many cases, we can develop two attitude-measuring instruments to measure the same attitude. We may then administer the first instrument at time 1 and the second at time 2. We may then obtain the reliability coefficient for the two forms. Reliability coefficients for the alternate forms are normally somewhat lower than reliability coefficients developed through the test–retest procedure. The reason for this is that with the test–retest procedure there is no variety in the items administered from time 1 to time 2. No matter how carefully two forms of the same test are developed, there is always some variability in the items from time 1 to time 2. Thus, slightly lower reliability estimates should be expected.

Split-Half Reliability

In many instances it is impossible or economically infeasible to administer instruments to the same people on two occasions. Therefore, we need to be able to estimate the reliability of our measuring instrument with only one administration. The split-half approach to reliability is very similar to the test–retest and alternate forms procedures except that there is only one measurement period so there is no time delay that could be accompanied by changes in the subjects, which would be reflected in lower reliability estimates. The split-half reliability procedure involves computing two scores for each participant on the basis of one administration of the test. One of the scores comes from one half of the test and other score comes from the other half.

Several methods can be employed to divide the test in half in order to obtain the two scores. A common one is to have all the odd-numbered items compose one half of the test and the even-numbered items the other half. Alternatively, if we had 20 items in our test, we could take the first 10 items as one half of the test and the last 10 items as the other half of the test. A somewhat less frequently employed method is to randomly select half of the items on the test to compose the first half and employ the remainder to represent the second half. The reliability coefficients that are produced by correlating the two scores of the two halves of the test must be corrected before they are interpreted. In essence, we have the reliability for only half of the test, e.g., if we administered half of the items at time 1 and the other half at time 2 we would be presuming that we had a 10-item test at each time, but we have a 20-item test.

Hoyt Analysis of Variance Reliability

The test–retest and alternate forms reliability approaches have been referred to as *external* reliability estimates. The split-halves and Hoyt analysis of variance reliability procedures have been referred to as *internal* reliability estimates. Cyril Hoyt's (1941) procedure is another method of computing essentially the same type of reliability estimate as the split halves. While the Hoyt procedure is less frequently employed by most researchers than the split-halves procedure, it is generally considered to be a superior procedure on statistical grounds. In actual practice, there is usually little difference between the reliability coefficients produced by the two procedures, but the Hoyt estimates tend to be slightly lower.

CRONBACH'S ALPHA RELIABILITY

The type of scalar reliability most commonly used by social scientists is the single administration reliability, and the most popular single administration reliability test is the Cronbach Alpha Reliability test (Cronbach, 1951). The Cronbach Alpha Reliability test is probably the most consistently reported reliability test in the social sciences, including communication. Since Cronbach's alpha is the most commonly used form of reliability testing, we will discuss how to go about determining a scale's Cronbach's alpha and how you report alpha in a research project.

For the purposes of this analysis, we will use the Generalized Attitude Scale data gathered for this book. As we saw in Figure 10.1, the Generalized Attitude Scale has six bipolar items with a 7-step scale between the two adjectives. To determine the alpha reliability, all of the items need to be recoded so that all of the positively worded items with low scores (good, fair, and wise) are scored with a 7 instead of a 1. For example, if a participant circled a "2" on the first row (Good), that number would be reflected as a "6." We do this recoding so that all of the positive words (good, right, beneficial, fair, wise, and positive) receive high scores of "7" and all of the negative words (bad, wrong, harmful, unfair, foolish, and negative) receive low scores of "1." You cannot determine the alpha reliability of a scale until this recoding has occurred.

We introduced in Chapter 8 two basic statistical packages commonly used by communication researchers: SPSS and SAS. We should note that both SPSS and SAS have very different methods for recoding items, so please read the individual instruction books for each software package to learn how to recode items for your own research purposes.

COMPUTER PRINTOUTS OF CRONBACH'S ALPHA

Most researchers no longer compute statistics by hand. Computing statistics by hand is very dangerous because humans make errors very easily when handling large quantities of data. To avoid simple computational mistakes, a variety of computer programs have been created to aid in this process. The two most commonly used statistical software packages used by communication researchers are SPSS and SAS. If you look on the CD-ROM that came with this book, you will find a folder marked "Book Data Sets." In this folder you will find folders for SPSS data sets, SAS data sets, and Note Pad Data sets. The SPSS and SAS data sets can be used only by SPSS and SAS software packages. If you do not have SPSS or SAS but have a different statistical software package, you can use the Note Pad Data sets to import the data into whatever program you prefer to use. However, we will only be discussing how to read and interpret results from SPSS and SAS in this book. To calculate your own alpha reliability, open the file called "Recoded Data Set." The "Recoded Data Set" has already recoded all of the scales using the coding schemes discussed in Chapter 7.

SPSS and Cronbach's Alpha

After opening SPSS, a window will pop up called "SPSS for Windows." In this window, you will notice that the "Open an existing data source" button is preselected, so you can either scroll through a list of previously used data files or select "More Files . . . " to find the data file you are attempting to find. Once you have either selected the correct data file or the "More Files" option, click "OK." If you chose "More Files" before you clicked "OK" in the previous box, the "Open File" window will appear on your screen. At this point you just need to search your computer (hard drive or CD-ROM) to find the data file you are attempting to use. If you do not know how to look for a file on your hard drive or CD-ROM, you may want to pick up a simple MS Windows manual at your local bookstore.

If you are looking on the CD-ROM that came with this book, you will find a folder called "Book Data Sets." You can then select the SPSS Data Sets folder. You can either double click the SPSS Data Sets folder or single click the folder and then click Open to open this folder. Once you are inside the SPSS Data Sets folder, you will find a number of different SPSS files that are designed to be used with your textbook. The "Main SPSS Data Set" is the collected data set without any changes or alterations to the data itself. The file marked "Recoded Data Set" is the file with the data that has already been recoded for your convenience, so the data can be easily manipulated in SPSS. When you finally open the file you want to work with, your computer will import the data into the SPSS window. If you encounter a problem opening the data file, go back to the beginning and repeat the steps or consult your computer's owner's manual for further instructions.

To conduct Cronbach's alpha, click on the drop-down menu under the word "Analyze." Then scroll over the word "Scale." When you scroll over "Scale," a menu will pop out to the left. You want to click on the word "Reliability Analysis." At this point, a window will open called "Reliability Analysis." If you did not get this window, backtrack and try to find out what went wrong. In the "Reliability Analysis" window, there are three major scroll- or drop-down boxes. On the upper left, you will find a scrolling box with all of the variables in the data set, and on the right you will see a scrolling box with nothing in it labeled "Items." Underneath the box with all of your variables is a drop-down box with different types of reliability formats. Notice that the screen comes up with Cronbach's alpha reliability preselected for use. To run a Cronbach's alpha, simply highlight the scale items that you are wanting to analyze. So, to run Cronbach's Reliability for the Attitude Scale you need to scroll down the list of variables until you find the variables listed as ATT1–ATT6. Depending on which version of SPSS you are using, ATT1 may come up as "Attitude About Higher Education" in the variable list. To highlight more items than can be seen at one time, click the first item and hold your "shift" button on your keyboard. Then scroll down to the last item and (still holding your shift button) click the last item, which will allow you to highlight all six attitude items. Now simply send the six items to the "Items" box by clicking the arrow in between the two boxes. If this has been done correctly, you will now see all six attitude variables in the box on the right-hand side of the screen. At this point you can do one of two things: you can click OK and get a simple printout of reliability (Figure 10.4), or you can click on the "Statistics" button at the bottom of the screen. Let's click on the Statistics button.

When you click on the Statistics button in the "Reliability Analysis" window, the "Reliability Analysis: Statistics" window will appear. You'll see lots of different types of tests that can be conducted. Most of these qualify as advanced statistical tests, so we will not explain what they mean in this book. However, in the upper left-hand corner, you will find the "Descriptives for" box. These statistics give basic information about each item, the overall reliability of the scale, and the reliability of the scale if we deleted one item. Once you have selected these three options, simply hit the Continue button. Once you have finished with the "Reliability Analysis: Statistics" window, you will be taken back to the "Reliability Analysis" window, and you are ready to run your Cronbach's alpha Reliability test, so simply hit OK on the right-hand side of the window. You will be given two different sets of information at this point. You will see the exact same reliability information that was given to you in Figure 10.4, plus you'll be given the information you asked for about the descriptive statistics for the scale and the alpha reliability if the scale is deleted (Figure 10.5).

In Figure 10.4 you will find three boxes. The first box is a warning that SPSS has opted not to show you the covariance matrix, which for our purposes in this textbook is perfectly

Reliability

Warnings

The space saver method is used. That is, the covariance matrix is not calculated or used in the analysis.

Case Processing Summary

		N	%
Cases	Valid	314	96.6
	Excluded[a]	11	3.4
	Total	325	100.0

[a] Listwise deletion based on all variables in the procedure.

Reliability Statistics

Cronbach's Alpha	N of Items
.915	6

Figure 10.4 SPSS Cronbach's Alpha Reliability

Item Statistics

	Mean	Std. Deviation	N
Attitude about "Higher Education"	6.2516	1.17362	314
att2	6.0924	1.22059	314
att3	6.2516	1.11785	314
att4	5.5796	1.39889	314
att5	6.0605	1.25101	314
att6	6.1656	1.08929	314

Item-Total Statistics

	Scale Mean if Item Deleted	Scale Variance if Item Deleted	Corrected Item-Total Correlation	Cronbach's Alpha if Item Deleted
Attitude about "Higher Education"	30.1497	26.690	.754	.901
att2	30.3089	25.882	.792	.896
att3	30.1497	27.073	.764	.900
att4	30.8217	26.013	.648	.920
att5	30.3408	25.446	.808	.893
att6	30.2357	26.570	.842	.891

Scale Statistics

Mean	Variance	Std. Deviation	N of Items
36.4013	37.212	6.10019	6

Figure 10.5 SPSS Cronbach's Alpha Reliability–Other Statistics

alright. The second box is the Case Process Summary box, which tells you how many participants have scores for the Generalized Attitude Measure that were used in the calculating of Cronbach's alpha ($N = 314$). The last box is the box with the reported reliability, 0.915, and the number of scale items ($N = 6$) that were used in the calculation of the reliability. Using the following information, the scales reliability can be interpreted:

0.90+	Excellent
0.80–0.90	Good
0.70–0.80	Respectable
0.65–070	Minimally acceptable
0.60–0.65	Undesirable
0.60 ↓	Unacceptable

In Figure 10.5 you are also presented with three boxes: Item Statistics, Item-Total Statistics, and Scale Statistics. The Item Statistics box presents you with the basic descriptive statistics (mean, standard deviation, and number of participants) for each individual scale item. The Item-Total Statistics box enables you to see what would happen to the overall scale if a single item from the scale was left out of the scale. The most important column in this box, for this discussion, is the last column (Cronbach's Alpha if Item Deleted), which is the column that let's us see if our alpha reliability can be helped if we drop an item from the scale. For example, if we dropped the first item from the scale, which would be the Good/Bad item, the alpha reliability would drop to 0.901, which is below the overall scale reliability of 0.915. In the world of reliability, the higher the reliability (the closer your score is to 1), the more consistent your participants have been when filling out the scale. So, when examining Figure 10.5, are there any items that, if we dropped them from the scale, would increase our overall reliability? The answer is yes. If you look in the Cronbach's Alpha if Item Deleted column next to Item 4, you will see that the overall reliability of the scale would increase from 0.915 (overall reliability with 6 items) to 0.92 (with item 4 dropped from the scale). Overall, the slight bump up in reliability is not going to be that meaningful, so the item should be kept. However, often you'll find that if you drop one item you'll get a significant bump in your reliability (e.g., 0.65 to 0.89), so dropping an item from a scale can often be necessary.

SAS and Cronbach's Alpha

To calculate a Cronbach's alpha using SAS, you will use a variation of the Procedure statement CORR. The PROC statement used to analyze this example using SAS is:

PROC CORR ALPHA NOMISS;

VAR ATT1—ATT6;

The information contained in Figure 10.6 is exactly the same as the information computed by SPSS in Figures 10.4 and 10.5, but presented in a different fashion. You'll notice that Figure 10.6 is presented in four different table blocks. You should be warned that SAS does not present information in clear tables, but we have opted to present it to you in this fashion to make it easier to understand here. The first box in Figure 10.6 contains all of the basic descriptive statistics of the individual items. This box does contain some additional information beyond N, Mean, and Standard Deviation. The fifth column contains the Sum of all of the participants' scores on this item. You should be able to divide the Sum for ATT1 (1963) by N (number of participants) and receive the mean for ATT1, or $1963/314 = 6.251592357$. SAS only rounds out five or six places, depending on the mathematical function. The last two columns present you with the minimum score seen for this item (1) and the maximum score seen for this item (7). You'll notice that on ATT3, the lowest reported score was a "2" instead of a "1."

```
                            The CORR Procedure

            6 Variables:  ATT1    ATT2    ATT3    ATT4    ATT5    ATT6

                           Simple Statistics

    Variable      N       Mean     Std Dev      Sum     Minimum    Maximum

    ATT1        314     6.25159    1.17362     1963     1.00000    7.00000
    ATT2        314     6.09236    1.22059     1913     1.00000    7.00000
    ATT3        314     6.25159    1.11785     1963     2.00000    7.00000
    ATT4        314     5.57962    1.39889     1752     1.00000    7.00000
    ATT5        314     6.06051    1.25101     1903     1.00000    7.00000
    ATT6        314     6.16561    1.08929     1936     1.00000    7.00000
```

```
                      Cronbach Coefficient Alpha

              Variables                    Alpha
              ƒƒƒƒƒƒƒƒƒƒƒƒƒƒƒƒƒƒƒƒƒƒƒƒƒƒƒƒƒƒƒƒƒ
              Raw                         0.915407
              Standardized                0.919153
```

```
                    Raw Variables              Standardized Variables

        Deleted      Correlation                 Correlation
        Variable     with Total      Alpha       with Total      Alpha
        ƒƒƒƒƒƒƒƒƒƒƒƒƒƒƒƒƒƒƒƒƒƒƒƒƒƒƒƒƒƒƒƒƒƒƒƒƒƒƒƒƒƒƒƒƒƒƒƒƒƒƒƒƒƒƒƒƒƒƒƒƒƒƒƒƒƒ
        ATT1          0.754128      0.901184      0.755499      0.906443
        ATT2          0.792354      0.895725      0.798538      0.900506
        ATT3          0.764154      0.900224      0.768055      0.904720
        ATT4          0.647715      0.919951      0.647516      0.920929
        ATT5          0.808284      0.893346      0.808427      0.899128
        ATT6          0.841978      0.890637      0.843664      0.894180
```

```
                            The CORR Procedure

                 Pearson Correlation Coefficients, N = 314
                       Prob > |r| under H0: Rho=0

              ATT1       ATT2       ATT3       ATT4       ATT5       ATT6

    ATT1    1.00000    0.69741    0.64808    0.52583    0.69899    0.65206
                       <.0001     <.0001     <.0001     <.0001     <.0001

    ATT2    0.69741    1.00000    0.70411    0.52427    0.68888    0.76221
            <.0001                <.0001     <.0001     <.0001     <.0001

    ATT3    0.64808    0.70411    1.00000    0.54185    0.62877    0.74494
            <.0001     <.0001                <.0001     <.0001     <.0001

    ATT4    0.52583    0.52427    0.54185    1.00000    0.62434    0.60564
            <.0001     <.0001     <.0001                <.0001     <.0001

    ATT5    0.69899    0.68888    0.62877    0.62434    1.00000    0.77100
            <.0001     <.0001     <.0001     <.0001                <.0001

    ATT6    0.65206    0.76221    0.74494    0.60564    0.77100    1.00000
            <.0001     <.0001     <.0001     <.0001     <.0001
```

Figure 10.6 SAS Cronbach's Alpha Reliability

The second box in Figure 10.6 represents Cronbach's alpha. You'll see two different alpha reliabilities reported: one raw and one standardized. While there are times when the standardized can be appropriate, the raw reliability (0.915407) is most generally reported for alpha.

In the third box you will see the same information for determining if an item should be removed from your scale to increase the reliability. You'll see that SAS separates these out into two columns: one for increasing your raw reliability and one for increasing your standardized reliability. Again, you'll notice that if you drop item 4 you will receive a small increase in your scale's reliability.

The fourth box contains the correlations between all of the items on the scale itself. (We will discuss correlations later in Chapter 19.) Now that we've shown you the basic printouts for Cronbach's alpha, let's see how you can write up this information using APA style.

APA Write-Up

The Generalized Attitude Measure is a scale originally created by McCroskey (1966) and later validated by McCroskey (2006) as a tool for determining someone's overall attitude about a specific subject. The Generalized Attitude Measure is measured using a six-item bipolar adjective scale with seven steps, which gives the scale a range from 6 to 42. For the purposes of this study, the Generalized Attitude Measure was utilized to determine the attitude of participants about higher education. The scale is coded so that higher scores represent more positive attitudes about higher education. The alpha reliability found for the Generalized Attitude Measure in the current study was 0.92 ($M = 36.40$, $SD = 6.10$).

APA Discussion

The first part of the APA write-up is a simple description of the scale itself. In this case, the scale was originally created by McCroskey in 1966 as part of his dissertation, but was then later validated and used in more research by McCroskey (2006). The second part of the APA write-up clearly explains what kind of scale is being used. In this case, the scale consists of six bipolar items with a seven-step scale in between the adjectives (1, 2, 3, 4, 5, 6, 7). The next part of the write-up explains to the reader that higher scores represent more positive attitudes about higher education. This step is often skipped by researchers and can end up leading to results that are extremely confusing to interpret. Finally, the scale's reliability is presented to the reader. Immediately after the reliability is presented, you'll notice that the mean (M) and standard deviation (SD) are presented as well. (Notice that "M" and "SD" are italicized, but the equal signs and numbers are not.)

Alpha Reliabilities from This Book

Now that we've looked at the reporting of attitude scale used in the creation of the data set for this book, you might be wondering what all of the reliabilities are for the various scales used in this book. Figure 10.7 has all of the alpha reliability information for every scale used in the creation of the data set that accompanies this book along with the means and standard deviations. In Figure 10.8, you will see the corresponding APA write-ups for each scale.

Reliabilities in the Real World

This book comes with a CD-ROM that has a number of different research articles on it published in *Communication Research Reports* and *Communication Quarterly* to help you

Variable	Alpha reliability	Mean	Standard deviation
Communication apprehension			
Group CA	.87	15.41	5.08
Meeting CA	.86	15.71	5.06
Interpersonal CA	.81	14.98	4.46
Public CA	.86	18.44	5.68
Total CA	.94	64.54	17.17
Ethnocentrism	.85	37.54	8.77
Humor assessment	.91	62.06	9.82
Nonverbal Immediacy Scale—Self-Report	.90	95.23	13.19
Sociocommunicative orientation			
Assertiveness	.82	36.29	5.95
Responsiveness	.89	39.39	6.20
Willingness to communicate			
Contexts			
Group WTC	.52	74.85	16.24
Meeting WTC	.59	68.74	19.17
Interpersonal WTC	.50	74.68	16.59
Public WTC	.65	67.25	19.72
Audience			
Stranger WTC	.88	48.29	25.66
Acquaintance WTC	.78	77.43	18.62
Friend WTC	.71	88.45	13.56
Overall WTC	.87	71.36	15.66
Belief that every college student should take public speaking	.98	20.44	10.01
Attitude towards higher education	.92	36.40	6.10

Figure 10.7 Reliabilities for Book Variables

PRCA-24. The Personal Report of Communication Apprehension-24 was created by McCroskey (1982) to measure an individual's level of fear or anxiety associated with either real or anticipated communication with another person or persons. The scale consists of 24 Likert items ranging from (1) *strongly agree* to (5) *strongly disagree*. This scale has a range from 24 to 120 with higher scores indicating stronger levels of anxiety associated with communication. The alpha reliability found for the PRCA-24 in the current study was .94 ($M = 64.54$, $SD = 17.17$).

Ethnocentrism. The Ethnocentrism Scale was created by Neuliep and McCroskey (1997) to measure an individual's tendency to feel that her or his culture is the center of the universe. The revised version of the scale employed here (Neuliep & McCroskey, 2000; McCroskey, 2001) consists of 22 Likert items ranging from (1) *strongly disagree* to (5) *strongly agree*. Fifteen of the items are scored; the remaining items are used as distracters. This scale has a range from 15 to 75, with higher scores indicating stronger ethnocentric attitudes. The alpha reliability found for the Ethnocentrism scale in the current study was .85 ($M = 37.54$, $SD = 8.77$).

Humor Assessment. The Humor Assessment instrument was created by Wrench and Richmond (2004) to measure an individual's use of humor as a communicative device in interpersonal relationships. The scale was originally published in Richmond, Wrench, and Gorham (2001) as a tool for teachers to assess their own use of humor in the classroom. The HA was then validated by Wrench and McCroskey (2001), who found that it functioned distinctly different from M. Booth-Butterfield and S. Booth-Butterfield's (1991) Humor

Figure 10.8 APA Write-Ups for Reliabilities

Orientation scale. The HA consists of 16 Likert-type items range from (1) *strongly disagree* to (5) *strongly agree*. This scale has a range from 16 to 80, with higher scores indicating higher usage of humor as a communicative tactic. The alpha reliability found for the HA in the current study was .91 ($M = 62.06$, $SD = 9.82$).

Nonverbal Immediacy Scale. The Nonverbal Immediacy Scale was created by Richmond, McCroskey, and Johnson (2003) to measure a receiver's perceived nonverbal immediacy between a her or himself and a source. The scale consists of 26 Likert type items ranging from (1) *strongly disagree* to (5) *strongly agree*. This scale has a range from 26 to 130, with higher scores indicating stronger degrees of nonverbal immediacy. The alpha reliability found for the Nonverbal Immediacy Scale in the current study was .90 ($M = 95.22$, $SD = 13.19$).

Sociocommunicative Orientation. The Sociocommunicative Orientation scale was created by Richmond and McCroskey (1985) as an instructional tool to examine the extent to which individuals use assertive or responsive communication. The instrument was first utilized in research by Thompson, Ishii, and Klopf (1990) and Ishii, Thompson, and Klopf (1990) to examine cultural differences in assertive and responsive communication. After the publication of these two articles, Richmond and McCroskey (1990) demonstrated the reliability and dimensionality of the measure itself. The sociocommunicative orientation scale consists of 10 items on each factor for a total of 20 items. Participants are asked to respond to short descriptive phrases that range from one to five words in length that indicate ways in which they may communicate. The measure asks a participant to respond in terms of how well the item applies to her or him using a Likert scale from (1) *strongly disagree that it applies* to (5) *strongly agree that it applies*. Each subscale has a range from 10 to 50. The alpha reliability found for assertiveness in the current study was .82 ($M = 36.29$, $SD = 5.95$), and the alpha reliability for responsiveness was .89 ($M = 39.39$, $SD = 6.20$). Higher scores for each subscale represent higher levels of that concept.

Willingness to Communicate. The Willingness to Communication instrument was devised by McCroskey (1992) to measures a person's willingness to initiate communication with another person or persons. The scale consists of 20 items. Each of the items is designed to measure whether an individual would initiate communication in a specific situation or with a specific individual. Eight of the items are fillers and 12 are scored as part of the scale. Using a 101-point range from 0 (never) to 100 (always), participants are asked to indicate the percentage of time they would choose to communicate in each type of situation. Ultimately, the scores on the 12 items are added together to create a composite score with higher scores indicating a higher willingness to communicate. The alpha reliability found for Willingness to Communicate Scale in the current study was .87 ($M = 71.36$, $SD = 15.66$).

Generalized Belief Scale. The Generalized Belief Scale was created by McCroskey (1966) and validated by McCroskey and Richmond (1996). The Generalized Belief Measure was created by McCroskey (1966) as a way to measure beliefs about specific concepts. By attaining an individual's general belief about a given topic, the researcher can measure the degree to which an individual believes in a given statement. The statement measured in this study was "Everyone Should Be Required to Take Public Speaking in College." The belief statement is then measured using a five-item semantic differential scale with seven steps, which gives the scale a range from 5 to 35. The scale is coded so that higher scores represent stronger beliefs. The alpha reliability found for Generalized Belief Scale in the current study was .98 ($M = 20.44$, $SD = 10.01$).

Generalized Attitude Measure. The Generalized Attitude Measure was a scale originally created by McCroskey (1966) and later validated by McCroskey and Richmond (1989) as a tool for determining someone's overall attitude about a specific subject. The Generalized Attitude Measure is measured using a six- item semantic differential scale with seven steps, which gives the scale a range from 6 to 42. For the purposes of this study, the Generalized Attitude Measure was utilized to determine the attitude of participants about higher education. The scale is coded so that higher scores represent more positive attitudes about higher education. The alpha reliability found for Generalized Attitude Scale in the current study was .92 ($M = 36.40$, $SD = 6.10$).

Scale tested	Alpha reliabilities
McCroskey, Richmond, Johnson, & Smith (2004)	
Study #1 (Organizational Orientations Scales)	
Ambivalent	.91
Indifferent	.79
Upward Mobile	.66
Study #2 (Initial Validation)	
Job Satisfaction	.97
Personal Report of Communication Apprehension–24	.95
Self Report of Immediacy Behaviors	.84
Assertiveness	.86
Responsiveness	.88
Study #3 (Measurement Improvement)	
Upward Mobile	.84
Ambivalent	.89
Indifferent	.79
Study #4 (Etiology and Outcomes)	
Organizational Orientations	
Upward Mobile	.85
Ambivalent	.88
Indifferentw	.80
Job Satisfaction	.96
Source Credibility	
Competence	.89
Caring/Goodwill	.94
Trustworthiness	.93
Eysenck's Big Three	
Extraversion	.78
Neuroticism	.82
Psychoticism	.65
Thomas, Richmond, & McCroskey (1994)	
Perceived Nonverbal Immediacy Behavior Scale	.83
Assertiveness	.90
Responsiveness	.91
Wrench & Richmond (2004)	
Humor Assessment	
Student Affective Learning	.95
Teacher Evaluation	
Affective Learning	.87
Nonverbal Immediacy Measure	.81
Student Motivation	.81
Teacher Credibility	.89
Competence	
Trustworthiness	.80
Caring/Goodwill	.86
	.86
Weber, Fornash, Corrigan, & Neupauer (2003)	
7-Item Multiple Choice Quiz	
Learner Empowerment Scale	.73
Impact	
Competence	.71
Meaningfulness	.85
Nonverbal Immediacy Scale	.85
	Not reported

Figure 10.9 Article Alpha Reliabilities

Cheseboro (1999)	
Listening Style	
People	.61
Action	.61
Time	.66
Content	.54
Conversational Sensitivity	.85
Punyanunt (2000)	
Behavior Alteration Techniques	
Effectiveness of Humor	.92
Uses of Humor	.94
	.95
Wrench & Booth-Butterfield (2003)	
Humor Orientation	.91
Source Credibility	
Competence	.86
Trustworthiness	.90
Caring/Goodwill	.88
Compliance Gaining Questionnaire	
Expectancies/Consequences	.69
Relationship/Identification	.82
Values/Obligations	.74
Patient Satisfaction	
Cognitive	.89
Affective	.92
Behavioral	.85
Rocca & Vogl-Bauer (1999)	
Verbal Aggression Scale	.81
Sports Spectator Identification Scale	.93
Sports Identification Behavior Scale	
Fan Display	.78
Verbal Response	.93
Violent Response	.85

further understand how research actually happens. Figure 10.9 contains the alpha reliabilities for every scale used in any of the articles on the CD-ROM itself.

You'll notice that not all of the reported reliabilities are either good (0.80–0.90) or excellent (0.90+). In fact, if you look at the Cheseboro (1999) article reliability results, the listening style scale clearly has a reliability problem. On this scale, the content factor is below 0.60, so it's unacceptable; people and action are between 0.60 and 0.65, so they're undesirable; and time is 0.66, which is minimally acceptable. In essence, people are not very consistent when filling out this scale, so the scale clearly has some problems and is not very reliable. So, how can someone make a scale more reliable?

Improving Reliability of Measurement

We measure things because we want to know what they "are." Thus, we measure attitude because we want to know what it is. Reliability is crucial to our measurement. If we measure something on several different occasions and never get anywhere near the same score, there are only two conclusions that we may draw: either the thing we are measuring is constantly changing or our measuring instrument is worthless. Presuming that we are attempting to measure a reasonably stable characteristic, the latter conclusion is probably the most appropriate. Reliability is absolutely crucial to measurement. Because there are excellent methods of estimating the reliability of our measuring instruments and because there are ways of improving instruments that lack reliability, there is no excuse for the social scientist to employ measures that lack adequate reliability. Let us consider a few of the ways in which reliability may be increased.

1. *Item construction*. Nothing contributes more to unreliability in a measuring instrument than bad items. If an item is ambiguous, it will produce variable responses both among people and with the same person on different occasions. At this point, we will merely suggest that the best way to improve reliability is to improve your items using the suggestions for scale item writing from the previous chapter.

2. *Length of the Instrument*. Reliability is directly associated with the number of items included in the measuring instrument. Other things being equal, a twenty-item test will be more reliable than a ten-item test. If everything possible has been done to improve the quality of individual items and the reliability is still somewhat below the level desired, creation of more items of the same type should increase the reliability of the instrument. Obviously, there are limitations normally imposed on the length that an instrument may be. Extreme increases in the length of the instrument may actually increase unreliability because subjects may become fatigued and merely record responses at random.

3. *Administration of the Test*. Measures should always be administered under standard, well-controlled conditions. If the instructions that are given the subjects are ambiguous, the subjects may interpret how they are supposed to respond differentially and thus, contribute to unreliability. Similarly, if the psychological conditions surrounding the subjects differ, this may influence the way the subjects respond. For example, one group of subjects may be in a friendly environment and do their best to record accurate responses while another group of subjects may take a dislike to the person administering the instrument and give random responses. In such cases, the reliability of the instrument will be estimated at much below what the actual reliability of the instrument could be.

Validity

In the first part of this chapter, we introduced the concept of reliability; in the last half of this chapter, we will discuss another extremely important concept in measurement, validity. Validity *is the degree to which the instrument measures what it is intended to measure.* For example, would you look at a clock and say, "It's 50° outside"? Of course not, because a clock is a measurement of time, not a measurement of temperature. If you want to know how hot it is outside, you look at a thermometer. In social scientific research, we must be equally concerned with whether or not our measuring instruments actually measure what they are intended to measure. Let's look at a Likert-type item (1, *strongly disagree*, to 5, *strongly agree*), "Children should be seen and not heard." Would you expect to see this item on a scale intended to measure happiness? Of course you wouldn't. However, this item could be on a scale designed to measure people's traditional views of children. Ultimately, when researchers talk about a scale's validity, we are discussing whether or not a created scale actually measures what we say we're measuring. Now that we've explained the general concept of validity, let's look at some examples of validity issues in communication research.

A communication researcher is in the process of creating a new measure to examine individuals who experience apprehension during social settings. Because she wants to assess the efficacy of helping people who experience this form of communication apprehension, she creates a physiological tool that can measure blood pressure, heart rate, and galvanic skin responses. She then takes to a bar some participants who she knows experience communication apprehension and some people who do not. If her new device is valid, the participants who are most afraid of communicating in social settings should register the highest ratings (increased blood pressure, heart rates, and galvanic skin responses) on her new device.

Another researcher is in the process of creating a new test for measuring nonverbal responses during greetings. Rather than creating a survey and asking people how they interact with people when they greet them, he develops an observational checklist for measuring greeting behaviors. He believes that greeting behaviors will be distinctly more intimate depending on the length of time people have known each other. He then trains a few coders to use the checklist and brings in pairs of people (strangers, acquaintances, friends, family members, and romantic partners) into a lab. After separating the pairs for an hour, he brings the two people back together in a room with a one-way mirror, and the coders watch how the two people interact when they see each other again using the newly design observational checklist.

A third research team, Sandy and William, are in the process of trying to create a new scale to examine different forms of communicative humor in the classroom. Based on research by Wanzer and Frymier (1999), Sandy and William know that students perceive humor as either appropriate or inappropriate. Wanzer and Frymier designated appropriate classroom humor as content-related humor, humor not related to content, impersonation, nonverbal behaviors, disparaging humor, humorous props, sarcasm, and unintentional humor; inappropriate classroom humor was designated as humor that makes fun of a student, humor-based stereotypes, failed humor, sexual humor, irrelevant humor, sarcasm, swearing, joking about serious issues, personal humor (inside jokes), and sick humor. Sandy and William used this typology of humor behaviors from Wanzer and Frymier (1999) to create a new scale to measure appropriate and inappropriate classroom humor and then distribute the scales to a large group of undergraduates, asking them to rate a professor in whose classroom the students had been that day or the day before.

The question that you may be asking by this point is, "How good will these new measures be?" Are they accurate measures for examining anxiety, nonverbal greetings, and classroom humor? What if the anxiety measure ends up measuring sexual attraction or drinking behavior, of which there is a lot in a bar setting? Maybe the greeting checklist is incomplete and only has a handful of behaviors on it, like hand shaking, hugging, and kissing, which are predominant greeting patterns in the United States, but it may not include greeting patterns between people who come from other cultures. Maybe the new classroom humor scale ends up measuring quantity of humor used and not appropriate versus inappropriate humor in the classroom setting. In essence, how can we determine if a new measure employed in research is actually measuring what it alleges to be measuring? Social scientists have been examining these types of questions for years and have devised a number of strategies for combating these problems. But ultimately, these questions concern what researchers call a measure's validity.

As important as reliability is to measurement, validity is even more important. Validity may be defined simply as the degree to which the measuring instrument measures what it is intended to measure. If we wish to measure the number of apples produced in a county, it will do us no good whatsoever to count the number of oranges produced in that county. Similarly, if we want to know a person's attitude toward rap music, it will probably do us little good to ask him questions about his relationship with his mother. There are three primary approaches to validity: face or content validity, predictive or concurrent validity, and construct or factorial validity. Let us consider each in turn.

FACE OR CONTENT VALIDITY

Face or content validity does not involve the use of correlation coefficients. Rather, it is a subjective type of validity criterion. The researcher or someone he or she employs for the task examines the content of the measuring instrument to see whether on its "face" it appears to be related to that which the researcher wished to measure. In addition, it is asked whether or not the items on the measure are reasonably representative of the universe of possible items that could be included. Unfortunately, because of its inherently subjective nature, face or content validity is the validity approach most commonly employed by researchers. In some circumstances this is not as serious a drawback as in others. As long as her or his measure is susceptible to influence as a result of the message manipulations, the instrument is "valid" for his purposes. However, when the social scientist is concerned with predicting behaviors, there is no true test of validity except how well it predicts those behaviors.

CRITERION VALIDITY

Criterion validity is concerned with how accurately a new measure can predict a well-accepted criterion or previously validated concept. For example, imagine if we wanted to test a newly developed anxiety tool, we could have people fill out the Personal Report of Communication Apprehension-24 (PRCA-24) and then give a speech. People who register the highest on our new anxiety tool should also have higher scores on the PRCA-24. To determine whether or not the anxiety tool corresponds with scores on the PRCA-24, we calculate the correlation between the two measures, and the end result would be a correlation coefficient. The coefficient estimates the degree to which a measuring instrument will predict a value on some outside criterion. That criterion might be the behavior of the person whose attitude was measured, or it might be some other measure of attitude. If our theory suggests that a high attitude score should be accompanied by a given behavior whereas a moderate score would be less associated with that behavior and a low score would not be associated with that behavior, then we can obtain a correlation between the attitude score obtained by subjects on our instrument and their subsequent behaviors. That correlation coefficient is referred to as a validity coefficient, and if it is reasonably high, we may suggest that our measure is a valid one. On the other hand, if there is no correlation or very low correlation, we have an indication that our instrument is invalid for making this kind of prediction. Few attitude-measuring instruments are actually submitted to the test of predictive validity. This is because, in most cases, we are not interested in predicting a specific behavior. If the scores are highly correlated, we have an indication that one is to the degree of the correlation as valid as the other. There are three subtypes of criterion validity that we should discuss briefly: predictive, concurrent, and retrospective.

Predictive

Predictive or prospective validity is a subset of criterion validity and is concerned with whether or not a person's score on a new measure can be used to predict future scores on another measure. For example, maybe we have 10 teachers all teaching the same class and using the same textbook, syllabus, and tests. We measure students' perceptions of teacher use of appropriate and inappropriate humor utilizing our new measure. Previous research has shown that the use of humor in the classroom can lead to higher levels of learning. If our new tool is truly measuring the use of appropriate and inappropriate humor in the classroom, we could predict that teachers who use the most appropriate humor and the least amounts of inappropriate humor should have students who perform better on the final examination. In essence, we are using our newly created scale to predict scores on a future scale.

Concurrent

An alternative to predictive validity when examining criterion validity is to examine a measure's concurrent validity. In concurrent validity, a researcher obtains the score for the new measure and the score for the criterion measure at the same point and then determines how strongly the two scores correlate. For example, if we are testing our new apprehension-measuring tool, we could have people fill out the State Communication Apprehension Measure (SCAM), a previously validated scale for examining state levels of communication apprehension, while wearing the new apprehension-measuring tool in a social setting. In essence, if our new apprehension-measuring tool is an accurate measure, it should strongly relate to an individual's score on the SCAM.

Retrospective

The last way to examine criterion validity is to examine a newly developed scales retro spective or postdictive validity. Retrospective validity occurs when a researcher has previously measured the criterion and then attempts to relate it to a newly developed measure at a later point. For example, maybe in a previous study a researcher examined the level of intimacy between different pairs of people. Later he develops the new checklist for greeting behaviors and has all of those individuals come back together and watches how they interact with each other when they enter into the laboratory setting. In essence, the researcher is using the previously collected measure (perceived intimacy between two people) and correlating it with the new measure (observational greeting checklist). Another way to do retrospective validity is to have people recall information from an earlier time or use previous record searches. Maybe a researcher wants to determine if a person's level of communication apprehension as a child correlates with her or his level of communication apprehension as an adult, so the researcher will have the participants' parents rate their level of communication apprehension as a child and then correlate that with a newly developed measure in the present. Maybe a researcher will look through old report cards looking for incidents of "doesn't talk," "is very shy," or "is very quiet" in report card notes and then quantify these and correlate them with the newly developed apprehension measure. In essence, there are multiple ways that retrospective validity can be accomplished, as long as the criterion was previously collected and is being used at a later point to relate to the newly developed measure.

CONSTRUCT OR FACTORIAL VALIDITY

An important property of all hypothetical constructs is that they are a result of theoretical development. In Chapter 9 we discussed the development of theoretical constructs, and construct validity therefore is a validity test of the theoretical construct itself. If we theorize, for example, that people with highly intense attitudes are less subject to influence by a persuader than are people with moderately intense attitudes, we must develop an attitude measure that taps the intensity dimension. We may then engage in an experiment in which we administer a persuasive treatment to subjects with an intense attitude and to subjects with only a moderately intense attitude. If the predicted difference in amount of attitude change is observed on our measure, we have not only confirmed our theory, but also have an indication that our measuring instrument validly taps the intensity dimension. The difficulty with this approach to validity is that if our predicted effects do not obtain, we don't know whether it is because of our faulty theory or because our instrument is invalid.

Another approach to construct validity that is less susceptible to the confounding with theory than the approach just mentioned is the measurement of known groups. If we are trying to develop an instrument to measure ethnic intolerance, we may administer that measure to members of the Ku Klux Klan (a group known for intolerance) and members of B'nai B'rith (a Jewish organization that fights anti-Semitism, racism, and bigotry while striving for human rights and peace throughout the world). If our measure is reasonably valid we should observe very large differences in the scores between these two groups, unless the former group was much more tolerant than is customarily presumed or the latter group is much less tolerant than is customarily presumed.

A third approach to construct validity that almost deserves a category to itself is factorial validity. Factorial validity is based on the statistical technique known as "factor analysis." Factor analysis is a highly sophisticated statistical technique for examining a series of items to see which items correlate well with one another but are not highly correlated with other items or groups of items. Simply put, factor analysis can tell us how many groups of items, or factors, there are in our instrument. This approach to validity was employed by McCroskey (1966) in the development of measuring instruments to tap source credibility (the attitude of communication receivers toward communication sources). At the outset, McCroskey presumed that this attitude was like other attitudes, i.e., unidimensional. He therefore developed a set of items to measure this attitude. However, when he subjected these items to factor analysis, he found that there were two dimensions to this attitude rather than one. More simply put, he thought he was measuring "apples," but he found that he was measuring "granny smith apples" and "red delicious apples." In essence, there were two parts (competence and trustworthiness) that created participants' perceptions of credibility. Just like granny smith and red delicious are two different types of apples. As a result, he was forced to develop two separate measures to measure these two new constructs. The only serious problem with the approach to validity through factor analysis is that it is a strictly negative approach. That is, factor analysis can tell someone that she is not measuring her construct, but cannot tell her that she is at least independent of other considerations.

In a more recent study, McCroskey, Richmond, and Johnson (2003) worked with the Nonverbal Immediacy Scale to improve reliability and validity. Since nonverbal immediacy is such a strong concept in the field now and wasn't 30 years ago, it was determined that the 14-item scale did not have high enough reliability and validity to continue using it. Thus, McCroskey, Richmond, and Johnson completed a study in which the reliability and validity of the Nonverbal Immediacy Scale was substantially improved. In Appendix C, there is a portion of the 2003 study that produced the new Nonverbal Immediacy Scales. Additionally, for a review of the measure of verbal immediacy, read the Robinson and Richmond (1995) article in which we prove the unreliability and the absence of validity of the verbal immediacy as defined by Gorham (1988).

In conclusion, many social scientists are concerned with which approach to validity they should employ in the development of measuring instruments. The answer to this is very simple. Do not choose among the approaches to validity. Rather, we should employ all of the approaches to validity that can be employed in the given case. If any one of the approaches indicates that the instrument is invalid, this is sufficient ground for substantial revision in the instrument that has been developed.

Validity Threats

A number of problems can occur when one is attempting to determine whether or not a newly developed measure is valid. In this section we will examine seven categories of threats to a newly developed measure's validity.

1. Inadequate Preoperational Explication of Concepts. The first threat that can befall a new measure's validity can occur when an individual really hasn't determined what a scale was supposed to measure in the first place. For example, if a researcher wants to create a scale about humor but has questions about communication apprehension thrown in the scale, the scale is going to have validity problems. Would you use a wrist watch to tell you how hot it is outside? Too often researchers just write countless numbers of scale items and then throw them against a statistical wall to see what sticks, which is not a good practice when writing a research scale. The more concrete your purpose is for creating a scale from the onset, the more valid your scale can be in the long run.

2. Mono-operation Bias. Another problem that can affect the validity of a newly developed measure can occur when you only administer the measure once. If you only measure something once, it's really hard to determine whether you're truly measuring the variable you intend to or just a portion of the variable. It is also possible that there will be some form of error that prevents you from accurately testing a newly developed measure's validity the first time you use it, so multiple administrations will enable you to get a much clearer picture of your scale's overall validity.

3. Interaction of Different Treatments. Often in research we want to determine if a newly developed treatment for something is effective. For example, maybe we create a new way to reduce students' levels of public speaking anxiety. To determine whether or not our treatment is effective, we have to know whether or not the measure we are using to determine public speaking anxiety is valid. Unfortunately, there are intervening variables that could prevent you from getting an accurate measure of the effectiveness of your treatment. For example, maybe one of your participants has hired a speech coach, and the individual attention has helped the participant lower her or his level of public speaking anxiety with no change occurring from your treatment. It's also possible that one of your participants could have a horrible public speaking experience which causes her or his public speaking anxiety to rise despite your treatment. In essence, one threat to validity is whether or not the results you are seeing are yours or whether they are the result of multiple treatments by yourself and others?

4. Interaction of Testing and Treatment. Often the combined effect of being measured multiple times along with receiving a treatment can cause someone to be more aware of the measurement process and alter her or his scores as a result of this awareness and not the treatment itself. Basically, when participants are aware of what is going on in an experiment, they are often more sensitive and/or receptive to future measures of a particular variable.

5. Restricted Generalizability Across Constructs. Another threat to the validity of a newly developed measure is how restricted that measure is across differing constructs.

In the example given at the beginning of this chapter about the newly developed scale for examining appropriate and inappropriate humor in the classroom, is this measure generalizable to elementary school teachers, junior high/middle school teachers, high school teachers, and college professors, or is this tool only useful in the college classroom? It is possible that Wanzer and Frymier's (1999) appropriate and inappropriate categories of humor are only true in the college setting, so the scale could not be applied to lower levels of education and the results from the newly developed scale found in college classrooms could not be cross-applied to elementary, junior high/middle school, and high school classrooms.

6. Confounding Constructs and Levels of Constructs. Another problem that can affect the validity of a measure is whether or not you are measuring a single construct, multiple constructs, or multiple levels of one construct in a given measure. Often one of the biggest problems that newly developed measures have is that they are measuring more than one construct at a time or multiple levels of the same construct. For example, in the PRCA-24, the overall construct of communication apprehension has been found to have four basic subconstructs within it: meeting, group, interpersonal, and public. Statisticians often call subconstructs factors, as discussed earlier in this chapter. Unfortunately, researchers often do not know which subconstructs or even multiple constructs exist in a set of scale items until he or she has collected the appropriate data to examine the validity of the scale.

7. Social Threats to Validity. In addition to the above threats to validity, there are also four social threats that can affect a measure's validity. The first social validity threat is hypothesis guessing. Often participants will guess what a researcher is attempting to measure and then respond to a measure accordingly. When a person guesses your hypothesis (either correctly or incorrectly), it can skew how he or she responds to your survey. A second social validity threat is evaluation apprehension. Many people experience anxiety when they know they are being evaluated, which can cause them to give responses that they might not have normally. A third social threat to validity involves experimenter expectancies. Often experimenters will unknowingly influence a participant's scores when the experimenter encourages the participant to respond in a specific manner. Experimenters should be trained to avoid influencing a participant's answers and behaviors as much as humanly possible to prevent this validity threat. Finally, social desirability bias can be a threat to a measure's validity. Social desirability bias is the term used by researchers for when a participant changes how he or she scores on a measure to be perceived in a "better light" than her or his actual scores would reveal. For example, maybe you are asking your participants how often they drink alcohol and a participant who normally drinks a case a day says he or she drinks a couple of beers a week for fear of being perceived as an alcoholic. While social desirability bias cannot be completely avoided, explaining that responses are confidential or ensuring anonymity should lessen social threats to a measure's validity.

Now that we have examined some threats to a measurement's validity, let's examine some general problems with measurement as a whole.

Problems with Measurement

The two most commonly discussed problems of measurement are reliability and validity, which are actually parts of one problem. Researchers are only concerned with reliability because of its implications for validity. A measure can be perfectly reliable and have absolute zero validity for the purpose for which a researcher created the measure. On the other hand, a measure cannot be valid unless it is also reliable. This may be better understood if we think in terms of reliability and validity coefficients for a moment. Presume we have two separate measures and are concerned with the ability of one measure to predict scores on the other measure. Through our research we obtain a Cronbach's alpha reliability coefficient for the first measure of 0.65 (minimally acceptable) and a Cronbach's alpha reliability coefficient for the second measure of 0.30 (unacceptable). To obtain the maximum possible validity coefficient for the predictability of one of these measures for the other we can multiply the two reliability coefficients by each other ($0.30 \times 0.65 = 0.195$). This does not give us the actual validity coefficient; rather it indicates the *absolute maximum* validity coefficient that we could obtain. Thus, if either of our measures is unreliable, we will have little or no validity. In the example we have just considered, one measure is minimally acceptable (0.65) and the other is simply unacceptable (0.30). Even if we increase the reliability of our most reliable instrument to the point of perfection, the highest validity coefficient we could obtain would be 0.30. Thus, we should not be overly concerned about the lack of high validity coefficients between our attitude measures and overt behaviors in the real world. This probably does not indicate that our attitude measure in itself is invalid. Rather, this is influenced by the extremely unreliable methods we have developed to measure behaviors in the real world. These measures tend to have two major problems accompanying them: the difficulty in obtaining agreement among observers and the very low level of potential measurement, seldom even ordinal, of such behaviors. Thus, even with a perfectly valid measure we are unlikely to get a high validity coefficient because of the unreliability of our criterion measure. We must be extremely concerned with reliability and the less precise estimates of validity such as content and construct validity rather than predictive validity. For example, it may be that attitudes toward federal finance of education and federal control of education are related to federal assistance to our local schools. These two attitudes may not simply add together to produce our behaviors—more likely they interact. Thus, in order to predict that particular behavior, we need to be able to measure these two attitudes separately. The two procedures most commonly employed to determine whether or not a measure is tapping more than one variable are factor analysis, as discussed above, and "scalogram analysis," as described by Guttman (1945).

A third problem to which measurement is particularly susceptible is what we shall call "faking." This is actually a broad title for several types of problems. Faking refers to any circumstance in which a respondent to our instrument deliberately attempts to alter the results in some specific way. Whenever faking is present, the validity of our instrument is not. One type of faking can be referred to as "acquiescence." The acquiescent individual wishes to cooperate with the investigator and give her or him what she or he wants. Thus, the respondent tries to determine the kind of response the investigator wishes and produce it. Another type of acquiescence that is somewhat different is produced by a personality type that merely tends to say "yes" to anything.

A second type of faking is produced by the influence of perception of social desirability. Often a respondent will not indicate his true beliefs, but rather will indicate beliefs that he thinks society accepts. This is particularly a problem when we are attempting to measure socially sensitive attitudes toward racial intolerance and toward morality. For example, a woman may indicate that she strongly disapproves of premarital intercourse because society opposes it. Her private behavior, however, may be quite the contrary of this response. This type of faking can be overcome to a considerable extent by insuring the respondent that her or his responses will be anonymous.

A third type of faking has been referred to by researchers by several very colorful terms. For the sake of propriety we shall refer to it as the "nuts-to-you" response, for as Joseph

Masling (1966) described it, the "screw you" effect. This is the almost exact opposite of acquiescence. Rather than attempting to give the researcher what he wants, the individual engaging in "nuts-to-you" behavior may attempt either to give him the exact opposite of what he wants or to give a completely random response.

All of these faking behaviors have implications for reliability, but their main impact is upon validity. Whenever faking is present, validity isn't.

The fourth problem that affects measurement, unless carefully avoided, is response set. A response set is *any tendency that causes a person to give different responses to test items than he or she would if the item was presented in a different form.* Response set, while severely reducing the validity of any instrument, may actually increase the obtained reliability estimate for the instrument. Response set is more often observed when all of the items in an instrument are worked in much the same way. For example, if all of the items are worded positively or negatively, response set is likely to be present. In such cases, if the subject indicates the fifth response to the first question, he or she is likely to continue to make the fifth response to the rest of the questions. This problem may be overcome by including an equal or nearly equal number of positively and negatively worded items and then arrange the items in random order.

The fifth and final major problem that affects measurement we have saved until last because it is the worst. This is the problem of bad items on the measure. In the development of any measure it is almost certain that some bad items will be included, but there is no excuse for them continuing to be included. A technique known as item analysis can be employed that will help to identify bad items in a group of items. Simply put, item analysis produces a correlation between an individual item and a total score across all items. A bad item will have a negative or low positive correlation, whereas a good item will tend to have a high positive correlation. The solution to the problem of bad items is very simple—identify them, throw them out, and develop good items.

Within the notable exception of the semantic differential as developed by Osgood (1957), almost all of the techniques for attitude measurement that have been developed employ the use of declarative statements or questions as items. The most important part of attitude scale construction is creating items that reflect both a balanced and a representative set of opinions about the issue at hand. The question of which scaling technique to use is of secondary importance despite the emphasis that differences in these techniques have received in the professional literature over the years. Using essentially the same set of items, researchers have found that the various techniques place individuals at the same locations on attitude scales relative to each other (i.e., individual A is more liberal than B, but only slightly more liberal than C.) That is to say, there is very little statistically one can gain from reliability or validity beyond what is already inherent in item content. A number of elements need to be taken into consideration when developing items in order to reduce sources of spurious response, and these will be considered in another chapter.

Conclusion

This chapter has focused on how we can be sure that people answer our research scales consistently and how to make sure we are measuring what we say we are measuring. Reliability and validity are extremely important for researchers because if your measures are not reliable and valid, your results are not meaningful. Now that we've discussed the measurement process, reliability, and validity, we will examine how research is conducted using three research techniques—survey, content analysis, and experimental—in the next three chapters.

KEY TERMS

Acquiescence
Alternate Forms Reliability
Concurrent Validity
Construct Validity
Criterion Validity
Cronbach's Alpha
  Reliability

Face/Content Validity
Faking Responses
Hoyt Analysis of Variance
  Reliability
Mono-operation Bias
Predictive Validity
Reliability

Response Set
Retrospective Validity
Screw You Effect
Social Desirability Bias
Split-Half Reliability
Test–Retest Reliability
Validity

REFERENCES

Cheseboro, J. (1999). The relationship between listening styles and conversational sensitivity. *Communication Research Reports, 16*, 233–238.

Cronbach, L. J. (1951). Coefficient alpha and the internal structure of tests. *Psychometrika, 16*, 297–333.

Gorham, J. S. (1988). The relationship between verbal teacher immediacy behaviors and student learning. *Communication Education, 37*, 40–53.

Guttman, L. (1945). A basis for analyzing test-retest reliability. *Psychometrika, 10*, 255–282.

Hoyt, C. (1941). Test reliability estimated by analysis of variance. *Psychometrika, 6*, 153–160.

Masling, J. (1966). Role related behavior of the subject and psychologist and its effects upon psychological data. In D. Levine (Ed.), *Symposium on Motivation* (pp. 67–103). *Lincoln, NB. University of Nebraska Press.*

McCroskey, J. C. (1966). *Experimental studies of the effects of ethos and evidence in persuasive communication.* Unpublished doctoral dissertation. University Park, PA: Pennsylvania State University.

McCroskey, J. C. (2006). Reliability and validity of the Generalized Attitude Measure and Generalized Belief Measure. *Communication Quarterly, 54*, 265–274.

Osgood, C. E. (1957). *The measurement of meaning.* Urbana, IL: University of Illinois Press.

Richmond, V. P., McCroskey, J. C., & Johnson, A. D. (2003). Development of the nonverbal immediacy scale (NIS): Measures of self- and other-perceived nonverbal immediacy. *Communication Quarterly, 51*, 504–517.

Robinson, R. Y., & Richmond, V. P. (1995). Validity of the verbal immediacy scale. *Communication Research Reports, 12*, 80–84.

Wanzer, M. B., & Frymier, A. B. (1999, April). *Being funny in the classroom: Appropriate and inappropriate humor behaviors.* Paper presented at the Eastern Communication Association's Convention, Charleston, WV.

FURTHER READING

DeVellis, R. F. (1991). *Scale development: Theory and applications* (Applied Social Research Methods Series, Vol. 26). Newbury Park, CA: Sage.

Dillman, D. A. (2000). Mail and internet surveys: The tailored design method (2nd ed.). New York: Wiley.

Fowler, F. J., Jr. (1993). Survey research methods (2nd ed.) (Applied Social Research Methods Series, Vol. 1). Newbury Park, CA: Sage.

Green, S. B., & Salkind, N. J. (2004). *Using SPSS for Windows and Macintosh: Analyzing and understanding data* (4th ed.). Upper Saddle River, NJ: Prentice Hall.

Grimm, L. G., & Yarnold, P. R. (Eds.). (2000). *Reading and understanding more multivariate statistics*. Washington, DC: American Psychological Association.

Singleton, R. A., Jr., & Straits, B. C. (1999). *Approach to social research* (3rd ed.). New York: Oxford University Press.

Tabachnick, B. G., & Fidell, L. S. (2007). *Using multivariate statistics* (5th ed.). Boston: Allyn and Bacon.

Survey Research

1   Distinguish between surveys, questionnaires, and interview schedules.
2   Know the four questions a researcher should ask to determine if a survey is the most appropriate research method.
3   Understand Fink's (2006) five steps for conducting a survey.
4   Understand the purpose of open-ended questions in survey research.
5   Understand the difference between cross-sectional, longitudinal, and accelerated longitudinal survey designs.
6   Explain the guidelines for pilot testing a survey.
7   Be able to explain the positive and negative aspects of the different ways to disseminate questionnaires.
8   Be able to define *response rate*.
9   Know the two types of nonresponses (unit and item) and how they affect surveys.
10 Explain some general ways to increase response rates.
11 Understand the three types of equivalence one must consider when translating survey items from one language to another language.
12 Understand the five different ways a research can translate a survey from one language to another language.

Chances are by this point in your academic career you have participated in some form of survey research. Whether filling out a questionnaire in class or being interviewed about our political views by a pollster, we are constantly completing surveys. You can't even register a recently purchased product these days without filling out a questionnaire. Since the moment James Cattell (1890) started discussing the notion of mental measures and using them to examine college students, the art and science of surveying has become a mainstay of our cultural reality. Before we can really discuss what a survey is, we first need to distinguish between three terms that often prove confusing for people: survey, questionnaire, and interview schedule. A survey is *a social scientific method for gathering quantifiable information about a specific group of people by asking the group members questions about their individual attitudes, values, beliefs, behaviors, knowledge, and perceptions.* There are two basic types of survey a researcher may conduct. First a researcher may conduct a descriptive survey, which is designed to find out how common a phenomenon is within a given group of people. For example, a researcher investigating how widespread communication apprehension (CA) is across the United States would be an example using a survey to examine a specific phenomenon within a given group of people (people living in the United States). The second type of survey is an analytical or explanatory survey. The purpose of analytical surveys is "to explain why people think or act as they do by identifying likely causal influences on their attitudes and behavior" (Buckingham & Saunders, 2004, p. 13). A questionnaire, on the other hand, is *a form containing a series of questions and mental measures that is given to a group of people in an attempt to gain statistical information about the group as part of a survey.* In other words, a questionnaire is a tool that a researcher who is conducting a survey uses to get data from the group of interest. The third term we use when discussing surveys in this chapter is interview schedule. An interview schedule is *the list of survey questions an interviewer reads an interviewee when conducting an oral survey.* While some people will discuss interview schedules as questionnaires, we prefer to differentiate between the two terms: paper-and-pencil methods (questionnaire) and oral interviewing (interview schedule). Later in this chapter we will discuss specific issues related to survey formation, but for now we are going to focus on when a survey is appropriate.

When to Use a Survey

People utilize surveys for a number of different projects, but you should never just jump into a survey project without knowing why you're conducting the survey in the first place. Buckingham and Saunders (2004) believe there are four questions a researcher must ask before conducting a survey.

DO YOU KNOW WHAT YOU WANT TO ASK?

First, does a researcher know what he or she wants to ask? Because of the physical need to generate a questionnaire or list of interview questions before a survey can occur, a researcher must know what he or she wants to study. Whether the researcher wants to conduct a descriptive survey or analytical survey, he or she must have some kind of a priori (before the fact) notion of what is being studied. Qualitative and rhetorical researchers have the ability to conduct exploratory research where they go in and start organically observing a phenomenon without any preconceived notions, but quantitative researchers simply do not have this luxury because of the nature of quantitative information.

DO YOU REALLY NEED TO COLLECT NEW DATA?

Second, researchers need to ask themselves if they really need to collect new data on a specific phenomenon. In certain types of research, performing a survey would be meaningless, if not impossible. For example, we cannot exactly conduct a survey of Irish American immigrants during the potato famine, because they're all dead now, and for some reason, dead people don't like filling out questionnaires. If the lives of immigrants during the potato famine is your research topic, conducting a survey just isn't going to help you get at anything. While there are research methods to study the lives of Irish immigrants during the potato famine, they are beyond the scope of this book.

A second reason why a researcher may not need to conduct a survey is if a more observational method is available that does not interfere with how people live their daily lives. For example, one common type of research conducted, often without your knowledge, pertains to shopping behavior. Retail stores often hire consulting firms to study shopping behaviors within a store for the purpose of determining the best way to lay out the store to maximize profits. While some scholars say this research is unethical because it invades your privacy, others say that it is perfectly ethical because the researcher is unobtrusively watching a shopper's behavior without direct contact or interference.

A third reason why a researcher may not need to collect data is if existing data are available. There are many organizations devoted to the collection and dissemination of information about people. In these cases, it's not that a survey wasn't conducted—it's that the survey was conducted by a third party for the purpose of disseminating the data to other researchers. The Journal of Statistics Education (http://www.amstat.org/publications/jse/) has numerous datasets that people can use to learn statistics, and many of them are based on actual collected survey data. The dataset provided with this textbook is another example of a preexisting dataset that could be used for analysis. Furthermore, check out organizations like the Centers for Disease Control and Prevention (http://www.cdc.gov/) and First Gov (http://www.firstgov.gov/) to find a wide variety of datasets at your fingertips.

Do Your Participants Know Anything or Will They Even Tell You?

Third, researchers must ask themselves how much their group of interest will know about what the researchers are interested in analyzing and whether or not the group members will even tell the researcher. Let's go ahead and break this one down into some simple chunks. First, as a researcher you need to ask yourself whether or not your future participants will even know about the topic you are studying. For example, if you want to examine the lasting impact of memorable messages after the Challenger explosion, using a group of freshmen probably would not be very useful since most of them were born after the accident in 1986. Furthermore, the types of questions you are interested in may also be problematic. Let's say you are interested in the media's effect on perceptions of terrorism, so you ask a group of participants how many news stories about terrorism they remember seeing the week after the 9/11 attacks. If you're like us, we couldn't even tell you how many news stories on terrorism we saw in the last week let alone 6 years ago. Asking people questions about events that have happened in the past is always problematic. However, the closer you can get to the event in quetion, the stronger your data will actually be.

The flip side of this issue deals with whether or not participants will be willing to tell you information about themselves. There are some issues that frankly make people very antsy, and they often will not want to discuss these issues openly. There are three basic reasons people may have for not wanting to disclose information. First, some people may simply be embarrassed by certain information. For example, researchers who study issues involving sexual communication often find that people are a little embarrassed by some of the questions asked on a questionnaire or during an interview. For some people, filling out a questionnaire about human sexuality is as close to openly discussing sexuality as they will ever get, so this could really make them feel embarrassed, which could lead to socially desirable responding. Socially desirable responding occurs when a participant fills out a questionnaire or responds to interview questions in a way that the participant thinks makes her or him look better.

The second reason some people may be hesitant to disclose information is shame. In research that has been conducted looking at people who are victims of violent crimes, especially sex crimes, many victims feel shame for having been violated. When people experience deep shame, they are much less likely to open up about the topic that is causing the shame.

The third reason some people may be hesitant to disclose information during a survey is because they fear some kind of retribution for their answers. For example, if a manager hands out a survey to subordinates on her or his managerial skills and then has the subordinates turn the survey back into the manager, people are going to be very hesitant to say anything negative for fear that the manager will hold their responses against them. Other people are simply hesitant to disclose information for fear that their disclosure will get them into legal trouble. Many researchers study illegal behaviors, and many people will either not participate in a study or will lie during a study about illegal behaviors for fear that their answers will get them thrown in jail.

We are not suggesting that you should never use surveys with people who might be embarrassed, shamed, or fearful. In fact, researchers have used survey methods with all kinds of people who experience embarrassment, shame, and fear as a result of the information discussed during a survey. However, it is extremely important that you ensure confidentiality and anonymity. The more certain people feel that their answers will not be used against them or traced back to them, the more honest they are going to be while filling out a questionnaire or answering a series of interview questions.

IS YOUR GOAL GENERALIZABILITY?

The last question a researcher should ask her- or himself is whether or not the goal of the study is generalizability. When discussing generalizability, there are two important terms to understand: populations and samples. A population is an entire set of objects, observations, or scores that have some characteristic in common. In the case of survey research, a population is everyone that has a specific characteristic in common that a researcher is attempting to study. For example, if you want to examine television-viewing patterns among college females, your population consists of every female who is in college. A sample, on the other hand, is a subset of the larger population. So instead of attempting to survey the entire female population on television-viewing patterns, you decide to survey 300 females at a local university. When researchers discuss the concept of generalizability, we are basically questioning whether the results of a sample (the 300 female students at a local college) mirror the results that would be found in the larger population (all college females). To make sure that your end results are generalizable, that is, your sample can be said to reflect the population correctly, you should randomly (i.e., every unit of analysis that exists within your population has an equal chance for inclusion in your sample) select your sample. We will discuss random sampling in much more detail in Chapter 14.

Now that we've discussed the four primary reasons researchers have for conducting a survey, we can switch gears and discuss the process one goes through when conducting survey research.

How to Conduct Survey Research

Many young scholars will simply find a series of random scales and throw them together to create a survey research project, but this is not only ineffective for hypothesis testing, it is also a waste of time. First, randomly throwing scales together with no theoretical reason enables you to find results that may not really mean anything. Randomly putting together a survey is kind of like throwing a vat of spaghetti against a wall—something will stick, but you're left with a mess. If you create a large dataset for no other purpose than seeing what relationships and differences might exist, you'll most definitely find statistical relationships and differences just by chance. But being haphazard in one's approach to research is not science. For this reason, the authors of this textbook have stated from the beginning that you should start with an overarching research question and then determine the most appropriate ways to go about measuring that communication phenomenon. Overall, use previously existing research scales wisely. The temptation to just throw a handful of research scales together is great, but the end result is generally substandard research that isn't publishable. To make sure that you design a good survey study, you might use Fink's (2006) five steps for conducting a good survey.

STEP 1: PICKING YOUR QUESTIONS

First and foremost there is no single way to go about picking the types of questions to include in a research survey. We wish we could tell you there was a magic bullet, but there simply isn't. Ultimately, the types of questions you will need to ask will be dictated by the hypotheses and research questions you want to examine in your study. As Converse and Presser (1986) wrote, "Every questionnaire must, finally, be handcrafted. It is not only that questionnaire writing must be 'artful'; each questionnaire is also unique, an original. A designer must cut and try, see how it looks and sounds, see how people react to it, and then cut again, and try again" (p. 48). While Converse and Presser are specifically talking about questionnaire development, the same is also true for developing an interview schedule. In this section we will discuss a number of commonly used question formats used on questionnaires by examining the types of variable levels.

Nominal Level Questions

Many questionnaires will have a series of nominal level questions like biological sex, ethnicity, religious affiliation, political party, etc. These questions are great for determining descriptive statistics of your research sample. When deciding which questions to actually include on your questionnaire, you need to ask yourself which questions are actually related to the current study. If you are not planning on examining your participants' political affiliations, then you have no need to include the variable on your questionnaire. You may also find yourself at some point needing to ask a series of Yes/No questions. Often having a "don't know" category is also useful. You may want to ask your participants, "Have you ever lived in a country other than the United States?" In this case, you probably don't need the "don't know" category because some people will ultimately check off "don't know" just to say "screw you." Ultimately, when dealing with nominal level variables on a questionnaire, you really want to make sure that you follow the guidelines for creating nominal variables discussed in Chapter 6.

One big question that is difficult to answer is where to place nominal level variables in the overall flow of a questionnaire. We would recommend keeping participant demographics until the very end because in longer surveys you may end up with participant fatigue and participants can generally recall their own demographic information without much cognitive expenditure. As for other types of nominal level questions, place the questions where they will be the most beneficial for your participants. For example, if you are having participants fill out a questionnaire examining their supervisor's communicative behavior, you may want to start by getting participants thinking about their supervisor before you jump into any mental measures related to the supervisor. To do this, place any nominal level demographic variables related to the supervisor before you have them fill out the more complex measures. Ultimately, when participants have to tell you their supervisor's biological sex up front, it forces the participant to start thinking about that specific supervisor, which will help the participant keep that supervisor in mind as they are responding to the rest of the survey.

Ordinal Level Questions

Just like nominal level variables, there are numerous ordinal level variables that are commonly used in research (year in school, social economic status group, level of education, etc.). Any time someone uses a single Likert-type question or semantic differential question, those function as ordinal level questions as well. One example of an ordinal variable discussed by Hildebrand, Laing, and Rosenthal (1977) related to political ideology is: *left*, *left-center*, *center*, *right-center*, and *right*. While these categories may not be measurable using a ruler, we can say that those categories clearly differ from each other qualitatively and quantitatively.

When it comes to using an ordinal level variable on a survey, the biggest question to ask yourself is what types of statistical tests you plan on conducting. While it is possible to use ordinal data in both relationship and difference tests, the results are based on one-shot questions, which leads to serious reliability and validity issues. While an ordinal question may be useful for determining someone's socioeconomic status (lower, middle, upper), an ordinal question would not be useful for measuring someone's level of communication apprehension.

Interval Level Questions

The most common type of question seen on questionnaires involves interval level variables. For example, all of the mental measures discussed in Chapter 7 are interval level variables. All of your Likert and semantic differential/bipolar adjective scales are interval variables, so a great deal of communication research involves interval level variables.

One of the biggest questions involving interval variables is really where to place them in your overall questionnaire. Especially if you have multiple interval variables, how should you order the mental measures so that you have a sequence that easily flows from one scale to the next and doesn't end up confusing your participants? While there are no steadfast rules on this, here are some general guidelines you may want to consider.

First, group items with like anchors together. An anchor is the technical term used for the words that you give people on a questionnaire and ask them to pick one (e.g., Disagree, Neither Agree or Disagree, Agree; Ineffective, Neutral, Effective; Unsatisfied, Neutral, Satisfied; etc.). Many types of anchors exist in mental measures, so you want to make sure that you group measures that have similar anchors together to avoid confusion. You may also want to point out in your instructions if you are using multiple anchoring systems so your participants don't think the new anchor is a typo.

Second, do not start a study with the most controversial questions right off the bat. For example, Wrench, Corrigan, McCroskey, and Punyanunt-Carter (2006) conducted a study examining numerous variables including religious fundamentalism, ethnocentrism, intercultural communication apprehension, tolerance for religious disagreements, and homonegativity. In the initial version of the questionnaire the homonegativity scale, which measures negative perceptions people have about bisexual, gay, and lesbian people, was one of the first scales. However, the researchers started discussing whether having that scale up front would actually end up biasing the way the participants might end up responding to the other questions. People tend to assume that the first scale you have on a questionnaire reflects what the study is about as a whole. In public speaking we talk about the concept of primacy—people remember the information at the beginning of a speech. People also tend to remember what the first set of scale items were asking, which can definitely slant how they respond to the rest of the study.

Third, keep like questions together. When we say like questions, we're talking about questions asking about the same target (as in a teacher or supervisor). When conducting survey research you may have questions the participant is supposed to respond to about her- or himself (e.g., participant's level of communication apprehension, ethnocentrism, sense of humor, etc.) and questions that the participant is supposed to respond to about a specific target (e.g., supervisor's nonverbal immediacy, teacher's use of humor, physician's credibility, etc.). Our recommendation is to keep questions about the participant together and questions about the target together to avoid confusion. If your survey jumps back and forth between the two, you may end up with some participants responding about themselves when they should be responding about the target, and vice versa.

Fourth, keep like contexts together. Often when conducting a survey we may be interested in comparing more than one communicative context. For example, maybe you want to compare participants' reported use of compliance-gaining strategies with both Internet and face-to-face friends. In this example, you would have survey questions relating to both the Internet communicative context and the face-to-face communicative context on your questionnaire. Just to make sure that your participants aren't confusing the two contexts, you should keep them separate on your survey.

Fifth, place very sensitive questions toward the end of a survey. If you start by asking for a participant's deepest, darkest secret, the chances that they will either start lying or will start answering in a socially desirable manner increase. Asking more benign questions initially allows the participant to become more comfortable with the questions. Ultimately, if your participants are comfortable with the earlier questions, they will be much more willing to divulge more private and personal information later in the survey.

Ratio Level Questions

Overall, there really are not that many questions that a researcher will ask using ratio level questions. The most common ratio level question asked on a survey is a participant's age. However, there are other types of ratio questions that may be asked during a survey that involve a number range that starts with a possible zero. How many visits to your doctor have you made this year? How many times a week do you eat breakfast? How many different sexual partners have you had in the last month? How many children do you have? All of these questions start with a possible zero and then escalate in an actual numerical fashion from there.

Another very common form of ratio level questions that appear on surveys is cognitive based questions. When creating tests that are designed to measure an individual's cognitive understanding of something, we rely on a number of different measurement mechanisms: matching, multiple choice, and true or false. All of these start with an absolute zero score (the participant got none of the answers correct), and then we can mathematically compare participants' scores as they go up from zero.

Open-Ended Questions

The final type of question commonly asked during a survey is open-ended questions. Open-ended questions are designed to allow respondents to further explore a concept. Instead of limiting the possible number of choices like we do with nominal, ordinal, interval, and ratio level questions, the answers given during open-ended questions are realistically limitless. For example, an open-ended question might ask, "How do you think you can improve your interpersonal communication with your spouse?" This question could receive one-sentence-long answers or pages of information. Open-ended questions can be very useful because they often present you with information that you did not expect to receive from your respondents. You may be wondering how an open-ended question can be quantitative, and you're right to ask this question because the responses are not innately quantitative. However, there are quantitative tools that we have at our disposal that can be used to analyze open-ended questions; we'll discuss the most common one, content analysis, in the next chapter.

As for placing open-ended questions on an actual questionnaire, the biggest consideration is providing enough space for your respondents to answer. People's handwriting differs in size, so you need to make sure that you allow the participants enough room to adequately answer a question. We generally recommend at least half a page for an open-ended answer. The more complex your question is, the more space your respondents may need to answer the question.

STEP 2: CREATING CLEAR INSTRUCTIONS

Murphy's Law: If people can find a unique and creative way for screwing something up, they will. Over the years all of the authors of this text have received a wide range of unique answers on questionnaires. We have also learned that if our instructions are very clear, we can avoid some of the ambiguity people may have while filling out a questionnaire or responding during an interview. One of the easiest ways to avoid ambiguity during the first part of an interview questionnaire is to offer your participants dummy questions and walk them through how to correctly answer the question.

In Figure 11.1 we have examples from an actual study that included dummy questions to walk participants through how to fill out the scales correctly. In our experience, college students tend to know how to correctly fill out research surveys, but the general public tends

---

Weight Locus of Control

Directions: The following questions are concerned with how you perceive yourself across a variety of issues. For each statement, place an "X" in the box that corresponds with your perception of the item based on the following scale: SD = Strongly Disagree, D = Disagree, N = Neutral, A = Agree, and SA = Strongly Agree.

For example, if given the sentence "I like peanut butter," if you only agree with the statement, but do not strongly agree with the statement, you would place an "X" in the column marked "A" for Agree (See example below).

		SD	D	N	A	SA
Ex.	I like peanut butter.				**X**	
1.	Being the ideal weight is a matter of luck.					

Generalized Attitude Measure

Directions: On the scales below, please indicate your feelings about **"Restaurant X."** Circle the number between the adjectives which best represent your feelings about **"Restaurant X."** Numbers "1" and "7" indicate a very strong feeling. Numbers "2" and "6" indicate a strong feeling. Numbers "3" and "5" indicate a fairly weak feeling. Number "4" indicates you are undecided or do not understand the adjectives themselves. There are no right or wrong answers. Circle only ONE number per row.

For example, if you were given a pair of adjectives (cheap and expensive) and you felt the program was reasonably priced, you might circle 1 or 2.

```
Ex.                    Cheap  ①  2  3  4  5  6  7  Expensive
1.                     Good   1  2  3  4  5  6  7  Bad
```

Figure 11.1 Sample Questionnaire Questions

to be more likely to need extra help, probably because they do not fill out as many question-naires. When looking at your instructions you should ask yourself a very simple question: "Will these instructions make sense to my intended participants?" If you want to survey people in a nursing home, you may want to show your instructions to someone who is elderly and get their feedback before moving on to pilot-testing the questionnaire.

STEP 3: STUDY DESIGN

When designing a survey research study, we typically talk about two types of designs: cross-sectional and longitudinal (Fowler, 1993). A *cross-sectional survey design* is used when a researcher wants to get information from a group of participants at a given point in time. For example, maybe you want to conduct a study like Rocca and Vogl-Bauer (1999), who stud-ied sports team identification and verbal aggression. In their study, the researchers asked a series of participants to fill out a scale containing items for sports team identification, verbal aggression, and sports spectator identification. In this study, the researchers simply wanted to get people's perceptions at the time they had filled out the scale. When using a cross-sectional survey design, researchers can examine many things like relationships between variables and differences between groups that exist within the research sample, but you can-not study changes that occur over time.

To examine how people change over time, one needs to employ a *longitudinal survey design*. While a longitudinal design cannot be used to make causal conclusions about rela-tionships and differences, it can allow you to make statements about variable order. The first type of longitudinal design is a trend design. A *trend design* is used to examine differ-ent samples of people at different points in time. For example, many researchers collected research data within the week prior to the 9/11 terrorist attacks in the United States. These same researchers were then able to collect data immediately after 9/11 using completely dif-ferent samples to see whether or not changes had a occurred within that short time period. While it is possible that preexisting differences between the two groups caused the change to occur, there is no way to know this in a trend design.

Another way to conduct a survey study longitudinally is to employ a *panel design*. A panel design is when a research recruits a series of participants who agree to be surveyed periodically over a given period of time. Some researchers have used this type of design to examine marital conflict. Researchers recruit participants when they get married and agree to pay them a certain amount of money if they will agree to be surveyed every 6 months. Then every 6 moths the researchers survey the couple about how they are handling conflict and the types of conflicts they are having. By surveying a panel over and over again like this, researchers can see how marital conflict strategies and themes change over time.

The last design is actually a combination of the first two types, which is called an *acceler-ated longitudinal design*. An accelerated longitudinal design is employed when a researcher wants to see how things change over a long period of time during a short period of time. We know this sounds a little odd, so let's use an illustration for clarification. Maybe a researcher wants to see how perceptions of situation comedies on television change over the course of one's adult life until retirement. In essence the researcher wants to see how people's percep-tions change from 18 to 65. To complete this study using a traditional longitudinal study, it would take a researcher 47 years, or most of his or her career. For this reason, this type of study is not very realistic. Instead, the researcher decides to recruit people in 5-year intervals starting at age 20, so they recruit 20-year-olds, 25-year-olds, 30-year-olds...all the way to 60-year-olds. The researcher then tracks these groups for 5 years. The idea here is that we are seeing changes over 5 years from participants who started the project at 20 and ended at 25 to participants who started when they were 60 and ended at 65. Ultimately, this type of design allows researchers to track how time affects the individual age groups over time, as well as how the differing age groups change.

STEP 4: DATA PROCESSING AND ANALYSIS

One of the areas the authors of this book have consistently realized is problematic for new researchers involves making sure the hypotheses and research questions can be answered by the information on the questionnaire. After you are done collecting data is not the time to realize that you should have asked another question(s). For this reason, before you ever set out to distribute your survey, you need to make sure that you can statistically answer your hypotheses and research questions based on the questions you actually have on your questionnaire. For example, last year one of the authors of this text had a group of students conducting a project in organizational communication. At the end of the project, the students realized they had measured employee motivation and not employee satisfaction. One of the students said, "Well if they're motivated, they're satisfied, right?" Nope! While research has shown the two variables to be positively related, they are not synonymous. If a researcher does not measure employee satisfaction, he or she cannot answer hypotheses or research questions about satisfaction.

In other words, you need to know exactly how you plan on analyzing your data when you are finished with the study itself. Figure 6.9 contains a chart that helps you determine which tests are most appropriate to conduct. For example, if you have two interval level variables (like communication apprehension and ethnocentrism) and you want to find the relationship between these two variables, you would use a correlation to test for a statistical relationship. If you had one nominal variable (female and male), and you wanted to test for a possible difference between these two categories on an interval level variable (willingness to communicate), the appropriate test would be an independent samples *t*-test. The last part of this book will go into more detail examining each of these different types of tests.

STEP 5: PILOT TESTING

The only way a researcher can really ever know how her or his respondents will provide answers to a survey is give it to people and find out directly. You may think your instructions were crystal clear and your survey questions all made sense, but once you give your survey to real people that can all change very quickly. In the study mentioned earlier in this chapter conducted by Wrench et al. (2006) examining religion, the researchers had listed as one of the possible religious affiliation categories (nominal variable) Protestant. Protestants are any Christian groups who are not Roman Catholic, Eastern Orthodox, or Anglican. In other words, Baptists, Methodists, Disciples of Christ, etc. are all Protestants. However, the researchers ended up with more people selecting "other" and defining themselves by their individual denominational names instead of as Protestant. Many respondents simply didn't know that they were Protestants, so they answered the best way they could. Unfortunately, this particular survey had not been adequately pilot tested, so this problem didn't arise until after the study was completed. Thankfully, changing the respondents' answers to Protestant in this case was very easy, but this could have been a much bigger problem. One way to prevent problems like this from occurring is to administer a pilot study. According to Buckingham and Saunders (2004), a pilot study is a "small-scale test-run for a planned piece of empirical research" (p. 294). We use pilot studies to make sure our instructions are easy to follow and our survey questions make sense to potential respondents. The following are some basic guidelines to follow when piloting a survey. These guidelines are applicable whether you are piloting a questionnaire or an interview schedule, the series of questions an interviewer asks during an interview.

Use Actual Survey Population Members

First and foremost, when you are pilot testing a survey you want to actually use the people you plan on surveying to test the survey. For example, if you're going to be surveying people in a retirement village, you don't want to pilot test your survey instrument on college students because they simply will not respond the same way.

Anticipate Survey Context

When piloting a survey, you should attempt to pilot the survey using the same conditions that people actually responding to the survey items will experience. For example, if you are going to be surveying people using an interview schedule over the phone, you would not want to pilot your survey using college students sitting in a lecture hall. While it may not be able to anticipate every possible survey context (e.g., person filling out a questionnaire in her or his car), you should at least try to approximate the general conditions under which most of your respondents will be participating.

Test Parts of the Survey

Another idea that can be very helpful when developing a survey is to pilot test parts of your survey instead of the whole thing. Often you have used parts of a survey in the past with the same population, so you do not need to retest those sections of the survey. Instead, you may want to test a newly developed section to make sure respondents understand the new instructions or questions.

Determining a Pilot Sample Size

Is there a magical number one should attempt to have in a pilot study? Not really. However, we do recommend that you attempt to pilot your questionnaire or interview schedule using at lest 5–10% of your target sample size. So if you are planning on surveying 200 participants, you should pilot your questionnaire or interview schedule with at least 10–20 people. The larger your pilot study is, the more likely you will find potential problems with your questionnaire or interview schedule.

Ask Questions After Someone Completes the Survey

One common practice that you can use during the pilot testing phase of a survey is to interview the respondents about their experience after they have completed the survey. Ask the respondents if they found any instructions confusing, were the questions clear, did they guess on any items, was the survey too long, could they physically read the survey (especially important when working with elderly populations). The more you know about how your participants felt while taking the survey, the more appropriate your revisions will be before disseminating your survey to your target sample.

Once you have pilot tested your survey, you are ready to hand out your survey to potential participants.

Disseminating Your Surveys

In the previous section we discussed the creation of research scales or measures. In this section we are going to discuss the dissemination of a research survey or questionnaire. While many different people use all five terms (scale, measure, research instrument, survey, and questionnaire) interchangeably, for the purpose of this book we are delineating a difference between scales/measures/research instruments and surveys/questionnaires. The first group is a single set of items designed to measure a specific variable. Surveys and questionnaires, on the other hand, are the putting together of a series of scales/measures/research instruments in an attempt to examine how variables relate to or differ from each other. In essence, a survey or questionnaire is when you place a variety of scales together to examine statistical relationships and differences. For example, maybe you want to put together a survey to examine the variables sociocommunicative orientation, willingness to communicate, and humor assessment. To examine these three variables, you put the three scales together in one small packet and have each participant fill out all three scales. You may even include some basic demographic information like biological sex, ethnicity, sexual orientation, etc. Once you have created a survey/questionnaire, you then need to determine the best way to get your survey into the hands of your target population. There are two primary ways that people can go about disseminating a survey: interviewing and self-administration.

INTERVIEWING

Face-to-Face Interviewing

Face-to-face (FtF) interviewing occurs when an interviewer asks an interviewee a set of questions. There are some clear advantages and disadvantages to FtF interviewing. The first advantage is that you tend to get a very high response rate. People have a hard tendency to tell people "no, I don't want to participate" when they are looking at them. FtF interviews also tend to be very beneficial for very long surveys where fatigue might be a problem because the interviewer can encourage the interviewee to continue answering questions at a point where they would stop answering them in other formats. The interviewer can also answer questions about the survey items if an interviewee is having problems understanding the questions, which can be very important when an interviewee's language skills are not high. FtF interviewing is also the best format in which to ask open-ended questions. In the first part of this chapter we focused on asking closed-ended questions or questions that have a clearly defined set of possible choices. In a Likert scale with a range from 1 (*strongly disagree*) to 5 (*strongly agree*), the person is not given the option of 9. There is a clearly defined set of permissible answers. However, open-ended questions are questions that allow for a wide variety of different answers. For example, maybe you want to know how someone perceives the federal government's propaganda about a new piece of legislation, so you ask, "How would you characterize the information you are receiving from Washington, DC, about this piece of legislation?" This enables the interviewee to express her or his thoughts in a very open fashion. While these open-ended responses can be coded and quantified, open-ended questions typically fall under the heading of qualitative rather than quantitative.

While there are some clear advantages to completing FtF interviews, there are also some rather important disadvantages as well. First, the cost of FtF interviewing is very high. You need teams of trained interviewers who go out and interview people in the sample you are intending to examine. These teams of trained interviewers cost a lot of money, not including the expense of travel, food, and hotels that may be incurred. Another disadvantage is that the interviewer can inadvertently affect how an interviewee responds to the questions. A simple sidewise glance from an interviewer that says "I can't believe you just answered that way" can cause the interviewee to start censoring her- or himself and start feeding responses to the interviewer that the interviewer wants to hear. Another problem caused by interviewers can be slight changes in how the questions are asked with regard to the actual text of the question; how a question is asked can change how people respond to questions either randomly or systematically. Even the biological sex or ethnicity of an interviewer can affect how some people will respond to an interviewer. While it is impossible to negate the effect that an interviewer can have on an interviewee, training interviewers to deliver questions in a systematic fashion and not outwardly respond to the answers they are given can help prevent interviewer effects from occurring.

One of the most famous social scientists to use interviewing as his primary form of research was a university professor at Indiana University named Alfred Kinsey. Kinsey initiated a line of research in the 1940s examining human sexuality in both females and males (Kinsey, Pomeroy, & Martin, 1948; Kinsey, Pomeroy, Martin, & Gebhard, 1953). Prior to Kinsey's studies, very little research had been conducted about human sexuality in the United States. Kinsey and a group of highly trained interviewers set out to interview a wide variety of different people around the country about their sexual histories. Kinsey realized early on that face-to-face interviewing enabled people to be more honest and forthright about their current and past sexual behaviors. Based on their research, Kinsey and his team revolutionized the discussion of sexuality in the United States and around the world.

Telephone Interviewing

The second way to disseminate a survey to a specific population is through the use of telephone interviewing. Telephone interviews are similar to FtF interviews in that an interviewer can clarify questions that interviewees have about the survey, and interviewers can ask more probing, open-ended questions. Telephones interviews are also considerably cheaper and quicker than face-to-face interviews. A researcher no longer needs to send someone to interview a person, so researchers cut down on travel, lodging, and meal expenses, which drastically reduces your overall research budget. In fact, telephone surveys actually enable researchers to include responses from geographically remote locations that they couldn't afford to visit, which makes a sample more representative of the total population.

While there are some clear advantages to telephone interviewing, there are some major drawbacks as well. First, a telephone interview cannot be as long as a FtF interview. In fact, a telephone interview that lasts 15 minutes is pretty long. Interviewers are also more likely to have people tell them that they are not interested in participating or just hanging up on the interviewer altogether, which can randomly or systematically skew a sample. People also tend to trust telephone interviewers less than they do FtF interviewers because there's always the perception in the back on the interviewee's mind that an interviewer is trying to sell them something. Unfortunately for academic researchers, there are less than scrupulous people out in the world who do attempt to disguise product sales as telephone research, which confuses the public and makes them less trustworthy of legitimate research endeavors as a whole. As with FtF interviewing, interviewers still run the risk of inadvertently affecting the responses received from an interviewee, so again training is extremely important to prevent this from occurring. One major limitation with phone surveys is that not everyone has a phone, so a group of people who could be a part of our research sample is not reached. When we exclude people who do not have or have less access to a phone, we bias our sample in the direction of people with phone access. While the bias caused by the lack of phone service is generally not a big deal, for some research projects this could be very problematic. If you wanted to determine people's perceptions of the phone as a communicative tool, you will get a very slanted population if you're surveying only people you can reach by phone because these people already clearly use the tool for communication purposes.

Self-Administration

The final way to get your survey into the hands of your targeted research sample is through self-administration. Self-administration is when an individual receives the survey and then fills out the survey without the help of an interviewer. There are three basic ways to administer a self-administered survey: mass administration, mailed administration, and Internet administration.

Mass Administration Mass administration occurs when you have a large group of people in a stable environment where you can pass out surveys. For example, if you want to examine religious communication, maybe you'll hand out surveys in a large church and have a collection box where people can place the surveys when they are done filling them out. Mass administrations are great when you have a large group of possible participants in a single location. One group that is consistently used in mass administration surveys are college students because they are conveniently available and do not cost researchers a lot of money to use since college students are most commonly paid for their participation in the form of class credit or extra credit.

Mailed Administration A mailed administration survey is when you mail an individual a survey to fill out, and then that individual sends the completed survey back to you. Say you wanted to survey all of the members of your state government on their use of persuasion during political campaigns. You could get a list of addresses for every elected state official and send them your survey, and when they are done filling it out they could send it back to you. Mailing surveys, however, is extremely expensive, and often people you have asked to participate won't send the survey back.

There are some techniques that have been shown to help increase the number of participants you can acquire during mail administered surveys. First, send a postcard to your potential participants letting them know that a survey is coming and why you are conducting your survey. This postcard hopefully will encourage people to participate, or at least be on the lookout for the survey packet itself. Second, send the survey packet with a self-addressed stamped envelope. You may even provide some kind of compensation in the envelope to provide incentive to the participant. One of the coauthors of this book remembers receiving a $1 bill in a survey he received in the mail. Even the $1 bill made our coauthor feel somewhat obligated to participate, so he did. Finally, if you have not received a survey packet back from a particular participant, you may want to follow up with a second postcard reminding the participant to participate. Some scholars will even send another copy of the survey packet to the potential participant through certified mail to ensure that the participant is actually receiving the survey. However, the more mailings you send as a researcher, the more costly mail surveys will become.

Internet Administration Internet administered surveys is the newest form of research and can be used as a replacement for mass administered and mail surveys or as a unique form unto itself (Best & Krueger, 2004; Dillman, 2000). As a way to replace traditional pen-and-paper surveys, many researchers opt to put surveys online because it saves the killing of many trees on an annual basis. Instead of having church members fill out a survey and turn it in, you ask them to go to the website and fill out the survey there. Or instead of mailing your survey to the members of your state government, you e-mail them asking them to fill out the survey online instead. These are two examples of how the Internet can replace pen-and-paper studies; however, the Internet can also be used to gain access to populations that you may not be able to reach using traditional means. For example, maybe you wanted to research the impact that image fixation has on female Buddhists. In the United States, finding a large enough sample of female Buddhists may be very difficult, but could be considerably easier to find online. All you would have to do is find a series of Buddhist websites and ask them if they would post your call for research. Many groups will agree to help a researcher if they can sense that what is being studied is not derogatory towards their group and could possibly benefit their group in the long run.

Advantages and Disadvantages of Self-Administered Surveying

Like other forms of surveying, self-administered surveys have some basic advantages and disadvantages. First, self-administered surveying is by far the cheapest form of surveying. With the exclusion of mail surveys, which can cost a few thousand dollars as a result of postage, most self-administered surveys do not cost more than a few hundred dollars in photocopying expenses or software and website development. The one nice thing about Internet surveys is that once a website has been developed and the software purchased, you can run countless numbers of surveys at one time without any additional expense. Another advantage of self-administered surveys is that you can reach a large cross section of people in a very short period of time. If you have a solid research strategy, getting 200 research participants can be achieved in a very short period of time if you utilize a self-administered technique. Furthermore, you do not have to worry about an interviewer affecting your sample inadvertently as well.

However, there are some clear disadvantages as well. First, participants do not have the ability to seek clarification when they do not understand a question on your survey. In fact, you may end up with serious problems at the end of a study because you did not see an inherent flaw in the design that could have been picked up on and corrected if you were interviewing people face-to-face. Second, you also do not have the ability to check to see if people are randomly answering your survey until the survey is entered into a data set and drops your reliability. Third, people may not take the survey as seriously if they are filling it out alone than if they are being asked the questions with the interviewer sitting in front of them or on the telephone. This problem is often seen in some of the questionnaire responses given by college students. There are some patterns of response that clearly fall into the "screw-you" category. For example, if you are using a 5-point Likert scale and you receive a survey that reads "123451234512345" or "12345432123454321," you can be guaranteed that the person just randomly filled out the survey because he or she obviously didn't care. When we come across a survey where the respondent just randomly filled in responses like this, we consider the survey as a unit nonresponse (discussed below) and eliminate the survey from the dataset.

Problem Areas Associated with Survey Research

As a whole, there are always disadvantages one must be aware of when conducting any specific type of research. This section will discuss a series of situations that can be problematic for researchers.

Response Rate

One of the biggest questions a researcher needs to be worried about when conducting research is her or his response rate. A researcher's response rate is the percentage of surveys returned compared to the percentage of surveys distributed. For example, if you initially hand out 100 surveys and 95 are returned, your response rate is 95%. However, in the real world of research it is not unheard of to receive a response rate under 50%. One of the authors of this book completed a two-part study examining parent–adolescent conflict. The first part of the study was completed and the researcher had around 200 participants. The second part of the study was to be completed 6 months later, and all of the participants in the first part had agreed to participate in the second. Unfortunately, the researcher only received 26 surveys back during the second stage of the research, which is a response rate of only 13%. Ultimately, this entire project had to be scrapped because of the low response rate from the participants. This study fell victim to the problem of nonresponse. According to

Dillman, Eltinge, Groves, and Little (2002), "Nonresponse occurs when a sampled unit does not respond to the request to be surveyed or to particular survey questions" (p. 3). Based on this definition, we can see that there are two types of nonresponse problems that can affect a researcher's survey: unit nonresponse and item nonresponse.

Unit Nonresponse

In the example above that yielded a 13% response rate, we can say that the other 87% of the sample falls into the category of unit nonresponse. Unit nonresponse is defined as the "failure to obtain any survey measurements on a sample unit" (Dillman et al., 2002, p. 6). There are three reasons why people do not participate. First, some participants may never receive the invitation to participate. For example, if you use the National Communication Association's database of members, there are going to be some people who have moved and not updated their information. So if you randomly select any these people to participate in a study, they may never receive the invitation to participate. The second group of people who do not respond simply refuse to do so. These people actually receive the request and basically ignore your request. The last group who do not respond are people who are either physically or mentally unable to do so. Maybe you send out an e-mail survey, and one of the people you asked to participate is ill in the hospital. He or she may even get the e-mail request, but not be in a position physically or mentally to respond.

Now that we've examined why people don't participate, you may be wondering why a participant agrees to participate in a study. Well, Dillman et al. (2002) argue that there are three basic reasons why people will agree to participate in a research survey, but this information is also true for getting people to participate in any type of research. First, participants will weigh the potential costs and rewards of participating in the survey. If a respondent sees her or his participation as a huge waste of time, he or she will be unlikely to participate unless the researcher can adequately entice the respondent to participate. While there are some people who will believe participating in research is part of her or his "civic duty," most people feel the need to be compensated in some way for their participation. This "compensation" can come in many different forms, from monetary incentives to personalized letters asking for cooperation. If the participant feels that the researcher is at least attempting to provide some benefit for participation, the participant is much more likely to participate. This is the real reason why researchers offer college students extra credit to participate in research projects.

Second, the more interesting the topic of research is to the participant, the more likely he or she will want to participate in your study. For example, if a potential participant could care less about politics, he or she will not be very likely to participate in a survey examining political communication. This is especially true in self-administered surveys because respondents can preview the types of questions asked on the survey prior to actually filling out the survey. For this reason, the more mundane a research study is, the more likely it will be that the researcher will need to provide adequate compensation to get participants. However, if you land on a really "sexy" topic, people will be likely to participate without expecting compensation. Unfortunately, as a researcher you often do not know if your topic is going to be seen as salient to people until after you begin collecting your data.

Finally, many participants are influenced to participate in a research project based on their previous participation in research. This is true for both new projects and continuing projects. For example, if a person feels he or she was treated poorly by a researcher in the past, he or she will be very unlikely to participate in future research studies when asked. Also, if a participant feels he or she is being mistreated during a research project, he or she may decide to leave the study. For these reasons, it is very important that researchers attempt to make the survey experience as interesting and harmless as humanly possible.

Item Nonresponse

Item nonresponse occurs when an individual participant fails to answer individual or groups of questions on a survey. According to Dillman et al. (2002), there are seven causes of item nonresponse: survey mode, interviewer training, question topics, question structure, question difficulty, institutional requirements and policies, and respondent attributes.

The first reason participants may not respond to specific items on a survey deals with the nature of surveying. In a self-administered survey, individual participants are ultimately responsible for reading and responding to all of the questions on the survey. One of the simplest reasons some people do not respond to an item is that their eyes visually skip an item whereas, during an interview an interviewer is responsible for making sure the participant responds to the survey questions. In fact, if a participant is hesitant to respond to a question, the interviewer can even encourage the interviewee to answer, which is not possible during a self-administered survey.

The second reason participants may not respond relates specifically to surveys that rely on interviewers. The interviewer can either help foster answers or actually cause participants to not answer survey questions. If an interviewer can develop a positive, friendly relationship with a participant, the interviewer is more likely to get the participant to answer survey questions. If, however, the interviewer is either unfriendly or very bland, the interviewee will be more likely to not answer questions. Also, interviewers have the ability to coax answers out of participants who may not otherwise answer a specific question.

The third reason participants may not respond to survey questions relates to the topics of the questions themselves. As discussed earlier in this chapter, many topics make people feel embarrassed, shamed, or fearful. When topics evoke these emotional responses, people may feel the questions are psychologically or physically threatening and just avoid answering the questions altogether.

The fourth reason people may not respond to survey questions involves the actual structure of the survey questions themselves. Basically, certain types of questions are more likely to be answered than other types of questions. For example, in self-administered surveys, open-ended questions are considerably more likely to be left unanswered when compared to closed-ended questions like Likert and semantic differential/bipolar adjective scales. Also, if you have questions that do not pertain to specific participants, they may skip those questions and skip more relevant questions at the same time. Again, if you have properly pilot tested a survey, this is much less likely to be a cause of nonresponse.

The fifth reason some people may not answer questions involves the difficulty of the question itself. Sometimes questions are either too difficult to answer or are too confusing for participants to answer. If you follow the general requirements for writing Likert scales in Chapter 9, you are less likely to run into this problem. Other questions may just ask participants to recall information they simply can't remember. For instance, if you ask a participant to recall the number of times he or she communicated with a family member in the past month, this may be impossible for some people to answer, so they just leave the item blank. Yet again, if you properly pilot test a study, this problem should take care of itself prior to administering your survey to your entire sample.

The sixth reason some people may not answer questions relates to institutional requirements and policies. First, some participants will not respond to items because they are legally allowed to not answer all of the questions. Institutional review boards will often require researchers to include a statement that the participant may stop her or his participation at any time, or that the participant does not have to answer all of the questions on the questionnaire. Other participants may not answer specific questions because they consider the information private or proprietary. An example of information that may be considered private is someone's salary, whereas information that is proprietary is information over which an individual or group exercises private ownership. For example, if you are surveying organizational members about organizational coaching practices, some may see you as trying to steal their organization's information, so they will just refuse to answer questions. The easiest way to alleviate this problem is to simply reassure the participants that all information is confidential or anonymous and will not be seen by anyone outside the research team.

The last reason some people do not respond to surveys is more of a personal issue than one the researcher can control. Dillaman et al. (2002) note that "older people and those with less education are less likely to provide answers in many surveys" (p. 14). Mason, Lesser, and Traugott (2002) also found that people who are reluctant participants in the first place are much more likely to not respond to individual items during the study. This is yet another reason to make sure that you attempt to get participants to see their participation as beneficial.

Effects of Nonresponse

Every survey is going to have some level of nonresponse associated with it. However, the question is whether this nonresponse actually alters the results of your survey in some meaningful way. The question then becomes, "Are those who are not responding distinctly different in some manner from those who are responding?" Fowler (1993) noted that in mail research "people who have a particular interest in the subject matter or the research itself are more likely to return mail questionnaires than those who are less interested" (p. 41). In other words, if a mail survey has a very low response rate, as a researcher you must question the generalizablity of your results to the whole population. Low response rates can also cause a specific type of error to enter into your study called nonresponse bias. In essence, the people who did not participate are different enough from the people who did participate that it skews your results.

While we know that nonresponse bias is extremely detrimental to a study, we really do not know how much of a bias there actually is. When you cannot get individuals to participate in the first place, it's hard to find out why they didn't respond later on as well. For this reason, we often have no way of quantifying the actual bias within a dataset due to nonresponse. The fact is there is no way to prevent nonresponse in survey research. Some people, for whatever reason, simply will either not participate or not answer specific questions in a research study. However, the research can improve the response rate by making sure the survey, whether a questionnaire or interview, is presented in a clear and logical manner.

Improving Response Rates

Now that we've looked at some of the disadvantages to mass administered surveys, here are some suggestions for how you can overcome some of these problems.

1. Make the Survey Easy to Fill Out. The more confusing a survey is for a participant, the more likely that participant is going to quit. Make sure that your font is large enough to be read by an average audience. Make sure your directions are very clear. I even suggest adding sample questions that clearly illustrate how items in your study should be answered. For example, if you have a Likert scale, add a fake item and explain how the item could be answered. In our experience, the one survey format that is often the most confusing is the bipolar adjectives format. Too many people believe they need to select a step on the scale for each adjective. For example, if your adjectives are "Yes 1, 2, 3, 4, 5, 6, 7 No," many people will circle 2 for "Yes" and 6 for "No." It does not matter if you bold, italicize, or underline the phrase "circle only one letter per adjective pair," people will still make mistakes filling out your survey. Having a sample question has been shown to alleviate some of the more common mistakes.

2. *Keep It Short.* Short surveys will always result in more participants, but longer surveys give you more information to analyze. While there is no magical formula, it is recommended that a pen-and-paper survey be no longer than three to four pages in length. It does not matter whether your survey is single or double sided. In essence, people tend to view four pages single sided and four pages double sided as being equal in length because it's still four pages. You should also vary the types of questions you have on a survey. Too often people will have page after page of Likert scale items, which can cause people to become bored and tired and not complete the study.

3. *Include an SASE.* This particular hint is primarily for mail-administered surveys. SASE is the acronym for self-addressed stamped envelope. If you do not include a self-addressed envelope and put postage on the envelope, people will not be very likely to return your survey. People generally believe that they are doing you a favor by filling out your survey, so the least you can do is make the filling out and returning experience as easy as humanly possible.

4. *Include a Good Cover Letter.* The cover letter should explain to potential participants who you are and why you are conducting the research along with any legal notifications related to compliance as established by both the federal government and your university. While the goal of the cover letter is to first and foremost convince people that they want to participate in your project, the letter is also a legal notification to participants of their rights as a participant. Some universities have very simple guidelines for what must be in a cover letter, and other universities have very specific guidelines for what must be in a cover letter. If you have any questions about what your university wants to see in a cover letter, contact your institutional review board.

5. *Use Multiple Administration Techniques.* The concept of multiple administration techniques can be broken down into two categories: (1) options of survey method and (2) multiple contacts. The first multiple administration technique is to allow participants the option to fill out a survey by pen and paper or by Internet. When you allow people this option, people who may not be likely to fill out the pen-and-paper survey may jump online and fill out the survey. The second aspect of the multiple administration technique is to use the multiple contact method. In essence, you contact a potential participant about your study through a quick e-mail or postcard to let them know you are sending them a survey. Next, you send them your survey. Two or three weeks later you send a follow-up letter or e-mail either thanking them for participating or reminding them that you still need their participation. Some scholars even suggest sending a final survey through certified mail, but this can get very expensive in the long run.

Translating Surveys into Other Languages

One area where researchers conducting survey research may have a great amount of trouble occurs when they conduct surveys using samples from multiple intercultural groups. Often researchers want to conduct surveys of people who do not speak English as their native language or even speak English at all. For this reason, researchers have had to devise a range of different techniques for translating surveys into other languages. However, translating a survey into another language is easier said than done. Translating surveys into different languages involves three key equivalence issues: semantic, conceptual, and normative (Behling & Law, 2000; Gudykunst, 2002).

Semantic Equivalence

The first major issue involved in translating surveys into other languages involves issues of semantics. The simple fact of the matter is that languages are semantically different from each other. Semantics is the study of meaning. So when we say that there is a problem with semantics, we are describing a language problem where a word in one language may not have an equivalent word with the same meaning in a different language. Words that exist in English may have no direct translation in Mandarin, which is going to cause problems if you attempt to translate a survey from one language to the other.

Conceptual Equivalence

Often when we create mental measures that are designed to measure one specific construct in one culture, the construct will not hold true in another culture. In other words, does the basic concept a researcher is attempting to study in one culture even exist within another culture? For example, one area where we tend to see conceptual problems is family communication. In some cultures the very notion that a child would be allowed to speak her or his mind to elders is absurd. If you have a mental measure that examines openness of ideas shared within the family, the basic concept will not translate to some other cultures. In other words, just because we can study a concept in the United States does not mean that the concept is able to be studied within other cultures. Zhang (2005a, 2005b, 2006) has examined the notion of nonverbal immediacy and how U.S. students and Chinese students perceive nonverbal immediacy different. In this case we have a concept that has been regularly studied within the United States that Zhang has shown does not translate for Chinese students. For this reason, Zhang (2006) has created a new mental measure specifically designed to measure Chinese students' perceptions of teacher nonverbal immediacy.

Normative Equivalence

Every cultural group has its own set of norms or social conventions. These norms do not translate from one culture to the next because they are culturally dependent. For this reason, survey questions are often very culturally specific. Behling and Law (2000) note that there are three behaviors that can impact the translating of research instruments: willingness to discuss certain topics, manner in which ideas are expressed, and treatment of strangers.

The first behavior that can impact the translating of research instruments is whether or not people in a specific culture are open to discussing certain topics. Different cultures have different norms when it comes to discussing specific topics. While the U.S. culture has no problem with gossiping about the sex lives of our political figures, other cultures tend to be less likely to discuss sexuality as a general concept (Frayser, 2002). For this reason, if you're conducting a survey on sexual communication in another culture, you may find that your non-response rate escalates because your participants do not like openly discussing the subject.

The second behavior that can affect the translating of research instruments deals with how participants may respond to questions. In some cultures, people are less likely to engage in self-aggrandizement or to make themselves appear better or greater than they actually are. For instance, if you're conducting a study on willingness to communicate, you may find cultural differences. Barraclough, Christophel, and McCroskey (1988) found that American students reported having higher levels of willingness to communicate and higher levels of self-perceived communication competence when compared to Australian students. When results like this are found, we could be looking at actual differences between cultures or just differences in how people in different cultures rate themselves on mental measures. Lonner and Ibrahim (1996) note that it is common for people in different cultures to respond to mental measures differently. In essence, Lonner and Ibrahim believe that people in different cultures have different positional response styles, i.e., people within cultures respond to scales in similar patterns that are representative of cultural test taking and not the differences on the measures themselves. In other words, people may be more or less likely to use the extremes on mental measures, or they are more likely to go for the neutral option on mental measures, based on their culture rather than their actual perceptions of their own attitudes, behaviors, beliefs, cognitive knowledge, personality traits, and values.

The final behavior that can impact the translating of research instruments deals with different cultures' handling of strangers. As noted by Behling and Law (2000), "Reactions to strangers—particularly to strangers asking questions—also vary from society to society" (p. 6). Different people in different cultures will have widely different reactions to people attempting to conduct research. Some people may attempt to give answers to a researcher that they perceive the researcher wants. Or the respondent may simply go along with the survey out of politeness, but not actually give the researcher any useful information. For this reason, we always recommend having at least one person on your research team who is from the target culture. If you are going to conduct research in Zimbabwe, you should have at least one researcher on your project who is from Zimbabwe to prevent the issue of being a stranger conducting research in another culture.

Now that we understand some of the problems that researchers face when translating surveys from one language to another, we need to discuss the ways in which researchers can successfully complete a survey translation. Behling and Law (2000) expanded on Guthery and Lowe's (1992) original ideas for translating surveys and came up with five unique methods researchers can employ for translating surveys.

Simple Direct Translation

The first method a researcher can employ for translating scales from one language to a secondary language is the simple direct translation. In this method of translating, a researcher recruits a bilingual individual, who takes the original survey and then translates this survey from the primary language to the secondary language. However, there are some problems with this method. First, when conducting a simple direct translation, the translator is only paying attention to semantic issues of translation. In essence, the translator is making sure the survey can be read and understood by people in the secondary language, but does not pay attention to conceptual or normative issues. Furthermore, the translator is not really being double checked. We already know that people make mistakes, so relying on one person to conduct a translation automatically opens your research projects to translation errors.

Modified Direct Translation

The second method a researcher can employ for translating scales from one language to a secondary language is the modified direct translation. In this version of survey translation, a translator performs the same translation he or she did in the simple direct translation, but with the addition of one step. After the translation process is completed, the translation is given to a panel of experts who know the primary and secondary languages, and the group decides whether or not the individual item translations are appropriate or not. While this sounds better than a simple direct translation, this method also opens itself up to a number of problems. First, the panel may be no more knowledgeable about translating information from one language to another language than the original translator is. Second, this method is very time consuming and really doesn't provide the researcher any information that he or she could not get from the original translation about the quality. If anything, the translation may end up making less sense after a group of people attempt to translate the survey.

Translation/Back-translation

The third method a researcher can employ for translating scales from one language to a secondary language is the translation/back-translation method. In this method, a researcher has a translator complete the same steps he or she would complete in the simple direct translation. After the initial translation is complete, the researcher then provides the new translation to another bilingual individual who has not seen the original survey, and then the second translator attempts to translate the work back into the first language. If the original survey and the retranslated survey are very similar, then the translation is semantically successful. If, however, the two translations are very different, the original and secondary translator can discuss possible problematic areas and a new translation can be completed. While this definitely provides great semantic verifiability, the researcher cannot be sure that the translator is actually paying attention to conceptual or normative issues. Furthermore, utilizing two translators can be quite expensive if they must be hired for the study.

Parallel Blind Technique

The fourth method a researcher can employ for translating scales from one language to a secondary language is the parallel blind technique. In this method of translation, a researcher has two independent translators translate the survey in the same way as described in the simple direct translation. After both researchers complete their independent translations, the two translators then compare their translations and ultimately agree upon a third translation that is given to the researcher. Ultimately, the researcher must trust her or his translators in this technique. However, the researcher cannot be sure that the translation is actually paying attention to conceptual or normative issues. Furthermore, utilizing two translators can be quite expensive if they must be hired for the study. On the plus side of this method, it tends to be quite fast.

Random Probe

The fifth method a researcher can employ for translating scales from one language to a secondary language is the random probe technique. In this method, a researcher has a translator complete the same steps he or she would complete in the simple direct translation. After the researcher has the translation in hand, he or she then pilot tests the translation with a group of bilingual participants. After the participants complete the survey, the researcher then asks a series of open-ended questions examining why the participants answered questions in a specific manner. The goal of this process is to ascertain whether or not the participants understand the questions in a manner that is similar to the researcher's own understanding of the mental measure. This method can actually help a researcher test for conceptual and normative issues of translating during the open-ended question interview portion of the pilot test. Behling and Law (2000) suggest using this approach in combination with the modified direct translation, translation/back-translation, or the parallel blind technique to make sure that the survey's translation is equivalent on all three levels (semantic, conceptual, and normative).

Using the Research Project Worksheet

The last part of this chapter contains what we call the Designing a Research Project Worksheet (Figure 11.2). This worksheet was originally designed by Dr. Jason Wrench (one of the text's coauthors) while he was working for a medical school and teaching biostatistics. This worksheet is very useful when either planning your own research projects or analyzing someone else's study. This worksheet contains components from this chapter and the next two chapters (content analysis and experimental research). The rest this chapter is going to walk through a sample survey research project and demonstrate how you could fill out the Designing a Research Project Worksheet. You can find an MS Word document file containing this worksheet on the CD-ROM that accompanies this book in the Workbook folder.

Question (In a single sentence, what would you like to know when your project is done?)

Design (Check one): ( ) Survey ( ) Content Analysis ( ) Data Mining ( ) Randomized Study ( ) Nonrandom Study

If a self-administered survey, how?	( ) Mass Administered	( ) Mail	( ) Web Based	
If an interview-based survey, how?	( ) Phone	( ) In Person		
If a content analysis, what type?	( ) Mediated	( ) Interactional	( ) Microlevel	( ) Macrolevel
If using preexisting data?	( ) Personally Collected	( ) Governmental Agency	( ) Other Records	( ) Other
Type of randomization?	( ) Nonblind	( ) Single Blind	( ) Double Blind	
Type of nonrandomized study?	( ) Case-Control	( ) Cohort		

Type of Experimental Design:

Quasi Experimental Design			
( ) Pretest–Posttest	( ) Time Series	( ) Multiple Time Series	( ) Switching Replications
True Experimental Design			
( ) Pretest–Posttest	( ) Two-Group Posttest Only	( ) Randomized Switching Replications	( ) Solomon Four-Group

Setting (Where will the survey/study be conducted?)

Participants
1. Do your participants need to possess any specific characteristics (high levels of communication apprehension, users of instant messaging, relational partner, age grouping, biological sex, etc.)? ( ) YES ( ) NO
    If Yes, explain:

2. How are you going to select/acquire participants?

3. Do you need a letter of consent for participation? (NOTE: All survey and experimentally based studies must have a letter of consent.) ( ) YES ( ) NO
    If No, explain why not:

Variables (What are your IVs/DVs, how are they measured, and what level of measurement are they?)

1. Independent Variables (label as nominal, ordinal, interval, or ratio):

Figure 11.2 Designing a Research Project Worksheet (Developed by Dr. Jason S. Wrench)

Continued

Continued

---

2. Dependent Variables (label as nominal, ordinal, interval, or ratio):

Hypotheses/Research Questions

Statistical Testing (Using the above Hypos/RQs, what statistical tests will you use to answer each question?)

Tentative Study Title:

Principal Researcher(s):

QUESTION

The first section of the Designing a Research Project Worksheet asks a researcher to explain in a single sentence what he or she would like to know when the project is done. Researchers need to have the ability to concisely explain the purpose of a research project, so forcing yourself to explain the project in one sentence will help keep you focused as you design your project.

For our example study, let's look for a possible difference between females and males in their levels of communication apprehension (CA) and willingness to communicate (WTC) and for a relationship between CA and WTC. Therefore, our one-sentence question could be, "Do females and males differ in their level of CA and WTC, and is there a relationship between CA and WTC?" This sentence is short, sweet, and very much to the point.

DESIGN

The second section of the Designing a Research Project Worksheet is concerned with the basic study design. The design section has components for surveys, content analysis, and experimental designs. Depending on which type of study you are planning on conducting, you should focus on those design aspects.

For our example study, we are planning on conducting a survey, so we would place an "X" next to Survey. Once you've determined that you're conducting a survey, you need to decide whether this survey will be self-administered (mass, mail, or web) or interview based (phone or in person). For our study, let's go ahead and do a mass-administered survey, so put an "X" next to Mass Administered. This is the last thing we must check in the Design section, since the rest of this section is either for content analysis studies or experimental studies.

SETTING

The third section of the Designing a Research Project Worksheet is concerned with the physical location you plan to use for your study. While this section is not very useful for a content analysis study, it is extremely important when conducting both survey research and experiments.

For our example study, let's pretend that we've gotten permission to hand out questionnaires at a local business club. For our setting, we may include information like where the club meets, what time the meeting is, and the appropriate dress. When thinking about the setting, you need to think about the context of the setting (a business club) and how this context will affect how you should present yourself as a researcher. If you're studying a sports team, you may present yourself in a very different manner than you would at a business club. Your goal for this section is to be as detailed as possible. Here's an example of what you might end up writing, "We will be handing out questionnaires at the local American Business Club meeting, which meets in Civic Center room 3-A on Mondays at noon. The researchers should be in professional dress since most of the potential participants are at the meeting during their lunch hour."

PARTICIPANTS

The fourth section of the Designing a Research Project Worksheet is concerned with the actual participants you are planning to collect during your study. Typically, there are three basic items you should know when thinking about potential participants: specific characteristics, how to recruit, and how to gain consent.

Specific Characteristics

The first question you need to ask yourself as a researcher is whether there are any specific characteristics your participants should have for recruitment into a study. For example, if you're conducting a survey of physicians, one of the characteristics your participants must possess is an MD or DO. For our example study, we really have no specific characteristics in mind, so place an "X" next to the word NO.

Recruitment

The second question to ask yourself related to participants is how are you going to get your participants. Throughout this chapter we've discussed many ways you can recruit participants, whether in the college classroom, by random phone surveying, or asking people at a business club meeting. The clearer your recruitment plan is up front, the easier it will be to actually recruit participants later on in your study. Also, if you have a unique group you want to study, you will have more time to determine how to best target those participants.

Consent

The next question you need to think about is whether or not you will need to attach a cover letter explaining consent. You should also decide whether or not the consent form needs to be signed or not. Of course, these are decisions that you cannot ultimately make yourself because you must get approval from the institutional review board to conduct any survey research study.

VARIABLES

Independent Variables

The next thing you want to have for your study is all of your independent variables. In our study, the only truly independent variable is biological sex.

Dependent Variables

Next you want to list all of your study-dependent variables. For our study, we have two dependent variables: CA and WTC. If you are testing for relationships, you can list the variables where most appropriate for your study. This will be discussed further in Chapter 20 when we talk about regressions.

HYPOTHESES/RESEARCH QUESTIONS

In the next section you should list any hypotheses and research questions. Obviously, these should relate directly to your independent and dependent variables. Remember, if you do not list a variable on your independent variable or dependent variable list, you cannot have a hypothesis or research question that involves that variable. In our sample study we list three variables (biological sex, CA, and WTC); therefore, I could not have a hypothesis that predicts that people who have been in their jobs longer will have lower levels of CA because we are not measuring how long someone has been in her or his job. If you find you want to measure a variable not listed as an IV or DV, you should add that variable to your study.

STATISTICAL TESTING

Once you know what your hypotheses and research questions are going to be, you can decide which statistical tests will be the most appropriate tests to conduct. While we will discuss how to determine which statistical tests to use in Chapters 16 through 21, you can always go back and use the chart in Chapter 6 (Figure 6.9).

For our current study, we know we are examining a difference between two groups (female and male participants) on one interval variable (communication apprehension/willingness to communicate), so we would use a t-test to analyze this hypothesis. Our second hypothesis tests for a relationship between two interval/ratio level variables, so we would use a correlation to analyze this hypothesis.

TENTATIVE STUDY TITLE

Every study needs to be called something. While the title you create at this stage in your research project will probably not be the title at the end of your project, you should go ahead and give your study a title just so you have something to call the study while you're working. There is no clear-cut way to title a study. The only real rule is that your title relate to your study itself. Our example study may be titled "Sex Differences and Communication Apprehension and Willingness to Communicate."

PRINCIPAL RESEARCHER(S)

The last part of the Designing a Research Project Worksheet is a list of all those involved in your project. Make sure you list all of the principal investigators and your advisor if you have one for this study. If you need to remember the appropriate method for listing authors for a study, reread the section in Chapter 3 on ethics related to authorship.

A completed version of the Designing a Research Project Worksheet can be seen in Figure 11.3.

Question (In a single sentence, what would you like to know when your project is done?)

Do females and males differ in on their level of CA & WTC, and is there a relationship between CA and WTC?

Design   (X) Survey   ( ) Content   ( ) Data Mining   ( ) Randomized   ( ) Nonrandom
(Check one):   Analysis   Study   Study

If a self-administered survey, how?	(X) Mass Administered	( ) Mail	( ) Web Based	
If an interview based survey, how?	( ) Phone	( ) In Person		
If a content analysis, what type?	( ) Mediated	( ) Interactional	( ) Microlevel	( ) Macrolevel
If using preexisting data?	( ) Personally Collected	( ) Governmental Agency	( ) Other Records	( ) Other
Type of randomization?	( ) Nonblind	( ) Single Blind	( ) Double Blind	
Type of nonrandomized study?	( ) Case-Control	( ) Cohort		

Type of Experimental Design:

Quasi-Experimental Design			
( ) Pretest–Posttest	( ) Time Series	( ) Multiple Time Series	( ) Switching Replications
True Experimental Design			
( ) Pretest–Posttest	( ) Two-Group Posttest Only	( ) Randomized Switching Replications	( ) Solomon Four-Group

Setting (Where will the survey/study be conducted?)
We will be handing out questionnaires at the local American Business Club meeting, which meets in Civic Center room 3-A on Mondays at noon. The researchers should be in professional dress since most of the potential participants are at the meeting during their lunch hour.

Participants
1. Do your participants need to possess any specific characteristics (high levels of communication apprehension, users of instant messaging, relational partner, age grouping, biological sex, etc.)? ( ) YES (X) NO
   If Yes, explain:

2. How are you going to select/acquire participants?
   Participants will be recruited during the American Business Club meeting. Participants will be handed a questionnaire as they arrive to the luncheon and asked to turn the questionnaires back in to one of the researchers at the end of the luncheon.

3. Do you need a letter of consent for participation? (NOTE: All survey and experimentally based studies must have a letter of consent.) (X) YES ( ) NO
   If No, explain why not:

Figure 11.3 Completed Project Worksheet

Continued

Variables (What are your IVs/DVs, how are they measured, and what level of measurement are they?)

3. Independent Variables (label as nominal, ordinal, interval, or ratio):
   Biological Sex (Nominal Variable)

4. Dependent Variables (label as nominal, ordinal, interval, or ratio):
   Communication Apprehension (Interval Variable)
   Willingness to Communicate (Interval Variable)

Hypotheses/Research Questions

H1: There will be a difference between men and women in their levels of communication apprehension.

H2: There will be a difference between men and women in their willingness to communicate.

H3: There will be a negative relationship between communication apprehension and willingness to communicate.

Statistical Testing (Using the above Hypos/RQs, what statistical tests will you use to answer each question?)

H1: There will be a difference between men and women in their levels of communication apprehension.
A t-test will be conducted using biological sex as the independent variable and communication apprehension as the dependent variable.

H2: There will be a difference between men and women in their willingness to communicate.
A t-test will be conducted using biological sex as the independent variable and willingness to communicate as the dependent variable.

H3: There will be a negative relationship between communication apprehension and willingness to communicate.
A correlation will be conducted between communication apprehension and willingness to communicate.

Tentative Study Title:
Sex Differences and Communication Apprehension and Willingness to Communicate

Principal Researcher(s):
Jason S. Wrench, Candice Thomas-Maddox, Virginia Peck Richmond, & James C. McCroskey

Conclusion

This chapter has examined some of the basic concepts related to survey research. In the next chapter we will discuss a second research method technique called content analysis.

KEY TERMS

Accelerated Longitudinal
  Survey Design
Analytical Survey
Conceptual Equivalence

Cross-Sectional Survey
  Design
Descriptive Survey
Generalizablity

Interview Schedule
Longitudinal Survey Design
Modified Direct Translation
Nonresponse

Nonresponse Bias
Normative Equivalence
Panel Design
Parallel Blind Technique
Pilot Test

Questionnaire
Random Probe Translation
Response Rate
Semantic Equivalence
Simple Direct Translation

Socially Desirable
 Responding
Survey
Translation/Back-translation
Trend Design

REFERENCES

Barraclough, R. A., Christophel, D. M., & McCroskey, J. C. (1988). Willingness to communicate: A cross-cultural investigation. *Communication Research Reports, 5(2)*, 187–192.

Behling, O., & Law, K. S. (2000). *Translating questionnaires and other research instruments: Problems and solutions.* Thousand Oaks, CA: Sage.

Best, S. J., & Krueger, B. S. (2004). *Internet data collection.* Thousand Oaks, CA: Sage.

Buckingham, A., & Saunders, P. (2004). *The survey methods workbook: From design to analysis.* Malden, MA: Polity Press.

Cattell, J. M. (1890). Mental tests and measurements. *Mind, 15*, 373–381.

Converse, J. M., & Presser, S. (1986). *Survey questions: Handcrafting the standardized questionnaire.* Thousand Oaks, CA: Sage.

Dillman, D. A. (2000). *Mail and internet surveys: The tailored design method* (2nd ed.). New York: Wiley.

Dillman, D. A., Eltinge, J. L., Groves, R. M., & Little, R. J. A. (2002). Survey nonresponse in design, data collection, and analysis. In R. M. Groves, D. A. Dillman, J. L. Eltinge, & R. J. A. Little (Eds.), *Survey nonresponse* (pp. 3–26). New York: John Wiley & Sons.

Fink, A. (2006). *How to conduct surveys: A step-by-step guide* (3rd ed.). Thousand Oaks, CA: Sage.

Fowler, F. J., Jr. (1993). *Survey research methods* (2nd ed.). Newbury Park, CA: Sage.

Frayser, S. G. (2002). Discovering the value of cross-cultural research on human sexuality. In M. W. Wiederman & B. E. Whitley, Jr. (Ed.), *Handbook for conducting research on human sexuality* (pp. 425–453). Mahwah, NJ: Lawrence Erlbaum.

Gudykunst, W. B. (2002). Issues in cross-cultural communication research. In W. B. Gudykunst & B. Mody (Eds.), *Handbook of international and intercultural communication* (2nd ed., pp. 165–177). Thousand Oaks, CA: Sage.

Guthery, D., & Lowe, B. A. (1992). Translation problems in international marketing research. *Journal of Language and International Business, 4*, 1–14.

Hildebrand, D. K., Laing, J. D., Rosenthal, H. (1977). *Analysis of ordinal data.* Newbury Park, CA: Sage.

Kinsey, A. C., Pomeroy, W. B., & Martin, C. E. (1948). *Sexual behavior in the human male.* Philadelphia: Saunders.

Kinsey, A. C., Pomeroy, W. B., Martin, C. E., Gebhard, P. H. (1953). *Sexual behavior in the human female.* Philadelphia: Saunders.

Lonner, W. J., & Ibrahim, F. A. (1996). Appraisal and assessment in cross-cultural counseling. In P. B. Pedersen, J. G. Draguns, W. J. Lonner, & J. E. Trimble (Eds.), *Counseling across cultures* (4th ed., pp. 292–322). Newbury Park, CA: Sage.

Mason, R., Lesser, V., & Traugott, M. W. (2002). Effect of item nonresponse on nonresponse error and inference. In R. M. Groves, D. A. Dillman, J. L. Eltinge, & R. J. A. Little (Eds.), *Survey nonresponse* (pp. 149–161). New York: John Wiley & Sons.

Rocca, K. A., & Vogl-Bauer, S. (1999). Trait verbal aggression, sports fan identification, and perceptions of appropriate sports fan communication. *Communication Research Reports, 16*, 239–248.

Wrench, J. S., Corrigan, M. W., McCroskey, J. C., & Punyanunt-Carter N. M. (2006). Religious fundamentalism and intercultural communication: The relationships among ethnocentrism, intercultural communication apprehension, religious fundamentalism, homonegativity, and tolerance for religious disagreements. *Journal of Intercultural Communication Research, 35*, 23–44.

Zhang, Q. (2005a). Immediacy, humor, power distance, and classroom communication apprehension in Chinese college classrooms. *Communication Quarterly, 53*, 109–124.

Zhang, Q. (2005b). Teacher immediacy and classroom communication apprehension: A cross-cultural investigation. *Journal of Intercultural Communication Research, 34*, 50–64.

Zhang, Q. (2006). Constructing and validating a Teacher Immediacy Scale: A Chinese perspective. *Communication Education, 55*, 218–241.

FURTHER READING

Groves, R. M. (2004). *Survey errors and survey costs.* Hoboken, NJ: John Wiley & Sons.

Lee, E. S., & Forthofer, R., N. (2006). *Analyzing complex survey data* (2nd ed.). Thousand Oaks, CA: Sage.

Patten, M. L. (2001). *Questionnaire research: A practical guide* (2nd ed.). Los Angeles: Pyrczak.

Punch, K. F. (2003). *Survey research: The basics.* Thousand Oaks, CA: Sage.

Rea, L. M., & Parker, R. A. (2005). *Designing and conducting survey research: A comprehensive guide* (3rd ed.). San Francisco: Jossey-Bass.

Singleton, R. A., Jr., & Straits, B. C. (1999). *Approach to social research* (3rd ed.). New York: Oxford University Press.

CHAPTER 12

Content Analysis

1 Understand the basic principles underlying the use of content analysis.

2 Know the different types of research studies that can be conducted using content analysis methods.

3 Explain the basic steps necessary to conduct a content analysis.

4 Explain the relationship between conceptualization, operationalization, and unit of analysis.

5 Understand the types of units of analysis often studied in content analysis.

6 Explain what coding is and how one creates a codebook and coding form.

7 Understand the training process necessary for training and evaluating coders.

8 Know what *intercoder reliability* is and how to calculate Cohen's kappa.

9 Understand the four problems a researcher may face with her or his coders (coder misinterpretations, coder in attention, coder fatigue, and recording errors).

In Chapter 11 we disussed how communication researchers go about studying a communicative phenomenon (surveying). In the next two chapters we will focus on two other methods that communication researchers can use to learn about human communication: content analysis and experimental research. Before delving into how communication researchers actually use content analysis, we will first explain what content analysis is and how it can be applied to a variety of communicative contexts.

According to Neuendorf (2002) *content analysis* is a "summarizing, quantitative analysis of messages that relies on the scientific method (including attention to objectivity–intersubjectivity, a priori design, reliability, validity, generalizability, replicability, and hypothesis testing) and is not limited as to the types of variables that may be measured or the context in which the messages are created or presented" (p. 10). When we look at this definition there are a number of important parts to understand. First, content analysis attempts to quantitatively summarize different messages. These messages may be verbal (e.g., types of jokes told by comedians), nonverbal (e.g., incidence of facial expressions during conversations), or mediated (e.g., portrayal of global warming in magazines). In each of these three cases, a researcher using content analysis would attempt to understand how various messages function.

Second, Neuendorf's (2002) definition of content analysis is dependent upon the scientific method. While we are not going to rehash our discussion of the scientific method here (see Chapter 2 to refresh your memory), we do want to emphasize that the empirical use of content analysis should conform to the traditional norms of scientific research. In other words, researchers should not randomly opt to use content analysis, but should have very specific reasons for believing that content analysis is the most appropriate method to examine communicative phenomena.

Finally, Neuendorf (2002) notes that content analysis can be applied to a wide range of differing communicative contexts: "Content analysis may be conducted on written text, transcribed speech, verbal interactions, visual images, characterizations, nonverbal behaviors, sound events, or any other type of message" (p. 24). Neuendorf does acknowledge that the notion of content analysis started by specifically examining textual works. One of the earliest examples of a content analysis occurred during the 1770s in Sweden. In Sweden, a hymnal entitled *Songs of Zion* was published and republished in multiple editions. At first, the Swedish authorities granted permission to publish the volume of songs, but then fear that the songs contained unorthodox (i.e., not approved by the Swedish Church) teachings began to arise. A well-read orthodox clergyman named Kumblaeus attempted to solve the debate through a simple textual analysis of the hymnal itself. Kumblaeus counted various orthodox themes in the hymnal and compared them to the number of unorthodox themes, and "concluded on the basis of his analysis that the exclusion of certain Christian themes and emphasis on certain others tended to create new conceptions which threatened the doctrine of the established church" (Dovring, 1954–55, p. 392). Overall, Kumblaeus was able to quantitatively examine the text and determine that the hymnal was indeed a clear source of unorthodox teachings. Not only did Kumblaeus complete a quantitative analysis of the themes within the text, he further suggested that these themes indicate that the editor of the volume clearly had an underlying motivation to spread unorthodox themes in the hopes of converting more followers. This example clearly illustrates how content analysis can be used to show how sources of messages construct messages and have motivations underlying the messages sent and how a source's message is intended to influence a specific receiver.

In modern scholarship, content analysis has been used to examine a wide range of different communication phenomena. In the context of mass-mediated messages, content analysis has been used to examine advertisers' use of product pricing (Howard & Kerin, 2006), physical attributes of violent video game characters (Lachlan, Smith, & Tamborini, 2005), candidate blogs during a presidential election (Bichard, 2006), differences in television reporting between embedded and nonembedded journalists in the Iraq war (Pfau, Haigh, Logsdon, Perrine, Baldwin, et al., 2005), coverage of the SARS outbreak in Chinese newspapers (Zhang & Flemming, 2005), portrayals of models over 50 years old in the United Kingdom (Simcock & Sudbury, 2006), and types of advertising found in New York City newspapers after 9/11 (McMellon & Long, 2006). This list of content analyses in mass-mediated communication represents only a small selection of studies published in 2005 and 2006, but it gives a general portrayal of the types of studies being conducted in this area. Overall, media researchers have historically been the primary group to utilize content analysis methods (Riffe, Lacy, & Fico, 2005), but they are not the only communication researchers to do so.

Many communication scholars conduct research that falls under the content analysis umbrella related to nonmediated messages. Some nonmediated messages have asked participants to write out how they perceived interactions would go: parent–adolescent conflict (Comstock & Buller, 1991), young adults' views of intergenerational communication

(Harwood, 1998), and heterosexuals' perceptions of interactions with gay, lesbian, and bisexual people (Hajek, & Giles, 2005, 2006). Other studies have attempted to code actual human interaction: communication strategies between patients and physicians (Roter, Lipkin, & Dorsgaard, 1991), gesturing (Feyereisen & Harvard, 1999), dominance and control between husbands and wives (Ayres & Miura, 1980; Courtright, Millar, & Rogers-Millar, 1979), facial expressions (Ekman & Rosenberg, 2005), self-disclosure (Shaffer, Pegalis, & Cornell, 1991), and speech rate (Feyereisen & Harvard, 1999). When we use the word "code" in content analysis, we simply mean to group one's findings in a consistent way. For example, maybe you're conducting a study on the incidence of biological sex in speakers at political conventions. For every speaker who speaks at the Democratic and Republican national conventions, you code the speakers as being either female or male. Overall, content analysis can be used in a variety of unique and interesting ways.

Conducting a Content Analysis

Now that we've explained what content analysis is and how the technique can be used in a variety of different research studies, we can focus our attention on the process one goes through when completing a content analysis. For this analysis, let's pretend that we want to conduct a study examining the level of physical attraction of lead characters in situation comedies during prime-time television. According to Neuendorf (2002), there are nine steps that a content analyst must complete to correctly conduct a content analysis: (1) theory and rationale, (2) conceptualization, (3) operationalization, (4) coding schemes, (5) sampling, (6) training and pilot reliability, (7) coding, (8) final reliability, and (9) tabulation and reporting. To help us understand the content analysis process, let's examine each of these areas individually.

THEORY AND RATIONALE

Like previous research we've discussed in this book, research in content analysis should be conducted using the scientific method. For this reason, a good content analysis should be theoretically based. The only way to make sure that you can create a strong rationale for your study is to do the library legwork necessary.

In Chapter 2 and Chapter 5 we discussed how to create a rationale for hypotheses and research questions, and this discussion cross-applies when conducting a content analysis as well. If you're going to conduct a content analysis, your hypotheses and research questions must stem from the work previously conducted by other researchers.

For our example of attractiveness of sitcom actors, there's a wealth of information about body shapes, facial characteristics, and even clothing choices of actors. Clearly, there is no lack of information to help you formulate theoretically based hypotheses and research questions about this topic.

CONCEPTUALIZATION

In Chapter 9 we defined conceptualization as the development and clarification of concepts of your germinal idea (the spark that causes an individual to realize that something new can be researched or measured). This definition is also relevant to our discussion of content analysis. When we conceptualize something, we must determine what variables we want to study and how we can define those variables combining all the necessary characteristics or particulars. There are many ways a researcher can go about defining a specific concept, so you must make sure that your definition is clear from the very beginning. The more ambiguous your attempt to define your research variables, the more likely you will finish conducting a study only to realize that you have ended up with absolutely nothing to show for your work.

For our example study (attractiveness of sitcom actors), one of the primary concepts a researcher must define is "attractiveness." Should a researcher rate individual actors on a scale of 0 (someone hit every rung on the ugly tree) to 100 (Oh Wow, Baby!!!!), which would be a ratio variable? Or should a researcher create more of an ordinal variable where people are separated into three categories: unattractive, average, very attractive? Ultimately, whichever conceptualization a researcher decides to utilize, he or she must be very clear about how an actor is categorized. Furthermore, in a study examining the attractiveness of television personalities, one must realize that all sitcom stars are fairly attractive by society standards. Let's face the fact, television networks aren't going to be starring Quasi Motto in the fall lineup anytime soon. For this reason, your conceptualization of attractiveness may be a little skewed because of the context itself. In essence, you need to determine what "attractiveness" means in the context of television sitcoms. Obviously, more traditional ways of defining attractiveness can't be used in this study because everyone would fall into the upper end of attraction. So a conceptualization of attractiveness of sitcom actors needs to take into account that everyone is attractive, but some actors are more attractive than others.

OPERATIONALIZATION

In Chapter 9 we defined operationalization as the detailed description of the research operations or procedures necessary to assign units of analysis to the categories of a variable in order to represent conceptual properties. When we operationalize a variable in a content analysis, many different questions need to be asked. First, a content analyst must determine whether her or his operationalization is consistent with her or his conceptualization of the variable itself. If a researcher's operationalization and conceptualization differ, then he or she will have problems with internal validity as discussed in Chapter 10. Second, researchers must determine their unit of analysis or the major phenomenon that is being analyzed within a study. In a content analysis, the unit of analysis is generally the specific message(s) that a content analyst is coding. There are many different typical units of analysis that a content analyst may opt to use. Keyton (2006) notes that words or phrases; complete thoughts or sentences; themes or a single assertion about some subject; paragraphs in text; message sources (both real and actors); communication acts, behaviors, or processes; advertisements; and television programs, films, or scenes have all been used in mediated research as units of analysis (p. 237). For studies that are more focused on interactional analysis, it's possible that a variety of units of analysis are also going to be utilized: nonverbal behaviors, turns in a conversation, an entire interaction sequence. Ultimately, when determining the appropriate unit of analysis, you need to think about how your operationalization determines which unit of analysis is the most appropriate for your specific hypotheses and research questions. For example, maybe you're coding videos of marital conflicts. Do you code each sentence of the conflict, or do you code each spouse's turn during a conflict? Ultimately, if you want to look at microlevel functions of conflicts (i.e., how people interact on a moment-to-moment basis during a conflict), coding each sentence or turn may be useful. However, if you want to code macrolevel themes (more overarching themes about conflict in general, not specific behaviors), coding each conflict interaction as one unit of analysis may be useful. Overall, determining your unit of analysis is all part of successful operationalization. You also need to determine which level of measurement (nominal, ordinal, interval, or ratio) is the most appropriate for your conceptualization. Whichever level of measurement you decide to use, you must be very clear about how the rating process occurs.

For example, maybe you'll define "unattractive" as someone who is overweight, is sporting out-of-date or plain clothing, and/or looks messy or dirty. While we are not suggesting that people who are overweight are unattractive, we will argue that the lack of portrayals of overweight people in Hollywood indicates that there is this perception among entertainment executives (just think how nasty Simon Cowell has been on *American Idol* to overweight contestants). You may define someone who is "average" as someone who is physically in shape and healthy looking, wears normal clothing, and is clean and kept. Finally, you may define someone who is "very attractive" as someone who has clear muscular definition, wears high-end fashions, and is meticulously groomed (i.e., not a hair is out of place, eyebrows perfectly plucked, and cuticles cut). Once you have a working operationalization of your variable (attractiveness), you can move on to the next stage of a content analysis—creating coding schemes.

CODING SCHEMES

Previously in this chapter we defined "coding" as *the process a researcher goes through to group one's variable of interest in a consistent way.* Your coding scheme should stem directly from your operationalization. As a content analyst you will need to create two products to help you with your content analysis: a codebook and a coding form. A codebook is a book that a researcher creates to explain the operationalization in a very clear and succinct way. The codebook should be so clear that even a stranger could pick it up and accurately code the phenomenon of interest. Second, you need to create a coding form. A coding form is a form that contains all of the information in the codebook in a simple check-off sheet to make it easier for coders to code information quickly.

In our example of sitcom attractiveness, Figure 12.1 represents what our codebook may look like. You'll notice that our codebook has the operationalization discussed in the previous step to help coders understand exactly what we are looking for in our coding of sitcom actors' attractiveness. The codebook also asks for the show's identification number

---

Sitcom Attractiveness Study

Unit of Data Collection: Each individual who is the lead in a situation comedy.

Show ID: Fill in the show's ID number, as indicated on the television show list provided.

Coder ID: Each coder has received an individual number, please write this number on every sheet.

Character Name: Please provide the name of the character you listed as the lead in each television show.

Character Attractiveness: Please rate each character's physical attractiveness using the following rating scheme:

1. Unattractive: Someone who is overweight, sporting out-of-date or plain clothing, or looks messy or dirty.

2. Average: Someone who is physically in-shape and healthy looking, wears normal clothing, and is clean and kept.

3. Very Attractive: Someone who has clear muscular definition, wears high-end fashions, and is meticulously groomed (i.e., not a hair is out of place, eyebrow not teased, or cuticle uncut).

Figure 12.1 Codebook

(we'll discuss this in more detail in the next step), and for the coder's ID. When conducting a content analysis, it is always important to have multiple coders looking at a set of data. Multiple coders will help you determine if your codebook is actually useful when coding the communicative phenomenon of interest. Often the coders will read your codebook and have wildly different perceptions of the communicative phenomenon because your codebook is simply not clear, so you may need to spell some things out more clearly and revise the codebook, which is why we have a training stage in content analysis (more on this in a moment).

The blank coding form (Figure 12.2a) quickly summarizes the information in the codebook. In this case, we have spots for the Show ID, Coder ID, Character Name, and the coding of attractiveness (unattractive, average, and very attractive). Each coding form will look different depending on the codebook used in a given study. Some content analysis codebooks could contain 15–20 pages of information being coded, so the corresponding coding forms could be 5–8 pages in length as well. Since our example study is very simple, the coding form is also very short and sweet. In Figure 12.2b and 12.2c, we see two completed coding forms. In both cases the coders indicate the Show ID (in this case 3 for *Reba*); the coders indicate their individual coder numbers; the coders indicate the lead actor (Reba McEntire); and the coders rate Reba's level of attractiveness. This example illustrates how a coding form is used. In the long run, coding forms make entering data into a statistical software program much faster.

a) Coding form

Sitcom Attractiveness Study			
Show ID: _____	Coder: _____		
Character Name	Attraction Level		
	Unattractive	Average	Very Attractive

b) Coder 1

Sitcom Attractiveness Study			
Show ID: _____3_____	Coder: _____1_____		
Character Name	Attraction Level		
	Unattractive	Average	Very Attractive
Reba McEntire			X

c) Coder 2

Sitcom Attractiveness Study			
Show ID: _____3_____	Coder: _____2_____		
Character Name	Attraction Level		
	Unattractive	Average	Very Attractive
Reba McEntire		X	

Figure 12.2 Coding Form

SAMPLING

One of the hardest tasks for content analysts is determining the sample necessary to conduct a study. While we will discuss the nature of sampling in much greater detail in Chapter 14, we do want to discuss some pertinent sampling issues related to content analysis here. When discussing sampling, there are two important terms to understand: populations and samples. A population is an entire set of objects, observations, or scores that have some characteristic in common. For example, in our example study, the population would include every sitcom that is on television, whereas a sample is a subset of the larger population. For example, maybe there are 20 sitcoms on television (whole population) and you want to only analyze half of those sitcoms, so you would need to take a sample of 10 sitcoms for your study. While there are numerous methods for sampling, there is no one way that is the best. However, to make sure that your end results are generalizable, that is, your sample can be said to reflect your population correctly, you should randomly (i.e., every unit of analysis that exists within your population has an equal chance for inclusion in your sample) select your sample. We will discuss random sampling in much more detail in Chapter 14.

TRAINING AND PILOT RELIABILITY

Researchers use coders for a wide variety of different reasons, but primarily because it helps maintain objectivity within the study. As researchers, we often spend many hours working on a study prior to the point where we start coding our data. For this reason, we may get to the point where we have spent so much time working on the project that we lose sight of some of the more simple aspects of the project. In other words, we may be so focused looking at the forest (our overall study) that we completely miss the trees (individual pieces of data). For this reason, researchers use coders to look at the data for them. If you have completed the previous step (codebook and coding form) accurately, training your coders should be very easy. However, just because we train our coders to examine individual pieces of data doesn't mean that our data will be coded correctly; for this reason the training process should always include some specific steps: introduction to coding book, sample coding, coding of initial data, initial reliability, retraining, final coding, and final reliability.

Introduction to Coding Book

The first part of coder training is to introduce your coders to the codebook and coding form. You should make sure that you go through the codebook, explaining how each part of the codebook should be used on the coding form. This process should be fairly comprehensive because you want to make sure that your coders will be able to use the codebook accurately.

Sample Coding

Once you have completed your codebook and coding form instruction, it's time to let your coders practice. We recommend having a number of sample pieces of data prepared prior to the coding session that can be used to allow your coders to practice using the coding form. For example, in our sitcom study, maybe you'll bring in snippets from dramatic shows instead of sitcoms and have the coders rate the dramatic actors' levels of attraction. Once your coders have completed the sample coding, it's time to go over the results from the sample coding and determine if everyone is coding the data the same way. For example, if someone codes *Boston Legal*'s William Shatner as "very attractive" and someone codes him as "unattractive," you need to discuss which one you (as the researcher) would classify him as according to the information in the codebook. These practice sessions are very important because it allows the researcher to see where any misunderstandings in the coding process are occurring and correct them.

Coding of Initial Data

Once everyone has coded the practice data, it's time to let your coders work on some real data. However, you do not let them code all of the data initially. You should tell your coders to code a specific number of pieces of data and make sure that they are coding the same pieces of data. Depending on how large your sample is, you may end up needing to have your coders code a few hundred pieces of data initially, or as few as 10.

Initial Reliability

Once your coders have had a chance to code some of the initial pieces of data, you need to determine whether or not they are coding the data in a reliable way. In Chapter 10 we focused on the concept of reliability and on determining if participants fill out a survey in a consistent fashion, but reliability is equally important in determining if coders are consistent. In content analysis we need to determine if multiple coders are actually perceiving the data in the same way.

Your two research assistants are asked to rate the same sitcom actors as being unattractive, average, or very attractive. As shown in Figure 12.2, Reba McEntire could be rated by one coder as "very attractive" and by the other coder as "average." How do you determine if the two coders are using the same coding system to determine attractiveness? If the first coder only finds redheads attractive and the second coder does not find redheads attractive, then you will end up with vastly different perspectives on attraction. While some problems may be corrected during training and practice coding, some issues will only surface once actively coding begins. For this reason, researchers have created a range of different statistical devices to help us determine if coders are coding information in consistent ways.

So, you ask your two coders to code 10 sitcom actors using the coding form. In Figure 12.3, you can see that your coders coded each of the 10 sitcom actors people as either "V" very attractive, "A" average, or "U" unattractive. The first sitcom actor was coded as "V" very attractive by Coder 1 and Coder 2, so you have agreement. If both coders find someone very attractive, then we have a match and we can count that as 1 match on our tally board (seen in Figure 12.3. in the 3 × 3 matrix).

Unfortunately, our coders did not always agree with each other. In fact, the fourth sitcom actor was rated as "A" by Coder 1 and "U" by Coder 2. In this case, you need to mark that

Here are our results from the study. U = Unattractive, A = Average, and V = Very Attractive.

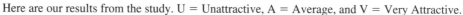
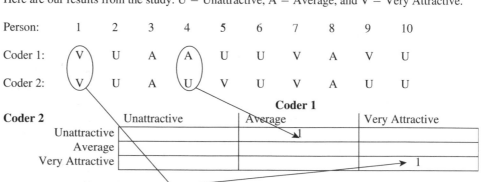

Person:	1	2	3	4	5	6	7	8	9	10
Coder 1:	V	U	A	A	U	U	V	A	V	U
Coder 2:	V	U	A	U	V	U	V	A	U	U

Coder 2	Unattractive	Average	Very Attractive
Unattractive		1	
Average			
Very Attractive			1

Figure 12.3 Coding Example

as a miss in the appropriate box. To do this, you would go to Coder One (the columns) and find the "A" column, then go to Coder Two (the rows) and find the "U" row, and where the two intersect you count that as one occurrence. Ultimately, you will have placed all 10 of the matches or mismatches in the appropriate places on the 3 × 3 grid, which can be seen in Figure 12.4.

Step One Once you have all of the matches and mismatches in place, you are ready to calculate the intercoder reliability. Start by adding the columns separately. In the first column (Coder 1 "Unattractive"), Coder 1 agreed with Coder 2 three times about people who were "unattractive," Coder 1 found no one "unattractive" that Coder 2 found "average," and Coder 1 found one person "unattractive" that Coder 2 found "very attractive." In other words, $3+0+1=4$ is the column total. You can then repeat this process for all of the columns and then for the rows as well. After you have done the simple addition, you should have a chart that looks like Figure 12.5.

Step Two Next you need to compute the total number of times your two coders agreed, or down the center diagonal (3, 2, 2):

$$\Sigma a = 3 + 2 + 2 = 7$$

Based on this, the percent of agreement would be 7/10, or 70%. If you only use the percentile agreement, then you are using an inflated agreement because it does not take into account the possibility that some of those agreements occurred by chance. To find out what is occurring by chance, you need to use the formula in Figure 12.6.

This formula is very easy to compute. First, you take the row total and then multiply it by the column total. For the first column total (5) and first row total (4), you simply multiply the

Coder 2	Coder 1		
	Unattractive	Average	Very Attractive
Unattractive	3	1	1
Average	0	2	0
Very Attractive	1	0	2

Figure 12.4 Coder Totals

Coder 2	Coder 1			
	Unattractive	Average	Very Attractive	SUMS
Unattractive	3	1	1	5
Average	0	2	0	2
Very Attractive	1	0	2	3
SUMS	4	3	3	TOTAL 10

Figure 12.5 Coder Totals

$$\text{Expected Frequency (ef)} = \frac{\text{Row Total} \times \text{Column Total}}{\text{Overall Total}}$$

Figure 12.6 Expected Frequency Formula

totals by each other ($5 \times 4 = 20$), and then divide that number by the overall total or N (10), so: $20/10 = 2$. This process than can then be repeated for the second column total (3) and second row total (2), so: $(3 \times 2)/10 = 0.6$. You repeat the process for the third column total (3) and third row total (3), so: $(3 \times 3)/10 = 0.9$. Finally, you simply add the three values together to get the "sum of expected frequencies" (Σef) value, so: Σef $= 2 + 0.6 + 0.9 = 3.5$.

Step 3 Once you have obtained your sum of expected frequencies value, you can simply plug everything into the formula in Figure 12.7:

Earlier in this section we calculated the sum of a (Σa) as being 7, we've calculated the sum of expected frequencies (Σef) as 4.1, and we know that number of participants observed (N) in this study was 10. At this point, we have all of the parts we need to complete the formula:

$$K = \frac{\Sigma a - \Sigma ef}{N - \Sigma ef}$$

$$K = \frac{7 - 3.5}{10 - 3.5}$$

$$K = \frac{3.5}{6.5}$$

$$K = 0.5384615385 \text{ or } 0.54$$

So, for this study the consistency to which the two coders rated the attractiveness of people in the mall was 0.54. According to Cohen (1960, 1968) if Cohen's kappa is greater than 0.70, the intercoder reliability is satisfactory, and if K is less than 0.70, the intercoder reliability is not satisfactory. In this example, Cohen's K $= 0.54$, so the intercoder reliability is not considered satisfactory. Here is how you would write up this result using APA.

APA Write-Up

Two coders were asked to rate a series of television situation comedy leads using the categories not attractive, average, and very attractive. A total of 10 observations were made. To determine if our two coders were assessing attraction uniformly, a Cohen's kappa was calculated, K $= 0.54$, which is not considered satisfactory.

Clearly, if you get an initial Cohen's kappa that is unsatisfactory there could be a number of problems causing this to occur. First, your codebook could be flawed at either the conceptual or operational level. If this is the case, you should rethink how you are conceptualizing and/or operationalizing your variables in the study. Second, your codebook could be confusing your coders, which could be causing them to miscode specific communicative behaviors. If this is the case, you may need to revise the codebook to make it clearer for your coders. Third, one of your coders could simply not be following the codebook or misusing the coding form. If your low intercoder reliability results from either the second or third problem, retraining is probably necessary.

Figure 12.7 Cohen's Kappa Formula

$$\text{Cohen's Kappa (K)} = \frac{\Sigma a - \Sigma ef}{N - \Sigma ef}$$

Retraining

Once you have determined where the coding problem is occurring (if you have a low intercoder reliability), you need to retrain your coders to correct any mistakes. If one of your coders is simply refusing to follow the codebook, you may want to consider simply removing the coder from the project. During the retraining, you should go through all of the data that have been coded and discuss why the coders coded the data the way they have. In other words, ask Coder 1 why he finds Reba McEntire "very attractive," and then ask Coder 2 why she finds Reba McEntire only "average." Often during the retraining phase you will realize that there could be legitimate reasons why your coders disagree. If you end up in a situation where your coders disagree about a coding, you may need to utilize a third coder to break the tie. Often, the researcher functions as the third coder. Once you have everyone back on the same track, it's time to let your coders finish coding all of the data.

Final Coding

The final coding of the data should be overseen closely by the researcher to ensure the most accurate results. Neuendorf (2002) warns that four problems may surface during coding: coder misinterpretations, coder inattention, coder fatigue, and recording errors. First, despite all of your training and the exactness of your codebook, it is always possible that a *coder may misinterpret a piece of data.* While you do not want to influence a coder's decision about her or his coding, you may want to have them re-heck the data to see if they coded it accurately without telling the coder where you think the problem lies. Second, a *coder may simply wander off mentally while coding,* which can cause errors in her or his coding. We all have moments when our minds wander for a second. If a coder is coding long, detailed conversations, he or she may miss something because he or she simply stops paying attention. Coder inattention often goes along with *coder fatigue,* when a coder gets too tired from coding that he or she starts to simply lose track of what he or she is doing. You may walk into the room where your coders are hard at work and see one of your coders coding the same piece of data for the third time. Coders often wish to finish the coding more than they desire to do the coding correctly. As the researcher, you may have to tell your coder to stop coding for the day or at least take a break and get some caffeine. Finally, all *coders will make mistakes when coding.* The mistake could be as simple as placing their Coder number in the spot where the Episode number should be. Other coders may skip a question on the coding form, which throws off all of their codes by one question. As the researcher in charge, your job is to make sure that the coding is done as consistently as humanly possible.

Final Reliability

Once your coders have coded all of the data in your study, it's time to find the final intercoder reliability. To find the intercoder reliability, you simply follow the steps utilized for Cohen's kappa discussed earlier in this chapter. In this chapter, we have used Cohen's kappa, which is useful if you have two coders with no missing data. However, often researchers will opt to use more than two coders, so they would want to use Krippendorff's alpha (Hayes & Krippendorff, 2007).

On the CD-ROM that accompanies this book there are two articles that utilized forms of content analysis (Boiarsky, Long, & Thayer, 1999; Brummans & Miller, 2004). While only two articles relied on coding observations, both articles reported Cohen's kappa to demonstrate that the people who were coding behaviors were coding these behaviors consistently. Figure 12.8 is the reporting of Cohen's kappas from the articles on the CD-ROM included with this book.

Coding Tested	Reliability
Brummans & Miller (2004) Independent Variable (High vs. Low Ambiguity) Dependent Variable (Effects of Ambiguity on Initiative Success)	Cohen's Kappa = 0.86 Cohen's Kappa = 0.70
Boiarsky, Long, & Thayer (1999) Content Pacing (Existence of a topic shift) Sound Effects (Counted number of effects) Visual Pacing (Counted number of cuts, wipes, and fads/dissolves)	Cohen's Kappa = 0.77–0.87 Pearson Correlation = 0.83–0.97 Pearson Correlation = 0.85–1.0

Figure 12.8 Cohen's Kappa in Articles

You'll notice that all of the reported Cohen's kappas fall into the satisfactory range, so you can say that the coders in both studies consistently coded the same observations. You'll also notice that Boiarsky, Long, and Thayer (1999) reported Pearson correlations for sound effects and visual pacing, since those were not categorical observations but were the number of times those occurred. We will discuss how to interpret correlations in detail in Chapter 19.

TABULATION AND REPORTING

Once a researcher has completed her or his basic reliability analysis, he or she is ready to summarize the information and place it into a statistical program like SPSS or SAS. There are many different ways that information can be presented, which will depend largely on the types of variables that you have collected. The last part of this book includes information on how to properly analyze statistical information. All of these different statistical techniques can be used to examine the data collected in a content analysis. To see how various types of content analyses analyze data, check out the various examples discussed in the early part of this book.

Conclusion

Overall, content analysis is one of the most unique and interesting methodologies that communication scholars have developed. Whether you are using content analysis to answer questions related to mass communications or human communication, the technique can be very telling about how communication occurs. In the next chapter we will look at the third type of quantitative study design, the experiment.

KEY TERMS

Coder	Cohen's Kappa (K)	Operationalization
Coding	Conceptualization	Unit of Analysis
Codebook	Content Analysis	
Coding Form	Intercoder Reliability	

REFERENCES

Ayres, J., & Miura, S. Y. (1981). Construct and predictive validity of instruments for coding relational control communication. *The Western Journal of Speech Communication, 45*, 159–171.

Bichard, S. L. (2006). Building blogs: A multi-dimensional analysis of the distribution of frames on the 2004 presidential candidate web sites. *Journal of Mass Communication Quarterly, 83*, 329–345.

Cohen, J. (1960). A coefficient of agreement for nominal scales. *Educational and Psychological Measurement, 20*, 37–46.

Cohen, J. (1968). Weighted kappa: Nominal scale agreement with provision for scaled disagreement of partial credit. *Psychological Bulletin, 70*, 213–220.

Comstock, J. M., & Buller, D. B. (1991). Conflict strategies adolescents use with their parents: Testing the cognitive communicator characteristics model. *Journal of Language and Social Psychology, 10*, 47–59.

Courtright, J. A., Millar, F. E., & Rogers-Millar, E. (1979). Domineeringness and dominance: Replication and expansion. *Communication Monographs, 46*, 179–192.

Dovring, K. (1954–1955). Quantiative semantics in 18th century Sweden. *Public Opinion Quarterly, 18*, 389–394.

Ekman, P., & Rosenberg, E. L. (Eds.). (2005). *What the face reveals: Basic and applied studies of spontaneous expression using the Facial Action Coding System (FACS)* (2nd ed.). New York: Oxford.

Feyereisen, P., & Harbard, I. (1999). Mental imagery and production of gestures while speaking in younger and older adults. *Journal of Nonverbal Behavior, 23*, 153–171.

Hajek, C., & Giles, H. (2005). Intergroup communication schemas: Cognitive representations of talk with gay men. *Language and Communication, 25*, 161–181.

Hajek, C., & Giles, H. (2006). On communicating pride, crying in moves, and recruiting innocent bystanders: The effect of sex on communication schemas activated with gay and heterosexual targets. *Communication Research Reports, 23*, 77–84.

Harwood, J. (1998). Young adults' cognitive representations of intergenerational conversations. *Journal of Applied Communication Research, 26*, 13–31.

Hayes, A. F., & Krippendorff, K. (2007). Answering the call for a standard reliability measure for coding data. *Communication Methods and Measures, 1*, 77–89.

Hickson, M., III, Turner, J., & Bodon, J. (2003). Research productivity in communication: An analysis, 1996–2001. *Communication Research Reports, 20*, 308–319.

Howard, D. J., & Kerin, R. A. (2006). Broadening the scope of reference price advertising research: A field study of consumer shopping involvement. *Journal of Marketing, 70*, 185–204.

Keyton, J. (2006). *Communication research: Asking questions, finding answers* (2nd ed.). Boston: McGraw-Hill.

Krippendorff, K. (2004). *Content analysis: An introduction to its methodology* (2nd ed.). Thousand Oaks: Sage.

Lachlan, K. A., Smith, S. L., & Tamborini, R. (2005). Models for aggressive behavior: The attributes of violent characters in popular video games. *Communication Studies, 56*, 313–329.

McMellon, C. A., & Long, M. (2006). Sympathy, patriotism, and cynicism: Post-9/11 New York City newspaper advertising content and consumer reactions. *Journal of Current Issues and Research in Advertising, 28*, 1–18.

Neuendorf, K. A. (2002). *The content analysis guidebook*. Thousand Oaks, CA: Sage.

Pfau, M., Haigh, M. M., Logsdon, L., Perrine C., Baldwin, J. P., et al. (2005). Embedded reporting during the invasion and occupation of Iraq: How the embedding of journalists affects television news reports. *Journal of Broadcasting & Electronic Media, 49*, 468–487.

Riffe, D., Lacy, S., & Fico, F.G. (2005). *Analyzing media messages: Using quantitative content analysis in research* (2nd ed.). Mahwah, NJ: Lawrence Erlbaum.

Roter, D., Lipkin, M. Jr., & Dorsgaard, A. (1991). Sex differences in patients' and physicians' communication during primary care medical visits. *Medical Care, 29,* 1083–1093.

Shaffer, D. R., Pegalis, L., & Connell, D. P. (1991). Interactive effects of social context and sex role identity on female self-disclosure during the acquaintance process. *Sex Roles, 24,* 1–19.

Simcock, P., & Sudbury, L. (2006). The invisible majority? Older models in UK television advertising. *International Journal of Advertising, 25,* 87–106.

Weber, R. P. (1990). *Basic content analysis* (2nd ed.). Newbury Park, CA: Sage.

Zhang, E., & Flemming K. (2005). Examination of characteristics of news media under censorship: A content analysis of selected Chinese newspapers' SARS coverage. *Asian Journal of Communication, 15,* 319–339.

CHAPTER 13

Experimental Design

> ### CHAPTER OBJECTIVES
>
> **1** Understand how experiments show time order.
>
> **2** Know the basic reasons researchers conduct experiments.
>
> **3** Explain the basic parts of an experiment (random assignment, manipulation of the independent variable, measurement of the dependent variable, and control).
>
> **4** Know the different ways a researcher can go about manipulating an independent variable.
>
> **5** Understand how factorial experimental designs are created.
>
> **6** Explain different measurement options for the dependent variable.
>
> **7** Understand the four issues researchers need to be aware of when attempting to control an experiment (threshold effects, experimenter effects, Hawthorne effect, and intervening variables).
>
> **8** Differentiate among the three types of confounding variables (suppressor, reinforcer, and lurker).
>
> **9** Explain the stages necessary to conduct an experiment.
>
> **10** Understand the six external threats to validity associated with experiments (historical flaw, maturation, testing flaw, regression to the mean, selection threat, and attrition).
>
> **11** Recognize and explain preexperimental designs.
>
> **12** Recognize and explain true experimental designs.

Whether the experiment consisted of adding two chemicals together in a chemistry class to see what would happen or you attempted to make a trash bag float using straws, tape, and birthday candles, we all conducted experiments in our physical science classes in grade school, but most people aren't as familiar with the purpose of experiments. The general reason scientists perform experiments is to establish *time* order, or *the idea that researchers can establish an exact order to when things occur—T_1 occurred and then T_2 occurred.*

For example, in a chemistry class you must first combine baking soda and vinegar together (T_1) to get the "volcanic reaction" (T_2) we all remember as children. If you just set the box of baking soda and the bottle of vinegar on the counter side-by-side without combining the two, you'll never get the volcanic reaction. While the social sciences may not be as exact as the physical sciences, social scientists also use experiments in research, so this chapter will examine how communication researchers can use experiments. Time order for experimental research is very akin to the age-old question, "Which came first, the chicken or the egg?" Imagine you're a researcher who took on this question. If at the end of your study you have a chicken and you have an egg, would you know which came first? Nope! If, however, you can show scientifically that it is a necessity for an egg to exist prior to a chicken's existence, then you can establish the "time order" of events—first egg, then chicken.

Communication researchers may not be interested in chickens and eggs, but we are interested in whether specific phenomena need to occur prior to exhibited communication behaviors. For example, imagine you wanted to find out whether children playing violent video games will exhibit increased antisocial behavior. In essence, you want to find a time order between playing violent video games (first instance of time) and its effect on antisocial behaviors (second instance of time). While you could ask for self-reports of video game playing and antisocial behavior, these reports may not be completely accurate and could only show a relationship between the two variables, not a time order between the two variables. For this reason, techniques beyond surveying (as discussed in Chapter 11) have been created to help researchers answer causal relationship questions. In this chapter we will examine what experiments are and why we do them and explore a series of common experimental designs.

What Are Experiments and Why Do We Do Them?

An experiment occurs when a researcher purposefully manipulates one or more variables in the hope of seeing how this manipulation affects other variables of interest. In the physical sciences, manipulating a variable is quite easy. If I want to see the effects of liquid nitrogen on a blown-up balloon, I simply submerge the inflated balloon in liquid nitrogen and watch what happens. While some communication experiments can be designed in this fashion (placing doughnuts in a room full of people and watching what happens), most communication experiments require considerably more complicated methods. In this section we will explore three important aspects of experiments: rationale, experimental design aspects, and experimental process.

RATIONALE FOR EXPERIMENTAL RESEARCH

Researchers use experimental research for a variety of reasons, all of which come back to one basic notion: experiments allow for demonstration of causal relationships. In essence, a researcher will conduct an experiment because it allows her or him to establish whether or not an independent variable causes a change in the dependent variable. In survey-based research, researchers essentially examine differences and relationships that individuals perceive, whereas in experimental research, researchers can examine differences and relationships that they manipulate. This process of examining how independent variables affect dependent variables is called "time order." As discussed above, time order is the idea that researchers can establish an exact order as to when things occur. For example, to determine whether playing violent video games leads to antisocial behavior, a researcher could use two groups. One group, the control group, plays a video game that does not contain violence.

In the experimental group, the researcher has the participants play a video game that has notable amounts of violence within the game. If the control group's antisocial behavior does not change from a pre- to a posttest but the experimental group's antisocial behavior increases from a pre- to a posttest, then we can ascertain that a time order occurred (first test of antisocial behavior, playing a violent video game, and then second test of antisocial behavior).

Experiments also allow researchers to rule out alternative explanations for their research findings. By having a baseline score (or pretest), the researchers in our video game study are able to know whether the playing of the violent video game led to violence. If the researchers did not have an initial score of antisocial behavior, the antisocial behavior seen after playing the video game could occur for a number of reasons. If the children placed in the nonviolent video game condition have already been exposed to lots of violent video game images, the results of antisocial behavior between those playing violent versus nonviolent video games may not be different at all. Furthermore, exposure to other violent media could also cause a difference in antisocial behavior. All in all, experiments enable researchers to control what occurs within the testing situation in a way that the researchers can either prevent or rule out other explanations for changes seen.

Another reason for performing experiments is to determine if intervening and antecedent variables are influencing the results. An antecedent variable is a variable that occurs prior to the experiment that could impact the way an independent variable or dependent variable functions. For example, maybe you want to determine if the type of school a student went to in college affects her or his earning potential after college. While this may seem fairly straightforward, what you may forget is that an individual's socioeconomic status (SES) could impact both her or his choice in colleges and her or his earning potential after college. In other words, there is a third variable that exists outside the simple linear model of college affects earning potential. As mentioned above, another variable that can influence the results is an intervening variable. An intervening variable occurs between an independent variable and a dependent variable. We'll discuss these in more detail later in this chapter. Since life is often very complex and requires complex questions and answers, experiments allow researchers to attempt to find underlying antecedent and intervening variables. If a researcher thinks that socioeconomic status may affect choices of colleges and earning potentials, then he or she could control for socioeconomic status to see how much impact the variable actually has.

The last reason we conduct experiments is to determine whether or not phenomena happen for some underlying reason or simply by chance. Often when researchers rely solely on survey research they will find relationships between variables that simply do not mean much. For example, maybe a researcher found a relationship between a physician's use of touch and a patient's perception of that physician's physical attractiveness. In other words, a patient finds a physician more physically attractive if the physician touches them (in a nonsexual way). When another researcher reads these results, he or she may be puzzled as to why such a relationship exists. In order to determine if this relationship truly exists or occurred by chance, the researcher may perform an experiment to determine causal relationships. The researcher could train a series of physicians to randomly use touch with some patients (condition one) and not use touch with other patients (condition two). The researcher could have participants rate the physicians' physical attractiveness and test if physicians' use of touch during medical interviews increases patients' perceptions of the physician physical attractiveness.

ASPECTS OF EXPERIMENTAL DESIGN

When looking at experimental designs, there are a number of aspects that a researcher must constantly attend to while doing research: random assignment, manipulation of the independent variable, measurement of the dependent variable, and control.

Random Assignment

Imagine we want to determine if an individual's use of verbal aggression affects an interaction partner's perception of the verbally aggressive person's likability. We may train a group of people called confederates (individuals who pretend to be researchers or research participants but are really part of the experimental manipulation) to use or not use specific verbal aggression strategies, and then have the confederates interact with the study participants in one-on-one interactions to see if the participant perceives highly verbally aggressive people differently than people who are not verbally aggressive. If we let people choose whether they wanted to interact with a high versus low verbally aggressive person, we may see some outcomes that are not real. Maybe participants who are verbally aggressive themselves enjoy other verbally aggressive people, so they would flock to the higher verbally aggressive interactant and purposefully rate these people highly likeable. People who are not verbally aggressive may avoid the verbally aggressive condition completely. For this reason, randomly

156	675	878	553	748	187	979	592
443	930	530	144	612	638	365	615
523	180	420	666	633	808	839	688
451	487	355	478	604	877	144	810
231	108	790	870	788	805	167	356
607	673	294	674	718	590	892	805
159	326	996	778	216	801	521	598
915	355	275	590	703	315	729	886
221	558	220	223	442	400	993	434
218	780	463	153	399	337	790	619
597	732	240	793	764	807	954	845
773	939	452	524	304	466	291	522
652	256	655	250	574	892	347	835
977	155	481	867	946	533	605	998
865	950	104	605	418	251	439	479
577	107	187	761	410	607	521	481
417	622	607	583	242	995	363	891
510	992	583	246	804	998	134	942
536	437	126	679	619	865	184	315
347	417	879	336	628	375	734	845
499	629	470	452	804	840	814	361
142	486	621	947	128	137	231	478
844	745	872	866	725	297	945	494
543	988	471	207	857	746	694	636
722	978	611	283	907	233	769	442
238	633	576	305	947	105	439	420
505	387	572	733	419	793	170	938
596	302	436	307	674	764	411	940
435	911	107	756	596	211	782	383
612	423	877	240	995	263	586	710
686	811	164	154	924	999	784	539
713	184	310	935	562	328	309	917
303	873	700	393	672	170	490	538
439	301	662	684	898	742	699	149
912	462	111	334	546	271	545	682
706	308	792	134	461	985	330	576
326	797	652	678	743	565	277	354

Figure 13.1 Random Number Table

placing participants into experimental conditions becomes extremely important for research to enable an accurate time order of experimental events. Random assignment comprises the procedures experimenters use for placing participants into a research condition that ensures that every participant in the sample has an equal chance to be in a research condition. For example, in this case everyone in our sample would have an equal chance of interacting with a highly verbally aggressive partner or a minimally verbally aggressive partner, and it is the experimenter's job to make sure that this randomization occurs.

So, how does one randomly assign people into experimental conditions? Well, there are a number of ways. Maybe for each participant you flip a coin—participants who land on heads interact with the verbally aggressive individual, and participants who land on tails interact with the nonverbally aggressive individual. Maybe you have participants draw a condition out of a hat. You have equal numbers of pieces of paper in a hat labeled "A" for the verbally aggressive condition and "B" for the nonverbally aggressive condition. If a person draws the letter "B," he or she is taken to the room where a nonverbally aggressive interactant is waiting. A third possible way is to use a random number generator or a random number table. Figure 13.1 was created by using a random number generator located at www.random.org.

One way to use a random number generator is to create a single column of random numbers and place the estimated number of participants needed in each experimental condition next to the same number of random numbers. For example, if I needed 20 participants in the first condition (verbally aggressive interactant) and 20 participants in the second condition (nonverbally aggressive interactant), then I would place a VA (verbally aggressive) next to the first 20 random numbers and NVA (nonverbally aggressive) next to the second 20 random numbers (Figure 13.2).

1	156	VA	21	499	NVA
2	443	VA	22	142	NVA
3	523	VA	23	844	NVA
4	451	VA	24	543	NVA
5	231	VA	25	722	NVA
6	607	VA	26	238	NVA
7	159	VA	27	505	NVA
8	915	VA	28	596	NVA
9	221	VA	29	435	NVA
10	218	VA	30	612	NVA
11	597	VA	31	686	NVA
12	773	VA	32	713	NVA
13	652	VA	33	303	NVA
14	977	VA	34	439	NVA
15	865	VA	35	912	NVA
16	577	VA	36	706	NVA
17	417	VA	37	326	NVA
18	510	VA	38	984	NVA
19	536	VA	39	675	NVA
20	347	VA	40	930	NVA

Figure 13.2 Random Number Table

If I then took the random numbers and ordered them numerically, I would effectively randomize the order in which we assign people into one of the two conditions. In our example, the first participant in the study is placed in the nonverbally aggressive condition (as seen in Figure 13.3), and then the next five are randomly assigned to the verbally aggressive condition. This trend continues until we have placed 40 participants into one of the two conditions.

Manipulation of the Independent Variable

The second major component of experimental design is the manipulation of the independent variable. Before defining what we mean by "manipulation of the independent variable," let's look at an example. In Chapter 2 we discussed an experiment conducted by Wrench, Millhouse, and Sharp (in press). In this study the researchers wanted to see if the inclusion of humor in preflight safety briefings influenced how people saw the flight attendants. To determine if humor had an effect on people's perceptions of flight attendants, the researchers created two preflight safety briefing scripts—one with humor and one without humor. In the experiment itself, participants were exposed to either one script or the other and then asked about their perceptions of the flight attendant. Let's break this experiment down for you. In this study, Time 1 occurs when the participants are exposed to the preflight safety briefing (humorous vs. standard), and Time 2 occurs as the participants responded to a series of survey questions about the flight attendants.

Ultimately, experimental designs are about manipulating an independent variable and seeing how that manipulation affects a dependent variable. By manipulating we mean that a researcher purposefully alters or changes the independent variable (IV) to see if this alteration in the IV

1	142	NVA	21	543	NVA
2	156	VA	22	577	VA
3	159	VA	23	596	NVA
4	218	VA	24	597	VA
5	221	VA	25	607	VA
6	231	VA	26	612	NVA
7	238	NVA	27	652	VA
8	303	NVA	28	675	NVA
9	326	NVA	29	686	NVA
10	347	VA	30	706	NVA
11	417	VA	31	713	NVA
12	435	NVA	32	722	NVA
13	439	NVA	33	773	VA
14	443	VA	34	844	NVA
15	451	VA	35	865	VA
16	499	NVA	36	912	NVA
17	505	NVA	37	915	VA
18	510	VA	38	930	NVA
19	523	VA	39	977	VA
20	536	VA	40	984	NVA

Figure 13.3 Randomized Conditions

has an effect on the dependent variable (DV). In our example in the previous paragraph, the researchers "altered" a standard preflight safety briefing to include humor. By creating one preflight safety briefing with humor and one without humor (manipulation of the IV), the researchers could see if the inclusion of humor could affect people's perceptions of their flight attendants (DV). The goal of this experiment is to test for differences between the two experimental conditions (humorous preflight safety briefing and standard preflight safety briefing). Now that we've introduced you to the basic components of IV manipulation, let's look at a number of ways that communication researchers can manipulate an independent variable.

First, researchers can provide some participants a specific stimulus or phenomenon (experimental group) and not give the same stimulus or phenomenon to the other participants (control group). In a study conducted by Tamborini, Eastin, Skalski, Lachlan, Fediuk, and Brady (2004), the researchers wanted to examine the effect that video games had on hostile thoughts. At the beginning of the semester, participants completed a self-report questionnaire designed to measure prior video game use and hostile thoughts. Participants were then randomly assigned to one of four conditions: (1) playing a violent virtual reality video game, (2) playing a standard violent video game, (3) observing a violent video game, and (4) observing a nonviolent video game. Ultimately, people in the first three conditions all experienced elevated hostile thoughts after engaging with or watching violent video games but not in the fourth condition where a nonviolent video game was observed.

Second, researchers can rely on written materials to manipulate people. For example, Stewart (1994) wanted to examine if an individual's expressed religious identity would add credibility to a speaker. To examine this research question, Stewart used written texts to introduce participants to a potential speaker. In one of the texts, Stewart mentioned that the speaker was "a regular churchgoer, is very active in church functions, and often publicly expresses his belief that prayer is important in achieving one's professional goals," whereas in the second introduction no mention of religion was made at all. Stewart ultimately found that participants perceived the potential speaker whose introduction contained religious content as more credible.

A third way of manipulating an independent variable in communication research is similar to the written method, but instead of using a written text you record (using either audio or video) the manipulation. In the article by Weber, Fornash, Corrigan, and Neupauer (2003) contained on the CD-ROM that came with this book, the researchers recorded two public relations lectures. In the first lecture (the control), the researchers used examples that are traditionally found in public relations textbooks. In the second lecture (the experimental condition), the researchers used more modern examples of public relations that are not typically found in textbooks. The goal of this study was to determine if the use of more modern, updated examples helps students score higher on a quiz.

Another prominent way of manipulating an independent variable is the use of confederates. A confederate is an individual who, without the participants' knowledge, is actually part of the experiment being conducted. An example of confederate use was founding a study conducted by Guéguen and De Gail (2003). Guéguen and De Gail had eight confederates (4 females and 4 males) randomly walk by 800 customers in a supermarket (400 females and 400 males) and randomly smile or not smile at the person. Immediately after this interaction, a second confederate (who was blind to whether smiling or not smiling had occurred) holding a portfolio and package of computer disks would "accidentally" drop the disks. Ultimately, the study wanted to determine if the smiling of the first confederate would lead the participant to help the second confederate. Overall, this study did find that smiling led to an increase in helping behavior.

The last major way in which communication researchers manipulate independent variables is through hypothetical scenarios and role-playing activities. In this type of manipulation, researchers give the participants a scenario and then the participants are asked to role-play a situation as if they actually were taking part in the fictionalized scenario. In a study by Wiener and Doescher (1994), the researchers wanted to determine the effect that expectation would have on willingness to comply with a request. The researchers placed 84 undergraduates into one of two conditions—high expectation or low expectation. The scenario given to the participants was the need to put an energy-regulating device on their apartment air-conditioning unit. In the high expectation group, the participants were told that 70% of the people within their state had already indicated a willingness to add the energy-regulating device to their air conditioning units; the low expectation group was told that only 15% would add the device. The participants were then asked if they would be willing to add the device to their air conditioners. Of the participants in the high-expectation condition, 84% said they would add the device, compared to only 59% of the participants in the low-expectation group.

Typically, when people think about independent variable manipulation it is easy to think of putting people into either an experimental condition or a control condition. However, as we saw in the above examples, a wide variety of different experimental forms are possible. Some experiments have more than two levels (control vs. experimental), and other experiments manipulate more than one independent variable. When an individual attempts to manipulate more than one independent variable, he or she is conducting a factorial design experiment. In the study by Guéguen and De Gail (2003), the researchers examined one dependent variable, smiling versus nonsmiling, but they also examined the impact of the biological sex of the confederate who smiled and the biological sex of the confederate who dropped her or his portfolio and disks. In this case, we have what is called a $2 \times 2 \times 2$ factorial experimental design. Each variable in this study (smiling, confederate who smiles biological sex, and confederate who drops materials biological sex) is represented by one of the 2s in the factorial design. The numeral 2 is used because each variable only has two levels (smiling vs. not smiling, female vs. male for confederate 1, and female vs. male for confederate 2). If we broadened this study to examine the impact that a third smiling characteristic, frowning, has on the study, then the study would become a $3 \times 2 \times 2$ factorial experimental design because the smiling variable would be manipulated three different ways (frowning, smiling, and nonemotion). If this had been the case, our experimental design would look like Figure 13.4.

In essence, we end up with 12 experimental conditions being compared to each other. The more independent variables a researcher utilizes, the more participants he or she needs to have in a study. For statistical purposes, each experimental condition should have no fewer than

	Female Confederate Smiling Condition		Male Confederate Smiling Condition	
	Female Confederate Dropping Condition	Male Confederate Dropping Condition	Female Confederate Dropping Condition	Male Confederate Dropping Condition
Smile at Participant				
Frown at Participant				
Show no Emotion Towards Participant				

Figure 13.4 Factorial Design

10 participants, but it is safer to have closer to 50 participants in each condition. Obviously, the more factors (independent variables) a researcher wants to examine, the more complicated the design will become and the more participants a researcher will ultimately need to complete the experiment. For example, if we then decide to add another independent variable to the study (participant's biological sex), we now have 24 experimental conditions in this example. For this reason, most experiments are greatly limited in the number of independent variables studied because it is not always realistic to recruit enormous samples for research.

Measurement of the Dependent Variable

The third major component of experimental designs is the measurement of the dependent variable. In all three of the previous experiments discussed in this chapter (video game violence and antisocial behavior; verbal aggression and likability; and medication and communication apprehension), the dependent variable could easily be measured by having a participant fill out a research scale. In the impact of violent video games on antisocial behavior, after a participant is exposed to the video game we could have the participant fill out a research measure examining levels of desire to engage in antisocial behavior. In the impact of verbal aggression on likability, after a participant interacted with the verbally aggressive or the nonverbally aggressive person the researchers could have the participant fill out a scale measuring their interactant's likability. By doing this, researchers can measure the extent to which participants like both verbally aggressive and non–verbally aggressive people. In the second example, the dependent variable is communication apprehension and can easily be measured by having participants fill out the Personal Report of Communication Apprehension–24 (PRCA-24) before the participants take the medication or placebo and then fill out the PRCA-24 again after they have been on the medication or placebo for a month. In both of these studies, the dependent variable was measured by having the participants fill out a pen-and-paper scale.

However, there are other, more observational ways to measure dependent variables. In the first example, after exposing a group of kids to both violent and nonviolent video games we could place all of them in a room together and watch for antisocial interaction behaviors. If the participants exposed to the violent video games are more likely to initiate antisocial behavioral patterns than those participants exposed to nonviolent video games, we would establish a time order between exposure and outcome. If you wanted to measure likability of verbally aggressive versus nonverbally aggressive interactants, you could watch the participants' nonverbal communicative behavior during the interaction. Participants who are attracted to their interaction partners will exhibit more nonverbally immediate behaviors than those participants who are not attracted to their interaction partners. Finally, maybe you want to examine if being on an antianxiety medication or a placebo changes a person's heart rate while giving an impromptu speech. In this case, you would simply hook a person up to a heart monitor and record her or his heart rate while giving the impromptu speech before and after the manipulation of the independent variable. Ultimately, when determining how to measure a dependent variable, a researcher needs to ask her- or himself what the basic purpose of the study is and what would be the most efficient way to determine if the independent variable manipulation is causing a change in the dependent variable.

One extremely important concept needs to be discussed with reference to measuring dependent variables. If a dependent variable is to change as a result of time order, the manipulation of the independent variable must be substantial enough to cause a change. For example, some people may argue that video games like Frogger and PacMan are violent. However, will exposing children to Frogger and PacMan lead to increases in antisocial behavior? Probably not. If exposing children to Frogger and PacMan are not adequate independent variable manipulations to cause a change in the dependent variable, exposing children to more obviously violent games like Dume, Duke Nukem, and Mortal Combat may be necessary to see changes in the dependent variable. Ultimately, if the manipulation of the independent variable is not substantial, the experiment will fail to see changes in the dependent variable that may actually exist.

Controlling an Experiment

One of the most difficult aspects of conducting experiments is attempting to make sure that what a researcher is examining with an experiment is actually being examined. For example, what if you are trying to manipulate the types of conflicts a married couple engages in only to find out that you're actually manipulating the compliance-gaining strategies a couple uses instead. For this reason, researchers must be very careful to avoid influencing an experiment in a way not being measured in the experiment itself. Researchers must be aware of a number of different issues that can affect the outcome of an experiment: threshold effects, experimenter effects, the Hawthorne effect, and intervening variables.

The first issue that researchers must be keenly aware of is the possibility of threshold effects. A threshold effect occurs when changes in a specific dependent variable are only seen after an independent variable reaches a certain level. For example, maybe a person only decreases her or his perception of an interactant's likability when the interactant becomes absurdly verbally aggressive, so low levels of verbal aggression do not impact the interactant's likability at all. Maybe high levels of antianxiety medication decrease an individual's level of communication apprehension but low dosages change nothing. In both of these examples there is a threshold or minimum level that the independent variable must meet before it will affect the dependent variable.

The second, and often the most problematic, issue that can affect the outcome of an experiment is experimenter effects. Experimenter effects are effects caused unknowingly by the experimenter on the participants. Experimenters often will accidentally influence research results without even knowing that they are doing so. For example, in the placebo versus antianxiety medicine study, it is possible that a researcher actually informs the participants slightly differently. This is not to say that the experimenter is purposefully trying to slant the results in one way or the other, but people often unconsciously change their behavior in ways that can affect the results of an experiment. For this reason, a technique has been developed by researchers called the double-blind study. In a double-blind study, neither the researcher nor the participant knows whether or not the participant is receiving the actual manipulation (antianxiety medication) or a fake manipulation (placebo).

The third problematic area researchers need to be aware of is called the Hawthorne effect. The Hawthorne effect gets its name from a series of experiments conducted at the Hawthorne Works of Western Electric Company in Chicago from 1924 to 1932. In this set of studies, the researchers wanted to initially determine if the level of lighting in an electric company affected the productivity level of the employees. In the original study, the researchers manipulated the lighting in the electric company (independent variable) to see if it influenced worker output (dependent variable). Ultimately, the researchers were astonished when they determined that their manipulation of the lighting did absolutely nothing to affect productivity because worker output increased in all of the lighting conditions. When the experiment was complete, the researchers realized that the lighting had not changed the worker output, but hovering over the workers and watching what they were doing had increased the worker output. This same problem can exist in other experiments as well, so researchers have adopted a number of safeguards to help prevent the Hawthorne effect from occurring in an experiment. First, researchers will often try to observe participants through video monitoring systems or one-way mirrors, so the participants do not know when they are being watched. Researchers will also deceive participants about the actual nature of the study being conducted. While there are clearly ethical issues that must be addressed (in Chapter 14), deception can be very useful when used in a fashion to help a researcher attain clear and consistent results. Other researchers will throw in blank or dummy experiments to throw a participant off the actual nature of the study. In the verbal aggression study, maybe the researcher will have the participants fill out a wide range of scales about the personality of the confederate interactant. While the researcher is attempting to look at likability, the researcher may also ask questions about the use of humor, immediacy, etc.

The last problem that needs to be overcome when conducting experiments is to be aware that other variables may be influencing the outcome of your experiment. In any experiment there can be a series of what are called extraneous variables—variables not being measured in your study but affecting your results. There are two major categories of extraneous variable: intervening and confounding. Intervening or mediating variables, often called latent variables, are variables that intervene between the independent variable and the dependent variable. For example, if you want to determine the effects of drinking in college on grades, it's possible that the two variables are not going to tell you the complete picture. While it's true that there may be a negative relationship between alcohol consumption in college and grades, it's also possible that what is really being seen is that alcohol consumption is a measure of partying at school, which means that a person is spending less time going to class and studying. As a result of spending less time in class and studying, then the participants' grades may start to suffer. In other words, alcohol consumption does not necessarily cause grades to slip in college, but it may create the circumstances (not going to class and not studying) that lead to slipping grades. In this example, the variables identified as not going to class and not studying are examples of intervening variables.

Confounding variables, on the other hand, are variables that obscure the effects of your independent variable. There are three types of confounding variables that often occur in research: suppressor, reinforcer, and lurker. Suppressor variables are variables that suppress or reduce the effect of the independent variable on the dependent variable. For example, research has shown us that introverts are more likely to have higher scores of communication apprehension than extraverted people. One cause of this could be that introverts are less likely to communicate with other people innately, so they do not end up gaining as much experience communicating with other people. This lack of experience could be a factor in causing introverts to be anxious when interacting with people. The variable "lack of experience" could be seen as a suppressor variable.

The second category of confounding variable is a reinforcer variable. For example, research has shown that extraverted people are more communicatively competent. Does this mean that extraverts are born with more information on how to communicate in a competent way than introverts? Probably not. However, extraverted people do probably have more experience interacting with other people, so they have more opportunities to develop competent communicative behaviors. In this case, experience is seen as a reinforcer variable.

The final type of confounding variable is a lurker variable, or a variable that explains both the independent variable and the dependent variable. For example, maybe a study finds that there is a relationship between communication apprehension and the number of friends a person has. However, it is possible that a third variable, introversion, is actually causing the other two variables to occur in the first place. In this example, introversion is a lurker variable because it is not a variable being directly studied, but is ultimately responsible for the scores of both the independent variable (communication apprehension) and the dependent variable (number of friends).

CONDUCTING AN EXPERIMENT

Now that we have examined the key components of experiments and the rationale for experiments, we can focus on the basic process of performing an experiment. The basic process that all researchers go through when conducting an experiment is as follows: introduce the experiment to the participant and obtain consent, randomly assign people to different conditions, manipulate the independent variable, measure the dependent variable, and debrief the participants when the experiment is completed.

Introducing the Experiment and Obtaining Consent

The first part of any actual experiment involves explaining to a participant what an experiment will actually entail. While researchers may use deception to prevent the participants from knowing what the researcher is actually examining, some cover story will be given to the participants. One reason researchers use deception when explaining what an experiment is examining is to prevent what Joseph Masling (1966) calls the "screw-you" effect. When participants know what a researcher is looking for, many participants will try to answer questions contrary to how they feel in order to throw off the experiment. We'll talk more about the ethical issues of deception in the next chapter.

The second part of the initial part of an experiment is obtaining consent. In the United States, the federal government has mandated that anyone used in a research experiment should giver her or his consent, and if someone cannot give consent (e.g., children or mentally impaired individuals), a legal guardian is needed to give consent. Obtaining consent entails explaining any actual risks involved in a study. For the most part, communication research does not involve physical risks, but many researchers examine sensitive topics that could cause people psychological distress. To avoid putting participants in a situation that would make them feel uncomfortable, participants must be informed of their legal rights (e.g., ability to leave the experiment at any time) and the risks involved with the study. As discussed in Chapter 3, every university has an institutional review board (IRB) that researchers must comply with in order to carry out research of any kind (both experimental and nonexperimental).

Random Assignment

The second part to conducting an experiment is to randomly assign people to a treatment group. Earlier in this chapter we discussed in much greater detail a number of ways to randomly assign people to different treatment groups. Once the participants are in a group any pretesting of the dependent variable that is necessary for the experiment will be conducted.

Manipulate the Independent Variable

Once participants have been placed into the different conditions of an experiment, a researcher will manipulate the independent variable. All of the experimental examples discussed in this chapter thus far have involved the manipulating of an independent variable. Whether studying interactions with verbally aggressive or non–verbally aggressive persons or the effects of being given a placebo or antianxiety medication, a researcher will attempt to alter the independent variable in a way that could cause a change in the dependent variable. One way to make sure that the participants are actually seeing the manipulation of the dependent variable is to perform a manipulation check.

A manipulation check is a procedure where a researcher inserts a quantitative measurement into a study to determine whether or not different conditions portray the independent variable differently. For example, in a study that had participants interacting with confederates who did or did not communicate verbally aggressively, a researcher could have the participants fill out the verbal aggression scale on the confederates. If the researcher found that the participants did not perceive the verbal aggression and nonverbal aggression interactants differently with regard to the verbal aggression levels, then the results of the study will be flawed. If, however, your participants rate the verbally aggressive confederate as being more verbally aggressive than the nonverbally aggressive confederate, then you can say that your manipulation of verbal aggression was good.

For example, in the Wrench, Millhouse, and Sharp (in press) study examining humorous versus standard preflight safety briefings, the researchers created the two scripts, but how do they know people perceive the humorous script as actually humorous? The three authors of the study could all have the same sense of humor, which could be different from their participants' senses of humor. To make sure that the participants perceived the humorous script as funny and the standard script as not funny, the researchers asked a single question that participants answered at the end of the survey, "On a scale of '0' not humorous to '9' very humorous, indicate how humorous you found the flight attendant's preflight briefing." By including this question, the researchers could then determine if the two groups actually viewed the humorousness of the script differently. By checking to see if the manipulation occurred, the researchers are able to know if the results they receive are actually a result of their manipulation of the independent variable (in this case the preflight safety briefing).

Measure the Dependent Variable

Once you have manipulated the independent variable, the next step in performing an experiment is to measure the dependent variable. As mentioned previously, there are a number of ways to measure a dependent variable, and a researcher must be careful when measuring a dependent variable that the measure is both reliable and valid (as discussed in Chapter 10).

Debriefing

The last part of an experiment occurs after a dependent variable has been measured for the last time. The debriefing part of an experiment is where a researcher first corrects any deception that was used at the beginning of an experiment. Researchers realize that it is unethical to let a research participant complete a study and not know what was done to them. In addition to correcting deception, researchers should also reaffirm the value of the research study and the participants' addition to the research process. Finally, a researcher may ask a couple of pointed question to determine if a participant knowingly changed her or his results based on what he or she thought the experiment was testing. After a participant has been debriefed, participants are usually very open to admitting that they may have slanted their answers in a particular direction because they thought it was what the researcher actually wanted to know ("demand characteristics"). Another problem that can also be noted during an experimental debriefing is whether or not a participant was more anxious than usual because he or she knew that the researcher was evaluating her or his behavior. Many people behave abnormally as a result of the contrived evaluation situation that many research projects create (remember the Hawthorne effect). By simply listening to participants' thoughts about the research process after the fact, a researcher can determine if either of these problems has occurred.

Threats to Experimental Validity

In this section we will examine six threats to the validity of an experiment, derived from the work by Campbell and Stanley (1963): historical flaw, maturation, testing flaw, regression to the mean, selection threat, and attrition.

HISTORICAL FLAW

The first validity threat that can affect an experiment is the historical flaw. When a historical flaw occurs, some historical event has caused the sample to change in a way that is not measurable. For example, in a study conducted after September 11, 2001, terrorist attacks in the United States, a researcher who wanted to see how attuned participants were to crisis communication could have a sample more attuned to crisis communication than would have occurred normally. Often historical flaws can be mentioned as a limitation, but other times the historical flaw may not even be known to the researcher.

MATURATION

A second threat to a study's validity is called maturation. Maturation involves changes to a sample that occur naturally as a result of time. In essence, the maturation threat occurs because it is possible that a portion of the estimated change is not as a result of our independent variable manipulations, but as a result of the passage of time between the first measure of a dependent variable and following measures. Many experiments can last for decades as a researcher collects pertinent data. If a researcher has a sample over a long period of time, some natural changes may occur that are outside the scope of the experiment. For example, many studies that involved large-scale pharmaceutical variables last from 5 to 10 years. In a 10-year period, people naturally change. A person who was active and fit at 30 may have gained weight and be a coach potato at 40 and skew the results of the study. Overall, researchers need to collect a number of data indicators at the beginning of a study to determine if the participants have drastically changed by the time they reached the end of the study.

TESTING FLAW

The third threat to validity that can exist in an experiment is what is called a testing flaw. As we have discussed previously in this chapter, one way to determine if an independent variable alters a dependent variable is to get a baseline score of the dependent variable at Time 1, manipulate the independent variable, and then get a second score of the dependent variable at Time 2. Unfortunately, changes in the score at Time 2 can occur simply because a score was taken at Time 1. So a researcher must be concerned with whether or not a score on a dependent variable occurs as a result of multiple administration of the dependent variable. We will look at a couple of experimental designs that attempt to control for this problem later in this chapter.

REGRESSION TO THE MEAN

The fourth validity threat that can occur in an experiment is referred to as a regression to the mean. A regression to the mean is the tendency for extreme scorers on one measurement to move (regress) closer to the mean on a later measurement, causing a change that would normally not happen in the population. For example, imagine you're teaching a class; you have 10 students take a midterm examination (Time 1) and you get the following scores: 0, 84, 85, 79, 89, 85, 86, 87, 82, 100. You would have a mean of 77.7 and a standard deviation of 27.86. If you then gave the test a second time a week later (Time 2), you may naturally see a shift in the scores towards the mean (72, 85, 86, 79, 89, 86, 86, 88, 82, 100), which would give you a mean of 85.3 and a standard deviation of 7.20. You'll notice that from Time 1 to Time 2 the standard deviation got smaller; this occurs because the scores on the test started to clump more around the mean, or regressed to the mean.

In Figure 13.5 you can see the example in graph form. In the first graph, you'll notice that the sample is left skewed, whereas the second graph looks more bell shaped. The first time the students took the test, their scores were further apart from the mean and regressed toward the mean the second time they took the test.

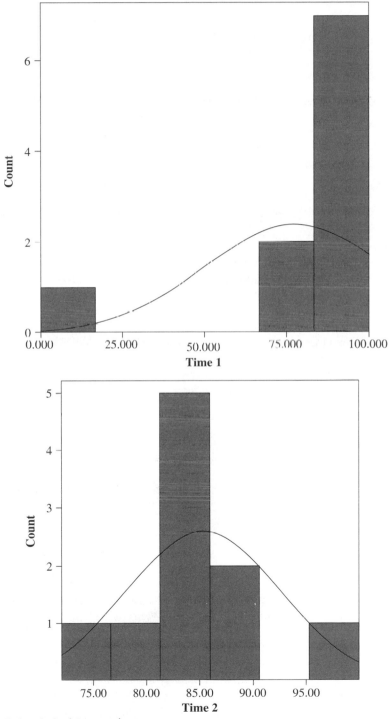

Figure 13.5 Statistical Regression

SELECTION THREAT

The fifth threat to experimental validity is the selection threat. The selection validity threat asks whether or not the participants who have selected to participate in an experiment have some characteristic that could slant the findings of the study. For example, a lot of researchers rely on college students in need of extra credit for participation in research studies. Are people who desperately need extra credit the most accurate sample when trying to make generalizations about the general population?

ATTRITION

The last validity threat that experiments can have is called attrition. Attrition is simply the number of participants who have left a study since it began. While short-term studies are not generally affected by attrition, long-term studies can often be greatly affected by the drop-out rate of the participants in a study. One of the authors of this book started a study with 200 participants at Time 1 and was only able to get 36 participants to continue the study at Time 2. Obviously, a researcher cannot generalize results from 36 participants accurately since only 16% of the initial sample still agreed to participate at Time 2. Attrition is one of those factors that cannot be accurately predicted, but can often have a devastating impact on the overall outcome of a study. One of the major problems with attrition occurs if the participants who dropped out of a study are systematically different from those participants who remained in the study.

While these six validity threats are specifically related to experimental procedures, we should remind you that we discussed a number of other validity threats in Chapter 10. All of the major threats to validity discussed in Chapter 10 (inadequate preoperational explication of concepts, mono-operation bias, interaction of different treatments, interaction of testing and treatment, restricted generalizability across constructs, confounding constructs and levels of constructs, and social threats to validity) are also validity threats to experiments as well. Now that we've explored some of the threats validity experiments can face, let's focus our attention on some common experimental designs.

Common Experimental Designs

We can now examine the three types of experimental designs that researchers work with (pre-experimental, quasi-experimental, and true experimental). However, we need to introduce a few notation devices that researchers commonly use to aid a discussion of research designs. Over the next few pages you will be shown a series of characters that look like mathematical formulas followed by a paragraph example. The characters in the "formula" are there to help illustrate how a specific experimental design is conducted. The characters we will use to illustrate the experimental designs are "O," "X," "R," "N," and "C." When you see the letter "O" in an illustrated experimental design, the "O" is an observation of the dependent variable being made by a researcher. When you see the letter "X" in an illustrated experimental design, the "X" is any time a researcher has manipulated the independent variable. You will often see "X" followed by a subscript 1 or 0. If the X is followed by a subscript 1 (X_1), then the independent variable has been manipulated and that line represents an experimental condition. If the X is followed by a subscript 0 (X_0), then the independent variable has not been manipulated. When you see the letter "R" in an illustrated experimental design, the "R" illustrates the fact that people within that experimental design have been randomized into the different treatment conditions. When you see the letter "N" in an illustrated experimental design, the "N" illustrates the fact that people within that experimental design have not been randomized into the different treatment conditions. Finally, when you see the letter "C" in an illustrated experimental design, the "C" represents the idea that participants have been placed into groups based on a cutoff score. For example, everyone above the mean is in group one and everyone below the mean is in group two (this could also be done by using the median). Now that we have the basic terminology necessary for examining the different experimental designs, we can start by looking at the preexperimental designs. We will demonstrate how each different design can be used to answer one common research question in many different ways. The example used in the next few pages will be as follows: a researcher wants to find out if attending a 6-hour workshop on using humor in the classroom will affect how students perceive their teacher's communication competence.

PREEXPERIMENTAL DESIGNS

One-Shot Case Study

$$NX_1 \rightarrow O$$

In the one-shot case study design, a researcher uses a nonrandomized sample (N), manipulates the independent variable (X_1), and then measures how people score on the dependent variable (O). In this first example, the researcher would send a group of teachers to a 6-hour workshop on using humor in the classroom (X_1) and then have the teachers' students fill out a communication competence scale on the teachers (O). The problem with this design is that we can never say with complete confidence that our manipulation of the independent variable caused the measurement of the dependent variable.

One-Group Pretest Posttest Design

$$NO_1 \rightarrow X_1 \rightarrow O_2$$

In the one-group pretest–posttest design, a researcher uses a nonrandomized sample (N), gives the sample a pretest (O_1), manipulates the independent variable (X_1), and then gives the sample a posttest (O_2). In this example, a researcher would have a teacher's students fill out the communication competence (O_1), then send the teacher to the 6-hour workshop on how to use humor in training (X_1), and then resurvey the students to see if their perception of the teacher has changed (O_2). This design is also somewhat problematic because it is easy for a researcher to miss intervening and confounding variables in this design of testing effects.

Static Group Comparisons

$$NX_1 \rightarrow O_1$$
$$NX_0 \rightarrow O_1$$

In the static group comparisons design, a researcher uses a nonrandomized sample (N), manipulates the independent variable (X_1), and then measures how people score on the dependent variable (O). Furthermore, the researcher does not manipulate the independent variable of a second group or the control group (X_0), but does measure the dependent variable (O_1).

In this example, a researcher has two groups: an experimental group and a control group. The researcher would send one teacher through the 6-hour workshop on using humor in the classroom (X_1) and not send another teacher through the 6-hour workshop (X_0). After the teacher in the first group has gone through the workshop, the researcher has the students in both groups fill out a communication competence scale on both teachers (O_1). This manipulation is called a static group comparison because the two groups already exist and were not created for the experimental purpose. The problem with this design is that there exists the possibility of prior relationships between the teacher and students, a history of maturation, and other experimental flaws that could prevent a researcher from attaining clear, useful results. For example, if the teacher sent to the workshop was more communicatively competent to begin with, there would be no way to determine that if one uses this preexperimental design.

QUASI-EXPERIMENTAL DESIGNS

A quasi-experimental design mirrors an experimental design but lacks randomization (Cook & Campbell, 1979). The next four types of designs are different perspectives on how to design a quasi-experiment.

Pretest–Posttest Design

$$NO_1 \rightarrow X_1 \rightarrow O_2$$
$$NO_1 \qquad\qquad O_2$$

The purpose of this design is to determine whether or not the effect of a pretest can account for the scores a person may achieve on a posttest. In this design, a researcher either creates two groups or uses two stagnant groups. In the manipulation group, a researcher measures the dependent variable (O_1), followed by a manipulation of the independent variable (X_1), and follows that by another measurement of the dependent variable (O_2). In the control group, a researcher measures the dependent variable (O_1), and then measures the dependent variable (O_2) a second time without any kind of manipulation in between.

In the first group, the researcher measures the student perceptions of the teacher's communication competence (O_1), sends the teacher to the 6-hour workshop on humor (X_1), and retests the student perceptions of the teacher's communication competence (O_2). In the control group, the teacher is not sent to the workshop on humor. After the teacher in the first group has gone through the 6-hour workshop, the researcher has the students in the control group fill out a communication competence scale again on the teacher (O_2) who had not attended the workshop. Notice that these are all issues previously discussed in this chapter looking at the validity of a study.

Time Series

$$NO_1 \rightarrow O_2 \rightarrow O_3 \rightarrow X_1 \rightarrow O_4 \rightarrow O_5 \rightarrow O_6$$

The time series design is a way for researchers to establish a clear baseline score on a specific dependent variable and then determine if the manipulation of the independent variable has lasting effects. In the time series design, one group is nonrandomly established. The researcher measures the dependent variable the first time (O_1), measures the dependent variable a second time (O_2), and measures the dependent variable a third time (O_3). The researcher then performs the manipulation of the independent variable (X_1). After the manipulation of the independent variable, the researcher then measures the dependent variable a fourth time (O_4), followed by a fifth measurement of the dependent variable (O_5), and then followed by a sixth measurement of the dependent variable (O_6). A time series experimental design is not limited to six measurements of the dependent variable—it could just as easily have been eight or ten measurements of the dependent variable. Multiple measurements of the dependent variable are useful because it helps decrease the chance of a statistical regression to the mean validity threat by stabilizing outliers (participants with extreme scores).

In our example experiment, a researcher could measure a group of students' perceptions of the teacher's communication competence three times, then send the teacher to the 6-hour workshop on how to use humor during training, and then measure the student's perception of the teacher's communication competence three more times. All in all, the teacher's communication competence would be measured six times. The major problem with this experimental design is that the researcher cannot determine whether or not the use of the same method for measuring the dependent variable (communication competence scale) is causing a change or the manipulation of the independent variable.

Multiple Time Series

$$NO_1 \rightarrow O_2 \rightarrow O_3 \rightarrow X_1 \rightarrow O_4 \rightarrow O_5 \rightarrow O_6$$
$$NO_1 \rightarrow O_2 \rightarrow O_3 \rightarrow X_0 \rightarrow O_4 \rightarrow O_5 \rightarrow O_6$$

The multiple time series design is a way for researchers to establish a clear baseline score on a specific dependent variable and then determine if the manipulation of the independent variable has lasting effects while controlling for multiple testing effects. In the multiple time series design, two groups are nonrandomly established (N). In the first group, the researcher measures the dependent variable the first time (O_1), measures the dependent variable a second time (O_2), and measures the dependent variable a third time (O_3). The researcher then performs the manipulation of the independent variable (X_1). After the manipulation of the independent variable, the researcher then measures the dependent variable a fourth time (O_4), followed by a fifth measurement of the dependent variable (O_5), and then followed by a sixth measurement of the dependent variable (O_6). In the second group, the researcher simply measures the dependent variable six separate times ($O_1, O_2, O_3, O_4, O_5, O_6$), but does not attempt to manipulate the independent variable (X_0).

In our example experiment, a researcher could measure the experimental group of student's perception of the teacher's communication competence three times, then send the teacher to the 6-hour workshop on how to use humor during training, and then measure the students' perception of the teacher's communication competence three more times. In the control group, the researcher simply measures the students' perception of the teacher's communication competence six different times. The purpose of the control group in this design is to determine if the effect of measuring the dependent variable six different times causes any of the changes noted in the dependent variable. However, since this design is not random, it is always possible that the two groups had preexisting characteristics that could lead to a change seen in the experiment.

Switching Replications Design

$$NO_1 \rightarrow X_1 \rightarrow O_2 \qquad O_3$$
$$NO_1 \qquad O_2 \rightarrow X_1 \rightarrow O_3$$

The switching replications design solves one of the basic problems that many people have with experimental designs—the need to exclude some participants from the independent variable manipulation. For example, maybe you find that a treatment for public speaking anxiety. You wouldn't want to turn down people who could benefit from the treatment, would you? While the new treatment clearly needs to be researched, you could give one half or your participants the treatment to begin with and then give the other half the treatment later, but both groups would still receive the treatment. In this design, researchers create two nonrandom groups. The researcher starts off by observing the dependent variable in both groups (O_1), followed by a manipulation of the independent variable in the first group (X_1) while doing nothing in the second group, followed by an observation of the dependent variable a second time for both groups (O_2). At this point the researcher switches gears and manipulates the independent variable for the second group (X_1) while doing nothing in the first group. This is followed by a third observation of the dependent variable for both groups (O_3).

In our experimental example, we could use two groups that we create or that are previously established. To start our experiment, we would measure how the students in both groups perceive their teachers' communication competence. We then send the first teacher to the workshop on how to use humor in the classroom. After the workshop, we then measure perceived teacher communication competence for both groups. At this point, we send the second teacher to the workshop on how to use humor in the classroom. After the workshop, we then measure perceived teacher communication competence for both groups for the third, and final, time. This design is very good and can really determine whether or not changes in the independent variable are happening by chance or as a result of the researcher's manipulation of the dependent variable. While this is a strong design, because of its lack of randomization it still can succumb to the validity threats discussed earlier in this chapter.

TRUE EXPERIMENTAL DESIGNS

True experimental designs are considered such because participants in the study are randomly placed into an experimental condition and the independent variable is actively manipulated (not just observed). In this section we will examine four different experimental designs.

Pretest–Posttest Design

$$R\,O_1 \rightarrow X_1 \rightarrow O_2$$
$$R\,O_1 \qquad\qquad O_2$$

The purpose of this design is to determine whether or not the effect of a pretest can account for the scores a person may achieve on a posttest. In this design a researcher randomly assigns a larger group of participants into two groups (R). In the first group, a researcher measures the dependent variable (O_1), followed by a manipulation of the independent variable (X_1), and then by another measurement of the dependent variable (O_2). In the control group, a researcher measures the dependent variable (O_1) the first time and then measures the dependent variable (O_2) a second time without any kind of manipulation in between.

In our example experiment, a researcher would recruit a sample of research participants and then randomly assign the participants to be in one of two training conditions (use of humor or control). In the first group, you measure the student perceptions of the teacher's communication competence (O_1), then send the teacher to the 6-hour workshop on humor (X_1), and then retest the student perceptions of the teacher's communication competence (O_2). In the control group, the teacher is not sent to the workshop on humor. After the teacher in the first group has gone through the workshop, the researcher has the students in the control group fill out a communication competence scale again (O_2). There still exists a possibility of a threat to the validity of the study caused by the pretest. Theoretically, the effect of the independent variable could be different when a pretest is present compared to when it is not.

Two-Group Posttest-Only Design

$$R\,X_1 \rightarrow O_1$$
$$R \quad\;\; O_1$$

In the two-group posttest-only design, a researcher uses a randomized sample (R), manipulates the independent variable (X_1), and then measures how people score on the dependent variable (O_1). Furthermore, the researcher only measures the dependent variable (O_1) for the second group. In this example, a researcher has two groups: an experimental group and a control group.

Using our example, the researcher would send one teacher through the 6-hour workshop on using humor in training sessions (X_1) and not send another teacher through the 6-hour workshop. After the teacher in the first group has gone through the workshop, the researcher would then have the students in both groups fill out a communication competence scale on both the teachers (O_1). This experimental design is very economical, which is why it is often used in research. This experiment also eliminates the possibility of pre- and posttest interactions. However, without a baseline observance of the dependent variable, you always run the risk that the two groups were different to begin with.

Randomized Switching Replications Design

$$R\,O_1 \rightarrow X_1 \rightarrow O_2 \qquad\qquad O_3$$
$$R\,O_1 \qquad\qquad O_2 \rightarrow X_1 \rightarrow O_3$$

The randomized switching replications design solves one of the basic problems of experimental designs—the need to exclude some participants from the independent variable manipulation. In this design, researchers randomly place participants into one of two groups. In this design, the researcher starts off by observing the dependent variable in both groups (O_1), followed by a manipulation of the independent variable in the first group (X_1) while doing nothing in the second group, and then by an observation of the dependent variable a second time for both groups (O_2). At this point the researcher switches gears and manipulates the independent variable for the second group (X_1) while doing nothing in the first group. This is followed by a third observation of the dependent variable for both groups (O_3).

In our experimental example, we could use two groups that we create or that are previously established. To start our experiment, we found how the students in both groups perceive their teachers' communication competence. We then send the first teacher to the workshop on how to use humor in the classroom. After the workshop, we measure perceived teacher communication competence for both groups. At this point we send the second teacher to the workshop on how to use humor in the classroom. After the workshop, we then measure perceived teacher communication competence for both groups for the third, and final, time. This design is very good and can determine whether or not changes in the dependent variable are happening by chance or as a result of the researcher's manipulation of the dependent variable.

Solomon Four-Group Design

$$RO_1 \rightarrow X_1 \rightarrow O_2$$
$$RO_1 \qquad\qquad O_2$$
$$R \qquad X_1 \rightarrow O_2$$
$$R \qquad\qquad O_2$$

The Solomon Four-Group Design is considered the "granddaddy" of all experimental research designs because it attempts to control for any major experimental flaws. In the Solomon Four-Group, a researcher separates her or his participants into a series of four different groups (R). In the first group, the research measures the dependent variable (O_1) at Time 1, manipulates the independent variable (X_1), and then measures the dependent variable (O_2) at Time 2. In the second group, the researcher observes the dependent variable (O_1) at Time 1 and then measures the dependent variable (O_2) at Time 2, but does not manipulate the independent variable. In the third group, the researcher does not measure the dependent variable at Time 1. Instead, the researcher starts the third group by manipulating the independent variable (X_1) and then measuring the dependent variable at Time 2 (O_2). In the fourth and final group, the research does not measure the dependent variable at Time 1 or manipulate the independent variable. The only thing the researcher receives from the fourth group is a measure of the dependent variable (O_2) at Time 2. In essence, the first group in the Solomon Four-Group Design measures the traditional pre- and posttest experimental design. The second group helps a researcher know if there is a difference between a pretest and posttest score in general. The third group determines if a pretest influences the outcome of the posttest. And the final group helps to determine if a maturation effect is occurring and the change is a result of time and not the independent variable manipulation.

Final Thoughts on Experiments

Experiments are very useful and can definitely help researchers determine the time effects or causal relationships between two variables. However, there are some problems with the experimental process in general. First, a researcher can only examine a small number of independent variables in any given experiment. The more independent variables a researcher attempts to manipulate, the more complex the design must become and the more participants a researcher will need. We suggest a bare minimum of 30 participants in each experimental condition. All of the experimental designs examined above were for one independent variable manipulation with two nominal levels. If an experimenter is conducting a factorial experimental design (e.g., a 2×3 design), the experimental design becomes even more complex and cumbersome. Furthermore, the more advanced the statistical tests a researcher wants to, the more participants a researcher needs. For example, it is recommended that a researcher have a minimum of 300 participants to run multivariate statistical tests, or statistical tests that use more than one dependent variable.

A second major problem that occurs with experimental designs relates to the overall generalizability of the findings in an experiment. One of the basic questions that all researchers must ask themselves is whether or not their results can be generalized to the larger population. Can the results from one study be generalized to similar subject areas, time periods, or contexts? If an experiment is so finite in its generalizability, then its usefulness and meaning can be seriously called into question. Three factors have been shown to limit the generalizability of experimental research. First, researchers in every social scientific field have overly relied upon college students as participant populations. Everyone will admit that college students are easy to get their hands on and fairly cooperative (especially when extra credit is offered). For this reason, college students are the single most overstudied population in the United States. This is not to say that college students should not be studied, but researchers need to think outside of the box and find participant populations outside the university walls.

Second, there exists an overreliance on laboratory settings when conducting experiments. There is a long-held belief that participants being studied in a laboratory environment will act differently than they would in a more natural environment. For this reason, researchers need to start creating more experimental designs employing natural environments instead of laboratory ones.

The third reason many experiments have generalizability problems is that many experimental tasks are low in mundane realism. In one rather famous study, participants were asked to persuade people to sit in a room and turn pegs on a pegboard clockwise 25 degrees. As far as we can tell, there is no practical application of this experimental task. While the finding from this study demonstrated that people commit to the persuasion task differently based on how much they were being paid to persuade someone to turn the pegs, the task cannot be generalized to any other task in the "real" world. Researchers need to create experimental tasks that are similar to real tasks a participant could face in her or his daily life.

We've looked at three ways in which generalizability is limited, and we can now discuss two ways to enhance generalizability. First, more researchers should attempt to conduct field experiments. Field experiments happen in the real world outside the confines of a laboratory. They are much more likely to reveal real behavior than laboratory experiments. Also, researchers should use more complex studies examining multiple independent variable manipulations. In most real world phenomena, the effect of a single independent variable manipulation will not be that big. For this reason, researchers need to develop more complex research designs to enable researchers to develop better understandings of how human communicative behavior occurs. Ultimately, complexity in research design is a matter of sample size. Researchers and statistical tests can handle complex designs, but as designs become more complicated, more research conditions are needed, which requires an ever-increasing sample size.

Conclusion

In this chapter we have examined what experiments are and why we do them while exploring a variety of preexperimental, quasi-experimental, and true experimental study designs. In the next chapter we will explore how to best sample a population to attain the most generalizable results possible.

KEY TERMS

Antecedent Variable	Experiment	Lurker Variable
Attrition	Experimental Group(s)	Manipulation Check
Baseline	Experimenter Effects	Manipulation of
Confederate	Factorial Experimental	Independent Variables
Confounding Variable	Design	Maturation
Control	Hawthorne Effect	Quasi-Experimental Design
Control Group	Historical Flaw	Random Assignment
Debriefing	Intervening Variable	Regression to the Mean

Reinforcer Variable   Testing Flaw   Time Order
Selection Threat   Threshold Effect

REFERENCES

Campbell, D. T., & Stanley, J. C. (1963). *Experimental and quasi-experimental designs for research.* Skokie, IL: Rand McNally.

Cook, T. D., & Campbell, D. T. (1979). *Quasi-experimental design and analysis issues for field settings.* Boston: Houghton Mifflin Company.

Guéguen, N., & De Gail, M. A. (2003). The effect of smiling on helping behavior: Smiling and good Samaritan behavior. *Communication Reports, 16*, 133–140.

Masling, J. (1966). Role-related behavior of the subject and psychologist and its effects upon psychological data. In D. Levine (Ed.), *Nebraska Symposium on Motivation* (pp. 67–103). Lincoln, NB: University of Nebraska Press.

Stewart, R. A. (1994). Perceptions of a speaker's initial credibility as a function of religious involvement and religious disclosiveness. *Communication Research Reports, 11*, 169–176.

Tamborini, R., Eastin, M. S., Skalski, P., Lachlan, K., Fediuk, T. A., & Brady, R. (2004). Violent virtual video games and hostile thoughts. *Journal of Broadcasting & Electronic Media, 48*, 335–357.

Weber, K., Fornash, B., Corrigan, M, & Neupauer, N. C. (2003). The effect of interest on recall: An experiment. *Communication Research Reports, 20*, 116–123.

Wiener, J. L., & Doescher, T. A. (1994). Cooperation and expectations of cooperation. *Journal of Public Policy & Marketing, 13*, 559–270.

Wrench, J. S., Millhouse, B., & Sharp, D. (in press). Laughing before takeoff: Humor, sex, and the preflight safety briefing. *Human Communication.*

FURTHER READING

Brown, S. R., & Melamed, L. E. (1990). *Experimental design and analysis.* Thousand Oaks, CA: Sage.

Field, A., & Hole, G. J. (2003). *How to design and report experiments.* Thousand Oaks, CA: Sage.

Levin, I. P. (2004). *Relating statistics and experimental design: An introduction.* Thousand Oaks, CA: Sage.

Ryan, T. P. (2007). *Modern experimental design.* New York: John Wiley & Sons.

Shadish, W. R., Cook, T. D., & Campbell, D. T. (2002). *Experimental and quasi-experimental designs for generalized causal inference.* Boston: Houghton Mifflin Company.

Singleton, R. A., Jr., & Straits, B. C. (1999). *Approaches to social research* (3rd ed.). New York: Oxford University Press.

Spector, P. E. (1981). *Research designs.* Newbury Park, CA: Sage.

CHAPTER 14

Sampling Methods

CHAPTER OBJECTIVES

1. Understand what sampling is and why we use samples instead of populations.
2. Be able to explain the sampling process.
3. Be able to explain the central limits theorem.
4. Be able to differentiate among the different probability samples (simple random samples, stratified random samples, cluster samples, and systematic samples).
5. Understand the importance of sampling error and its relation to probability samples.
6. Be able to differentiate among the different nonprobability samples (convenience samples, volunteer samples, purposive samples, quota samples, and network samples).
7. Understand the general rules discussed in this chapter for determining a necessary sample size.
8. Understand the relationship between confidence intervals and sample sizes.
9. Be able to explain why we replicate studies and the four methods researchers can use to replicate a study.

Selecting participants for a research study is the perhaps one of the most crucial elements for the success of the project. Suppose a researcher wanted to answer the question, "What is the level of communication satisfaction between teachers and principals?" Who would you suggest that the researcher approach to be included in this study? The obvious answer is teachers and principals. However, there could be other characteristics of these two groups of participants that guide the research design. It would be important to include teachers from private and public schools, as well as those at the elementary, junior high, and high school levels. Perhaps selecting teachers with a variety of years of teaching experience would be important in answering the question. As you can see, there are numerous factors to consider when selecting a sample for your research design.

Consider this: every time you complete an exam for a class, you are responding to questions that address a sample of the information learned in the class. If the instructor were to test you on each and every thing you had learned, the exam might be extremely long. Instead, a sample of concepts is selected to assess your knowledge. In this chapter we will discuss the various sampling methods used to identify who should be included in the research project. Different types of samples will be identified, and questions regarding how many participants to include will be answered.

Why Use a Sample?

Sampling is the term used to refer to selecting people or units for inclusion in a research study. Scholars use samples because including all possible persons or units for a study is a virtually impossible task. Of course, since it is not possible to include every person or unit in the research project, it is important that the sample chosen be representative of the entire group. To begin our discussion, let's identify some key terms that will guide your understanding of the sampling process.

POPULATION

Population refers to an entire set of objects, observations, or scores that have some characteristic in common. For example, all registered voters between the ages of 18 and 25 could be considered a population. In this instance, all members of the population have two characteristics of interest in common: voter eligibility and age. Suppose the purpose of your research study is to identify the communication motives of college students who have visited their academic advisors. The population for this study would be extremely large. Thus, a sample of the population should be selected for the study to make data collection more manageable.

SAMPLE

Sample is the term used to refer to the people or units that a researcher actually includes in the study. Researchers choose samples because including all members of the population can be very costly and extremely time-consuming. Have you ever wondered how the marketers of Trident concluded that four out of five dentists whose patients chew gum recommend Trident? They probably didn't interview every dentist in the United States, so it is more likely that they contacted a sample from the population of dentists and calculated a statistic that could be generalized. Consider our earlier example of the population of college students who have visited their academic advisors. Since it is impossible to contact all of the college students who have done so, a researcher could select a sample of students and ask them to complete a survey about their communication motives. Furthermore, not all members of your sample will necessarily participate in the study. Sample members may choose to drop out of the study, they may refuse to participate, or they may not respond to every item. At times, the terms "population" and "sample" may be confusing. To review, population refers to all possible people or units that could be included, and sample refers to those people or units who are selected for inclusion in the study. The question becomes: How does a researcher identify the population and select the sample to include in the study?

THE SAMPLING PROCESS

Ask any researcher what her or his ultimate goal is when selecting a sample for inclusion in a study, and he or she will likely respond that he or she wants a sample that will produce results that are generalizable to the population. The term "generalizable" refers to the notion that the results of studying a sample can be assumed to be true of the entire population. To ensure generalizability, the researcher must take specific steps to ensure that the characteristics of the sample closely resemble those of the population. As you can see, the primary task at this stage of the research process involves identifying the appropriate sample. The sampling process involves several steps. Often the population that is the focus of a study is not accessible. For example, conducting a study on the aggressive communication behaviors encountered by women in abusive relationships would be difficult. Because many women in the population are apprehensive about reporting the abuse, while they are members of the theoretical population they may not be accessible for the study. So the first step in sampling involves identifying the theoretical population that the researcher would like to generalize the results of the study to and then identifying the actual study population that includes participants that the researcher could realistically contact.

After selecting the study population, the second step involves identifying all members of that group and determining how each one could be contacted for inclusion in the study. Recall our earlier example regarding the communication motives of students who have visited their academic advisors. Suppose a researcher has determined that the accessible population includes students attending Eastern University. Members of the population could be identified by asking all academic advisors on campus to provide a list of the students who had visited their offices during the previous two semesters. The list of all potential participants in the study population (students attending Eastern University) that are accessible to the researcher is referred to as the sampling frame. Remember, the sampling frame includes all members of the population accessible to the researcher, not all possible members of the theoretical population.

Say a study requires a researcher to conduct a survey inquiring about citizens' opinions about the credibility of a local politician. The local phone book could be used as a listing of the accessible population. Why couldn't this be considered representative of the theoretical population? Keep in mind that there are various things that could preclude a person from being listed in the phone book. Phone numbers may be unlisted, some members of the theoretical population may only use cell phones, and the listing typically only includes the name of one member of a household. Thus, while the phone book can be used to provide contact information for the accessible population, it does not provide information for the theoretical population.

The final step of the sampling process involves identifying the method that will be used to select members of the accessible population for inclusion in the sample that is contacted for the study. Suppose Eastern University is a large school and the academic advisors provided you with a list of over 15,000 names. Contacting everyone on the list would be very time-consuming, not to mention expensive. Thus, the researcher must identify the sample of students to be included in the study. A variety of sampling designs can be used to determine who will be contacted to participate in the study. Two primary designs involve probability sampling and nonprobability sampling. Each of these designs has a variety of sample methods available for a researcher to use.

SELECTING A SAMPLE DESIGN

When selecting the sample for a study, the researcher needs to decide whether to use probability or nonprobability designs when choosing participants. Probability designs involve the random selection of participants that guarantees that each member of the population has an equal chance of being selected (as discussed in Chapter 13). Examples of probability methods for selecting participants include simple random samples, stratified random samples, cluster samples, and systematic samples. Nonprobability designs involve selecting members of the accessible population in a nonrandom manner. Examples of nonprobability methods include convenience samples, volunteer samples, purposive samples, quota samples, and network samples.

Your decision of which design to use should consider your desire to predict the sampling error associated with the study. "Sampling error" refers to the random differences that exist between the sample and the population. By selecting a probability design, a researcher can calculate the sampling error or the degree to which the sample might be different from the population it was selected to represent. Nonprobability samples do not enable a researcher to calculate the degree to which the sample differs from the population. Let's take a closer look at these sample designs and discuss how a researcher decides which sampling method to use.

PROBABILITY SAMPLING

Probability sampling involves randomly selecting participants from the population so that all potential participants have an equal chance of being selected for the study. Random selection methods eliminate any potential bias by ensuring that each person in the population has an equal chance of being chosen. Chances are that you have used probability sampling at various times in your life and not realized it. The strategy of "drawing straws" for a task is one that involves random selection. Since the length of the straws is concealed from view and selection of straws is random, each person who takes a turn at selecting a straw has an equal chance of drawing the short straw.

As we emphasized earlier, probability designs are used in situations where the researcher wants to calculate and report the sampling error. It makes sense that probability theory holds true in situations where probability samples are used—the score that occurs most frequently in the sample will also be the score that should occur most frequently in the population. Probability samples produce scores that accurately reflect the most and the least common scores in the population. Recall the normal distribution curve we discussed in Chapter 8. Probability methods allow the researcher to select a sample whose scores will be distributed in the shape of a normal distribution curve. The central limits theorem is used to explain the relationship between probability samples and the population. According to the central limits theorem, collecting data from repeated samples within the same population will produce a distribution of scores in the shape of a normal curve. More specifically, the central limits theorem states that the mean of the scores obtained from the probability sample will be equal to the mean of the scores obtained from the population. Further, the central limits theorem states that the variance of the sample mean is equal to the variance of the population mean divided by the sample size (N). Thus, the more variance that exists between scores in the population, the more variance that will exist between scores in the sample used to represent that population. Finally, the central limits theorem states that the distribution of mean scores from the sample will more closely represent the distribution of mean scores of the population as the sample size (N) increases, which makes sense because probability samples provide equal opportunity for selection, and the results are more likely to reflect the population.

As mentioned earlier, an advantage of probability sampling is that it enables the researcher to calculate sampling error, or how likely it is that the population mean differs from the sample mean. We will address the concept of sampling error in more detail later in this chapter. Once the researcher determines that probability designs are preferred, the next step involves selecting the specific method that will be used to choose participants for the sample.

SIMPLE RANDOM SAMPLES

As discussed in Chapter 13, random sampling is considered by many to be the "purest" method for collecting a probability sample. It ensures that each member of the population has an equal chance of being selected for the study. The researcher makes a random decision of who will be included in the sample. Various methods of randomization are used to select sample members, and these methods are selected to ensure the validity of the study. Two forms of randomization can be used in research: random samples and random assignment. "Random sample" refers to the selection of study participants from the population. "Random assignment" is a term used to refer to how the researcher assigns the sample drawn from the population to various groups within the study. Suppose a researcher wants to examine the persuasive effect of language used in fear appeals. To ensure a truly representative sample, a researcher might select a simple random sample of 150 people from the target population. Next, members of the sample would be randomly assigned in groups of 50 to one of three conditions—high-, medium-, and low-intensity fear appeals. Thus, it is possible to design a study that utilizes both random sampling and random assignment. Random sampling allows a researcher to generalize the results to the population, thus enhancing the external validity of the study. Random assignment allows the researcher to strengthen the internal validity of the study by ensuring that participants are randomly assigned to the conditions being examined.

So how do researchers identify a simple random sample for a study? This task is often completed by using a table of random numbers or some other computer-generated list that ensures random selection (see Figure 14.1 for an example from www.random.org). Recall our earlier example of students who meet with academic advisors. The first step in securing a random sample requires the identification of the accessible population. To accomplish this, we would ask academic advisors to provide lists of students who had visited their office during the past two semesters. In the next step, we would identify the sample size desired for the project. Sample size will be discussed later in this chapter, but for now let's assume that we want to survey 100 students out of the 850 students included on the lists provided by advisors. One method for randomly selecting the participants might involve placing all 850 names in a hat and drawing 100 names to contact. While this method would ensure that each person had an equal chance of being selected, it would be extremely time-consuming. A more efficient method for randomly selecting participants involves using a table of random numbers. Computers have made the task of random number assignment much easier. In the previous chapter we presented how to use an electronic random number generator—let's now look at an example using a random number table (Figure 14.1).

Using this table of random numbers, we can collect a random sample for our study. Step one involves assigning each student on the list a number between 1 and 850. Next, refer to the first three digits of each number listed on the chart of random numbers, since 850 is a three-digit number. Step three involves closing your eyes and randomly pointing to a spot on the chart. Suppose you randomly selected 46882 in Figure 14.1. Next, we read the number as 468 (the first three digits). Thus, the student who was assigned the number of 468 is included in

61424	20419	86546	00517
46882	27993	04952	66762
02429	71146	97668	86523
85676	10005	07216	25906
19761	50349	15370	90222
78733	16447	27932	89990

Figure 14.1 Sample Table of Random Numbers

our sample list. Continue down the column to the next number, which is 02429. This is interpreted a 024, which means that student 24 is selected for the sample. Our next number on the chart is 85676. However, we only have 850 students on our list. Not a problem—simply skip that number and continue to the next number in the column. Continue through the chart until 100 students have been randomly selected for the sample.

As you can see, this task can be particularly time-consuming for drawing large samples. Computers have enabled researchers to accomplish this task more efficiently. Yet another method for assigning random numbers to a list generated from the population can be accomplished using Microsoft Excel. For our study of students who visit advisors, we would simply copy and paste the list of names into an Excel spreadsheet. In the column next to the list of names, the formula "=RAND()" is inserted in the cell to instruct Excel to assign a random number between 0 and 1 beside each name on the list. Be sure to copy and paste this formula throughout the entire selection of cells. Next, conduct a sort of both columns by instructing Excel to sort and arrange the list of random numbers from lowest to highest (or vice versa). Once this is completed, you simply need to select the first 100 names from your list of 850.

So what are the advantages and disadvantages of random samples? The primary advantage is the ability to calculate the statistical sampling error. Disadvantages include the need to have accurate lists representing the entire population and the time involved in the process of random selection. In addition, by sheer luck a researcher may find that the sample selected randomly does not provide an accurate representation of the population. Other probability sampling methods can be used combat these concerns.

STRATIFIED RANDOM SAMPLES

In some instances where the population is extremely large, researchers may want to select participants based on criteria chosen specifically for the study. Stratified random samples enable researchers to divide the population into specific strata, also known as subsets of the population that have a common characteristic. Participants are randomly selected from the strata that have been identified. Some examples of strata that could be examined in a study include males and females; full-time and part-time students; or Democrats, Republicans, and Independents. Once the strata have been identified, conduct a simple random sample of each group.

Stratified sampling is the preferred method in some studies because it reduces the potential for sampling error. Researchers often use this sampling method in situations where there is unequal representation of one group or stratum of a population compared to other groups. Consider our example of student motives for visiting academic advisors. If the list of names provided by advisors was disproportionate in terms of the number of freshmen, sophomores, juniors, and seniors, the researcher might decide to conduct a stratified random sample to ensure that information is gathered from all class ranks.

Once the strata have been identified, the next task involves determining the sample size for each group. As a general rule, the researcher should ensure that the number of participants selected from each stratum is proportionate to the group's size in the population. Suppose we know that of the 850 students included on the list, 300 are freshmen, 275 are sophomores, 175 are juniors, and 100 are seniors. Since there is a disproportionate amount of seniors in the population, it would be important to conduct a stratified sample to determine if communication motives of seniors differ from those of freshmen and sophomores. To calculate the proportionate sample size for each stratum, we first need to determine what percentage of the overall population is represented by each group. To determine the percentage, you divide the number of people in a group by the total number of students. For example, to find the percentage of freshman we need to divide the number of freshmen (300) by the total number of students

(850), or 300 / 850 = 35.29 (when rounded). The population is comprised of 35.29% freshman, 30.24% sophomores, 20.59% juniors, and 11.76% seniors. This means that out of our sample of 100, we should survey 36 freshmen, 31 sophomores, 21 juniors, and 12 seniors.

The obvious advantage to stratified samples is their ability to ensure that various sub-groups in the population are included in the study, which is especially important in instances where there are minority groups who may not be selected for the study if simple random selection methods are used. Disadvantages to stratified sampling include the difficulty in identifying nonoverlapping strata and the additional time needed to organize groups for simple random selection.

CLUSTER SAMPLES

Cluster sampling allows a researcher to identify naturally occurring clusters of participants who have a variable in common within the target population. Suppose in your study of college students you want to collect information from colleges across the country. You would need a lot of time and money to complete the project if you began in California and surveyed students at colleges until you arrived in Maine. An alternative method for ensuring that colleges have an equal chance of being selected would involve using the cluster sample method. This method requires the researcher to first divide the country into regions: west, southwest, midwest, east, and so forth. Once all the colleges within each region are selected, the cluster sample method is used to randomly select the region of the country from which to select participants. Once the region is randomly selected, random sampling is conducted within each region to ensure that a probability sample is obtained. Another instance where cluster sampling could be useful is if a researcher wanted to interview employees of an organization with offices around the nation or the world.

One apparent advantage of cluster sampling is the money and time that can be saved by contacting participants in a few areas rather than gathering data from all possible regions. A disadvantage of the method is that participants in the same geographical area or same organizational region might be very similar to one another, thus they could be less representative of the population than the researcher originally anticipated. A second, very important disadvantage to cluster samples is that the chance of sampling error (*the random differences that exist between the sample and the population*) will increase with each step (we'll discuss this idea in more detail in a moment).

SYSTEMATIC SAMPLES

A final probability sampling method involves selecting a sample by determining the sample size needed from the population and selecting every "*n*th" person from the population for inclusion in the study. This method is just as effective as simple random sampling as long as there is no systematic order to the listing of a population. In our earlier example, systematic sampling could be used as long as advisors were not instructed to submit their lists in order of class rank or grade point average. If any of the lists include a method for organizing or ordering population members, systematic sampling cannot be used.

Suppose you want to conduct interviews with 15 employees from a population of 200. Simply divide 200 by 15 and you would discover that every thirteenth employee on the list should be included in your sample. To ensure that every employee has an equal chance of being chosen, choose a random number between 1 and 15 to determine your starting point. Then select every 13th name on the employee list. If number 7 is the random number selected to start, employees 7, 20, 33, 46, and so forth would be included in the sample.

Systematic samples are often used because they are much easier to conduct compared to simple random samples. However, a potential disadvantage of this method is that results could be biased if there is a hidden order to the list of population members used to generate the sample. For example, let's say you get a list of addresses and you select every tenth house. If a city block has 10 houses, then you may be selecting every house that is right on a corner. If you want to ask people about noise problems, people living in a corner house may experience more noise than people who live in the middle of the block. In other words, you've actually built into your design error unknowingly.

Sampling Error

As stated earlier, one of the primary advantages of selecting probability sampling methods over nonprobability methods is the opportunity they afford the researcher to calculate the sampling error. Sampling error statistics provide the researcher with an idea of how accurate the sample will be in predicting similar results in the population. When the results of a study produce a low sampling error score, this indicates that there is little range or variability in the sample distribution of scores. A high sampling error score indicates wide variability. How do you know what the sampling error is for the study? You can get a good idea by reviewing the sample standard deviation. The larger the standard deviation score is for the sample, the larger the sampling error that is present. This translates into a greater chance that discrepancies will be found when trying to generalize the results from the sample to the population. Later in this chapter we will discuss how to calculate sample size. Sample size is directly related to sampling error in that the larger the sample size, the less chance that sampling errors have occurred. It makes sense—the larger the sample size, the greater chance that you have captured the characteristics representative of the population.

Nonprobability Samples

Samples that are not randomly selected are known as nonprobability samples. Because selection is not random, there is a greater chance for bias to exist in the results. While nonprobability samples do not involve random selection, it is not necessarily the case that nonprobability samples are not representative of the population. Nonprobability samples may represent the population just as accurately as a probability sample. However, a researcher is not able to provide statistical support for the sampling error of a nonprobability sample. As a result, it is difficult to determine whether the results generated from the sample can be generalized to the population. So why would a researcher choose to use nonprobability samples in lieu of a random sample? Several explanations might be offered for such a decision. In some instances a study might be examining a variable or phenomenon that is new. In this situation it may be difficult to determine which population is most appropriate for the study. Other studies may focus on variables or characteristics that make it difficult to find participants. Recall the earlier example of a study designed to examine the verbal aggressiveness of women in abusive relationships. Finding participants for this sensitive topic may be difficult, thus a researcher might be forced to engage in nonprobability sampling. A third reason for selecting this sampling method is related to the efficiency of cost and time associated with finding participants. Finally, nonprobability samples are used in instances where the characteristic being studied is not easily found.

Even though these are all legitimate reasons for selecting nonrandom methods of sampling, the researcher needs to be aware of several cautions with their use. As we've already discussed, the chance of sampling error increases with nonprobability sampling. Of course, we can never be sure exactly what the error is due to the fact that random methods were not employed. As a result of higher sampling error, the ability to generalize results to the population is limited. In these instances, the researcher needs to pay careful attention to addressing the sampling issues in the discussion section of the research paper when identifying limitations of the study. Finally, sampling bias is often associated with nonprobability samples. This bias is defined as a systematic difference between the population and the sample that results from failing to select representative cases. There are five primary types of nonprobability sampling methods employed by communication scholars: convenience samples, volunteer samples, purposive samples, quota samples, and network samples. Let's begin by exploring the selection of convenience samples.

CONVENIENCE SAMPLES

Convenience samples involve the selection of participants for the sample based on their availability. If you've ever been asked to complete a survey during class for a research project, chances are you were part of a convenience sample. Are the results biased using this method? Absolutely! After all, only individuals who are enrolled in the class are included in the sample. Is this necessarily a bad thing? Not if the variable being examined is only applicable to those who are enrolled in the class.

While some scholars may perceive results produced by convenience samples with skepticism, there are instances where these samples can produce useful information. In a study designed to examine the nonverbal behaviors displayed in physician–patient interactions, Riddle et al. (2002) used a convenience sample of patients and physicians. Forty-seven patients who sought care at various clinics were approached and asked if they would be willing to participate in the study. Their medical oncologists also agreed to participate. In this instance, the clinic afforded the researcher the opportunity to solicit a convenience sample of the target population in an environment that ensured they met criteria necessary for inclusion in the study. Soliciting a sample by randomly calling names in a phone book would be less efficient since one criterion for inclusion in the sample was that participants should have engaged in an interaction with a physician.

As stated earlier, the major disadvantage with convenience sampling lies in the inability to generalize the results to the population. However, this method can be particularly useful in exploratory studies when a researcher has limited time or money to compile a random sample.

VOLUNTEER SAMPLES

In some instances, participants may volunteer to participate to be a part of the study sample. Volunteer samples are often recruited by offering participants a reward in exchange for their time. Fans who cast their votes each week via phone on *American Idol* or *Dancing with the Stars* are examples of volunteer samples. The participants choose whether or not to be part of the sample of the population that selects the winner. Many media studies employ this method to obtain feedback from the population. Researchers find that it is often easier to have people volunteer to be a part of the study than to engage in other methods to locate participants.

An obvious disadvantage of this type of sampling method is that only those who are aware of the study would be available to volunteer. There is no mechanism for collecting information from those who are either unaware of the study or who choose not to participate. Advantages to volunteer sampling are that it is efficient to conduct the study in terms of cost and time, and it is more likely that participants who choose to participate have some level of knowledge or interest in the topic.

PURPOSIVE SAMPLES

Purposive sampling involves nonrandomly selecting participants to fulfill or meet a specific purpose the researcher has in mind. The sample is selected based on specific characteristics the researcher is investigating—generally the participants meet some predetermined criteria that the researcher has used to determine eligibility. Purposive sampling is a method that is used in both quantitative and qualitative studies. A primary strength of the purposive sample lies in its ability to select participants or cases who meet the criteria being examined in the study. Suppose a researcher wanted to explore the perceived communication effectiveness of an organization following a crisis situation. It would make perfect sense to select a purposive sample of workers and businesses in the Gulf Coast region that were displaced from their facilities following Hurricane Katrina.

In a study examining intercultural perspectives taught in public relations courses, Bardhan (2003) used a purposive sample of students enrolled in his public relations course and asked them to provide responses to three open-ended questions. Since the goal was to examine perspectives taught in a public relations class, it is only logical that public relations students would be recruited for the purposive sample. In another study that examined the causes of job satisfaction among public relations practitioners, Grunig (1990) selected a total of 87 practitioners from 48 organizations, which represented one of four structural typologies. These organizations and their members were purposely selected so that there would be 12 organizations representing each of the four types of organization. In order to ensure that all four organization types would be equally represented in the study, a purposive sample of practitioners and organizations was chosen.

The primary advantage of purposive sampling is that it enables the researcher to collect information from the target sample more efficiently. Further, it ensures that all participants selected for the study have a study variable in common. Disadvantages include the overrepresentation of the sample more easily accessed in the population and the tendency to obtain sample sizes that are not proportionate to the population size.

QUOTA SAMPLES

To obtain a quota sample, participants are separated into strata or groups based on a common characteristic or variable, and then participants from each group are selected nonrandomly for inclusion in the study. It is important to note that while both quota and stratified samples identify strata for participant classification, one uses random methods for selecting participants from each group while the other does not.

Quota samples can be proportionate or nonproportionate in relation to the population. Nonproportionate quota samples recruit volunteers until the determined number of participants has been recruited. Suppose you were conducting a study of 100 male and female employees to examine perceptions of their manager's communication style. Even though the population of the organization consists of 80% females and 20% males, a nonproportionate quota sample could be drawn by simply interviewing the first 100 employees who enter the company cafeteria. Doing so may result in a sample population comprised of 60% females and 40% males, but they all meet the group criteria of being an employee in the organization.

Proportionate quota samples are chosen to ensure that the number of volunteers recruited for the study is proportionate or equal to the number of group members in the population. Consider our earlier sample of 100 employees. Since the population consists of 80% women and 20% men and a total of 100 employees is needed for the sample, the researcher will continue to select participants until the percentage in each group matches the population percentage. In this instance the researcher will stop interviewing women when 80 have been included in the sample. Even if additional female employees come along prior to soliciting 20 male employees, they will be excluded from the study because a proportionate quota has been met.

The primary distinction between quota and stratified samples is their use of random or nonrandom procedures for selecting participants for the sample. Recall our earlier study of student motives for communicating with their advisor. A total of 100 students were identified as the target sample size for the study. While stratified sampling methods might utilize a table of random numbers to select students from the list to fill the determined number of participants for each category, quota sampling methods might simply take the first 20 juniors and the first 11 seniors they contacted.

Many communication studies have employed quota sampling methods to identify samples. In a study examining children's comprehension of television advertising, Chan (2000) selected a quota sample of boys and girls to represent each class level from kindergarten to sixth grade. To ensure that each grade level included an equal number of boys and girls, a total of 32 boys and 32 girls were selected from each grade. Thus, participants were selected to participate until the predetermined number in each group was obtained.

An advantage of quota samples is that they enable the researcher to identify a target number for each group or category of a population, thus ensuring that each group is equally represented. Further, this sampling method is less costly and less time-consuming than stratified sampling. The obvious disadvantage lies in the nonprobability methods used for selecting participants. Not everyone has an equal chance of being selected for the study, and thus the study may produce results that are potentially biased.

NETWORK SAMPLE

A final nonprobability sampling method used involves asking participants to refer researchers to other people who could serve as participants. Network sampling is often used in instances where a variable or characteristic being studied is rare or difficult to identify in a population. Referrals from participants provide the researcher with a cost and time-effective method for locating others who meet the study criteria. Earlier we discussed a study that might examine the verbal aggressiveness of victims of domestic abuse. Since many victims are not willing to openly disclose their situation, a researcher might have to obtain a sample by asking each participant to refer another person who has experienced a similar situation.

Bruess and Pearson (2002) identified participants for their study examining the functions of rituals in friendships and marriages by using the network sampling method. They asked undergraduate students to assist them in recruiting married couples to complete questionnaires and participate in interviews. Students volunteered to assist the researchers, resulting in a total of 494 surveys from married individuals and a total of 489 surveys on friendships. Bruess and Pearson would have spent a considerable amount of time soliciting a sample size that large and that diverse without the assistance of network sampling.

One advantage of the network sample is that it enables researchers to recruit members of populations that are not easily identifiable (e.g., gay, lesbian, bisexual, and transgendered people; internet porn addicts; people with an identical twin; etc.). Another advantage is that it enables researchers to obtain larger sample sizes more quickly. The obvious disadvantage of the network sample lies in the inability to generalize findings to the population.

Determining Sample Size

Perhaps one of the first questions asked by students in research methods classes is, "How many participants should I recruit for my sample?" As we discussed earlier, larger sample sizes typically produce results that are more generalizable to the population. However, it is important to assess your study. Samples that are too large could end up wasting the researcher's time and money. On the other hand, a sample size that is too small can produce results that do not accurately reflect the larger population.

A quick analysis of the research design can help answer some initial questions regarding sample size. The more the population varies with respect to the characteristics being examined, the larger the sample size should be to account for the variance. Suppose you wanted to do a study on Internet use in a region of the United States Chances are that the patterns and motives for use would vary greatly depending on a person's age, sex, and employment or education status. Teens may be more likely to access the Internet than the elderly, and students may use their computers more for class research purposes than do stay-at-home mothers. It is likely that the population will vary greatly, and thus a larger sample size is needed.

The first question a researcher must answer in determining the appropriate sample size is to identify the confidence level with which you want to report your results. Confidence levels tell you how confident or sure you can be that the results are generalizable to the population and not due to chance. As a general rule, if you want to produce results that are more precise, a larger sample size should be selected. The most frequently used confidence level in research is 95%. This means that the sample results should predict the population results with 95% accuracy.

A confidence interval provides additional information to interpret results. Confidence intervals are typically expressed in terms of plus or minus a specific number. Consider the following example. When reporting on election exit poll results, television networks may report that the polls indicate that 62% of the population support Candidate A and cite a confidence interval (also referred to as the margin of error) of plus or minus 3%. This lets the audience know that between 59 and 65% of the population will likely vote for Candidate A. The range (59–65) is the confidence interval. The researchers can be 95% sure that the actual percentage of people voting for Candidate A will fall between 59 and 65%. Obviously, that's very good news for Candidate A! It is important to note that the relationship between sample size and confidence interval is not necessarily linear in nature. Simply doubling the sample size will not necessarily reduce the confidence interval by half.

Many online and print resources are available to assist researchers in calculating sample size. Figure 14.2 shows a table for determining the sample size of a given population. In order to perform online calculations (http://statpages.org/javastat.html has many links to online calculators that could be useful), the researcher typically needs to identify specific criteria: the desired confidence level (typically either 95% or 99%), the desired confidence interval, and an estimate of the population size. It is important to remember that sample size calculators assume that random sampling methods are used in the study. Results obtained from the calculators cannot be used for nonrandom samples. Remember—random samples produce results that enhance the external validity of your study.

Replication

At times researchers may identify a study that produced results inconsistent with other studies or they may want to apply a theory to new contexts or populations to determine the generalizability to other groups or settings. Replication involves conducting additional research

N	*S	N	S	N	S
10	10	220	140	1,200	291
15	14	230	144	1,300	297
20	19	240	148	1,400	302
25	24	250	152	1,500	306
30	28	260	155	1,600	310
35	32	270	159	1,700	313
40	36	280	162	1,800	317
45	40	290	165	1,900	320
50	44	300	169	2,000	322
55	48	320	175	2,200	327
60	52	340	181	2,400	331
65	56	360	186	2,600	335
70	59	380	191	2,800	338
75	63	400	196	3,000	341
80	66	420	201	3,500	346
85	70	440	205	4,000	351
90	73	460	210	4,500	354
95	76	480	214	5,000	357
100	80	500	217	6,000	361
110	86	550	226	7,000	364
120	92	600	234	8,000	367
130	97	650	242	9,000	368
140	103	700	248	10,000	370
150	108	750	254	15,000	375
160	113	800	260	20,000	377
170	118	850	265	30,000	379
180	123	900	269	40,000	380
190	127	950	274	50,000	382
200	132	1,000	278	75,000	382
210	136	1,100	285	100,000	383

N = population size.

S = sample size.

* Confidence Interval = 5 & Confidence Level = 95%.

The entries in this table were computed by the authors.

Figure 14.2 Determining Sample Size from a Given Population

on an existing topic for one of several reasons: (1) to determine if the original results were by error or remain constant; (2) to examine the variable using new population characteristics; (3) to apply results from previous studies to new situations; and (4) to combine the results of two or more previous studies in developing new research directions.

Four primary types of replication are conducted. Each is distinguished by the researcher's decision to alter instrumentation or methods, samples, and data analysis procedures. *Literal replication* involves duplicating a previous study by keeping the instrumentation, experimental procedures, and the sample as similar as possible to the original study. In *operational replication*, the researcher maintains similar samples and methods, but the instrumentation or surveys used in the study are changed. *Instrumental replication* involves measuring the dependent variable the same way as in the initial study, but changes in the independent variable are made to see if a different operationalization of experimental procedures will yield similar results. Finally, *constructive replication* refers to a researcher's decision to use entirely new instrumentation, methods or procedures, sample, and data analysis techniques to duplicate the conceptual foundation of a previous study.

Replication is essential for testing and supporting various communication theories. Recall the discussion of central limits theorem earlier in this chapter. We pointed out that data collected from multiple samples will yield results that are more generalizable to the population. The sample principle of probability applies to replication. Repeated studies focusing on the same variable or phenomenon assist communication scholars in building strong theoretical foundations for our discipline. Authors often provide suggestions for ways in which their studies can be replicated when discussing the limitations. However, very few researchers attempt to replicate original studies. As students of research methods, you may want to consider ways in which you can replicate and build on previous research as you define your own interests.

Conclusion

There are many decisions that researchers need to consider when identifying which sampling method to use. In this chapter we have introduced you to a variety of sampling methods that can be used in designing your own research study. Probability and nonprobability sampling methods were discussed. As you decide which of these methods is most appropriate for your own research, it is important to consider the steps you can take to ensure that the results obtained from your sample are generalizable to the target population being examined. An important element in determining the generalizability focuses on the selection of random or nonrandom samples in addition to the size of the sample selected for the study. We concluded this chapter with a discussion of the importance of replication. As you begin studying communication research methods, consider utilizing one of the four methods of replication to build on the research of others and test theories using new populations.

KEY TERMS

Central limits theorem	Operational Replication	Sampling
Cluster Samples	Population	Sampling Error
Confidence Interval	Probability Sampling	Sampling Frame
Constructive Replication	Probability Theory	Simple Random Samples
Convenience Samples	Purposive Samples	Stratified Random Samples
Instrumental Replication	Quota Samples	Systematic Samples
Literal Replication	Replication	Theoretical Population
Network Samples	Sample	Volunteer Samples

REFERENCES

Bardhan, N. (2003). Creating spaces for international and multi(inter)cultural perspectives in undergraduate public relations education. *Communication Education, 52*, 164–172.

Bruess, C. J., & Pearson, J. C. (2002). The function of mundane ritualizing in adult friendship and marriage. *Communication Research Reports, 19*, 314–326.

Chan, K. (2000). Hong Kong children's understanding of television advertising. *Journal of Marketing Communications, 6*, 37–52.

Grunig, L. A. (1990). An exploration of the causes of job satisfaction in public relations. *Management Communication Quarterly, 3*, 355–375.

Krejcie, R. V., & D. W. Morgan. (1970). Determining sample size for research activities. *Educational and Psychological Measurement, 30*, 607–610.

Riddle, D. L., Albrecht, T. L., Coovert, M. D., Penner, L. A., Ruckdeschel, J. C., Blanchard, C. G., Quinn, G., & Urbizu, D. (2002). Differences in audiotaped versus videotaped physician-patient interactions. *Journal of Nonverbal Behavior, 26*, 219–239.

FURTHER READING

Fink, A. (2002). *How to sample in surveys* (2nd ed.). Thousand Oaks, CA: Sage.

Henry, G. T. (1990). *Practical sampling.* Thousand Oaks, CA: Sage.

Kalton, G. (1983). *Introduction to survey sampling.* Newbury Park, CA: Sage.

Thompson, S. K. (2002). *Sampling* (rev. ed.). New York: Wiley, John & Sons.

Thompson, S. K., & Seber, G. A. F. (1996). *Adaptive sampling.* New York: Wiley, John & Sons.

CHAPTER 15

Hypothesis Testing

CHAPTER OBJECTIVES

1 Be able to differentiate between alternative and null hypotheses.
2 Understand the mathematical nature of sampling error.
3 Understand the importance of a 95% confidence interval in scientific research.
4 Know the process a researcher goes through for significance testing.
5 Understand the nature of probability levels and their relationships with confidence intervals.
6 Understand the relationship between calculated and critical values.
7 Understand the relationship between null hypotheses and statistical power.
8 Understand the relationship between null hypotheses and statistical significance.
9 Understand the affect that one-tailed and two-tailed hypotheses have on statistical significance.
10 Be able to explain the importance of effect sizes in statistical research.
11 Be able to describe both Type I (α) and Type II (β) errors.

In Chapter 8 we started a discussion comparing descriptive statistics (statistics used to describe data—mean, median, mode, skewness, kurtosis, range, sum of squares, variance, and standard deviation) and inferential statistics (statistics used by a researcher to make predictions). These predictions alluded to in the definition of inferential statistics stem out of a study's research hypotheses and research questions:

H_1: There will be a negative relationship between communication apprehension and an individual's belief that all students should take public speaking in college.

or

RQ_1: Do females and males differ in their willingness to communicate?

Of course, as we discussed in Chapter 5, whether one forms hypotheses or research questions depends on whether or not a researcher can find support to form logical arguments that lead to a logical hypothesis. If one cannot find the research to logically support a hypothesis, a researcher can opt to ask a research question instead.

The above hypothesis and research question represent to statisticians two *alternative hypotheses*. An alternative hypothesis is *the prediction that there is a relationship or there is a difference that has not occurred by chance or random error*. While we differentiate between hypotheses and research questions in the creation of theoretical predictions based on previous research, there are no mathematical differences in how they are perceived. For this reason, both of the above predictions can be represented as alternative hypotheses:

H_1:   There is a negative relationship between communication apprehension and an individual's belief that all students should take public speaking in college.

or

H_1:   Females and males differ in their willingness to communicate.

In Chapter 5 we also mentioned another important component we need to review before discussing significance testing, the null hypothesis. The null hypothesis is generally expressed as the "nil" hypothesis—there are zero differences or zero relationships (Cohen, 1994). The hypothesis and research question presented above are considered the "alternative hypotheses" and their null hypothesis counterparts would be the following:

H_0:   There is no relationship between communication apprehension and an individual's belief that all students should take public speaking in college.

or

H_0:   There is no difference between females and males and their willingness to communicate.

You'll notice here that both hypotheses and research questions that are generated for a study in one's rationale section have null hypothesis counterparts that say either there isn't a relationship or there isn't a difference. In Chapter 14 we discussed that our goal in research is to be able to determine whether or not our samples are consistent with their populations. The null hypothesis expresses expectations for what should occur within the population, so the null hypothesis allows researchers to determine the probability of the results we find in our samples are consistent with the overall population.

While we have talked about the null hypothesis as being something generally researchers avoid, this isn't always the case. Researchers often hope that there isn't a relationship or difference in a study, or they want to accept the null hypothesis. For example, you may theorize that there is no relationship between an individual's communication apprehension and her or his IQ and form a hypothesis in a study predicting a lack of relationship. However, the alternative hypothesis always predicts that there is a relationship or difference:

H_1:   There is a relationship between an individual's communication apprehension and her or his IQ.

However, the null hypothesis would predict that there is not a relationship:

H_0:   There is no relationship between an individual's communication apprehension and her or his IQ.

In this case, the theoretical hypothesis made in our study suggests that we need to accept the null hypothesis, which would have us reject the alternative hypothesis. Hypothesis testing then is *the process a researcher goes through using inferential statistics to determine whether or not we reject or accept the null hypothesis.* Now that we've explained the general concept of hypothesis testing, let's look at a case study to help us further understand the hypothesis-testing process.

Hypothesis Testing Case Study

A team of researchers wanted to determine if viewing of televangelists positively or negatively influenced nonreligious individuals' perceptions of religion. The researchers used a phone bank that randomly called people in a large city. A large number of potential participants were contacted via telephone and asked if they would participate in a study, and 80% agreed to help. The researchers mailed the participants a series of scales and asked the participants to fill out the scales and return them in the stamped envelope with the researcher's mailing address preprinted on the envelope. The initial survey packet contained a short survey asking the participants about their perceptions of various religious organizations. After completing the initial survey, the participants sent the researchers back the first survey packet.

When the researchers received the first survey packet, the participant was sent a second survey packet (sealed in a secondary envelope) with a set of instructions attached. The researchers asked the participants to refrain from opening the survey packet until the participants watched a televangelist from a religion not their own on television. Once a participant had watched a televangelist, he or she opened the secondary survey packet and filled out the survey that asked the participants to rate their attitudes towards the religion of the televangelist on the television show they had watched. The participants also supplied information about the television show they had watched. When the survey was completed, the participants sent the survey back to the researchers.

In essence, each participant rated the televangelist's religion two different times. The measurement of the dependent variable (perception of a religion) occurred in the first survey packet, since participants supplied their attitudes about a wide range of religious groups. The second measurement of the dependent variable (perception of religion) occurred more specifically toward the specific religion. However, since attitudes about a religious faith were gathered at both Time 1 (T_1; first survey packet) and at Time 2 (T_2; second survey packet), this is a clear experimental procedure. To make sure that the study didn't have a time effect on the participants' filling out the surveys, the researchers also had a control group that just filled out the survey packet in T_1 and again in T_2, but were not asked to watch a televangelist from a differing religion. In the control group, the means on the religious attitude scales were virtually identical ($MT_1 = 53.69$; $MT_2 = 53.56$). In the manipulation group (filled out the scales in Time 1, watched the televangelist, and then filled out the survey packet in Time 2), the means are a little different ($MT_1 = 52.9$; $MT_2 = 48.9$). If we were just eyeballing this finding, we might say that there is almost a four-point drop from Time 1 to Time 2, so clearly people end up not liking a religion after viewing a televangelist. However, in statistics we simply cannot eyeball a difference in means and say that the change is statistically meaningful. For this reason, a process has been created called hypothesis testing to determine if a difference or relationship between two means is meaningful or is occurring as a result of random chance.

HYPOTHESIS TESTING IN THE CASE STUDY

As defined in Chapter 2, a hypothesis is a tentative statement about the relationship between independent and dependent variables. In this chapter we clump both of these concepts together under the heading of "hypothesis testing" because we are talking about mathematical hypothesis testing not a hypothesis derived at as a result of your literature review. For our case study, the alternative and null hypotheses would be:

H_1:   There is a difference between people who view a televangelist and people who do not and their perceptions of a televangelist's religion.

H_0:   There is no difference between people who view a televangelist and people who do not and their perceptions of a televangelist's religion.

In this example we want to determine if there is a difference between the mean score on the religious attitude scale for Time 1 (before they watched the televangelist) and the mean score on the religious attitude scale for Time 2 (after they watched the televangelist). The mathematical notion for this would then be:

$$H_1: \mu_{\text{Time1}} \neq \mu_{\text{Time2}}$$

This statement says that the mean of Time 1 is not equal to (or there is a difference between) the mean of Time 2.

In our example above, our null hypothesis would state that the mean score on the religious attitude scale for Time 1 (before they watched the televangelist) and the mean score on the religious attitude scale for Time 2 (after they watched the televangelist) were the same, or no difference exists. The mathematical notion for this would then be:

$$H_0: \mu_{\text{Time1}} = \mu_{\text{Time2}}$$

This statement basically says that the mean of Time 1 is equal to (or there is not a difference between) the mean of Time 2. Notice how the alternative hypothesis and null hypothesis would be the same whether you developed a hypothesis or research question out of your literature review.

From Random Samples to a Whole Population

One of the most interesting and complex aspects of empirical social scientific research is that researchers must deal with people and numbers. As a result of dealing with people and numbers, there is a certain amount of error that naturally occurs. Ideally, researchers would be able to gather data from an entire population, but this is not realistic so we must rely on samples as discussed in Chapter 14. When researchers rely on samples, a certain amount of error occurs called sampling error, or *the degree to which a sample* probably *differs with respect to a specific variable from a population.* For example, imagine our example study in this chapter had only 10 participants. If we attained the mean on the religious attitude scale for each of the 10 participants, we would see that not everyone's score was identical, so we would have what is called a sampling distribution. And as we know, the mean of a sampling distribution can be calculated by adding up all of the 10 individual scores on the religious attitude scale and dividing by 10 (number of participants; $N = 10$). If in our sample we got the 10 following scores—57, 58, 62, 23, 54, 56, 55, 54, 51, and 59—Time 1 and 55, 57, 60, 20, 50, 52, 53, 55, 48, and 39 at Time 2, you would get means and standard deviations for Time 1 of ($MT_1 = 52.9$, $SD = 10.94$) and for Time 2 of ($MT_2 = 48.90$, $SD = 11.67$). If we wanted to determine how much error was in our sampling distribution (how much our random sample means differ from the overall mean of 52.9), we simply divide the standard deviation by the square root of N (sample size or 10). So first, we need to calculate the square root of 10, which is 3.16227766. We can then divide our standard deviation (10.94) by 3.16227766 and we get 3.45953176. In other words, the standard error of the mean (SE$_M$) in our example is roughly 3.46. In other words, our sample has an inherent amount of error, which is always expected in statistics.

Ultimately, sampling error must be taken into account when attempting to determine whether or not a statistical difference or relationship exists. Since we calculated that our sample has a standard error of the mean of 3.46 in the first mean, this indicates that we can guess that the actual population mean (everyone who could have participated in the study) should exist between 56.36 and 49.44. We get this interval of possible choices because we take the calculated mean we had in our sample (52.9) and then add and subtract the SE$_M$ (3.46) from that mean. As we learned from Chapter 8, anything that falls within ± 1 standard deviation of the mean (10.94 in our example) is said to account for approximately 68.26% of the individual means in a sample. In other words, using our SE$_M$ of ± 3.46, we know that our population mean will fall between 56.36 and 49.44, but this also means that about 31.74% of the time the actual population mean will not fall between 56.36 and 49.44. I don't know about you, but I clearly want something that will be accurate more than 65.26% of the time. For this reason, researchers have decided that for something to be considered statistically significant, an interval of numbers (e.g., 56.36 to 49.44) should be at least accurate 95% of the time. As we know from Chapter 8, 95.44% of all sample means will fall between two standard deviations away from the mean or ± 2SD; the same is also true for the standard error mean. In our example, the SE$_M$ is ± 3.46, so if we multiply 3.46 × 2 we get 6.92. If we take this number and add it to and subtract it from our mean 52.90, we can say that 95% of all of our scores fall between 45.98 and 59.82, which is a range of 13.84. This range of scores of random sample means associated with a confidence level is called a confidence interval, so at the 95% confidence level (or possibility of 5% chance we're wrong), our population mean would fall between 45.98 and 59.82. So all in all, how confident should a researcher be?

Researchers generally agree that we should be at least 95% confident or have a 95% confidence interval, which means that researchers expect their results to be inaccurate 5% of the time. To achieve a confidence interval of 95%, we know that the SE$_M$ (3.46) must be multiplied by ± 1.96 (see Chapter 8 for a discussion of this), which would be 5.8474. In other words, we can be 95% confident that the population mean from which our sample mean (the 10 people in the study, $M = 52.9$) will lie between 47.0526 and 58.7474.

You may be wondering if this is something that only social scientific researchers do—it's not. In fact, most research—from medicine to physics to communication—uses the 95% confidence interval as the standard to judge statistics. Think of it like this: imagine a drug company wants to find out whether or not their drug kills people. At the 95% confidence rate, the drug would kill 1 in 20 people. For this reason, occasionally medical studies will increase the confidence rate to 99.99%, which would mean that only 1 out of every 10,000 people who take the drug would die as a result. However, the 95% confidence interval is still standard for most statistically based research.

Most research studies do not rely on just one variable's confidence interval, so other techniques have been developed to help us determine how confident researchers are when examining multiple variable means. When researchers are examining multiple variables, researchers pool these individual variables and use them as a single random sample (both Time 1 and Time 2 together) to stand for the large number of random samples that are being examined (both Time 1 and Time 2 separately). By doing this and following the same steps that we performed above looking at the combined ± 1.96SE$_M$, researchers can create a confidence interval, and this confidence interval allows researchers to know what kind of sampling error or "margin of error" actually exists. For example, what if we found out that in our example the means for Time 1 (before watching the televangelist) and Time 2 (after watching the televangelist) were different only at a confidence interval of ± 20%? Would you then be willing to say that these two means were different from each other? If you said a 60% confidence interval is fine, then you're basically saying that 40 times out of 100 the findings of your study would be false. In other words, your study's results are meaningless. If however, we found that the mean for Time 1 and Time 2 were different with a confidence interval of ± 2.5%, then we could say that the two variables were different at a 95% confidence level.

Testing for Significance

In the previous section we introduced the concept of confidence intervals and the importance of a 95% confidence level. In this section we are going to see how we can determine if a difference or relationship between two variables has occurred by chance. The process to determine if chance causes a difference or relationship is called "significance testing." In significance testing, the goal is to determine if our null hypothesis (H_0: $\mu_{Time1} = \mu_{Time2}$) is accurate. As mentioned above, in significance testing, we are always concerned with testing the null hypothesis, so significance testing is the process of analyzing quantitative data to determine if a null hypothesis is probably either true or false. Notice that in this definition we are examining whether the null is *probably* true or false, which indicates that there is always a possibility of error occurring when conducting a significance test. Significance testing then is determining whether you can accept the null hypothesis (there is no difference between the participants' religious attitudes before they watched a televangelist and after they watched a televangelist) or you have to reject the null hypothesis (there is a difference between the participants' religious attitudes before they watched a televangelist and after they watched a televangelist).

After you have collected data from a sample, the first step in significance testing is determining a significance level. In other words, a researcher must determine how large a relationship or difference must be before it is considered significant. Just like we discussed above in confidence intervals, researchers prefer to be at least 95% confident. 95% confidence in significance testing indicates that a researcher could expect to see a difference or relationship occurring in her or his results by accident as a result of chance about 5 times out of 100. Again, that may sound like a lot, but it is the standard used by all scientists when determining if something is an actual difference or relationship.

In significance testing, we often refer to the "probability level" when discussing how confident we are about our results. To determine the "probability level," simply take the percentile number (95) and subtract it from 1, or $1 - 0.95 = 0.05$. The probability level is also sometimes called a *p*-value, probability value, or even referred to by the Greek letter alpha (α). So if you wanted to be 99% confident, your *p*-value would be 0.01 ($1 - 0.99 = 0.01$), and so on. As a quick side note to the use of the Greek letter α, this is not the same alpha referred to earlier in this book with regards to scale reliability. Often in statistics, statisticians will use the same Greek letter to represent a number of different functions depending on what statistical formula is being discussed.

We should also note that sampling error is also one of the major reasons why replication of studies is important. If a study's findings are accurate 95% of the time, then there is a 5% chance that the results obtained in a study happen because of error. For this reason, scientists often will replicate a study or research the same patterns of variables multiple times to make sure the results are consistent. Often researchers find contradictory results even when the research process, measures, and participants are identical. There is an advanced statistical procedure, meta-analysis, that can be used to combine a number of different studies looking at the same phenomenon to achieve stronger support for the existence of a relationship or difference or the lack of a relationship or difference. Now that we've explained what a probability value is, let's examine the steps necessary in significance testing.

STEP 1: SET THE PROBABILITY LEVEL

Before you can perform any statistical tests to determine if there are differences or relationships in your study, you must first decide how confident you need to be. As noted above, the standard probability level is always going to be 0.05, or we are sure that if we ran the same test 100 different times only 5 tests would yield inaccurate results. If you're researching a study that could have greater chances of killing someone (like many pharmaceutical studies), you may want to be more than 95% confident in your results. Maybe in a pharmaceutical company you would pick a probability level of 0.0005 indicating that you are 99.95% confident in the finding of a difference or a relationship between a set of variables. Ultimately, what level of probability you establish for your study will determine whether or not a difference exists. The lower your p-value, the harder it is to be significant at that level. For example, in our study maybe we find out that we are significant at $p < .10$ but are not significant at $p < .05$. In this case, if we had previously established that for a difference to exist we would have to be 95% confident that it exists, then the difference found between the pretest (before the participant watched the televangelist) and the post test (after the participant watched the televangelist) would not be statistically significant. If, however, we had established a 90% confidence interval, then our study would be significant at $p < .10$. While some researchers will raise their confidence interval to .90, we strongly encourage you not to do this because you increase the probability of Type II error (we accept the null hypothesis based on our sample, but the null hypothesis is actually false in the population), which we will examine in the last part of this chapter.

STEP 2: CONDUCT A STATISTICAL TEST

The second part of significance testing is conducting a statistical test. Every statistical test ultimately generates a value called the "calculated value," which is simply the end result that a researcher receives when he or she has completed a mathematical formula related to a specific statistical test. This part of significance testing is often the most complicated and time-consuming part if completed by hand. For this reason, researchers often prefer to work with computer packages (e.g., SPSS, SAS, etc.) that calculate the calculated value for them.

STEP 3: COMPARING CALCULATED AND CRITICAL VALUES

The third part of conducting a significance test is to compare the calculated value (the answer one achieves through arithmetic) to a critical value (a predetermined value calculated by statisticians that a calculated value must be greater than). For example, in the example in this chapter (Is there a difference between in an individual's perception of a televangelist's religion after seeing the televangelist in action?), if we obtained a calculated value of 2.176 and the critical value associated with the .05 probability level we had to beat was 2.262, our calculated value is smaller, so it does not beat the threshold. If our calculated value is not greater than the critical value, then we cannot say that we are significant at that level, or the probability of a relationship or difference existing is less than the probability level (less than 95%).

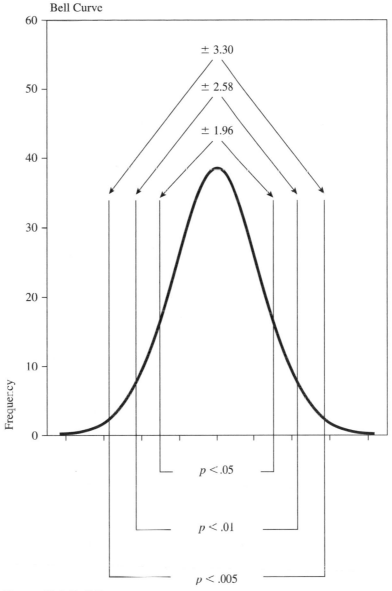

Figure 15.1 Bell Curve

We will spend a lot more time exploring this concept as we look at various statistical tests in the next five chapters.

Critical values are determined based on the size of sample a person has, the number of variables being compared, and the type of statistical test. Each statistical test has its own unique set of critical values. These critical values ultimately allow researchers to determine if a calculated value is greater than a specific critical value that indicates that it is significant at the ±1.96 *SD* away from the mean. Remember that we can be 95% confident in a result if that result beats the ±1.96 *SD* threshold for determining if something is confident at that level. In Figure 15.1 is the bell curve with the standard deviation estimates for determining the critical values at $p < .05$, $p < .01$, and $p < .005$ levels.

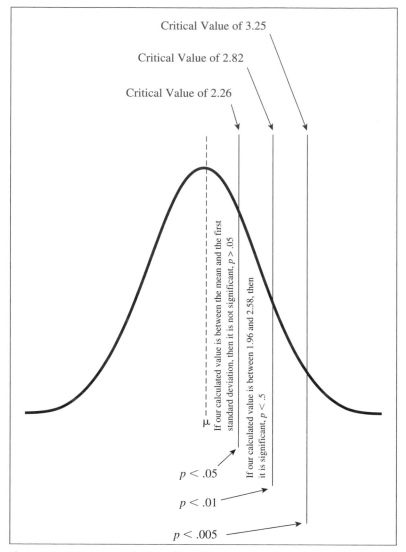

Figure 15.2 Curve with Significant Values

As we know from our example, the critical value to beat to obtain a 95% confidence in our results is 2.262 and the value we calculated was 2.176. (We used a paired *t*-test to statistically test for a significant difference between the two means. Paired *t*-tests are discussed later in Chapter 17.) If you look at Figure 15.2, you'll see three sets of critical values to beat to obtain significance at $p < .05$, $p < .01$, and $p < .005$. With our calculated value of 2.176, we fall between the mean and the first critical value (±1.96 or 2.262). If, however, we had a calculated value of 2.367, we would have fallen between the .05 and .01 confidence intervals and, thus, would have been significant at $p < .05$. Ultimately, this is how significance testing is completed.

Testing for Power

In addition to making sure that a difference or relationship is statistically significant, it is also important to make sure that a statistical test has power. The purpose of statistical power is to determine whether or not a researcher can reject a false null hypothesis. Power allows a researcher to determine how sensitive a statistical test will be in detecting relationships and differences of a specific size. If a study is powerful, then a researcher will be able to correctly find even small differences and relationships, but if a study is not powerful a researcher may miss small differences and relationships. In other words, a researcher could conclude that there is no relationship between an individual's level of communication apprehension (anxiety about real or perceived communication) and her or his willingness to communicate (desire to initiate communication) based on her or his sample. However, previous research consistently shows that there should be a negative relationship between communication apprehension (CA) and willingness to communicate (WTC), or, as someone's CA goes up, her or his WTC goes down. There are three reasons why a researcher may accept a false null hypothesis (i.e., there is no relationship between CA and WTC).

First, the type of test a researcher uses to examine the relationship is relevant. Some tests are less "sensitive," or less likely to notice actual relationships or differences even when they do exist. We will talk about some of these issues in the next six chapters.

Second, two-tailed hypotheses are harder to attain statistical differences. As we talked about in Chapter 5, two-tailed hypotheses leave open the direction of a difference or relationship; whereas a one-tailed hypothesis is specific about the direction of the difference or relationship. In Figure 15.3 we see the problem that can often occur when examining one- and two-tailed hypotheses. To be significant at the 0.05 probability level using a one-tailed test, a calculated value has to be greater than a lower critical value (located + or −1.65, but not ±1.65, standard deviations away from the mean); however, to be significant at the .05 probability level using a two-tailed test we test in both directions on the number line so the critical value is higher (±1.96).

If you have a clear reason for using a one-tailed test, it is perfectly appropriate to do so. However, one-tailed hypothesis testing is often misused as a way of gaining significance even when a research question does not warrant the test. In other words, use one-tailed hypothesis testing sparingly, but understand that there are circumstances that do warrant its use.

Finally, small sample sizes often make it impossible for a statistical device to determine when a null hypothesis should be rejected. Many researchers attempt to calculate complicated statistics based on very small sample sizes. A lot of medical and social scientific research is conducted with sample sizes of less than 20 participants. Ideally, no sample should be smaller than 200 unless the entire population from which the sample is drawn is smaller than 200. When a sample has 200 or more participants, the likelihood of finding statistically significant small differences and relationships increases, which decreases the incidence of Type II error as we will see in a moment.

To increase the likelihood that a statistical test will be able to reject a null hypothesis when it should, a researcher should use appropriate statistical tests, use one- and two-tailed tests appropriately, and have a large sample. Power, when it is measured, exists on a continuum from 0 to 1. However, statistical power should never be lower than 0.8, or you risk the chance of missing actual relationships and differences that really exist.

Effect Sizes

Along with power, another extremely important characteristic to understand is the effect size of a statistical finding (as discussed in Chapter 6). An effect size is like a thermometer. If there's been a change to one or two degrees cooler, you may not even notice that it's gotten

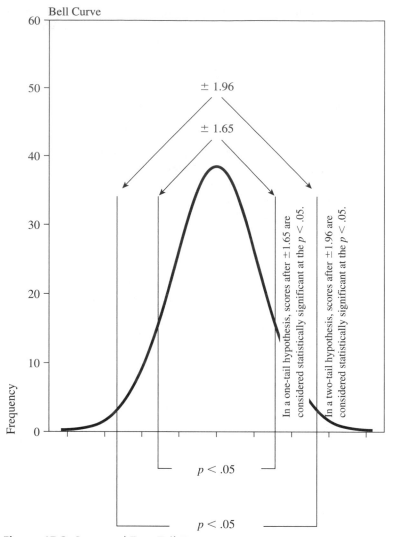

Figure 15.3 One- and Two-Tail Tests

colder. While there may be a significant difference in the heat, it may not be large enough for it to really matter. If the temperature decreases by 50 degrees, you'll be hunting around your house for an electric blanket. In other words, an effect size is the strength of a relationship or the magnitude of a difference occurring between two variables, or the degree to which a null hypothesis is false. There are three types of effect sizes that can be seen in statistics (small, medium, and large). Each difference test discussed in this book has a corresponding effect size that is important to understand, so we will discuss this concept in greater detail later in the book.

In Figure 15.4, the first set of bell curves illustrates what we mean by a small effect size. In this case, we are examining the difference between two means (noted by the dashed lines). This is similar to the example we looked at in the first part of this chapter where we wanted to see if an individual's attitude about a religion changes after he or she sees a televangelist in action (Time 1 = 52.9; Time 2 = 48.9). In the first case, notice that the means are closer together. While the means may be significantly different, researchers cannot conclude that

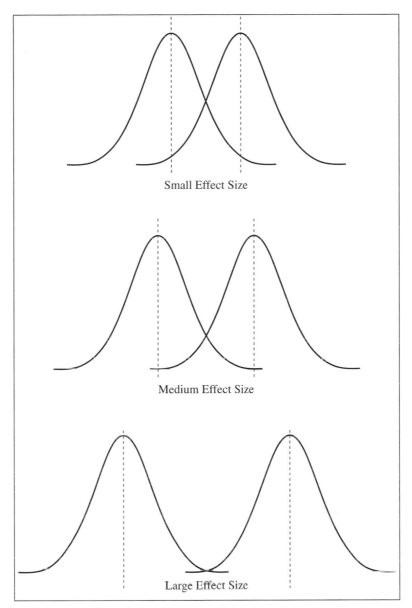

Figure 15.4 Effect Size

means are drastically different. A lot of research done on sex differences runs into this problem. Basically, very little research that examines differences between male and female behavior (if the difference is significant) is beyond a small effect. In case of small effects, researchers have to be honest about these effect sizes. While the difference may be significant, it simply may not mean much.

The second graph in the chart in Figure 15.4 represents what a medium effect may look like if we graphed it. In this case, the mean differences are further apart than we saw in the first graph, but still closer together than we see in the third graph, which represents a large effect. All in all, it's important to realize that while something may be statistically significant, the effect size associated with that significance is also extremely important.

Understanding Error

The last part of this chapter is going to explore a concept that we have already hinted at in the previous sections in this chapter—error. The chart we are going to use to explain error can be seen in Figure 15.5.

To understand this chart, we're going to look at each aspect clearly and then give an example to illustrate each part. Along the top of the chart are two columns: "Null Is True" and "Null Is False." These two columns are referring to what actually happens in the real world. In other words, the "Null Is True" column refers to the notion that in the real world your null hypothesis is true, or your hypothesis is false. Maybe you predicted that men and women will have differing levels of humor, but in reality there is no difference between men and women and their use of humor. In this case, the null hypothesis is true in the real world.

In the whole Population ⟶ ↓ What We conclude Based on our Sample	**Null Hypothesis Is True** In reality… • There is no difference or relationship • Our theory is wrong	**Null Hypothesis Is False** In reality… • There is a difference or relationship • Our theory is correct
Accept the Null Hypothesis We <u>say</u>… • There is no difference or relationship • Our theory is wrong	$1 - \alpha$ The Confidence Interval The odds of saying there is <u>no</u> effect or gain when in fact there is none No. of times out of 100 when there is no effect, we'll say there is none	β Type II Error The odds of saying there is <u>no</u> effect or gain when in fact there is one No. of times out of 100 when there <u>is</u> an effect, we'll say there is none
Reject the Null Hypothesis We <u>say</u>… • There is a difference or relationship • Our theory is correct	α Type I Error The odds of saying there <u>is</u> an effect or gain when in fact there is none. No. of times out of 100 when there is <u>no</u> effect, we'll say there is one	$1 - \beta$ Power The odds of saying there <u>is</u> an effect or gain when in fact there is one. No. of times out of 100 when there <u>is</u> an effect, we'll say there is one

Figure 15.5 α and β Errors

On the other hand, often a null hypothesis is false. If you were examining men and women and differing levels of verbal aggression, men are more verbally aggressive in the real world, so the null hypothesis is false in the real world (or your actual hypothesis—that men have higher verbal aggression scores than women—is true).

As mentioned in both of these examples, often what we expect to happen when we create a mathematical hypothesis is correct and often it's wrong. For this reason, we have to understand whether or not we have accepted the null hypothesis after we get our results. If we accept the null hypothesis, we're basically saying that our original hypothesis was incorrect. If we had predicted that there would be a positive relationship between nonverbal immediacy and assertiveness, and the results indicated that there was not a significant relationship, then we would accept the null hypothesis. On the other hand, if we had predicted that there was a relationship between humor assessment and nonverbal immediacy, and we found a significant relationship, then we could reject the null hypothesis (or affirm our actual hypothesis).

We realize that this sounds very backwards and almost like we're talking out of both sides of our mouths, but remember what we said in the beginning of this chapter—in statistics we are not testing hypotheses, we are testing null hypotheses. For this reason, when we talk about error, many people get confused because it sounds logically backward compared to how most people think. Now that we've looked at what the columns mean and what the rows mean, we can examine the four quadrants indicated by both reality and what we conclude.

In the first quadrant, "The Confidence Interval," we have a case where in "reality" (or in the actual population) the null hypothesis is true and through our statistical testing we accept the null hypothesis. Imagine you predicted there would be a relationship between responsiveness and the attitude people have towards college. However, when you conduct a test with your sample to see if this relationship exists, you do not find a significant relationship. At the same time, in the larger population this relationship does not exist as well. In other words, first you accepted the null (there is no relationship between responsiveness and attitude towards college) and the null is true (in the real world, there is no relationship between responsiveness and attitude towards college); you get a confidence interval. As discussed earlier in this chapter, a confidence interval lets you know how many times out of 100 your results will say there is no effect (difference or relationship) and there is no effect (difference or relationship) in the real world. The confidence interval is represented by $1 - $ alpha (α). If your alpha reliability (or p-value) is .0001, then your confidence interval is $1 - 0.0001 = 0.9999$ or a 99.99% confidence interval. Generally speaking, when reporting alphas it's always important to round up and not down. For example, if you found that a statistical test was significant at .052, then this test would not be considered significant at .05 because .052 is greater than .05. Also, it's often best to report alpha levels on half step intervals like .05, .01, .005, .001, .0005, and .0001. So if you found that the calculated value for p was .0047, the easiest way to report this alpha would be to say that the test was significant at .005, since this is the nearest half-step interval rounded up. When looking at computer printouts, SPSS and SAS will both provide you with calculated alpha levels. However, there is some disagreement as to how to report alpha levels that are below .000. Levine and Atkin (2004) argue that when a computer printout prints a .000 alpha level (this occurs with SPSS), it is most correct to report this alpha level as .0005 (99.95% confident). SAS, on the other hand, will actually report alpha levels down to .0001 (99.99% confident).

In the quadrant diagonal to "The Confidence Interval" is the quadrant labeled "Power." Power is the odds of saying there is a difference or relationship when in fact there is one. In this case, you reject the null hypothesis based on the results from your statistical analysis and the null hypothesis is actually rejected in the real world. For example, maybe you predicted that there would be a positive relationship between nonverbal immediacy and responsiveness. To test this question, you run a statistical analysis and find out that there is a relationship, and then this relationship actually exists in the real world. In this case, your statistical test rejected the null hypothesis and the null hypothesis should be rejected in the world. When this occurs, the result is called power. In essence, power is the number of times out of 100 when there is a relationship or difference in a study and there is a relationship or difference that exists in the real world. Power is represented by $1 - $ beta (β). If your beta is equal to 0.05, then your power is $1 - 0.05 = 0.95$. As we mentioned above when we discussed power, power should be above 0.80 to successfully reject the null hypothesis when the null hypothesis is rejected in the larger population. These first two quadrants represent what we hope will happen when we use statistics to analyze quantitative data. However, there are two types of errors that occur when people use statistics to analyze quantitative data.

The first type of error (Type I error or α error) occurs when a researcher rejects a null hypothesis (says their alternative hypothesis was true) based on a sample when the null should be accepted (alternative hypothesis was false in the real world). In other words, you run a test to see if an individual's level of interpersonal humor (humor assessment) is related to nonverbal sensitivity (ability to pick up on other people's nonverbal behavior). You find a positive relationship between humor assessment and nonverbal sensitivity in your sample, but in the real world this relationship does not exist. When this occurs, you have a Type I error. A Type I error is the odds of finding a difference or relationship when in fact there is not one. This probability is represented by alpha or your probability value. If a finding is significant at $p < .05$, then there is a 5% chance that you will reject your null hypothesis (or affirming your hypothesis or research question) when in the actual population you would not reject your null hypothesis.

The second type of error (Type II error or β error) occurs when a researcher accepts a null hypothesis (says their alternative hypothesis was not true) based on a sample when the null should be rejected (says their alternative hypothesis was true in the real world). We can take the flip side of the example discussed under Type I Error. You run a test to see if an individual's level of interpersonal humor (humor assessment) is related to nonverbal sensitivity (ability to pick up on other people's nonverbal behavior). You do not find a relationship between humor assessment and nonverbal sensitivity in your sample, but in the real world (or actual population) this relationship exists. When this occurs, you have a Type II error. A Type II error is the odds of finding there is no difference or relationship when in fact there is one. Type II error is represented by the Greek letter β. If in a study you find that $\beta = 0.05$, then there is a 5% chance that you will accept the null hypothesis (or reject your hypothesis or research question) when in the actual population you would reject your null hypothesis (or affirming your hypothesis or research question).

One of the basic goals of empirical research is to limit both Type I and II errors as much as humanly possible. To limit Type I error, the best thing to do is to increase your confidence interval from say 95% confidence (5 times out 100 you're wrong) to say 99% confidence (1 time out of 100 you're wrong). However, you might think that this means that researchers should just neglect the 95% confidence interval for a more conservative 99% confidence interval all the time. Unfortunately, if you try to protect against Type I errors (rejecting a null hypothesis that is probably true, a false positive), you often enable the committing of Type II errors instead (accepting a null hypothesis that is probably false, a false negative). In other words, Type I errors (alpha errors) and Type II errors (beta errors) are inversely related. The more stringent the probability level, the more likely you'll commit a Type II error, and the more stringent the power, the more likely you'll commit a Type I error. In an ideal world, a fair balance can be struck between Type I and Type II errors, but often researchers must error on one side or the other. However, increasing the sample size one obtains does allow a research to achieve both low alpha and high beta values. To prevent both Type I and Type II errors, researchers are encouraged to recruit fairly large samples (at least 200 participants).

Ultimately, the number of participants needed for a study is based on a variety of factors related to how many groups you want to compare, and the size of the differences and relationships you hope to obtain.

Conclusion

This chapter has introduced you to three major concepts that will be seen again and again during the next five chapters (significance, power, and effect size). Remember, just because two means may appear different does not indicate that the difference is statistically significant. For instance, we have used an example throughout the entire chapter about 10 participants who agreed to participate in a study to determine if a difference occurs in an individual's attitude toward a religion after watching a televangelist. Based on the numbers described in the first part of a chapter, there was not a significant difference between Time 1 (before watching the televangelist) and Time 2 (after watching the televangelist). In fact, the calculated p-value was .052, so the difference was not significant at the .05 level. (How this was tested will be discussed in Chapter 18.)

KEY TERMS

Alternative Hypothesis	Hypothesis Testing	Probability Value (p-Value)
Calculated Value	Null Hypothesis	Sampling Error
Critical Value	One-Tailed Hypothesis	Significance Testing
Confidence Interval	Power	Two-Tailed Hypothesis
Confidence Level	Probability	Type I Error (α Error)
Effect Size	Probability Level	Type II Error (β Error)

REFERENCES

Cohen, J. (1994). The earth is round ($p < .05$). *American Psychologist, 49,* 997–1003.

Levine, T. R., & Atkin, C. (2004). The accurate reporting of software-generated p-values: A cautionary research note. *Communication Research Reports, 21,* 324–327.

FURTHER READING

Chow, S. L. (1997). *Statistical significance: Rationale, validity, and utility.* Thousand Oaks, CA: Sage.

Gravetter, F. J., & Wallnau, L. B. (2000). *Statistics for the behavioral sciences* (5th ed.). Belmont, CA: Wadsworth/Thomson Learning.

Howell, D. C. (1997). *Statistical methods for psychology* (4th ed.). Belmont, CA: Duxbury Press.

Huff, D. (1954). *How to lie with statistics.* New York: W. W. Norton & Company.

Keller, D. K. (2006). *The Tao of statistics: A path to understanding (with no math).* Thousand Oaks, CA: Sage.

Lehmann, E. L. L., & Romano, J. P. (2005). *Testing statistical hypothesis* (3rd ed.). New York: Springer-Verlag.

Mohr, L. B., & Lewis-Beck, M. S. (1990). *Understanding significance testing.* Thousand Oaks, CA: Sage.

Salkind, N. J. (2004). *Statistics for people who (think they) hate statistics* (2nd ed.). Thousand Oaks, CA: Sage.

Singleton, R. A., Jr., & Straits, B. C. (1999). *Approach to social research* (3rd ed.). New York: Oxford University Press.

Tabachnick, B. G., & Fidell, L. S. (2001). *Using multivariate statistics* (4th ed.). Boston: Allyn and Bacon.

Trochim, W. M. K. (2000). *The research methods knowledge base* (2nd ed.). Cincinnati, OH: Atomic Dog. Online available at: http://www.socialresearchmethods.net/

Chi-Square (χ^2) Test of Independence

In this chapter we will explore the chi-square (χ^2) test of independence. The term chi-square actually has two different meanings in statistics, which often leads to confusion for new researchers. First, researchers refer to a specific type of mathematical distribution that occurs without any necessary referent outside of mathematics. While this distribution is beyond the scope of this textbook, understand that this distribution is important to a number of statistical tests. In this chapter we are more concerned with the second meaning of a chi-square, which is a specific statistical test. However, this statistical test (χ^2 test of independence) is related to the first definition. In essence, the chi-square test examines whether scores obtained from a group of people is similar to, or different from, the scores expected if the numbers were evenly distributed along the chi-square distribution. Let's say you want to determine if females and males differ in their preference for two soft drinks (A and B). In an ideal world, we would have four categories (females who like soft drink A, females who like soft drink B, males who like soft drink A, and males who like soft drink B). Notice that both categories (biological sex and soft drink preference) are nominal variables. If we set up a taste test using 200 people (100 females and 100 males), in an ideal world we would expect that there would be 50 people in each of the four categories. Unfortunately, the "ideal world" rarely happens and often scores are not evenly distributed among available categories. Maybe 70 females prefer soft drink A and only 30 females prefer soft drink B. When this lopsidedness happens, the question becomes one of what researchers would expect to see versus what researchers are actually seeing.

The purpose then of a chi-square is to examine the balance between observed frequencies—number of times participants fell into a specific category (how many females and males picked each of the soft drinks)—and expected frequencies—(number of times one would expect participants to fall into a specific category). If the observed and expected frequencies are equal, then the chi-square statistic will always equal zero because there isn't a difference between the two numbers. The greater the difference between observed and expected frequencies, the larger the chi-square statistic will be. And as the chi-square statistic increases, so does the likelihood that there is a statistically significant difference between observed and expected frequencies. Now that we've explained the basic purpose of a chi-square statistic, let's examine an example of a chi-square statistic.

Case Study Introduction

For the first part of this chapter, we're going to pretend that you are working in a Communication Studies department and have been asked to analyze when females and males take public speaking during their academic careers. If you remember back to Chapter 6, female and male is an example of a nominal variable. Remember, nominal variables are categorical or people that can be clearly placed into one category (female) or the other (male), but not both. Your department chair has also given you another variable to examine—school classification. For school classification, your department chair has given you five categories: precollege, first-year student, sophomore, junior, and senior. Yet again, the school classification variable is also a nominal variable because you cannot be a sophomore and a senior at the same time. If you look at figure 6.9 earlier in this book, you'll notice that if you have two nominal variables the appropriate statistic to examine differences is a chi-square test for independence.

After discussing this project with you, your department chair hands you a table of when students are taking public speaking in the department (Figure 16.1). In this table, we have what is called a 2 × 5 table. This means that we have 2 rows (male and female) by 5 columns (precollege, first-year student, sophomore, junior, and senior). Where a row intersects with a column we have cells. For example, on row "female" in column "junior" the number 8 appears in the cell. This chapter will illustrate how you can use the chi-square test for independence to determine if females and males differ in their school classification when they take public speaking.

	Precollege students	First-year students	Sophomores	Juniors	Seniors	*N*
Male	6	8	10	1	25	50
Female	7	20	9	8	6	50

Figure 16.1 When Students Take Public Speaking

Chi-Square Background Information

The one-sample chi-square test evaluates whether the proportions of individuals who fall into categories of two or more nominal variables are equal to hypothesized values. In other words, in an ideal world you would have equal numbers of females and males taking public speaking in each school classification category. For example, if you had 50 females and 50 males in a school, you would expect that there would be 10 females and 10 males taking public speaking in the precollege category, 10 females and 10 males taking public speaking in the first-year student category, and so on. However, the real world rarely works this smoothly. Maybe 15 male students were all friends and decided to sign up to take public speaking together during one semester or quarter. If this occurred, then it would prevent our perfect world of 10 females and 10 males in every class.

To be able to use the chi-square test for independence there are some basic assumptions that must be met before you can use the test:

1. Both variables being analyzed must be nominal in nature (biological sex, school classification, etc.).

2. Participants contributing data should represent a random sample drawn from the population of interest (this is an assumption of most statistical tests—see Chapter 13 for an explanation of the importance randomization).

3. One participant's appearance in a category (female taking public speaking during her senior year) should not affect the probability of another participant's appearance in another cell (male taking public speaking during his sophomore year).

4. If you have a 2 × 2 table, there should be no fewer than 5 cases in every cell. However, if you have a larger table (such as the 2 × 5 table like the one in our example), 20% of the cells should be no fewer than 5 cases in every cell.

The one-sample chi-square test is more likely to yield significance if the sample proportions for the categories differ greatly from the hypothesized proportions and if the sample size is large. If all the females were able to take public speaking in the first two and half years and all the males took public speaking in the last two and a half years, we would see a very large difference. However, as we see in Figure 16.1, there are differences, but whether or not these differences are truly statistically significant is not known. For this reason, the chi-square test of independence was created to help us determine if statistically significant differences do exist in examples such as the one we have here.

Before a researcher ever starts calculating a statistical test, he or she must first set the significance level of the test. In Chapter 15, we discussed why researchers set the significance level at 95% confidence level or $p = 0.05$. The reason we set the significance level prior to conducting the test is for ethical reasons. There have been cases where less than scrupulous researchers have lowered their significance level to 90% or $p = 0.10$ because their results were not significant at the 95% confidence level. If you remember back to our discussion of research ethics in Chapter 3, we discussed the problem of post hoc revisions of hypotheses (changing your hypothesis when the study was completed to match the results you found). In many ways, the discussion we had for post hoc revisions of hypotheses is akin to changing our confidence level after the fact. The need for setting your confidence level prior to conducting a statistical test is true for all statistical tests. Once you've set your confidence level, you can then begin calculating your chi-square.

$$\chi^2 = \sum \frac{(f_o - f_e)^2}{f_e}$$

Figure 16.2 Chi-Square Formula

Let's go ahead and look at Figure 16.2, which depicts the mathematical formula for completing the chi-square test of independence. We know this formula looks pretty scary, but it really is not hard to understand what it is saying. f_o stands for the frequency observed. "Frequency observed" is the technical term for what was discussed in Figure 16.1. f_e stands for the frequency expected. But before we can discuss frequency expected, we really need to start going step by step in our computation of the chi-square statistic.

Step-by-Step Approach to the Chi-Square Test of Independence

Step One. The first step in computing the chi-square test of independence is to add the totals from each row separately. For example, to obtain the total for the male row, you need to add $6 + 8 + 10 + 1 + 25$, which gives you a row total of 50. You then repeat the same thing for the female row ($7 + 20 + 9 + 8 + 6$), which also gives you a row total of 50. You then repeat this process for each of the five columns (precollege, first-year student, sophomore, junior, and senior) as well. For the pre-college column, you will add $6 + 7$, which gives you a total of 13. In Figure 16.3, you can see that we have provided row and column totals for you in an easy-to-use table because we will need these numbers in the next step.

Step Two. The second step is slightly more complicated than the first two steps and requires that you keep track of where you are getting your numbers from carefully. As mentioned above, the second part of the formula requires us to examine the expected frequency (f_e), so this step is going to help us generate these numbers. The expected frequency is a simple calculation to help define an ideal hypothetical distribution that would be in agreement with the null hypothesis. In other words, based on the data that you have, what is the frequency for upholding the null hypothesis (that there is no difference between females and males and when they take public speaking in college). To obtain these values, you use the following simple formula:

Expected frequency = (total column × total row) / overall total

So, let's compute the first expected frequency for males in pre-college. The column total for pre-college, as seen in Figure 16.3, is 13. The row total for males is 50. And the overall total for the population or N, is 100. So to obtain the expected frequency for males in pre-college, we then plug these numbers into the formula: $(13 \times 50) / 100 = 6.5$. Based on this result, we can say that to reject the null hypothesis that females and males take public speaking at different points in college, the expected frequency for males in pre-college would have to be 6.5. Obviously, you can't have a 0.5 person, so this number is very hypothetical. In reality, we need to look at all of the expected frequencies for each biological sex in each school classification to get a full picture of the numbers necessary to reject the null hypothesis. In Figure 16.4, we have gone ahead and computed all of the expected frequencies for you just repeating the computational process for each category.

	Precollege students	First year students	Sophomores	Juniors	Seniors	TOTAL
Male	6	8	10	1	25	50
Female	7	20	9	8	6	50
Total	13	28	19	9	31	100

Figure 16.3 Adding Row and Column Totals (Step One)

Step Three. At this point we can once again look at the formula given in Figure 16.2. The basic formula for the chi-square test of independence can be said to be the following:

Chi-square = sum of ((observed frequencies − expected frequencies)^2
/ expected frequencies)

Notice that we are looking at the Σ, or sum of the equation. This basically means that we need to compute that formula for each and every one of the cells in the table and then add up the values that we obtain. Let's compute the first portion of the chi-square statistic for males in pre-college. The observed frequency score for males, as seen in Figure 16.1, is 6. And the expected frequency score for males, as seen in Figure 16.4, is 6.5. So to obtain the portion of the chi-square statistic represented by males in pre-college we then plug these numbers into the formula: $(6 − 6.5)^2 / 6.5 = 0.038462$. In Figure 16.5, we have gone ahead and computed all of the parts of the chi-square statistic.

Step Four. And since the sigma was in front of the formula, now we just add all of the values from Step Three together:

$$0.038462 + 2.571429 + 0.026316 + 2.722222 + 5.822581 + 0.038462$$
$$+ 2.571429 + 0.026316 + 2.722222 + 5.822581$$

	Total column		Total row		Overall total		Expected frequency
Males in precollege	13	*	50	/	100	=	6.5
Male first year students	28	*	50	/	100	=	14.0
Male sophomores	19	*	50	/	100	=	9.5
Male juniors	9	*	50	/	100	−	4.5
Male seniors	31	*	50	/	100	=	15.5
Females in precollege	13	*	50	/	100	=	6.5
Female First-year students	28	*	50	/	100	=	14.0
Female sophomores	19	*	50	/	100	=	9.5
Female juniors	9	*	50	/	100	=	4.5
Female seniors	31	*	50	/	100	=	15.5

Figure 16.4 Expected Frequencies

	Observed frequency		Expected frequency			Expected frequency		Chi-square (χ^2) statistic
Males in precollege	(6	−	6.5)	^{2}	/	6.5	=	0.038462
Male first year students	(8	−	14)	^{2}	/	14.0	=	2.571429
Male sophomores	(10	−	9.5)	^{2}	/	9.5	=	0.026316
Male juniors	(1	−	4.5)	^{2}	/	4.5	=	2.722222
Male seniors	(25	−	15.5)	^{2}	/	15.5	=	5.822581
Females in precollege	(7	−	6.5)	^{2}	/	6.5	=	0.038462
Female first year students	(20	−	14)	^{2}	/	14.0	=	2.571429
Female sophomores	(9	−	9.5)	^{2}	/	9.5	=	0.026316
Female juniors	(8	−	4.5)	^{2}	/	4.5	=	2.722222
Female seniors	(6	−	15.5)	^{2}	/	15.5	=	5.822581
					χ^2 Calculated value		=	22.362

Figure 16.5 Chi-Square (χ^2) Statistics

This sum indicates that the calculated value that we obtained for chi-square is 22.362. However, we still have a couple of steps to go before we can say that we are truly finished with this example.

Step Five. In this step we need to calculate the degrees of freedom for the chi-square computed in this example. The "degrees of freedom" is defined as the number of participant scores in a sample that can or are free to vary. Since this is an important concept, let's think of this in terms of a car lot. Imagine you're a car salesperson and you have five cars to sell. All of the cars are the same make and model, but are different colors: yellow, blue, green, red, and white. On one day five customers come to your showroom to buy cars. The first person looks at the five cars and selects the blue one. This person had the ability to choose between five cars, but the next person who comes to the dealership can only choose among four cars (yellow, green, red, and white) because the blue car has already been sold. The second person picks the yellow car. The third person only has three choices then and picks the red car. The fourth person who comes in now only has the freedom to choose between two cars and selects the white car. The fifth person who comes into the showroom now has no ability to vary at all and must select the green car or go elsewhere. Each of these customers had the ability to vary her or his choice until the last customer. Generally speaking, degrees of freedom is seen as the number of options a person has (five cars) minus one, or 5 − 1.

However, since in the chi-square example we are dealing with two different nominal variables (sex and classification in school), the formula is a little different: (r − 1)(c − 1) or (number of rows − 1)(number of columns − 1). In this example, we had two rows (male and female) and five columns (pre-college, first-year student, sophomore, junior, and senior). So the degrees of freedom for our chi-square example would be (2 − 1)(5 − 1) or (1)(4), which is equal to 4. So in our example, the degree to which the frequencies had the freedom to vary was 4.

Step Six. Figure 16.6 is what is called a critical value table. A critical value table is a table that has been previously created to determine where specific chi-square calculated values are

df	0.10	0.05	0.01	0.005	0.001
1	2.71	3.84	6.64	7.88	10.83
2	4.61	5.99	9.21	10.60	13.82
3	6.25	7.82	11.34	12.84	16.27
4	7.78	9.49	13.28	14.87	18.47
5	9.24	11.07	15.09	16.75	20.52
6	10.65	12.59	16.81	18.55	22.46
7	12.02	14.07	18.48	20.28	24.32
8	13.36	15.51	20.09	21.95	26.12
9	14.68	16.92	21.67	23.59	27.88
10	15.99	18.31	23.21	25.19	29.59
11	17.28	19.68	24.72	26.76	31.26
12	18.55	21.03	26.22	28.30	32.91
13	19.81	22.36	27.69	29.82	34.53
14	21.06	23.69	29.14	31.32	36.13
15	22.31	24.99	30.58	32.80	37.70
16	23.54	26.30	32.00	34.27	39.26
17	24.77	27.59	33.41	35.72	40.80
18	25.99	28.87	34.81	37.16	42.32
19	27.20	30.14	36.20	38.59	43.83
20	28.41	31.41	37.57	40.00	45.32

If the observed chi-square is greater than or equal to the tabled value for the desired probability level and degrees of freedom, we should reject the null hypothesis.

The entries in this table were computed by the authors.

Figure 16.6 Probability Values of the Chi-Square Distribution

statistically significant (for a discussion of statistical significance, see Chapter 15). On the left-hand side is the column for the degrees of freedom. In our study, our degrees of freedom value, as calculated in Step Five, was 4, so we need to compare the number we calculated for the chi-square statistic in Step Four, 22.362, against the numbers in row 4 on this chart. If 22.362 is greater than the number listed in the columns, our chi-square is statistically significant at that p-value level (shown at the top of each column). The first column represents $p < .10$, which is not statistically significant, as discussed in Chapter 15. The critical value in this column was 7.779, and our calculated chi-square statistic was 22.362, which is greater than 7.779, so we would consider our chi-square significant at the $p < .10$ level. However, .10 does not meet the 95% confidence interval discussed in the previous chapter, so we would not consider a chi-square statistically significant at this p-value. The second column represents $p < .05$, which meets the 95% confidence interval discussed in the previous chapter, so if our computed value is greater than the critical value, we would consider a chi-square statistically significant at this p-value. The critical value in the $p = .05$ column was 9.488, and our calculated chi-square statistic was 22.362, which is greater than 9.488, so we would consider our chi-square significant at the $p < .05$ level. Our example is clearly larger than the critical value of 9.49 shown in the table, so we can reject the null hypothesis and affirm the claim that female and male undergraduates differ in the year in college when they take public speaking. In fact, if you examine the critical values table further, we can reject the null hypothesis at both the $p < .02$ and $p < .01$ levels as well.

Computer Printouts of the Chi-Square Test of Independence

Now that we have examined how the chi-square test of independence can be calculated by hand, we will examine what output from two statistical computer programs, SPSS and SAS, looks like as well. Most researchers no longer compute statistics by hand. Computing statistics by hand is very dangerous because humans make errors very easily when handling large quantities of data. In this example, we only had 100 people in the 10 cells in the 2 × 5 table. Imagine if we had used 4000 people. While the statistics could be computed by hand like we did above, it just isn't very time efficient to do so. For this reason, a variety of computer programs have been created to aid in this process. The two most commonly used statistical software packages used by communication researchers are SPSS and SAS. If you look on the CD-ROM that came with this textbook, you will find a folder marked "Book Data Sets." In this folder you will find folders for SPSS data sets, SAS data sets, and Note Pad Data sets. The SPSS and SAS data sets can be used only by SPSS and SAS software packages. If you do not have SPSS or SAS but have a different statistical software package, you can use the Note Pad Data sets to import the data into whatever program you prefer to use. For example, if you would prefer to use Microsoft Excel, we would recommend reading Salkind (2007). However, we will only be discussing how to read an interpret results from SPSS and SAS in this book. We should mention that we specifically used SPSS 14.0 and SAS 9.1 in the conducting of the statistical tests in this book. We mention this because previous versions of the software may display more or less information in similar or different ways. While the steps in conducting the tests will be the same for various versions of the software packages, often the display does get altered. For this reason, if you are utilizing an earlier version (or later version) of either SPSS or SAS, you may want to consult the software guide that accompanied the software package. For the most part, these changes are minor, but for students new to dealing with statistical software packages the changes may be confusing.

SPSS AND CHI-SQUARES

For this section, open the SPSS data sets folder and select the file "chi-square." *When you select this file, SPSS will automatically import the data into the front page of the software program.* When using SPSS to calculate a chi-square, you use the "crosstabs" function. To get to the crosstabs function, go to the menu bar at the top of your screen and click on "Analyze." When you click on "Analyze," a dropdown menu will appear. Go to the second category on this menu, "Descriptive Statistics," and scroll over the arrow and another menu will appear to the right. The last choice on this menu is "Crosstabs"; click on it. When you do this, the crosstabs dialogue box appears. On the left side of the screen you will find a box that lists all of the variables in the data set. If you have opened the chi-square file from the CD-ROM, you will see two variables listed (sex and class). To compute a chi-square using SPSS, highlight the sex variable and click on the right arrow to the left of the box labeled "Row(s)." If you have done this correctly, you will see the sex variable has no been placed in the "Row(s)" box on the right side of the dialogue box. Next, highlight the class variable and click on the right arrow to the left of the box labeled "Column(s)." If you have done this correctly, you will see the class variable has been placed in the "Column(s)" box on the right side of the dialogue box.

At the bottom of the crosstabs dialogue box you will see three buttons: "Statistics," "Cells," and "Format." Click on the "Statistics" button. A new dialogue box called "Cross-tabs: Statistics" will appear. In this box, you will see a variety of different statistical procedures that can be completed using the crosstabs procedure. However, we are only interested in the one on the top left side called "Chi-square." When you click on the white box next to the words "Chi-square," you will see a little black checkmark appear in the box. Now go click the button "Continue" on the opposite side of the "Statistics" dialogue box.

Next, we're going to go click on the button "Cells." A new dialogue box will open called "Crosstabs: Cell Display." When this dialogue box first appears, the only box that will have a checkmark in it is next to the word "Observed," which is the same thing as frequency observed. Right under "Observed" is "Expected"; go ahead and click on this as well, and then click "Continue."

At this point you can go ahead and click "OK" in the upper right-hand side of the cross-tabs dialogue box. Figure 16.7 shows the actual results you will see from SPSS.

When looking at the SPSS printouts, you'll notice three boxes. The first box is labeled the "Case Processing Summary" box, and lets you know how many cases (or participants) were used in this test. Just like when we did it by hand, 100 participants were used in this statistical test. The second box is the "Sex × Class Crosstabultation" box. This box is similar to the box seen in Figure 16.3, but it also has both the observed and expected values. Go through and notice that all of the numbers we calculated by hand match up perfectly to those in this box. The third box in the SPSS printouts, the "Chi-Square Tests" box, is the box that is important for understanding whether or not the chi-square was statistically significant. While there are three tests represented in this box, the one to be concerned about for a basic chi-square is the first test, the "Pearson Chi-Square." Look at the "Pearson Chi-Square" row, which has been bolded, and you will see three columns: "Value," "df," and "Asymp. Sig. (2-sided)." The first column is the calculated value for the chi-square. And just like the calculated value we obtained when we calculated chi-square by hand, the computer also found the calculated value to be 22.362 and the degrees of freedom to be 4. However, the computer is able to obtain a much more exact p-value than we could by looking at a critical value chart. In this case, the chi-square was found to be significant at the $p < .0005$ level. You'll notice that the printout just says that the significance is .000; however, this means that the significance is lower than this level, so adding a 5 to the end of it is the most appropriate thing to do (Levine & Atkin, 2004).

Crosstabs

Case Processing Summary

	Cases					
	Valid		Missing		Total	
	N	Percent	N	Percent	N	Percent
SEX * CLASS	100	100.0%	0	.0%	100	100.0%

SEX * CLASS Crosstabulation

			CLASS					
			Pre-college	First Year Student	Sophomore	Junior	Senior	Total
SEX	male	Count	6	8	10	1	25	50
		Expected Count	6.5	14.0	9.5	4.5	15.5	50.0
	female	Count	7	20	9	8	6	50
		Expected Count	6.5	14.0	9.5	4.5	15.5	50.0
Total		Count	13	28	19	9	31	100
		Expected Count	13.0	28.0	19.0	9.0	31.0	100.0

Chi-Square Tests

	Value	df	Asymp. Sig. (2-sided)
Pearson Chi-Square	**22.362**[a]	**4**	**.000**
Likelihood Ratio	24.153	4	.000
Linear-by-Linear Association	9.541	1	.002
N of Valid Cases	100		

[a] 2 cells (20.0%) have expected count less than 5. The minimum expected count is 4.50.

Figure 16.7 SPSS Printout

SAS AND CHI-SQUARES

Unlike the simple Windows-based operating system that SPSS uses, SAS tends to be designed for those people have a stronger computer background—especially in the old DOS operating world. While anyone can use SAS after a little time, it is very different in its approach to data entry and computation. When using SAS, all commands are called "PROC" or Procedure commands. For more information on using SAS, we recommend Delwiche and Slaughter (2003). To calculate a chi-square using SAS, you use the "PROC FREQ" or Procedure Frequency. The exact SAS code needed to run the chi-square for the example in this chapter would be:

```
PROC FREQ;
    TABLES SEX*CLASS / ALL;
```

```
                         The FREQ Procedure

                       Table of SEX by CLASS

      SEX         CLASS

      Frequency,
      Percent   ,
      Row Pct   ,
      Col Pct   ,        1,        2,        3,        4,        5,   Total
      ƒƒƒƒƒƒƒƒƒ^ƒƒƒƒƒƒƒƒ^ƒƒƒƒƒƒƒƒ^ƒƒƒƒƒƒƒƒ^ƒƒƒƒƒƒƒƒ^ƒƒƒƒƒƒƒƒ^
           1 ,        6 ,        8 ,       10 ,        1 ,       25 ,       50
             ,     6.00 ,     8.00 ,    10.00 ,     1.00 ,    25.00 ,    50.00
             ,    12.00 ,    16.00 ,    20.00 ,     2.00 ,    50.00 ,
             ,    46.15 ,    28.57 ,    52.63 ,    11.11 ,    80.65 ,
      ƒƒƒƒƒƒƒƒƒ^ƒƒƒƒƒƒƒƒ^ƒƒƒƒƒƒƒƒ^ƒƒƒƒƒƒƒƒ^ƒƒƒƒƒƒƒƒ^ƒƒƒƒƒƒƒƒ^
           2 ,        7 ,       20 ,        9 ,        8 ,        6 ,       50
             ,     7.00 ,    20.00 ,     9.00 ,     8.00 ,     6.00 ,    50.00
             ,    14.00 ,    40.00 ,    18.00 ,    16.00 ,    12.00 ,
             ,    53.85 ,    71.43 ,    47.37 ,    88.89 ,    19.35 ,
      ƒƒƒƒƒƒƒƒƒ^ƒƒƒƒƒƒƒƒ^ƒƒƒƒƒƒƒƒ^ƒƒƒƒƒƒƒƒ^ƒƒƒƒƒƒƒƒ^ƒƒƒƒƒƒƒƒ^
      Total           13        28        19         9        31       100
                   13.00     28.00     19.00      9.00     31.00    100.00


             Statistics for Table of SEX by CLASS

       Statistic                     DF       Value       Prob
       ƒƒƒƒƒƒƒƒƒƒƒƒƒƒƒƒƒƒƒƒƒƒƒƒƒƒƒƒƒƒƒƒƒƒƒƒƒƒƒƒƒƒƒƒƒƒƒƒƒƒƒƒƒ
       Chi-Square                     4       22.3620      0.0002
       Likelihood Ratio Chi-Square    4       24.1533      <.0001
       Mantel-Haenszel Chi-Square     1        9.5414      0.0020
       Phi Coefficient                         0.4729
       Contingency Coefficient                 0.4275
       Cramer's V                              0.4729
```

Figure 16.8 SAS Printout

You'll notice that each line of this code is followed by a semicolon. In SAS, if you miss one semicolon or put something in the wrong place, the program will not run. If you ever have a program that will not run, we strongly suggest you first start by making sure all of the semicolons are typed in your input file correctly. Figure 16.8 is the SAS printout for the chi-square example in this chapter.

Again, the SAS printouts are not as graphically appealing as the SPSS printouts, but the information is identical if you know where to look. In SAS, you'll notice that there are numbers in the "Table of Sex by Class" chart but named labels in the SPSS chart. In this chart, 1 = male and 2 = female for the rows, and 1 = pre-college, 2 = first-year student, 3 = sophomore, 4= junior, and 5 = senior for the columns. The information is set up in an identical manner, it's just presented in the numbers that were originally entered into the computer. In the second chart, the "Statistics for Table of Sex by Class" chart, you will notice that a number of different statistical tests were conducted using the PROC FREQ procedure. The first test conducted is the chi-square test of independence. Again, we have bolded this result to make it easier to see in this example. Notice that the results from both SPSS and SAS are identical in their presentation of the chi-square test. Now that we have examined the chi-square test itself, let's see how a researcher would write up this finding using APA style in a results section of an article.

APA WRITE-UP

A chi-square was conducted to assess whether females and males take public speaking at different stages in their educational career. The result for this test was significant: $\chi^2(4, N = 100) = 22.36, p < .0005$.

You'll notice that in this APA write-up, everything is very simply stated. The actual statement written is very simple: χ^2 = (degrees of freedom, number of people in sample) = calculated value, level of statistical significance. In the future, when analyzing a chi-square, all you really need to see is this one line to determine what was done and what were the results found by the researchers. Make sure that you also note that APA requires that we round results to the nearest hundredth (two decimal places) for all results except your p-value.

DISCUSSION OF FINDINGS

By this point you're probably wondering what the result actually means. To really grasp what we've found in this chi-square, you really must go back to what we said about the chi-square in the very beginning of this chapter. A chi-square is a difference test. All you basically get in a chi-square test is whether or not a difference occurs between the two groups. In this example, based on the basic chi-square, we can say that a statistically significant difference occurs between females and males and when they take public speaking in college. We cannot say exactly when that difference occurs. In other words, we cannot eyeball Figure 16.1 and say that more females take public speaking during their first year in college than men because we did not conduct a test to determine if this is true. Based on a simple chi-square test of independence, all you can legitimately say is that a difference exists.

To ascertain where this difference exists, you need to conduct a multiple comparison procedure. You only need to conduct a multiple comparison procedure if the overall chi-square is significant. While a chi-square multiple comparison procedure is useful, it is not the most statistically accurate way to obtain results. In a chi-square multiple comparison procedure, you compare all of the parts of the smaller variable (sex) with all of the parts of the larger variable (year in school). Since sex only has two levels (male and female), we really do not have to worry about changing anything for sex. However, since year in school has five levels, we have to conduct 10 comparison tests. To determine how many comparison tests are necessary, you can use the following formula: $(K(K-1))/2$, with K being the number of groups being compared. In this case, we have five groups being compared (precollege, first year student, sophomore, junior, and senior). So the formula would be solved like this:

$$(5(5-1))/2$$

$$(5(4))/2$$

$$20 / 2$$

$$10$$

To perform a multiple comparison test, you simply select two categories from the larger variable (year in school) you want to compare (e.g., pre-college and first-year student) and then compare them by conducting a chi-square. In SPSS, you open the chi-square file and go to the menu bar on the top of your screen and click on "Data." When you click on "Data," a dropdown menu will appear. Scroll down and click on "Select Cases." The "Select Cases" dialogue box will appear. On the left-hand side of the box you will see your variables listed, and on the right-hand side you will see that the radio button "All Cases" currently has a black dot filling the button. Click on the second radio button down, or the radio button that corresponds with the phrase "If condition is satisfied." Once you have clicked "If condition is satisfied," click on the bottom "If" immediately below. When you click on this button, the "Select Cases: If" dialogue box will appear. In this window, you will see your variables in a box on a left-hand side, an empty box on the top right-hand side, a calculator in the center, and some mathematical expressions on the bottom right. The only box you will need to be worried about at this time is the empty box on the top right-hand side. Type in this empty box *class = 1 or class = 2*. Then click the "Continue" button at the bottom of the "Select Cases: If" dialogue box. And click the "OK" button at the bottom of the "Select Cases" dialogue box. When you do this, you will notice that a new variable appears called "filter_$." Furthermore, you will notice that many of your cases now have a slash mark through the case number on the left-hand side of the main SPSS screen. In essence, you have told SPSS that you are only going to pay attention to the first two parts of the "class" variable (pre-college and first-year students). You then will compute a chi-square test of independence just like we did above. Only this time, the only variables being compared will be a 2 × 2 table or sex (male and female) by class (pre-college and first-year students). This process will then be repeated nine more times comparing each set of variables in the chi-square itself (e.g., pre-college with sophomores, pre-college with juniors, pre-college with seniors, sophomores with juniors, etc.). When all 10 chi-square have been calculated, you end up with the results shown in Figure 16.9.

Based on the above results, we can safely say that females and males differ when they take public speaking between pre-college and seniors, first-year students and seniors, sophomores and juniors, sophomores and seniors, and juniors and seniors. We can make these claims because the chi-square tests of independence were significant for these pairwise comparisons. However, this is a very liberal or loose conclusion. With any statistical test there occurs a certain amount of error as discussed in Chapter 15. The more statistical tests one runs, the more the error is compounded, and the is an increased chance of Type I error. For this reason, statisticians recommend being very conservative. One way to be conservative and prevent Type I error is to lower the significance level. While there are many tests to help you lower your significance level, one we commonly use is the Dunn-Sidak test. Using the formula $1 - (1 - \alpha)^{1/k}$, where k is the number of comparisons being made (which as we discussed above is 10 in this case), a lower alpha level can be calculated. Since this hypothesis was examining 10 different chi-square tests, k was equal to 10 and alpha as discussed in Chapter 15 is usually set at $p < .05$, so the Dunn-Sidak test would look something like this:

$$1 - (1 - 0.05)^{1/10}$$

$$1 - (0.95)^{1/10}$$

$$1 - (0.9916965052)$$

$$0.0051161969$$

In other words, for the 10 pairwise comparisons to be considered statistically significant, the computed alpha level must now be less than .005. For example, by normal standards there is a significant difference between precollege and seniors because alpha was computed at $p = .022$, however, at the new alpha level of .005, $p = .022$ is not considered significant because it is greater than $p < .005$. With this more conservative alpha level, only two pairwise comparisons are now significant (first-year students and seniors) and (juniors and seniors). Here is how you would write up this portion of your report in APA:

Post Hoc APA Write-Up

As a post hoc analysis, 10 pairwise comparisons were calculated to determine where the actual differences are. To correct for Type I error in this procedure, a Dunn-Sidak procedure

Chi-Square Tests - Pre-College vs. First Year

	Value	df	Asymp. Sig. (2-sided)	Exact Sig. (2-sided)	Exact Sig. (1-sided)
Pearson Chi-Square	1.221[b]	1	.269		
Continuity Correction[a]	.564	1	.453		
Likelihood Ratio	1.196	1	.274		
Fisher's Exact Test				.307	.225
Linear-by-Linear Association	1.191	1	.275		
N of Valid Cases	41				

[a.] Computed only for a 2 × 2 table

[b.] 1 cells (25.0%) have expected count less than 5. The minimum expected count is 4.44.

Chi-Square Tests - Pre-College vs. Sophomore

	Value	df	Asymp. Sig. (2-sided)	Exact Sig. (2-sided)	Exact Sig. (1-sided)
Pearson Chi-Square	.130[b]	1	.719		
Continuity Correction[a]	.000	1	1.000		
Likelihood Ratio	.130	1	.719		
Fisher's Exact Test				1.000	.500
Linear-by-Linear Association	.126	1	.723		
N of Valid Cases	32				

[a.] Computed only for a 2 × 2 table

[b.] 0 cells (.0%) have expected count less than 5. The minimum expected count is 6.50.

Chi-Square Tests - Pre-College vs. Junior

	Value	df	Asymp. Sig. (2-sided)	Exact Sig. (2-sided)	Exact Sig. (1-sided)
Pearson Chi-Square	3.010[b]	1	.083		
Continuity Correction[a]	1.612	1	.204		
Likelihood Ratio	3.298	1	.069		
Fisher's Exact Test				.165	.101
Linear-by-Linear Association	2.874	1	.090		
N of Valid Cases	22				

[a.] Computed only for a 2 × 2 table

[b.] 2 cells (50.0%) have expected count less than 5. The minimum expected count is 2.86.

Figure 16.9 Multiple Comparison Tests

Continued

Continued

Chi-Square Tests - Pre-College vs. Senior

	Value	df	Asymp. Sig. (2-sided)	Exact Sig. (2-sided)	Exact Sig. (1-sided)
Pearson Chi-Square	5.234[b]	1	.022		
Continuity Correction[a]	3.709	1	.054		
Likelihood Ratio	5.006	1	.025		
Fisher's Exact Test				.033	.029
Linear-by-Linear Association	5.115	1	.024		
N of Valid Cases	44				

[a.] Computed only for a 2 × 2 table
[b.] 1 cells (25.0%) have expected count less than 5. The minimum expected count is 3.84.

Chi-Square Tests - First Year vs. Sophomore

	Value	df	Asymp. Sig. (2-sided)	Exact Sig. (2-sided)	Exact Sig. (1-sided)
Pearson Chi-Square	2.773[b]	1	.096		
Continuity Correction[a]	1.848	1	.174		
Likelihood Ratio	2.767	1	.096		
Fisher's Exact Test				.130	.087
Linear-by-Linear Association	2.714	1	.099		
N of Valid Cases	47				

[a.] Computed only for a 2 × 2 table
[b.] 0 cells (.0%) have expected count less than 5. The minimum expected count is 7.28.

Chi-Square Tests - First Year vs. Junior

	Value	df	Asymp. Sig. (2-sided)	Exact Sig. (2-sided)	Exact Sig. (1-sided)
Pearson Chi-Square	1.128[b]	1	.288		
Continuity Correction[a]	.379	1	.538		
Likelihood Ratio	1.272	1	.259		
Fisher's Exact Test				.403	.280
Linear-by-Linear Association	1.098	1	.295		
N of Valid Cases	37				

[a.] Computed only for a 2 × 2 table
[b.] 1 cells (25.0%) have expected count less than 5. The minimum expected count is 2.19.

Continued

Chi-Square Tests - First Year vs. Senior

	Value	df	Asymp. Sig. (2-sided)	Exact Sig. (2-sided)	Exact Sig. (1-sided)
Pearson Chi-Square	16.185[b]	1	.000		
Continuity Correction[a]	14.142	1	.000		
Likelihood Ratio	16.994	1	.000		
Fisher's Exact Test				.000	.000
Linear-by-Linear Association	15.911	1	.000		
N of Valid Cases	59				

[a.] Computed only for a 2×2 table
[b.] 0 cells (.0%) have expected count less than 5. The minimum expected count is 12.34.

Chi-Square Tests - Sophomore vs. Junior

	Value	df	Asymp. Sig. (2-sided)	Exact Sig. (2-sided)	Exact Sig. (1-sided)
Pearson Chi-Square	4.414[b]	1	.036		
Continuity Correction[a]	2.845	1	.092		
Likelihood Ratio	4.955	1	.026		
Fisher's Exact Test				.049	.042
Linear-by-Linear Association	4.256	1	.039		
N of Valid Cases	28				

[a.] Computed only for a 2×2 table
[b.] 1 cells (25.0%) have expected count less than 5. The minimum expected count is 3.54.

Chi Square Tests - Sophomore vs. Senior

	Value	df	Asymp. Sig. (2-sided)	Exact Sig. (2-sided)	Exact Sig. (1-sided)
Pearson Chi-Square	4.402[b]	1	.036		
Continuity Correction[a]	3.169	1	.075		
Likelihood Ratio	4.337	1	.037		
Fisher's Exact Test				.056	.038
Linear-by-Linear Association	4.314	1	.038		
N of Valid Cases	50				

[a.] Computed only for a 2×2 table
[b.] 0 cells (.0%) have expected count less than 5. The minimum expected count is 5.70.

Continued

Continued

Chi-Square Tests - Junior vs. Senior

	Value	df	Asymp. Sig. (2-sided)	Exact Sig. (2-sided)	Exact Sig. (1-sided)
Pearson Chi-Square	14.824[b]	1	.000		
Continuity Correction[a]	11.925	1	.001		
Likelihood Ratio	15.054	1	.000		
Fisher's Exact Test				.000	.000
Linear-by-Linear Association	14.453	1	.000		
N of Valid Cases	40				

[a.] Computed only for a 2 × 2 table

[b.] 1 cells (25.0%) have expected count less than 5. The minimum expected count is 3.15.

Figure 16.9

Pairwise Comparison	*N*	df	χ^2	*p*
Precollege vs. First-Year Student	41	1	1.22	.27
Precollege vs. Sophomore	32	1	1.30	.72
Precollege vs. Junior	22	1	3.01	.08
Precollege vs. Senior	44	1	5.23	.02
First-Year Student vs. Sophomore	47	1	2.77	.10
First-Year Student vs. Junior	37	1	1.23	.29
First-Year Student vs. Senior	59	1	16.19	.0005*
Sophomore vs. Junior	28	1	4.41	.04
Sophomore vs. Senior	50	1	4.40	.04
Junior vs. Senior	40	1	14.82	.0005*

Significant at the .005 level after a Dunn-Sidak correction.

Figure 16.10 Pairwise Comparisons

was conducted to correct for possible compounded error due to the 10 pairwise comparisons. The new calculated alpha value is $p < .005$. Based on the new alpha value, only two pairwise comparisons were found to be statistically significant: first-year students and seniors, and juniors and seniors. Figure 16.10 contains the chi-square statistics for all of the pairwise comparisons.

Now that we have calculated a complete chi-square by hand, let's examine a real chi-square based on data actually collected with a real sample population.

Biological Sex and Political Affiliation

In this example, we wanted to see whether or not females and males differed in their political affiliation. In this case, we created a nominal variable for political affiliation consisting of the following categories: Democrat, Republican, other, not registered to vote. Ultimately, we had a 2 × 4 design (sex ×, politics). Figure 16.11 represents the findings from the SPSS results and Figure 16.12 represents the findings from the SAS results.

Crosstabs

Case Processing Summary

	Cases					
	Valid		Missing		Total	
	N	Percent	N	Percent	N	Percent
Biological Sex * Political Affiliation	321	98.8%	4	1.2%	325	100.0%

Biological Sex * Political Affiliation Crosstabulation

			Political Affiliation				Total
			Democrat	Republican	Other	Not Registered to Vote	
Biological Sex	Male	Count	57	85	27	14	183
		Expected Count	66.7	82.1	22.2	12.0	183.0
	Female	Count	60	59	12	7	138
		Expected Count	50.3	61.9	16.8	9.0	138.0
Total		Count	117	144	39	21	321
		Expected Count	117.0	144.0	39.0	21.0	321.0

Chi-Square Tests

	Value	df	Asymp. Sig. (2-sided)
Pearson Chi-Square	6.697[a]	**3**	**.082**
Likelihood Ratio	6.767	3	.080
Linear-by-Linear Association	5.915	1	.015
N of Valid Cases	321		

[a] 0 cells (.0%) have expected count less than 5. The minimum expected count is 9.03.

Figure 16.11 SPSS Printout for Sex × Politics

Again, notice that the results you get from SPSS and SAS are identical. For the most part, the results from these two programs are identical until you get into some of the formulas used for advanced statistical techniques.

APA Write-Up

A chi-square was conducted to assess whether females and males differ in their political affiliation (Democrat, Republican, other, and not registered to vote). The result for this test was not significant: $\chi^2(3, N = 321) = 6.70$, $p > .05$.

```
                              CHI-SQUARE

                            The SAS System

                          The FREQ Procedure

                        Table of SEX by POLITICS

              SEX        POLITICS

              Frequency,
              Percent  ,
              Row Pct  ,
              Col Pct  ,        1,        2,        3,        4,   Total
              ƒƒƒƒƒƒƒƒƒ^ƒƒƒƒƒƒƒƒ^ƒƒƒƒƒƒƒƒ^ƒƒƒƒƒƒƒƒ^ƒƒƒƒƒƒƒƒ^
                    1 ,       57 ,      85 ,      27 ,      14 ,     183
                      ,    17.76 ,   26.48 ,    8.41 ,    4.36 ,   57.01
                      ,    31.15 ,   46.45 ,   14.75 ,    7.65 ,
                      ,    48.72 ,   59.03 ,   69.23 ,   66.67 ,
              ƒƒƒƒƒƒƒƒƒ^ƒƒƒƒƒƒƒƒ^ƒƒƒƒƒƒƒƒ^ƒƒƒƒƒƒƒƒ^ƒƒƒƒƒƒƒƒ^
                    2 ,       60 ,      59 ,      12 ,       7 ,     138
                      ,    18.69 ,   18.38 ,    3.74 ,    2.18 ,   42.99
                      ,    43.48 ,   42.75 ,    8.70 ,    5.07 ,
                      ,    51.28 ,   40.97 ,   30.77 ,   33.33 ,
              ƒƒƒƒƒƒƒƒƒ^ƒƒƒƒƒƒƒƒ^ƒƒƒƒƒƒƒƒ^ƒƒƒƒƒƒƒƒ^ƒƒƒƒƒƒƒƒ^
              Total          117      144       39       21      321
                            36.45    44.86    12.15     6.54   100.00

                         Frequency Missing = 4


                   Statistics for Table of SEX by POLITICS

              Statistic                      DF      Value      Prob
              ƒƒƒƒƒƒƒƒƒƒƒƒƒƒƒƒƒƒƒƒƒƒƒƒƒƒƒƒƒƒƒƒƒƒƒƒƒƒƒƒƒƒƒƒƒƒƒƒƒƒƒƒƒƒƒ
              Chi-Square                      3      6.6971    0.0822
              Likelihood Ratio Chi-Square     3      6.7672    0.0797
              Mantel-Haenszel Chi-Square      1      5.9145    0.0150
              Phi Coefficient                        0.1444
              Contingency Coefficient                0.1430
              Cramer's V                             0.1444
```

Figure 16.12 SAS Printout for Sex × Politics

Discussion of Brummans and Miller's Article

To help further your understanding of chi-square tests for independence, the 2004 article by Boris Brummans and Katherine Miller entitled "The Effect of Ambiguity on the Implementation of Social Change Initiative" can be found on the CD-ROM that accompanied this textbook in the folder titled "articles." To view this article, you will need to download a copy of the Adobe Acrobat Reader (http://www.adobe.com/products/acrobat/readermain.html) if you do not already have this program installed on your computer. We strongly encourage you to read the article first and then read our analysis of the article. The goal of this process is to make sure you understand how to read and interpret research results related to chi-squares.

ARTICLE PURPOSE

In 1992, the Kellogg Foundation's set out to influence health care in three Michigan communities through its Comprehensive Community Health Models Initiative (CCHM). To do this, the Kellogg Foundatoin sought to "legitimize the problem of community health" and "provide resources and infrastructure for change" (Brummans & Miller, 2004, p. 4). The goal of the Brummans and Miller (2004) article was to see if people involved with the implementation of the initiative found the ambiguity of the term "collaborative community health improvement" as detrimental or beneficial to the implementation of the initiative.

METHODOLOGY

The research team involved in this project interviewed 48 "key participants" in three small group settings. After the interviews, the research team searched for specific ambiguity oriented language (see last sentence of the first paragraph on page 6 in the article) and broke the dialogue into research units. These units were then classified as either high ambiguity or low ambiguity by two independent coders, which is the independent variable in this study. If you'll remember the section on Cohen's kappa from Chapter 12, you'll notice that 0.86 is above the 0.70 designation described as necessary to be considered satisfactorily reliable for coders. The coders also determined whether the participant perceived the ambiguity as either beneficial or detrimental to the CCHM initiative's implementation, which is the dependent variable in this study. Ultimately, the coders created a 2 × 2 table (high ambiguity and low ambiguity) × (detrimental effects and beneficial effects). The actual 2 × 2 table can be seen on page 7 of the article.

RESULTS

The goal of this study was to see if there was a difference in perception of the effects based on the level ambiguity. The Pearson's chi-square was reported as ($\chi^2 = 117.05$, 1 df, $p < .01$). Notice that this format for presenting the chi-square information is slightly different than the one discussed in the APA write-ups. However, all of the same information is presented (N can be found in the table on page 7). So based on the results, people do perceive the effects of the implementation with regard to their perception of the ambiguity of the term "collaborative community health improvement."

One other statistic is also presented here that we have not discussed—is Cramér's phi (Φ). All a chi-square test of independence can do is tell you that a difference exists, Cramér's phi is used to determine how much of the difference in one variable can be accounted for by the variance in another variable. In other words, how much an individual's level of the effects of the implementation can be caused by her or his perceptions of the ambiguity of the term "collaborative community health improvement." To obtain Cramér's phi, the formula in Figure 16.13 is used.

To understand this formula, you need to have a calculated value for a chi-square (117.05) and remember that N = total number of observations ($N = 263$) and k = the smaller of the number of rows or columns ($k = 2$). In other words:

$\Phi = \sqrt{(117.05 / (263 (2 - 1)))}$,

$\Phi = \sqrt{(117.05 / (263 (1)))}$,

$\Phi = \sqrt{(117.05 / (263))}$

$\Phi = \sqrt{(117.05 / (263 (2 - 1)))}$

$$\Phi = \sqrt{\frac{X^2}{N (k - 1)}}$$

Figure 16.13 Cramér's Phi Statistic

$\Phi = \sqrt{0.4450570342}$ ← This number is the % of variability in the dependent variable (effect) was accounted for by the independent variable (ambiguity).

$\Phi = 0.6671259508$ ← This is the number that is reported in the article.

Cramer's phi in this article was 0.67, and the level of ambiguity of the term "collaborative community health improvement" (high and low) accounted for approximately 45% of the variability in a person's perception of detrimental or beneficial effects of the initiative. Overall, this article is a good example of how the chi-square test of independence can be used to answer a research question.

Conclusion

In this chapter we have examined how to compute a chi-square statistic by hand, how to compute and interpret computer results of a chi-square statistic in both SPSS and SAS, and how to write up a chi-square tests using APA style. We have seen the chi-square statistic used in three different examples. In the next chapter we will discuss how to calculate t-tests.

KEY TERMS

Calculated Value	Cramer's Phi (Φ)	Degrees of Freedom
Chi-Square (χ^2)	Critical Value	Dunn-Sidak Test

REFERENCES

Brummans, B. H. J. M., & Miller, K. (2004). The effect of ambiguity on the implementation of a social change initiative. *Communication Research Reports, 21,* 1–10.

Dunn, O. J. (1991). Multiple comparisons among means. *Journal of the American Statistical Association, 56,* 52–64.

Levine, T. R., & Atkin, C. (2004). The accurate reporting of software-generated p-values: A cautionary research note. *Communication Research Reports, 21,* 324–327.

Fisher, R. A. (1970). *Statistical methods for research workers* (14th ed.). New York: Macmillan Publishing.

Salkind, N. J. (2007). *Statistics for people who (think they) hate statistics: The Excel® edition.* Thousand Oaks, CA: Sage.

FURTHER READING

Abramson, J. H., & Abramson, Z. H. (2001). *Making sense of data: A self-instruction manual on the interpretation of epidemiological data* (3rd ed.). New York: Oxford.

Bruning, J. L., & Kintz, B. L. (1997). *Computational handbook of statistics* (4th ed.). New York: Longman.

Delwiche, L. D., & Slaughter, S. J. (2003). *The little SAS book: A primer* (3rd ed.). Cary, NC: SAS Press.

Gravetter, F. J., & Wallnau, L. B. (2000). *Statistics for the behavioral sciences* (5th ed.). Belmont, CA: Wadsworth/Thomson Learning.

Green, S. B., & Salkind, N. J. (2004). *Using SPSS for Windows and Macintosh: Analyzing and understanding data* (4th ed.). Upper Saddle River, NJ: Prentice Hall.

Greenwood, P. E., & Nikulin, M. S. (2004). *A guide to chi-square testing*. New York: John Wiley & Sons.

Hocking, J. E., Stacks, D. W., & McDermott, S. T. (2003). *Communication research* (3rd ed.). Boston: Allyn and Bacon.

Howell, D. C. (1997). *Statistical methods for psychology* (4th ed.). Belmont, CA: Duxbury Press.

Huff, D. (1954). *How to lie with statistics*. New York: W. W. Norton & Company.

Keller, D. K. (2006). *The Tao of statistics: A path to understanding (with no math)*. Thousand Oaks, CA: Sage.

Pyrczak, F. (1999). *Statistics with a sense of humor: A humorous workbook and guide to study skills* (2nd ed.). Los Angeles: Pyrczak.

Reynolds, H. T. (1984). *Analysis of nominal data* (2nd ed.). Newbury Park, CA: Sage.

Salkind, N. J. (2004). *Statistics for people who (think they) hate statistics* (2nd ed.). Thousand Oaks, CA: Sage.

SAS Institute. (2004). *SAS 9.1 Companion for Windows*. Cary, NC: SAS Press.

Singleton, R. A., Jr., & Straits, B. C. (1999). *Approach to social research* (3rd ed.). New York: Oxford University Press.

Trochim, W. M. K. (2000). *The research methods knowledge base* (2nd ed.). Cincinnati, OH: Atomic Dog. Online available at: http://www.socialresearchmethods.net/

CHAPTER 17

Independent Samples *t*-Tests

When we conducted a chi-square in the last chapter, both of the variables we analyzed had to be nominal or categorical variables (if you don't remember what this means, please reread Chapter 6 before continuing). A *t*-test, on the other hand, examines one nominal variable with two categories (two independent groups) and their scores on one dependent interval/ratio variable. The nominal variable in a *t*-test is the independent variable and the interval/ratio variable is the dependent variable. A group is considered independent when one participant's place in one group does not influence anyone else's placement within that group or another group. In essence, the two groups are not related to each other. For example, one common nominal variable used in *t*-tests is biological sex. With the nominal variable, biological sex, we have two groups: females and males. If the first participant in the sample is male, then the second participant in the sample could equally be either female or male because the first participant's biological sex has no impact on the second participant's biological sex. In addition to the two groups being independent from each other, every participant should have scores on two variables: the grouping/nominal variable (biological sex) and a test/dependent variable. In the case of an independent samples *t*-test, the goal is to determine if two groups' means differ on an interval/ratio variable of some kind. The groups function as the independent variable, and the interval/ratio variable is the dependent variable. For example, maybe we wanted to determine if females and males (independent variable) differ in their levels of nonverbal sensitivity (dependent variable). Now that we've explained the basic purpose of an independent *t*-test, let's examine an example of an independent samples *t*-test.

Case Study Introduction

Imagine you're a teacher teaching an interpersonal communication seminar to two different classes with five students in each class ($n = 5$). In one class, you wear stylish clothing (Class A), and in the other class you wear clothes from the 1970s (Class B). You want to determine if the style of clothing you wear affects the performance of your class on a test. You formulate a hypothesis that predicts that your wardrobe (stylish clothing vs. outdated clothing) influences the midterm examination grades of Class A and Class B.

Based on the above description, you have one nominal variable (stylish clothing vs. outdated clothing) and one ratio variable (grades on a midterm). You might ask yourself why the grades on the midterm variable is considered a ratio variable. If a student answers none of the questions correctly on a test, then he or she could receive an absolute zero (assuming the professor does not give points for correctly spelling one's name). If you look on the chart at the end of Chapter 6 in this book, you'll notice that if you have one nominal variable and one interval/ratio variable, the correct statistical test to determine if a difference exists is an independent *t*-test. Let's now examine a handful of important assumptions about the independent samples *t*-test.

Independent Samples *t*-Test Background Information

The independent samples *t*-test allows a researcher to examine the differences on an interval or ratio variable between two nominal variables. The nominal variables always function as the independent variables in the *t*-test. For example, maybe you wanted to determine the level of communication apprehension between females and males. The biological sex nominal variable (females and males) would be the independent variable and communication apprehension would be the dependent variable. If your nominal variable has more than two levels (e.g., political affiliation—Democrat, Republican, independent voter, not registered to vote), you cannot use an independent samples *t*-test to ascertain differences, instead the one-way ANOVA, which will be discussed in the next chapter, should be used.

Now that we've discussed a couple of the basic aspects of the independent samples *t*-test itself, let's look at the underlying assumptions of the independent samples *t*-test:

1. The dependent variable must be an interval or ratio variable.
2. The independent variable must be a nominal variable.
3. The dependent variable (grade) should be normally distributed in both of the independent variable levels (stylish clothing vs. outdated clothing). Specifically, the distributions for both populations should not have a high skewness or kurtosis. In a real world situation, it is recommended that each nominal category have at least 30 participants. (Since we are only performing an example in this chapter, we do not have 30 participants in each category to make the math easier to compute.)
4. A sample should be drawn from populations with equal variances on the dependent variable (midterm grade). Variance in the *t*-statistic formula is obtained by averaging the variance for both of the independent variables (stylish clothing vs. outdated clothing). Since the variance is obtained by averaging the variance of both independent variables,

$$t = \cfrac{(\overline{X}_1 - \overline{X}_2) - (\mu_1 - \mu_2)}{\sqrt{\left[\cfrac{\Sigma X^2_1 - \cfrac{(\Sigma X_1)^2}{n_1} + \Sigma X^2_2 - \cfrac{(\Sigma X_2)^2}{n_2}}{n_1 + n_2 - 2}\right]\left(\cfrac{1}{n_1} + \cfrac{1}{n_2}\right)}}$$

Figure 17.1 *t*-test Formula

it makes sense that both values should be estimating the same population variance. If the independent variables are both estimating the same population variance, then you are said to have achieved the homogeneity of variance assumption (we will see this assumption again in the next chapter).

5. Finally, the participants contributing data should represent a random sample drawn from the population of interest (this is an assumption of most statistical tests).

The above assumptions are extremely important because if one assumption is violated, the meaning of the *t*-test is lost. Now that we've explained what a *t*-test is and what the basic assumptions of the *t*-test are, we can look at the basic *t*-test formula given in Figure 17.1.

For some, this formula is very scary looking. However, most of the formula is simply computing some basic descriptive statistics like we did in Chapter 8 and then plugging those answers into the formula as we go along.

Step-by-Step Approach to the Independent *t*-Test

As we discussed above, the basic hypothesis being examined in this example is that there is a difference between Class A (fashionable dress) and Class B (outdated dress) and student performance on their midterm examinations. Figure 17.2 portrays the midterm test scores from all 12 student participants.

Step One. The first step to solving the independent *t*-test is to find the ΣX_1 (all five grades in Class A added together), $\overline{X}_1$ (the average for Class A), and the ΣX_1^2 (sum of squares for Class A). To find the ΣX_1, you need to add all five scores for the midterm examination for Class A together ($90 + 85 + 88 + 98 + 90 = 451$). To find $\overline{X}_1$, take the sum you found for ΣX_1 (451) and divide it by *n*, which is the number of people in Class A ($451 / 5 = 90.2$). To get the ΣX_1^2 value (student grades in class A) you start by first squaring each *X* value on the chart. For example, Natalie got a 90 on her test, so you take 90^2 or 90×90 and get 8100. You then repeat this process for each student in Class A. Louise obtained an X^2 value of 7225, Jimmy had a 7744, Tika had a 9604, and Kristen had a 8100. You then add all of these X^2 values together to obtain the ΣX_1^2 ($8100 + 7225 + 7744 + 9604 + 8100 = 40773$). Once you have completed this process for Class A or X_1, you then repeat the process for Class B or X_2. Figure 17.3 contains the mathematical values for Class A (X_1) and Class B (X_2) necessary for computing the *t*-test.

Step Two. As with any formula, you need to start by doing things within parentheses and brackets first. The part we are going to solve for in Step Two is bolded in Figure 17.4.

Both of these portions of the formula involve the ΣX_1 (451) and the ΣX_2 (364). The actual formula for this part is $(\Sigma X_1)^2 / n_1$. Remember, the lowercase *n* stands for the number of students in each class, or the number 5 in this example. So the solution for this part of the formula would be this:

$$(\Sigma X_1)^2 / n_1$$

$$(451)^2 / 5$$

| Summary of Data (Scores Out of 100) | | | |
| Class A (Fashionable Dress) Condition$_1$ ($n = 5$) | | Class B (1970s Dress) Condition$_2$ ($n = 5$) | |
Participant	X	Participant	X
1. Natalie	90	1. Dave	83
2. Louise	85	2. Tad	71
3. Jimmy	88	3. Penny	96
4. Tika	98	4. Kevin	52
5. Kirsten	90	5. Brenda	62

Figure 17.2 *t*-Test Sample Data

| Summary of Data (Scores Out of 100) | | | | | |
| Class A (Fashionable Dress) Condition$_1$ ($n = 5$) | | | Class B (1970s Dress) Condition$_2$ ($n = 5$) | | |
Participant	X	X^2	Participant	X	X^2
1. Natalie	90	8100	1. Dave	83	6889
2. Louise	85	7225	2. Tad	71	5041
3. Jimmy	88	7744	3. Penny	96	9216
4. Tika	98	9604	4. Kevin	52	2704
5. Kirsten	90	8100	5. Brenda	62	3844
	$\Sigma X_1 = 451$	$\Sigma X_1^2 = 40773$		$\Sigma X_2 = 364$	$\Sigma X_2^2 = 27694$
	$\overline{X}_1 = 90.2$			$\overline{X}_2 = 72.8$	

Figure 17.3 Summary Data Table for *t*-Test Example

$$t = \frac{(\overline{X}_1 - \overline{X}_2) - (\mu_1 - \mu_2)}{\sqrt{\left[\dfrac{\Sigma X_1^2 - \dfrac{(\Sigma X_1)^2}{n_1} + \Sigma X_2^2 - \dfrac{(\Sigma X_2)^2}{n_2}}{n_1 + n_2 - 2} \right] \left(\dfrac{1}{n_1} + \dfrac{1}{n_2} \right)}}$$

Figure 17.4 Step Two *t*-Test Computation

$$(203,401) / 5$$

$$40,680.2$$

So, $(\Sigma X_1)^2 / n_1 = 40,680.20$.

We can now just repeat these steps for $(\Sigma X_2)^2 / n_2$ to find the result:

$$(\Sigma X_2)^2 / n_2$$

$$(364)^2 / 5$$

$$(132,496) / 5$$

$$26,499.20$$

So, $(\Sigma X_2)^2 / n_2 = 26,499.20$.

$$t = \frac{(\overline{X}_1 - \overline{X}_2) - (\mu_1 - \mu_2)}{\sqrt{\left[\dfrac{\Sigma X_1^2 - \dfrac{(\Sigma X_1)^2}{n_1} + \Sigma X_2^2 - \dfrac{(\Sigma X_2)^2}{n_2}}{n_1 + n_2 - 2} \right] \left(\dfrac{1}{n_1} + \dfrac{1}{n_2} \right)}}$$

Figure 17.5 Step Three *t*-Test Computation

Step Three. At this point, we can do everything within the brackets on the top side of the numerator bar, which is shown in bold in Figure 17.5:

Now we need to bring back our sum of square calculations for both Class A (X_1) and Class B (X_2). The sum of square calculation for Class A was $\Sigma X_1^2 = 40{,}773$. And the sum of square calculation for Class B was $\Sigma X_2^2 = 27{,}694$. In this part of the formula, we are subtracting the sum of square for X_1 from the portion of the formula for X_1 that was computed in Step Two [$(\Sigma X_1)^2 / n_1 = 40{,}680.20$]. In other words, we are subtracting 40,680.20 from 40,773:

$$\Sigma X_1^2 - [(\Sigma X_1)^2 / n_1]$$

$$40{,}773 - 40{,}680.20 =$$

$$92.8.$$

We then repeat this part of the formula for X_2. We are now going to subtract the sum of square for X_2 from the portion of the formula for X_2 that was computed in Step Two [$(\Sigma X_2)^2 / n_2 = 26{,}499.20$]. In other words, we are subtracting 26,499.20 from 27,694.

$$\Sigma X_2^2 - [(\Sigma X_2)^2 / n_2]$$

$$27{,}694 - 26{,}499.20 =$$

$$1194.8$$

Step Four. Step Four is threefold, but very easy. First, we need to add both of the numbers calculated in Step Three together ($92.8 + 1194.8 = 1287.6$). Second, we need to complete the formula immediately below what we just completed doing ($n_1 + n_2 - 2$). If you remember from above, $n_1 = 5$, which indicates that there are five students in Class A; and $n_2 = 5$, which indicates that there are five students in Class B. To complete the formula you do the mathematical computation ($5 + 5 - 2 = 8$). Finally, we need to divide the first number calculated in this step (1287.6) by the second number calculated in this step (8): $1287.6 / 8 = 160.95$.

Step Five. In the fifth step of this equation, we need to calculate everything in the big parentheses to the right of the part of the equation we just finished computing. This part of the equation reads $(1 / n_1) + (1 / n_2)$. As we already know, $n_1 = 5$ and $n_2 = 5$, so we just need to compute the formula:

$$(1 / n_1) + (1 / n_2)$$

$$(1 / 5) + (1 / 5)$$

$$(.2) + (.2)$$

$$0.4$$

So, $(1 / n_1) + (1 / n_2) = 0.4$.

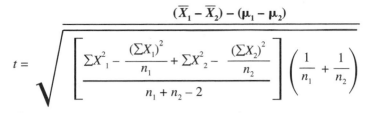

Figure 17.6 Step Seven *t*-Test Computation

Step Six. In this step, take the number calculated in the third part of Step Four (160.95) and multiply it by the number calculated in Step Five (0.4):

$$160.95 * 0.4 = 64.38$$

We now take this newly calculated number (64.38) and find its square root: $\sqrt{64.38} = 8.0237$. At this point, we have calculated everything on the bottom part of this formula.

Step Seven. The seventh step is going to calculate the top portion of the formula, or the part that is bolded in Figure 17.6

This part of the formula $(\overline{X}_1 - \overline{X}_2) - (\mu_1 - \mu_2)$ can be understood as the sample mean difference minus the population mean difference. As was previously explained, one of the assumptions of the basic *t*-test is the homogeneity of variance, so the population mean difference should equal 0. In essence, all that must be computed in this part is $(\overline{X}_1 - \overline{X}_2)$. As stated in Figure 17.3, $\overline{X}_1 = 90.2$ and $\overline{X}_2 = 72.8$. At this point, we can complete this part of the formula:

$$(\overline{X}_1 \quad \overline{X}_2) - (\mu_1 - \mu_2)$$

$$(90.2 - 72.8) - (0)$$

$$17.4 - 0$$

$$17.4$$

So, $(\overline{X}_1 - \overline{X}_2) - (\mu_1 - \mu_2) = 17.4$.

Step Eight. The final step in computing the *t*-statistic is to simply divide the calculated value from Step Six (8.0237) from the calculated value in Step Seven (17.4) or:

$$17.4 / 8.0237 =$$

$$2.168575595 \text{ or } 2.169$$

This indicates that the calculated value that we obtained for *t* is 2.169. However, we still have a couple of steps to go before we can say that we are truly finished with this example.

Step Nine. In this step we need to calculate the degrees of freedom for the *t* computed in this example. The formula for the degrees of freedom for the *t*-test is very simple. In fact, we've already computed it as part of the formula of the *t*-test in Step Four. The formula for the *t*-test df is (df = $n_1 + n_2 - 2$), or (df = 5 + 5 − 2), or 8.

Step Ten. Figure 17.7 contains the independent samples *t*-test critical value table. You'll notice that this critical value table is different from the table used to test for chi-square significance in the previous chapter. On the left-hand side is the column for the degrees of freedom. In our study, our degrees of freedom value, as calculated in Step Nine, was 8, so we need to compare the number we calculated for the *t* statistic in Step Eight, 2.169, against

df	0.10	0.05	0.01	0.005	0.001
1	6.31	12.71	63.66	636.62	363.62
2	2.92	4.30	9.93	31.60	31.60
3	2.35	3.18	5.84	12.94	12.92
4	2.13	2.78	4.60	8.61	8.61
5	2.02	2.57	4.03	6.86	6.87
6	1.94	2.45	3.71	5.96	5.96
7	1.90	2.37	3.50	5.41	5.41
8	1.86	2.31	3.36	5.04	5.04
9	1.83	2.26	3.25	4.78	4.78
10	1.81	2.27	3.17	4.59	4.59
11	1.80	2.20	3.12	4.44	4.44
12	1.78	2.18	3.06	4.32	4.32
13	1.77	2.16	3.01	4.22	4.22
14	1.76	2.15	2.98	4.14	4.14
15	1.75	2.13	2.95	4.07	4.07
16	1.75	2.12	2.92	4.02	4.02
17	1.74	2.11	2.90	3.97	3.97
18	1.73	2.10	2.88	3.92	3.92
19	1.73	2.09	2.86	3.88	3.88
20	1.73	2.09	2.85	3.85	3.85

The entries in this table were computed by the authors.

Figure 17.7 *t*-Test Critical Value Table (Two-Tailed Test)

the numbers in row 8 on this chart. If 2.169 (calculated value) is greater than the number listed in the columns (critical values), our *t*-test is statistically significant at that *p*-value level (shown at the top of each column). The first column represents $p < .10$, which is not statistically significant as discussed in Chapter 15. The critical value in this column was 1.860, and our calculated *t* statistic was 2.169, which is greater than 1.860, so we would consider our *t* significant at the $p < .10$ level. However, .10 does not meet the 95% confidence interval discussed in the previous chapter, so we would not consider a *t*-test statistically significant at this *p*-value. The second column represents $p < .05$, which is statistically significant as discussed in Chapter 15. The critical value in this column was 2.306, and our calculated *t* statistic was 2.169, which is not greater than 2.306, so our *t*-test is not statistically significant at the $p < .05$ level. In essence, our *t*-test is not statistically significant. We cannot be 95% confident that there is a difference between the two classes and their midterm examination scores, which means we must accept the null hypothesis that style of dress (fashionable and 1970s dress) did not affect the students' scores on the midterm examination.

Computer Printouts of the Independent *t*-Test

Now that we have examined how independent *t*-test can be calculated by hand, we will examine what output from two statistical computer programs, SPSS and SAS, looks like as well.

SPSS AND *t*-TESTS

Using SPSS to compute an independent *t*-test is fairly easy as long as you know how to follow instructions, so let's get started. First, open up your SPSS student version and then locate the file on the CD-ROM in the SPSS folder called "*t*-test." When you open this file you will see two variables listed "class" and "score." Class is the variable name given to either Class A (fashionable dress) or Class B (1970s dress). You'll notice though that the Classes are only represented by the numbers 1 (Class A) and 2 (Class B). Remember, a statistics program can only understand numbers, so it's up to you as a researcher to remember how you classified the two groups when you are inputting the data. The "score" variable is the score that each participant received on the midterm examination.

To conduct the *t*-test, go to the menu bar at the top of your screen and click on "Analyze." When you click on "Analyze," a dropdown menu will appear. Go to the fourth category on this menu, "Compare Means," and scroll over the arrow and another menu will appear to the right. The third option on the "Compare Means" menu is "Independent Samples T-Test"; click on it. At this point, the "Independent Samples T-Test" dialogue box will appear on your screen. You'll notice that the screen has three major boxes on it. On the left-hand side is a box with your variables listed in it already. On the upper right is a box labeled "Test Variable(s)," and below that box is a small box labeled "Grouping Variable." Any dependent variables that you are attempting to analyze are placed in the "Test Variable(s)" box. Click on the dependent variable for this example "scores." When "scores" is highlighted blue, click the right arrow between the variable list box and the "Test Variable(s)" box. After clicking the right arrow, "scores" should now appear in the "Test Variable(s)" box. Next, we need to send our independent variable "class" to the "Grouping Variable" box as well. When conducting a *t*-test, your independent variable will always be placed in the "Grouping Variable" box and your dependent variable(s) will always be placed in the "Test Variable(s)" box.

You will notice at this point that you cannot click OK yet because you have not completely finished telling the computer what to do. Click on the word "class" in the "Grouping Variable" box if it is not already highlighted blue. In the "Grouping Variable" box, click the button labeled "Define Groups." When you click on "Define Groups," the "Define Groups" dialogue box will pop-up. In the "Define Groups" dialogue box you need to tell the computer which two numbers in the variable "class" you are comparing. Remember, a *t*-test can only be used if a nominal variable has two levels, so you need to tell your computer what numbers you chose to represent those two levels. As mentioned above, we have chosen the numbers 1 and 2 to represent Class A (1) and Class B (2). We could have chosen 0 and 1 or 8 and 9—the numbers don't matter to the computer—what matters is that we clearly identify them to the computer. So, in the "Define Groups" dialogue box, you'll notice two places for you to enter information beside "Group 1" and "Group 2." Next to "Group 1" type the number "1" in the box, and next to "Group 2" type the number "2" in the box. Once you have clearly labeled the groups, you can then click on the "Continue" button. You will now be looking again at the "Independent Samples T-Test" dialogue box. At this point, you can click "OK." If for some reason you cannot click "OK," you have not entered your grouping variables correctly, so repeat the steps above and attempt to find out where you made your mistake. The results from SPSS in Figure 17.8 will appear when you have clicked "OK."

The first box that you will see in the results is simply a "Group Statistics" box. In this box you will see that the N, mean, standard deviation, and standard error means are listed for you for both Class A and Class B. The second box, or the "Independent Samples Test" box, is where the primary information about the *t*-test itself is located. The first thing we have to do when analyzing our computer printouts is to determine if we have met the assumption discussed earlier called the "homogeneity of variance" assumption for *t*-tests.

The second column in the "Independent Samples Test" box is labeled "Levene's Test for Equality of Variances." The Levene's Test for Equality of Variances tests the homogeneity of variance assumption. If the Levene's test is statistically significant, then the assumption has not been met. Remember, the assumption states that the variances would be equal, so

T-Test

Group Statistics

	Class	N	Mean	Std. Deviation	Std. Error Mean
Test Scores	Class A	5	90.2000	4.8166	2.1541
	Class B	5	72.8000	17.2829	7.7292

Independent Samples Test

		Levene's Test for Equality of Variances		t-test for Equality of Means					95% Confidence Interval of the Difference	
		F	Sig.	t	df	Sig. (2-tailed)	Mean Difference	Std. Error Difference	Lower	Upper
Test Scores	Equal variances assumed	6.053	.039	2.169	8	.062	17.4000	8.0237	−1.1027	35.9027
	Equal variances not assumed			2.169	4.618	.087	17.4000	8.0237	−3.7501	38.5501

Figure 17.8 SPSS Results for *t*-Test Example

when the two groups' variances are not equal, the assumption is not met. In the "Levene's Test for Equality of Variances" column, you will notice two subcolumns "F" and "Sig." If "Sig." is below .05, then the Levene's test for equality of variances is significant and the basic assumption of the *t*-test has been violated, so equal variances cannot be assumed, which is the second row listed.

So, what does it mean when your *t*-test that equal variances cannot be assumed? Well, it means that the *t*-test that we calculated by hand in the example has to be tweaked since this assumption was violated. If you look at the "Independent Samples Test" box, you'll notice that there are *t*-test results for both "equal variances assumed" and "equal variances cannot be assumed." If our Levene's test for equal variances is statistically significant ($p < .05$), we must report the *t*-test on the lower level. The biggest change that occurs is how we report our degrees of freedom. By lowering the degrees of freedom from 8 (like we calculated) to 4.618 (as seen for the "equal variances cannot be assumed"), we make it harder for a *t*-test to be statistically significant to protect against possible Type I errors. If you look at the significance levels for "equal variances assumed" ($p = .062$) and "equal variances cannot be assumed" ($p = .087$), you'll notice that the *p*-value for equal variances being assumed is lower (greater chance of reaching statistical significance) than the *p*-value for equal variances cannot be assumed (less of a chance of reaching statistical significance). You'll notice that the *t*-value, the "Mean Difference," and the "Standard Error Difference" are all identical; the only values that are affected by the homogeneity of variance assumption are the "df" and "Sig." values.

SAS AND *t*-TESTS

When using SAS, all commands are called "PROC" or procedure commands. To calculate a *t*-test using SAS, you use the "PROC TTEST" or Procedure T-Test. The exact SAS code needed to run the *t*-test for the example in this chapter would be:

PROC TTEST;

CLASS CLASS;

VAR SCORE;

SAS calls the independent variable a "CLASS" or classification variable, so seeing the two CLASS statements may look odd, but that was just because we labeled the variable CLASS as well. The dependent variables go after the VAR statement in SAS. The SAS printout for our example can be seen in Figure 17.9

You will find all of the same information on the SAS printout that you did on the SPSS printout, but in a slightly different order. Since it is a little hard to find specific information on the printout, we've bolded the information you need to report to make it easier to find the information. In the first set of SAS printouts, you'll notice the basic descriptive statistics. Once again you can see the N, mean, standard deviation, and standard error. At the bottom of the SAS printout you can find a test for equality of variance. You'll notice that the test SPSS and SAS come up with different calculated values for this test because they use two different tests. SPSS uses the Levene test for equality of variances and SAS uses what is called a Folded F' test to examine the equality of variances. Despite the fact that SAS and SPSS use two different tests, both came up with the same conclusion—the homogeneity of variance assumption for the *t*-test was not met.

```
                        The TTEST Procedure

                           Statistics

                     Lower CL          Upper CL  Lower CL           Upper CL
Variable  CLASS       N     Mean    Mean    Mean   Std Dev  Std Dev  Std Dev  Std Err

SCORE            1    5   84.219   90.2   96.181   2.8858   4.8166   13.841   2.1541
SCORE            2    5   51.34    72.8   94.26    10.355   17.283   49.663   7.7292
SCORE     Diff (1-2)     -1.103   17.4   35.903   8.5693   12.687   24.305   8.0237


                             T-Tests

        Variable   Method        Variances    DF   t Value   Pr > |t|

        SCORE      Pooled        Equal         8     2.17     0.0620
        SCORE      Satterthwaite Unequal     4.62     2.17     0.0868


                      Equality of Variances

        Variable   Method      Num DF   Den DF   F Value   Pr > F

        SCORE      Folded F       4        4      12.88     0.0297
```

Figure 17.9 SAS Results for *t*-Test Example

Above the "Equality of Variances" SAS results are the two sets of *t*-tests (one for variances equal and one for variances unequal). You'll notice that the unequal variances option for the *t*-test is the same for both SPSS and SAS. Once again, notice that the ultimate results from both SPSS and SAS are identical in their presentation of the *t*-test although they use different statistical tests to determine the homogeneity of variance assumption for the *t*-test. Now that we have examined the *t*-test test itself, let's see how a researcher would writeup this finding using APA style in a results section of an article.

APA Write-Up (SPSS)

An independent *t*-test was conducted to determine if an instructor's dress in a classroom (fashionable vs. out-of-date dress) affected the scores students received on their midterm examinations. The Levene's test for equality of variances was significant ($F = 6.05$, $p < .04$), so equality of variances cannot be assumed, $t(4.62) = 2.17$, $p > .05$.

APA Write-Up (SAS)

An independent *t*-test was conducted to determine if an instructor's dress in a classroom (fashionable vs. 1970s dress) affected the scores students received on their midterm examinations. The Folded F' test was significant, $F(4, 4) = 12.88$, $p < .03$. Since the Folded F' test was significant, equality of variances cannot be assumed: $t(4.62) = 2.17$, $p > .05$.

Discussion of Findings

So now that we have completed the APA write-ups you may be wondering what they actually tell us. To understand what the *t*-test tell us, we must go back to the original purpose we had for conducting the *t*-test. In our example, we had a school teacher who wanted to determine if altering her dress between modern fashions in one class and outdated clothing from the 1970s in the other class would affect student learning. To test student learning, the teacher used the midterm examination as a benchmark. Based on the *t*-test that we conducted, no difference was noticed on the students' midterm examinations between the two classes. In a difference test, when we say that something is not significant or greater than .05, we're saying that a difference did not occur within our sample. In this case, the teacher's dress, whether fashionable or from the 1970s, did not change how students performed on the midterm examination.

Biological Sex and Communication Apprehension

In this example we wanted to determine if females and males differed in their reported communication apprehension levels. To test for a possible difference between females and males on the Personal Report of Communication Apprehension-24, we used the nominal variable biological sex and the interval variable communication apprehension. Figure 17.10 shows the findings from the SPSS results, and Figure 17.11 shows the findings from the SAS results.

Again, notice that the values calculated for *t* are identical in both the SPSS and SAS printouts. Also, notice that SPSS and SAS use two different tests when testing for the homogeneity of variance. You'll notice that once again the equal variances assumption cannot be assumed in this example either, so when reporting the *t*-test it is necessary to report the test with the revised degrees of freedom for unequal variances.

T-Test

Group Statistics

	Biological Sex	N	Mean	Std. Deviation	Std. Error Mean
bigca	Male	177	62.7910	15.19406	1.14206
	Female	137	66.3504	19.04738	1.62733

Independent Samples Test

		Levene's Test for Equality of Variances		t-test for Equality of Means						95% Confidence Interval of the Difference	
		F	Sig.	t	df	Sig. (2-tailed)	Mean Difference	Std. Error Difference	Lower	Upper	
bigca	Equal variances assumed	6.164	.014	−1.842	312	.066	−3.55940	1.93239	−7.36157	.24276	
	Equal variances not assumed			−1.790	255.133	.075	−3.55940	1.98809	−7.47455	.35574	

Figure 17.10 SPSS Results of Sex and CA *t*-Test

```
                          The TTEST Procedure

                              Statistics

                               Lower CI            Upper CL  Lower CI              Upper CL
Variable  SEX          N      Mean      Mean       Mean      Std Dev  Std Dev      Std Dev  Std Err

BIGCA                1 177    60.537    62.791     65.045    13.759   15.194       16.966   1.1421
BIGCA                2 137    63.132    66.35      69.569    17.028   19.047       21.615   1.6273
BIGCA     Diff (1-2)          -7.362    -3.559     0.2428    15.747   16.982       18.427   1.9324


                              T-Tests

          Variable   Method        Variances    DF    t Value   Pr > |t|

          BIGCA      Pooled        Equal        312    -1.84     0.0664
          BIGCA      Satterthwaite Unequal      255    -1.79     0.0746


                          Equality of Variances

          Variable   Method     Num DF    Den DF    F Value    Pr > F

          BIGCA      Folded F      136       176      1.57     0.0048
```

Figure 17.11 SAS Results of Sex and CA *t*-Test

APA WRITE-UP (SPSS)

An independent *t*-test was conducted to determine if an individual's level of reported communication apprehension differed based on biological sex (male and female). The Levene's test for equality of variances was significant ($F = 6.14$, $p < .05$), so equality of variances cannot be assumed: $t(255.13) = -1.79$, $p > .05$.

APA WRITE-UP (SAS)

An independent *t*-test was conducted to determine if an individual's level of reported communication apprehension differed based on biological sex (male and female). The Folded F' test was significant: $F(136, 176) = 1.57$, $p < .005$. Since the Folded F' test was significant, equality of variances cannot be assumed: $t(255) = -1.79$, $p > .05$.

Discussion of the Weber, Fornash, Corrigan, and Neupauer Article

To help you further understand the concept of the independent samples *t*-test, we have included an article on the CD-ROM that accompanies this textbook that utilizes the statistical test. The 2004 article by Keith Weber, Bennie Fornash, Michael Corrigan, and Nicholas Neupauer entitled "The Effect of Interest on Recall: An Experiment" can be found in the folder titled "articles." To view this article, you will need to download a copy of the Adobe Acrobat Reader (http://www.adobe.com/products/acrobat/readermain.html) if you do not already have this program installed on your computer. We strongly encourage you to read the article first and then read our analysis of the article. The goal of this process is to make sure you understand how to read and interpret research results related to *t*-tests.

ARTICLE PURPOSE

Have you ever had to sit through a lecture where the professor used examples that were very outdated and didn't mean a lot to you? Apparently these researchers had as well, and they wanted to determine if these outdated examples affected student learning. The basic goal of this project was to determine if presenting interest-based examples (examples that are meaningful to the student, are something the students know about so they can actually discuss the examples openly, and are examples that clearly make a difference in everyday life) create more interested students in the classroom and end up with students who perform better on subsequent tests.

METHODOLOGY

In this study, the researchers divided participants into two groups and showed them a 10-minute video with a lecturer talking about public relations. In one video, the instructor (a male in his mid-30s) used examples that are not current but exist in most public relations textbooks (P. T. Barnum, Edward Bernays, and Ivy Ledbetter Lee). In the second video, the instructor (the same person as in the first video) used contemporary personalities such as Vince McMahon (wrestling promoter), Ray Lewis (professional football player), and Sean "Puffy" Combs (musician/entertainer/entrepreneur). The goal of this second video was to use examples that students would be familiar with and therefore, theoretically, cause them to be more interested in the course content as well.

After both groups watched the 10-minute videos, the groups were given a seven-item multiple choice "quiz" to test their ability to understand the actual content from the videos. The groups also filled out a learner empowerment scale that measured the three concepts that represent interest-based examples (meaningfulness, competence, and impact).

The participants also filled out a nonverbal immediacy test to determine if one group perceived the lecturer from the video as being more nonverbally immediate (and thus skewing the results from the examples). To test this notion, the researchers conducted an independent *t*-test and did not find a significant difference between the textbook example and modern example lecturer's nonverbal immediacy. This indicates that the lecturer did not alter his nonverbal communication significantly between the taping of one video to the next.

RESULTS

The first hypothesis in this study stated that "Lectures utilizing interest-based examples should result in more interested participants" (p. 118). To examine this hypothesis, the researchers conducted an independent *t*-test to determine if students' interest in the videos (dependent variable) was different based on whether they watched the textbook based examples lecture versus the contemporary examples lecture (independent variable). The researchers reported that the students who watched the video with the contemporary examples scored significantly higher on the interest scale than those students who watched the video with the traditional textbook examples. In other words, students are more interested in lectures that have examples they can relate to in a classroom. If you look at the way the authors of the article presented their results, you'll notice that they presented the *t*-test as we previously discussed in this chapter and then presented the actual means for each group since the difference was significant. While presenting the means is necessary, we strongly encourage you to always present both the mean and the standard deviation because they influence the meaningfulness of the findings. When presenting means in an article, it should look something like this (*M* = #, *SD* = #). Notice that "M" and "SD" are both capitalized and italicized when presenting them in a research article.

The second hypothesis in this study predicted that "Lectures utilizing interest-based examples should result in participants with higher scores on subsequent tests of cognitive recall" (p. 118). To examine this hypothesis, the researchers conducted an independent *t*-test to determine if students' scores on the seven-item quiz (dependent variable) was different based on whether they watched the textbook-based examples lecture versus the contemporary examples lecture (independent variable). The researchers reported that the students who watched the video with the contemporary examples scored significantly higher on the quiz than those students who watched the video with the traditional textbook examples. In other words, students will remember more and be able to recall it on a quiz when they listen to lectures that have examples they can relate to in a classroom.

The researchers then break the first hypothesis down and look at all three aspects of interest separately in three post hoc (after the fact) tests. In the post hoc analysis, the researchers conducted three more independent *t*-tests examining the three factors of interest-based examples (competence, meaningfulness, and impact). The researchers report that they found differences between the two lecture groups on competence and meaningfulness, but not on impact. In other words, these results indicate that students in classrooms with modern examples feel that the examples are more meaningful to them and therefore are more competent to discuss these examples than students who listened to examples that came from traditional textbooks. However, the impact of both the contemporary and textbook examples did not differ between the two groups.

Overall, this article is very helpful because it emphasizes that college professors must stay on top of current events if they are going to be effective and affective teachers in the classroom. Sticking with examples that exist in the textbook and dismissing the notion that modern examples are needed will only do a disservice to the learning environment.

Calculating Effect Sizes

As mentioned in both Chapters 6 and 15, one of the most important aspects related to difference research is the effect size, or the magnitude of the difference. While statistics allows researchers to find very small differences between two groups, the magnitude of this difference is not always known. In the Weber et al. (2003) article, the researchers report that there was a statistically significant difference between the two groups (modern vs. textbook examples) and how they performed on a 10-item quiz. The experimental group (modern examples) had a mean of 4.6, and the control group (textbook examples) had a mean of 3.1. As researchers we have to ask ourselves: is a difference between 4.6 and 3.1 that big? Statistically, the relationship may be meaningful, but how big a difference are we talking about here? For this reason it is important to calculate an effect size any time one is calculating a difference using an independent *t*-test. To test for an independent samples effect size, we use this formula:

$$d = t \sqrt{\frac{N_1 + N_2}{N_1 N_2}}$$

t-Test Effect Size Formula

You'll notice that all of the information we need to compute the effect size for the *t*-test from the Weber et al. (2003) article is located within the article itself. First, we need the computed *t*-value, which was 4.8 in the study. Second, we need the number of participants in the study ($N = 122$). The researchers say in their article that every participant was randomly put into either the experimental condition or the control condition, so we can surmise that each group had 61 participants. Often group sizes are varied, so knowing how many people were in each group is important because we are able to determine our N variables that way: $N_1 = 61$ and $N_2 = 61$. Once we have both of these pieces of information, it's simply a matter of completing the formula.

Step 1. The first step for computing d is to handle everything within the square-root function first. First, let's solve the information in the numerator ($N_1 + N_2$):

$$N_1 + N_2$$
$$61 + 61 = 122$$

Second, we want to solve the information within the denominator ($N_1 N_2$):

$$N_1 N_2$$
$$61 \times 61 = 3721$$

Third, we divide the result from step 1 (122) by the result from step 2 (3721):

$$(N_1 + N_2) / (N_1 N_2)$$
$$122 / 3721 = 0.0327868852$$

Finally, we take the square root of the result we found in the third step (0.0327868852):

$$\sqrt{(N_1 + N_2) / (N_1 N_2)}$$

$$\sqrt{0.0327868852} = 0.181071492$$

Step 2. The second step is to take the calculated *t*-test value reported in the article (4.8) and multiply it by the number we found in step last part of Step 1

(0.181071492):

$$t\sqrt{(N_1 + N_2) / (N_1 N_2)}$$

$$4.8 \times 0.181071492 = 0.869143162$$

or, Cohen's *d* = 0.87

To interpret *t*-test effect sizes, use the following scale (Green & Salkind, 2004):

0.2—small effect size

0.5—medium effect size

0.8—large effect size

Based on this scale, the effect found (Cohen's *d* = 0.87) for the quiz scores differences between the group who had modern examples (*M* = 4.6) and the group who had the standard textbook examples (*M* = 3.1) is large.

Conclusion

In this chapter we have examined how to compute a *t*-test by hand, how to compute and interpret computer results of a *t*-test in both SPSS and SAS, and how to write up a *t*-test using APA style. We have seen the *t*-test used in four different examples, and finally discussed how to compute a *t*-test effect size.

KEY TERMS

Cohen's *d*   *t*-Test

REFERENCES

Cohen, J. (1988). *Statistical power analysis for the behavioral sciences* (2nd ed.). Hillsdale, NJ: Lawrence Erlbaum.

Weber, K., Fornash, B., Corrigan, M, & Neupauer, N. C. (2003). The effect of interest on recall: An experiment. *Communication Research Reports, 20*, 116–123.

FURTHER READING

Abramson, J. H., & Abramson, Z. H. (2001). *Making sense of data: A self-instruction manual on the interpretation of epidemiological data* (3rd ed.). New York: Oxford.

Bruning, J. L., & Kintz, B. L. (1997). *Computational handbook of statistics* (4th ed.). New York: Longman.

Delwiche, L. D., & Slaughter, S. J. (2003). *The little SAS book: A primer* (3rd ed.). Cary, NC: SAS Press.

Gravetter, F. J., & Wallnau, L. B. (2000). *Statistics for the behavioral sciences* (5th ed.). Belmont, CA: Wadsworth/Thomson Learning.

Green, S. B., & Salkind, N. J. (2004). *Using SPSS for Windows and Macintosh: Analyzing and understanding data* (4th ed.). Upper Saddle River, NJ: Prentice Hall.

Hocking, J. E., Stacks, D. W., & McDermott, S. T. (2003). *Communication research* (3rd ed.). Boston: Allyn and Bacon.

Howell, D. C. (1997). *Statistical methods for psychology* (4th ed.). Belmont, CA: Duxbury Press.

Huff, D. (1954). *How to lie with statistics.* New York: W. W. Norton & Company.

Keller, D. K. (2006). *The Tao of statistics: A path to understanding (with no math).* Thousand Oaks, CA: Sage.

Pyrczak, F. (1999). *Statistics with a sense of humor: A humorous workbook and guide to study skills* (2nd ed.). Los Angeles: Pyrczak.

Salkind, N. J. (2004). *Statistics for people who (think they) hate statistics* (2nd ed.). Thousand Oaks, CA: Sage.

SAS Institute. (2004). *SAS 9.1 Companion for Windows.* Cary, NC: SAS Press.

Singleton, R. A., Jr., & Straits, B. C. (1999). *Approach to social research* (3rd ed.). New York: Oxford University Press.

Tabachnick, B. G., & Fidell, L. S. (2001). *Using multivariate statistics* (4th ed.). Boston: Allyn and Bacon.

Trochim, W. M. K. (2000). *The research methods knowledge base* (2nd ed.). Cincinnati, OH: Atomic Dog. Online available at: http://www.socialresearchmethods.net/

One-Way Analysis of Variance (ANOVA)

When we conducted a *t*-test in the last chapter, one variable had to be nominal with no more than two independent groups and their scores on one dependent interval/ratio variable. A one-way ANOVA, on the other hand, has one nominal variable with two or more independent groups and their scores on one dependent interval/ratio variable. Once again the nominal variable (with two or more groups) is the independent variable, and the interval/ratio variable is the dependent variable. A group is considered independent when one participant's place in one of the groups being tested does not influence anyone else's placement within that group or another group. In essence, the groups being tested are not related to each other. For example, one common nominal variable used in one-way ANOVA is political affiliation. With the nominal variable, political affiliation, as we have defined it in this text, there are four groups: Democrat, Republican, other political party affiliation, and not registered to vote. If the first participant in the sample is a Democrat, then the second participant in the sample could equally be a Democrat, Republican, other political party affiliation, or not registered to vote because the first participant's political affiliation has no impact on the second participant's political affiliation at all. In addition to the two or more groups being independent from each other, every participant should have scores on two variables: the grouping/nominal variable (political affiliation) and a test/dependent variable. In the case of a one-way ANOVA, the goal is to determine if the two or more groups' means differ on an interval/ratio variable of some kind.

The groups function as the independent variable, and the interval/ratio variable is the dependent variable. For example, maybe we wanted to determine if people differ based on political affiliation (independent variable) in their levels of ethnocentrism (dependent variable).

The one-way analysis of variance is part of the family of statistical tests that belong to the general linear model (GLM) family. While we wanted to mention here that the one-way ANOVA is a GLM test, we will discuss what the GLM is and how it functions when we talk about regressions in Chapter 20. Now that we've explained the basic purpose of a one-way ANOVA, let's examine an example of a one-way ANOVA.

Case Study Introduction

Have you ever noticed how some rooms just make you feel very sleepy or physically drained? What if the color of the room caused this kind of reaction? In this example, a nonverbal communication researcher wants to find out if the color of a room affects the speed with which a person can take a standard 10-item test. Using the same 10-item test, the researcher places 12 participants randomly into one of three rooms: white, yellow, and blue. When all was said and done, the researcher tested the time (in minutes) for the four participants in the white room, the four participants in the yellow room, and the four participants in the blue room.

In the previous chapter, we examined what was necessary to find a difference between a nominal variable with two levels (e.g., female and male) on an interval/ratio variable (communication apprehension). In this chapter, we will examine what is necessary to find a difference between a nominal variable with two or more levels (white, yellow, and blue) on an interval or ratio variable of some kind (time in minutes to complete the test). To perform this type of test, we calculate what is called a one-way analysis of variance (ANOVA).

One-Way ANOVA Background Information

The one-way ANOVA allows researchers to compare two or more groups on an interval variable using one test. If we attempted to do the example here using t-tests, we would have to conduct three t-tests with three unique null hypotheses:

H_o: $\mu_{white} = \mu_{yellow}$ ← mean time (in minutes) to take a test in the white room is equal to the mean time (in minutes) to take a test in the yellow room

H_o: $\mu_{white} = \mu_{blue}$ ← mean time (in minutes) to take a test in the white room is equal to the mean time (in minutes) to take a test in the blue room

H_o: $\mu_{yellow} = \mu_{blue}$ ← mean time (in minutes) to take a test in the yellow room is equal to the mean time (in minutes) to take a test in the blue room

While three groups and three t-tests may not sound like a bad proposition, if we were comparing seven groups we would need 21 separate t-tests. Not only would 21 tests be time-consuming, but, more important, it would also be inherently flawed because in each t-test we accept a 5% chance of our conclusion being wrong (when we test for $p = .05$). So, in 21 tests we would *expect* (by probability) that one test would give us a false result. And frankly, we don't like those odds at all. In a one-way ANOVA, the null hypothesis reads like this:

H_o: $\mu_{white} = \mu_{yellow} = \mu_{blue}$ ← mean time (in minutes) to take a test in the white room is equal to the mean time (in minutes) to take a test in the yellow room, which is equal to the mean time (in minutes) to take a test in the blue room.

$$SS_{total} = \sum x^2 - \frac{G^2}{N} \qquad\qquad df_{total} = N - 1$$

$$SS_{between} = \frac{\sum T^2}{n} - \frac{G^2}{N} \qquad df_{between} = k - 1$$

$$SS_{within} = \sum SS_{inside\ each\ treatment} \qquad df_{within} = N - k$$

$$F = \frac{MS_{between}}{MS_{within}} \quad \text{Where each } MS = \frac{SS}{df}$$

Figure 18.1 One-Way ANOVA Formula

Your hypothesis would then predict that at least one of the pairs (white and yellow, white and blue, and yellow and blue) is not equal, or:

$$H_1: \mu_{white} \neq \mu_{yellow} \neq \mu_{blue}$$

Instead of doing three tests or 21 tests, the one-way ANOVA lets us perform one simple test to examine differences.

Now that we've discussed a couple of the basic aspects of the one-way ANOVA itself, let's look at the underlying assumptions of the one-way ANOVA:

1. The dependent variable must be an interval/ratio variable.

2. The independent variable must be a nominal variable.

3. The dependent variable (time to take the test in minutes) should be normally distributed in the independent variable levels (white room, yellow room, and blue room). Specifically, the distributions for all of the populations should not have a high skewness or kurtosis. In a real world situation, it is recommended that each nominal category have at least 30 participants. (Since we are only performing an example in this chapter, we do not have 30 participants in each category to make the math easier to compute.)

4. The populations for all groupings in the independent variable (white room, yellow room, and blue room) should have equal variances. If the population in the largest group has no more than 1.5 times the number of participants than the number of participants in the smallest group, you will not violate the homogeneity assumption (Stevens, 1986).

5. Finally, the participants contributing data should represent a random sample drawn from the population of interest.

The above assumptions are extremely important because if one assumption is violated, the meaning of the one-way ANOVA is lost. Now that we've explained what a one-way ANOVA is and what the basic assumptions of the one-way ANOVA are, we can look at the basic one-way ANOVA formula given in Figure 18.1.

Do not be scared by the formula, it is just as easy to calculate the one-way ANOVA as it was to calculate a chi-square or t-test. Most of the one-way ANOVA formula is simply computing some basic descriptive statistics like we did in Chapter 8 and then plugging those answers into the formula as we go along.

Step-by-Step Approach to the One-Way ANOVA

As we discussed above, the basic hypothesis being examined in this example is that there is a difference in the time it takes participants to take a test in a white room versus a yellow

White	Yellow	Blue
5	5	8
6	6	10
5	10	10
4	7	8

Figure 18.2 Participant Scores from Chapter Example

White	Yellow	Blue
5	5	8
6	6	10
5	10	10
4	7	8
T = 5 + 6 + 5 + 4 = 20	5 + 6 + 10 + 7 = 28	8 + 10 + 10 + 8 = 36

Figure 18.3 Step One One-Way ANOVA

$$SS_{between} = \frac{\sum T^2}{n} - \frac{G^2}{N} \qquad df_{between} = k - 1$$

Figure 18.4 Sum of Squares Between Formula

room versus a blue room. Figure 18.2 portrays the raw data from all 12 participants in this study.

Step One. The first step in computing a one-way ANOVA is to determine the $\sum X$ for each of the three groups. To find the $\sum X$ or T for each group, you add up each participant's score (in minutes). Figure 18.3 illustrates how this is accomplished.

Step Two. In the next two steps you will calculate the part of the formula represented in Figure 18.4.

The computed value you will attain in this step is called the sum of squares between (SSB). The SSB measures two different phenomena: (1) the differences between the groups that have been caused by the treatment effects (i.e., the difference in time it takes the participants to take the 10-item test caused by being either in a white, yellow, or blue room) and (2) the differences between the treatments that are simply due to chance. In this step we will calculate the first part of the SSB formula ($\sum T^2 / n$). To compute this formula, simply take the T values computed in Figure 18.4 and then square them and divide them by the number of participants in each column (4). So to compute the formula (T^2 / n) for the white room group, you take the T value found in Step One (20) and square that value ($20 \times 20 = 400$). You then take 400 and divide it by n (the number of participants in the group or 4), or $400 / 4 = 100$. So, for the white group $T^2 / n = 100$. You now compute this number for the other two groups as well:

$$\sum T^2 / n$$

$$((20)^2 / 4) + ((28)^2 / 4) + ((36)^2 / 4)$$

$$(400 / 4) + (784 / 4) + (1296 / 4)$$

$$100 + 196 + 324$$

$$620$$

So, $\sum T^2 / n = 620$.

Step Three. We now need to compute the part of the SSB formula that is represented by G^2 / N. G is represented by the formula ΣT, which is simply taking the T values found in Step One and adding them together to create a summed total. The T score for the white room group was 20; the T score for the yellow group was 28; and the T score for the blue group was 36. When you add these three numbers together (20 + 28 + 36), you get a total of 84. Now that we have attained G, we need to square that number ($84^2 = 7056$). The number we get for G^2 is then divided by the total number of participants in the study ($N = 12$), or 7056 / 12 = 588.

Step Four. The next step of the one-way ANOVA will give us the actual value for the SSB. To compute the SSB, you have to take the value created in Step Two (620) and subtract it from the value created in Step Three (588):

$$(\Sigma T^2 / n) - (G^2 / N)$$

$$620 - 588 = 32$$

So for our example the SSB is equal to 32.

Step Five. In this step we will determine another very important part of the one-way ANOVA puzzle called the sum of squares within (SSW). Figure 18.5 represents the formula portion for the SS_{within}.

Inside each condition or group tested in a one-way ANOVA we have participants who are treated exactly the same. In other words, the researcher treats all of the participants who take the test in the white room the same, so the researcher does nothing that could cause the individuals to have different scores within that room. When you look at the scores from Figure 18.2, you will notice that people in the white room took the test at different speeds. Why did the four people in the white room take the test at different speeds? Well, the only answer that is plausible is that the people in the white room took the test at different speeds purely by chance. In other words, the SSW provides a measure of how much difference in the time it took to take the 10-item test used in this study is simply due to chance.

To find the SSW, you have to compute a simple formula which we have done before $\Sigma SS_{inside\ each\ treatment}$. In other words, for each group of participants, we are going to determine the sum of squares for that group (white, yellow, and blue), and then add the three scores together to come up with the SSW.

To calculate the SSW, you must first find the mean for each group. In Figure 18.3, you take the T value computed for each group and then divide the T value by the number of participants in that group (n = 4). For example, in the white group the T value is equal to 20 and there were 4 participants in the group, so to find the mean you simply divide 20 by 4 (20 / 4 = 5). You then repeat this procedure for the other two groups: yellow (28 / 4 = 7) and blue (36 / 4 = 9).

Once you have the averages computed, you then subtract the individual scores for each participant in a group from the group average and then square that number (just like we did in Chapter 8 when we first introduced the sum of squares concept). So, for the white group you take the first participant's score (5) and subtract that score from the mean score (5), or 5 – 5 = 0. You then take this score (0) and square it. Of course, 0×0 is always going to equal 0. Let's follow the same procedure for the second participant in the white group. Take the second participant's score (6) and subtract that from the mean score (5), or 5 – 6 = –1. You then take this score (–1) and square it. Of course, $–1 \times –1$ is always going to equal 1. Don't forget, when

$$SS_{within} = \Sigma SS_{inside\ each\ treatment} \qquad df_{within} = N - k$$

Figure 18.5 Sum of Squares Within Formula

you multiply a negative number by a negative number the two negatives cancel each other out. Let's now take the third participant's score (5) in the white group and subtract that from the mean score (5), or $5 - 5 = 0$. You then take this score (0) and square it. Of course, 0×0 is always going to equal 0. Lastly, we can take the fifth participant's score (4) in the white group and subtract it from the mean score (5), or $5 - 4 = 1$. You then take this score (1) and square it. Of course, 1×1 is always going to equal 1. You then add these four scores together: $0 + 1 + 0 + 1 = 2$, so the sum of squares for the white room is 2. You can now repeat these steps for both the yellow and blue room groups. This process has been completed in Figure 18.6.

To compute the overall score for the SSW, you simply take the four scores calculated in Figure 18.5 and add them together $(2 + 14 + 4 = 20)$. In our example, the SSW = 20.

Step Six. In this step we will determine the Sum of Squares Total (SS_{total}). To calculate the SS_{total}, you simply add the $SS_{between}$ from Step Four (32) and the SS_{within} from Step Five (20) together:

$$SS_{total} = SS_{between} + SS_{within}$$
$$32 + 20 = 52$$

So for this example, the $SS_{total} = 52$.

Step Seven. At this point, we need to compute the degrees of freedom for the one-way ANOVA. The one-way ANOVA has two different types of degrees of freedom (between and within). To calculate the between df, the formula is $K - 1$, or the number of groups (white, yellow, and blue) being examined in your study minus one $(3 - 1 = 2)$. In this example, the between df = 2. To calculate the within df, the formula is $N - K$, or the total number of participants in a study (12 in our example) minus the number of groups (3 in our example) being examined in your study $(12 - 3 = 9)$. In this example, the within df = 9.

	Group Average		Participant's Score				
White Room	5	–	5	=	0^2	=	0
	5	–	6	=	-1^2	=	1
	5	–	5	=	0^2	=	0
	5	–	4	=	1^2	=	1
					Sum		2

	Group Average		Participant's Score				
Yellow Room	7	–	5	=	2^2	=	4
	7	–	6	=	1^2	=	1
	7	–	10	=	-3^2	=	9
	7	–	7	=	0^2	=	0
					Sum		14

	Group Average		Participant's Score				
Blue Room	9	–	8	=	1^2	=	1
	9	–	10	=	-1^2	=	1
	9	–	10	=	-1^2	=	1
	9	–	8	=	1^2	=	1
					Sum		4

Figure 18.6 Computing the Sum of Squares Within

On this chart, you will notice that the df numbers run along the top and down the lefthand side of the table. The df numbers that run along the top of the chart (columns) represent the degrees of freedom numerator (df between), and the df numbers that are on the left hand side of the chart (rows) represent the degrees of freedom denominator (df within).

$\alpha = .05$									
1	**2**	**3**	**4**	**5**	**6**	**7**	**8**	**9**	**10**

	1	2	3	4	5	6	7	8	9	10
1	161.00	200.00	216.00	225.00	230.00	234.00	237.00	239.00	241.00	242.00
2	18.51	19.00	19.16	19.25	19.30	19.33	19.36	19.37	19.38	19.39
3	10.13	9.55	9.28	9.12	9.01	8.94	8.88	8.84	8.81	8.78
4	7.71	6.94	6.59	6.39	6.26	6.16	6.09	6.04	6.00	5.96
5	6.61	5.79	5.41	5.19	5.05	4.95	4.88	4.82	4.78	4.74
6	5.99	5.14	4.76	4.53	4.39	4.28	4.21	4.15	4.10	4.06
7	5.59	4.74	4.35	4.12	3.97	3.87	3.79	3.73	3.68	3.63
8	5.32	4.46	4.07	3.84	3.69	3.58	3.50	3.44	3.39	3.34
9	5.12	4.26	3.86	3.63	3.48	3.37	3.29	3.23	3.18	3.13
10	4.96	4.10	3.71	3.48	3.33	3.22	3.14	3.07	3.02	2.97
11	4.84	3.98	3.59	3.36	3.20	3.09	3.01	2.95	2.90	2.86
12	4.75	3.88	3.49	3.26	3.11	3.00	2.92	2.85	2.80	2.76
13	4.67	3.80	3.41	3.18	3.02	2.92	2.84	2.77	2.72	2.67
14	4.60	3.74	3.34	3.11	2.96	2.85	2.77	2.70	2.65	2.60
15	4.54	3.68	3.29	3.06	2.90	2.79	2.70	2.64	2.59	2.55
16	4.49	3.63	3.24	3.01	2.85	2.74	2.66	2.59	2.54	2.49
17	4.45	3.59	3.20	2.96	2.81	2.70	2.62	2.55	2.50	2.45
18	4.41	3.55	3.16	2.93	2.77	2.66	2.58	2.51	2.46	2.41
19	4.38	3.52	3.13	2.90	2.74	2.63	2.55	2.48	2.43	2.38
20	4.35	3.49	3.10	2.87	2.71	2.60	2.52	2.45	2.40	2.35

$\alpha = .01$									
1	**2**	**3**	**4**	**5**	**6**	**7**	**8**	**9**	**10**

	1	2	3	4	5	6	7	8	9	10
1	4052.00	4999.00	5403.00	5625.00	5764.00	5859.00	928.00	5981.00	6022.00	6056.00
2	98.49	99.01	99.17	99.25	99.30	99.33	99.34	99.36	99.38	99.40
3	34.12	30.81	29.46	28.71	28.24	27.91	27.67	27.49	27.34	27.23
4	21.20	18.00	16.69	15.98	15.52	15.21	14.98	14.80	14.66	14.54
5	16.26	13.27	12.06	11.39	10.97	10.67	10.45	10.27	10.15	10.05
6	13.74	10.92	9.78	9.15	8.75	8.47	8.26	8.10	7.98	7.87
7	12.25	9.55	8.45	7.85	7.46	7.19	7.00	6.84	6.71	6.62
8	11.26	8.65	7.59	7.01	6.63	6.37	6.19	6.03	5.91	5.82
9	10.56	8.02	6.99	6.42	6.06	5.80	5.62	5.47	5.35	5.26
10	10.04	7.56	6.55	5.99	5.64	5.39	5.21	5.06	4.95	4.85
11	9.65	7.20	6.22	5.67	5.32	5.07	4.88	4.74	4.63	4.54
12	9.33	6.93	5.95	5.41	5.06	4.82	4.65	4.50	4.39	4.30
13	9.07	6.70	5.74	5.20	4.86	4.62	4.44	4.30	4.19	4.10
14	8.86	6.51	5.56	5.03	4.69	4.46	4.28	4.14	4.03	3.94
15	8.68	6.36	5.42	4.89	4.56	4.32	4.14	4.00	3.89	3.80
16	8.53	6.23	5.29	4.77	4.44	4.20	4.03	3.89	3.78	3.69
17	8.40	6.11	5.18	4.67	4.34	4.10	3.93	3.79	3.68	3.59
18	8.28	6.01	5.09	4.58	4.25	4.01	3.85	3.71	3.60	3.51
19	8.18	5.93	5.01	4.50	4.17	3.94	3.77	3.63	3.52	3.43
20	8.10	5.85	4.94	4.43	4.10	3.87	3.71	3.56	3.45	3.37

The entries in this table were computed by the authors.

Figure 18.7 Critical Values of the *F*-Distribution

Step Eight. We can now calculate the two mean squares (MS) in this example. To calculate the $MS_{between}$, you divide the $SS_{between}$ calculated in Step Four (32) by the between df calculated in Step Seven (2), or 32 / 2 = 16. So, in this example the $MS_{between}$ = 16. To calculate the MS_{within}, you divide the SS_{within} calculated in Step Five (20) by the between df calculated in Step Seven (9), or 20 / 9 = 2.22. So, in this example the MS_{within} = 2.22.

Step Nine. Once we have the $MS_{between}$ and the MS_{within} we can calculate what is called the *F*-ratio or *F* value. To calculate the *F*-ratio we simply divide the MS_{within} (2.22) from the $MS_{between}$ (16):

$$F = MS_{between} / MS_{within}$$

$$16 / 2.22 = 7.20$$

So for our current example the *F* value = 7.20. The *F* value lets us know that the differences between the three groups (white room, yellow room, and blue room) and the time it took the participants to take a 10-item test is more than 7% bigger than we would expect to see randomly occurring. This could indicate that, yes, the participants did take the test at different speeds in the differently colored rooms (white, yellow, and blue). However, to truly determine if a difference exists, we must determine whether or not the one-way ANOVA is statistically significant.

Step Ten. Figure 18.7 contains the *F* value critical value table. You'll notice that this critical value table is different than the other critical value tables we've already seen. On this chart, you will notice that the df numbers run along the top and down the left-hand side of the table. The df numbers that run along the top of the chart (or the columns) represent the degrees of freedom numerator (df between), and the df numbers that are on the left-hand side of the chart (or the rows) represent the degrees of freedom denominator (df within). You'll notice that there are two separate charts presented in Figure 18.7. The first chart examines the critical values at $p < .05$, and the second chart examines the critical values at $p < .01$. To analyze this chart, we need to remember the $df_{between}$ (2) and df_{within} (9) we calculated in Step Seven. To determine our critical value for to compare to our calculated value (7.20), we need to go to the second column ($df_{between}$) and then go down to the ninth row (df_{within}). The critical value for *F* at $p < .05$ is 4.26. Since our calculated *F* value (7.20) is larger than the critical value of 4.26, we are statistically significant at the $p < .05$ level. To determine if we are statistically significant at the $p < .01$ significance level (the second chart in Figure 18.7), we need to go to the second column ($df_{between}$) and then go down to the ninth row (df_{within}) to find the critical value, which is 8.02. Since our calculated *F* value (7.20) is smaller than the critical value of 8.02, we are not statistically significant at the $p < .01$ level.

Step Eleven. The last step of the one-way ANOVA calculation is to create what is called an ANOVA summary table. Figure 18.8 is the ANOVA summary table for this example.

The ANOVA summary table arranges information that you have calculated in a very easy-to-understand chart format. All of the basic information you need about the calculation of a one-way ANOVA can be found on this chart.

Source	df	SS	MS	F	p
Between	2	32	16	7.20	.05
Within	9	20	2.22		
Total	11	108			

Figure 18.8 ANOVA Summary Table

Computer Printouts of the One-Way ANOVA

Now that we have examined how a one-way ANOVA can be calculated by hand, we will examine what output from two statistical computer programs, SPSS and SAS, looks like as well.

SPSS and One-Way ANOVAs

Using SPSS to compute a one-way ANOVA is fairly easy as long as you follow the instructions, so let's get started. First, open up your SPSS student version and then locate the file on the CD-ROM in the SPSS folder called "one-way anova." When you open this file you will see two variables listed: "color" and "time." Color is the variable name given to the variable that contains the three room colors. You'll notice though that the colors are only represented by the numbers 1 (white), 2 (yellow), and 3 (blue). Remember, a statistics program can only understand numbers, so it's up to you as a researcher to remember how you classified the two groups when you are inputting the data. The "time" variable is the amount of time in minutes it took each participant to complete the 10-item quiz.

To conduct the one-way ANOVA, go to the menu bar at the top of your screen and click on "Analyze." When you click on "Analyze," a dropdown menu will appear. Go to the fifth category on this menu, "General Linear Model," and scroll over the arrow and another menu will appear to the right. The first option on the "General Linear Model" menu is "Univariate"; click on it. At this point, the "Univariate" dialogue box will appear on your screen. On this screen you will see six boxes. The first box, on the left-hand side of the "Univariate" dialogue box, will contain your variables. To the right, on top is the "Dependent Variable" box, which is where dependent variables are placed (time). To place the variable "time" in this box, click and highlight in blue the variable time. When time is highlighted blue, click the right arrow button next to the "Dependent Variable" box. Below that box is the "Fixed Factor(s)" box, which is where you place your nominal independent variable (color). To place the variable "color" in this box, click and highlight in blue the variable color. When color is highlighted blue, click the right arrow button next to the "Fixed Factor(s)" box.

To the right of those boxes, you will see six buttons: "Model," "Contrasts," "Plots," "Post Hoc," "Save," and "Options." Click on the button called "Post Hoc." The "Univariate: Post Hoc Multiple Comparisons for Observed Means" dialogue box will appear on your screen. First, you need to select the Factor(s) you want to compute a post hoc analysis for by selecting the variable (color) and clicking the arrow between the "Factor(s)" box and the "Post Hoc Tests for" box. After you have sent your Factor variable over to the "Post Hoc Tests for" box you will notice that the various post hoc tests are now active. In this box, there are two groupings for post hoc tests. One grouping is for "Equal Variances Assumed" and one is for "Equal Variances Not Assumed." We will go into more detail in a few minutes about post hoc tests, but for now go ahead and put a checkmark in the box next to the "Tukey" post hoc test under the "Equal Variances Assumed" list (it's the second one in the second column). Once "Tukey" is checked, you can push the button at the bottom of the screen marked "Continue."

You should now have returned to the "Univariate" dialogue box. Now press the sixth button at the bottom of the dialogue box marked "Options." In the "Options" dialogue box, you will find two boxes on top and a variety of options at the bottom. To have any options performed, you need to select the variable (politics) you want options for on the left in the "Factor(s) and Factor Interactions" box and send the variable over to the right box "Display Means for" by selecting the variable and pushing the arrow button between the two boxes. Once "color" is in the "Display Means for" box, we can then select a variety of options at the bottom of the page. The bottom box is called the "Display" box and contains two items we need to check at this point: "Descriptive statistics" and "Estimates of effect size." Once you have selected "Descriptive statistics" and "Estimates of effect size," click on the "Continue" button. Once you are back to the "Univariate" dialogue box, click the "OK" button to run the results. The results (excluding the post hoc) can be seen in Figure 18.9.

The results for the SPSS printouts are very straightforward at this point. If you examine the three tables printed in Figure 18.9, you will see that the first table contains information about the independent variable, the second table contains simple descriptive statistics for the dependent variable, and the third table contains much of the same information as the ANOVA summary table we created in Step Eleven earlier in this chapter. The third row "COLOR" is the row that contains the information we calculated by hand earlier in this chapter. The major difference between the information contained in the SPSS ANOVA Summary Table and the one in Figure 18.8 is that the SPSS table gives you an exact calculation of the significance level ($p = .014$) and SPSS also calculates the effect size for the difference seen in the test

Univariate Analysis of Variance

Between-Subjects Factors

		Value Label	N
Room	1.00	White	4
Color	2.00	Yellow	4
	3.00	Blue	4

Descriptive Statistics

Dependent Variable: Time (in minutes) to finish the test.

Room Color	Mean	Std. Deviation	N
White	5.0000	.8165	4
Yellow	7.0000	2.1602	4
Blue	9.0000	1.1547	4
Total	7.0000	2.1742	12

Test of Between-Subjects Effects

Dependent Variable: Time (in minutes) to finish the test.

Source	Type III Sum of Squares	df	Mean Square	F	Sig.	Eta Squares
Corrected Model	32.000[a]	2	16.000	7.200	.014	.615
Intercept	588.000	1	588.000	264.600	.000	.967
COLOR	32.000	2	16.000	7.200	.014	.615
Error	20.000	9	2.222			
Total	640.000	12				
Corrected Total	52.000	11				

[a.] R Squared = .615 (Adjusted R Squared = .530)

Figure 18.9 SPSS One-Way ANOVA Results

($\eta^2 = 0.615$). Eta square (η^2) ranges from 0 to 1, with 0 indicating that there is no difference at all and 1 indicating that there is a difference between the groups but not a difference in scores within the groups. To interpret η^2, researchers rely on the following interpretation:

0.01—small effect size

0.06—medium effect size

0.14—large effect size

In this example, our effect size was 0.62, so we could say that there is a large proportion of the variance within the dependent variable (time it took to take the test) related to one of the groups (white, yellow, or blue). Based on this, we can conclude that a large portion of the time it took someone to fill out the survey was dependent upon the color of room the participant was in. However, at this point we cannot say which room had the most impact, so a multiple comparison test is needed.

One part of the one-way ANOVA that we did not calculate by hand is the multiple comparison test. As of this point, all we know is that our one-way ANOVA test is significant (people take tests in different colored rooms at different speeds), but we don't know where those differences are. Maybe people in white rooms take tests slower than people in blue rooms but not slower than people in yellow rooms. Maybe yellow people take tests at similar speeds to people in white and blue rooms, but people in white rooms take tests faster than people in blue rooms. If you remember the null hypothesis we created at the beginning of this chapter, we wrote: "H_o: $\mu_{white} = \mu_{yellow} = \mu_{blue}$ ◄ mean time (in minutes) to take a test in the white room is equal to the mean time (in minutes) to take a test in the yellow room, which is equal to the mean time (in minutes) to take a test in the blue room. Your hypothesis would then predict that **at least one of the pairs** (white and yellow, white and blue, and yellow and blue) is not equal, or H_1: $\mu_{white} \neq \mu_{yellow} \neq \mu_{blue}$." Notice that the boldfaced portion emphasizes that at least one pair will be different, but not all three different from each other. For this reason, when conducting a one-way ANOVA with an independent variable that has three or more levels (white, yellow, and blue), we need to find out where the difference(s) actually exists. Since based on a simple one-way ANOVA we cannot make these judgments, we have to conduct a post hoc (after the fact) multiple comparison test.

Multiple Comparison Tests

In the t-test we were able to compare the two groups directly to each other, which we can also do with a one-way ANOVA if, and only if, the nominal variable being used as the independent variable has two groups (such as females and males). If the nominal variable has more than two groups (like our example), the one-way ANOVA will determine if at least one pair within a group is different from each other, but we will not know which pair is different until we perform a multiple comparison test. For example, if we are comparing three groups (white, yellow, and blue), a statistically significant one-way ANOVA will let us know whether these three groups differ in their means on a dependent variable. However, a one-way ANOVA will not say that people in the white room took more time to take the test than people in the blue room. To determine where the difference lies, a second test, the multiple comparison test, is conducted, which compares white and yellow, white and blue, and yellow and blue. The multiple comparison test then tells us where the specific difference actually lies.

If you remember from the SPSS steps above, when you entered into the "One-Way ANOVA: Post Hoc Multiple Comparisons" dialogue box, SPSS provides you with 18 different types of multiple comparison tests broken into two groups "Equal Variances Assumed" and "Equal Variances Not Assumed." The four most common post hoc tests for a one-way ANOVA are Fisher's Least Significant Difference (LSD), Student Newman-Keuls (SNK), Tukey's Honestly Significance Difference Test (Tukey), and Scheffé (Scheffe). The order presented above (LSD, SNK, Tukey, and Scheffe) is a continuum from liberal to conservative post hoc tests. Liberal tests are called such because they make it easier to find significant differences between groups (white room, yellow room, and blue room). However, with a liberal test your chance of Type I error also increases, so they should always be used with caution. Conservative tests make it harder to find significant differences between groups, and you have less of a chance of Type I error. Let's briefly explain the four post hoc tests. First, Fisher's LSD is the equivalent of running a series of paired t-tests, but the alpha level is not controlled for, so the chance of compounded error is great. Second, SNK is a stepwise test for ordered means where the alpha level depends upon the number of "steps apart" each of the means are from each other. This test is great when your data consists of ranges, but isn't very useful for pairwise comparisons. Furthermore, the SNK post hoc has more power, so you are more likely to find significant pairwise comparisons (Seaman, Levin, & Serlin, 1991). However, when you attempt to increase power, you run the risk of increasing your Type I risk. Third, unlike the SNK, the Tukey HSD is able to test for pairwise comparisons while controlling your Type I error and generating confidence intervals (Seaman, Levin, & Serlin, 1991). Finally, the Scheffé post hoc test assumes you wish to test all possible pairs and all possible combinations of means. For example, if you have three means, then there are six possible comparisons (white vs. blue, white vs. yellow, blue vs. yellow, white + blue vs. yellow, white + yellow vs. blue, and yellow + blue vs. white). The only real reason to use the Scheffé post hoc test is if you really need to examine all six possible combinations. For these reasons, we generally recommend using the Tukey HSD. The results for the post hoc analysis we selected earlier (Tukey HSD) can be seen in Figure 18.10.

In the "Multiple Comparisons" box in Figure 18.10, we see that the three colors are compared to each other. The first row compares people who took the test in the white room to people who took the test in the yellow and blue rooms. The second column in the "Multiple Comparisons" box is labeled "Mean Difference I-J," with "I" being the white room and "J" being both people in the yellow and blue rooms. In essence, what this first row is testing is whether people in the white room took longer or less time to take the 10-item test than people in the yellow room, and whether people in the white room took longer or less time to take the 10-item test than people in the blue room. The first room that the white room is compared to is the yellow room. If you look in the "Mean Difference" column, you will notice that there is a mean difference between the two of -2.000. If a mean difference is negative, then the mean time spent taking the 10-item test in the group in the "I" column (in this case people in the white room) is less than the group it is being compared to in the "J" column (or yellow). However, while people in the white room took less time to complete the test than people in the yellow room. The fourth column in the "Multiple Comparisons" SPSS printout box indicates that the significance is $p = .195$, which is not statistically significant. In other words, there is not a significant difference between the time it took people in the white and yellow rooms to complete the 10-item test.

At this point we have used the first row on the "Multiple Comparisons" SPSS printout box to compare people in white rooms with people in yellow rooms. We now need to compare people in white rooms with people in blue rooms. On the first row, the second variable listed under the "J-Room Color" is blue. If you look in the "Mean Difference" column, you will notice that there is a mean difference between white and blue of −4.000. Again this means

Post Hoc Tests

Room Color

Multiple Comparisons

Dependent Variable: Time (in minutes) to finish the test.
Tukey HSD

(I) Room Color	(J) Room Color	Mean Difference (I-J)	Std. Error	Sig.	95% Confidence Interval	
					Lower Bound	Upper Bound
White	Yellow	-2.0000	1.0541	.195	-4.9431	.9431
	Blue	-4.0000*	1.0541	.011	-6.9431	-1.0569
Yellow	White	2.0000	1.0541	.195	-.9431	4.9431
	Blue	-2.0000	1.0541	.195	-4.9431	.9431
Blue	White	4.0000*	1.0541	.011	1.0569	6.9431
	Yellow	2.0000	1.0541	.195	-.9431	4.9431

Based on observed means.
 *. The mean difference is significant at the .05 level.

Homogeneous Subsets

Time (in minutes) to finish the test.

Tukey HSD[a,b]

Room Color	N	Subset 1	Subset 2
White	4	5.0000	
Yellow	4	7.0000	7.0000
Blue	4		9.0000
Sig.		.195	.195

Means for groups in homogeneous subsets are displayed.
Based on Type III Sum of Squares
The error term is Mean Square(Error) = 2.222.
 a. Uses Harmonic Mean Sample Size = 4.000.
 b. Alpha = .05.

Figure 18.10 SPSS One-Way ANOVA Post Hoc Test

that people in the white room took the test 4 minutes faster than the people in the blue room. You'll notice that next to the −4.000 beside blue in the "Mean Difference" column is an asterisk (*) next to the number. SPSS automatically flags significant multiple comparisons if they are at the $p < .05$ level. In this case, the significance level listed in the fourth column of the "Multiple Comparisons" SPSS printout box was $p = .011$. At this point we have found out that people in the white and yellow rooms did not complete the test at significantly different rates, but people in the white room did complete the test significantly faster than people in the blue room. At this point, there is only one other pairing that we have not examined; we have not examined if people in yellow and blue rooms took the test at different speeds.

The second row in the "Multiple Comparisons" SPSS printout box now has yellow in the "(I) Room Color" column and white and blue in the "(J) Room Color" column. The first comparison that can be made compares yellow to white, but we did this comparison already so we are not concerned with it here. All of the comparisons are done twice in the printout, so be careful not to report both sets of multiple comparisons. Once you have reported the comparison between white and yellow, you do not need to report it a second time. In this case we are only interested in the comparison between yellow and blue. Yet again, the mean difference between yellow and blue is –2.000, which indicates that people in the yellow room took the test on average 2 minutes faster than people in the blue room; however, this is not a significant difference, $p = .195$.

SAS AND ONE-WAY ANOVAs

To calculate a one-way ANOVA using SAS you use what is called the general linear model (GLM). Most statistics are based on the GLM. However, since it is a regression-based model, some of the information in the printouts is extraneous to what we are examining in this chapter. The PROC statement used to analyze a one-way ANOVA using SAS is:

PROC GLM;
CLASS COLOR;
MODEL TIME = COLOR;
MEANS COLOR / TUKEY;
MEANS COLOR;

The printouts for the GLM Procedure statement can be found in Figure 18.11.

To make the SAS printout easier to read, we've separated the printouts into four sections. When you actually input the PROC statement into SAS, you will not get your printout in a nice table format with four distinct sections like we have done in Figure 18.11. The information contained in the first row of the results is basic information. The table lists the variable "COLOR" as the classification variable (independent variable), and noticed that it has three levels, the values of which are "1," "2," and "3." Of course, this is another good example of how you have to remember what you label categories when inputting data. In this example 1 = white, 2 = yellow, and 3 = blue. This section also lets you know how many observations (participants) the program read and used. In this study, we have 12 participants and the computer was able to use the data from all 12 participants when conducting the one-way ANOVA.

In the second grouping of the SAS printout, you will find the traditional ANOVA summary table like we created in Step Eleven above during the hand-computation part of this chapter. The only visual difference between the SPSS and SAS ANOVA summary tables is that SAS takes the significance level out one more decimal place to .0136; whereas SPSS lists $p = .014$. Again, this is not a computation difference; just a difference in how the programs opt to round numbers.

The third part of the SAS printout will look very foreign to you because it involves the regression aspect of the GLM. For that reason, we will not discuss this part in this chapter. Instead, we will look at the fourth part of the SAS printout, which examines the Tukey Studentized Range (HSD). Reading the Tukey HSD in the SAS printout can be somewhat confusing. The first section of the SAS printout gives the researcher some basic statistics (alpha, error degrees of freedom, error mean square, critical value of studentized range, and minimum significant difference) that the computer used in determining where the differences existed. The section we are interested in here is the one we have boldfaced for you on

```
                          The GLM Procedure

                       Class Level Information

                   Class         Levels     Values

                   COLOR             3       1 2 3

                Number of Observations Read          12
                Number of Observations Used          12
```

Dependent Variable: TIME

Source	DF	Sum of Squares	Mean Square	F Value	Pr > F
Model	2	32.00000000	16.00000000	7.20	0.0136
Error	9	20.00000000	2.22222222		
Corrected Total	11	52.00000000			

R-Square	Coeff Var	Root MSE	TIME Mean
0.615385	21.29589	1.490712	7.000000

Source	DF	Type I SS	Mean Square	F Value	Pr > F
COLOR	2	32.00000000	16.00000000	7.20	0.0136

Source	DF	Type III SS	Mean Square	F Value	Pr > F
COLOR	2	32.00000000	16.00000000	7.20	0.0136

```
              Tukey's Studentized Range (HSD) Test for TIME

NOTE: This test controls the Type I experimentwise error rate, but it generally has a higher
                Type II error rate than REGWQ.

              Alpha                                    0.05
              Error Degrees of Freedom                    9
              Error Mean Square                     2.222222
              Critical Value of Studentized Range   3.94850
              Minimum Significant Difference          2.943
          Means with the same letter are not significantly different.
```

Tukey Grouping		Mean	N	COLOR
	A	9.000	4	3
	A			
B	A	7.000	4	2
B				
B		5.000	4	1

Level of COLOR	N	Mean	Std Dev
1	4	5.00000000	0.81649658
2	4	7.00000000	2.16024690
3	4	9.00000000	1.15470054

Figure 18.11 SAS One-Way ANOVA Results

the printout. If you read the disclaimer above the bolded section, it reads "Means with the same letter are not significantly different." You'll then notice that there is a small chart with four columns: "Tukey Grouping," "Mean," "N," and "COLOR." The first column is the column that lists what is and is not different. The disclaimer states that if a group has the same letter, then those groups are not significantly different from each other. The letter "A" is seen next to the COLOR numbers 3 (blue) and 2 (yellow), which indicates that blue and yellow are not significantly different from each other. The letter "B" is seen next to the COLOR numbers 2 (yellow) and 1 (white), which indicates that yellow and white are not significantly different from each other. However, there is not a letter "A" in front of COLOR 1 (white) or a "B" in front of COLOR 3 (blue), which indicates that there *is* a significant difference between 3 (blue) and 1 (white). Again, this is the exact same result that the SPSS Tukey post hoc determined, it's just a little more confusing when examining the printouts.

APA Write-Up (Without Chart)

This research question wanted to determine if there was a significant difference in the color of a room (white, yellow, and blue) and the length of time (in minutes) it took the participant to finish a 10-item test. A one-way Analysis of Variance (ANOVA) was calculated using the color of the room as the independent variable and length of time to finish the test (in minutes) as the dependent variable. A significant difference was noted: $F(2, 9) = 7.20$, $p < .05$, $\eta^2 = 0.62$. In a follow-up to this question, a Tukey HSD post hoc was conducted. The Tukey HSD post hoc indicated that there was a significant difference between people in the white room ($M = 5$, $SD = 0.82$) and people in the blue room ($M = 9$, $SD = 1.15$). However, the Tukey HSD post hoc test did not find a significant difference between people who took the test in the white room ($M = 5$, $SD = 0.82$) and people who took the test in the yellow room ($M = 7$, $SD = 2.16$), and the Tukey HSD also did not find a significant difference between people in the yellow room ($M = 7$, $SD = 2.16$) and people in the blue room ($M = 9$, $SD = 1.15$).

APA Write-Up (with Chart)

This research question wanted to determine if there was a significant difference in the color of a room (white, yellow, and blue) and the length of time (in minutes) it took the participant to finish a 10-item test. A one-way Analysis of Variance (ANOVA) was calculated using the color of the room as the independent variable and length of time to finish the test (in minutes) as the dependent variable. A significant difference was noted: $F(2, 9) = 7.20$, $p < .05$, $\eta^2 = 0.62$. In a follow-up to this question, a Tukey HSD post hoc was conducted. Figure 18.12 examines the exact differences that were noted.

Discussion of Findings

After all of the work that we have done so far in this chapter, this is the point where we get to try to make some sense out of the results. To do this, let's go back to the initial question we

Room Color	N	M	SD	White	Yellow
White	4	5.0	0.82		
Yellow	4	7.0	2.16	NS	
Blue	4	9.0	2.17	*	NS

*Note: NS = nonsignificant differences between pair means; * = significance using the Tukey HSD procedure.*

Figure 18.12 Post Hoc Analysis of Test Time and Room Color

asked. We wanted to determine if the color of a room (white, yellow, or blue) caused people to take a 10-item test at different speeds. After calculating the one-way ANOVA, we found that the color of a room does cause people to take a 10-item test at different speeds. Based on this information, we performed a Tukey HSD post hoc analysis to see where that difference actually existed. Based on the Tukey HSD, we can say that people in white rooms and yellow rooms will take tests at roughly the same speed. We can also say that people in yellow rooms and blue rooms will take tests at roughly the same speed. However, we found out that people in white rooms finish tests faster than people in blue rooms. Now that we've completed a hypothetical example of a one-way ANOVA, let's examine results from an actual sample.

Political Affiliation and Humor Assessment

The purpose of this example was to see if differences existed among political affiliations (Democrat, Republican, other, or not registered to vote) and an individual's humor assessment. Call this an "Are Democrats really funnier than Republicans?" question. To test for a possible difference between Democrats, Republicans, people belonging to other political parties, and people not registered to vote on the humor assessment inventory, we used the nominal variable politics (independent variable) and the interval variable humor assessment (dependent variable). Figure 18.13 represents the findings from the SPSS results, and Figure 18.14 represents the findings from the SAS results.

In this example, you'll notice that both SPSS and SAS indicated that there were no differences between the basic statistics computed. If you examine the Tukey test in SAS, you'll notice that it has laid out the multiple comparisons slightly differently. Since the test was not significant, none of the post hoc tests will be either, but you can see that SAS has presented the comparisons in a fashion that is more akin to SPSS when you have more than four or more levels to a group (Democrats, Republicans, people belonging to other political parties, and people not registered to vote).

APA Write-Up

This research question tests for a possible difference between Democrats, Republicans, people belonging to other political parties, and people not registered to vote on their reported levels of humor assessment. A one-way Analysis of Variance (ANOVA) was calculated using the four political party groupings as the independent variable and humor assessment as the dependent variable. The test was not significant: $F(3, 312) = 0.36$, $p > .05$.

Discussion of the Boiarsky, Long, and Thayer Article

To help you further understand the concept of the one-way ANVOA, we have included an article on the CD-ROM that accompanies this textbook that utilizes the one-way ANOVA in a unique way. The 1999 article by Greg Boiarsky, Marilee Long, and Greg Thayer entitled "Formal Features in Children's Science Television: Sound Effects, Visual Pace, and Topic Shifts" can be found in the folder titled "articles." To view this article, you will need to download a copy of the Adobe Acrobat Reader (http://www.adobe.com/products/acrobat/readermain.html) if you do not already have this program installed on your computer. We strongly encourage you to read the article first and then read our analysis of the article. The goal of this process is to make sure you understand how to read and interpret research results related to one-way ANOVAs.

Univariate Analysis of Variance

Between-Subjects Factors

		Value Label	N
Political	1.00	Democrat	116
Affiliation	2.00	Republican	141
	3.00	Other	39
	4.00	Not Registered to Vote	20

Descriptive Statistics

Dependent Variable: Humor Assessment

Political Affiliation	Mean	Std. Deviation	N
Democrat	62.4138	9.7223	116
Republican	62.2979	10.2510	141
Other	61.9744	8.1127	39
Not Registered to Vote	60.0000	10.4630	20
Total	62.1551	9.8024	316

Test of Between-Subjects Effects

Dependent Variable: Humor Assessment

Source	Type III Sum of Squares	df	Mean Square	F	Sig.	Eta Squares
Corrected Model	104.800[a]	3	34.933	.361	.781	.003
Intercept	666134.510	1	666134.510	6890.452	.000	.957
POLITICS	104.800	3	34.933	.361	.781	.003
Error	30162.602	312	96.675			
Total	1251055.000	316				
Corrected Total	30267.402	315				

[a.] R Squared = .003 (Adjusted R Squared = -.006)

Estimated Marginal Means

Political Affiliation

Dependent Variable: Humor Assessment

Political Affiliation	Mean	Std. Error	95% Confidence Interval	
			Lower Bound	Upper Bound
Democrat	62.414	.913	60.618	64.210
Republican	62.298	.828	60.669	63.927
Other	61.974	1.574	58.877	65.072
Not Registered to Vote	60.000	2.199	55.674	64.326

Figure 18.13 SPSS Results of Political Affiliation with Humor Assessment

Post Hoc Tests

Political Affiliation

Multiple Comparisons

Dependent Variable: Humor Assessment
Tukey HSD

(I) Political Affiliation	(J) Political Affiliation	Mean Difference (I-J)	Std. Error	Sig.	95% Confidence Interval Lower Bound	95% Confidence Interval Upper Bound
Democrat	Republican	.1159	1.2325	1.000	-3.0504	3.2822
	Other	.4394	1.8200	.995	4.2361	5.1150
	Not Registered to Vote	2.4138	2.3806	.741	-3.7020	8.5296
Republican	Democrat	-.1159	1.2325	1.000	-3.2822	3.0504
	Other	.3235	1.7789	.998	-4.2465	4.8936
	Not Registered to Vote	2.2979	2.3493	.762	-3.7377	8.3334
Other	Democrat	-.4394	1.8200	.995	-5.1150	4.2361
	Republican	-.3235	1.7789	.998	-4.8936	4.2465
	Not Registered to Vote	1.9744	2.7042	.885	-4.9728	8.9215
Not Registered to Vote	Democrat	-2.4138	2.3806	.741	-8.5296	3.7020
	Republican	-2.2979	2.3493	.762	-8.3334	3.7377
	Other	-1.9744	2.7042	.885	-8.9215	4.9728

Based on observed means.

Homogeneous Subsets

Humor Assessment

Tukey HSD[a,b,c]

Political Affiliation	N	Subset 1
Not Registered to Vote	20	60.0000
Other	39	61.9744
Republican	141	62.2979
Democrat	116	62.4138
Sig.		.659

Means for groups in homogeneous subsets are displayed.
Based on Type III Sum of Squares
The error term in Mean Square(Error) = 96.675.

a. Uses Harmonic Mean Sample Size = 43.786.

b. The group sizes are unequal. The harmonic mean of the group sizes is used. Type I error levels are not guaranteed.

c. Alpha = .05.

```
                          ONE-WAY ANOVA

                        The GLM Procedure

                     Class Level Information

                  Class        Levels    Values

                  POLITICS        4      1 2 3 4


               Number of Observations Read        325
               Number of Observations Used        316
```

Dependent Variable: BIGHA

Source	DF	Sum of Squares	Mean Square	F Value	Pr > F
Model	3	104.80025	34.93342	0.36	0.7810
Error	312	30162.60165	96.67501		
Corrected Total	315	30267.40190			

R-Square	Coeff Var	Root MSE	BIGHA Mean
0.003462	15.81906	9.832345	62.15506

Source	DF	Type I SS	Mean Square	F Value	Pr > F
POLITICS	3	104.8002470	34.9334157	0.36	0.7810

Source	DF	Type III SS	Mean Square	F Value	Pr > F
POLITICS	3	104.8002470	34.9334157	0.36	0.7810

```
            Tukey's Studentized Range (HSD) Test for BIGHA

         NOTE: This test controls the Type I experimentwise error rate.


               Alpha                                  0.05
               Error Degrees of Freedom                312
               Error Mean Square                   96.67501
               Critical Value of Studentized Range 3.65285


         Comparisons significant at the 0.05 level are indicated by ***.
```

Figure 18.14 SAS Results of Political Affiliation with Humor Assessment

POLITICS Comparison	Difference Between Means	Simultaneous 95% Confidence Limits	
1 - 2	0.116	-3.068	3.299
1 - 3	0.439	-4.261	5.140
1 - 4	2.414	-3.735	8.563
2 - 1	-0.116	-3.299	3.068
2 - 3	0.324	-4.271	4.918
2 - 4	2.298	-3.770	8.366
3 - 1	-0.439	-5.140	4.261
3 - 2	-0.324	-4.918	4.271
3 - 4	1.974	-5.010	8.959
4 - 1	-2.414	-8.563	3.735
4 - 2	-2.298	-8.366	3.770
4 - 3	-1.974	-8.959	5.010

The GLM Procedure

Level of POLITICS	N	BIGHA Mean	Std Dev
1	116	62.4137931	9.7222908
2	141	62.2978723	10.2509544
3	39	61.9743590	8.1126515
4	20	60.0000000	10.4629673

ARTICLE PURPOSE

Children love television. Most of us have been raised on some form of child-centric television. Whether it was the Muppets, Sesame Street, Mr. Rogers, or Captain Kangaroo, we all enjoyed entertainment with a lesson. More recently, a new breed of children's television has surfaced known as children's science television. The purpose of this study was to determine if four different children's television shows (*Beakman's World*, *Bill Nye the Science Guy*, *Magic School Bus*, and *Newton's Apple*) differed in their use of sound effects per minute, cuts per minute, fades/dissolves per minute, wipes per minute, and topic shifts per minute.

METHODOLOGY

In this study, the researchers analyzed a sampling the four children's science television shows during the 1995–96 season. The shows were then coded to examine sound effects per minute, cuts per minute, fades/dissolves per minute, wipes per minute, and topic shifts per minute. To test for reliable program attribute coding, two independent researchers coded content pacing, sound effects, and visual pacing with Cohen's kappas ranging from 0.77 to 1.0. While the 0.77 (content pacing's Cohen's kappas ranged from 0.77 to 0.87) is somewhat suspect (see Chapter 12 for information on intercoder reliability), all of the other coding was strong.

RESULTS

The researchers ran a series of five one-way ANOVAs using the four children's television shows (*Beakman's World*, *Bill Nye the Science Guy*, *Magic School Bus*, and *Newton's Apple*) as the independent variable and the program attributes (sound effects per minute, cuts per minute, fades/dissolves per minute, wipes per minute, and topic shifts per minute) as the dependent variables. All five of their one-way ANOVAs were significant. One problem with this article is seen in the reporting of the post hoc analyses. While the authors do a good job explaining which television shows they perceive to have higher levels of specific program attributes, they do not explain what type of post hoc analysis was completed. While this article was set up very nicely overall, its discussion of the post hoc analyses used needed some help.

Conclusion

In this chapter we have examined how to compute a one-way ANOVA by hand, how to compute and interpret computer results of a one-way ANOVA in both SPSS and SAS, and how to write up a one-way ANOVA using APA style. We have seen the one-way ANOVA used in three different examples. Later on in this book we will discuss different types of ANOVAs (Chapter 21). For now, we are going to turn our attention to the next statistical test in this book, the correlation.

KEY TERMS

Degrees of Freedom (df) Between

Degrees of Freedom (df) Within

Eta-Square (η^2)

F Test

Fisher's Least Significant Difference (LSD)

General Linear Model

Mean Squares Between

Mean Squares Within

Multiple Comparison Tests

One-Way Analysis of Variance

Scheffé

Student Newman-Keuls (SNK)

Sum of Squares Between

Sum of Squares Within

Tukey's Honestly Significant Difference Test (Tukey HSD)

REFERENCES

Boiarsky, G., Long, M., Thayer, G. (1999). Formal features in children's science television: Sound effects, visual pace, and topic shifts. *Communication Research Reports, 16*, 185–192.

Green, S. B., & Salkind, N. J. (2004). *Using SPSS for Windows and Macintosh: Analyzing and understanding data* (4th ed.). Upper Saddle River, NJ: Prentice Hall.

Seaman, M. A., Levin, J. R., & Serlin, R. C. (1991). New Developments in pairwise multiple comparisons: Some powerful and practicable procedures. *Psychological Bulletin, 110*, 577–586.

FURTHER READING

Abramson, J. H., & Abramson, Z. H. (2001). *Making sense of data: A self-instruction manual on the interpretation of epidemiological data* (3rd ed.). New York: Oxford.

Bruning, J. L., & Kintz, B. L. (1997). *Computational handbook of statistics* (4th ed.). New York: Longman.

Cortina, J. M., & Nouri, H. (1999). *Effect size for ANOVA designs*. Thousand Oaks, CA: Sage.

Delwiche, L. D., & Slaughter, S. J. (2003). *The little SAS book: A primer* (3rd ed.). Cary, NC: SAS Press.

Gravetter, F. J., & Wallnau, L. B. (2000). *Statistics for the behavioral sciences* (5th ed.). Belmont, CA: Wadsworth/Thomson Learning.

Green, S. B., & Salkind, N. J. (2004). *Using SPSS for Windows and Macintosh: Analyzing and understanding data* (4th ed.). Upper Saddle River, NJ: Prentice Hall.

Hocking, J. E., Stacks, D. W., & McDermott, S. T. (2003). *Communication research* (3rd ed.). Boston: Allyn and Bacon.

Howell, D. C. (1997). *Statistical methods for psychology* (4th ed.). Belmont, CA: Duxbury Press.

Iversen, G. R., & Norpoth, H. (2004). *Analysis of variance* (2nd ed.). Thousand Oaks, CA: Sage.

Keller, D. K. (2006). *The Tao of statistics: A path to understanding (with no math)*. Thousand Oaks, CA: Sage.

Salkind, N. J. (2004). *Statistics for people who (think they) hate statistics* (2nd ed.). Thousand Oaks, CA: Sage.

SAS Institute. (2004). *SAS 9.1 Companion for Windows*. Cary, NC: SAS Press.

Scheffé, H. (1959). *The analysis of variance*. New York: John Wiley & Sons.

Singleton, R. A., Jr., & Straits, B. C. (1999). *Approach to social research* (3rd ed.). New York: Oxford University Press.

Stevens, J. (1986). *Applied multivariate statistics for the social sciences*. Hillsdale, NJ: Lawrence Erlbaum Associates.

Tabachnick, B. G., & Fidell, L. S. (2001). *Using multivariate statistics* (4th ed.). Boston: Allyn and Bacon.

Trochim, W. M. K. (2000). *The research methods knowledge base* (2nd ed.). Cincinnati, OH: Atomic Dog. Online available at: http://www.socialresearchmethods.net/

Turner, J. R., & Thayer, J. (2001). *Introduction to analysis of variance: Design, analysis, & interpretation*. Thousand Oaks, CA: Sage.

Weiss, D. J. (2005). *Analysis of variance and functional measurement: A practical guide*. New York: Oxford.

Correlation

1   Understand the different types of relationships (positive, negative, curvilinear, and neutral).
2   Explain the purposes of a correlation.
3   Understand that correlation does not equal causation.
4   Understand how to calculate a correlation by hand.
5   Know how to conduct a correlation using both SPSS and SAS.
6   Be able to interpret the print-outs associated with a correlation.
7   Examine a real-world correlation analysis using the textbook's data set.
8   Be able to correctly interpret large correlation tables.
9   Be able to analyze the use of the correlations in the articles by Cheseboro (1999) and Punyanunt (2000).

In the previous chapter we examined one-way ANOVA, which utilized one nominal variable (with two or more groups) and one interval/ratio variable. In fact, the first three tests examined (chi-square, t-test, and one-way ANOVA) all utilized nominal variables to examine differences between groups. The correlation is not a difference test, so it does not utilize nominal variables at all. Instead, the Pearson product-moment correlation uses two interval/ratio variables.

The Pearson product-moment correlation coefficient (r) is a measure of the degree to which two quantitative variables (Likert/ratio) are linearly related in a sample (changes in one variable correspond to changes in another variable). To conduct a Pearson product-moment correlation, a researcher needs to obtain two scores (one for each variable) from each participant. If the correlation coefficient (r) is significant, there exists some type of relationship between the two variables. However, if the correlation coefficient (r) is not significant, then we cannot draw any conclusions about the nature of the relationship between the two variables. Let's look at a communication-related example where the Pearson product-moment correlation could be used.

Correlation Background Information

The basic purpose of a correlation is to determine the relationship between two independent variables. In statistics, four types of relationships are theoretically possible. The purpose of a correlation is to measure whether as the score on one variable changes (goes up or down), the score on a second variable also changes (goes up or down). The four types of relationships are illustrated in Figure 19.1.

The first type of relationship a researcher can find between two variables is called a positive relationship or positive correlation. Figure 19.1a is an example of a positive correlation. In this example you have the two variables: humor assessment and popularity. This example is a positive relationship because as a person's use of interpersonal humor increases, so does her or his popularity. This relationship indicates that the more humorous a person is, the more popular he or she will be, which is a positive relationship or correlation.

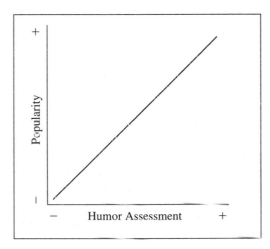

(a) Positive Relationship

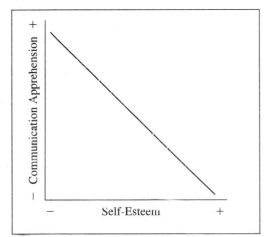

(b) Negative Relationship

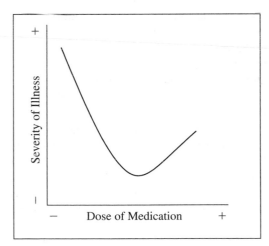

(c) Curvilinear Relationship

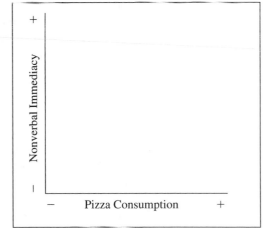

(d) No Relationship

Figure 19.1 Four Types of Relationships

The second type of relationship, seen in Figure 19.1b, is a negative relationship. A negative relationship exists when the score on one variable goes up and the score on the other variable goes down. In the example in Figure 19.1b, we are examining the relationship between communication apprehension and self-esteem. As a person's level of communication apprehension goes up, her or his self-esteem goes down. The converse is also true; as a person's level of self-esteem goes up, her or his level of communication apprehension goes down.

The third example of a relationship, seen in Figure 19.1c, is called a curvilinear relationship. A curvilinear relationship is a relationship that is either positive or negative to a certain point and then starts to go in the other direction. In the example in Figure 19.1c, we have the severity of an illness and dose of medication. In an ideal world, the severity of an illness will go down as the dose of medication goes up. However, there does come a point when you can actually take too much medication for an illness (called an overdose) and the severity of your illness will go up. This is a good example of a curvilinear relationship.

Finally, as seen in Figure 19.1d, some variables are simply not related to each other at all. In this example we are looking at an individual's pizza consumption and her or his nonverbal immediacy. These two variables simply don't make sense together in the first place, so clearly as one variable's score goes up or down, there should be no clear change in the score of the other variable.

Now that we've explained what the four basic types of relationships are, we need to make one thing very clear—correlation does not mean causation. In other words, being more humorous does not cause popularity, low self-esteem does not cause high levels of communication apprehension, and more medication does not cause the severity of the illness to change. You might be thinking "of course medication causes the severity of the illness to change," which might be very true. However, the statistical tool called a correlation only examines whether or not two variables are linearly related to each other, *not* if one causes the change to occur in the other variable.

A published example of the "relationship versus causation" issue came from Eugene Volokh (2004), a professor in the UCLA School of Law, who conducted a study examining the relationship between ice cream consumption and the incidence of rape. In his study, Volokh (2004) used data from the international Dairy Foods Association's Dairy Facts (2000) publication to find out the monthly average of ice cream eaten (in millions of gallons). He then used data from the Federal Bureau of Investigation's Uniform Crime Reports (2000) to find out the number of rapes (percentage of 2000 rapes) that occurred monthly as well. The two variables were shown be strongly related to each other. An untrained person might say that this finding indicates that eating ice cream causes people to go out and rape others, but this is obviously a fairly idiotic statement. Instead, when one looks at the data more closely, there is a clear spike in the amount of ice cream consumed and the number of rapes that occur during the summer months. People eat more ice cream when it's hot, and people are outside more during the summer, which makes them more vulnerable to rape.

Another example of the problem of trying to create causation from correlation can be found in the study conducted by Janis Walworth (2001), who wanted to see if there was a relationship between the number of Protestants live in a state and the incidence of tornados. While there was no relationship between the number of Jews and Catholics living in a state and the number of tornados a state reports, this could not be said for Protestants. The relationship between the number of self-reported Protestants in a state and the number of tornados was quite strong ($r = .71$ for the statistically inclined). She further analyzed this phenomenon by examining the differences between reported categories of Protestantism (Lutheran, Methodist, and Baptist) and the number of tornados. Lutherans apparently did not annoy God enough to spite them with a natural disaster because there was not a statistical relationship between the number of Lutherans live in a state and the number of tornados a

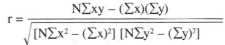

$$r = \frac{N\Sigma xy - (\Sigma x)(\Sigma y)}{\sqrt{[N\Sigma x^2 - (\Sigma x)^2] [N\Sigma y^2 - (\Sigma y)^2]}}$$

Figure 19.2 Pearson Product-Moment Correlation Formula

state experiences. However, the numbers of both Methodists (r = .52) and Baptists (r = .68) positively related to the number of tornados a state has annually. Walworth concludes by saying, "this means that Texas could cut its average of 139 tornados per year in half by sending a few hundred thousand Baptists elsewhere (Alaska maybe?)" (p. 5), which has no tornados. Obviously, Walworth is joking in this article. However, we do see the interesting phenomenon that can occur if someone tries to create causal inferences from statistical relationships. One reason there may be a strong relationship between the number of Methodists and Baptists and the number of tornados is that more Methodists and Baptists live in the region of the United States known as tornado alley. While there is a strong relationship, clearly having Methodists and Baptists in a state does not cause tornado activity.

Now that we have examined some basic information about what a correlation is, we can turn our attention to the basic assumptions of the correlation:

1. Both the independent variable and the dependent variable should be interval (communication apprehension) or ratio (heart rate change).
2. A sample should be random.
3. Scores for both variables being compared must be obtained from each participant.
4. The relationship between the two scores should be linear (positive or negative) because the Pearson product-moment correlation (the test we will be conducting) does not test for curvilinear relationships.
5. To avoid having an abnormal distribution, the Pearson product-moment correlation should have no fewer than 25 participants. (To make the math easy for this example, our example has fewer than 25 participants.)

The above assumptions are extremely important, because if one assumption is violated, the meaning of the Pearson product-moment correlation is lost. Now that we've explained what a correlation is and what the basic assumptions of the correlation are, we can look at the basic correlation formula given in Figure 19.2.

You'll notice that in this formula we are solving for the mysterious "r" value. When you see an "r" reported in research, you can be guaranteed that you are seeing a Pearson product-moment correlation. While the formula may look somewhat scary, it is just as easy as the other formulas previously computed in this book.

Case Study Introduction

Many people around the world suffer from communication apprehension. As we talked about in Chapter 7, communication apprehension can affect people in their interpersonal relationships, in health care, in organizations, and in intimate relationships. One area that communication apprehension clearly affects is one's ability to give speeches in a public setting. In this example we have a researcher who is studying the relationship between a participant's score on the Personal Report of Communication Apprehension-24 (PRCA-24) and her or his change in heart rate while giving a an impromptu speech—a speech without any time for preparation.

The researcher first has the participants fill out the PRCA-24. Then the participants are hooked up to a machine that monitors and records their heart rates. The participants are then asked to speak for 5 minutes about why they did or did not vote in the last election. The researcher records the participants' heart rate at the beginning of their speeches and throughout the speech, recording the highest heart rate achieved while speaking. After the fact, the researcher takes the highest heart rate and subtracts the baseline heart rate to obtain a figure called heart rate change. In essence, they are determining if people who have higher scores on the PRCA-24 (interval variable) have faster heart rates (ratio variable because heart rate change could be equal to 0) while giving a speech than people who have lower levels of CA while giving a speech. Before we can calculate the correlation, some basic concepts related to correlations must be discussed.

Step-by-Step Approach to the Pearson Product-Moment Correlation

In our example a researcher wants to determine if an individual's level of communication apprehension (independent variable) relates positively or negatively to a participant's change in heart rate during an impromptu speaking situation. Figure 19.3 represents the raw data for this study. In this figure, PRCA scores are referred to as "x" scores and heart rate change as "y" scores.

Step One. Before we can start completing any of the parts of the formula, we must do some simple descriptive statistics. First, we need to find the sum of x multiplied by y (Σxy). To do this, we multiply everyone's x score (PRCA-24 score) by her or his y score (heart rate change). For example, the first participant's x score is 120 and her or his y score is 5.5. To obtain xy we simply multiply 120 times 5.5, or $120 \times 5.5 = 660$. We have gone ahead and multiplied all of the xy scores in Figure 19.4 (as seen in the third column). Once you have computed all of the xy scores, you simply add them up to achieve the Σxy, which is equal to 5698.5.

Participant	Communication Apprehension (X)	Change in Heart Rate (Y)
1	120	5.5
2	71	4.6
3	72	3.8
4	118	5
5	58	3.2
6	60	3.1
7	72	3.8
8	55	2
9	115	4.9
10	70	3.7
11	68	3.5
12	24	0
13	72	3.7
14	65	3.3
15	70	3.4
16	92	4
17	95	4.1
18	90	3.8
19	63	3.4
20	24	0

Figure 19.3 Raw Data for Correlation Example

Participant	CA (x)	HR Change (y)	x*y	x*x	y*y
1	120	5.5	660	14400	30.25
2	71	4.6	326.6	5041	21.16
3	72	3.8	273.6	5184	14.44
4	118	5	590	13924	25
5	58	3.2	185.6	3364	10.24
6	60	3.1	186	3600	9.61
7	72	3.8	273.6	5184	14.44
8	55	2	10	3025	4
9	115	4.9	563.5	13225	24.01
10	70	3.7	259	4900	13.69
11	68	3.5	238	4624	12.25
12	24	0	0	576	0
13	72	3.7	266.4	5184	13.69
14	65	3.3	214.5	4225	10.89
15	70	3.4	238	4900	11.56
16	92	4	368	8464	16
17	95	4.1	389.5	9025	16.81
18	90	3.8	342	8100	14.44
19	63	3.4	214.2	3969	11.56
20	24	0	0	576	0
Sum =	**1474**	**68.8**	**5698.5** $= \Sigma xy$	**121490** $= \Sigma x^2$	**274.04** $= \Sigma y^2$
Mean =	**73.7**	**3.44**	**284.925** $= \Sigma xy$	**6074.5** $= \Sigma x^2$	**13.702** $= \Sigma y^2$

Figure 19.4 Descriptive Statistics for the Correlation Formula

Next, we need to determine the sum of squares x and then the sum of squares y. As discussed in Chapter 8, to find the sum of squares x (Σx^2) you simply square each x value (individual's PRCA score) and then add those values. For example, to square the first participants score you simply take her or his PRCA-24 score (120) and multiply it by itself ($120 \times 120 = 14400$). After you have done this for all of the participants' x scores, you simply add the scores up to obtain the sum of squares x (Σx^2), which can be seen in the fourth column in Figure 19.4. Finally, you repeat the process for each participant's y scores (heart rate change) and then add these totals together to obtain the sum of squares y (Σy^2).

Figure 19.4 has all of these totals for us. To complete the Pearson product-moment correlation formula, we need to know the sum of X ($\Sigma x = 1474$), the sum of X-squared ($\Sigma x^2 = 121,490$), the sum of Y ($\Sigma y = 68.8$), the sum of Y-squared ($\Sigma y^2 = 274.04$), the sum of X × Y ($\Sigma xy = 5698.5$), and the number of participants ($N = 20$). With these six numbers, we can now fill in every part of the correlation formula.

Step Two. The first part of the formula in Figure 19.2 we are going to complete is the part above the division line, $N\Sigma xy - (\Sigma x)(\Sigma y)$. At this point, we simply have to plug in the results from Step One into the formula and perform the calculation. Specifically, this formula asks us to multiply the number of participants ($N = 20$) by the sum of xy ($\Sigma xy = 5698.5$) and then subtract this total from the sum of x ($\Sigma x = 1474$) multiplied by the sum of y ($\Sigma y = 68.8$).

$$(20 \times 5,698.5) - (1474 \times 68.8)$$

$$(113,970) - (101,411.2)$$

$$12,558.8$$

So, the $N\Sigma xy - (\Sigma x)(\Sigma y) = 12,558.8$.

Step Three. Next, we are now going to start computing the formula under the division line. To start with, let's work on the part of the formula under the division line that appears in the left bracket, $[N\Sigma x^2 - (\Sigma x)^2]$. Once again, this is simply a matter of plugging in the results we computed in Step One. For this equation, we need to multiply the number of participants ($N = 20$) by the sum of x-squared ($\Sigma x^2 = 121,490$) and then subtract this total from the sum of x ($\Sigma x = 1474$) squared.

$$(20 \times 121,490) - (1,474)^2$$

$$(2,429,800) - (2,172,676)$$

$$257,124$$

So, $[N\Sigma x^2 - (\Sigma x)^2] = 257,124$.

Step Four. Next, we are now going to continue computing the formula under the division line, by working on the part of the formula that appears in the right bracket, $[N\Sigma y^2 - (\Sigma y)^2]$. Once again, this is simply a matter of plugging in the results we computed in Step One. For this equation, we need to multiply the number of participants ($N = 20$) by the Sum of y-squared ($\Sigma y^2 = 274.04$) and then subtract this total from the sum of y ($\Sigma y = 68.8$) squared.

$$(20 * 274.04) - (68.8)^2$$

$$(5,480.8) - (4,733.44)$$

$$747.36$$

So, $[N\Sigma y^2 - (\Sigma y)^2] = 747.36$

Step Five. In this step, we are going to do two basic computations. First we need to multiply the answer from Step Three (257,124) by the answer from Step Four (747.36): $257,124 \times 747.36 = 192,164,192.6$. Once you have done that, you simply take the square root of that number, $\sqrt{192,164,192.6} = 13,862.32998$.

Step Six. At this point, we have no calculated everything above the division line (Step Two = 12,558.8) and everything below the division line (Step Five = 13,862.32998). All we have to do now to obtain our *r* value is to divide 12,558.2 by 13,862.32998:

$$12,558.2 / 13,862.32998 = .905922743$$

So, for this example $r = .91$.

All Pearson product moment correlation coefficients (*r*) exist on a scale from 0 to 1 or 0 to –1. The closer a correlation coefficient is to 1 or –1, the stronger the relationship is. To understand what *r* means, we need to explore a concept called practical significance. Practical significance is not the same thing as statistical significance. Practical significance is an indicator of the strength of the relationship. The general agreed-upon practical significance for an *r* value is that if it is under .30 (or –.30) then it is a weak relationship (and somewhat questionable), if *r* is between .30 and .59 (or –.30 to –.59) then it is a moderate relationship (there is a clear relationship, but it's not strong), and if *r* is above .60 (or –.60) it is a strong relationship (there is a clear, strong relationship between the two variables). In our example, we achieved an *r* value of .91, so there is a clear, strong, positive relationship between the two variables. However, practical significance does not mean anything unless it is statistically significant.

Step Six. In this step we are going to determine if our *r* value (.91) is statistically significant. Before we can determine this, we need to calculate the degrees of freedom for the correlation. The formula for calculating the Pearson product moment correlation degrees of freedom is *N*-2, or the number of participants in a study (20) minus 2 ($20 - 2 = 18$). So for our example, the degree of freedom is 18.

| df | Level of Significance for a nondirectional two-tailed test | | | |
N − 2	0.10	0.05	0.01	0.001
1	0.9877	0.9969	0.9999	1.0000
2	0.9000	0.9500	0.9900	0.9990
3	0.8054	0.8783	0.9587	0.9912
4	0.7293	0.8114	0.9172	0.9741
5	0.6694	0.7545	0.8745	0.9507
6	0.6215	0.7067	0.8343	0.9249
7	0.5822	0.6664	0.7977	0.8982
8	0.5494	0.6319	0.7646	0.8721
9	0.5214	0.6021	0.7348	0.8471
10	0.4973	0.5760	0.7079	0.8233
11	0.4762	0.5529	0.6835	0.8010
12	0.4575	0.5324	0.6614	0.7800
13	0.4409	0.5139	0.6411	0.7603
14	0.4259	0.4973	0.6226	0.7420
15	0.4124	0.4821	0.6055	0.7246
16	0.4000	0.4683	0.5897	0.7084
17	0.3887	0.4555	0.5751	0.6932
18	0.3783	0.4438	0.5614	0.6787
19	0.3687	0.4329	0.5487	0.6652
20	0.3598	0.4227	0.5368	0.6524
25	0.3233	0.3809	0.4451	0.5974
30	0.2960	0.3494	0.4093	0.5541
35	0.2746	0.3246	0.3810	0.5189
40	0.2573	0.3044	0.3578	0.4896
45	0.2428	0.2875	0.3384	0.4648
50	0.2306	0.2732	0.3218	0.4433
60	0.2108	0.2500	0.2948	0.4078
70	0.1954	0.2319	0.2737	0.3799
80	0.1829	0.2172	0.2565	0.3568
90	0.1726	0.2050	0.2422	0.3375
100	0.1638	0.1946	0.2301	0.3211

The entries in this table were computed by the authors.

Figure 19.5 Critical Values Table for the Pearson Product-Moment Correlation

On the left-hand side of Figure 19.5 runs the df for the Pearson product-moment correlation. Since our df calculated for this example was 18, we need to go to the row with the number 18 listed as the df. In this row you will see the critical values listed for the calculated *r* value. As we have seen in previous chapters when examining a critical value table, if the *r* calculated is larger than the value in a column at a specific *p*-value, then the *r* value is significant at that *p*-value. For example, in the first column in row 18 is the critical value 0.3783. Since the calculated value for *r* (.91) is larger than the critical value (0.3783), then we can say the correlation is significant at *p* < .10. However, .10 does not meet the 95% confidence interval discussed in Chapter 15, so we would not consider a correlation statistically significant at this *p*-value. However, if you look across the entire row of *p*-values listed on the critical value chart (0.05, 0.01, and 0.001), the calculated *r* in this example (.91) is larger than all three of the critical values (0.4438, 0.5614, and 0.6787, respectively). The lowest *p*-value listed in the chart is .001, so we would have to declare .001 as the significance level since we do not have a more accurate significance level. However, it is probably significant at an even lower significance level, so let's examine how correlations are reported by SPSS and SAS.

Computer Printouts of the Pearson Product-Moment Correlation

Now that we have examined how the Pearson product-moment correlation can be calculated by hand, we will examine output from two statistical computer programs: SPSS and SAS.

SPSS AND PEARSON PRODUCT-MOMENT CORRELATIONS

Using SPSS to compute a Pearson product-moment correlation is fairly easy as long as you follow instructions, so let's get started. First, open up your SPSS student version and locate the file on the CD-ROM in the SPSS folder called "correlation." When you open this file you will see two variables listed: "ca" and "hrchange." "CA" is the variable name for the participants' scores on the PRCA-24, and "HRChange" is the variable name for the participants' change in heart rates while giving the impromptu speech.

To conduct a Pearson product-moment correlation using SPSS, go to the menu bar at the top of your screen and click on "Analyze." When you click on "Analyze," a dropdown menu will appear. Go to the sixth category on this menu, "Correlate," and scroll over the arrow; another menu will appear to the right. Scroll over the first option in this list, "Bivariate," and click on it. The "Bivariate Correlations" dialogue box will appear. You'll notice that there are two white boxes, one on the left-hand side of the screen (with your variables listed) and an empty one on the right-hand side of the screen labeled "Variables." You'll also notice that some correlation functions have been preselected. The SPSS "Bivariate Correlations" dialogue box allows you to perform three different types of correlations (Pearson's product-moment, Kendall's tau-b, and Spearman's rho). When you enter into the "Bivariate Correlations" dialogue box, "Pearson" is automatically checked because it is the most common form of correlation conducted by researchers. Below the three types of correlations, you'll notice that you can choose either a two-tailed significance test or a one-tailed significance test. If you remember from our discussion of significance in Chapter 15, you can use a one-tailed test if you have made a prediction about the direction of a correlation; however, it is recommended that you always use a two-tailed test since it is more conservative and less likely to cause Type I errors. For this reason, SPSS automatically selects a two-tailed significance test unless told otherwise. Finally, you'll see that SPSS has selected the "Flag significant correlations" box. When you look at the SPSS correlation printout, you'll see an asterisk (*) next to any significant correlation.

To actually run the correlation using SPSS, simply highlight the variables you want to correlate. When the variables are highlighted in blue, hit the right arrow button and the variables will transfer to the "Variables" box. At this point, simply hit "OK." The results for the SPSS results can be seen in Figure 19.6.

Correlations

Correlations

		Communication Apprehension	Heart Rate Change
Communication Apprehension	Pearson Correlation Sig. (2-tailed) N	1.000 . 20	**.906** .000 20
Heart Rate Change	Pearson Correlation Sig. (2-tailed) N	.906** .000 20	1.000 . 20

** Correlation is significant at the 0.01 level (2-tailed).

Figure 19.6 SPSS Results for CA and HR Change

When SPSS produces a correlation result, it correlates all of the variables listed as both the independent variable and as the dependent variable. For this reason, in a correlation table each result will be presented twice. Furthermore, the computer program also correlates each variable with itself. If you correlate a thing with itself, then you will have a perfect correlation of 1.0. If you look at the answer listed in the first column and the first row (CA correlated with CA), you'll notice that they list 1.0 as the correlation coefficient. You'll also notice that in column 2 / row 2 SPSS correlated HR Change with HR Change and reported a 1.0 correlation coefficient. For this reason, you will always end up with a diagonal line going through a correlation table where the program has correlated each variable with itself. On either side of that diagonal of 1.0 correlation coefficients will appear the exact same set of results. For this reason, it is recommended that you select one side of the line just to make sure you only report correlation results once.

In this example, you'll notice that the r-value listed in the SPSS chart is identical to the one we computed by hand earlier in this chapter. You'll also notice immediately under the r-value is the significance (.000) level, and immediately under that is the number of participants used in the correlation (20). The computer is able to obtain a much more exact p-value than we could by looking at a critical value chart. In this case, the correlation was found to be significant at the $p < .0005$ level. You'll notice that the printout just says that the significance is .000; however, this means that the significance is lower than this level, so adding a 5 to the end of it is the most appropriate thing to do (Levine & Atkin, 2004).

SAS AND PEARSON PRODUCT-MOMENT CORRELATIONS

To calculate a Pearson product-moment correlation you will use the Procedure statement CORR. The PROC statement used to analyze this example using SAS is:

PROC CORR;

VAR CA HRCHANGE;

The results in Figure 19.7 are exactly like those found in both our hand calculation and the results reported by SPSS. The PROC CORR procedure first provides the descriptive statistics of the two variables (CA and HRCHANGE). Again, you'll notice we've bolded the significant correlation on the results to make it stand out more easily here. SAS correlation tables can become somewhat confusing because they are not placed in a nice chart format like in SPSS. While you may not notice this problem here, in a few minutes when we look at a larger example you'll see this problem more clearly. Again, to make these tables easier to understand, we recommend finding the diagonal lines of 1.0 and marking a line through them with a highlighter to make it easier to view.

Notice that SAS reports a significance level lower than .000 (as was done in SPSS). SAS actually reports significance levels out to .0001. In the SPSS printout, we have no way of knowing if the significance level is .0005 or .0004, so reporting it at the .0005 level is the most accurate way to report the SPSS significance (Levine & Atkin, 2004). However, since SAS does report the significance level out to .0001, you may report significance levels as .0001 if they are indicated as such on the computer printouts.

APA WRITE-UP FOR SPSS

This research question tested for a relationship between an individual's level of communication apprehension and her or his increase in heart rate during an impromptu speaking situation, $r(20) = .91$, $p < .0005$, which is considered to be a strong relationship.

The CORR Procedure

2 Variables:　CA　　　　HRCHANGE

Simple Statistics

Variable	N	Mean	Std Dev	Sum	Minimum	Maximum
CA	20	73.70000	26.01235	1474	24.00000	120.00000
HRCHANGE	20	3.44000	1.40240	68.80000	0	5.50000

Pearson Correlation Coefficients, N = 20
Prob > |r| under H0: Rho=0

	CA	HRCHANGE
CA	1.00000	**0.90597** **<.0001**
HRCHANGE	0.90597 <.0001	1.00000

Figure 19.7 SAS Results for CA and HR Change

APA WRITE-UP FOR SAS

This research question tested for a relationship between an individual's level of communication apprehension and her or his increase in heart rate during an impromptu speaking situation, $r(20) = .91$, $p < .0001$, which is considered to be a strong relationship.

DISCUSSION

After all of the work we have done so far in this chapter, this is the point where we get to try to make some sense out of our results. Let's go back to the initial research question we asked. The goal of this example was to see if a person's level of communication apprehension (CA) related to a person's heart rate change (HR change) while giving an impromptu speech. We found a strong, significant relationship between CA and HR change, which means that as a person's level of CA goes up, so did her or his heart rate while giving a speech. Remember, this does not mean that an individual's CA caused the heart rate change, only that the two variables are positively related to each other. Just as another reminder, when dealing with numbers in APA style, we always round to the hundredth, or two numbers following the decimal. The only exception to this rule is the reporting of your p-value.

Relationships Between Communication Apprehension, Willingness to Communicate, and Beliefs About Public Speaking

The purpose of this example is to determine the relationships between an individual's communication apprehension (CA), willingness to communication (WTC), and their belief that all students should be required to take public speaking in college (BELIEF). To analyze this question, we conducted three correlations: CA with WTC, CA with BELIEF, and WTC with BELIEF. Since we can calculate all of these correlations in one printout, Figure 19.8 shows the SPSS printout and Figure 19.9 the SAS printout.

Correlations

Correlations

		Communication Apprehension Total	Willingness to Communicate	Everyone should be required to take public speaking in college
Communication Apprehension Total	Pearson Correlation	**1.000**	-.464**	-.345
	Sig. (2-tailed)	.	.000	.000
	N	**317**	299	305
Willingness to Communicate	Pearson Correlation	-.464**	**1.000**	.248**
	Sig. (2-tailed)	.000	.	.000
	N	299	**306**	298
Everyone should be required to take public speaking in college	Pearson Correlation	-.345	.248**	**1.000**
	Sig. (2-tailed)	.000	.000	.
	N	305	298	**312**

**Correlation is significant at the 0.01 level (2-tailed).

Figure 19.8 SPSS Results for WTC, CA, and BELIEF

```
                    The CORR Procedure

        3  Variables:  BIGCA    BIGWTC    BELIEF


                    Simple Statistics

Variable        N        Mean      Std Dev       Sum    Minimum      Maximum

BIGCA         317    64.53628     17.16919     20458   24.00000    120.00000
BIGWTC        306    71.36329     15.65637     21837   18.25000    100.00000
BELIEF        312    20.44231     10.00883      6378    5.00000     35.00000


               Pearson Correlation Coefficients
                  Prob > |r| under H0: Rho=0
                    Number of Observations

                        BIGCA       BIGWTC       BELIEF

          BIGCA       1.00000     -0.46399     -0.34504
                                   <.0001       <.0001
                          317          299          305


          BIGWTC     -0.46399      1.00000      0.24831
                       <.0001                    <.0001
                          299          306          298


          BELIEF     -0.34504      0.24831      1.00000
                       <.0001       <.0001
                          305          298          312
```

Figure 19.9 SAS Results for WTC, CA, and BELIEF

In this example, you'll notice that both SPSS and SAS indicated that there were significant relationships between the three variables. To make it somewhat easier to see the results, we boldfaced the diagonal line of 1.0 correlation coefficients where the program correlates each variable with itself. You should only look at the results either to the right of the diagonal line or the left of the diagonal line to make it easier to interpret your results. It does not matter if you look to the left or right of the diagonal line because the results are identical.

APA WRITE-UP FOR SPSS

This research question was intended to examine the relationships between an individual's communication apprehension, willingness to communication, and the belief that all students should be required to take public speaking in college. To conduct this analysis, three Pearson product-moment correlations were conducted. Communication apprehension was found to be negatively related to an individual's willingness to communicate, $r(299) = -.46$, $p < .0005$, which is considered a moderate relationship. Communication apprehension was found to be negatively related to an individual's belief that all students should be required to take public speaking in college, $r(305) = -.35$, $p < .0005$, which is considered a moderate relationship. Finally, willingness to communicate was found to positively relate to an individual's belief that all students should be required to take public speaking in college, $r(298) = .35$, $p < .0005$, which is considered a minimal relationship.

APA WRITE-UP FOR SAS

This research question was intended to examine the relationships between an individual's communication apprehension, willingness to communicate, and belief that all students should be required to take public speaking in college. To conduct this analysis, three Pearson product-moment correlations were conducted. Communication apprehension was found to be negatively related to an individual's willingness to communicate, $r(299) = -.46$, $p < .0001$, which is considered a moderate relationship. Communication apprehension was found to be negatively related to an individual's belief that all students should be required to take public speaking in college, $r(305) = -.35$, $p < .0001$, which is considered a moderate relationship. Finally, willingness to communicate was found to positively relate to an individual's belief that all students should be required to take public speaking in college, $r(298) = .35$, $p < .0001$, which is considered a minimal relationship.

Reading Large Correlation Tables

Since correlations are probably the most common statistical tool used by social scientists, understanding how to read a correlation table is extremely important. For this reason, we have taken all of the variables from the real sample data set on the CD-ROM that accompanied your textbook (communication apprehension, ethnocentrism, humor assessment, nonverbal immediacy, assertiveness, responsiveness, willingness to communicate, belief that everyone should take public speaking in college, and attitude towards higher education) and run the correlations. To determine how many correlations you will actually need to report, you can use the following formula: $[(N \times (N - 1)) / 2]$, with N being the number of variables you want to correlate. In the sample data set, we have nine unique variables, so the formula would be:

Correlations

		Communication Apprehension Total	Ethnocentrism	Humor Assessment	Nonverbal Immediacy	Assertiveness	Responsiveness	Willingness to Communicate	Everyone should be required to take public speaking in college	Attitude about Higher Education
Communication Apprehension Total	Pearson Correlation	1.000	.165**	-.248**	-.235**	-.322**	-.125*	-.464**	-.345**	-.077
	Sig. (2-tailed)	.	.003	.000	.000	.000	.026	.000	.000	.181
	N	317	316	311	311	314	314	299	305	307
Ethnocentrism	Pearson Correlation	.165**	1.000	-.322**	-.379**	.013	-.329**	-.233**	-.012	-.278
	Sig. (2-tailed)	.003	.	.000	.000	.814	.000	.000	.838	.000
	N	316	324	318	318	321	321	305	311	313
Humor Assessment	Pearson Correlation	-.248**	-.322**	1.000	.467**	.232**	.291**	.272**	.064	.382**
	Sig. (2-tailed)	.000	.000	.	.000	.000	.000	.000	.266	.000
	N	311	318	319	318	319	319	302	307	309
Nonverbal Immediacy	Pearson Correlation	-.235**	-.379**	.467**	1.000	.148**	.462**	.285**	.049	.405**
	Sig. (2-tailed)	.000	.000	.000	.	.008	.000	.000	.388	.000
	N	311	318	318	319	319	319	302	307	309
Assertiveness	Pearson Correlation	-.322**	.013	.232**	.148**	1.000	.270**	.317**	.153**	.182**
	Sig. (2-tailed)	.000	.814	.000	.008	.	.000	.000	.007	.001
	N	314	321	319	319	322	322	305	310	312
Responsiveness	Pearson Correlation	-.125*	-.329**	.291**	.462**	.270**	1.000	.265**	.050	.333**
	Sig. (2-tailed)	.026	.000	.000	.000	.000	.	.000	.385	.000
	N	314	321	319	319	322	322	305	310	312
Willingness to Communicate	Pearson Correlation	-.464**	-.233**	.272**	.285**	.317**	.265**	1.000	.248**	.135*
	Sig. (2-tailed)	.000	.000	.000	.000	.000	.000	.	.000	.019
	N	299	305	302	302	305	305	306	298	298
Everyone should be required to take public speaking in college	Pearson Correlation	-.345**	-.012	.064	.049	.153**	.050	.248**	1.000	.000
	Sig. (2-tailed)	.000	.838	.266	.388	.007	.385	.000	.	1.000
	N	305	311	307	307	310	310	298	312	311
Attitude about Higher Education	Pearson Correlation	-.077	-.278	.382**	.405**	.182**	.333**	.135*	.000	1.000
	Sig. (2-tailed)	.181	.000	.000	.000	.001	.000	.019	1.000	.
	N	307	313	309	309	312	312	298	311	314

**. Correlation is significant at the 0.01 level (2-tailed).

*. Correlation is significant at the 0.05 level (2-tailed).

Figure 19.10 Reading Large SPSS Correlation Tables

The CORR Procedure

9 Variables: BIGCA   BIGETHNO BIGHA   BIGIMM   ASSERT   RESPON   BIGWTC   BELIEF
               ATTITUDE

Simple Statistics

Variable	N	Mean	Std Dev	Sum	Minimum	Maximum
BIGCA	317	64.53628	17.16919	20458	24.00000	120.00000
BIGETHNO	324	37.53704	8.76677	12162	16.00000	61.00000
BIGHA	319	62.06270	9.82084	19798	34.00000	80.00000
BIGIMM	319	95.22571	13.19016	30377	63.00000	130.00000
ASSERT	322	36.28571	5.95249	11684	19.00000	50.00000
RESPON	322	39.39441	6.19941	12685	20.00000	50.00000
BIGWTC	306	71.36329	15.65637	21837	18.25000	100.00000
BELIEF	312	20.44231	10.00883	6378	5.00000	35.00000
ATTITUDE	314	36.40127	6.10019	11430	19.00000	42.00000

Pearson Correlation Coefficients
Prob > |r| under H0: Rho=0
Number of Observations

	BIGCA	BIGETHNO	BIGHA	BIGIMM	ASSERT
BIGCA	**1.00000**	0.16464	-0.24840	-0.23510	-0.32202
		0.0033	<.0001	<.0001	<.0001
	317	316	311	311	314
BIGETHNO	0.16464	**1.00000**	-0.32240	-0.37938	0.01319
	0.0033		<.0001	<.0001	0.8139
	316	**324**	318	318	321

Pearson Correlation Coefficients
Prob > |r| under H0: Rho=0
Number of Observations

	RESPON	BIGWTC	BELIEF	ATTITUDE
BIGCA	-0.12529	-0.46399	-0.34504	-0.07651
	0.0264	<.0001	<.0001	0.1812
	314	299	305	307
BIGETHNO	-0.32897	-0.23349	-0.01163	-0.27833
	<.0001	<.0001	0.8381	<.0001
	321	305	311	313

Figure 19.10 Reading Large SPSS Correlation Tables

The SAS System   09:50 Thursday, December 9, 2004   35

The CORR Procedure

Pearson Correlation Coefficients
Prob > |r| under H0: Rho=0
Number of Observations

	BIGCA	BIGETHNO	BIGHA	BIGIMM	ASSERT
BIGHA	-0.24840	-0.32240	**1.00000**	0.46660	0.23169
	<.0001	<.0001		<.0001	<.0001
	311	318	**319**	310	319
BIGIMM	-0.23510	-0.37938	0.46660	**1.00000**	0.14768
	<.0001	<.0001	<.0001		0.0082
	311	318	318	**319**	319
ASSERT	-0.32202	0.01319	0.23169	0.14768	**1.00000**
	<.0001	0.8139	<.0001	0.0082	
	314	321	319	319	**322**
RESPON	-0.12529	-0.32897	0.29150	0.46217	0.27020
	0.0264	<.0001	<.0001	<.0001	<.0001
	314	321	319	319	322
BIGWTC	-0.46399	-0.23349	0.27247	0.28456	0.31749
	<.0001	<.0001	<.0001	<.0001	<.0001
	299	305	302	302	305
BELIEF	-0.34504	-0.01163	0.06364	0.04942	0.15326
	<.0001	0.8381	0.2663	0.3882	0.0069
	305	311	307	307	310
ATTITUDE	-0.07651	-0.27833	0.38236	0.40515	0.18194
	0.1812	<.0001	<.0001	<.0001	0.0012
	307	313	309	309	312

Pearson Correlation Coefficients
Prob > |r| under H0: Rho=0
Number of Observations

	RESPON	BIGWTC	BELIEF	ATTITUDE
BIGHA	0.29150	0.27247	0.06364	0.38236
	<.0001	<.0001	0.2663	<.0001
	319	302	307	309
BIGIMM	0.46217	0.28456	0.04942	0.40515
	<.0001	<.0001	0.3882	<.0001
	319	302	307	309
ASSERT	0.27020	0.31749	0.15326	0.18194
	<.0001	<.0001	0.0069	0.0012
	322	305	310	312

Continued

Continued

```
                    The CORR Procedure

                Pearson Correlation Coefficients
                 Prob > |r| under H0: Rho=0
                    Number of Observations

            RESPON          BIGWTC          BELIEF         ATTITUDE

RESPON      1.00000        0.26521         0.04954         0.33268
                           <.0001          0.3847          <.0001
              322            305             310             312


BIGWTC     0.26521         1.00000         0.24831         0.13544
           <.0001                          <.0001          0.0193
              305            306             298             298


BELIEF     0.04954         0.24831         1.00000         0.00002
           0.3847          <.0001                          0.9997
              310            298             312             311


ATTITUDE   0.33268         0.13544         0.00002         1.00000
           <.0001          0.0193          0.9997
              312            298             311             314
```

Figure 19.10

$$(9 \times (9 - 1)) / 2$$

$$(9 \times 8) / 2$$

$$72 / 2$$

$$36$$

So, the correlation table will have 81 (36 correlations you need to report on one side of the diagonal, 36 correlations that are replicated on the other side of the diagonal, and 9 correlations where the variable is correlated with itself), but only 36 of them are unique correlations. Figure 19.10 contains the SPSS results, and Figure 19.11 contains the SAS results.

On the SPSS printout, to make it easier, we placed a big black line down the diagonal to point this out clearly. Also, we put a big black "X" through the left side of the diagonal, so we will only focus on those results found on the right side of the "X." Remember, the results on the left and right side of the diagonal of 1.0 are identical. To find the relationship between two variables, select a variable name from the top (columns) and one from the right side (rows). Where the column and row intersect, you will find the correlation information for the relationship between those two variables. For example, let's find the relationship between ethnocentrism and responsiveness. To do this, find the ethnocentrism row and then find the responsiveness column. The correlation you find at this intersect is $r(321) = -.33$, $p < .0005$. In other words, there is a moderate, but negative, relationship between ethnocentrism and responsiveness. Therefore, as a person's ethnocentrism goes up, her or his responsiveness goes down.

As we warned you earlier, the SAS printouts are not as easy to interpret, but they do function in the same way. SAS printouts are designed for a standard piece of paper, so the results are printed with 1-inch margins, so there is no way all of the results can be printed in a single box as with SPSS. For this reason, keeping track of the diagonal line of 1.0 is extremely important. In Figure 19.11, we have boldfaced the diagonal to make it jump more than the printouts reveal. You'll notice that the SAS printouts are broken into groupings of a handful of columns with a handful of rows For example, the first two chunks of printouts examines BIGCA and BIGETHNO with all nine variables, but the printouts are broken into two groups: (1) BIGCA, BIGETHNO, BIGHA, BIGIMM, and BIGASSERT and (2) RESPON, BIGWTC, BELIEF, and ATTITUDE. By breaking what would otherwise be one continuous line into two truncated lines, SAS presents the information in exactly the same way that SPSS does. The most important thing to remember is where the diagonal line of 1.0 is located, so you don't lose any of your actual results or replicate your results. So, let's find the relationship between an individual's humor assessment and her or his belief that everyone should take a public speaking class in college. In the four groupings of SAS results, you find the row "BIGHA" and the column "BELIEF," which indicates that these results are to the right of the diagonal line. The results for the relationship between BIGHA and BELIEF are $r(307) = .06$, $p > .05$. This finding is not significant, which indicates that an individual's level of humor assessment does not relate to her or his belief about the notion that everyone should take public speaking in college.

Discussion of the Chesebro Article

To help you understand how correlations appear in research, this section will examine two articles (both of which can be found on the CD-ROM accompanying this textbook). The first article, by Joe Chesebro, "The Relationship Between Listening Styles and Conversational Sensitivity," can be found in the folder titled "articles." To view this article, you will need to download a copy of the Adobe Acrobat Reader (http://www.adobe.com/products/acrobat/readermain.html) if you do not already have this program installed on your computer. We strongly encourage you to read the article first and then read our analysis of the article. The goal of this process is to make sure you understand how to read and interpret research results related to the Pearson product-moment correlation.

ARTICLE PURPOSE

Have you ever noticed that you can let a group of people watch a video and everyone will come away with something completely different? One reason this occurs is because of listening styles. In the Chesebro article, he talks about four listening styles (people, action, content, and time). People-oriented listeners listen for information-related feelings and emotions and areas of common interest. Action-oriented listeners like short and simple messages where people get to the point. Content oriented listeners enjoy complex messages that they can evaluate and sink their teeth into. Finally, time-oriented listeners are more focused on their watches than on the messages. The purpose of this study was to see if the four types of listener styles (people, action, content, and time) related to an individual's conversational sensitivity, or the degree to which an individual is attentive and responsive during a conversation.

METHODOLOGY

Chesebro had 239 participants in an introduction to communication course fill out scales. The set of scales the participants filled out measured listening styles and conversational sensitivity along with basic demographic information.

RESULTS

If you look at the results on page 236 in Chesebro, they are very straightforward. Chesebro used two different types of correlation (Pearson and partial correlations) in the article.

A partial correlation is an advanced correlation tool. It (r_p) allows a researcher to determine actual relationships between variables that are highly interrelated. For example, the four listening styles are highly related constructs because they all involve listening and are measured using the same scale. To control for interference between the measurement of conversational sensitivity and one listening type (people), you can rule out the interference of the other variables (action, content, and time). While this is by no means a complete description of what a partial correlation is, it should suffice to examine the results of this study.

The goal of this study was to examine the relationship between the independent variables (people, action, content, and time) and the dependent variable (conversational sensitivity). Looking at just the Pearson product-moment correlations, the people listening style is the only listening style that significantly relates to conversational sensitivity. While two of the other listening styles did relate significantly when examining the partial correlations, the correlations were minimal, and so probably not overwhelmingly meaningful.

Discussion of the Punyanunt Article

The 2000 article by Narissra Punyanunt entitled "The Effects of Humor on Perceptions of Compliance-Gaining in the College Classroom" can be found on the CD-ROM that accompanied this textbook in the folder titled "articles." To view this article, you will need to download a copy of the Adobe Acrobat Reader (http://www.adobe.com/products/acrobat/readermain.html) if you do not already have this program installed on your computer. We strongly encourage you to read the article first and then read our analysis of the article. The goal of this process is to make sure you understand how to read and interpret research results related to the Pearson product-moment correlation.

ARTICLE PURPOSE

The purpose of this article was to find the relationships between a teacher's use of humor, whether the teacher was effective at it, and how the teacher attempts to gain compliance and change behavior through communication in the college classroom. According to the article, a teacher in a college classroom can use 22 possible behavioral alteration techniques (BATs) to gain compliance and change behavior. The BATs are listed on page 34 of the Punyanunt article. The purpose of this article was to see if there were relationships between students' perception of a teacher's use of humor in the classroom and the 22 BATs and to see if a student's perception of a teacher's effectiveness at using humor in the classroom related to the 22 BATs.

METHODOLOGY

The 428 participants in this study were all students attending a large southwestern university. The participants were asked to fill out a modified version of the behavioral alteration techniques scale with one column asking participants to rate whether or not they thought their teacher used humor when using a specific behavioral alteration technique. This was measured using a five-point Likert scale from 1 *never* to 5 *always*. The second column added to the BAT scale asked participants if they thought their instructor was effective at using humor to deliver the specific behavioral alteration technique. This was measured using a five-point Likert scale from 1 *very ineffective* to 5 *very effective*.

RESULTS

To examine the relationship between a teacher's use of humor, its effectiveness, and the use of a specific behavior alteration technique, Punyanunt correlated the BAT scores for each BAT with the use of humor and effectiveness use of humor questions. The results from these analyses can be seen in the charts on pages 34–55. These results demonstrated that teachers do use humor when trying to alter students' behavior in the classroom. For example, these results indicate that when using humor to guilt students into doing something, it may not be as effective as using humor to enhance a student's self-esteem.

Conclusion

In this chapter we have examined how to compute a Pearson product-moment correlation by hand, how to compute and interpret computer results of a Pearson product-moment correlation in both SPSS and SAS, and how to write-up a Pearson product-moment correlation using APA style. We have also seen the Pearson product-moment correlation used in four different examples.

KEY TERMS

Causation	Curvilinear Relationship	Neutral Relationship
Correlation (*r*)	Negative Relationship	Positive Relationship

REFERENCES

Cheseboro, J. (1999). The relationship between listening styles and conversational sensitivity. *Communication Research Reports, 16,* 233–238.

Fisher, R. A. (1970). *Statistical methods for research workers* (14th ed.). New York: Macmillan Publishing.

Levine, T. R., & Atkin, C. (2004). The accurate reporting of software-generated *p*-values: A cautionary research note. *Communication Research Reports, 21,* 324–327.

Punyanunt, N. M. (2000). The effects of humor on perceptions of compliance-gaining in the college classroom. *Communication Research Reports, 176,* 30–38.

Volokh, E. (2004, July 13). Ice cream production is closely correlated with the rate of forcible rape [blog]. Message posted to http://volokh.com/archives/archive_2004_07 07.shtm

Walworth, J. (2001, September/October). Does God Punish Gays? A Statistical Approach. *Gay & Lesbian Review Worldwide, 8* (5), 5.

FURTHER READING

Abramson, J. H., & Abramson, Z. H. (2001). *Making sense of data: A self-instruction manual on the interpretation of epidemiological data* (3rd ed.). New York: Oxford.

Bruning, J. L., & Kintz, B. L. (1997). *Computational handbook of statistics* (4th ed.). New York: Longman.

Chen, P. Y., & Popovich, P. M. (2002). *Correlation: Parametric and nonparametric measures.* Thousand Oaks, CA: Sage.

Delwiche, L. D., & Slaughter, S. J. (2003). *The little SAS book: A primer* (3rd ed.). Cary, NC: SAS Press.

Gravetter, F. J., & Wallnau, L. B. (2000). *Statistics for the behavioral sciences* (5th ed.). Belmont, CA: Wadsworth/Thomson Learning.

Green, S. B., & Salkind, N. J. (2004). *Using SPSS for Windows and Macintosh: Analyzing and understanding data* (4th ed.). Upper Saddle River, NJ: Prentice Hall.

Hocking, J. E., Stacks, D. W., & McDermott, S. T. (2003). *Communication research* (3rd ed.). Boston: Allyn and Bacon.

Howell, D. C. (1997). *Statistical methods for psychology* (4th ed.). Belmont, CA: Duxbury Press.

Huff, D. (1954). *How to lie with statistics.* New York: W. W. Norton & Company.

Keller, D. K. (2006). *The Tao of statistics: A path to understanding (with no math).* Thousand Oaks, CA: Sage.

Pyrczak, F. (1999). *Statistics with a sense of humor: A humorous workbook and guide to study skills* (2nd ed.). Los Angeles: Pyrczak.

Salkind, N. J. (2004). *Statistics for people who (think they) hate statistics* (2nd ed.). Thousand Oaks, CA: Sage.

SAS Institute. (2004). *SAS 9.1 Companion for Windows.* Cary, NC: SAS Press.

Singleton, R. A., Jr., & Straits, B. C. (1999). *Approach to social research* (3rd ed.). New York: Oxford University Press.

Trochim, W. M. K. (2000). *The research methods knowledge base* (2nd ed.). Cincinnati, OH: Atomic Dog. Online available at: http://www.socialresearchmethods.net/

Regression

Remember when you first learned how to graph a line in high school algebra? We all learned that the formula for graphing a line is $Y = mX + b$. For example, imagine you've been asked to tutor students in public speaking during the next semester/quarter. Before you will tutor anyone, you get paid $20 to assess their skills, and then you charge $10 per hour of tutoring there after. One student, Fatwah, comes to you and wants you to tutor her for 5 hours. To determine how much you would get paid, you can plug it into the linear formula, with m equaling the charge per hour, X equaling the number of hours, and b equaling your $20 assessment fee, $Y = (10 \times 5) + 20$, or $70. If your next student, Bob, comes in and wants to be tutored for 8 hours you can still use the same formula, $Y = (10 \times 8) + 20$, or $100. And the relationship between Fatwah's cost and Bob's cost would be a perfect relationship ($r = 1.0$). Furthermore, both scores would exist on a straight line if you graphed them because you're using the same formula to determine their overall cost. If Tika then comes to you and only wants to receive 2 hours of tutoring, you can once again use the formula to determine how much she would be charged, $Y = (10 \times 2) + 20$, or $40. Figure 20.1 shows these three situations on a graph. Remember, b values are points where the line intercepts the Y-axis. Notice in this

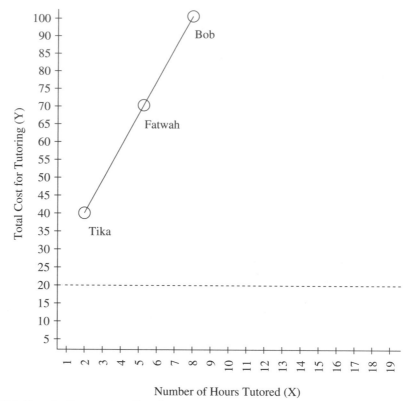

Figure 20.1 Simple Regression Graph

graph that the three points form a perfect line or have an *r*-value of 1.0. Unfortunately, most relationships are not perfect (*r* = 1.0), so seeing perfect lines does not happen very often in research. However, a simple linear regression can let us know how close to the perfect line the relationship between two variables is.

As mentioned in the chapter on one-way ANOVA, there is a series of statistical tests that all fall in the general category of general linear models (GLM), which includes regression. The easiest way to start understanding the general linear model is through the discussion we had earlier looking at how two variables (time tutoring and amount paid) are linearly related to each other. Throughout this entire chapter we will be discussing the importance of linearity with reference to bivariate regression and multiple regression equations. Before we get into too much detail about linear equations, let's revisit the example from the previous chapter.

Case Study Introduction

In the previous chapter we examined the relationship between an individual's score on the Personal Report of Communication Apprehension–24 (PRCA-24) and her or his change in heart rate while giving an impromptu speech in public. We found that there was a significant correlation between the two variables: *r*(20) = .91 and *p* < .0005. This finding indicates that there is a strong, positive linear relationship between an individual's level of communication apprehension (CA) and her or his increase in heart rate (HR change) while giving an impromptu speech. This chapter is going to take the same example, but further develop the nature of the linear relationship between CA and HR change.

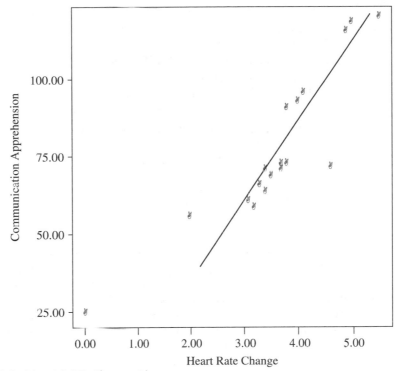

Figure 20.2 CA with HR Change Line

$$Y = m_{slope} X + b_{constant}$$ **Figure 20.3** Regression Equation

$$m = \frac{\Sigma xy - (N * \mu_x * \mu_y)}{\Sigma X^2 - N\mu_x^2}$$

$$b = \mu_y - b\mu_x$$

Let's compare the perfect line seen in Figure 20.1 to the line between CA and HR change from Chapter 19, which can be seen in Figure 20.2. The line drawn in on top of the scatterplot (type of graph that illustrates where participants scores on the x-axis value [HR change] and the y-axis value [CA] intersect) runs through the means of both variables to demonstrate w h e r e the linear relationship exists. Notice that most of the participants' scores for CA and HR change do not fall on the line perfectly. When this occurs, the predictive nature of the linear relationship is not perfect and we have some amount of error. Therefore, the formula for examining regressions must include an error term as seen in Figure 20.3.

Regression Background Information

Now that we have examined some basic information about what a regression is, we can turn our attention to the basic assumptions of the regression:

1. Both the independent variable(s) and the dependent variable should be interval (communication apprehension) or ratio (heart rate change).

2. Your sample should be random.

3. Scores for both variables being compared must be obtained from each participant.

4. The cases represent scores (on CA and HR change) that are independent of each other from one participant in your sample to the next participant. In other words, Jerry's level of CA cannot impact Heather's HR change.

5. The dependent variable (HR change) must be normally distributed in the population for each level of the independent variable. To ensure normal distributions, adequate sample sizes are necessary. Small samples may produce *p*-values that are invalid.

6. The population variances of the dependent variable (HR change) are the same for all levels of the independent variable. If this assumption is violated, then the resulting *p*-value for the overall *F* test is not trustworthy.

The above assumptions are extremely important because if one assumption is violated, the meaning of the linear regression is lost.

While a correlation does not require that you specifically determine independent and dependent variables, a regression requires that you know which variable is independent and which variable is dependent. In our example we are predicting that a person's communication apprehension (independent variable) can account for why a person's heart rate increases while giving an impromptu speech (dependent variable). You should also remember that independent variables and dependent variables often are not interchangeable. For example, it would not make sense to say that a person's change in heart rate while giving an impromptu speech causes her or his preexisting level of communication apprehension. With these two variables, there is clearly only one direction in which the linear equation can occur. Remember, correlations just test for relationships—regressions are creating predictive equation lines. It is the hope of the regression that if you are able to supply a person's CA score—then you can determine how much her or his heart rate will increase. If the correlation between two variables was 1.0, then the predictive nature of the line would be perfect. However, since our correlation between CA and HR change was .91, there is going to be some amount of error in our ability to predict a person's HR change from her or his CA score.

Step-by-Step Approach to a Linear Regression

In our example, a researcher wants to determine the nature of the linear relationship between an individual's level of communication apprehension (independent variable) and her or his change in heart rate during an impromptu speaking situation. In essence, the goal is to find the "best fitting" straight line that was drawn in Figure 20.2 for the correlation data discussed in Chapter 19. This line is called a regression line. So what do we mean by "best fit?" For any set of data, it is possible to draw hundreds of lines that will pass through the data and appear meaningful. However, only one line is the best line to represent the relationship between the data and the actual relationship between the two variables, and this line is said to provide the "best fit" for the actual data points in a study. Before we can complete the linear aspect of the regression equation, we need to retrieve some information from Chapter 19. We need to know the sum of x ($\Sigma x = 1474$), the sum of x-squared ($\Sigma x^2 = 121{,}490$), the sum of y ($\Sigma y = 68.8$), the sum of y-squared ($\Sigma y^2 = 274.04$), the sum of X × Y ($\Sigma xy = 5698.5$), and the number of participants (N = 20). If you forgot how these numbers were calculated, please refresh your memory by rereading the first part of Chapter 19.

Step One. In this step we need to find the mean of x (CA) and the mean of y (HR Change). To find the mean of x (μ_x), we simply take the sum of x (1,474) and divide it by N (20), or $1{,}474/20 = 73.7$. Next we just repeat this process for the mean of y(μ_y), or $68.8/20 = 3.44$.

Step Two. In this step we are going to compute the top portion of the formula for b, $\Sigma xy - (n \times \Sigma\mu_x \times \Sigma\mu_y)$. We already know the sum of x × y ($\Sigma xy = 5698.5$), the number of participants in the study ($N = 20$), the mean of x ($\mu_x = 73.7$), and the mean of y ($\mu_y = 3.44$). Since we have already calculated each of these numbers, all we have to do is complete the formula as follows:

$$\Sigma xy - (n \times \mu_x \times \mu_y)$$

$$5698.5 - (20 \times 73.7 \times 3.44)$$

$$5698.5 - 5070.56$$

$$627.94$$

So, $\Sigma xy - (n \times \mu_x \times \mu_y) = 627.94$

Step Three. Now we need to calculate the part of the equation under the division bar, $\Sigma x^2 - N\mu_x^2$. Again, we have already calculated the sum of x-squared ($\Sigma x^2 = 121,490$), the number of people in the sample ($N = 20$), and the mean of x ($\mu_x = 73.7$). Since we have already calculated each of these numbers, all we have to do is complete the formula as follows:

$$\Sigma x^2 - N\mu_x^2$$

$$121,490 - (20 \times 73.7^2)$$

$$121,490 - (20 \times 5431.69)$$

$$121,490 - 108,633.8$$

$$12,856.2$$

So, $\Sigma x^2 - N\mu_x^2 = 12,856.2$

Step Four. In this step, we simply need to complete the equation by dividing the finding for Step Two (627.94) by the finding in Step Three (12,856.2), or 627.94/12,856.2 = 0.048433596. In other words, the slope of the linear relationship between CA and HR change is $m = 0.048433596$.

Step Five. Now that we have found m we need switch gears and find the constant or m. To find b we simply have to fill in the following equation: $b = \mu_y - b\mu_x$. At this point we already know the mean of y ($\mu_y = 3.44$), the slope of the line ($m = 0.048433596$), and the mean of x ($\mu_x = 73.7$), so we just need to fill in the formula:

$$\mu_y - b\mu_x$$

$$3.44 - (0.048433596 \times 73.7)$$

$$3.44 - (0.048433596 \times 73.7)$$

$$3.44 - 3.599755603$$

$$-0.159755603$$

So, $b = -0.159755603$

Now we have all of the parts needed to complete the linear equation of $Y = mX + b$. So, the linear equation for the "best-fit" line between CA and HR change is:

$$Y = mX + b$$

$$Y = 0.048433596X + -0.159755603$$

At this point, we can turn our attention to the results from the computer to determine if this "best-fit" line between CA and HR change is significant.

Computer Printouts of the Linear Regression

Now that we have examined how the linear regression line can be calculated by hand, we will examine the output from SPSS and SAS.

SPSS AND SIMPLE LINEAR REGRESSIONS

Using SPSS to compute a simple linear regression is very easy, so let's get started. First, open up your SPSS student version and then locate the file on the CD-ROM in the SPSS folder called "regression." When you open this file, you will see two variables listed "ca" and "hrchange." "CA" is the variable name for individual's scores on the PRCA-24, and "HR Change" is the variable name for an individual's change in heart rate while giving the impromptu speech. You could also use the file from the last chapter labeled "Correlation" since the data is identical.

To conduct a linear regression, go to the menu bar at the top of your screen and click on "Analyze." When you click on "Analyze," a dropdown menu will appear. Go to the seventh category on this menu "Regression" and scroll over the arrow and another menu will appear to the right. Scroll over the first option in this list "Linear" and click on it. The "Linear Regression" dialogue box will appear. As we have previously noted, in this example a person's CA is the independent variable, so it should be placed in the second box down, labeled "Independent(s)." To do this, highlight the variable "ca" and then click the right arrow next to the box labeled "Independent(s)." Next, we need to place the "hrchange" variable in the "Dependent" box by highlighting the variable "hrchange" and then click the right arrow next to the box labeled "Dependent." Once you have moved the variables, simply click "OK," and SPSS will produce the results that you see in Figure 20.4.

In the first box, SPSS tells you which variable(s) are the independent variables (in the "Variables Entered" box) and which variable was the dependent variable listed as "b" under the box itself. The second box of statistics is extremely important. The first column of results reports the "R" value for this linear regression. Since this is a bivariate linear regression (meaning we only looked at two variables—CA and HR change), the R value is the same computational value received for r in the last chapter, so R = .91. The second box indicates the R^2 value. R^2 is a very important concept to understand when talking about regressions. R^2 is a coefficient of determination, which means that R^2 determines what proportion of the variability in Y or your dependent variable (HR change) can be predicted by its relationship with X or your independent variable (CA). In our example, $R^2 = .821$, which indicates that 82% of the variance in an individual's heart rate changes while giving an impromptu speech can be predicted by an individual's level of communication apprehension. With that said, we should remember that to find out how much of the variance is not accounted for by our linear regression, we simply subtract R^2 from 1 ($1 - 0.821 = 0.179$). In other words, 17.9% of an individual's change in her or his heart rate while giving an impromptu speech can not be predicted by the linear relationship with communication apprehension. In essence, not all of the increase in an individual's heart rate during an impromptu speech can be accounted for by her or his level communication apprehension. The next column, "Adjust R Square," is a mathematical adjustment to R^2 that attempts to more accurately reflect the goodness of fit in the overall linear regression. In essence, researchers may attempt to conduct a regression when they have enough participants to justify the number of independent variables they

Regression

Variables Entered/Removed[b]

Model	Variables Entered	Variables Removed	Method
1	Communication Apprehension[a]		Enter

[a.] All requested variables entered.
[b.] Dependent Variable: Heart Rate Change

Model Summary

Model	R	R Square	Adjusted R Square	Std. Error of the Estimate
1	.906[a]	.821	.811	.6100

[a.] Predictors: (Constant), Communication Apprehension

ANOVA[b]

Model		Sum of Squares	df	Mean Square	F	Sig.
1	Regression	30.671	1	30.671	82.432	.000[a]
	Residual	6.697	18	.372		
	Total	37.368	19			

[a.] Predictors: (Constant), Communication Apprehension
[b.] Dependent Variable: Heart Rate Change

Coefficients[a]

Model		Unstandardized Coefficients		Standardized Coefficients	t	Sig.
		B	Std. Error	Beta		
1	(Constant)	-.160	.419		-.381	.708
	Communication Apprehension	4.884E-02	.005	.906	9.079	.000

[a.] Dependent Variable: Heart Rate Change

Figure 20.4 SPSS Regression Results for CA and HR Change

are using. When this happens, the adjusted R^2 is a more accurate portrayal of the variance accounted for. Datasets that use small samples and a large number of independent variables will see the greatest differences between R^2 and adjusted R^2. The last column, the "Standard Error of Estimate," provides a measure of how accurately the regression equation predicts dependent variable values. The smaller your standard error of estimate is, the better you can predict that the independent variable(s) accounts for variance in the dependent variable. In this case, the standard distance between the actual data points seen in this example and the regression line is 0.61, which would indicate that the actual data points are fairly close to the regression line. The higher the standard error, the lower your R value will be.

The next table of results is also important because it is a traditional ANOVA summary table akin to the one we saw in Chapter 18 when we examined one-way ANOVAs. The reason we get an ANOVA summary table for a regression is because regressions, like one-way ANOVAs, are based on the general linear model, so the F test allows us to determine whether or not our linear regression was statistically significant. If you need a refresher course in reading an ANOVA summary table, reread the discussion in Chapter 18 on how to create them.

The fourth box in the SPSS results, "Coefficients," is extremely important for regressions, but not necessarily for a simple linear bivariate regression like the example we used above. We will examine a more complicated regression model called a multiple linear regression later in this chapter and spend more time discussing this box at that point. However, we do want to point out it contains the information you need for creating your line formula $Y = mX + b$. The second column in this box is labeled "Unstandardized Coefficients," and in this column is the letter B. The first number listed under "B" is your constant (b) or y-axis number (-0.160). The second number needed to create your linear equation is in the "Communication Apprehension" row (4.884E-02), which is scientific notation for 0.04884. When you put these two numbers together you achieve the same linear formula that we calculated by hand earlier, $Y = 0.04X + -0.16$.

SAS AND THE SIMPLE LINEAR REGRESSION

To calculate a linear regression you will use the procedure statement REG. The PROC statement used to analyze this example using SAS is:

PROC REG;

MODEL HRCHANGE=CA / STB;

The results in Figure 20.5 are exactly like those found in both our hand calculation and the results reported by SPSS. You'll notice that we have separated the results into four rows of information to make it easier to explain. However, when SAS actually displays these printouts, the results are displayed as a single file without the clear separation of parts. In the first section of results, the SAS program let's you know which procedure has been conducted—"The REG Procedure"—what type of model was used—"MODEL1"—what your dependent variable was—"HRCHANGE"—and the number of observations read and used to calculate your linear regression. The second box is the ANOVA summary table, just like we saw in the chapter on one-way ANOVAs and above in the SPSS results. If you compare the SAS and SPSS results, you'll notice that the rounding may be slightly different, but the overall results are identical.

In the third grouping, you will see the term root MSE. The root MSE is a different way of saying standard error of estimate, and the root MSE is the identical calculation that was presented by the SPSS results earlier. To the right of the root MSE is the value for R-square (.8208) and below the R-square number is the adjusted R-square (.8108), which we also saw above in the SPSS printouts. You'll notice that SAS does not print out your R value for you. As always, to find R from R^2, simply take the square root of R^2.

The last set of results is called parameter estimates and is similar to the SPSS "Coefficients" box. You'll notice that in the bottom right-hand corner of this set of results under the column heading "Standardized Estimate" is the value 0.90597, which is the R value (this is only true in a bivariate linear regression). You'll also notice that under the "Parameter Estimate" column is the information needed to form the linear equation we calculated by hand earlier in this example. We will discuss the other parts of the parameter estimates SAS results later in this chapter.

APA WRITE-UP

A bivariate linear regression was conducted to evaluate the prediction of heart rate change during an impromptu speech from an individual's level of communication apprehension. The regression equation for predicting an individual's hear rate change is

Change in heart rate = (0.04 × communication apprehension) + −0.16

```
                        The REG Procedure
                          Model: MODEL1
                   Dependent Variable: HRCHANGE

               Number of Observations Read        20
               Number of Observations Used        20
```

Analysis of Variance

Source	DF	Sum of Squares	Mean Square	F Value	Pr > F
Model	1	30.67070	30.67070	82.43	<.0001
Error	18	6.69730	0.37207		
Corrected Total	19	37.36800			

Root MSE	0.60998	R-Square	0.8208	
Dependent Mean	3.44000	Adj R-Sq	0.8108	
Coeff Var	17.73190			

Parameter Estimates

Variable	DF	Parameter Estimate	Standard Error	t Value	Pr > |t|	Standardized Estimate
Intercept	1	-0.15976	0.41929	-0.38	0.7077	0
CA	1	0.04884	0.00538	9.08	<.0001	0.90597

Figure 20.5 SAS Regression Results for CA and HR Change

The linear combination of communication apprehension and heart rate change was significant: $F(1, 18) = 82.43$, $p < .0001$. The sample multiple correlation coefficient (R) was .91, which indicates that approximately 82% of the variance in heart rate change in the sample can be accounted for by an individual's level of communication apprehension.

DISCUSSION

We have now looked at this example for two complete chapters, so you are probably getting somewhat tired of trying to further your understanding of communication apprehension and the effect it has on heart rate change while a person delivers an impromptu speech. However, this simple example has illustrated how both a Pearson product-moment correlation could be conducted and how a bivariate linear regression could be conducted. The regression finding indicates that there is a certain predictive nature between a person's level of CA and the change we could expect to see in her or his heart rate during an impromptu speech. Let's pretend that Pam has a CA score of 90. Using the equation generated by this example, we can actually predict how much Pam's heart rate will increase while giving an impromptu speech. We simply plug in Pam's CA score for X:

Change in heart rate = (0.04 × communication apprehension) + −0.16

Change in heart rate = (0.04 × 90) + −0.16

Change in heart rate = (3.6) + −0.16

Change in heart rate = 3.44

Given this finding, we would expect that Pam's heart rate would increase by 3.44 beats per minute during an impromptu speech. Admittedly, this is just an example and not based on actual research findings, but it does illustrate how regression equations can be used to make predictions.

Relationships Between Communication Apprehension and Beliefs About Public Speaking

Here we present an example based on actual research collected from a college sample. In this research question, we want to see if an individual's level of communication apprehension (independent variable) can predict an individual's belief that public speaking should be

Regression

Variables Entered/Removed[b]

Model	Variables Entered	Variables Removed	Method
1	bigca[a]		Enter

[a] All requested variables entered.
[b] Dependent Variable: belief

Model Summary

Model	R	R Square	Adjusted R Square	Std. Error of the Estimate
1	.345[a]	.119	.116	9.40001

[a] Predictors: (Constant), bigca

ANOVA[b]

Model		Sum of Squares	df	Mean Square	F	Sig.
1	Regression	3618.233	1	3618.233	40.949	.000[a]
	Residual	26773.164	303	88.360		
	Total	30391.397	304			

[a] Predictors: (Constant), bigca
[b] Dependent Variable: belief

Coefficients[a]

Model		Unstandarized Coefficients		Standardized Coefficients		
		B	Std. Error	Beta	t	Sig.
1	(Constant)	33.369	2.097		15.917	.000
	bigca	-.201	.031	-.345	-6.399	.000

[a] Dependent Variable: belief

Figure 20.6 SPSS Results for Linear Regression of CA and Belief

```
                        The REG Procedure
                        Model: MODEL1
                    Dependent Variable: BELIEF

         Number of Observations Read              325
         Number of Observations Used              305
         Number of Observations with Missing Values  20

                        Analysis of Variance

                              Sum of        Mean
    Source            DF      Squares       Square    F Value   Pr > F

    Model              1    3618.23300   3618.23300    40.95   <.0001
    Error            303       26773      88.36028
    Corrected Total  304       30391

              Root MSE            9.40001   R-Square    0.1191
              Dependent Mean     20.40328   Adj R-Sq    0.1161
              Coeff Var          46.07110

                        Parameter Estimates

                   Parameter    Standard                        Standardized
    Variable   DF   Estimate      Error    t Value   Pr > |t|     Estimate

    Intercept   1   33.36941     2.09651    15.92     <.0001             0
    BIGCA       1   -0.20115     0.03143    -6.40     <.0001      -0.34504
```

Figure 20.7 SAS Results for Linear Regression of CA and Belief

a required course for all college students. The findings for this linear regression can be seen in Figure 20.6 for the SPSS printout and Figure 20.7 for the SAS printout.

In this example, you'll notice that both SPSS and SAS results are basically identical in the linear regression equation, so let's look at the APA write-up.

APA WRITE-UP

A bivariate linear regression was conducted to evaluate the prediction of an individual's belief that all college students should be required to take public speaking from her or his level of communication apprehension. The regression equation for predicting an individual's belief that all college students should be required to take public speaking is:

Belief about public speaking = (−0.20 × communication apprehension) + 33.37

The linear combination of communication apprehension and belief about public speaking was significant: $F(1, 303) = 40.95$, $p < .0001$. The sample multiple correlation coefficient (R) was .35, which indicates that approximately 12% of the variance in a person's belief that all college students should be required to take public speaking in the sample can be accounted for by an individual's level of communication apprehension.

Understanding Multiple Linear Regressions

Multiple linear regressions allow researchers to determine how a number of independent variables collectively account for the variance in a single dependent variable. For example, perhaps we wanted to go further than just communication apprehension and see how an individual's level of willingness to communicate, assertiveness, responsiveness, and communication apprehension accounted for the variance in her or his belief that all college students should take public speaking. Figure 20.8 is a pictorial representation of what we're asking in a multiple linear regression.

When we ran this research question in SPSS or SAS, we indicated that there were multiple independent variables (CA, WTC, assertiveness, and responsiveness) instead of just one, like we did in the previous two examples in this chapter, and one dependent variable (student belief about college). The results for what a multiple linear regression would look like can be seen in Figures 20.9 (SPSS) and 20.10 (SAS).

Notice that the output has not changed in how it is presented, but there is now more information presented in the "Coefficients" box in SPSS or the "Parameter Estimates" section in SAS. For this reason we need to discuss what the results in the "Coefficients" box in SPSS or the "Parameter Estimates" section in SAS mean. First, the column marked "B" in SPSS and "Parameter Estimate" in SAS represents the same linear equation as seen in the bivariate linear regression in the previous two examples, but this one is more complex.

$$Y = -0.17X_{CA} + 0.09X_{WTC} + -0.02X_{ASSERTIVENESS} + -0.04X_{RESPONSIVENESS} + 27.25$$

It's still the same linear $Y = mX + b$, but now you have four mX statements—one for each independent variable you are examining. Ultimately, this is where the true power of the general linear model comes into play for researchers. The next column is your standardized error for the "Unstandardized Coefficients" in SPSS and "Parameter Estimates" in SAS.

This is followed by the "Standardized Coefficients" column in SPSS and the t-value column in SAS. In SAS, the "Standardized Estimate" column, which is the last column in the "Parameter Estimates" section, is the same thing as the "Standardized Coefficients" column in SPSS. The values represented in this column can be interpreted as correlation coefficients

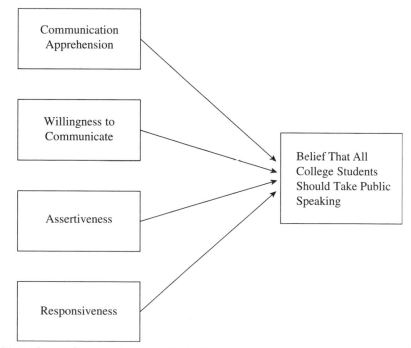

Figure 20.8 Pictorial Example of Multiple Linear Regression

Regression

Variables Entered/Removed[b]

Model	Variables Entered	Variables Removed	Method
1	respon, bigca, assert, bigwtc[a]		Enter

[a.] All requested variables entered.
[b.] Dependent Variable: belief

Model Summary

Model	R	R Square	Adjusted R Square	Std. Error of the Estimate
1	.367[a]	.135	.123	9.41036

[a.] Predictors: (Constant), respon, bigca, assert, bigwtc

ANOVA[b]

Model		Sum of Squares	df	Mean Square	F	Sig.
1	Regression	3946.475	4	986.619	11.141	.000[a]
	Residual	25326.687	286	88.555		
	Total	29273.162	290			

[a.] Predictors: (Constant), respon, bigca, assert, bigwtc
[b.] Dependent Variable: belief

Coefficients[a]

Model		Unstandardized Coefficients		Standardized Coefficients		
		B	Std. Error	Beta	t	Sig.
1	(Constant)	27.250	6.459		4.219	.000
	bigca	-.168	.036	-.292	-4.608	.000
	bigwtc	.088	.041	.136	2.124	.035
	assert	-.024	.106	-.014	-.230	.819
	respon	-.036	.097	-.022	-.376	.707

[a.] Dependent Variable: belief

Figure 20.9 SPSS Results for Multiple Linear Regression

and are called beta weights. However, for a beta weight to be significant, the t-value must be significant. For example, communication apprehension has a beta weight of -0.292, a t-value of 4.22, and a p-value of .0001. In essence, this indicates that communication apprehension significantly accounts for a portion of the unique variance in a person's belief that public speaking should be required of all college students. However, if you look at responsiveness, the results indicate that it has a beta weight of -.022, a t-value of -0.38, and a p-value of .7075, which would indicate that responsiveness does not account for a portion of the unique variance in a person's belief that public speaking should be required for all college students. Beta weights are actually just standardized ways of examining the "Standardized Coefficients"

```
                        The REG Procedure
                          Model: MODEL1
                     Dependent Variable: BELIEF

          Number of Observations Read                  325
          Number of Observations Used                  291
          Number of Observations with Missing Values    34

                         Analysis of Variance

                            Sum of         Mean
     Source          DF    Squares        Square    F Value    Pr > F

     Model            4   3946.47496   986.61874     11.14    <.0001
     Error          286      25327      88.55485
     Corrected Total 290      29273

              Root MSE            9.41036   R-Square    0.1348
              Dependent Mean     20.42612   Adj R-Sq    0.1227
              Coeff Var          46.07023

                        Parameter Estimates

                    Parameter     Standard                          Standardized
     Variable    DF   Estimate       Error    t Value  Pr > |t|       Estimate

     Intercept    1   27.24966     6.45921      4.22   <.0001                0
     BIGCA        1   -0.16811     0.03648     -4.61   <.0001         -0.29233
     BIGWTC       1    0.08812     0.04148      2.12    0.0345         0.13635
     ASSERT       1   -0.02425     0.10561     -0.23    0.8186         -0.01365
     RESPON       1   -0.03632     0.09669     -0.38    0.7075         -0.02151
```

Figure 20.10 SAS Results for Multiple Linear Regression

or "Parameter Estimates," which are actually unstandardized regression coefficients (*B*) or partial regression coefficients.

APA WRITE-UP

A multiple regression was conducted to evaluate how well the independent variables (communication apprehension, willingness to communicate, assertiveness, and responsiveness) could predict the dependent variable (an individual's belief that all college students should be required to take public speaking). The linear combination of the independent variables was significantly related to an individual's belief that all college students should be required to take public speaking: $F(4, 286) = 11.14$, $p < .0001$. The sample multiple correlation coefficient, R, was .37, which indicates that approximately 13% of the variance of an individual's belief that all college students should be required to take public speaking could be accounted for by the linear combination of communication apprehension, willingness to communicate, assertiveness, and responsiveness. However, only communication apprehension ($t = -4.61$, $p < .0001$, $\beta = -.29$) and willingness to communicate ($t = 2.12$, $p < .05$, $\beta = .14$) account for any of the unique variance in an individual's belief that all college students should be required to take public speaking.

DISCUSSION

So, what does this actually mean? Well, a multiple regression allows us to see whether the linear combination of a variety of variables (CA, WTC, assertiveness, and responsiveness) can help predict a dependent variable (belief that all college students should be required to take public speaking). In this case we found that only an individual's CA and her or his WTC actually helps to predict her or his belief that all college students should be required to take public speaking. Assertiveness and responsiveness, on the other hand, were not shown to add anything to one's ability to predict a person's belief that all college students should be required to take public speaking. As usual, the statistical process may be complex and unnerving at times, but the findings are generally fairly straightforward.

Discussion of the Wrench and Booth-Butterfield Article

Because regressions are very commonly used in communication research, we are going to examine two studies that have utilized regressions in this chapter. The article by Jason Wrench and Melanie Booth-Butterfield (2003) entitled "Increasing Patient Satisfaction and Compliance: An Examination of Physician Humor Orientation, Compliance-Gaining Strategies, and Perceived Credibility" can be found on the CD-ROM that accompanied this textbook in the folder titled "articles." To view this article, you will need to download a copy of the Adobe Acrobat Reader (http://www.adobe.com/products/acrobat/readermain.html) if you do not already have this program installed on your computer. We strongly encourage you to read the article first and then read our analysis. The goal of this process is to make sure you understand how to read and interpret research results related to the linear and multiple linear regressions.

ARTICLE PURPOSE

Have you ever noticed that some physicians have a good sense of humor when interacting with their patients and some simply do not? Well, this is what the authors of this study had noticed, and they wanted to determine how a physician's humor orientation (use of jokes and humorous story telling during interpersonal interactions) related to patient perceptions of credibility (competence, caring/goodwill and trustworthiness), patient satisfaction (affective, behavioral, and cognitive), use of compliance-gaining strategies (expectancies/consequences, relationship/identification, and values/obligations), and actual patient compliance. (See the original article for a more detailed explanation of what each of these variables actually entails.)

METHODOLOGY

Participants in this study were college students ($N = 44$), professional educators in a masters' program ($N = 48$), people shopping at a mall ($N = 142$), and people online ($N = 26$). All participants were asked to fill out a variety of scales measuring the study variables using either a pen-and-paper test or an Internet-based survey.

RESULTS

The results from this study indicated that physician humor can help predict a patient's satisfaction (affective, behavioral, and cognitive) and a patient's perception of a physician's credibility (competence, trustworthiness, and caring/goodwill). In a multiple regression analysis using physician humor orientation, credibility, use of compliance gaining strategies, and patient satisfaction as the independent variables and actual patient compliance as the dependent variable, 11% of the variance in compliance was accounted for by two compliance-gaining strategies (expectancies/consequences and values/obligations) and two forms of patient satisfaction (cognitive and behavioral).

While humor was shown to be a strong predictor of satisfaction and patients' perceptions of physician credibility, it did not affect whether or not a patient would actually comply with a physician's treatment plan. We chose this article because the regression analyses are very straightforward and are designed in a way that follows the reporting format that we have shown you in this chapter. You'll also notice that this article reported results for correlations and a one-way ANOVA as well, which is often the case in actual research. Most research does not rely on single statistical tests like the majority of the articles we have selected for inclusion on the CD-ROM that accompanies this book.

Discussion of the Rocca and Vogl-Bauer Article

The 1999 article by Kelly Rocca and Sally Vogl-Bauer entitled "Trait Verbal Aggression, Sports Fan Identification, and Perceptions of Appropriate Sports Fan communication" can be found on the CD-ROM that accompanied this textbook in the folder titled "articles." To view this article, you will need to download a copy of the Adobe Acrobat Reader (http://www.adobe.com/products/acrobat/readermain.html) if you do not already have this program installed on your computer. We strongly encourage you to read the article first and then read our analysis. The goal of this process is to make sure you understand how to read and interpret research results related to the linear and multiple linear regressions.

ARTICLE PURPOSE

Let's face it, sports fans are nuts!!! Now, we're not talking about the average sports enthusiast (the person who enjoys a good game on a Sunday afternoon or Monday night). No, we're talking about the cheese-head–wearing, body-painting, screaming and yelling types that are often broadcast into our living rooms while we're watching any kind of athletic competition. Sometimes these sports fans can get really out of control. Fans have been known to assault fans from other teams, destroy property, cause riots, and exhibit other antisocial forms of behavior. After noticing this phenomenon, Rocca and Vogl-Bauer wanted to determine what fans saw as appropriate forms of sports fan communication.

To examine appropriate fan behavior, Rocca and Vogl-Bauer created a new scale for measuring fan behavior. The scale consists of three sub-scales: verbal response (yelling at officials, taunting the opposing team, openly criticizing players and coaches, etc.), fan display (wearing clothing with team logos, wearing jewelry with team logos, buying a news paper to read about the team, etc.), and violent response (destroying objects while watching a game, hitting someone during an intense game, being more violent than normal during a game, etc.). Ultimately, Rocca and Vogl-Bauer wanted to determine how fan display, verbal response, and physical response related to sports spectator identification (degree of connection a person feels with a specific sports team) and verbal aggression (personality construct where people use character attacks, competence attacks, insults, maledictions, teasing, profanity, and threats to attack the self-concept or self-esteem of another person).

METHODOLOGY

Participants in this study were undergraduates from either a large Eastern university ($N = 213$) or a medium-sized Midwestern university ($N = 194$). The participants were asked to fill out three scales (verbal aggression, fan identification, a revised version of the sports identification behavior scale).

RESULTS

In this study there are only two basic research questions. The first research question examined the relationship between sports fans' verbal aggression and sports fans perceptions of appropriate communicative messages at a sporting event (behavioral identification, verbal response, and physical violence). The researchers examined how participants' perceptions of appropriateness of communicative behavior (behavioral identification, verbal harassment, and physical violence) could account for an individual's level verbal aggression (dependent variable). The independent variables accounted for 12% of the variance in an individual's verbal aggression. Rocca and Vogl-Bauer found that fan display related negatively to verbal aggression ($\beta = -.12$) and verbal response related positively to verbal aggression ($\beta = .28$), but violence did not significantly account for any of the unique variance in an individual's level of verbal aggression.

Next, Rocca and Vogl-Bauer examined how participants' perceptions of appropriateness of communicative behavior (behavioral identification, verbal harassment, and physical violence) could account for an individual's sport spectator identification (dependent variable). The independent variables accounted for 9% of the variance in an individual's sport spectator identification. Both verbal response ($\beta = .27$) and fan display ($\beta = .17$) related positively to sports spectator identification, but violence did not significantly account for any of the unique variance in an individual's level of sport spectator identification.

The regression equations used in this article are written up using APA style, which is slightly different from those used in the Wrench and Booth-Butterfield article discussed. This does not mean that one format is better than another, just different. One of the things you will learn as you continue doing social scientific research is that there are a variety of ways to present the same information.

Conclusion

In this chapter we have used simple and complete ways of presenting information to educate you about all of the major facets of the tests we have studied in the past five chapters. This is not to say that we have taught you everything there is to know about any one test. In fact, there are graduate-level courses in ANOVAs and regressions alone, so the information presented here is to help you learn the basic terminology of statistics, see how simple statistics can be employed to answer real research questions, and provide you with enough information to allow you to read actual research in any field that employs social scientific statistical procedures. In the next chapter, we will explain a variety of more advanced statistical procedures.

KEY TERMS

Beta (β) Weights
General Linear Model
Regression (R)
R-Squared (R^2)

References

Rocca, K. A., & Vogl-Bauer, S. (1999). Trait verbal aggression, sports fan identification, and perceptions of appropriate sports fan communication. *Communication Research Reports, 16,* 239–248.

Wrench, J. S., & Booth-Butterfield, M. (2003). Increasing patient satisfaction and compliance: An examination of physician humor orientation, compliance-gaining strategies, and perceived credibility. *Communication Quarterly, 51,* 482–503.

Further Reading

Abramson, J. H., & Abramson, Z. H. (2001). *Making sense of data: A self-instruction manual on the interpretation of epidemiological data* (3rd ed.). New York: Oxford.

Achen, C. H. (1982). *Interpreting and using regression.* Newbury Park, CA: Sage.

Bruning, J. L., & Kintz, B. L. (1997). *Computational handbook of statistics* (4th ed.). New York: Longman.

Chatterjee, S., Hadi, A. S., & Price, B. (2000). *Regression analysis by example* (3rd ed.). New York: John Wiley & Sons.

Delwiche, L. D., & Slaughter, S. J. (2003). *The little SAS book: A primer* (3rd ed.). Cary, NC: SAS Press.

Gravetter, F. J., & Wallnau, L. B. (2000). *Statistics for the behavioral sciences* (5th ed.). Belmont, CA: Wadsworth/Thomson Learning.

Green, S. B., & Salkind, N. J. (2004). *Using SPSS for Windows and Macintosh: Analyzing and understanding data* (4th ed.). Upper Saddle River, NJ: Prentice Hall.

Hocking, J. E., Stacks, D. W., & McDermott, S. T. (2003). *Communication research* (3rd ed.). Boston: Allyn and Bacon.

Howell, D. C. (1997). *Statistical methods for psychology* (4th ed.). Belmont, CA: Duxbury Press.

Huff, D. (1954). *How to lie with statistics.* New York: W. W. Norton & Company.

Keith, T. Z. (2006). *Multiple regression and beyond.* Boston: Allyn & Bacon.

Keller, D. K. (2006). *The Tao of statistics: A path to understanding (with no math).* Thousand Oaks, CA: Sage.

Pyrczak, F. (1999). *Statistics with a sense of humor: A humorous workbook and guide to study skills* (2nd ed.). Los Angeles: Pyrczak.

Salkind, N. J. (2004). *Statistics for people who (think they) hate statistics* (2nd ed.). Thousand Oaks, CA: Sage.

Schroeder, L. D., Sjoquist, D. L., & Stephan, P. E. (1986). *Understanding regression analysis: An introductory guide.* Newbury Park, CA: Sage.

SAS Institute. (2004). *SAS 9.1 Companion for Windows.* Cary, NC: SAS Press.

Seber, G. A. F., & Lee, A. J. (2003). *Linear regression analysis* (rev. ed.). John Wiley & Sons, New York.

Singleton, R. A., Jr., & Straits, B. C. (1999). *Approach to social research* (3rd ed.). New York: Oxford University Press.

Tabachnick, B. G., & Fidell, L. S. (2001). *Using multivariate statistics* (4th ed.). Boston: Allyn and Bacon.

Trochim, W. M. K. (2000). *The research methods knowledge base* (2nd ed.). Cincinnati, OH: Atomic Dog. Online available at: http://www.socialresearchmethods.net/ Achen, C. H. (1982). *Understanding and using regression.* Newbury Park, CA: Sage.

Advanced Statistical Procedures

In the previous five chapters we have explained in great detail five common statistical procedures that communication researchers employ when doing social scientific empirical research. However, many research articles utilize a wide range of statistical tests, so this chapter is going to introduce you to four difference tests and four relationship tests that are currently found in communication journals. Most of these tests are useful because they allow researchers to be parsimonious. The law of parsimony states that scientists should look *for the simplest assumption in the formulation of a theory and the simplest test to interpret data*. While we are not as concerned with the first part of this definition (theory), we are very interested in the second part because of its depiction of how researchers should carry data analysis. In essence, the law of parsimony states that researchers should find the simplest way to analyze their data. We've actually already conducted one statistical test in this book because of the law of parsimony, but we didn't tell you so at the time. When someone conducts a one-way ANOVA that has an independent variable with three categories (A, B, and C), he or she could easily run one one-way ANOVA or three independent *t*-tests (A and B; B and C; A and C). However, when we run three independent *t*-tests, our error is compounded for each test, so the likelihood of Type I error rises. Furthermore, conducting one one-way ANOVA is more frugal than running three *t*-tests, so a one-way ANOVA is more parsimonious in this case. All of the advanced statistics could be conducted using the tests previously described in this text, but these tests are more parsimonious. Additionally, these advanced tests generally perform computations that the less parsimonious tests would not be able to compute, so we are able to ask more advanced questions about our data using a single test.

This chapter is not going to give you computer printouts or make you compute things by hand. If you would like to learn more about how to run these tests in SPSS, we encourage you to read Mertler and Vannatta (2005), and if you want to run these tests in SAS, we encourage you to read Hatcher and Stepanski (1994). If you want to see how many of these tests are calculated by hand, please read Bruning and Kintz (1997). Instead, this chapter will introduce you to a variety of advanced statistical procedures you may encounter while reading communication journals. While there are literally hundreds of statistical tests that can be used, there are a handful of very common statistical tests that you should at least be aware of at this point. To examine these tests, we're going to group them into two categories: difference tests and relationship tests. In the difference tests section, we will examine factorial ANOVAs, analysis of covariance (ANCOVA), multivariate analysis of variance (MANOVA), and repeated measures ANOVA. In the relationship tests section, we will examine canonical correlations, path analysis, structural equation modeling, and factor analysis.

Difference Tests

FACTORIAL ANOVA

Example

Suppose you wanted to find out if there were differences between males and females and differences between political affiliations (Democrat, Republican, other, and not registered to vote) on college students' attitudes towards college. Well, we could run two one-way ANOVAS to answer this question using both sex and political affiliations as two separate independent variables (remember in a one-way ANOVA the IV is always a nominal variable) looking for differences in the dependent variable (college students' attitudes towards college). (This example is actually based on the data set found on the CD-ROM accompanying this book.) Unfortunately, one thing we know about statistics is that the more statistical tests a researcher runs to answer the question, the greater the chance he or she will run into Type I error. For this reason, running the two one-way ANOVAs is not considered parsimonious for this specific example. In statistics, we want the most frugal and simple (parsimonious) way to answer a single research question. For example, why run three linear regressions when one multiple linear regression will do the same thing? The same thing is true in this example as well. There is no need to run two separate one-way ANOVAs ("sex with attitude towards college" and "political affiliation with attitude towards college"). Instead, we simply run what is called a two-way or factorial ANOVA instead.

Explanation

When we originally talked about one-way ANOVAs, we mentioned that the independent variable is called a factor, so in a factorial ANOVA you're simply dealing with more than one factor. In the example above, we have two levels in the first factor (male and female) and four levels in the second factor (Democrat, Republican, other, and not registered to vote). This design then would be considered a 2 × 4 factorial ANOVA. In a factorial ANOVA there are three types of difference tests. The first two differences calculated look for what are called main effects because they look for differences between each of the nominal independent variable's categories separately. For example, the difference computed in a factorial ANOVA looks at the first independent variable (female vs. male) and the dependent variable (attitude toward college). The second difference computed in a factorial ANOVA looks for differences among the categories in the second nominal independent variable (Democrat, Republican, other, and not registered to vote) and the dependent variable (attitude towards college). Again, the first differences look for main effects, while the third difference looks for an interaction effect between the two independent variables (sex and political affiliation) and the dependent variable (attitude towards college). The third difference test examined in a two-way ANOVA is called an interaction test because it's looking for differences in the combination of the two factors (male Democrat, male Republican, male other, male not registered to vote, female Democrat, female Republican, female other, and female not registered to vote). In other words, the interaction test looks for differences between all of the following 8 groups (2 × 4 = 8): male Democrat, male Republican, male other, male not registered to vote, female Democrat, female Republican, female other, and female not registered to vote. So not only is a factorial ANOVA more parsimonious, but it also gives you a third type of difference test that cannot be done by simple one-way ANOVAs. You could even throw another factor into this study if you so desired, such as geographical location (north, south, east, or west), and get a 2 × 4 × 4. In this case you would end up with 32 comparisons being examined by the single interaction test and three main effect tests being reported by the factorial ANOVA test. Now that we've explained what a factorial ANOVA is, let's see how the APA write-up of a factorial ANOVA would appear in a journal.

APA Write-Up

A 2 × 4 ANOVA was conducted to evaluate the effects of biological sex (male and female) and political affiliation (Democrat, Republican, other, and not registered to vote) on college students' attitudes towards college. The means and standard deviations can be seen in Figure 21.1. The ANOVA indicated a significant main effect for sex with attitude towards college: $F(1, 304) = 4.45$, $p < .05$; did not indicate a significant main effect for political affiliation with attitude towards college: $F(3, 304) = 0.201$, $p > .05$; and did not indicate an interaction effect for sex by political affiliation with attitude towards college: $F(3, 304) = 0.144$, $p > .05$. The biological sex main effect indicated that females have more positive attitudes towards college than men.

Discussion

In this APA write-up we see that there were three separate F tests reported in the one factorial ANOVA conducted to analyze this research question: two main effects tests and one interaction test. One of the main effect tests was significant, indicating that females reported having more positive attitudes toward college than males do. The other main effect test indicated that people in the four political affiliations (Democrat, Republic, other, and not registered to vote) did not differ in their attitudes towards college. Finally, we found that there were no statistical differences between the eight combined groups (male Democrat, male Republican,

Biological Sex	Political Affiliation	Mean	SD
Male	Democrat	35.86	6.19
	Republican	35.17	6.51
	Other	36.37	6.10
	Not Registered to Vote	34.46	6.02
	Total	35.52	6.29
Female	Democrat	37.78	5.19
	Republican	37.57	5.89
	Other	37.45	5.07
	Not Registered to Vote	37.50	7.48
	Total	37.65	5.54

Figure 21.1 Factorial ANOVA Means and SDs

male other, male not registered to vote, female Democrat, female Republican, female other, and female not registered to vote) and their attitudes toward college. In other words, female Republicans did not differ from males not registered to vote and so on. Overall, the factorial ANOVA allows researchers to answer more complex questions than could be accomplished using a simple one-way ANOVA.

ANALYSIS OF COVARIANCE

Example

Suppose you want to determine if males and females differ in their level of communication apprehension. You have a group of college students fill out the Personal Report of Communication Apprehension–24. However, you realize that there is a fairly strong negative relationship between an individual's communication apprehension and her or his willingness to communicate. For this reason, you want to see if willingness to communicate is a confounding variable when determining if females and males have different levels of communication apprehension. (This example is actually based on the data set found on the CD-ROM accompanying this book.)

Explanation

The analysis of covariance (ANCOVA) is an extension of the one-way ANOVA discussed in Chapter 18. You may be wondering how someone knows if they should even look for a covariate in the first place. Well there are typically two reasons a researcher may opt to use an ANCOVA. First, the researcher may want to exclude the effect of a given independent variable. For example, maybe you're conducting a study looking at sex differences and perceptions of political speeches. However, when you collect your data you find a significant difference between the ages of the females and males in your sample. To prevent age from becoming a factor while you are looking at the sex differences, you decide to use age as a covariate to exclude the effect that age may have on your participants' perceptions of the political speeches.

The second reason a researcher may opt to use an ANCOVA is when there are two variables that are strongly related to each other. If someone is looking for a difference in a dependent variable, it is possible that the researcher will end up finding a difference in the variance accounted for by the dependent variable and another variable (the covariate). For this reason, the researcher may want to partial out the variance of the covariate, so he or she can only look for a difference in the variance not accounted for by the covariate. In our sample ANCOVA, we will test the second use of an ANCOVA. The purpose of our example ANCOVA is to allow a researcher to determine if a difference lies between groups (female and male) on a dependent variable (communication apprehension) after the dependent variable has been mathematically adjusted for differences associated with one or more covariates (willingness to communicate). The basic test analyzed in an ANCOVA is similar to the one-way ANOVA in that both look for differences between groups. The ANCOVA, however, increases the power of the F test for a main effect or interaction by removing the predictable variance associated with the covariate (willingness to communicate) from the error term for the F test. In essence, a covariate (willingness to communicate) is a variable related to the dependent variable that can cause the participants' scores on the dependent variable (communication apprehension) to be skewed or altered, so the ANCOVA readjusts the dependent variable scores to prevent this skewing from occurring.

APA Write-Up

The purpose of this research question was to examine the possibility of a significant difference in communication apprehension based on biological sex (male and female) while controlling for an individual's willingness to communicate. A one-way analysis of covariance was conducted using biological sex (male and female) as the independent variable, communication apprehension as the dependent variable, and willingness to communicate as the covariate. A significant relationship was found between the dependent variable (communication apprehension) and the covariate (willingness to communicate): $F(1, 295) = 86.41$, $p < .0001$, $\eta^2 = 0.23$. Furthermore, a significant difference was found between males ($M = 62.68$, $SD = 15.43$) and females ($M = 66.41$, $SD = 19.25$) on communication apprehension: $F(1, 295) = 8.78$, $p < .005$, $\eta^2 = 0.03$.

Discussion

The results above indicate that there is a significant difference between males and females and their levels of communication apprehension. In Chapter 17, we ran the exact same test using an independent t-test procedure and found no differences between males and females and communication apprehension. Since we used the exact same data off the CD-ROM sample to ask this question, what caused the difference to appear now? The correction of communication apprehension that occurred by the covariate willingness to communicate is what ultimately caused this difference to occur. You'll notice that two separate F tests are reported in the ANCOVA. The first F test indicated that there was a significant relationship between the dependent variable (communication apprehension) and the covariate (willingness to communicate). The eta-squared ($\eta^2 = 0.23$) indicates that approximately 23% of the variance in communication apprehension can be accounted for by willingness to communicate. In an ANCOVA, you can think of eta-squared as being similar to R^2 in a regression.

The second F test examines the differences between males and females on communication apprehension. This test indicated that females do have slightly higher levels of communication apprehension than males in the sample. Notice again that eta-squared is reported for this F test. While males and females differ in their communication apprehension in this sample, biological sex only accounts 2.9% of the variance, which is not that much when you really think about it.

MULTIVARIATE ANALYSIS OF VARIANCE

Example

A multivariate analysis of variance (MANOVA) allows a researcher to examine differences using one or more nominal independent variables with one or more dependent variables. Perhaps a researcher wants to see if males and females differ in their levels of ethnocentrism, but wants to also see if males and females differ in their levels of willingness to communicate with strangers as well. This could be answered using two one-way ANOVAs (sex with ethnocentrism and sex with willingness to communicate with strangers), but again the more tests you use, the greater the chance you will end up with Type I error. So in order to be parsimonious (simple and frugal), you would need to conduct a one-way MANOVA.

Explanation

A MANOVA, as discussed above, is considered a multivariate test because you have multiple dependent variables (ethnocentrism and willingness to communicate with strangers). A one-way ANOVA is considered a univariate test because you have one dependent variable. Often the dependent variables analyzed in a MANOVA are different measures of the same phenomenon. As in our example, we would think that people who have higher levels of ethnocentrism would be less willing to communicate with strangers, so these two variables could theoretically be related. However, the two do not need to be related, but should share a common conceptual meaning and some degree of linearity (remember all ANOVA tests are general linear model tests). In essence, the dependent variables in a MANOVA should go together in a way that makes sense, so you wouldn't put both apples and oranges as dependent variables in the same MANOVA. Again the purpose of this chapter is not to explain all of the mathematical aspects of the MANOVA procedure, but just to introduce you to the basic concept. For this reason, we strongly urge you to read more information about the MANOVA elsewhere since it is the basis of a number of advanced statistical procedures.

APA Write-Up

The goal of this research question was to determine if there was a difference between males and females on ethnocentrism and willingness to communicate with strangers. To analyze this question a one-way MANOVA was calculated using biological sex (female and male) as the independent variable and the participant's scores for ethnocentrism and willingness to communicate with strangers as the dependent variables. The Box's test (Box's M = 3.58) reveals that equal variances can be assumed: $F(3, 31993081) = 1.19$, $p > .05$; so Wilks' lambda (Λ) will be used as the test statistic. The Wilks' lmbda criteria indicates significant group differences in biological sex for the overall model: Wilks' $\Lambda = 0.975$, $F(2, 302) = 3.94$, $p < .02$, multivariate $\eta^2 = 0.03$. Univariate ANOVA results were interpreted using alpha at 0.05. Results reveal that males ($M = 38.43$, $SD = 9.08$) and females ($M = 35.63$, $SD = 8.08$) significantly differ on ethnocentrism: $F(1, 303) = 7.91$, $p < .005$, partial $\eta^2 = 0.03$. Results also revealed that males ($M = 47.86$, $SD = 24.86$) and females ($M = 48.86$, $SD = 26.67$) did not significantly differ on willingness to communicate with strangers: $F(1, 303) = 0.11$, $p > .05$.

Discussion

Let's start an analysis of these results by remembering the purpose of this research question. The goal was to use one independent variable (sex) to examine two dependent variables (ethnocentrism and willingness to communicate with strangers) using one test. The first result reported in the MANOVA is the test that measures for the equality of variances assumption. Just like in other tests we have examined, the MANOVA has a basic assumption that the variances from the groups being examined are equal. The Box's M test examines the equality of variances assumption and determines whether we can use the Wilks' lambda (if Box's M is not significant—we accept the equality of variances assumption) or Pillai's trace (if Box's M is significant— we reject the equality of variances assumption). In this example, Box's M was not significant, so we were able to utilize Wilks' lambda. The Wilks' lambda or Pillai's trace are two multivariate tests that examine statistical significance of the whole model (both Independent Variables—IVs and Dependent Variables—DVs).

The multivariate test is then followed by a series of univariate tests (F tests) for the IV (sex) with every dependent variable (ethnocentrism and willingness to communicate with strangers). The multivariate test essentially lets us know that a difference exists between the IV and DVs, but not where the difference actually is. In our example, the overall multivariate test was significant, so we needed to examine the univariate statistics (sex with ethnocentrism and sex with willingness to communicate with strangers). In our example, males had higher levels of ethnocentrism than females, but there was no difference between females and males in their willingness to communicate with strangers. However, once again, biological sex only accounted for a small amount of the variance in ethnocentrism (3%).

REPEATED MEASURES ANOVA

Example

Suppose you are a public speaking teacher and you want to determine if taking a public speaking course actually decreases a person's level of communication apprehension. One possible way to determine if a person's level of communication apprehension decreases over the course of a public speaking class would be to test their CA level at the beginning of the course, test it again halfway through the course, and test it a third time at the end of the course. You could calculate three paired t-tests to determine this research question (Time 1 to Time 2, Time 2 to Time 3, and Time 1 to Time 3), but again the more tests you run, the more error your findings will have. In order to avoid increasing your Type I error, you can run a procedure called a repeated measures ANOVA. (This example is hypothetical because the data on the textbook CD-ROM is not set up to answer a repeated measures ANOVA question.)

Explanation

A repeated measures ANOVA allows a researcher to determine if differences occur in a variable over time. In the example above, we measures these differences occurring over time by having students fill out the Personal Report of Communication 24 at the beginning of the semester/quarter, in the middle of the semester/quarter, and at the end of the semester/quarter. By having the students fill out the survey all three times, we have a way of mapping what happens to communication apprehension levels throughout the course of a public speaking class. In essence, what we are testing is the null hypothesis that $\text{Time}_1 = \text{Time}_2 = \text{Time}_3$.

APA Write-Up

The goal of this research question was to determine if a person's level of communication apprehension changes over the course of a public speaking class. A one-way within-subjects repeated measures ANOVA was conducted using three scores for communication apprehension taken at the beginning of the course ($M = 65.11$, $SD = 15.49$), the middle of the course ($M = 64.61$, $SD = 14.36$), and the end of the course ($M = 64.09$, $SD = 15.93$). This study found no significant differences between the measurements: Wilks' $\Lambda = 0.985$, $F(2, 125) = 0.96$, $p > .05$.

Discussion

In this APA write-up, we learned that there was not a significant difference among the beginning, middle, and end of the public speaking course and individual levels of communication apprehension. While this test is considered a univariate test, it still relies on a multivariate test (Wilks' Λ) to determine the overall significance of the model. If the test had been significant, then we could have used paired t-tests to determine where the actual difference existed (Time$_1$ to Time$_2$, Time$_1$ to Time$_3$, or Time$_2$ to Time$_3$).

It's also very easy to make the repeated measures ANOVA even more complicated by adding what is called a between groups aspect to the test. For example, perhaps you wanted to see if male and female levels of CA changed over the course of a public speaking course, which would give you one group within (everyone and CA) and one group between (males and females). Needless to say, more and more layers can be added to the repeated measures ANOVA by adding multiple dependent variables, which would create a repeated measures MANOVA.

Relationship Tests

CANONICAL CORRELATIONS

Example

In the variable communication apprehension, there are four subscales that can be examined: group CA, meeting CA, interpersonal CA, and public CA. There are also four subscales in willingness to communicate as well: group WTC, meeting WTC, interpersonal WTC, and public WTC. Suppose you wanted to determine the nature of the relationship between the four subscales of communication apprehension with the four subscales of willingness to communicate. Well, you could run a lot of correlations, or you could conduct one canonical correlation.

Explanation

A canonical correlation is a statistical tool that allows a researcher to investigate the relationships among two or more variable sets. In our example, we have two different variable sets: communication apprehension (group, meeting, interpersonal, and public) and willingness to communicate (group, meeting, interpersonal, and public). Variables in a canonical correlation must be either interval or ratio level variables. All of the variables used in our example are interval variables, so the canonical correlation is a good statistical tool to determine the interrelationships among the variables. Ultimately, a canonical analysis is the best test to use when examining statistical relationships between multiple interval/ratio independent variables with multiple interval/ratio dependent variables.

APA Write-Up

The goal of this research question was to examine the relationships among the four communication apprehension subscales (group, meeting, interpersonal, and public) and the four willingness to communicate subscales (group, meeting, interpersonal, and public). A canonical correlation was calculated using the four communication apprehension subscales as the predictors of the four willingness to communicate subscales. Using Wilks' Λ, the overall model was significant—Wilks' $\Lambda = .68$, $F(16, 889.66) = 7.54$, $p < .0001$—which indicates that the two variable sets are significantly associated by the canonical correlation. Only the first two canonical correlations were found to be significant in this study: canonical correlation 1,

Wilks' Λ = .68, F(16, 889.66) = 7.54, p < .0001; and canonical correlation 2, Wilks' Λ = .91, F(9, 710.80) = 3.10, p < .001. Canonical correlations 3 and 4 were not significant: canonical correlation 3, Wilks' Λ = .99, F(4, 586) = 0.94, p > .05; and canonical correlation 4, Wilks' Λ = .99, F(1, 294) = 0.07, p > .05. The first variate accounted for approximately 26% of the variance in the dependent variable (canonical correlation = .51), and the second variate accounted for approximately 7.84% of the variance in the dependent variable (canonical correlation = .28). The exact canonical loadings for each variable can be seen in Figure 21.2.

Discussion

When examining a canonical analysis, it's always important to remember what is actually being correlated. In this example, we were examining the relationships between the four communication apprehension subscales (group, meeting, interpersonal, and public) and the four willingness to communicate subscales (group, meeting, interpersonal, and public). The first statistic that is reported is the significance test for the whole model. You'll notice that since our independent variable (communication apprehension) had four variables (group, meeting, interpersonal, and public), we end up with four canonical correlations to be calculated. The results indicated that only the first two canonical correlations were significant. This does not mean that only the relationships between group CA and meeting CA are significant. Instead, in a canonical correlation, the model allows for the possibility that each independent variable may function uniquely and thus need its own variate. To understand what the two significant canonical correlations mean, you must look at how all of the variables (both independent and dependent) load on the significant variates (see Figure 21.2). When looking at Figure 21.2, you'll notice that the communication apprehension variables load negatively on the first variate and the willingness to communicate variables load positively on the first variate. This should be expected since CA and WTC are negatively related constructs. However, the story does not end there. When you look at the second variate, a new story is developing. The cutoff point for meaningfulness of a loaded variable on a variate is .30 (Tabachnick & Fidell, 2001), so in our example in Figure 21.2, group CA, meeting CA, meeting WTC, and public WTC did not load on the second variate at all. Most of the variables are loaded moderately on the variate (interpersonal CA, public CA, and group WTC). Interpersonal WTC is actually loaded negatively higher on the second variate than on the first variate. It should also be noted that interpersonal CA loads positively on the second variate.

So, what does all of this mean about the relationship between the CA subscale variables and WTC subscale variables? A lot actually. First, we learn that CA and WTC are clearly

Variable	Variate One	Variate Two
Group Communication Apprehension	−.81	.16
Meeting Communication Apprehension	−.94	−.13
Interpersonal Communication Apprehension	−.88	.41
Public Communication Apprehension	−.74	−.46
Group Willingness to Communicate	.81	−.41
Meeting Willingness to Communicate	.89	−.17
Interpersonal Willingness to Communicate	.61	−.67
Public Willingness to Communicate	.94	.08

Figure 21.2 Canonical Variate Loadings

negatively related. However, the exact nature of that relationship does depend on the subscales themselves because they do not simply negatively relate. The second variate indicates that while interpersonal WTC, public CA, and group WTC may be low, it is still possible for someone to have a higher level of interpersonal CA. In other words, there are some people that do not exhibit high levels of public speaking CA, but may still experience high levels of interpersonal CA.

PATH ANALYSIS

Example

Causal relationships are one of the areas that social scientific researchers are very hesitant discussing. One technique that has been developed to examine causal relationships is the path analysis. Perhaps you wanted to determine the causal relationships between communication apprehension, ethnocentrism, humor assessment, attitudes towards college, and people's belief that everyone should be required to take public speaking in college. You start doodling on a piece of paper and come up with a theoretical explanation for why people like college and others do not, and why some people think everyone should take public speaking and others do not (Figure 21.3). You believe that people with higher levels of communication apprehension are less likely to like college and are less likely to believe that everyone in college should take public speaking (represented by the minus sign next to the lines). Furthermore, you believe that people who are more humorous will enjoy college more and believe that everyone in college should take public speaking (represented by the plus sign next to the lines). Finally, you believe that people who are ethnocentric are going to have more negative attitudes about college, but you do not think that there will be a relationship between an individual's level of ethnocentrism and her or his belief that everyone should take a public speaking class in college.

Explanation

In a path analysis, two different types of variables need to be examined: endogenous and exogenous variables. Endogenous variables are explained by one or more of the other variables in

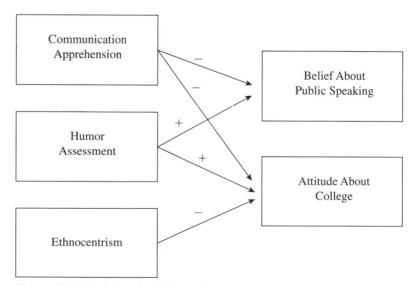

Figure 21.3 Path Analysis Example

the model (e.g., belief about public speaking and attitude about college). Exogenous variables are taken as a given, so the model does not try to explain them (CA, ethnocentrism, and HA). To calculate a path analysis, we calculate a series of multiple linear regressions using the exogenous variables as the independent variables (CA, ethnocentrism, and HA) and the endogenous variables as the dependent variables (belief about public speaking and attitude about college). From these regressions, you simply report the beta weights for each regression on the picture.

APA Write-Up

A path analysis was conducted to determine the causal effects among the variables communication apprehension, ethnocentrism, humor assessment, belief that everyone should take public speaking in college, and attitude about college. Prior to the analysis, an initial model was created (Figure 21.3). This model was not consistent with the empirical data. More specifically, two of the correlations exceeded a difference of .05, so the nonsignificant paths were removed from the model. Thus, a revised model was generated (Figure 21.4). Approximately 12% of the variance in a person's belief that a person should be required to take public speaking in college can be accounted for by the model, and approximately 17% of the variance in a person's attitude about college can be accounted for by the model.

Discussion

Overall, you can think of the path analysis as a pictorial way of presenting information about multiple regressions. The numbers shown to the left of the exogenous variables are Pearson product-moment correlations that were calculated among the exogenous variables. The numbers above the lines originating from an exogenous variable pointing toward an endogenous variable are beta weights calculated during multiple regressions and indicate whether there is a positive or negative relationship. What we can tell from these findings is that an individual's level of CA negatively relates to her or his belief that all college students should take public speaking. We also learned that there is a positive relationship between an individual's humor assessment and positive attitudes about college, and that there is a negative relationship between an individual's ethnocentrism and positive attitudes about college. In other words, people who are more humorous feel more positively about college; where as, people who are more ethnocentric feel less positively about college.

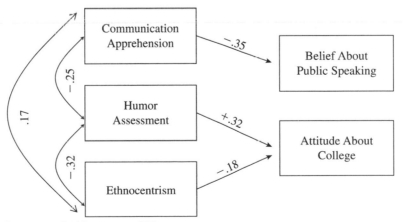

Betas were significant at $p < .005$.
Figure 21.4 Path Analysis Calculated

STRUCTURAL EQUATION MODELING

Example

As we have noticed throughout this chapter and in previous chapters, the data set that we collected for this textbook has indicated that there is a negative relationship between an individual's level of communication apprehension and her or his belief that all college students should be required to take public speaking. Suppose you wanted to examine this relationship in light of the four subscales that allegedly make up communication apprehension. We could run a path analysis like we did in the previous section, but the problem with a path analysis is that it relies on the use of a number of linear and multivariate regressions, which simply is not parsimonious. For this reason, a newer statistical technique has been created called structural equation modeling. In this example, we want to see how well the four subscales of communication apprehension create this variable known as communication apprehension and how communication apprehension relates to a participant's belief that all students in college should be required to take public speaking. Figure 21.5 shows how this question would look pictorially. You'll notice that in this drawing we have a variety of circles and squares instead of just boxes. To further understand this research question, let's examine what a structural equation actually is.

Explanation

Structural equation modeling is very similar in purpose to path analysis; however, the calculations are considerably more difficult but mathematically more meaningful. Ultimately,

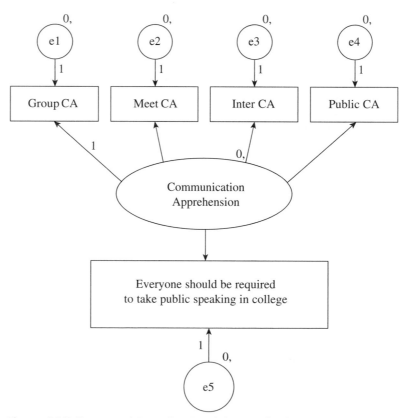

Figure 21.5 Structural Equation Model Hypothesis

structural equation modeling is concerned with observed and latent variables. An observed variable can be an observation that a researcher directly collects (self-reports on a survey, scores on an achievement test, coded responses to interview questions, etc.). Latent variables are variables that are not directly measured, but we believe that our measurements help us understand this variable. For example, we believe that communication apprehension is a product of four subscales (group CA, meeting CA, interpersonal CA, and public CA). We do not measure a variable called "communication apprehension," but rather the four subscales together, and then combine their results to create an overall score of communication apprehension. In essence, "communication apprehension" is the latent variable being measured by the four subscales (group CA, meeting CA, interpersonal CA, and public CA). As shown Figure 21.5, we measured each of the four subscales in a rectangular box indicating that these variables are directly measured by the researcher. However, the variable listed as "communication apprehension" is an oval, indicating that CA is a latent variable.

In structural equation modeling like we saw in path analysis, there are two types of variables discussed: exogenous and endogenous. Exogenous latent variables are similar to independent variables because they can account for some of the variance in other variables in the model. Endogenous latent variables are similar to dependent variables because they are influenced by the exogenous variables. In our example, communication apprehension is an example of an exogenous variable because it attempts to account for some of the variance in an individual's belief that all college students should be required to take public speaking.

APA Write-Up

Using structural equation modeling, the relationships were examined between communication apprehension, a latent variable with four indicators (group CA, meeting CA, interpersonal CA, and public CA), and an individual's belief that public speaking be a required course in college. The hypothesized model is presented in Figure 21.5. Circles represent latent variables, and rectangles represent measured variables. Absence of a line connecting variables implies lack of a hypothesized relationship. Results indicated that the proposed structural model was problematic: $\chi^2(5, N = 325) = 24.20$, $p < .0005$. However, since this model had more than 200 participants, other goodness-of-fit indices are necessary. All of the goodness-of-fit indices far exceeded the recommended levels: normed fit index (NFI) = .99, comparative fit index (CFI) = .99, relative fit index (RFI) = .98, incremental index of fit (IFI) = .99, and the Tucker-Lewis index (TLI) = .99. All of the indices of fit were over the .95 mark, which indicates that the model proposed is a superior fit. The final structural equation model can be seen in Figure 21.6.

Discussion

The goal of this research question was to see whether the four subscales of the PRCA-24 actually created a latent exogenous variable called communication apprehension and then to determine if this latent exogenous variable was related to an individual's belief that everyone in college should be required to take public speaking. To examine these findings, we'll first talk a little about the statistics involved and then examine the structural equation model in Figure 21.6. The first statistic that is reported is a chi-square test to determine whether or not the model is a good fit. When examining the chi-square test that is conducted for a structural equation model, there are two things that really should be examined: the chi-square statistic and the degrees of freedom. In an ideal test, the df is less than 5, and the closer the df is to the chi-square statistic, the stronger your model is said to be. However, the chi-square test of goodness-of-fit in the structural equation model is not always the best way to determine if you have a strong model, especially if a study has more than 200 participants (Boolen &

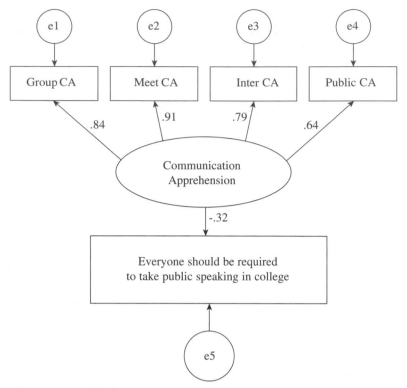

Figure 21.6 Calculated Structural Equation Model

Long, 1993). If your study has more than 200 participants, your chi-square is almost always going to be significant, which is an indication of poor fit. For this reason, a number of other indices have been developed such as the ones reported in the results above: normed fit index (NFI), comparative fit index (CFI), relative fit index (RFI), incremental index of fit (IFI), and the Tucker-Lewis index (TLI). Without going into the mathematical reasoning for each of these goodness-of-fit tests, each of theses tests is designed to explain to us mathematically whether our model makes sense the way we designed it. All of these goodness-of-fit indices can range from 0 to 1 with scores above .95 as generally being seen as acceptable (Byrne, 2001; Kelem, 2000). Overall, all of the goodness-fit-indices indicate that the model that we proposed in Figure 21.5 was a good model to explain the data.

Next to the goodness-of-fit indices, the most important part of the structural equation model is the standardized estimates seen in Figure 21.6. The standardized estimates can be seen as beta weights when determining the linearity of the relationship. In essence, all four subscales contribute to create the latent variable "communication apprehension" above .64, which indicates that the four subscales do actually measure the latent variable effectively. There is also a negative relationship between the latent exogenous variable "communication apprehension" and an individual's belief that all students should be required to take public speaking in college. While this resembles the path analysis results from the previous section examining this question, the biggest difference between a path analysis and a structural equation model is that the structural equation model is more parsimonious and accounts for possible error that a series of multiple linear regressions cannot. Attached to every observed variable (the rectangles in the model) you will notice that there is an error term (a small circle with the letter "e" followed by a number from 1 to 5). Again, to avoid going into the computational mathematics, understand that the error associated with observed variables (four CA subscales and belief about public speaking) accounts for measurement error. Measurement error can come from one of two places: random error and error uniqueness. Random error is simply random measurement error that occurs as a result of measuring things. Error uniqueness is a term that indicates that there was a form of error unique to a particular variable and which is considered nonrandom measurement error.

FACTOR ANALYSIS

Example

Factor analysis is an extremely important technique to master if you want to understand how to create survey research measures like the PRCA-24, WTC, sociocommunicative orientation scale, or any of the other scales we have used in this textbook. One of the problems when creating a new scale is that you never know if what you think you are measuring in your new scale is actually measuring what you say it should be measuring. While the primary way we examine problems like this is through validity testing (see Chapter 9), another way we can attempt to understand whether or not a scale is measuring what we say it is measuring is through a factor analysis. In 2001, Richmond, Wrench, and Gorham created a new research scale to measure an individual's use of humor during interpersonal interactions. The scale itself consists of 16 Likert-type items using a five-point scoring system from 1 *strongly disagree* to 5 *strongly agree*. How do we know that these 16 items actually measure anything? As discussed in Chapter 10, the HA has an alpha reliability of .92 ($M = 62.06$, $SD = 9.82$). So we know the scale is reliable, but do the 16 items in the HA actually measure just one thing? To determine if a set of scale items (like the 16 items on the HA) is measuring one concept or multiple concepts, we conduct a factor analysis.

Explanation

A factor analysis is a technique that enables researchers to determine variation and covariation among research measures. For example, suppose we had two items being measured on a Likert scale ranging from 1 *strongly disagree* to 5 *strongly agree*. The first item in the scale reads: "People are innately good," and the second item reads "Cats are the best animals." You give these two questions to a large sample and get the results back. Suppose you get an alpha reliability of .80, which is considered good. So your scale is reliable, but what is the scale measuring? Chances are your scale is not measuring one coherent concept, but rather measuring two concepts that happen to be related to each other. The purpose of a factor analysis is to determine how many different concepts are being measured by a set of questions on a research scale. If you recall the discussion from Chapter 10 on creating scales, we mentioned that a single research scale can only measure one thing. In the instance of the humor assessment, the purpose of the scale is to examine only an individual's use of humor during interpersonal interactions. The scale does not measure an individual's ability to use humor, an individual's sense of humor, or anything else. The scale has a single purpose, and all 16 scale items were written to reflect that conceptualization.

In the area of factor analysis, two basic types of factor analyses can be calculated. The first is called an exploratory factor analysis. Exploratory factor analysis occurs when a researcher has a set of scale items and wants to determine how many concepts the set of scale items is measuring. If you have 20 scale items, it's theoretically possible that each scale item is measuring a completely different concept and there is no unity between the set of scale items. However, it is also possible that all 20 items are only measuring a single variable. Most communication scales tend to measure between one and five distinct concepts. For example, of the scales used in this text book, only one scale measures two distinct variables. Know which scale it is? If you guessed the sociocommunicative orientation scale, then you were correct. The sociocommunicative orientation scale measures the degree to which an individual is assertive and the degree to which an individual is responsive. Each concept measured by a scale is called a factor. A factor analysis helps researchers group the individual scale items into coherent sets of concepts called factors. Sometimes you may think you've written 30 strong scale items to measure one single concept, cooperative communication, only to find out that your 30 items are actually measuring three different concepts—cooperative behavior, competitive behavior, and trust. Other times, the 30 items will hold strong and clearly measure one variable—cooperative communication.

The second type of factor analysis is called confirmatory factor analysis (CFA). Confirmatory factor analysis is when a researcher uses a factor analysis to make sure that a previously determined factor structure is consistent with present results. For example, in the last example looking at structural equation modeling, we used structural equation modeling to determine if the four subscales of communication apprehension actually measure a variable called "communication apprehension." While not an exact example of CFA, this is similar to what a CFA actually does, except in a true CFA we would have also tested whether each of the individual scale items clearly helps in creating the individual subscales (meeting CA, group CA, interpersonal CA, and public CA).

The last area of factor analysis that we need to explain here is what we refer to as extraction methods and rotation. Extraction refers to the specific type of factor analysis that an individual is conducting. The most basic factor analysis extraction method is called a principal component factor analysis. While we will not discuss the mathematical details of a principal component analysis, you should know that there are other forms of factor analysis, each of which is best used in different circumstances (unweighted least squares, generalized least squares, maximum likelihood, principal axis factor, etc.), and each factoring method contains differing mathematical reasoning and computations. For a good explanation of the different types of extraction methods and when to use one rather than another, we strongly encourage you to read Tabachnick and Fidell (2001) or Grimm and Yarnold (2000a,b).

Another important concept in the world of factor analysis is factor rotation. When researchers calculate factor analyses, it is often difficult to ascertain a clear factor structure for the scale items involved. Trying to find factor structures is akin to looking at Impressionist art. Sometimes you have to step back from the art piece to see what is actually on the canvas, or maybe you'll have to turn the canvass sideways to see what the artist intended her or his viewing audience to see. Examining factor structures often involves a certain amount of scrutiny and manipulation. Imagine we have all of the data points on a graph. If we look at the graph straight on we may not see much, but if we turn the page slightly, a clear linear structure may appear on the paper. When we rotate the data points along either the x or y axis, we have rotated the factor structure. This is a simplistic view of what happens in a factor analysis rotation, but it gives you a basic idea of what happens when a researcher needs to rotate a factor to determine the actual structure of the factor analysis.

APA Write-Up

The humor assessment instrument (HA) was developed to measure an individual's predisposition to use humor as a communicative tool during interpersonal situations. The HA is a 16-item, self-report measure that uses a 5-point Likert format ranging from 1 *strongly disagree* to 5 *strongly agree*.

The dimensionality of the 16 items for the HA was analyzed using an unrotated principal component factor analysis. Four criteria were used to determine the number of factors to rotate: sampling adequacy, the a priori hypothesis that the measure was unidimensional, the scree plot, and the interpretability of the factor solution. To examine sampling adequacy,

Kaiser's measure of sampling adequacy (MSA) was used. The MSA obtained was .92, which is considered "marvelous" for conducting a factor analysis (Kaiser, 1974). The scree plot indicated that our initial hypothesis of unidimensionality was correct. The principal component analysis revealed a strong primary factor. The factor loadings can be seen in Figure 21.7.

Discussion

First, let's remember the basic research question involved in calculating the factor analysis. Our goal was to determine if the 16 scale items created by Richmond, Wrench, and Gorham (2001) measure an individual's use of humor in interpersonal interactions using one factor. To analyze the above results, let's start by discussing some of the main features mentioned in the results section. First, the results mention that the researchers utilized an unrotated principal component analysis. In this example, there was no need to rotate the principal component analysis because the factor structure was clear without a rotation.

Second, Kaiser's MSA was used to determine if the sample was adequate for performing a factor analysis. The Kaiser's MSA is a tool to determine if your sample is sufficient (robust) enough to perform the factor analysis on the number of items in a scale. The way to interpret Kaiser's MSA is to use the system Kaiser (1974) created for determining if the data set is appropriate for the factor analysis: .9 and above is marvelous, .8–.9 is meritory, .7–.8 is middling, .6–.7 is mediocre, .5–.6 is miserable, and .5 and lower is unacceptable. As a general rule, Kaiser's MSA must be at least .6 or above, but most journals expect a Kaiser's MSA of .8 or above, with preference given to scores above .9.

1. I regularly communicate with others using humor.	.62
2. People usually laugh when I make a humorous remark.	.69
3. I am not funny or humorous.	-.66
4. I can be amusing or humorous without having to tell a joke.	.63
5. Being humorous is a natural communication orientation for me.	.70
6. I cannot relate an amusing idea well.	-.68
7. My friends would say that I am a humorous or funny person.	.68
8. People don't seem to pay close attention when I am being funny.	-.62
9. Even funny ideas and stories seem dull when I tell them.	-.67
10. I can easily relate funny or humorous ideas to the class.	.64
11. My friends would say that I am not a humorous person.	-.71
12. I cannot be funny, even when asked to do so.	-.68
13. I relate amusing stories, jokes, and funny things very well to others.	.64
14. Of all the people I know, I am one of the "least" amusing or funny persons.	-.65
15. I use humor to communicate in a variety of situations.	.68
16. On a regular basis, I do not communicate with others by being humorous or entertaining.	.61

Figure 21.7 Factor Analysis Humor Assessment

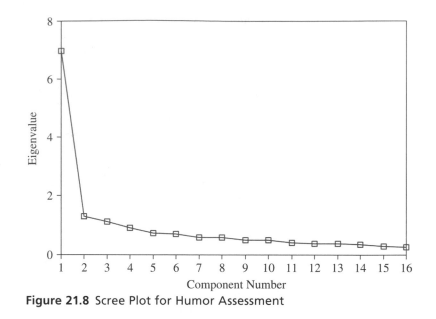

Figure 21.8 Scree Plot for Humor Assessment

The third part of the factor analysis results indicates that a scree plot was used to determine whether or not the model was unidimensional (contained only one factor). A scree plot is a plot of eigenvalues. Without going into detail, an eigenvalue describes the variance of the set of data points in a multivariate space that has one axis for each variable (Tabachnick & Fidell, 2001). You probably just hit your head on the table and think that sentence makes absolutely no sense whatsoever. Don't fear, we're here to help. In any data set, the maximum number of the eigenvalues is equal to the number of scale items being factor analyzed. For example, in the HA there are 16 scale items, so the combined eigenvalue for the scale is 16. The question becomes, can we minimize the eigenvalue sum (16) so that only one eigenvalue is above the number 1? For example, in our survey, the first component had an eigenvalue of 6.966, which accounted for 43.54% of the variance. In other words, one factor accounts for 43.54% of the variance in the HA scale. Ideally, for each eigenvalue above 1.0 in a factor analysis, you will extract one factor. In the example above, there were actually three factors that had eigenvalues above 1.0 (component 2, 1.30: and component 3, 1.12). However, researchers have shown that relying on the eigenvalues alone for extracting factors can be misleading. For this reason, it is also encouraged that you examine a scree plot when extracting factors (Figure 21.8).

In Figure 21.8, the scree plot is actually the plot of the eigenvalues themselves. The word "scree" is actually a geological term referring to the debris that collects towards the bottom of a rocky slope. If you look at Figure 21.8, the figure is kind of reminiscent of a rocky slope. The scree plot has a clear downward trajectory that then levels off and flattens out to the right. You'll notice that the first data point is placed at 6.966 and the second point is plotted at 1.30. To determine how many factors to extract using a scree plot, it is best to use the concept of looking at the elbow. On a scree plot there will always be at least one eigenvalue above 1.0. In our example, the first eigenvalue 6.966 is considerably larger than the rest of the eigenvalues. In fact, if you look at the scree plot, it's hard to clearly delineate the 15 eigenvalues from each other as far as how they are plotted. This leveling off of a scree plot is called the elbow of the plot. Any eigenvalues separated from the elbow are considered actual factors, and those eigenvalues in the elbow or in the tail of the scree plot are considered residuals of that primary factor. Figure 21.9 shows the scree plot associated with the factor analysis of

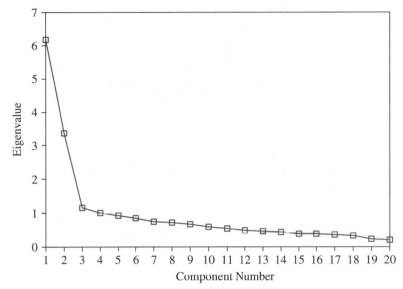

Figure 21.9 Scree Plot for Sociocommunicative Orientation

the sociocommunicative orientation scale. Remember, the sociocommunicative orientation measures two factors—assertiveness and responsiveness.

You'll notice that in Figure 21.9 that there are two clear eigenvalue plots—one at 6.17 and one at 3.36—and then you see a big dip and the creation of the elbow of the scree plot. This is an example of what it looks like when a factor analysis has two clear factors that need to be extracted from the data.

Once we have determined how many factors need to be extracted from the data, we can examine how the values actually load. In our example we only extracted one actual factor, which can be seen in Figure 21.7. When examining the factor loadings (number in the right column in Figure 21.7), you'll notice that all of the loadings are .61 and higher. Even if a number has a minus in front of it, it is considered a high loading on the factor analysis. If you look carefully, you'll notice that all of those items that have negative factor loadings are items that are reverse coded on the scale. A factor analysis has the ability to factor a set of variables even if items have not been reverse coded because the factor analysis is attempting to determine if people answer a set of scale items in a coherent fashion or whether participants respond one way to a certain type of questions and another way to a different type of question. As a rule of thumb, items should load on a single factor at .50 or higher and not load another factor at .30 or higher. Often, when more than one factor is extracted from a factor analysis, an item will load equally high for two different factors. In essence, this means that the scale item is actually not measuring either factor but is an index of both factors, and since a scale can only measure one thing, that scale item must be removed from the scale if it is to be statistically valid.

Conclusion

In this chapter we have introduced you to a variety of advanced statistical techniques, shown you how their results may appear in a research article, and discussed seven research questions (that could be answered using the data set on your CD-ROM) as well as one hypothetical research question. We have looked at four difference tests (factorial ANOVA, ANCOVA, MANOVA, and repeated measures ANOVA) and four relationship tests (canonical correlation, path analysis, structural equation modeling, and factor analysis). This chapter concludes our investigation of actual statistical techniques that communication researchers employ to answer social scientific research questions. The next chapter will examine what to do with your research study when you're done with the paper/project.

KEY TERMS

Analysis of Covariance (ANCOVA)

Canonical Correlation

Covariate

Factor Analysis

Factorial ANOVA

Interaction Effect

Law of Parsimony

Main Effect

Multivariate Analysis of Variance (MANOVA)

Multivariate Test

Path Analysis

Repeated Measures ANOVA

Structural Equation Model

Univariate Test

REFERENCES

Bollen, K. A., & Long, S. J. (1993). *Testing structural equation models.* Newbury Park, CA: Sage.

Byrne, B. M. (2001). *Structural equation modeling with AMOS: Basic concepts, applications and programming.* Mahwah, NJ: Lawrence Erlbaum Associates.

Grimm, L. G., & Yarnold, P. R. (Eds.). (2000a). *Reading and understanding multivariate statistics.* Washington, DC: American Psychological Association.

Grimm, L. G., & Yarnold, P. R. (Eds.). (2000b). *Reading and understanding more multivariate statistics.* Washington, DC: American Psychological Association.

Kaiser, H. F. (1974). An index of factorial simplicity. *Psychometrika, 39,* 401–415.

Klem, L. (2000). Structural equation modeling. In L. G. Grimm & P. R. Yarnold (Eds.), *Reading and understanding more multivariate statistics* (pp. 227–259). Washington, DC: American Psychological Association.

Mertler, C. A., & Vannatta, R. A. (2005). *Advanced and multivariate statistical methods* (3rd ed.). Glendale, CA: Pyrczak.

Richmond, V. P., Wrench, J. S., Gorham, J. (2001). *Communication, affect, and learning in the classroom.* Acton, MA: Tapestry Press.

Tabachnick, B. G., & Fidell, L. S. (2001). *Using multivariate statistics* (4th ed.). Boston: Allyn and Bacon.

FURTHER READING

Asher, H. B. (1983). *Causal modeling* (2nd ed.). Newbury Park, CA: Sage.

Bruning, J. L., & Kintz, B. L. (1997). *Computational handbook of statistics* (4th ed.). New York: Longman.

Hatcher, L., & Stepanski, E. J. (1994) *A step-by-step approach to using the SAS® System for univariate and multivariate statistics.* Cary, NC: SAS Institute.

22

Presenting Research

CHAPTER OBJECTIVES

1 Understand how a discussion section is written in response to the rest of the paper.

2 Be able to explain the five goals of a discussion section.

3 Know what goes into an abstract.

4 Understand the purposes of conference presentations.

5 Be able to differentiate between the three types of conference presentations (paper, poster, and panel).

6 Know the process one goes through for submitting a paper to a conference.

7 Know the process one goes through for submitting a paper to an academic journal.

8 Understand the three responses an author may receive from a journal editor (accept for publication, revise and resubmit, and reject).

This book has taken you on a journey to demonstrate how communication researchers conduct quantitative research. In the first three chapters we introduced you to the basic underlying assumptions in scientific communication research and how to conduct yourself ethically as a researcher. Chapters 4 and 5 then discussed how to go about searching for existing literature and then incorporate this literature into a *literature review*. This literature review then enabled you to create a series of arguments that formed hypotheses and research questions in your *rationale section*. Chapters 6 and 7 then explained what variables are and how communication researchers utilize variables. Chapters 9 and 10 discussed how we measure variables in communication, while Chapter 8 explained how mathematics can be used to describe collected variable data. Chapter 11 introduced us to conducting survey research, while Chapter 12 introduced content analysis, and Chapter 13 introduced experimental research. Chapter 14 then explained the different types of samples that researchers could utilize while conducting research. Basically, Chapters 6 through 14 provided you with the nuts and bolts of conduct quantitative research, which is the information one generally provides in her or his *method section*. Chapter 15 then introduced you to the theoretical premises behind hypothesis testing before actually showing you a variety of statistical tests, covered in Chapters 16 through 21. In those chapters we provided you with numerous examples of how to write up research results using APA style. The results section of a research paper consists of conducting the most parsimonious tests to answer the hypotheses and research questions you formulated in your rationale section at the end of the literature review. In other words, for every hypothesis or research question you posed in your rationale section, you should have a corresponding section in your *results section*. But we do not stop the research process just because we've written our results.

By this point in your research project, you have completed your data analysis and are probably ready to exhale a huge sigh of relief. But what good are results for a study if the author fails to explain what the information means for the reader? In this chapter we will describe the process of writing the discussion section of a research paper, presenting at conferences, and publishing your research.

Writing a Discussion Section

Too often, students or authors spend countless hours completing a research project only to have it sit in a file folder. Our purpose in conducting research is to share our knowledge and expand our understanding of phenomena in our discipline. In this chapter we will describe the steps involved in preparing your work for conference presentations and publication. After all, it would be a shame to keep your research findings on a shelf.

WRITING THE DISCUSSION

The six previous chapters have been dedicated to the data analysis phase of the research project. Each chapter has provided you with information on how to present the findings of your analyses in the results section using APA format guidelines. But do you recall our instructions to provide "just the facts" in the results section and resist the temptation to engage in any interpretation of the data? There was a reason for that—each research project concludes with a discussion section, and this section provides the author with the opportunity to provide an interpretation of the findings.

Students often report that they find the discussion section to be the most interesting part of a journal article. After all, this is where the author's own voice is heard. The discussion section allows the researcher to create links between the study and previous work, discuss any roadblocks that were encountered during the research process, and provide suggestions as to how other scholars can build upon this new information. In essence, the discussion section is like the last chapter in a good book. It provides a conclusion to the research project.

Depending on the type of research methodology employed, the format of the discussion section could vary. Qualitative studies sometimes combine results and discussion sections together since it is difficult to present findings without simultaneously interpreting them for the reader. The focus of this chapter will be on writing the discussion section for quantitative studies. As a general rule, there are typically five goals for this section:

1. Provide the reader with a summary of the major results or findings of the study.
2. Provide an interpretation or the meaning of these findings.
3. Discuss the relationship between the findings and previous research.
4. Acknowledge any limitations of the study.
5. Discuss the implications of the findings and suggest future research directions.

PROVIDING A SUMMARY OF MAJOR FINDINGS

Discussion sections begin with one or two paragraphs summarizing the major findings of the study. In essence, the introductory paragraph serves as an abstract for the discussion section. If the results section is strong, the reader already has the statistical information and knows whether the research questions and hypotheses were supported, so this is not the place to reiterate statistics. Instead, a clear and succinct summary of the results should be presented. Figure 22.1 shows the introductory paragraph from the discussion section of Wrench and Booth-Butterfield's (2003) study on patient compliance. Notice how the authors succinctly summarize the major findings of the study and transition into an interpretation of these results:

They begin the discussion by stating the primary goal for the study. This information creates the foundation for the remainder of the section by reminding the reader of the overall purpose for the project. Next, a concise summary of the overall findings is presented. This statement is especially important in studies where extensive data analyses are conducted. It enables the reader, who may not have a strong grasp of statistical analyses, the opportunity to understand the overall results. Wrench and Booth-Butterfield conclude the paragraph with a preview of the information to be discussed in the section. Previews such as these allow the author to subtly remind the reader what research questions and hypotheses were proposed in the study.

PROVIDING AN INTERPRETATION OF FINDINGS

At this point in the research process, you have spent countless hours formulating, examining, and analyzing questions and data. Now is the time to present your interpretation of the study. The discussion section of the research report provides you with the opportunity to allow your voice to be heard. A second goal of the discussion section is to explain the meaning of the results and share insight into to why the findings are relevant or important. Typically, the author will devote a paragraph of discussion for each research question or hypothesis proposed in the study. A good way to start each paragraph is by paraphrasing the question or hypothesis being discussed. Follow this with a concise statement that clearly states the

> The primary goal of this study was to determine how physicians' humor orientation, credibility, and use of compliance-gaining strategies relate to patient satisfaction and compliance. The findings revealed significant relationships suggesting that better physician communication skills were associated with improved patient perceptions of physician credibility and patient satisfaction. The following paragraphs focus on the relationship that a physician's humor orientation has on patient satisfaction and physician credibility, the relationship between patient satisfaction and physician credibility, the relationship of compliance-gaining strategies with physician–patient interactions, and the post–hoc analysis of the data sources used.

Figure 22.1 Introducing the Discussion Section

direction of the relationship between the independent and dependent variables. Subsequent sentences focus on the author's interpretation of why the findings are important. The use of language in interpreting the results is particularly important in this section. Resist the temptation to use definitive language to describe your results. Rather than stating that "results proved" something, consider evaluating results by applying language such as "results suggest" or "indicate."

Review the Wrench and Booth-Butterfield (2003) article and note how each paragraph provides a succinct overview of the research question or hypothesis that was examined. No statistical information was included in the summaries. Rather, they summarize the statistical results by using descriptive terms such as "positive relationship," "negative relationship," and "statistically significant." Declarative statements are avoided. Instead, the language used to interpret their findings includes phrases such as "the results appear to show" and "suggest" to avoid making claims that may later need to be defended.

DISCUSSING THE RELATIONSHIP BETWEEN FINDINGS AND PREVIOUS STUDIES

Remember the review of literature that was completed at the beginning of the research project? While you may have thought the only purpose of the review was to provide information for formulating the research question or hypothesis, there is one more opportunity to incorporate the information in your paper. One of the primary goals of research is to build a body of knowledge. Since the review of literature serves as the foundation for a research project, it is important to show how the current study builds on the existing knowledge. A third goal of the discussion section is to discuss the relationship between the study's findings and previous studies. How do your findings compare with those of related studies? Discussing the relationship between the current study and previous studies creates a context for the results. If the current study was the result of an idea for future research proposed by a previous study, now is the opportunity to acknowledge this information. Some common phrases used to make connections between studies include "supports the findings of Smith (1998)" or "contribute to the differences found in the current study and those reported by Smith (1998)." The last goal of the discussion section is to demonstrate how your results support and build upon theory. As we mentioned in Chapter 4, one of the reasons many researchers conduct research is to test and extend existing theories. The discussion section is where a researcher is able to shed light on the theory he or she is examining based on the results in her or his study. Did the researcher's results support the assumptions of the theory, or did the results negate the assumptions of the theory? Ultimately, clearly demonstrating how one's results impact our understanding of theory is extremely important because your discussion will influence how other people understand the theory.

Wrench and Booth-Butterfield (2003) incorporate previous research findings to provide a rationale for their results. Several references are made throughout the discussion section to previous results to demonstrate that a pattern of similar findings exists across studies. This serves to strengthen the conclusions proposed by the authors. Notice that references to previous studies are separate from the discussion of the findings. Rather they are woven throughout the discussion to provide the reader with a "big picture" of the major findings and how they relate to earlier work.

ACKNOWLEDGING LIMITATIONS

Every research study is affected by limitations. It is better for the author to identify and address the limitations of the study in the discussion section than to have a reader or reviewer point them out later. You are not claiming that the study was poorly designed by pointing out these flaws; rather you are sharing the insight gained by looking at the "big picture." Later in this chapter we will provide recommendations for submitting research for presentation or publication. An author who points out the weaknesses in her or his study will enhance the author's credibility as a researcher. In addition to highlighting limitations, the discussion section provides the author with an opportunity to propose methods for overcoming these flaws in future studies. Examples of limitations often addressed in this section include inappropriateness in the design, population, methods, or instrumentation.

While the Wrench and Booth-Butterfield (2003) study provides valuable insight into understanding the relationship between physicians' use of humor and patient satisfaction, the study has limitations. The authors highlight these limitations through the use of the subheading "limitations" and devote two paragraphs to address the limitations with measurement instruments and sampling methods. Notice that they incorporate examples of previous research by other scholars to provide support for their recommendations.

Discussing Implications and Future Directions

The discussion section should conclude with a summary of the theoretical or practical implications of the study and recommendations for future research. If the study supports existing theory, it is appropriate to point out the contributions it makes in this section. Perhaps your results offer practical implications for the reader. Use this opportunity to discuss the benefits of the information. In their article, Wrench and Booth-Butterfield (2003) conclude by emphasizing the benefits of the study for enhancing interactions between patients and physicians and potentially decreasing the number of malpractice claims that are filed as a result of dissatisfaction.

While the research project is designed to answer questions, the end result may actually result in questions that are unanswered. Some of these questions may evolve because of the findings of your study. The concluding paragraphs of the discussion section provide the author with an opportunity to suggest directions for future research. Reflecting on the current study, ideas are proposed for the next step in research that examines similar variables. Some of these may evolve out of the limitations of the existing study. Others may be the result of comparing results with similar studies. The future directions provide other researchers with ideas to launch their own research projects.

Once the discussion section is finished, your research task may seem to be complete. But not so fast—after all, has the study contributed to the body of literature on a subject if it remains on your computer or in a file folder? Given the time and energy dedicated to the project, it is important to share the data with others. Several outlets for research exist. These include presenting your research at professional conferences or conventions and submitting your study for publication in an academic journal.

Writing the Abstract

Once you have concluded your discussion section, it is time to write your study's abstract. As we discussed in Chapter 5, the American Psychological Association's style manual (2001) says that an abstract should be accurate, self-contained, and concise/specific. To be accurate, an abstract should correctly reflect what occurs in the paper itself. To be self-contained, an abstract should not need any specialized information for the reader to understand what the abstract is communicating. Finally, a good abstract should be concise and specific. You should not attempt to retell your entire study, but you should give as much information to a potential reader that he or she understands what you did in your study by discussing any relevant results and conclusions. However, many research projects can have 10–20 results or major conclusions, so it is usually best to limit your number of conclusions in the abstract to the five most important findings, because in APA style your abstract is limited to 120 words.

Now that we've taken you through the world of creating, conducting, and writing quantitative research projects, it's time to talk about how to disseminate your findings to other researchers by both presenting at conferences and publishing.

Presenting at Conferences

Each professional discipline has its own associations that are designed to promote the research and scholarly activities of its members. In the communication discipline, there are associations at the state, regional, national, and international levels. Depending on your area of specialization, there may even be additional opportunities to network and share research. For example, if you completed a study examining humor in organizations, you could present your research at business conferences, psychology conferences, or humor conferences instead of communication conferences. Figure 22.2 lists the communication associations that host conventions or conferences where research is presented. The majority of these associations host annual conventions that feature research presentations by students and faculty. Some convention feature special preconferences, which focus on undergraduate and graduate research. Deadlines for conference submissions vary, and it is best to consult the organization's website for submission information.

As a student, there are many reasons why a communication conference should be of interest to you. Conferences provide students with an opportunity to meet and hear from scholars in the field, to learn about new methodologies and applications in research, and to present their own research. Networking and research presentation opportunities are the primary focus of these events. Faculty and alumni from various institutions catch up and share research and teaching ideas. Many schools recruit future graduate students at these events. After all, if an undergraduate student has an interest in presenting research and getting involved in professional associations, this is a good indicator of her or his potential as a graduate student. Before we continue, it is important to remember that conferences are professional events, so you should always dress appropriately. In other words, if you are presenting, you should be in formal business attire, and if you are just attending but not presenting, you can dress down slightly and go with business casual.

DIVISIONS AND INTEREST GROUPS

An important benefit provided by conferences is the opportunity provided to network with colleagues with similar interests. Perhaps the best way to meet other scholars with similar interests is to attend presentations sponsored by specific interest groups or divisions. Most associations provide their members with the opportunity to affiliate with several interest groups or divisions that represent various communication contexts. The National Communication Association currently has around 50 divisions and sections representing a variety of interests (the 2006 list of NCA divisions can be seen in Figure 22.3). Each of these groups schedules programs of research presentations at an annual convention, so whatever your interests are, there is an outlet for presentation.

INTERNATIONAL
International Communication Association
World Communication Association

NATIONAL
American Communication Association
National Communication Association

REGIONAL
Central States Communication Association
Eastern Communication Association
Southern States Communication Association
Western Communication Association

STATE
Arizona Communication Association
Arkansas Speech Communication Association
California Speech Communication Association
Carolinas Communication Association
Florida Communication Association
Georgia Communication Association
Illinois Speech & Theatre Association
Iowa Communication Association
Kansas Speech Communication Association
Kentucky Communication Association
Louisiana Communication Association
Maryland Communication Association
Michigan Association of Speech Communication
Minnesota, Communication and Theatre
     Association
Mississippi Speech Communication Association
Missouri, Speech and Theatre Association of
Nebraska Speech Communication and Theatre
     Association
New Jersey Communication Association
New York State Communication Association
North Dakota Speech and Theatre Association
North West Communication Association
Ohio Communication Association
Oklahoma Speech Theatre Communication
     Association
Oregon Speech Communication Association

Pennsylvania, Speech Communication
     Association of
Rocky Mountain Communication Association
South Dakota, Speech Communication
     Association
Tennessee Speech Communication Association
Texas Speech Communication Association
Virginia Association of Communication Arts
     and Sciences
Wisconsin Communication Association

**SAMPLE OF SPECIALIZED OR RELATED
     ASSOCIATIONS**
Academy of Management
American Association of Public Opinion Research
American College of Physicians
American Public Health Association
American Society for the History of Rhetoric
Association for Business Communication
Association for Women in Communications
Association for Education in Journalism and
     Mass Communication
Broadcast Education Association
Gerontological Society of America
International Association for Conflict Management
International Association for Humor Studies
International Association for Intercultural
     Communication Studies
International Association for Media and
     Communication Research
International Association for Relationship
     Research
International Listening Association
International Public Relations Association
Kenneth Burke Society
Media Ecology Association
National Council on Family Relations
Public Relations Society of America
Religious Communication Association
Rhetoric Society of America
Society for Personality and Social Psychology
Society for Risk Analysis

Figure 22.2 Professional Communication Associations

SUBMITTING RESEARCH FOR CONFERENCE REVIEW

Once you've decided to submit your research paper to a professional conference, you should consult the call for programs on the organization's website. The call for programs document provides important information on submitting your paper or proposal for review. Typically the deadlines for convention submissions are 6–9 months prior to the actual event. A sample of the call for papers for submissions to the Organizational Communication Division of NCA (Figure 22.4) illustrates many of the guidelines provided for submissions.

The call will specify whether the paper should be submitted in electronic format or mailed to the coordinator. Be sure to note what file format is preferred for submissions. Instructions

African American Communication & Culture Division
American Studies Division
Applied Communication Division
Argumentation and Forensics Division
Asian/Pacific American Communication Studies Division
Basic Course Division
Communication and Aging Division
Communication and the Future Division
Communication and Law Division
Communication Apprehension and Avoidance Division
Communication Assessment Division
Communication Centers Section
Communication Ethics Division
Community College Section
Critical and Cultural Studies Division
Elementary and Secondary Education Section
Emeritus/Retired Members Section
Environmental Communication Division
Ethnography Division
Experiential Learning in Communication Division
Family Communication Division
Feminist and Women's Studies Division
Freedom of Expression Division
Gay/Lesbian/Bisexual/Transgender Communication Studies Division
Group Communication Division
Health Communication Division
Human Communication and Technology Division
Instructional Development Division
Communication and Social Cognition Division
International and Intercultural Communication Division
Interpersonal Communication Division
Language and Social Interaction Division
Latino/Latina Communication Studies Division
Mass Communication Division
Nonverbal Communication Division
Organizational Communication Division
Peace and Conflict Communication Division
Performance Studies Division
Political Communication Division
Public Address Division
Public Relations Division
Rhetorical and Communication Theory Division
Semiotics and Communication Division
Spiritual Communication Division
Student Section
Theatre Division
Training and Development Division
Undergraduate College and University Section
Visual Communication Division

Figure 22.3 National Communication Association—2006 Divisions and Sections

NATIONAL COMMUNICATION ASSOCIATION

ORGANIZATIONAL COMMUNICATION DIVISION
Copies of Papers: 1 [in electronic form only; NO hard copies]
Deadline: February 15, 2006
Specify student papers: yes
Maximum length: 25 pages, excluding title page, abstract, references,
tables and figures

The Organizational Communication Division invites competitive papers and panel proposals on the
theory, research, and teaching of organizational communication. The Division embraces all theoretical and
methodological approaches to research. The submission of papers and panels pursuing the convention theme,
"Creating Sites for Connection and Action," is strongly encouraged.

PLEASE NOTE: Submitters must upload one copy of their paper to NCA's All Academic website. There
will be NO exceptions to the electronic submission process. Papers must be submitted online in one of
the following file formats: Microsoft Word, Word Perfect, PDF, RTF. Compressed or Zip files will not be
accepted.

Papers must include a title, an abstract of no more than 250 words, a list of important keywords
characterizing the paper, and any audio-visual presentation needs. Please also note on the title page if the
paper is a "student-authored" paper. Papers should not exceed 25 typed, double-spaced pages. To ensure
blind review, submitters should remove their names from their cover page before uploading the document,
and no information identifying the author may appear in the paper.

Please indicate if your paper would be appropriate for the new Scholar-to-Scholar: Interactive Media
Formats (Posters, Laptop Displays, Experiential Activities, etc.). Scholar-to-Scholar replaces the Poster
Sessions and has been redesigned to encourage alternative forms of presentation, one-on-one interaction, and
neighborhoods of knowledge. Your paper will be reviewed by the Division and, if you indicate an interest in
this format, it may then be scheduled during the Scholar-to-Scholar session. For more information, see the
Scholar-to-Scholar call for papers.

Panel proposals may be one of two types: 1) a group of panelists who discuss a specific topic that is
described in a 75-word abstract to be printed in the convention program; or 2) a group of panelists with titled
presentations centered on a common theme. For either type of panel proposal, submitters also must include
a statement that each participant agrees to attend, as well as participants' names, affiliations, and contact
information.

Figure 22.4 Sample Call for Convention Papers

provide guidelines as to page length limitations and deadlines for submission. Specific information on formatting of submission is included, and often items such as a title page, abstract,
key terms, and audiovisual needs are detailed. Some divisions schedule special panels or
present awards to the top papers authored by students. To be considered for these you should
include the phrase "Student Authored" or "Student Paper" on the title page.

All conference submissions are submitted to blind peer review to ensure that all papers are
given an equal opportunity for programming. The blind review process requires all authors
to remove any identifying information from the text of the paper to ensure that no preferen-
tial treatment will be shown in the evaluation. Most of the information that would need to
be changed is located in the methods section of the research paper, and changes are often
relatively simple. For example, if you initially reported in the paper that participants were
students enrolled in classes at Ohio University, the name of the institution could be concealed
by changing the description to students enrolled in classes at a large midwestern university.

TYPES OF CONFERENCE PRESENTATIONS

Paper Presentations

Presentations take one of three forms at a professional conference: paper presentations, poster presentations, or panel discussions. Paper presentations involve an oral report about the research project typically followed by a response from a scholar who has conducted research in the area. If time permits, the audience may choose to ask authors questions about their projects. Depending on the topic, an average of three to six papers may be scheduled to be presented during the same session. This typically means that an author can expect to have between 10 and 15 minutes to talk about the research project. That's not a lot of time, so if your paper is selected for presentation you will need to give careful consideration to what you will highlight in your presentation and rehearse to ensure that your presentation meets the time constraints.

If you have only 10–15 minutes, how do you condense a 25- to 30-page paper to that short period of time? Here is what we recommend. First, start your presentation by introducing your title and giving a short background about how the project was initiated. Did you see a hole in a theory? Did you notice that a communication variable hadn't been explored in a new context? Whatever the reasoning you have for your study, explain why you initiated the project in the first place. Explaining why you conducted your study should take no more than 1 minute. Second, introduce the bare minimal research background necessary for your audience to understand your research variables. If you're dealing with a widely known concept like communication apprehension, you may need to provide a quick definition and a review of one or two studies that set up how you are looking at communication apprehension in your study. Presenting your study's variables should take no more than 2–5 minutes. Third, explain the methods you used in your study. Start by giving a brief overview of how you collected your sample and any important demographics (sex, age, ethnicity, etc.). Next, explain the procedure that you used in your study as briefly as possible. If you conducted a complicated experiment, you may need to allow yourself a little more time to explain your experimental procedures. Then discuss the instrumentation used in your study. At this point, it is not really necessary to go into detail about alpha reliabilities, means, and standard deviations—just refer your audience to the paper for the specific statistical information. Presenting your methods should take only 1–4 minutes. Fourth, systematically deliver your results. We recommend telling your audience what a specific hypothesis or research question was, explaining how you tested the hypothesis or research question, and presenting the general result for the hypothesis or research question. You do not want to get yourself hung up on long strings of numbers that confuse your audience. For example, if you're reporting a regression, just say that the regression was significant, what R2 was, and if any beta weights accounted for unique variance. Do not attempt to read all of the numbers in the F-test, because saying that the regression was statistically significant will cover this in an oral presentation. You can also provide a basic interpretation of what each result means as you're discussing each finding. This section may take 2–5 minutes depending on your time limit, so keep it moving steadily. Fifth, explain your limitations very briefly (30 seconds max). Finally, explain why this research is important and where you see this line of research heading in the future.

After all of the presentations are complete, you may or may not have a respondent for your paper. A respondent is an academic who is trained in your area of research who will provide feedback on your manuscript's writing, analysis, and conclusions. The respondent will discuss each person's paper separately, so it's possible that it will feel like you're getting picked on during this process. The respondent is not trying to hurt your feelings or make you feel inferior, he or she really wants to offer you advice on how to make your paper stronger. While listening to the respondent, it is important not to become argumentative even if you think the respondent is wrong. Instead, listen and take notes about what the respondent is saying and then later decide if you agree or disagree. If you start arguing with the responding either out loud or inside your head, you may end up missing some very useful advice.

After the respondent is finished, the people who are attending the panel session are allowed to ask questions as time allows. As researchers, you should be ready for almost any type of question related to your study. People may ask you about why you used specific scales or why you chose your specific statistical analysis. If you are presented with a question that you're not completely sure you can answer, we recommend that you simply say that you're not sure, but you would be glad to find the answer for the questioner if he or she would provide you with an e-mail address at the conclusion of the session.

Poster Presentations

Poster presentations provide the presenter with an opportunity to talk with audience members one on one about their research. In 2006 the National Communication Association established Scholar-to-Scholar presentations, where top names in the field would roam around and interact with people presenting their posters. Typically, a large number of posters are displayed in a large exhibit area for each session. If your paper is programmed as a poster session, you will be notified of the size requirements for your poster. As a general rule, most posters are the size of a standard sheet of poster board. You should always ask how posters will be displayed. Many conferences expect free-standing posters that sit on top of a table, while others have easels available, and yet others expect you to attach your poster to some kind of partition. During the 1- to 2-hour session, audience members have an opportunity to view the displays and ask questions of the presenters. Since there is no "formal" presentation, discussions about the research project allow audience members to engage in more in-depth interaction in areas that are likely of common research interest. If your research is scheduled to be presented in poster format, guidelines for the poster will be included with your acceptance letter. As you prepare your poster, seven elements should be included:

1. Title of the research project, the author(s), and institutional affiliation(s)
2. A brief description (1–2 paragraphs) of the research. Consider using information similar to that included in an abstract to highlight the major findings of the study.
3. Use graphs, charts, and tables to present statistical results
4. Make your poster visually appealing—use color, clip art or photos, and fonts that are large enough to be seen from a distance.
5. Include headings on sections of your poster to highlight information in much the same way that you would use headings in a paper to guide your reader from one section to the next.
6. Remember, less is often more. While it may be difficult deciding what to include on your poster, consider ways that you can visually represent information or use bulleted lists to represent stages in your methodology.
7. Prepare at least 25 copies of your paper for distribution during the session. Since the presentation is more informal, this will provide the audience with an opportunity to review the complete paper at a later time. However, many people are opting to have a sign-up list available for papers instead of having the hardcopies available. People who are interested in your study can sign up for the paper, and you can e-mail them the paper after the conference.

Panel Presentations

Panel discussions are comprised of three or more individuals who discuss a common topic in an informal format. Rather than each presenter delivering a formal presentation, they may be asked to offer their insight or opinions while a facilitator guides the discussion. Audience members are often encouraged to participate during panel sessions by asking questions or offering comments.

While we wish we could say that all presentations are created equally, they really are not perceived this way in academia. Typically speaking, people who are presenting original research on a competitive panel generally are perceived as more prestigious than people presenting posters or sitting on panel discussions. In fact, some universities will not even count posters or panels as research presentations. We say this not to devalue posters and panels, but to warn you that you need to know how your academic institution places value on these different presentational formats, especially if you decide to make a career in academia. Now that you understand the opportunities offered by professional associations for young scholars, we hope that you will consider submitting your research projects for review. After all, the format of a convention paper is nearly identical to the format discussed for research papers in this text.

Publication

One of the best ways to ensure that your research study contributes to the body of knowledge in the field is to submit it for publication to an academic journal. Articles submitted to academic journals are scholarly in nature. "Scholarly" indicates that facts and information included in the study are documented by citing the author and date of publication for relevant research. It is important to note that while authors of convention papers often receive feedback in 2–3 months, the journal review process is considerably longer. It may take anywhere from 1–5 years before an article submitted for review actually ends up in print. To better understand the time required for publishing journal articles, let's take a closer look at the review process.

JOURNAL REVIEW PROCESS

All articles submitted to academic journals are peer-reviewed. The peer review process for academic journals is similar to that used by professional conventions with one notable exception. Feedback provided in a journal article review is much more comprehensive than the comments provided by a convention review panel. Whereas convention reviewers may simply rank papers they think should be presented, the process is much more rigorous when reviewing articles for publication. Journal review board members are often asked to provide one of four recommendations to the editor: (1) publish as is; (2) publish pending revisions; (3) revise and resubmit before a decision is made; or (4) reject the study. If the article is rejected, some editors and reviewers may offer suggestions for alternative outlets for the study to be considered for publication. Whether a study is accepted or rejected, authors typically receive extensive feedback from a panel of two or three anonymous reviewers. Let's take a look at the two processes involved in journal publication more closely: the submission process and the review process.

Submission Process

Once you have decided to submit your research for review, the next question is often, "Which journal is most appropriate for this study?" There are several options to choose from in determining which outlet is best for your research. Many of the associations listed in Figure 22.2 publish one or more academic journals, and the focus of each journal is unique in terms of the types of methodologies, communication contexts, and length of articles published. To determine which outlet is best suited for which your research, review the call for manuscripts for more detailed guidelines. Samples of call for manuscripts are provided in Figure 22.5 for two prominent communication journals: *Communication Education* (CE) and *Communication Research Reports* (CRR).

Each of these samples provides scholars with information on the types of articles that are typically published with regard to methodology and contextual focus. In addition, format guidelines are provided as well as information about page length and how to submit articles.

COMMUNICATION EDUCATION

Guidelines for manuscript submissions

Communication Education publishes original scholarship bearing on the intersections of communication, instruction, and human development. Within this broad purview, it welcomes diverse disciplinary, conceptual, and methodological perspectives, especially scholarship in the following areas:

- Classroom discourse
- Life-span development of communication competence
- Mediating instructional communication with technology
- Diverse backgrounds of learners and teachers in instructional interaction
- Interaction in informal education and in varied instructional settings
- Learning outcomes associated with instructional communication practices across disciplines
- Learning outcomes and processes in the discipline of communication studies
- Rhetorical and organizational aspects of communication among educational agencies, among policy-makers, and among their stakeholders

Manuscripts submitted to Communication Education must subscribe to the National Communication Association Code of Professional Ethics for Authors. (See *http://www.natcom.org/policies/Internal/code_of_professional_ethics.htm* or write NCA, 1765 N Street NW, Washington, DC 20036.) These guidelines enjoin authors to use inclusive and nondefamatory language. In addition, submissions should be accompanied by a cover letter attesting that the author has met professional standards for any of the following principles as may apply. (1) The manuscript is original work and proper publication credit is accorded to all authors. (2) Simultaneous editorial consideration of the manuscript at another publication venue is prohibited. (3) Any publication history of the manuscript is disclosed, indicating in particular whether the manuscript or another version of it has been presented at a conference, or published electronically, or whether portions of the manuscript have been published previously. (4) Duplicate publication of data is avoided; or if parts of the data have already been reported, then that fact is acknowledged. (5) All legal, institutional, and professional obligations for obtaining informed consent from research participants and for limiting their risk are honored. (6) The scholarship reported is authentic.

Full-length manuscripts of articles reporting empirical research, critical analyses, historical scholarship, or theoretic expositions should conform to the *Style Manual of the American Psychological Association*, 5th edition (2001). Article manuscripts should generally not exceed 30 double-spaced pages, except in cases in which "thick description" of qualitative data may require it. Authors are asked to submit three manuscript copies along with an electronic file on disk. (Rich Text Format is preferred for the electronic copy.) To facilitate masked review, the author's identity should not be discernible in the text, except on the title page. The title page should also state the history of the manuscript (i.e., whether it has been previously presented at a conference or derives from a thesis or dissertation) and any author acknowledgments. Authors should mail these materials to the Editor.

COMMUNCIATION RESEARCH REPORTS

Guidelines for Submission

A Publication of the Eastern Communication Association

Communication Research Reports publishes brief empirical articles (approximately 10–12 double-spaced pages or less including references) on a wide variety of topics pertaining to human communication. Appropriate topics include studies of small group, relational, political, persuasive, organizational, nonverbal, mass, interpersonal, intercultural, instructional, health, aging/life span, family, and computer mediated communication. Authors should provide a sentence to a paragraph outlining the theoretical framework guiding the brief empirical report. In sum, theoretical rationale should receive modest coverage in the research report (1–2 paragraphs) along with a brief review of the representative literature on the topic, with the main portion of the paper devoted to a thorough reporting and interpretation of the results.

Manuscript Preparation: After removing all identifiers in the properties of the document (go to File-Properties-Summary and delete your name and affiliation), authors should submit one electronic double-spaced copy of the manuscript and one separate title page in Microsoft Word (preferred) or WordPerfect conforming to the 5th edition of

Figure 22.5 Call for Manuscripts for *Communication Education* and *Communication Research Reports*

Continued

Continued

the *American Psychological Association Style Manual* and should also submit a hard copy to the editor at the address below. The detachable cover sheet must contain: (1) the title of the manuscript; (2) the author's name, mailing address and institutional affiliation; and (3) the author's phone number and email address. The first page of the manuscript must include the title and a 50 to 100-word abstract. Manuscripts should be emailed and mailed to the Editor.

The final version of a manuscript accepted for publication must be submitted and formatted in Word (6.0 or above) to the editor via email.

Review Policy: Manuscripts will be blind-reviewed by at least two members of the editorial board whose evaluations will provide the basis for the editor's publication decision. ***Communication Research Reports*** is committed to completing the review process as rapidly as possible, ideally within three months of the manuscript's receipt. Manuscripts that do not conform to the mission of the journal, or that do not comply with submission guidelines, will not be reviewed. No manuscript can be previously published or be under consideration by any other journal at the time of submission.

One obvious difference in the calls for CE and CRR is their page length requirements: CRR has a limit of 12 pages, while CE accepts manuscripts up to 30 pages in length. Another distinction can be found in the research contexts included in the journal: CE encourages manuscripts focusing on classroom communication phenomenon, while CRR welcomes manuscripts on a wide variety of topics focusing on human communication. Three basic factors will help guide your decision as to which journal is right for your research: (1) focus on communication context, (2) research methodologies, and (3) page length. To see a list of possible publication outlets that publish communication scholarship, review the chart of communication-related journals in Figure 4.6 from Chapter 4.

Once you have determined which journal is appropriate for your research, be sure to adhere to all instructions for manuscript preparation detailed in the call. In particular, pay close attention to guidelines for page length, limits on the number of words to be included in the abstract, and preferred style format (APA or MLA). Be sure to carefully edit the manuscript to avoid any embarrassing mistakes. When you submit your paper, it is often a good idea to draft a short cover letter to the editor pointing out the unique contributions of your paper and how it "fits" with the journal content. Some editors may request that you add a statement confirming that the article has not been published elsewhere and is not being submitted simultaneously for review by another journal.

Review Process

As discussed earlier, the journal review process is lengthy and sometimes frustrating. Once you've reached this point in the process, be prepared to wait. Journal editors will often review the list of references included in your article to identify potential reviewers. Throughout the entire process, the author(s) and reviewer(s) remain anonymous. However, authors often include information in the manuscript that provides the reviewer with clues as to their identity. To maintain your anonymity, refrain from including too many references to your own work, and be sure to remove any and all identifying information from the manuscript. Citing references from the journal to which you are submitting your article is another way of demonstrating to the reviewers and editor how your research fits with what the journal is already publishing.

Prepare yourself for the feedback you will receive. After all, reviewers often feel obligated to find some issues with your study. Rarely do papers get accepted on the initial submission. Many papers undergo two to three revisions before they are ready for publication. Editors

Communication and Critical/Cultural Studies (2003)	6%
Communication Education (2002–2003)	18.9%
Communication Monographs (2002–2003)	13.3%
Communication Teacher (2002–2003)	43%
Critical Studies in Media Communication (2002–2003)	10%
Journal of Applied Communication Research (2005)	12.84%
The Quarterly Journal of Speech (2003)	12.59%
Review of Communication (2003)	100%
Text and Performance Quarterly (2003)	16.67%

Acceptance rates are calculated on the three-year editorial term of the previous editor.
SOURCE. National Communication Association website
(http://www.natcom.org/nca/Template2.asp?bid=222)

Figure 22.6 NCA Journal Acceptance Rates

will send typed comments from the reviewers along with their anonymous recommendation for acceptance, revision, or rejection. If the recommendation from reviewers is to revise and resubmit your article, take heed and be sure to address the concerns identified in their reviews. Once you have made the recommended changes, it is a good idea to draft a letter to the reviewers letting them know that you have made the changes requested in their review. Address each recommendation made by the reviewer and explain how you responded to it in the revised manuscript. Doing so will communicate to the reviewers and the editor that you are committed to addressing their concerns and value their feedback.

Let's face it, not every manuscript that is submitted to a journal gets accepted. In fact, most communication journals average an acceptance rate of between 10 and 20%. That means that 80–90% of the articles are rejected. A summary of the rejection rates for journals published by NCA (Figure 22.6) should provide you with additional insight into journal acceptance rates.

If you decide to submit your research for publication, chances are that you'll experience rejections along the way. While rejection is frustrating, you can adopt a positive view of the process if you utilize the feedback provided by the reviewers to help you revise the paper for submission to a different journal. Ask a colleague or professor to read the paper and share the feedback provided by reviewers to get their suggestions. While nobody likes being rejected, it is important to remember that it is part of the publication process. Trust us—the satisfaction you will experience upon receiving your first acceptance letter will make this entire process worth the effort.

Conclusion

Throughout this text, we have described the process involved in writing and conducting scholarly research. As you have noticed, this process takes time, and it would be a shame not to share the results of your hard work with others. In this chapter we have provided information to assist you in writing up the discussion section of your paper. Various elements and suggestions for language use are provided to interpret results for the reader. We chose to conclude this text with an explanation of the options available and a description of the processes involved in submitting your research for conference presentation or journal publication. As you begin your journey as a communication scholar, we encourage you to share your work with others—after all, you are the future scholars of our field!

KEY TERMS

Academic Divisions/Interest Groups
Call for Papers
Discussion

Future Directions
Limitations
Panel Discussion
Paper Presentation

Peer Review
Poster Presentation
Research Implications

REFERENCES

Publication manual of the American Psychological Association (5th ed.). (2001). Washington, DC: American Psychological Association.

Wrench, J. S., & Booth-Butterfield, M. (2003). Increasing patient satisfaction and compliance: An examination of physician humor orientation, compliance-gaining strategies, and perceived credibility. *Communication Quarterly, 51,* 482–503.

FURTHER READING

Alexander, A., & Potter, W. J. (Eds.). (2001). *How to publish your communication research: An insider's guide.* Thousand Oaks, CA: Sage.

Kitchin, R., & Fuller, D. (2005). *Academics guide to publishing.* Thousand Oaks, CA: Sage.

Knapp, M. L., & Daly, J. A. (2004). *A guide to publishing in scholarly communication journals.* Mahwah, NJ: Lawrence Erlbaum.

McInerney, D. M. (2002). *Publishing your psychology research: A guide to writing for journals in psychology and related fields.* Thousand Oaks, CA: Sage.

Nicol, A. A. M., & Pexman, P. M. (2003a). *Displaying your findings: A practical guide for creating figures, posters, and presentations.* Washington, DC: American Psychological Association.

Nicol, A. A. M., & Pexman, P. M. (2003b). *Presenting your findings: A practical guide for creating tables.* Washington, DC: American Psychological Association.

Qualitative Research

James W. Chesebro and Deborah J. Borisoff

James W. Chesebro (PhD, University of Minnesota) is a professor in the Department of Communication at Indiana State University in Terre Haute, Indiana. Dr. Chesebro has specialized in the study of media as symbolic and cognitive systems. Since 1966, he has maintained a sustained focus on dramatistic theory, methods, and criticism with specific applications to television. Since 1981, this orientation has been extended to all media systems, with conceptual attention devoted to media literacy and media technologies as communication and cognitive systems, a perspective reflected in both his teaching and research. Dr. Chesebro has served as Editor of two National Communication Association (NCA) journals: *Critical Studies in Mass Communication* and the *Review of Communication*. In 1996, Dr. Chesebro served as President of NCA. Dr. Chesebro has published several books, including *Analyzing Media: Communication Technologies as Symbolic and Cognitive Systems*, *Extensions of the Burkeian System*, *Computer-Mediated Communication*, *Public Policy Decision-Making*, *Orientations to Public Communication*, and coedited the third edition of *Methods of Rhetorical Criticism: A Twentieth-Century Perspective*. He has published over 100 articles in communication journals.

Deborah J. Borisoff (PhD, New York University) is a professor in the Department of Culture and Communication in New York University's Steinhardt School of Education. Dr. Borisoff has been an active scholar in the areas of gender and communication, conflict management, organizational communication, cross-cultural communication, and listening. She has been the coauthor or coeditor of 10 published books, including *The Power to Communicate: Gender Differences as Barriers*, *Conflict Management: A Communication Approach*, *Listening in Everyday Life*, *Women and Men Communicating: Challenges and Changes*, and numerous book chapters and journal articles. Dr. Borisof has been named a Distinguished Research Fellow and Distinguished Teaching Fellow by the Eastern Communication Association and received New York University's Steinhardt School of Education Teaching Excellence Award. She was awarded NYU's Distinguished Teaching Medal in 2004.

CHAPTER OBJECTIVES

1 Differentiate between the three primary methods used by communication researchers—quantitative, critical, and qualitative.

2 Understand the six labels commonly used in qualitative research.

3 Know the five commonly shared characteristics of all forms of qualitative research—natural settings, researcher as participant, subject-based communication, subject intentionality, and pragmatism.

4 Understand the purpose of grounded theory in communication research.

5 Differentiate between the nine reactive effects that affect a study's validity.

6 Be able to explain the purposes of open-ended questions, when researchers should use this qualitative method, and what kinds of results are generated.

7 Be able to explain the purposes of focus groups, when researchers should use this qualitative method, and what kinds of results are generated.

8 Be able to explain the purposes of participant observation, when researchers should use this qualitative method, and what kinds of results are generated.

9 Be able to explain the purposes of unobtrusive measures, when researchers should use this qualitative method, and what kinds of results are generated.

10 Be able to explain the purposes of triangulation or multiple class measurements, when researchers should use this qualitative method, and what kinds of results are generated.

11 Explain the four ethical issues commonly discussed in qualitative research—informed consent, deception, privacy and confidentiality, and accuracy.

What meanings do college students give to the programs they watch on television or the lyrics they listen to in defining who they are as individuals? Why are over 100 million young people registered members of www.MySpace.com? How do working parents experience their companies' personnel policies on fulfilling their dual roles as professionals and parents? What sense do members of different races, cultures, and classes make of how they are treated in the public and private lives they lead? While numerous research methods are available to get at these questions, this supplemental chapter considers an approach to research that focuses primarily on the ways in which humans construct, understand, and convey their lived experiences. Before we examine this approach, it is important to distinguish it within three predominant threads of inquiry: *quantitative*, *critical*, and *qualitative*.

A wide variety of approaches are used to examine and systematically study human communication. Some prefer to observe what people do and the conditions under which they act as they do. Within this context, employing surveys and questionnaires, some communication scholars emphasize what people report they have done when communicating. Seeking to provide broad generalizations or theories about human communication over diverse situations, this behavioral orientation is typically identified as a *scientific*, *social scientific*, or *quantitative* approach to communication. Still another group focuses on the values and value judgments that always permeate and undergird all communicative experiences. Frequently, these scholars challenge our assumptions, and they even propose alternative ways of communicating. They goad and encourage us to aspire to more humane and responsible ends as communicators. This approach to the study of communication is predominantly identified as a *critical approach*. In this appenidx we examine yet another way in which to study human communication. We focus on how people communicate in their own natural environments, when they are guided by their own personal objectives, and how they give meaning to their communication, especially when they are using communication for those pragmatic objectives that determine and control day-to-day existence. This approach has had a host of different labels, but its central and most unifying label is *qualitative research.*

In this appendix, we develop this qualitative approach in six ways. First, we begin by recognizing the diverse ways in which qualitative research has been defined. Second, we isolate five common characteristics that ultimately constitute a unifying definition of qualitative research. Third, we identify some important kinds of questions and issues that define the concerns of qualitative researchers. Fourth, we examine the contributions of qualitative research to the study of human communication. Fifth, we identify five major methods that we think are particularly useful when conducting qualitative research. Finally, ethical issues involved in the use of qualitative research are identified.

Multiple Labels for One Research Method

In our view, qualitative research has been identified in a host of ways. We would like to dismiss these differences by merely claiming that different people in different situations merely identified and began to employ different labels for a common experience. Yet, in some ways, the labels reflect some important differences in how qualitative research is perceived, studied, and ultimately even understood. In some cases, diverse labels have emerged because a variety of different disciplines —such as sociology, anthropology, linguistics, and psychology—are involved, and over time, each discipline has selected and employed a different label to reflect its particular emphasis and spin on what is being observed. In other cases, different researchers have legitimately perceived and understood different things when they have been in the natural environments of human beings when they communicate. Or they believe that different motives and even theoretical orientations must be recognized, and identified in alternative ways, to account for why and how people communicate in their own environments.

We believe that six different labels have been used to deal with different dimensions and characteristics of qualitative research: naturalistic, qualitative, interpretive/interpretivist, ethnographic, field, and action/applied. Each of these labels deserves attention, and each begins to reveal an important feature of what we mean by qualitative research.

NATURALISTIC RESEARCH

Two dimensions have traditionally been used to define "naturalistic research."[1] First, the researcher seeks to make the research experience as much a part of the subjects' everyday environment as possible. A question of degree, the more a research project blends into and is a part of the daily experiences of subjects, the more the research findings are viewed as "naturalistic." Second, research is viewed as more "naturalistic" if the behavior studied is restricted as little as possible by the researcher or by the design of the research project. In this regard, if a researcher asks you to complete a questionnaire in classroom and the questionnaire provides you with only a limited number of responses to each question or statement on the questionnaire, the environment and the nature of the questionnaire itself would suggest the research project is extremely artificial rather than natural. On the other hand, if a rescarcher is one of your friends and you are unaware that he is observing your behaviors for a research project, you might believe your friend has been acting unethically and in a deceptive fashion, but the research project itself would be classified as "naturalistic" because the study was conducted in your everyday environment and the behaviors your displayed were not restricted in any way by the researcher or the design of the research project.

QUALITATIVE RESEARCH

Fundamentally, qualitative researchers seek to preserve and analyze the situated form, content, and experience of social action, rather than subject it to mathematical or other formal transformations....Unlike naturalistic inquiry, qualitative research is not always carried out in the habitat of cultural members....Unlike ethnography, qualitative research does not always immerse the researcher in the scene for a prolonged period, adopt a holistic view of social practices, or broadly consider their cultural and historical contexts....Most communication scholars, for example, consider *qualitative research* to be the broadest and most inclusive term for these phenomena.[2]

Others have argued that, "Qualitative data take the form of words rather than numbers. Qualitative data are analyzed and presented in the form of case studies, critiques, and sometimes verbal reports....Qualitative data are analyzed most often by rhetorical critics and ethnographers."[3]

INTERPRETATIVE RESEARCH OR INTERPRETIVIST EPISTEMOLOGY

Hafren has provided a set of terms for characterizing interpretative research in contrast to terms used to characterize positivist/empirical research (Figure A.1)[4]

ETHNOGRAPHIC RESEARCH

"[E]thnography is used to study people's behavior in specific, natural settings. Ethnographers try to capture as fully as possible, and from the research participant's perspective, the ways that people use symbols within specific contexts."[5]

FIELD RESEARCH

Academic/Scholarly Definition: "As the name implies, **field experiments** are like experiments in terms of researcher control over the manipulation of independent variables and random assignment of participants. However, the research environment is realistic and natural. Participants are not asked to come to a laboratory environment that is used exclusively for experimentation. Rather, the research is conducted in environments with which participants already are familiar."[6] As Frey, Botan, Friedman, and Kreps have aptly noted, "A *field experiment* is an experiment conducted in a natural setting."[7]

Vernacular Definition: In everyday use (not literary, cultured, or foreign uses), as reflected in dictionary definitions, the word *field* is not associated with experiments, manipulations of independent variables, or laboratory environments. For example, a "field test" is conducted "in a natural environment" to determine utility and acceptability. "Field work" involves "first hand observation" and interviewing "subjects in the field."[8] Indeed, the notion of a "field trip" suggests a "visit made by students and usually a teacher" out of the academic or scholarly environment and into a situation that allows for "firsthand observations" of events as they naturally occur.[9] Within this context, several academic and scholarly publications view field studies as "artistic," an "artistic challenge" to "preserve, convey, and celebrate" the "complexity" of the field "even to the point of messing science up the way humans seem capable of doing."[10]

	Interpretative	**Positivist/Empirical**
Key Terms	Phenomenology	Data
	Quality	Statistics
	Meaning	Positivist
	Process	Empirical
Thrust of Research	Feelings	Numbers
Methods	Unstructured interview	Questionnaire
	Observations	Measurements
Readability	Great fun	With a calculator
Scale of Work	Small scale	Lots of people
Ease of Research	One person	Team, big computer or secondary data
Fashionability	High among sociologists	Lower generally among experts
Validity	So-so, depends on your topic, but supplements positivist work.	Overestimated.
Reliability	Easy to cheat and select data.	Overestimated if you believe the nature of society is to change.
Perspective	Interactional.	Post-Durkheim and in the British tradition.
Problems to Consider	• Time factor. • Making notes. • Ethics. • Ease with which subjects can manipulate the image they project. • Possibility of becoming involved in criminal or deviant acts.	• Cost of research. • Time factor. • Possibility of creating 'leading' questions. • Reliability of responses. • Have the correct questions been asked? • Interpreting statistics is a specialized field. • People can read too much into results.

Figure A.1 Interpretative/Phenomenological and Positivist/Empirical Research Revision Checklist

Field Research as Both Participant and Nonparticipant: Douglas[11] has argued that there are two types of field research, one very consistent with the "academic/scholarly definition" above, and one with the "vernacular definition" above. At the same time, Douglas argues that each type employs different data-gathering techniques. The "participant field research" approach employs depth-probe field research, investigative reporting, detective work, covert field research, overt journalism and police work, and overt field research. The "nonparticipant field research" approach employs discussion (free-flowing), in-depth interviews, and in-depth interviews with flexible checklists of questions.

ACTION OR APPLIED RESEARCH

Action or applied research is "conducted for the purpose of solving a particular 'real-world,' socially relevant problem." Action or applied researchers "start with a perceived problem and conduct a study to solve it."[12]

Five Commonly Shared Characteristics of All Forms of Qualitative Research

The forms of qualitative research mentioned immediately above employ distinct approaches. However, they all share certain commonalities—natural settings, researcher as participant, subject-based communication, subject intentionality, and pragmatism.

NATURAL SETTING

Investigation and data collection are conducted in a geographic location, time, and set of rituals determined, if not controlled, by the subjects. The environment is not and was never intended for the investigations and data collection. Some argue that a simulation of a natural setting can be equivalent to and control symbol-using in the same way that a natural setting does.

RESEARCHER AS PARTICIPANT

The researcher is perceived by the subjects as a participant in some significant way. While the investigator may be known as a researcher, the verbal and nonverbal actions of the investigator are not perceived as stemming from the role of researcher.

SUBJECT-BASED COMMUNICATION

The subjects are allowed to identify and determine topics of communication, provide transitions from one topic to another, and provide any qualifiers they see fit. The researcher's objectives and research questions do not generate and guide the communication topics, transitions, and qualifiers of the subjects.

SUBJECT INTENTIONALITY

The researcher seeks to capture and preserve the communication and symbol-using of subjects as the subjects understand and intend them.

PRAGMATISM

The specific results obtained have immediate utility and/or produce direct and instant insight into ongoing social processes and outcomes; the research analysis resolves an existing social problem. It may or may not contribute to theory development.

Significant and Unique Research Goals, Questions, and Issues Guiding Qualitative Research

In their work on human communication theory and research, Robert Heath and Jennings Bryant argue that "[t]he word *theory* refers to the process of observing and speculating."[13] They further explain that "[a] theory is a systematic and plausible set of generalizations that explain some observable phenomena by linking concepts (constructs and variables) in terms of an organizing principle that is internally consistent."[14] Heath and Bryant's notion of theory has important implications for the area of qualitative research. The initial part of their definition includes "process" and appears at first glance to be open to interpretation. The second portion of their definition, however, makes certain assumptions regarding what this process ought to yield. First, it presupposes that full "explanation" is possible. Second, it presupposes that "internal consistency" inheres in all instances of the phenomena being observed. Third, the term "observable" suggests distance, or being apart, from that which is being observed.

Theory-building has been the abiding *sina qua non* (without which it could not be) of research. How we get at developing and generating theory, however, has been questioned and transformed. This transformation is the focus of this section. Within the field of communication as well as other disciplines, quantitative research has been long regarded as the predominant methodology to test and to generate theories. Qualitative research was viewed more as a precursor to rigorous (read quantitative) measures; it was seen as providing primarily impressionistic and unsystematic descriptions that produced mostly case studies with limited value. With the 1967 publication of their path-breaking *The Discovery of Grounded Theory*, sociologists Barney Glaser and Anselm Strauss challenged these assumptions about qualitative research and provided an approach to field research that effectively unseeded the quantitative paradigm as the only legitimate approach to research.[15] In the process, they situated field research as an "endeavor in its own right."[16]

What is grounded theory? Essentially, grounded theory suggests that theory emerges inductively from the data—that is, "from the ground up." This contrasts with the traditional inquiry characteristic of quantitative research, which posits a deductive approach (one begins with a theory and then tests or examines it). However, even among grounded research theorists there are divergent views regarding the process and goal this type of research ought to produce.

In her chapter on grounded theory, Kathy Charmaz explains how qualitative researchers (including Glaser and Strauss as well as subsequent adherents) came to embrace different approaches regarding the researcher's role and the goal of grounded theory research.[17] The traditional view follows the "objectivist" perspective (also identified as a "positivist" lens). The more recent perspective has been called the "constructivist" perspective (also identified as an "interpretive" lens). Figure A.2, "Objectivist and Constructivist Approaches to Qualitative Research," summarizes some of these differences.

Distinguishing Characteristics	Objectivist/Positivist Approach	Constructivist/Interpretative Approach
Conception of and Approach to *Real* World	The real world and the truths it holds are waiting to be discovered.	The world is made real through people's actions and thoughts—it emerges and does not exist in some external and readily discovered form.
Method for Analysis	The approach assumes a systematic set of methods that can lead ultimately to discovering truths about reality that will yield testable theories. *Truth*, in this context, is with a small letter t.	The approach assumes methods that are open to refinement that can illuminate how subjects construct reality; it does not presume a generalizable truth about reality. The aim is to identify the meaning people construct as they interact.
Role of Researcher	The researcher's stance is as observer, recorder, analyst of the data. The researcher stands apart from the research.	The researcher's interactions with subjects contribute to the emerging concepts and categories. The researcher functions as a participant as well as an observer. The data collected are co-constructed by the researchers and subjects studied.
Nature of Data	Rich data yields categories, ultimately categories that are privileged over experience.	Data includes the feelings and interpretations of what subjects reveal both explicitly as well as tacitly. Ultimately, it is possible that the data may remain at a more intuitive and impressionistic level.
Trustworthiness of the Findings	Reliability and validity can be achieved, allowing for the study to be replicated.	Hypotheses and concepts can be generated which other researchers can apply to similar research problems.

Figure A.2 Objectivist and Contructivist Approaches to Qualitative Research

The nuances reflected in Figure A.2 are profound. However, both approaches share the following six key aspects that guide grounded theory inquiry.[18]

Grounded Theory Must Be Applicable and Work

By "applicable" we mean that any findings generated from the study must connect to the actual data collected and should not be forced or superimposed by the researcher. By "work" we mean that the data collected should be both relevant and connected to the behaviors being studied. If, for example, a researcher is exploring how couples talk about dividing tasks in the home, the researcher should not assume that these couples talk or approach spending money in the same way.

Grounded Theory Is Localized

Because qualitative research focuses on how individuals communicate in their own natural environment, the researcher must be able to develop a cohesive representation and explanation of the data that has emerged within a particular context at a particular moment in time. For example, a researcher talking with students of a particular ethnic group about how they experience academic support at their institution needs to consider the particular institution (location, size, reputation, etc.) as well as the political and social events within the larger society.

Grounded Theory Is Patterned

The corpus of qualitative research emerges primarily through interaction in natural environments (or field situations). The researcher, therefore, needs to identify the patterns that emerge from the data collected. This process is inductive because the researcher is not conducting an experiment that controls or regulates behaviors and responses. A researcher looking at how stress is experienced in organizations, for example, might engage with a group of managers who are working for a particular company. Through a series of interviews it may emerge that "stress" is experienced differently by different age groups; it may be affected by marital status; it may be experienced differently by women and men; it may be informed by ethnicity, culture, or sexual orientation. The researcher must connect the dots, so to speak.

The Process of Grounded Theory Is Connected to Emergent Design

The naturalistic paradigm occurs in divergent settings with distinct subjects who hold multiple views on reality. Moreover, the process itself is affected by the relationship of the researcher to those in the study. The unique and idiosyncratic nature of both the context and the individuals involved, therefore, suggests that no single research design will be appropriate for all naturalistic inquiry.

Whereas conventional inquiry is based on the assumption that the investigator "knows what he or she doesn't know" and thus can use a defined methodology to approach the study deductively (e.g., formulate a hypothesis to be tested), naturalistic inquiry, in contrast, is rooted in the assumption that the investigator "does *not* know what he or she doesn't know." Under the latter conditions, a fully developed initial design would be suspect. Lincoln and Guba suggest, therefore, that in this type of research, the design must "unfold, cascade, roll, emerge."[19]

GROUNDED THEORY DESIGN IS REFINED AND NEGOTIATED

How, then, does a design "unfold" and "emerge"? Charmaz suggests that the power of grounded theory lies in methods that are "flexible," "heuristic" and ongoing, as opposed to formulaic.[20] Lincoln and Guba suggest the following aspects that comprise this ongoing process.[21] The researcher needs to engage in:

1. Continuous data analysis to review what has emerged through interviews or observations (the researcher interacts with the data rather than to map concepts onto the data)

2. Ongoing inductive data analysis so that any questions, insights, orgaps can be identified and pursued (constant comparison between the data collected and emergent themes)

3. Checking with interviewees/subjects (e.g., through debriefing interviews) to assure an accurate representation of their thoughts, ideas, and intentions and to prevent possible misinterpretation on the part of the researcher

4. Maintaining adequate and scrupulous records of the project—what is termed "audit-trail"

5. Maintaining a personal journal whereby the researcher can record personal insights, thoughts, and questions related to the data gathered

6. Being open to the potentiality for "milestones"—that is, key moments that may occur unpredictably

These aspects illustrate the process dimension of grounded-theory research. Moreover, they suggest that "indeed, tolerance of ambiguity may well be the most important personal characteristic the naturalistic investigator must possess."[22]

GROUNDED THEORY HAS PRESCRIBED APPLICATION

As the above aspects of grounded theory that guide qualitative research suggest, inquiry into *particular* individuals at a *moment in time* in a *discrete context* can provide enormous insight and understanding. It can illuminate powerfully how individuals or groups see themselves and others, make meaning of their experiences, and identify problems or issues that affect them deeply. This information, which can emerge only from the thick description obtained in the data-gathering process, can make a significant contribution in ways that are not the purview of quantitative research.

Yet it is precisely the specificity of naturalistic inquiry that gives rise to its limitation. No single study can be duplicated exactly. The people are different; the setting is not the same; changes in societal norms and values occur over time. Thus we cannot assume that findings from a particular study can necessarily be replicated precisely with identical findings in a later study. And yet, similar studies do occur. Researchers may take up anew earlier studies in different contexts and with different individuals. Often the experiences, problems, concerns, and feelings of individuals do recur across time and across contexts. There are resonances of themes, patterns, expressions, etc., that suggest consistency, relevance, and understanding. It is at these intersections of recurrence that the potential power and relevance of grounded theory in naturalistic research is revealed. When we begin to explore more formally the limits of research designs and to minimize explicitly the influence of a research design so that only the subjects' personal reactions can emerge, then we are turning our attention to the concept of *reactivism* as a standard for conducting research.

Reactivism: A Rationale for Qualitative Research

In the late 1950s, four psychologists—Sellitiz, Jahoda, Deutsch, and Cook[23]—recognized that the act of measuring, the measurement instruments used, who is examined, and how samples are selected can influence, if not determine, the results obtained during experiments and in surveys. These factors—identified as *reactive effects*—can raise questions about the validity and reliability of the data collected, suggesting that the results obtained stem not from the phenomena being investigated, but from how the phenomena were examined. A variety of reactive effects exist.[24]

GUINEA PIG EFFECT

If people feel they are "guinea pigs" being experimented with, or if they feel that they are being "tested" and must make a good impression, or if the method of data collection suggests or stimulates an interest the subject did not previously feel, the measurement process may be distorting the results.

ROLE SELECTION

Another way in which the respondent's awareness of the research process produces differential reaction involves not so much inaccuracy, defense, or dishonesty, but rather a specialized selection from among the many "true" selves or "proper" behaviors available to any respondent.

MEASUREMENT AS CHANGE AGENT

The initial measured activity introduces real changes in what is being measured. The "preamble effect" was studied by Jack Orr, who demonstrated that survey attribution affects responses to the questions asked on a survey.

RESPONSE SETS

A wide range of predetermined responses have been demonstrated including the fact that respondents will endorse a statement more frequently than disagree with it, a response that may be personality specific. Additionally, subjects have a preference for extreme rather than moderate statements. Moreover, if allowed, subjects will start to consistently select one answer (all true) unless their pattern of response is somehow disrupted.

INTERVIEWER EFFECTS

The interview can contribute a substantial amount of variance to a set of findings. An interviewer who is just beginning to ask subjects questions will possess an eagerness or freshness that someone conducting interviews for hours may not have. The eagerness or exhaustion of the interviewer affects how subjects respond. Likewise, for example, the degree of attractiveness of an interviewer affects subject responses.

CHANGE IN THE RESEARCH INSTRUMENT

The measuring (data-gathering) instrument is frequently an interviewer who may conduct the interview in different ways at different times. For example, an interviewer may become more competent later in the interview process rather than during early stages.

POPULATION RESTRICTIONS

Public opinion poll organizations seldom claim they have a random sample of an entire population. So many groups of people within a population are simply not available to pollsters, such as those in mental institutions, people and military forces overseas, those working unusual shifts, etc. In addition, the time of day when a survey is conducted, the use of the telephone (unlisted numbers, the time when people are at home, etc.), and the economic level of the neighborhood (e.g., extremely poor or extremely rich neighborhoods are avoided by door-to-door interviewers) are factors.

POPULATION STABILITY OVER TIME

The population available varies dramatically in terms of a host of factors, such as the weather (e.g., rain or snow days), seasonal layoffs, and summer and winter vacations.

DROSS RATE

Investigators avoid data-collection systems that generate a high rate of irrelevant-to-relevant information.

ABILITY TO REPLICATE

While one might feel confident that the interview style and questionnaire are reproduced in a replication, several factors can restrict the ability to conduct replications. Archives and physical evidence may be restricted or destroyed.

These 10 reactive effects are only illustrative. A host of additional reactive effects can also be identified and demonstrated to affect experimental and survey research.

Qualitative Research Methods

As you might have anticipated by this point, studying people in their natural environment may require devising a set of procedures that are particularly sensitive and appropriate to the unique kind of communication you are observing. At the same time, there are some more "standardized" methods you may wish to consider. These methods may provide you with some procedures that are especially useful to you for the task you encounter when you seek to describe and interpret, and perhaps even evaluate, the communication you find in natural human environments.

We examine five specific methods here and provide a brief example for each method: open-ended question, focus groups, participant observation, unobtrusive measures, and triangulation or multiple class measurements. We believe that each of these methods can be particularly useful to you as you formally study human communication as well as in your personal life. In all, these methods have utility in formal research studies but also in your everyday encounters with others.

THE OPEN-ENDED QUESTION

As a student about to embark on a full-time career, it might be useful to explore an aspect of the interview process: specifically, what criteria—including aspects of communication—are valued for entry-level positions in those organizations to which you may apply? Beyond visiting company websites, one way to get at these criteria—including the centrality of communication—would be to conduct interviews with actual individuals in several companies who are directly involved in the interview and hiring process.

Employing open-ended questions during the actual interview can provide you with some specific, accurate, and extremely useful information. There are a host of appropriate questions you can ask. Examples might include the following: "Over the course of the year, approximately how many applicants do you interview?" "What criteria are used to assess the suitability of applicants?" "How important is each of these criteria—for example, grades, prior experience, analytic skills, oral and written skills, the ability to work in teams, to work independently, etc.)?" "What are some typical questions that you ask that help you get at the abilities not reflected in the resume?" "What behaviors, in particular, contribute to a positive assessment of an applicant? to a negative assessment?"

This experience can be significant on many levels. You are able to engage in a natural setting with others. You are able to amass important information that connects with the literature on the interviewing process from first-hand interactions with those who are in the trenches making decisions on new hires. You are able to gain important insights into what is truly valued in your career, and those qualities will facilitate acclimating to organizational life.

In these ways, we begin here with the recognition that the wording of a question can influence how a question is answered. Indeed, this brings us back to the idea of *reactivism*, a concept we introduced earlier when we noted that how a researcher asks a question can dramatically influence the responses to that question. We also noted that when interviewing subjects, reactivism can exist in a host of ways, and efforts need to be made to reduce reactivism. For example, the wording of a question appears to make a profound difference in how subjects respond to a question. The Gallup Organization repeatedly devotes attention to issues regarding the wording of questions as an explanation for why people respond to surveys.[25] Accordingly, in face-to-face interviews, it is extremely likely that how questions are worded influences how subjects respond to questions.

Definition of the *Open-Ended Question*

An *open-ended question* is an interrogative sentence asked of subjects in a natural setting that is designed to permit spontaneous and unguided responses and that allows subjects to offer any qualifiers, contingencies, or introduce any situational variables they see fit to provide when answering the question.

Focal Points of the Open-Ended Question

1. *Natural Setting*: Especially in field research contexts, part of the context that defines an "open-ended question" is that subjects are interrogated in a personal environment. A personal environment is a situation or context of one's own creation or choice.

2. *Parasocial Relationship*: The relationship between the interrogator or researcher and subject should permit the most open and honest of responses. Hence, the researcher should establish a parasocial relationship with the subjects before beginning the formal interrogation process. In a parasocial relationship, the subjects feel that the researcher is a "friend" who is a part of the "circle of one's peers." In this regard, the researcher seeks to "achieve an intimacy" with those who are "literally a crowd of strangers," and the subjects feel as they "they 'know'" the researcher in the "same way they know their chosen friends."[26]

3. *No Time and Space Restrictions Built into the Question*: In its formulation, the interrogative sentence specifies a topic area, but it should not contain any specific time or space

context built into the question. Accordingly, interviewees, in order to answer the question, must provide a time and space definition when answering the question. For example, when interviewing a married couple, an open-ended question might be: "Of all of the millions of couples in the world, how did you two meet?"[27] Nonverbally, so that the interviewer does not direct the question to one member of the couple rather than the other, eye contact with either person should be avoided at the moment the question is asked.

4. *Subjects Feel They Can Qualify Their Answers as They Wish*: If open-ended questions are asked, subjects should feel and even report later that they were able to qualify any and all of their answers in any way they thought appropriate. In other words, the subjects should feel they are completely spontaneous and unguided when they answer questions. Ignoring interruptions is one measure of spontaneous answers. In this regard, one intriguing measure of this standard is whether or not subjects ignore interrogative questions that interrupt answers they have already begun.

Uses or Functions of the Open-Ended Question

1. Subjects say what they are thinking—they offer content they wish to provide. Focused questions elicit information which may or may not be relevant to the subjects.

2. Subjects reveal how they interact—they reveal interaction strategies as well as content. An effective use of the open-ended question should allow subjects to interact in any way they wish to when answering a question. They should use their own way or method for answering the question. Therefore, the researcher can focus not only on what is said, but how it is said. When interviewing a husband and wife couple, for example, it is frequently extremely important to note that the husband is always the first to answer an open-ended question.

Advantages and Disadvantages of the Open-Ended Question

1. Dross rate is high if the researcher is interested in a particular hypothesis. In this context, dross can be understood as "wasted information" or as "excessive information" or as "more information than you needed to know." Open-ended interviews allow subjects to say whatever *the subjects want to say*, which will not always be relevant to what the *researcher wants to know*. A high dross rate means that the researcher may be wasting time and energy in terms of answering a specific hypothesis.

2. Open-ended questions allow researchers to find out what they think as they think it. In this sense, open-ended questions reduce reactivism.

FOCUS GROUPS

During the past several decades there has been a concerted effort at many academic institutions to enhance their image and reputation at the international level—to establish a global presence. One way to achieve this recognition is by enhancing the visibility of international students on their campus.

Once students from other cultures arrive, academic institutions typically provide an array of orientations and events to help student acclimate to academic and social life in the United States, particularly on their campus. The goal is to facilitate their success while they are studying here.

If you are taking a class on cross-cultural or intercultural communication, for example, you might pose the following questions: "How easily do international students adapt to the education experience in the United States (particularly on your campus)?" "To what extent did their initial experiences and/or expectations on campus coincide with their actual experiences?"

The use of focus groups can provide a productive approach to get at these questions. Participants can be asked to talk about how they are currently experiencing their lives as students. What are some of their positive experiences? What challenges have they faced? Do they feel that they are welcome? Do they feel that they belong? If they could suggest strategies that might have helped them along the way or that might enhance the experiences of future students from their (or other countries), what would they recommend?

Although first discussed in mass communication research in 1946 by Merton, Fiske, and Curtis,[28] focus groups became more widely used in the 1970s and early 1980s. Lunt and Livingstone explain the increasing importance of the focus group for both media and communication research:

> The resurgence of interest in the focus group interview in social science research, including media and communications, is part of the move toward qualitative methods. Researchers increasingly prefer insightful findings and ecologically valid, interpretative techniques to the more experimental, quantitative, or supposedly scientific methods and their perceived limitations....The focus group has been used, variously, to discover consumer attitudes and motivations and to reveal public discourses and interpretative communities. It has also been used in a variety of theoretical contexts and with a range of methodological assumptions, providing both a source of ideas for quantitative testing and an instrument of discovery.[29]

While Lunt and Livingstone's observation applies more directly to consumer attitudes and behaviors, by 1999 Berke had argued that focus groups have become increasingly important in virtually all practical settings, and particularly to determine voters' attitudes and reactions to all potential issues in political campaigns.[30]

Definition of a Focus Group

While we might wish it otherwise, because focus groups have been so widely used for so many different purposes, they have varied in conception, form, and how they are conducted. In this context, Lunt and Livingstone have provided a useful initial definition of a focus group as well as noted the variance that can occur when a focus group is employed:

> Briefly, the focus group method involves bringing together a group, or, more often, a series of groups, of subjects to discuss an issue in the presence of a moderator. A moderator ensures that the discussion remains on the issue at hand, while eliciting a wide range of opinions on that issue. The usual considerations for conducting open-ended interviews apply; one of the commonly expressed advantages of the method is that of speeding up sampling for one-to-one interviews. Many parameters of the group discussion can be varied, and the decisions taken by the researcher may affect significantly the resulting discussion and have implications for sampling, setting, control, validity, and reliability.[31]

At the same time, it helpful to establish some basic guidelines for thinking about what a focus group can be. Some of these key operational features of a focus group can deal with the range, specificity, depth, and personal context,[32] which can take the following forms:

1. Traditionally, a group of people is selected to determine reactions to a service and/or product. But it is important to recognize that any kind of grouping can be selected to provide precision to what is to be understood and learned. Multiple criteria (such as age, gender, ethnicity, etc.) can be used to secure certain kinds of results about certain types of groups.

2. The group is aware of the advertising and marketing motives of the researchers. Paying them may increase their willingness to divulge.

3. Focus is on the group's interpretation of reality, not their judgment about the effects or influence of the service and/or product.

4. Typically, the researcher seeks the unstructured ideas (open-ended questions are employed) of group members as much as possible to find out how and why people feel as they do.

5. The conversation and dialogue of the group are also important information. In this sense, you would be asking how people arrive at conclusions and when do they think they have reached agreement.

Significance and Uniqueness of Focus Groups

The significance and uniqueness of focus groups emerges most clearly when compared to other research techniques such as survey questionnaires, participant observation, and content analysis.

Survey Questionnaires: The topic of a questionnaire and the prepared questions created by a researcher presume that the researcher already knows what an audience thinks is relevant and significant as well as how the audience wants to respond to these questions. However, the issues that a researcher has about a given topic may not reflect the concerns that a specific audience has or cares about when it comes to the topic the researcher is exploring. While the audience may respond to the specific items on a questionnaire, the items may not be that salient or relevant to the audience. For the audience, the questionnaire may not reflect the specific concerns and situations the audience faces in everyday life.

Participant Observation: While participant observation may be a technique that encourages a researcher to enter the everyday environments of audience members and detect what audiences are reacting to, the method is time-consuming, labor intensive, and requires access to private environments. If the researcher is to preserve the natural environment of the audience members, ethical issues may also emerge regarding full disclosure and honesty.

Content Analysis: While content may be extracted from an audience's natural environment, the analysis of such content does not explain the ideas isolated and identified nor does a content analysis reveal how and why the frequency of ideas occur as they do.

While the significance and uniqueness of focus groups might be readily recognized, nonetheless, we must also recognize that the quality of focus groups can vary dramatically. Some focus groups are far more useful than others. What makes the differences? What are some of the most decisive factors for successfully employing focus groups as a research technique?

To assure full and open participation, it is important to consider the following variables:

1. All members should feel encouraged to interact evenly and equally. The focus group should not be the platform for a few. The facilitator should let the group know "that it is acceptable—and in fact desirable—for them to disagree on issues."[33]

2. Minimize interviewer effects. The role of the interviewer is to facilitate, not control, the group. Training sessions are typically required, and at times mock sessions are desirable. Depending on the group composition and the nature of the topic, in some instances "[a] facilitator of the same racial or ethnic background contributes to participants' feelings that the facilitator shares with them common experiences."[34]

3. Minimize the guinea pig effect so that participants don't feel their responses and contributions will be a reflection on them. There are no right or wrong answers.

4. Group size affects group interaction and participation. Typical focus groups include four to eight members.

5. The typical duration of focus group sessions is 1–3 hours.

6. The interview setting and location should be appropriate (formal/informal; on- or off- site) to the purpose of the group. For example, a focus group with college students on alcohol abuse would not likely be productive if it were to be held in the dean's office.

7. Sequencing of topics and questions can facilitate the flow of interaction and responses. Generally, focus groups start with introductory remarks and move from general to specific questions.

8. Data recording (live recorders to capture the sense and meaning of the group interactions—ideas, interactions, and even the nonverbal reactions of groups members) is critical for the analysis and evaluation phase.

9. The focus group typically provides one dimension of several data bases prior to reaching conclusions. Multiple measurements are employed.

Limitations of the Focus Group as a Research Technique

It is equally useful to be aware of what focus groups cannot do as a research technique. No single research technique can accomplish everything that we might want to know about human communication. While the focus group is now one of the most frequently used and most economic techniques that can be used to understand human preferences and choices and ultimately future human behavior, nonetheless, the limits are appropriate to identify and to anticipate when conducting focus group research. These limitations include:

1. The qualitative findings obtained about a specific form or type of human communication behavior may not be reflected in the quantitative results obtained through focus groups. In one sense, it is frequently difficult to get from the qualitative to the quantitative. Accordingly, a researcher may be left with the question: How significant is a group interpretation?

2. Focus group data do not easily generate cause-to-effect relationships.

3. Difficult to get from interpretation to policy: There is no automatic link between a group's interpretation and appropriate policy.

4. For the researcher, there are real and significant costs in terms of subjects' time and payment, interviewer time and payment, and recorder time and payment. Additionally, subjects can get upset at the time and energy involved in the process.

5. The profit motive and politically oriented nature of focus groups frequently preclude theoretically rich data; the data derived frequently serve administrative and atheoretical ends rather than research objectives.

6. As the issues involved become increasingly complex, it becomes more difficult to derive clear findings from the focus group interactions.

7. The group is the context for focus group interviews, and the issue is whether or not the service and/or product involved will subsequently exist within such a context. Are the data constrained by the context in which they were collected?

8. Focus groups are unlikely to generate reliable data. Verification may be secured if "broad interpretations" are made, but a strict sense of reliability is unlikely to be provided. In all, while focus groups cannot do it all, they are now one of the most frequently employed and most powerful research techniques used by human communication researchers, especially for those conducting consumer preference and behavior research, those carrying out political campaigns, and those in the advertising and public relations industries. Understanding focus groups as a research technique, as well as having experience conducting focus groups, could easily become one of the most valuable skill sets you could possess.

PARTICIPANT OBSERVATION

Many undergraduate students are encouraged to engage in internships which provide immersive experiences. These internships provide students with intensive, work-related experiences in terms of the day-to-day workings of the careers they plan to enter. These field internships can also provide a learning opportunity about how communication is enacted, what is expected, and what is valued. Indeed, these experiences often provide a valuable glimpse into their futures.

During these internships, students may be able to observe dimensions of communication that connect directly to courses including organizational communication, interpersonal communication, conflict management, intercultural communication, gender and communication, and nonverbal communication. By maintaining a journal or log, insight into intersections of communication with one's role, with channels of interaction, and with the overall tone or climate of the unit can be, in part, ascertained. Who talks to whom? What topics are discussed—informally and formally? How is space used? How are tasks assigned? What type of work is addressed in groups? Individually? What types of conflicts typically occur? How are these conflicts addressed and/or resolved?

Examining the office environment through the lens of one of the aforementioned courses can provide an important learning experience. Students have the opportunity to connect the theories they are studying with their first-hand observations. Moreover, in the process they can learn a great deal about themselves: their aspirations, their own values, how they can contribute to create a product and positive professional life in the future.

Participant observation is a third method frequently used in qualitative research. There have been significant transformations in how this method has been conceptualized and utilized since its emergence in the nineteenth century. To get at these transformations, we discuss first its history. We then situate participant observation as a research technique in *natural* or everyday environments.

A History of the Methodology of Participant Observation—The Traditional Definition of Participant Observation

Participant observation as a methodology has a long legacy. It first emerged as a technique in a 1855 field study by anthropologist Frederick Leplay.[35] Nearly 45 years later (1918–1920), researchers William I. Thomas and Florian Znaniecki were the first researchers to apply this technique in a qualitative study of social values.[36] But it was not until 1924 that the first definition of participant observer actually appeared in a publication by Edward C. Lindeman:

> For experimental purposes the cooperating observers have been called "participant observers." The term implies not that the observers are participating in the activities of the group being observed. . . . There are few such persons available and those who are must be trained. Such training involves its own difficulties. Shall the participant observer be trained to look for exactly the same factors which are sought by the observer from the outside? This method would inevitably lead to error for the participant observer should be free to see many things which the outsider can never see.[37]

Lindeman's definition reveals a powerful benefit to the process of participant observation: Participant observation researchers are able to obtain *more* data in their dual role as participant and observer than would be possible by observation alone.

At the same time, however, we need to recognize some of the limitations that this research technique possesses. Three of these limitations are particularly noteworthy:

1. Because verification of the results of participant observation studies would be more difficult to accomplish than in empirical studies, it was initially regarded as an incomplete and less rigorous approach than traditional empirical approaches.

2. Because it was regarded as less rigorous, it was assumed that findings from participant observation studies would not likely produce enduring, representative, and significant statements about motives or values.

3. Participation observation, consequently, was initially perceived predominantly as an approach capable of producing only exploratory studies. This perception continues to exist among some researchers today, and these researchers are likely to perceive participantobservation itself as capable of generating only pretheoretical or speculative understandings. In this context, the results of participant observation analyses may be viewed as inherently incomplete. We reject such views, but we recognize that every research technique can possess an image or credibility based upon its earlier uses rather than how it has evolved into a more mature and competent research strategy. Accordingly, the evolution of participantobservation as a research technique is particularly important to note.

Additional studies over the next several decades helped to situate participant observation as a legitimate and powerful method of research.[38] By 1940, Florence Kluckohn provided what is considered "the original and now somewhat classic statement" on participant observation. She defines the process as follows:

> Participant observation is conscious and systematic sharing, in so far as circumstances permit, in the life-activities and, on occasion, in the interests and affects of a group of persons. Its purpose is to obtain data about behavior through direct contact and in terms of specific situations in which the distortion that results from the investigator's being an outside agent is reduced to a minimum.[39]

Importantly, Kluckhohn contends that less distortion is likely to occur when the researcher acts in the dual role of observer and participant. This addresses the concern of incompleteness mentioned above, especially as other studies began to emerge and illustrate the dual role of the researcher as both participant and observer throughout the 1940s and 1950s.[40]

In 1955, Morris S. Schwartz and Charlotte Green Schwartz[41] addressed methodology of participantobservation studies and included registering, interpreting, and recording of the data as part of the process. Howard Becker, in 1958, argued for sufficiency—that is, if the participant observer can vary the number and length of situations he or she is in, he or she can begin to assert that the data collected are enduring, representative, and can provide significant insight.[42] These contributions speak to the above-mentioned concerns about rigor and significance.

The importance of participant observation as a complete method was achieved, finally, in the 1960s. Berreman suggested that varying the number of kinds of situations the researcher is in can produce sufficient data to address concerns of validity and replication.[43] Gans focused on ethical questions and the process of note-taking.[44] But most significantly, Herbert Blumer's work on symbolic interactionism provided a new definition of participant observation based on its purpose, not its unique characteristics: *to capture the frame of reference of the people being examined in order to understand their meanings, values, and communicate those motives to outsiders.*[45] Blumer shifts the lens slightly, but this shift is significant. It moves the lens of participant observation away from *what* the researcher can achieve and *how* the researcher can function in this dual role and places the spotlight and emphasis on the *meaning-making* process of the individuals (the subjects) themselves. In 1966, Bruyn offered a complete analysis of participant observation as a complete method for studying human action.[46]

By the 1960s, then, participant observation came to be regarded as a complete method. We turn now to its application as a research technique in "natural" or everyday communication environments.

The Uses of Participant-Observation as a Research Technique in "Natural" or Everyday Communication Environments

Several research methods exist whenever we wish to understand how people communicate and with what effects. Traditionally, social scientists have maintained that the most reliable and valid way of studying communication is in a controlled environment, ideally a laboratory specifically designed to hold all variables equal except the one variable being studied. The variable being studied, it has been maintained, could be varied in different ways, and any audience responses and changes in an audience response should be due to the way in which the variable was manipulated. Such studies are designed to tell us, as clearly as possible, how a particular variable functions under different conditions. The laboratory design is also intended to allow a researcher to isolate a specific cause for a particular outcome. In all, this approach has been employed to study multiple variables in the communication process.

The approach has been lauded in several ways. Some have maintained that the approach is "objective" in the sense that the systematic nature of the experimental conditions precludes personal intuitive inferences. Indeed, some have maintained that the experimental and behavioral emphasis of the laboratory may preclude personal and intuitive inferences.

However, some have questioned whether or not we really understand the communication process if we ignore our personal and intuitive impulses as researchers or whether or not it is even possible to exclude such impulses in the design and execution of a laboratory study. Such questioning is not intended to deny the significance of laboratory experiments, for such experiments have introduced a sense of logical rigor, predictiveness, provocativeness, manageability, and comprehensiveness into the study of communication. Yet those who have questioned the use of laboratory experiments have asked whether or not a second approach cannot also be used to study human communication.

"Naturalistic" as an Alternative Research Strategy

The second approach might complement the kind of reasoning that controls the experimental-behavioral approach to the study of communication. This alternative approach suggests that it might also be valuable to study human communication in "natural" or everyday environments in which most human communication occurs. Indeed, there is some evidence that the research environment employed to study communication makes a difference in what kinds of results are obtained.

An extended example is instructive. In 1955, researchers Gump and Sutton-Smith[47] investigated the reactions of poorly skilled players when they were put in more or less difficult games positions or roles. For example, in the game of tag, the *it* position is more demanding than other roles. As children played the game experimentally, an *it* in the center of a rectangular playing field attempts to tag opponents who run to and from "safe" areas at each end of the rectangle. One variant of the game gives *high power* to the *it* position by permitting the child in that position to "call the turn" when runners may attempt to cross from one safe position to another. Another variant gives *low power* to the *it* by permitting players to run whenever they choose. In one phase of the experiment, slow runners were assigned to high-power *it* positions and, in another, to low-power *it* positions. The hypothesis—that poorly skilled boys would be more successful in high-power than low-power *it* positions and that scapegoating of these inept boys would be less frequent in the high- than in the lower-power positions—were unequivocally confirmed.

In contrast, some 5 years later, in 1961, researchers Gump and Kounin also observed boys in natural, rather than experimental situations, in gyms, playgrounds, and campuses, and obtained the following impressions: "(a) Poorly skilled boys do not often get involved in games they cannot manage; (b) if they do get involved, they often manage to avoid difficult roles by not trying to win such a position or by quitting if they cannot avoid it; and (c) if they occupy the role and are having trouble, the game often gets so boring to opponents that these opponents let themselves get caught in order to put the game back on a more zestful level."[48]

These two studies provide us with very different conceptions of the ways in which adolescent boys interact and what we can expect from boys of different skill levels. The 1955 study could certainly lead us to believe that poorly skilled boys can be successful in high-power positions and will not be scapegoated for their lack of skills if the proper conditions are created. Such a study might, then, encourage some to create high status expectations for boys with poor skills in a given area, and failure which results would be attributed to environmental conditions; a realistic assessment of the strengths and weaknesses of the boys is likely to be slighted. In the second study in 1960, however, we are more likely to recognize that human dynamics will encourage highly skilled boys to participate in those activities in which they might also be successful. We may not find the philosophy implied in either study especially desirable, but the overall point being made here is that experimental studies may suggest a perspective which is quite different from the kind of perspective created by a study of communication in natural or everyday settings.

Defining the Concept of Everyday Communication

A central key to or way of understanding participant observation is to focus on the unique object of study that focuses and directs the attention of researchers who function as participant observers. That unique object of study is what we call *everyday communication*.[49] The study of natural or everyday communication typically involves: (1) an attempt to capture or identify the central symbols of a community as they are conceived, used, and intended by the members of that community, (2) the collection of data in settings created and maintained by the community being studied, (3) a researcher functioning as both a participant in and observer of the ongoing activities of the community being studied, and (4) the attempt to minimize reactivism.[50]

The Dual Role of the Researcher

Everyday communication can be studied in any number of ways. As the word suggests, when a researcher employs participant observation as a method for studying everyday communication, the researcher adopts two roles simultaneously in order to obtain data regarding a particular community of subjects. The researcher enters the community to be studied, assumes roles specified by members of the community, and in this sense is a participant in the community. However, the researcher also adopts a second role of observer and systematically records interactions in a community, the concepts employed in a community, and the rules and norms used by members of the community. In most studies the researcher adopts the role of participant only to obtain data regarding the community, and in most studies the researcher does not tell members of the community that he or she is functioning as an observer and engaged in the study of communication. While there are certainly ethical issues that should be considered, the impression members of the community are to be left with is that the researcher is only a participant in their community.

Comparing Participant Observation and Experimental Observations

The early conceptions and modifications of participant observation—examined earlier—provide a foundation for attempting to clarify the role and function of the researcher who employs participant observation as a research method. One way of specifying the role and function of the participant observer is to emphasize the ways in which participant observers observe the object of their study compared to the observational concerns of the experimental behavioralist in a laboratory setting. Figure A.3 provides an indication of some of these differences.[51]

Criteria for Judging the Data of Participant Observation and Laboratory Experimentalism

These observational concerns of the participant observer and the laboratory experimentalist also generate a set of criteria that can be used to determine how meaningful reported data are. Again, we can contrast the criteria which are of concern to the participant observer and those which are of concern to the experimentalist–behavioralist in order to highlight the nature of participant observation. Figure A.4 provides a summary of this comparison.

Observational Concerns of the Participant Observer	Observational Concerns of the Laboratory Experimentalist
1. Investigate particular phenomena without definitive preconceptions of their nature.	1. Investigate particular phenomena with definitive preconceptions of their nature.
2. Observe in phenomena that which appears immediately to consciousness.	2. Observe in phenomena that which immediately appears to the senses.
3. Look for similarities in phenomena as given to consciousness; distinguish their essences and essential relations intuitively.	3. Look for similarities and differences between what is observed and what is operationally defined; distinguish their correlations statistically.
4. Explore how the phenomena constitute themselves in consciousness while continuing to suspend prior conceptions of their nature.	4. Explore how the phenomena constitute themselves in reason relative to social typologies.
5. Examine what concealed meanings may be discovered through the application of ontological conceptions [or socially created understandings] of reality.	5. Examine what concealed meanings may be discovered through the application of theoretical conceptions of social action.

Figure A.3 Observational Concerns of the Participant Observer and the Laboratory Experimentalist

Criteria for Judging the Data of the Participant Observer	Criteria for Judging the Data of the Laboratory Experimentalist
1. TIME: How long has the observer participated in the setting?	1. Does the observer relate his or her interpretations to empirical fact and structural theory?
2. PLACE: Where has the observer participated in the physical setting?	2. Does the observer relate his or her study to other culturally associated contexts?
3. CIRCUMSTANCES: In what social groups and social roles has he participated?	3. Does the observer manifest a lack of definition in his or her reporting and sufficient distance from his or her subjects?
4. LANGUAGE: How well does the observer know the language?	4. Does the observer manifest illustrativeness and an objective style in his or her description?
5. INTIMACY: In what private social arrangements does the observer participate?	
6. CONSENSUS: How does the observer confirm what meanings he or she finds existing in the culture?	

Figure A.4 Criteria for Judging the Data of the Participant Observer and Laboratory Experimentalist

Criteria for Judging Participant Observation Data

These criteria for judging the data of the participant observer suggest several directions and guidelines for how a participant observation study is carried out.

1. *Time*: Record the different temporal phases of data gathering which the observer experiences in becoming a natural part of the culture studied. We assume that the longer the participant observer remains in the social setting, the more knowledgeable he or she becomes about the people. We might even anticipate that as the observer studies a culture, the role occupied by the researcher may change from (1) newcomer, (2) provisional member, (3) categorical member, (4) personalized member (rapport), and (5) imminent migrant. Each of these roles carries its own perspective of what a cultural reality is, and correspondingly, by examining and reporting these time differentials carefully, the researcher may avoid gathering data that can easily be misinterpreted.

2. *Place*: Record the experience that people have with their physical environment. The personal relationships that people acquire in the context of their environment is a basic part of the record of the participant observer. In this regard, the researcher should appropriately recognize that at least three different levels of "experience-environment" conditions may exist: (1) the cultural experience of the subjects with their environments, (2) the experience of the observer with the environment, and (3) the conceptualization the observer makes of the cultural interpretation of the subject's contacts with the physical world.

3. *Social Circumstance*: Record the experiences of people under contrasting social circumstances. Inaccurate interpretations have been avoided and excellent insights added by researchers who have observed their subjects in contrasting social circumstances and environments. It is crucial for the observer to record what social position he or she occupies in the culture studied and what images others develop of him or her as he or she functions in this position. In most cases, a team approach becomes the best way to deal with the subtle problems of securing data on a large, complex social system, since the observer cannot assume all roles significant to the study simultaneously. However, it is possible in some cases to develop a generalized role that allows equal access to different portions of the population studied.

4. *Language*: Record the experience of learning the symbolic forms of language that bear upon the social meanings under study. The term *language* is considered here in its broadest sense as representing all those forms of communication that enter significantly into the lives of the people studied. The observer is interested in the part language plays in forming the meanings under investigation. As the participant observer becomes personally involved in the language of the culture studied, his or her own behavior changes accordingly. It then becomes very important to record these changes as they influence understanding of the culture. The observer should make a list of specific kinds of language/linguistic forms and factors that bear upon the interpretation of the subjects. The researcher may need to examine such matters as the length of sentences, the average number of syllables in words expressed, the words most often repeated, the concepts or ideas that do and do not dominate conversations, the degree to which unique or insider interpretations are used, favorite slang expression, and so forth.

5. *Intimacy*: Record how the observer experienced and encountered social openings and barriers in seeking accurate interpretations of privately held social meanings. Every formal structure has both a private and public aspect. Erving Goffman describes some of the sociological features of formal structures as constituting "back regions" to which access is difficult for outsiders.[52] Officials (these may not have formal titles at all) in such situations are preoccupied with what Goffman calls "impression management,"[53] and consequently

any invasion into what lies behind the scenes could be hazardous. It becomes important, then, for the observer to record the objective barriers which he or she finds between group communication in settings studied and the different ways he or she was able or unable to overcome them.

6. *Consensus*: Record how social meanings are confirmed in the context of the culture studied. Interpretations are often offered by researchers from a theoretical orientation rather than being a serious effort at confirming the original meaning in a culture. Confirmation of general social meanings is achieved when the researcher can observe repeated instances of expressed meanings over a period of time in different settings. The researcher may achieve a direct confirmation of specific meanings through consultation with those studied. In all cases, the researcher should (1) document the specific circumstances under which the meanings were confirmed, (2) indicate the number of people who confirm them, (3) describe the way in which they were confirmed, and (4) record the period of time in which the observations were made.

Verifying Participant Observation Data

After the criteria for collecting and judging data collected through participant observation are satisfied, the researcher may also wish to employ some standards for assessing and evaluating the quality of the data that has been collected. Figure A.5 provides a summary of six guidelines that can be employed for this purpose.[54]

Overview of the Major Features of Participant Observation

In the briefest fashion, the outline that follows illustrates and summarizes some of the major phases of participant observation. This outline is summarized in Figure A.6.[55]

	Categories of Data Collected		
Dimensions of Data	**Cognition** (How is the meaning made intelligible?)	**Cathexis** (What quality of feeling is associated with the meaning?)	**Conduct** (What kind of social action accompanies the meaning? How many people are involved?)
Time	How long has the meaning been intelligible?	How long has the sentiment been associated and does time change it?	How long have how many people participated?
Place	Is it cognitively associated with the environs? How?	Is the sentiment associated with the environs? How?	In what place do how many people act accordingly?
Circumstances	Is it associated with social roles and groups? How?	Is it felt differently in different roles and events?	How do people act in different groups?
Language	How is the meaning communicated?	How is the sentiment communicated?	How is it conveyed in action? (In sound or ritual?)
Intimacy	Is it expressed in private? How is it conveyed intelligibly?	How is it experienced privately?	How do people behave behind the scenes?
Consensus	How is it confirmed?	How is the sentiment confirmed?	How do people show agreement in action?

Figure A.5 Categories for Verifying Participant Observation Data

I. *Aim*:
To discover, describe, and explain the culture of the people encountered in the study

II. *Method*:
A. Discovery—
- To experience events that are important to the participants and realize how they interpret them.
- To imaginatively take the role of participants in the process of experiencing events through social action.

B. Description—
- To record the way events are interpreted by participants.
- To record the interpretations (meanings) of participants in eventful social action.

C. Explanation—
- To reveal how these events and meanings exhibit a cultural character as in themes and values.
- To reveal how this cultural character exhibits a configuration in action.
- To reveal how this configuration exhibits analytical character (having reference to other cases) in categories and theories of people in society.

III. *Procedures*:
A. Journal Record—
1. Describe the way (process) in which events are interpreted by participants.
2. Describe the interpretations (meanings) themselves. Include intersubjective interpretations (collective meanings).
3. Describe how the interpretations of participants and the observer compare within the context of time, place, circumstance, language, intimacy, and consensus.

B. Analysis (examples are drawn from the study of the culture of a mental hospital)[56]—
1. List categories representing significant areas of interpretations (meanings):
   a. Patient subculture.
   b. Professional subculture.
   c. Employees' subculture.
      (1) Patient-doctor contacts.
      (2) Controlling patient behavior.
      (3) Defining circumstances requiring punishment.
      (4) Carrying on ward routine with minimum effort.
2. Describe how interpretations exhibit a cultural character:
   a. *Hierarchy of values* in "patient subculture":
      (1) Going home.
      (2) Residence in certain wards.
      (3) Attention of doctors.
      (4) Preference for certain jobs in hospital:
         (a) Kitchen and dining jobs in hospital.
         (b) Jobs contributing toward discharge, etc.
   b. *Themes* in "professional subculture":
      (1) "All patients must be classified in two weeks."
      (2) "All patients must work inside the institution."
3. Describe the total configuration in action:
   a. The *formal* design of how the subculture and the organizations expressing them are an interrelated network of life-works and activities.
   b. The *dynamics* of the design as in professional and employee cultures conflicting in their separate orientations toward the patient; the professional orientation involves diagnostic treatment and release while the employees' orientation involves punishment and control of patients.
4. Describe the relationship of the design to analytical categories and theory:
   a. An appropriate analytical category having reference to the configuration would be *bureaucracy*; another analytical category having reference to the data would be *norms*.
   b. A general theory would be structural-functionalism; some of the explanatory elements of this theory would include the functional requirements for the survival of bureaucratic organizations in general (with specific reference in this case to psychiatric hospitals) and the general processes of institutionalization in society.

Figure A.6 Overview of the Major Features of Participant Observation: Aims, Methods, and Procedures

Unobtrusive Measures[57]

Beyond participant observation, an entire group or class of far less popular research strategies and measures have been created that are intended to allow a researcher to collect data in the natural settings of people without disrupting everyday communication. No one of these research techniques can be used in isolation to generate data that can be independently relied upon as a complete or valid conception of human communication. Yet these techniques possess tremendous heuristic value. They can encourage researchers to think about the study of human communication in more subtle and intriguing ways, ways that may reveal how people communicate when they are being studied. For our purposes, we will examine five of these techniques: physical trace analysis, running archive analysis, episodic and private record archives, simple observation, and contrived observations. Figure A.7 provides a convenient summary of these techniques.

At the same time, each of these unobtrusive measures can vary from one research situation to another. Additionally, a researcher might profitably presume that every unobtrusive measure is capable of undergoing a major transformation. For example, some of these measures, such as contrived observation, are particularly susceptible to changes in technological development. In this context, it may be especially useful to know what people look at when they watch a television or computer screen. One can easily imagine, for instance, that advertisers want to know if viewers are actually looking at their product or service's brand name when they watch television or computer ads. In this regard, eye-tracking devices have been employed to make such a determination, for the movement of the eyeball itself can be tracked. While these eye-tracking mechanisms were, for years, extremely awkward and obtrusive for subjects to wear, they have become increasingly unobtrusive. Indeed, eye-tracking systems can even be employed now without subjects even knowing that the systems are being used.[58] In all, developments—of all kinds—in any of these unobtrusive measures can change if and how these measures might be employed in a research endeavor.

Overall, from our perspective, we think an examination of these techniques might encourage you to consider unusual and novel ways of examining human beings as they communicate in their natural environments.

Triangulation or Multiple Class Measurements

In the earlier section on participant observation, the internship was examined as a vehicle for connecting communication research to one's field experience. Recording one's experiences and observations through a journal or log produces one kind of information. However, these recordings are decidedly one-sided—that is, they are viewed through the lens of the intern who is doing the observing. By introducing an additional dimension into the data-gathering process, initial observations may be confirmed, deepened, or challenged; additional aspects of the work–life experience may be generated as well.

On one level, we are only recognizing and drawing attention to what virtually everyone comes to know in everyday life and especially in an employment environment. Namely, you need to consider the inputs and understandings of others if you are to be successful. Accordingly, in an employment environment, selected interviews with other employees in a unit can augment the data gathered during the observation stage. Open-ended questions as well as some specifically focused questions can be used: How long has the person been with the company? In the specific field? What changes have they observed in how business is conducted? What has influenced this change? What aspects of their work do they find especially rewarding or engaging? What challenges do they (or have they) encountered and how do they deal with them? What metaphors would they use to describe their work and the organizational climate (e.g., family, balanced, pressure-cooker, 24/7, etc.), and what specifically contributes to this view?

Type of Unobtrusive Measure	Definition	Example
Physical Trace Analysis: Erosion and Accretion	Physical trace analysis involves the observation and assessment of "the degree of selective wear on some material yields the measure" (erosion) or "deposit of materials" (accretion) are measures of "past social behavior" (pp. 35–36). Because physical traces can be "a patently weak source of data" when used as a single measure, "physical evidence has greatest utility in consort with other methodological approaches" (p. 36).	* Vinyl tile replacements around different exhibits in a museum as a measure of the popularity of each exhibit (pp. 36–37). * Popularity of books by the number of times it is checked out in a library. * Wear and tear on specific pages of a book as a measure of the popularity of the sections or portions of a book.
Archive Analysis: The Running Archive	Running archive analysis involves the "examination and evaluation of some uses of data periodically produced for other than scholarly purposes, but which can be exploited by social scientists" (p. 53). In this sense, the records collected and maintained in virtually all literate cultures could provide a measure of how social practices and preferences vary from one community or society to another. Webb and his colleagues reasoned that, "Besides the low cost of acquiring a massive amount of pertinent data, one common advantage of archival material is its nonreactivity" (p. 53).	* Birth, marriage, and death records each constitute an example of a running archive. * Middleton (p. 58) proposed that the increase or decline of the number of children portrayed in families in magazine advertisements reflect preferred family sizes. * Reasoning that people might readily lie about it, Christensen (p. 59) suggested that a comparison of the dates of all marriages and the dates of all first born children could provide a measure of premarital sex within different communities.
Archive Analysis: Episodic and Private Archives	Episodic and private archive analysis involves the use and assessment of "discontinuous" materials preserved over time which are normally not part of the "public record" (p. 88). For example, the military maintains long-term archives that are normally not available to the public. Similar kinds of episodic and private records can exist in various sales records, particularly of items that people may not wish to discuss (e.g., drugs and alcohol). Correspondingly, vending machine sales might be examined and various measures employed to isolate a host of different social reactions to different kinds of stimuli (e.g., stress, package appeal, etc.).	* Using Air Force records, Lodge determined that pilots over 6 feet tall had more accidents. The finding encouraged the Air Force to reconsider the design of cockpit designs and visual angles of the instrument panel (p. 89). * Brown suggested that liquid soap usage in restrooms could be a measure of cleanliness in different restaurants (p. 89). * Hillebrandt argued that the sale of alcoholic drinks at Chicago airports could be used as a measure of "passenger anxiety produced by air crashes" (p. 90). * Chesebro systematically measured graffiti markings differences throughout the city of Philadelphia as a measure of racial and poverty disengagement and discrimination.[59]
Simple Observation	As a research technique, simple observation involves the examination in "situations in which the observer has no control over the behavior or sign in question, and plays an unobserved, passive, and nonintrusive role in the research situation" (p. 112). A host of factors are involved in designing simple observation studies, and controversies certainly exist in these studies. For example, regarding the issue of whether or not observers should be obvious or not, Arsenian has argued that "patently visible observers can produce changes in behavior that diminish the validity of comparisons," although Polansky has disagreed, while Deutsch has argued that the effect of observers "may erode over time" (p. 113).	* In one sense, all participant observation studies might be considered as examples of research involving the use of simple observation (p. 114). * Maintaining that it is a measure of anxiety, Conrad has argued that the length of a bullfighter's beard is longer on the day of the fight than any other day, although—as you might anticipate—the validity of that measure has been contested (pp. 115–116). * Reflecting how societies change, Burma reported in 1959 that tattoos were a indication of juvenile delinquency (p. 116). By contrast, tattoos today might be viewed as a measure of modest social protests for some, but a form of body art, beauty, and expression for others.

Figure A.7 Unobtrusive Measures[60]

| Contrived Observation | Contrived observation involves the study of human reactions when investigators intentionally intervene into the "observational setting." Recasting the "observational setting" into more of a laboratory condition, depending on the nature of the intervention, the observations following the intervention are best viewed as contrived observations. Various recording hardware or conspicuous observers can be employed as the stimuli for contrived observation. | * Marking a shift from private to public behavior, virtually all people shift and adapt their behaviors when they are asked to "speak clearly into the microphone, please" (p. 142).
* Different ethnic groups might be compared by examining the degree to which they use slang within intracultural settings compared to language use in cross-cultural settings (p. 143).
* At news stands, men are less likely to examine "sexy" magazines if women (research confederates) are present.
* People are more likely to sign a petition if the person (research confederates who are systematically changed) collecting signatures is perceived as more attractive or handsome (pp. 155–164). |

By supplementing the initial observations with detailed responses of organizational members, the opportunity to gain invaluable insight can occur. Importantly, points of confirmation (of initial observations) may be supported. Points where observations are not supported (i.e., the observer reads some interactions as disruptive whereas the interactants view the disruptions as a welcome respite from the job pressures) can also emerge in the process.

One final qualitative research method we consider here may well be the most important, but it must be considered last in our survey. We consider triangulation or the use of multiple class measurements as a research technique because we are convinced that new insights and new understandings about human communication can be generated by triangulation or the use of multiple class measurements.

Defining *Triangulation* or *Multiple Class Measurements*

In a nutshell, triangulation or the multiple class measurements means that a researcher will attempt to combine different research findings into one coherent explanation of human communication. In order words, as concepts, the terms *triangulation* or the *use of multiple classes* underscore an important objective for researchers; they suggest that a researcher will attempt to combine extremely different findings or results to provide new and more coherent understandings of a human communication experience or event. Particularly, triangulation or the use of multiple measurement classes means that a researcher generates new descriptions, interpretations, explanations, and even predictions about human communication from several different kinds of research findings. These different kinds of data-collection procedures are employed to generate different kinds of data about human communication that ultimately reflect different perspectives. More precisely, Frey, Botan, Friedman, and Kreps have aptly defined triangulation as the "use of multiple methodologies and/or techniques to study a phenomenon."[61]

The Rationale for Triangulation or the Use of Multiple Class Measurements

Arguing for the use of multiple measurement classes or different kinds of research findings, Webb, Campbell, Schwartz, and Sechrest begin with the proposition that "no single measurement class is perfect" and "neither is any scientifically useful." They specifically argue that a hypothesis should be a question that is answered only with a "series of complementary methods of testing," which provides a "degree of validity unattainable by one tested within the more constricted framework of a single method."

Needless to say, those who are "method-bound" may find such analyses problematic, but we are convinced that virtually every communication situation can be more comprehensively and coherently understood by employing, as Webb and his colleagues put it, "multiple operationalism." In this regard, Webb et al. aptly conclude: "It is through triangulation of data procured from different measurement classes that the investigator can most effectively strip of plausibility rival explanations." Accordingly, rather than ask "Which of the several available data-collection methods will be best for my research problem?" the researcher should ask "Which set of methods will be best?"[62]

Multitasking, Multifunctionalism, and Concurrent Media Exposure

Beyond the research issues involved in the study of human communication, triangulation or the use of multiple class measurements now appears appropriate, if not essential, because of some of the new transformations that are occurring in human communication. Particularly, when people communicate, our new media and technology now simultaneously employ a diverse set of different communication channels of communication that allows—if not encourages—people to communicate simultaneously with different people in different contexts. Identified as multitasking or multifunctionalism, this kind of communication behavior is actually different in kind than other forms of multitasking, simple because of the frequency and range of technologies and tasks involved. For example, rather than being unusual behavior, it is now common for a person to be both chatting on a telephone with a client while simultaneously searching for relevant information on a computer while referring to notes from a previous meeting with colleagues about this client. Even at home when we are relaxing, we may read a newspaper or magazine while simultaneously watching a television program. Or, if you are captivated by a TV program when your cell phone rings, you may continue watching television while also continuing to chat on the telephone.

Other studies are emerging that underscore the importance of multitasking in human communication. In an intriguing field study conducted from March through early June of 2005, Holmes, Papper, Popovich, and Bloxham[63] had 150 observers follow and record the communication behavior of over 400 people all day long, "starting as soon after someone got up in the morning and would allow us...and continuing until as close to bedtime as the person would allow us to stay." Observers employed a "Media Collector program run on a smart keyboard" (i.e., a small laptop-like computer running the Palm OS). This device allowed observers to record the starting time and end time for all media activity. Their findings suggest that people routinely employ multiple media technologies simultaneously. As the authors of the report put it, "[c]onsumers may choose to combine two or more media to gratify a particular need or accomplish a task." Additionally, people are also "subjected to 'environmental' media content in public places." And, more generally, "[i]f a medium is used frequently throughout the day, even in short episodes, it is more likely to be paired with other media" and "that medium's use will overlap with use of other media." In all, Holmes and colleagues coin the expression *concurrent media exposure* to describe this communication experience. The ambiguity of the word *exposure* seems particularly apt, for it is unclear if an individual's attention and comprehension of stimuli shift back and forth from one medium to another, if some individuals are capable to employing dual channels and processing diverse forms of different media stimuli simultaneously, or if some combination of stimuli merge to create yet another kind of apprehension, comprehension, and understanding. In this regard, after completing its survey of over 2200 adults, the Pew Internet & American Life Project concluded that Internet users are now "media multiplexers," and that the number and length of time of all of their interactions are longer and more significant than non-Internet users.[64] Similarly, Mark observed the behavior of employees in West Coast high-tech firms for over 1000 hours. In summarizing this study, Thompson reported:

> Each employee spends only 11 minutes on any given project before being interrupted and whisked off to do something else. What's more, each 11-minute project was itself fragmented into even shorter three-minute tasks, like answering email messages, reading a Web page or working on a spreadsheet. And each time a worker was distracted from a task, it would take, on average, 25 minutes to return to that task. To perform an office job today, it seems, your attention must skip like a stone across water all day long, touching down only periodically.
>
> Yet while interruptions are annoying, Mark's study also revealed their flip side: they are often crucial to office work. Sure, the high-tech workers grumbled and moaned about disruptions, and they all claimed that they preferred to work in long, luxurious stretches. But they grudgingly admitted that many of their daily distractions were essential to their jobs. When someone forwards you an urgent e-mail message, it's often something you really do need to see; if a cellphone call breaks through while you're desperately trying to solve a problem, it might be the call that saves your hide. In the language of computer sociology, our jobs are "interrupt driven." Distractions are not just a plague on our work—sometimes they *are* our work. To be cut off from other workers is to be cut off from everything.[65]

In our view, the existence of concurrent media exposures and the emergence of multitasking suggests that triangulation and the use of multiple class measurements will increase in the twenty-first century. We fully expect that communication interactions will become more complex and interrelated, that human communication will increasingly become mediated by an ever-increasing number of technologies, and that the only way to handle this emerging scenario will be to combine the results of a host of different research strategies and findings.

Promoting Triangulation and the Use of Multiple Class Measures

Specifically, as research strategies, designs, and methods evolve—as they continually do—we think it would be useful to consider the following six propositions as generative and formative in how questions of research method should be considered:

1. In entertainment, business, and even interpersonal and private arenas, human communication is becoming increasingly complex, mediated, multidimensional, multitasking, and multicontextual. Hypotheses about human communication are likely to reflect these complexities.
2. It is unlikely that a single method or type of method can respond comprehensively to all of the questions and dimensions affecting complex human communication systems.
3. In so far as research methods seek to be isomorphic or be "similar to the form or structure" of human communication in real environments,[66] different kinds of research methods will be required to deal with all of the different kinds of questions, qualities, and dimensions shaping and controlling the human communication process.
4. Qualitative research methods are becoming increasingly important when human communication processes are described by communication researchers. We think this increase is occurring, in part, because some of the particular research techniques associated with qualitative research—such as simple observation[67]—are perceived by communication researchers as increasingly important.
5. One of the most important gaps to overcome is how quantitative and qualitative research methods, designs, collected data, and interpretations can be made complementary. Several existing research methodologists have already identified techniques such as collaboration as one of the most important forms of triangulation.[68]

6. Communication researchers must go beyond reliability and validity standards when finding common ground in diverse research methods. They must also recognize that other forms of triangulation must be identified as goals for the discipline of communication. We certainly agree with Frey, Botan, Friedman, and Kreps when they argue that triangulation can provide an important means for "checking the validity of preliminary research with other findings to assess their consistency."[69]

At the same time, we think it may also be necessary to begin to attribute far more functions to triangulation. We are particularly impressed by Keyton when she recommends that multiple forms of triangulation be recognized, including *data triangulation,* or the use of a variety of data sources in one study, *investigator triangulation,* or when several different researchers or evaluators participate in the research, *theory triangulation,* which occurs when a research project uses multiple perspectives or multiple theories to interpret a single set of data, *methodological triangulation,* when the researcher uses multiple methods—quantitative and qualitative—to study a single problem, and *interdisciplinary triangulation,* when researchers from a variety of disciplines work together on a research project.[70]

In all, communication research and the methods employed to generate communication data constitute a dynamic and ever-changing area. We can each shape and influence that development. We would encourage you not only to employ the methods provided by qualitative researchers, but also to ask how those methods and the findings generated by these methods can be linked to the perspectives, theories, methods, data, and procedures of both quantitative as well as critical scholars of communication. Communication is now so complex, and growing increasingly multidimensional and intricate, that we now require the insights, capabilities, understandings, and procedures of all people involved in the study of human communication.

Ethical Issues

As we have shown in this appendix, there are multiple paths for conducting qualitative research. Many of these paths bring the researcher and his or her subjects in close proximity for intense periods of time to talk about topics, opinions, and feelings that are highly personal and often are felt intensely. This process can engender a close bond, albeit for limited duration and within a proscribed setting. Moreover, qualitative research can yield deep insights and unveil significant information about how subjects make meaning about their experiences, their relationships, their behaviors, and their places in the world.

Regardless of the approach used, however, it is expected that researchers will adhere to a code of ethics in conducting their work. This section presents ethical standards that have been widely adopted to guide empirical research and examines how each of these standards raises particular challenges for qualitative researchers.

In the chapter "Ethics and Politics in Qualitative Research," Clifford Christians traces transformations from the Enlightenment to today that have contributed to how empirical social science research, in particular, came to embrace as its goals the establishment of empirical facts and be both value-free and morally neutral.[71]

In pursuit of empirical facts, some studies used procedures that resulted in psychological or physical harm to the subjects involved. Yale psychologist Stanley Milgram's studies on obedience to authority was one notable example in the late 1960s and early 1970s.[72] In response to these occurrences, by the 1980s professional and academic associations developed and adopted their own codes of ethics by which researchers were expected to abide. In general, four overarching guidelines are included in these ethical codes: informed consent, deception, privacy and confidentiality, and accuracy.[73]

INFORMED CONSENT

Subjects have the right to be informed about the nature and potential consequences of any study prior to agreeing to participate. Moreover, agreeing to participate must be voluntary. That is, researchers are not permitted to use any forms of coercion to secure participation. Implicit in this guideline is that researchers make themselves known to the subjects. However, as Punch observes, often the very nature of fieldwork would be compromised and undermined by informed consent: "divulging one's identity and research purpose to all and sundry—will kill many a project."[74] Thus the degree to which adherence to the informed consent guideline would be practical and/or detrimental to both the study and to the subjects needs to be assessed carefully prior to engaging in research.

For instance, suppose you wanted to study under what conditions a person who has found cash on the sidewalk will "hand it over" to its' supposed owner. There is no way that research can be successful if the people who approach the "finder" to request the money back have to announce that they are conducting research on the return of found money. In order to conduct the research, the fact that research is being conducted has to be withheld.

DECEPTION

Deliberately deceiving subjects is considered especially egregious. Clearly, the Milgram experiments referred to above had powerful consequences for many of the subjects who were persuaded by presumed legitimate authorities to administer what they thought were electric shocks to others. The resultant harm to numerous subjects in the study gave rise to this code. And yet, again, nuance is important. In many medical studies, for example, understanding the efficacy of certain medications often requires the use of placebos for comparison. The severity of potential harm caused to the subject by the deception, then, is both nuanced and measured against the ultimate consequences of the study.

Similarly, in qualitative studies which rely on fieldwork, observation, or in-depth cases, the extent to which the research would be compromised must be measured against the potential harm to the subjects. Two recently published works relied on changing the authors' identities in order to gain first-hand experience and insight into the topics. In sociologist Barbara Ehrenreich's *Nickel and Dimed: On (Not) Getting By in America*,[75] the author worked in a series of low-paying jobs to understand more fully how class and income impact significant members of the U.S. culture. In Norah Vincent's *Self-Made Man: One Woman's Journey into Manhood and Back Again*,[76] the journalist–author takes on the persona of a male for 18 months in order to understand more fully how men think and act and to dispel long-held assumptions about the male experience. Neither of these projects could have been undertaken without deception, yet in both the value of their work was thought to outweigh the potential harm to the people who were deceived during the duration of the role-playings.

PRIVACY AND CONFIDENTIALITY

While researchers may sometimes choose to "make themselves known" after the research data has been collected, the identities of the research subjects are always sacrosanct. To safeguard exposing people's identities, personal data should be concealed "and made public only behind a shield of anonymity."[77] The danger of disseminating studies despite efforts to maintain confidentiality, Christians continues, is that "(p)seudonyms and disguised locations are often recognized by insiders. What researchers consider innocent is perceived by participants as misleading or even betrayal. What appears neutral on paper is often conflictual in practice."[78]

The implications for qualitative research are especially salient. In-depth interviews conducted with students at a college, with managers at a corporation, or with patients at a clinic can produce rich and meaningful data. While the names of the participants and the sites studied can be altered, the authors' names and affiliations are not.

How such works will be disseminated, then, is critical. The majority of such studies are published within the disciplinary academic journals and are not likely to directly affect the participants. Other works, however, are crossover works intended for public consumption. Arlie Hochschild's recently published *The Time Bind: Where Work Becomes Home and Home Becomes Work*, for example, situated the author in a fictitious company, Americo.[79] Her in-depth interviews with employees of a real company yielded compelling insights into how organizational life and policies are experienced across positions, how these policies are administered unevenly, and how changes in the family and home have produced a disconnect for many employees with their own families. The extent to which the participants recognize themselves and their colleagues in the book, and the potential repercussions such recognitions might have, remain unknowable to those outside the organization.

ACCURACY

It is expected that the data reported should accurately reflect the findings and not be altered. "Data that are internally and externally valid are the coin of the realm, experimentally and morally" according to Christians.[80] In their work on naturalistic inquiry, Lincoln and Guba suggest that an additional major step in qualitative research includes the decision process on the part of the researcher regarding what portions and/or details of the data are included and what portions are omitted in the reporting process.[81] Such decisions reflect active choices on the part of the researcher. The challenge, consequently, is to report responsibly information that maintains the integrity of the project and omitting that which—no matter how fascinating in its own right—is beyond the purview of the study.

The four aspects of ethical codes we have discussed initially were connected to empirical studies whose foci were presumably value-free and morally neutral. By the nature of the studies the researchers remained apart—separate from—those they were studying. While we have suggested how aspects of qualitative research relate to these codes, the final point we raise has to do with notions of positionality and what constitutes meaning-making.

During the past few decades there has been a growing recognition of contributions by interpretive researchers and an inclusion of the ethic of care, nurturance, empathy, and collaboration as significant (see Gilligan,[82] Steiner,[83] Wood[84]). There has been, under the rubric of "feminist communitarianism," the recognition that human identity is constituted through intersections between our places in society, by our interactions with others, by constructions of power, and by the lenses through which we see and are seen by others. These lenses are powerful and are informed by gender, race, culture, class, and sexual orientation as well as other influences.

Transforming the human condition is important, but acceptable transformation can occur only when multiple perspectives are given voice—when those participating in studies are afforded agency in the research process. This agency is possible by situating the researcher in a reciprocal relationship with the subject. In so doing, participants are given a powerful voice and share in identifying and articulating issues and problems that matter to them. In this way, interpretative discourse from a feminist communitarian view demands and encourages multiplicity (not precision), moral awareness (not neutrality), and transformation (not replication).

Ethics is an abiding issue in the research process. As what we understand and define as research has been transformed over time, there has been a simultaneous shift in how such inquiry comes to be proscribed and evaluated. As we have suggested in this appendix, qualitative research has assumed a key position in communication and other disciplinary research, and as it has done so it has affected the whole question of research ethics.

Conclusion

In this chapter, we have focused on how people communicate in their own natural environments when they are guided by their own personal objectives and when they are using communication for those pragmatic objectives that determine and control day-to-day existence. This approach has had a host of different labels, but its central and most unifying label is *qualitative research*. Regardless of its specific label, we have suggested that qualitative research examines human communication in natural settings in which the researcher functions as both an observer and participant. Within such contexts and in the role of participant–observer, the researcher examines subject-based communication and is guided by the intentions of those being observed and pragmatic ends of those being studied. This kind of research endeavor is guided by significant and unique research goals, questions, and issues, ultimately suggesting that grounded theory can be a powerful conceptual approach to the study of human communication. In all, we are convinced that qualitative research can avoid a host of reactive issues found in more formal social scientific research methods. Toward these ends, we have suggested that any one or more of five research techniques can be employed to complete qualitative research: open-ended questions, focus groups, participant observation, unobtrusive methods, and triangulation or multiple class measurements.

While these multiple paths for conducting qualitative research exist, many of these approaches bring the researcher and his or her subjects in close proximity for intense periods of time to talk about topics, opinions, and feelings that are highly personal and often intensely felt. Because these researcher–subject relationships can engender an extremely close bond—albeit for limited duration and within a proscribed setting—qualitative research can yield deep insights and unveil significant information about how subjects make meaning about their experiences, their relationships, their behaviors, and their places in the world. Such relationships require that ethics guide the entire relationship from start to finish.

At a minimum, ethical guidelines in qualitative research should involve informed consent, avoid the use of any kind of deception, maintain the privacy and confidentiality of every individual within the study, and particularly maintain an overwhelming commitment to accuracy when reporting all results. In all, while both social scientific and critical approaches to human communication are important, from our perspective, qualitative research provides equally important and powerful ways of understanding human communication.

Key Terms

Action/Applied Research
Critical Research Methods
Ethnographic Research
Field Research
Focus Groups
Grounded Theory

Interpretive/Interpretivist
   Research
Naturalistic Research
Open-Ended Question
Participant Observation
Qualitative Research
   Methods

Quantitative Research
   Methods
Triangulation/Multiple
   Class Measurements
Unobtrusive Measurements

NOTES

1. Edwin P. Willems, "Planning a Rationale for Naturalistic Research" (pp. 44–71) in E. P. Willems and H. L. Raush (Eds.), *Naturalistic Viewpoints in Psychological Research* (New York: Holt, Rinehart and Winston, Inc., 1969), p. 46.

2. Thomas R. Lindlof and Bryan C. Taylor, *Qualitative Communication Research Methods* (2nd ed.) (Thousand Oaks, CA: Sage Publications, 2002), p. 18. For an analysis of the rationale for and issues involved in qualitative research, see also Yvonna S. Lincoln and Norman K. Denzin, *Turning Points in Qualitative Research: Tying Knots in a Handkerchief* (Walnut Creek, CA: AltaMira Press/A Division of Rowman & Littlefield Publishers, Inc. 2003).

3. Lawrence R. Frey, Carl H. Botan, Paul G. Friedman, and Gary L. Kreps, *Interpreting Communication Research: A Case Study Approach* (Englewood Cliffs, NJ: Prentice Hall, 1992), p. 7.

4. See: Bryn Hafren, "Empirical and Interpretative Research," at: http://www.barrycomp.com/bhs/a_research.htm. We have made some adjustments in this table to reduce the complexity of the analysis in the table and to reflect the background of the readers of this chapter.

5. Lawrence R. Frey, Carl H. Botan, Paul G. Friedman, and Gary L. Kreps, *Interpreting Communication Research: A Case Study Approach* (Englewood Cliffs, NJ: Prentice Hall, 1992), p. 7. See also: Robin Patric Clair (Ed.), *Expressions of Ethnography: Novel Approaches to Qualitative Methods* (Albany, NY: State University of New York, 2005); Arthur P. Bochner and Carolyn Ellis (Eds.), *Ethnographically Speaking: Autoethnography, Literature, and Aesthetics* (Walnut Creek, CA: AltaMira Press/A Division of Rowman & Littlefield Publishers, Inc., 2002). Often viewed as art-based research, *ethnodrama* is often treated as an area of analysis related to ethnographic research; see Johnny Saldana (Ed.), *Ethnodrama: An Anthology of Reality Theatre* (Lanham, MD: Rowman & Littlefield Publishing Group, Inc., 2005).

6. Joann Keyton, *Communication Research: Asking Questions, Finding Answers* (Mountain View, CA: Mayfield Publishing Company, 2001), p. 161.

7. Lawrence R. Frey, Carl H. Botan, Paul G. Friedman, and Gary L. Kreps, *Interpreting Communication Research: A Case Study Approach* (Englewood Cliffs, NJ: Prentice Hall, 1992), p. 55.

8. *Webster's New Collegiate Dictionary* (Springfield, MA: G. & C. Merriam Company, 1981), p. 423.

9. *Webster's Third New International Dictionary Unabridged and Seven Language Dictionary* (Vol. 1) (Chicago: Encyclopaedia Britannica, Inc., 1986), p. 846.

10. Harry F. Wolcott, *The Art of Fieldwork* (2nd ed.) (Walnut Creek, CA: AltaMira Press/A Division of Rowman & Littlefield Publishers, Inc., 2005). See also John VanMaanen, *Tales of the Field: On Writing Ethnography* (Chicago, IL: The University of Chicago Press, 1988).

11. Jack D. Douglas, *Investigative Social Research: Individual and Team Field Research* (Beverly Hills, CA: Sage Publications, 1976), p. 15 provides a convenient overview of this analysis.

12. Lawrence R. Frey, Carl H. Botan, Paul G. Friedman, and Gary L. Kreps, *Interpreting Communication Research: A Case Study Approach* (Englewood Cliffs, NJ: Prentice Hall, 1992), pp. 4–5.

13. Robert L. Heath and Jennings Bryant, *Human Communication Theory and Research: Concepts, Contexts, and Challenges* (Mahwah, NJ: Lawrence Erlbaum Associates, Publishers, 2000), p. 10.

14. Robert L. Heath and Jennings Bryant, *Human Communication Theory and Research: Concepts, Contexts, and Challenges* (Mahwah, NJ: Lawrence Erlbaum Associates, Publishers, 2000), p. 10.

15. Barney Glaser and Anselm Strauss, *The Discovery of Grounded Theory* (Chicago, IL: Aldine, 1967).

16. Kathy Charmaz, "Grounded Theory: Objectivist and Constructivist Methods" (pp. 509–535) in Norman K. Denzin and Yvonna S. Lincoln (Eds.), *Handbook of Qualitative Research* (Thousand Oaks, CA: Sage, 2000), esp. p. 511.

17. Kathy Charmaz, "Grounded Theory: Objectivist and Constructivist Methods" (pp. 509–535) in Norman K. Denzin and Yvonna S. Lincoln (Eds.), *Handbook of Qualitative Research* (Thousand Oaks, CA: Sage, 2000), esp. p. 511.

18. For a more complete discussion of grounded theory, see Yvonna S. Lincoln and Egon G. Guba, *Naturalistic Inquiry* (Newbury Park, CA: Sage, 1985).

19. Yvonna S. Lincoln and Egon G. Guba, *Naturalistic Inquiry* (Newbury Park, CA: Sage, 1985), p. 209.

20. Kathy Charmaz, "Grounded Theory: Objectivist and Constructivist Methods" (pp. 509–535) in Norman K. Denzin and Yvonna S. Lincoln (Eds.), *Handbook of Qualitative Research* (Thousand Oaks, CA: Sage, 2000), esp. p. 510.

21. Yvonna S. Lincoln and Egon G. Guba, *Naturalistic Inquiry* (Newbury Park, CA: Sage, 1985), pp. 209–211.

22. Yvonna S. Lincoln and Egon G. Guba, *Naturalistic Inquiry* (Newbury Park, CA: Sage, 1985), p. 211.

23. Claire Selltiz, Marie Jahoda, Morton Deutsch, and Stuart W. Cook, *Research Methods in Social Relations* (New York: Holt, Rinehart & Winston, 1959) (published for the Society for the Psychological Study of Social Issues). See also: Donald T. Campbell, "Factors Relevant to the Validity of Experiments in Social Settings," *Psychological Bulletin, 54* (1957), pp. 297–312; Donald T. Campbell and J. C. Stanley, "Experimental and Quasi-Experimental Deigns for Research on Teaching" (pp. 171–246) in N. L. Gage (Ed.), *Handbook of Research on Teaching* (Chicago: Rand McNally, 1963).

24. At this juncture, we are summarizing the analysis of reactivism provided in Eugene J. Webb, Donald T. Campbell, Richard D. Schwartz, and Lee Sechrest, *Unobtrusive Measures: Nonreactive Research in the Social Sciences* (Chicago: Rand McNally College Publishing Company, 1966), pp. 12–34.

25. For example, see: David W. Moore, "Issue Framing in Polls," The Gallup Organization, July 12, 2005, http://www.gallup.com/poll/content/print.aspx?ci=17296.

26. For details regarding the parasocial relationship, see Donald Horton and R. Richard Wohl, "Mass Communication and Para-Social Interactions: Observations on Intimacy at a Distance," *Psychiatry, 19* (August 1956), pp. 215–229.

27. For details on the use of this question when interviewing couples, see Paul Watzlawick, Janet Beavin and Don D. Jackson, *Pragmatics of Human Communication: A Study of Interactional Patterns, Pathologies, and Paradoxes* (New York: W. W. Norton & Company, 1967).

28. Robert King Merton, Marjorie Fiske, and Alberta Curtis, *Mass Persuasion: The Social Psychology of a War Bond Drive* (New York: Harper, 1946). In 1956, Merton, Fiske, and Kendal provided the first comprehensive analysis was provided in a 1956 book entitled *The Focused Interview: A Manual of Problems and Procedures*; see Robert King Merton, Marjorie Fiske, and Patricia L. Kendall, *The Focused Interview: A Manual of Problems and Procedures* (Glencoe, IL: The Free Press, 1956).

29. Peter Lunt and Sonia Livingstone, "Rethinking the Focus Group in Media and Communications Research," *Journal of Communication, 46* (Spring 1996), pp. 79–80.

30. Richard L. Berke, "Focus Groups Sometimes Emphasize the Trivial," *The New York Times,* November 21, 1999, Section 4, page WK3.

31. Peter Lunt and Sonia Livingstone, "Rethinking the Focus Group in Media and Communications Research," *Journal of Communication, 46* (Spring 1996), p. 80.

32. For example, see R. K. Merton, M. Fiske, and A. Curtis. *The Focused Interview* (New York: Free Press, 1956). See also D. L. Morgan, *Focus Groups as Qualitative Research* (Newbury Park, CA: Sage, 1988).

33. Esther Madriz, "Focus Groups in Feminist Research" in Norman K. Denzin and Yvonna S. Lincoln (Eds.), *Collecting and Interpreting Qualitative Research* (Thousand Oaks, CA: Sage, 2003), p. 381.

34. Esther Madriz, "Focus Groups in Feminist Research" in Norman K. Denzin and Yvonna S. Lincoln (Eds.), *Collecting and Interpreting Qualitative Research* (Thousand Oaks, CA: Sage, 2003), p. 380.

35. [Pierre Guillaume] Frederick LePlay, *Les Ouvriers des deux mondes* (Paris: Société d'économie et de science socials, 1855).

36. William Isaac Thomas and Florian Znaniecki, *The Polish Peasant in Europe and America* (New York: Alfred A. Knopf, 1927).

37. Edward C. Lindeman, *Social Discovery: An Approach to the Study of Functional Groups* (New York: Republic Publishing Co., 1924), p. 191.

38. See Ruth Benedict, *Patterns of Culture* (Baltimore, MD: Penguin Books, Inc., 1934); Robert S. Lynd and Helen M. Lynd, *Middletown in Transition* (New York: Harcourt, Brace & World, Inc., 1937);

Robert Redfield, *Tepoztlan: A Mexican Village* (Chicago: University of Chicago Press, 1930); Hans Reimer, "Socialization in the Prison Community," *American Prison Association Proceedings* (1937), pp. 151–155.

39. Florence R. Kluckhorn, "The Participant-Observer Technique in Small Communities," *American Journal of Sociology*, *46* (November 1940), p. 331.

40. In the context of the dual role of the researcher we are discussing here, for example, see: George C. Homan, *The Human Group* (New York: Harcourt, Brace & World, Inc., 1950). [one section, on pages 53–54, is of particular interest in terms of participant observation]; John Dollard, *Caste and Class in a Southern Town* (Garden City, NY: Doubleday Anchor Books, 1949), especially p. 33; S. M. Miller, "The Participant Observer and Over-Rapport," *American Sociological Review*, *17* (February 1952), especially p. 98; and, Arthur J. Vidich, "Participant Observation and the Collection and Interpretation of Data," *American Journal of Sociology*, *60* (January 1955), especially p. 354.

41. Morris S. Schwartz and Charlotte Green Schwartz, "Problems in Participant Observation," *American Journal of Sociology*, *60* (January 1955), p. 343.

42. In 1958, Becker argued that if the participant observer can vary the number and length of situations he/she is in, she/he can begin to argue that the data collected is enduring, representative, and significant statements about a subculture. Becker's study provided the basis for a major analysis of verification in the method to be developed by Bruyn in 1966. For a specific discussion of Becker's contributions, see: Howard S. Becker, Blance Gerr, Everett C. Hughes, and Anselm L. Strauss, *Boys in White* (Chicago: University of Chicago Press, 1961); Howard S. Becker, *Outsiders* (New York: Free Press of Glencoe, Inc., 1963); Howard S. Becker, "Problems of Inference and Proof in Participant Observation," *American Sociological Review*, *23* (December 1958); and Howard S. Becker and Blanche Geer, "Participant Observation: The Analysis of Qualitative Field Data" in *Human Organization Research*, eds. Richard Adams and Jack J. Preiss (Homewood, IL: Richard D. Irwin, Inc., 1960).

43. Gerald D. Berreman, *Behind Many Masks*, Monograph No. 4 (Ithaca, NY: Cornell University Society for Applied Anthropology, 1962), p. 8.

44. Herbert J. Gans, *Urban Villagers* (New York: Free Press of Glencoe, Inc., 1962), pp. 344–345.

45. Herbert Blumer, "Society as Symbolic Interaction" in *Human Behavior and Social Processes: An Interactionist Approach*, ed. by Arnold Rose (Boston: Houghton Mifflin Company, 1962), p. 188. Emphasis and bold added by Chesebro.

46. Severyn T. Bruyn, *The Human Perspective in Sociology: The Methodology of Participant Observation* (Englewood Cliffs, NJ: Prentice-Hall, Inc., 1966).

47. Paul Gump and Brian Sutton-Smith, "Activity-Setting and Social Interaction: A Field Study" in "Therapeutic Play Techniques; Symposium," *American Journal of Orthopsychiatry*, *4* (October 1955), pp. 755–760.

48. Paul V. Gump and Jacob S. Kounin, "Milieu Influences in Children's Concepts of Misconduct," *Child Development*, *32* (December 1961), pp. 711–720.

49. In another context, Chesebro has defined *everyday communication* in these terms: "While the concept of everyday communication is seldom treated as a critical concept, we have conceived of the study of everyday communication to be the examination of: (1) particular intentions rather than intentionality as an epistemological issue; (2) settings in which agents assume that a single reality exists independent of perception; (3) agents who believe that imperative actions are required rather than dialectic exchanges; (4) imminent actions and face-to-face interactions possessing the full scope of all verbal and nonverbal stimuli in which immediate, flexible, continuous, and pre-reflective symbolic exchanges occur; (5) exchanges in which members of a communication system assume there is a correspondence among their meanings; and, (6) agents engaged in continuity in their interactions in terms of geography, time, and social relations. Thus, everyday communication is the study of autobiographical meanings or the pragmatics and self-serving understandings of an inner circle or symbolic enclave in which there is a high degree of dependency, interest, and intimacy. We would not, therefore, perceive formal speeches, academic debates, most written essays, or highly ceremonial occasions typically to be 'everyday communication.'" See: James W. Chesebro and Kenneth L. Klenk, "Gay Masculinity in the Gay Disco" in *Gayspeak: Gay Male and Lesbian Communication*, ed. by James W. Chesebro (New York: The Pilgrim Press of the United Church, 1981), pp. 327–328.

50. We have defined *reactivism* in detail earlier in this chapter. At this point we are suggesting that researchers seek to reduce or eliminate reactivism. In this context, reactivism can be the knowledge on the part of the members of the community that they are being studied. When researchers seek to reduce reactivism, more generally they seek to prevent any feature of the research design from influencing the results obtained.

51. While we have made some adjustments in these materials, Figures A.3 through A.6 are provided in: Severyn T. Bruyn, *The Human Perspective in Sociology: The Methodology of Participant Observation* (Englewood Cliffs, NJ: Prentice-Hall, Inc., 1966).

52. For example, see: Erving Goffman, *The Presentation of Self in Everyday Life* (Garden City, NY: Doubleday Anchor Books / Doubleday & Company, Inc., 1959); Erving Goffman, *Interaction Ritual: Essays on Face-to-Face Behavior* (Garden City, NY: Anchor Books / Doubleday & Company, Inc., 1967).

53. For an extension and development of Goffman's concept, see Barry R. Schlenker, *Impression Management: The Self-Concept, Social Identity, and Interpersonal Relations* (Monterey, CA: Brooks / Cole Publishing Company / A Division of Wadsworth, Inc., 1980).

54. Figure A.5 is provided in Severyn T. Bruyn, *The Human Perspective in Sociology: The Methodology of Participant Observation* (Englewood Cliffs, NJ: Prentice-Hall, Inc., 1966), p. 261.

55. Figure A.6 is provided in Severyn T. Bruyn, *The Human Perspective in Sociology: The Methodology of Participant Observation* (Englewood Cliffs, NJ: Prentice-Hall, Inc., 1966), pp. 268–270.

56. S. Kirson Weinberg and H. Warren Dunham, *The Culture of a Mental Hospital* (Detroit: Wayne State University Press, 1960).

57. At this juncture, we are summarizing the analysis provided in Eugene J. Webb, Donald T. Campbell, Richard D. Schwartz, and Lee Sechrest, *Unobtrusive Measures: Nonreactive Research in the Social Sciences* (Chicago: Rand McNally College Publishing Company, 1966).

58. For example, see Andrew T. Duchowski, *Eye Tracking Methodology: Theory and Practice* (New York: Springer Publishing Company, 2003).

59. James W. Chesebro, "Graffiti as Communication in the Popular Culture," paper presented at the meeting of the Central States Speech Association, April 1975, Kansas City, KS.

60. All of the concepts, definitions, and examples provided in this table are drawn from Eugene J. Webb, Donald T. Campbell, Richard D. Schwartz, and Lee Sechrest, *Unobtrusive Measures: Nonreactive Research in the Social Sciences* (Chicago: Rand McNally College Publishing Company, 1966), pp. 35–170.

61. Lawrence R. Frey, Carl H. Botan, Paul G. Friedman, and Gary L. Kreps, *Interpreting Communication Research: A Case Study Approach* (Englewood Cliffs, NJ: Prentice Hall, 1992), p. 323.

62. For a more complete discussion of the rationale for multiple class measurement, see Eugene J. Webb, Donald T. Campbell, Richard D. Schwartz, and Lee Sechrest, *Unobtrusive Measures: Nonreactive Research in the Social Sciences* (Chicago: Rand McNally College Publishing Company, 1966), Chapter 7, "A Final Note," pp. 171–183. Our quotations here are drawn from pp. 174 and 175.

63. Michael E. Holmes, Robert A. Papper, Mark N. Popovich, and Michael Bloxham, *Middletown Media Studies: Observing Consumers and Their Interactions with Media, Concurrent Media Exposure* (Muncie, IN: Center for Media Design of Ball State University, Fall 2005), pp. 12–15. In the context of the tradition of qualitative research, it should be noted that this research team focused on subjects in the Muncie and Indianapolis area, and the use of "Middletown" reflects their awareness of the studies completed in the 1930s in Muncie, Indiana, which was then identified as "Middletown" by the Lynds; for example, see Robert S. Lynd and Helen M. Lynd, *Middletown in Transition* (New York: Harcourt, Brace & World, Inc., 1937).

64. Jeffrey Boase, John B. Horrigan, Barry Wellman, and Lee Rainie, *The Strength of Internet Ties: The Internet and Email Aid Users in Maintaining Their Social Networks and Provide Pathways to Help When People Face Big Decisions* (Washington, DC: Pew Internet & American Life Project, January 25, 2006), esp. p. v, although the entire report is relevant to our discussion here. See: www.pewinternet.org.

65. Clive Thompson, "Meet the Life Hackers," *The New York Times Magazine*, October 16, 2005, pp. 40–46, especially pp. 40 and 42.

66. Roger D. Wimmer and Joseph R. Dominick, *Mass Media Research: An Introduction* (8th ed.) (Belmont, CA: Thomson Wadsworth / Part of Thomson Corporation, 2006), p. 51.

67. Wimmer and Dominick report that "field observation was rarely used in mass media research before 1980. Cooper, Potter, and Dupagne (1994) found that about 2% of all published studies from 1965 to 1989 relied on observation. Recently, however, field observations have become common in the research literature (Anderson 1987; Lindlof 1987, 1991, 1995); see Roger D. Wimmer and Joseph R. Dominick, *Mass Media Research: An Introduction* (7th ed.) (Belmont, CA: Thomson Wadsworth / Part of Thomson Corporation, 2003), p. 115. See also: J. A. Anderson, *Communication Research: Issues and Methods* (New York: Mc-Graw-Hill, 1987); R. Cooper, W. Potter, and M. Dupagne, "A Status Report on Methods Used in Mass Communication Research," *Journalism Educator, 48* (1994), 54–61; T. R. Lindlof, *Natural Audiences: Qualitative Research of Media Uses and Effects* (Norwood, NJ: Ablex, 1987); T. R. Lindlof, "The Qualitative Study of Media Audiences," *Journal of Broadcasting and Electronic Media, 35* (1991), pp. 23–42; and T. R. Lindlof, *Qualitative Communication Research Methods* (Thousand Oaks, CA: Sage, 1995).

68. For example, see: Roger D. Wimmer and Joseph R. Dominick, *Mass Media Research: An Introduction* (8th ed.) (Belmont, CA: Thomson Wadsworth / Part of Thomson Corporation, 2006), p. 50; Joann Keyton, *Communication Research: Asking Questions, Finding Answers* (Mountain View, CA: Mayfield Publishing Company, 2001), p. 77.

69. Lawrence R. Frey, Carl H. Botan, Paul G. Friedman, and Gary L. Kreps, *Interpreting Communication Research: A Case Study Approach* (Englewood Cliffs, NJ: Prentice Hall, 1992), p. 323.

70. Joann Keyton, *Communication Research: Asking Questions, Finding Answers* (Mountain View, CA: Mayfield Publishing Company, 2001), pp. 77–78. Bolding is in the original.

71. Clifford Christians, "Ethics and Politics in Qualitative Research" (pp. 133–155) in N. K. Denzin and Y. S. Lincoln (Eds.), *Handbook of Qualitative Research* (Thousand Oaks, CA: Sage, 2000).

72. Stanley Milgram, *Obedience to Authority* (New York: Harper & Row, 1974).

73. For a deeper discussion of how these codes developed over time, see Clifford Christians, "Ethics and Politics in Qualitative Research" in N. K. Denzin and Y. S. Lincoln (Eds.), *Handbook of Qualitative Research* (Thousand Oaks, CA: Sage, 2000), pp. 138–140.

74. M. Punch, "Politics and Ethics in Qualitative Research" in N. K. Denzin and Y. S. Lincoln (Eds.), *Handbook of Qualitative Research* (Thousand Oaks, CA: Sage, 1994), p. 90.

75. Barbara Ehrenreich, *Nickel and Dimed: On (Not) Getting By in America* (New York: Metropolitan Books, Henry Holt and Company, 2001),

76. Norah Vincent, *Self-Made Man: One Woman's Journey into Manhood and Back Again* (New York: Viking, 2006).

77. Clifford Christians, "Ethics and Politics in Qualitative Research" in N. K. Denzin and Y. S. Lincoln (Eds.), *Handbook of Qualitative Research* (Thousand Oaks, CA: Sage, 2000), p. 139.

78. Clifford Christians, "Ethics and Politics in Qualitative Research" in N. K. Denzin and Y. S. Lincoln (Eds.), *Handbook of Qualitative Research* (Thousand Oaks, CA: Sage, 2000), p. 139.

79. Arlie Hochschild (1997). *The Time Bind: Where Work Becomes Home and Home Becomes Work* (New York: Henry Holt and Company, 1997).

80. Clifford Christians, "Ethics and Politics in Qualitative Research" in N. K. Denzin and Y. S. Lincoln (Eds.), *Handbook of Qualitative Research* (Thousand Oaks, CA: Sage, 2000), p. 140.

81. Yvonna S. Lincoln and Egon G. Guba, *Naturalistic Inquiry* (Newbury Park, CA: Sage 1985).

82. Carol Gilligan, *In a Different Voice: Psychological Theory and Women's Development* (Cambridge, MA: Harvard University Press, 1982).

83. Linda Steiner, "Feminist Theorizing and Communication Ethics," *Communication, 12*, 3 (1991), pp. 157–174.

84. Julia T. Wood, *Who Cares? Women, Care and Culture* (Carbondale, IL: Southern Illinois University Press, 1994).

Textbook Questionnaire

Hello!

We are Drs. Jason Wrench, Virginia Peck-Richmond, Candice Thomas-Maddox, and James McCroskey, and we are creating a data set to include with a new quantitative research methods textbook being developed for Roxbury Publishers.

Completing this questionnaire should take approximately 30–40 minutes. There are no known risks to participation in this data collection. Your participation is completely voluntary, and you may end your participation at any time. Your responses will be kept completely anonymous. After your individual survey has been entered into a computer database, your survey will be destroyed.

If after reading this letter you decide to participate in this data collection, simply fill out the attached questionnaire. Please be honest and as complete as possible with your answers. The person proctoring this data collection will have further instructions for you on how he or she will collect the completed surveys.

Returning this questionnaire certifies that you have read and understand this consent form and agree to be a participant in the data collection described. Additionally, you agree that known risks for your participation have been explained to your satisfaction and you understand that no compensation is available from either West Virginia University or Ohio University and its employees for any injury resulting from your participation in this research. Participation in this data collection also certifies that you are 18 years of age or older. Please understand that you may discontinue participation at any time without penalty or loss of any benefits to which you may otherwise be entitled.

Thank you for your time. We greatly appreciate your willingness to complete this questionnaire.

Sincerely,

Jason S. Wrench, Ed.D.   Candice Thomas-Maddox, Ed.D.

Virginia Peck-Richmond, Ph.D.   James C. McCroskey, D. Ed.

Instructions: This instrument is composed of 24 statements concerning feelings about communicating with others. Please indicate the degree to which each statement applies to you by marking whether you:

Strongly Disagree	Disagree	Neutral	Agree	Strongly Agree
1	2	3	4	5

_____1. I dislike participating in group discussions.

_____2. Generally, I am comfortable while participating in group discussions.

_____3. I am tense and nervous while participating in group discussions.

_____4. I like to get involved in group discussions.

_____5. Engaging in a group discussion with new people makes me tense and nervous.

_____6. I am calm and relaxed while participating in group discussions.

_____7. Generally, I am nervous when I have to participate in a meeting.

_____8. Usually, I am comfortable when I have to participate in a meeting.

_____9. I am very calm and relaxed when I am called upon to express an opinion at a meeting.

_____10. I am afraid to express myself at meetings.

_____11. Communicating at meetings usually makes me uncomfortable.

_____12. I am very relaxed when answering questions at a meeting.

_____13. While participating in a conversation with a new acquaintance, I feel very nervous.

_____14. I have no fear of speaking up in conversations.

_____15. Ordinarily I am very tense and nervous in conversations.

_____16. Ordinarily I am very calm and relaxed in conversations.

_____17. While conversing with a new acquaintance, I feel very relaxed.

_____18. I'm afraid to speak up in conversations.

_____19. I have no fear of giving a speech.

_____20. Certain parts of my body feel very tense and rigid while giving a speech.

_____21. I feel relaxed while giving a speech.

_____22. My thoughts become confused and jumbled when I am giving a speech.

_____23. I face the prospect of giving a speech with confidence.

_____24. While giving a speech, I get so nervous I forget facts I really know.

Instructions: Below are items that relate to the cultures of different parts of the world. Work quickly and record your first reaction to each item. There are no right or wrong answers. Please indicate the degree to which you agree or disagree with each item using the following five-point scale:

Strongly Disagree	**Disagree**	**Neutral**	**Agree**	**Strongly Agree**
1	**2**	**3**	**4**	**5**

_____1. Most other cultures are backward compared to my culture.

_____2. My culture should be the role model for other cultures.

_____3. People from other cultures act strangely when they come to my culture.

_____4. Lifestyles in other cultures are just as valid as those in my culture.

_____5. Other cultures should try to be more like my culture.

_____6. I am not interested in the values and customs of other cultures.

_____7. People in my culture could learn a lot from people in other cultures.

_____8. Most people from other cultures just don't know what's good for them.

_____9. I respect the values and customs of other cultures.

_____10. Other cultures are smart to look up to our culture.

_____11. Most people would be happier if they lived like people in my culture.

_____12. I have many friends from different cultures.

_____13. People in my culture have just about the best lifestyles anywhere.

_____14. Lifestyles in other cultures are not as valid as those in my culture.

_____15. I am very interested in the values and customs of other cultures.

_____16. I apply my values when judging people who are different.

_____17. I see people who are similar to me as virtuous.

_____18. I do not cooperate with people who are different.

_____19. Most people in my culture just don't know what is good for them.

_____20. I do not trust people who are different.

_____21. I dislike interacting with people from different cultures.

_____22. I have little respect for the values and customs of other cultures.

Instructions: The following statements apply to how people communicate humor when relating to others. Indicate the degree to which each of these statements applies to you by filling in the number of your response in the blank before each item:

Strongly Disagree	Disagree	Neutral	Agree	Strongly Agree
1	2	3	4	5

_____1. I regularly communicate with others by joking with them.

_____2. People usually laugh when I make a humorous remark.

_____3. I am not funny or humorous.

_____4. I can be amusing or humorous without having to tell a joke.

_____5. Being humorous is a natural communication orientation for me.

_____6. I cannot relate an amusing idea well.

_____7. My friends would say that I am a humorous or funny person.

_____8. People don't seem to pay close attention when I am being funny.

_____9. Even funny ideas and stories seem dull when I tell them.

_____10. I can easily relate funny or humorous ideas to the class.

_____11. I would say that I am not a humorous person.

_____12. I cannot be funny, even when asked to do so.

_____13. I relate amusing stories, jokes, and funny things very well to others.

_____14. Of all the people I know, I am one of the "least" amusing or funny persons.

_____15. I use humor to communicate in a variety of situations.

_____16. On a regular basis, I do not communicate with others by being humorous or entertaining.

Instructions: The following statements describe the ways some people behave while talking with or to others. Please indicate in the space at the left of each item the degree to which you believe the statement applies **to you**. Please use the following 5-point scale:

Never	Rarely	Occasionally	Often	Very Often
1	2	3	4	5

_____1. I use my hands and arms to gesture while talking to people.

_____2. I touch others on the shoulder or arm while talking to them.

_____3. I use a monotone or dull voice while talking to people.

_____4. I look over or away from others while talking to them.

_____5. I move away from others when they touch me while we are talking.

_____6. I have a relaxed body position when I talk to people.

_____7. I frown while talking to people.

_____8. I avoid eye contact while talking to people.

_____9. I have a tense body position while talking to people.

_____10. I sit close or stand close to people while talking with them.

_____11. My voice is monotonous or dull when I talk to people.

_____12. I use a variety of vocal expressions when I talk to people.

_____13. I gesture when I talk to people.

_____14. I am animated when I talk to people.

_____15. I have a bland facial expression when I talk to people.

_____16. I move closer to people when I talk to them.

_____17. I look directly at people while talking to them.

_____18. I am stiff when I talk to people.

_____19. I have a lot of vocal variety when I talk to people.

_____20. I avoid gesturing while I am talking to people.

_____21. I lean toward people when I talk to them.

_____22. I maintain eye contact with people when I talk to them.

_____23. I try not to sit or stand close to people when I talk with them.

_____24. I lean away from people when I talk to them.

_____25. I smile when I talk to people.

_____26. I avoid touching people when I talk to them.

Instructions: The questionnaire below lists 20 personality characteristics. Please indicate the degree to which you believe each of these characteristics applies to you while interacting with others by marking whether you (5) strongly agree that it applies, (4) agree that it applies, (3) are undecided, (2) disagree that it applies, or (1) strongly disagree that it applies. There are no right or wrong answers. Work quickly; record your first impression.

_____1. helpful

_____2. defends own beliefs

_____3. independent

_____4. responsive to others

_____5. forceful

_____6. has strong personality

_____7. sympathetic

_____8. compassionate

_____9. assertive

_____10. sensitive to the needs of others

_____11. dominant

_____12. sincere

_____13. gentle

_____14. willing to take a stand

_____15. warm

_____16. tender

_____17. friendly

_____18. acts as a leader

_____19. aggressive

_____20. competitive

Instructions: Below are 20 situations in which a person might choose to communicate or not to communicate. Presume you have completely free choice. Indicate the percentage of times you would choose to communicate in each type of situation. Indicate in the space at the left of the item what percent of the time you would choose to communicate. (0 = Never to 100 = Always)

_____1. Talk with a service station attendant

_____2. Talk with a physician

_____3. Present a talk to a group of strangers

_____4. Talk with an acquaintance while standing in line

_____5. Talk with a salesperson in a store

_____6. Talk in a large meeting of friends

_____7. Talk with a police officer

_____8. Talk in a small group of strangers

_____9. Talk with a friend while standing in line

_____10. Talk with a waiter/waitress in a restaurant

_____11. Talk in a large meeting of acquaintances

_____12. Talk with a stranger while standing in line

_____13. Talk with a secretary

_____14. Present a talk to a group of friends

_____15. Talk in a small group of acquaintances

_____16. Talk with a garbage collector

_____17. Talk in a large meeting of strangers

_____18. Talk with a spouse (or girl/boyfriend)

_____19. Talk in a small group of friends

_____20. Present a talk to a group of acquaintances

Instructions: On the scales below, please indicate the degree to which you believe the following statement "Everyone should be required to take public speaking in xollege." Numbers "1" and "7" indicate a very strong feeling. Numbers "2" and "6" indicate a strong feeling. Numbers "3" and "5" indicate a fairly week feeling. Number "4" indicates you are undecided or do not understand the adjective pairs themselves. There are no right or wrong answers. *Only circle one number per line.*

1) Agree	1	2	3	4	5	6	7	Disagree
2) False	1	2	3	4	5	6	7	True
3) Incorrect	1	2	3	4	5	6	7	Correct
4) Right	1	2	3	4	5	6	7	Wrong
5) Yes	1	2	3	4	5	6	7	No

Instructions: On the scales below, please indicate your feelings about "higher education." Numbers "1" and "7" indicate a very strong feeling. Numbers "2" and "6" indicate a strong feeling. Numbers "3" and "5" indicate a fairly week feeling. Number "4" indicates you are undecided or do not understand the adjective pairs themselves. There are no right or wrong answer. *Only circle one number per line.*

1) Good	1	2	3	4	5	6	7	Bad
2) Wrong	1	2	3	4	5	6	7	Right
3) Harmful	1	2	3	4	5	6	7	Beneficial
4) Fair	1	2	3	4	5	6	7	Unfair
5) Wise	1	2	3	4	5	6	7	Foolish
6) Negative	1	2	3	4	5	6	7	Positive

Demographic Information

Biological sex: (circle one)   Male   Female

Political affiliation: (circle one)   Democrat   Republican   Other
Not Registered to Vote

Classification in school: (circle one)   Freshman   Sophomore   Junior
Senior   Graduate Student

How much time do you spend online every week: (circle one)

0–½ hour	½–1 hour	1–2 hours	2–5 hours
5–10 hours	10–15 hours	15–20 hours	25+ hours

Age: _____

Case Study: McCroskey, Richmond, and Johnson (2003)

Introduction

The evolution of measures of nonverbal immediacy was primarily within instructional communication research. In addition to the validity problems with these measures, there also has been a reliability problem. Both the 14- and 10-item NIM have provided a wide variety of reliability estimates—ranging from 0.67 to 0.89 (Hess & Smythe, 2001; McCroskey et al., 1995) with most of the estimates in the middle of this range, so the alpha reliabilities range from minimally acceptable (0.67) to good (0.89). An instrument developed by Burgoon, Buller, Hale, and deTurck (1984) produced similar reliability estimates (0.76), which is considered respectable. A self-report of immediacy developed by Richmond and McCroskey (2000a) has estimates that are considered good, 0.81, in three studies. However, the reliability for a version of this scale designed to be an other-report of immediacy (in this study, supervisors) generated a 0.87 reliability estimate, which is also good.

Even though numerous studies have shown nonverbal immediacy measures to be substantially correlated with a variety of outcome variables, the reliability issue is still important. In Chapter 10 we indicated that alpha reliabilities above 0.80 were considered good, and alpha reliabilities between 0.70 and .79 were considered respectable. However, generally speaking, researchers should avoid having scales with reliability coefficients less than 0.70 because low reliabilities negatively impact a measure's validity. Simply put, there is room for improvement. Given the inconsistent reliability estimates for nonverbal immediacy measures, it is likely that the degree of association of nonverbal immediacy with these other variables has been underestimated. As a consequence, the current study was designed to produce more reliable instruments which can be used in communication research to measure either self-reported nonverbal immediacy or other-reported nonverbal immediacy. If we were to fail in this endeavor, we hoped that we would at least be able to determine the source(s) of unreliability affecting nonverbal immediacy measures.

Participants were undergraduate students enrolled in mass lecture introductory courses in communication at a large mid-Atlantic university. The data were collected during the first week of classes to avoid the possibility that the participants' responses on the questionnaires would be influenced by content in the course. A total of 656 instruments were completed by males (53%) and 585 were completed by females (47%). The classes in which the participants were enrolled draw students from all colleges and departments in the university that enroll undergraduates. Although we did not collect direct reports concerning race or ethnicity from the participants, based on the enrollment data for the courses, they were predominately Caucasian (>95%), with the remainder being highly diverse. This is consistent with the overall enrollment in the university.

Nonverbal Immediacy Instrument

Since the purpose of this research was to develop a measure that could be employed either as a self-report or as an other-report, some items for the instrument were drawn from previously used measures of both types. These items were drawn primarily from instruments developed or revised by Andersen (1978, 1979), McCroskey, Richmond, Sallinen, Fayer, and Barraclough (1995), Richmond, Gorham, and McCroskey (1987), and Richmond and McCroskey (2000). Some additional items were generated by the researchers to balance the positively worded items (where agreement would indicate high immediacy) with negatively worded items (where agreement would indicate low immediacy).

A total of 26 items (13 positively worded, 13 negatively worded) were chosen to constitute the research instrument. These items are presented in Figure C.1 as a self-report of nonverbal immediacy and in Figure C.2 as an other-report of nonverbal immediacy.

The only differences between the two versions of the instrument are the designation of the target to be addressed (applies "to you" for self-report, applies to [a designated target] for other-report) and the wording of the items ("I use my hands . . ." for self-report, "He/She uses her/his hands . . ." for other-report).

The items were presented with a 5-point Likert-type response format (noted in Figures C.1 and C.2). Scores on the 13 negatively worded items were reflected prior to data analyses. These are items 3, 4, 5, 7, 8, 9, 11, 18, 20, 23, 24, 25, and 26.

Validation Instruments

Although additional validity tests for these instruments will come as a function of future research, two simple instruments were developed as a preliminary test of predictive validity. Since immediate communicators are often described as "warm" and "approachable," two-item instruments were developed for initial validity tests of the scales as predictors of warmth and approachability.

The items chosen for the measure of warmth were (in the form for other-perceived immediacy): He/She is a "warm" person when talking; He/She is a "cold" person when talking. The items chosen to measure approachability were (in the form for the self-report of immediacy): I am approachable; I am not approachable. The same type of response pattern used for the immediacy scale was employed for these measures. Again, the scoring of the negatively worded items was reflected prior to data analyses. Obtained alpha reliability for the warmth instrument was estimated at 0.65. For the approachability instrument the alpha estimate was 0.66. These were deemed less than fully satisfactory for an initial predictive validity test. Consequently, scores on these two instruments were added together to form a four-item measure of "warmth and approachability." This appeared justified by the substantial intercorrelations of the four items involved. The obtained alpha reliability for this combined instrument was 0.80. This was considered satisfactory for the initial predictive validity test.

DIRECTIONS: The following statements describe the ways some people behave while talking with or to others. Please indicate in the space at the left of each item the degree to which you believe the statement applies to yourself. Please use the following 5-point scale:

1 = Never; 2 = Rarely; 3 = Occasionally; 4 = Often; 5 = Very Often

_____1. I use my hands and arms to gesture while talking to people.
_____2. I touch others on the shoulder or arm while talking to them.
_____3. I use a monotone or dull voice while talking to people.
_____4. I look over or away from others while talking to them.
_____5. I move away from others when they touch her or him while talking.
_____6. I have a relaxed body position when talking to people.
_____7. I frown while talking to people.
_____8. I avoid eye contact while talking to people.
_____9. I have a tense body position while talking to people.
_____10. I sit close or stand close to people while talking with them.
_____11. My voice is monotonous or dull when talking to people.
_____12. I use a variety of vocal expressions when talking to people.
_____13. I gesture when talking to people.
_____14. I am animated when talking to people.
_____15. I have a bland facial expression when talking to people.
_____16. I move closer to people when talking to them.
_____17. I look directly at people while talking to them.
_____18. I am stiff when talking to people.
_____19. I have a lot of vocal variety when talking to people.
_____20. I avoid gesturing while talking to people.
_____21. I lean toward people when talking to them.
_____22. I maintain eye contact with people when talking to them.
_____23. I try not to sit or stand close to people when talking with them.
_____24. I lean away from people when talking to them.
_____25. I smile when talking to people.
_____26. I avoid touching people when talking to them.

SCORING: To compute your scores follow the instructions below:

1. Nonverbal Immediacy Scale – Self Report (NIS-S)
    Step One: Add scores for items 1, 2, 6, 10, 12, 13, 14, 16, 17, 19, 21, 22, and 25.
    Step Two: Add scores for items 3, 4, 5, 7, 8, 9, 11, 15, 18, 20, 23, 24, and 26.
    Step Three: Add 78 to Step One.
    Step Four: Subtract the score for Step Two from the score for Step Three.

Figure C.1 Nonverbal Immediacy Scale–Self Report (NIS-S)

Instruments were prepared to be either a self-report measure or an other-report measure. The target individual was varied across three types—teacher, supervisor, and date. These were chosen to represent the school environment, the work environment, and the social environment. These were believed to be a good cross section of the communication contexts the participants encounter. For the teacher condition, the participants were asked to respond to "the teacher you have in the class just before the one you are in." This is the most common method of assuring a broadly representative sample of teachers in instructional research. For the supervisor condition, the participants were asked to respond to "the supervisor you have in your current job, or had in your most recent job." Since the participants were all students and some were not employed while attending school, the latter portion of the instructions directed

DIRECTIONS: The following statements describe the ways some people behave while talking with or to others. Please indicate in the space at the left of each item the degree to which you believe the statement applies to (**fill in the target person's name or description**). Please use the following 5-point scale:

1 = Never; 2 = Rarely; 3 = Occasionally; 4 = Often; 5 = Very Often

_____1. He/She uses her or his hands and arms to gesture while talking to people.
_____2. He/She touches others on the shoulder or arm while talking to them.
_____3. He/She uses a monotone or dull voice while talking to people.
_____4. He/She looks over or away from others while talking to them.
_____5. He/She moves away from others when they touch her or him while talking.
_____6. He/She has a relaxed body position when talking to people.
_____7. He/She frowns while talking to people.
_____8. He/She avoids eye contact while talking to people.
_____9. He/She has a tense body position while talking to people.
_____10. He/She sits close or stands close to people while talking with them.
_____11. He/She's voice is monotonous or dull when talking to people.
_____12. He/She uses a variety of vocal expressions when talking to people.
_____13. He/She gestures when talking to people.
_____14. He/She is animated when talking to people.
_____15. He/She has a bland facial expression when talking to people.
_____16. He/She moves closer to people when talking to them.
_____17. He/She looks directly at people while talking to them.
_____18. He/She is stiff when talking to people.
_____19. He/She has a lot of vocal variety when talking to people.
_____20. He/She avoids gesturing while talking to people.
_____21. He/She leans toward people when talking to them.
_____22. He/She maintains eye contact with people when talking to them.
_____23. He/She tries not to sit or stand close to people when talking with them.
_____24. He/She leans away from people when talking to them.
_____25. He/She smiles when talking to people.
_____26. He/She avoids touching people when talking to them.

SCORING: To compute your scores follow the instructions below:

1.   Nonverbal Immediacy Scale–Other Report (NIS-O)
      Step One: Add scores for items 1, 2, 6, 10, 12, 13, 14, 16, 17, 19, 21, 22, and 25.
      Step Two: Add scores for items 3, 4, 5, 7, 8, 9, 11, 15, 18, 20, 23, 24, and 26.
      Step Three: Add 78 to Step One.
      Step Four: Subtract the score for Step Two from the score for Step Three.

Figure C.2 Nonverbal Immediacy Scale–Other Report (NIS-O)

them to a recent job. For the date condition, the participants were asked to respond to the person "you most recently dated, but are *not* dating now." A previous dating partner was chosen over a current one because the researchers believed that responses to this target would be less skewed than might be the case if participants were responding to a current significant other.

Instruments were distributed so that there would be as close as possible to an equal number of participants in each target condition and assure that there were at least 300 participants in each condition as recommended by Hatcher (1994). This resulted in 311 participants in the self-report condition, 310 in the teacher condition, 311 in the supervisor condition, and 309 in the date condition.

Data Analyses

All data analyses employed the appropriate SAS statistical software. The first set of analyses involved a series of principal components factor analyses (for an explanation of what a factor analysis is, please read the section on factor analysis in Chapter 21). Both unrotated factor loadings and loadings for two factors employing oblique (Promax) rotation were examined. Since our intent was to generate a single-dimensional scale, the unrotated factor loadings provided the first test of dimensionality. The second test of dimensionality was the rotated factor loadings and the relationship between the two factors obtained.

Once a scale was identified, the means, standard deviations, and score ranges for all measures were computed. In addition, possible sex effects were examined and tests of the significance of those effects was obtained through analyses of variance.

The third set of analyses focused on alpha reliabilities of the instrument in each of the conditions studied and the overall data set. In conjunction with these analyses, the SAS software employed automatically provided information that we could use to determine whether eliminating any item from the measure would result in increased reliability estimates. We also were provided information so that we could determine the level of association of each item on the scale with the total score of the scale.

The final data analyses focused on the predictive validity of the instrument. Correlations between scores on the research instrument and the criterion scale scores were obtained for each condition in the study and the overall data set.

Factor Analyses

The first data analysis focused on factor analyses. A separate factor analysis was conducted for each data set (self, teacher, supervisor, date) and the combined data set (including all four subsets). Kaiser's Measure of Sampling Adequacy (MSA) was calculated for each data set. The results indicate that all samples were adequate for analysis: overall data set, MSA = 0.93; self MSA = 0.86; teacher MSA = 0.91; supervisor MSA = 0.92; date MSA = 0.91.

Our first step in interpreting the factor analysis results was to examine the loadings of the items on the first factor in the unrotated factor pattern matrix. Using the criterion suggest by Hatcher (1994), we judged any item with a loading of at least 0.40 on the initial factor (and no other loading > 0.39) to be loaded on the first factor. When factoring a truly single-factor scale, if an item does not meet this criterion, it suggests either that a nonloading item represents another factor or that the item may simply not be a good item for measuring the intended construct. For the self, supervisor, and date data sets, all 26 items had a loading greater than 0.40 and no other loading that high. For the teacher and overall data sets, 24 items had a loading greater than 0.40 and no other loading that high. The remaining two items in both data sets had their highest loadings on the first factor and no other loading higher than that, but the loadings on the first factor were less than 0.40.

Since only two items out of 130 did not meet the test for loading on the first factor, the possibility that this observation was chance is high. However, they examined the two non-conforming items and found that both dealt with touch. We also examined the mean of each of these items in the teacher data set in comparison with other items in that data set and the touch means for the same items in the other data subsets. We determined that in the teacher data set, these two touch items had the lowest means of all the items on the measure. It was also observed that the means for these two items were much lower in the teacher data set than in the other subsets.

Items related to touch were present in the early measures of nonverbal immediacy of teachers (Andersen, 1978, 1979; Richmond, Gorham, & McCroskey, 1987). However, in measures developed later (which included efforts to produce shorter instruments) these items do not appear (McCroskey, Richmond, Sallinen, Fayer, & Barraclough, 1995). While teachers in early elementary schools frequently touch their students, it has been observed in studies involving college instructors that they are much less likely to do so for a variety of reasons (Richmond, Gorham, & McCroskey, 1987). We decided to retain these items in the scale since (as noted below) it was demonstrated that these items did not harm the reliability of the scale. However, they do enhance the content validity of the scale. From the earliest research with nonverbal immediacy in instruction, touch has been seen as a central element in nonverbal immediacy (Andersen, 1978). We believe that the reason these two items were weak in the teacher context is that the participants in this study were all college students. The fact that these participants reported that their teachers engaged in very few touching behaviors suggests the data from these items provided a restricted range, which very likely reduced the correlations between these items and the remaining items in the scale which did not have a restricted range. As a result, the obtained correlations between these items and the remainder of the items would not appear as equally strongly associated with the overall construct being measured.

Our second test of the dimensionality of the scale involved submitting the overall data set to factor analysis with oblique rotation. We first examined eigenvalues for all dimensions reported (scree test). It appeared that two factors might exist, but definitely no more than that. Hence, we examined results from the two-factor, oblique rotation. The correlation between the factors obtained was −0.61, with indicates a strong correlation between the factors. An examination of the items loading on the different factors indicates that one factor included positively worded items while the other included negatively worded items. We conducted similar analyses for each of the subsets and found essentially the same results, with only minor variation in the correlations between factors. These consistent results clearly indicated that the single-factor solution we obtained initially was the best interpretation of the data.

The outcomes of this research were the Nonverbal Immediacy Scale–Self (NIS-S) and the Nonverbal Immediacy Scale–Other (NIS-O). These instruments are presented in Figures C.1 and C.2.

The third set of data analyses focused on alpha reliability estimates. The reliability estimates for all of the data sets were at or above 0.90. The alpha analyses also indicated that in every data set every item was positively correlated with the total scores for both measures.

The final data analysis centered on obtaining predictive validity estimates for the nonverbal immediacy scale from each data set. The measure of warmth/approachability served as the criterion variable. The raw validity correlations ranged from 0.58 to 0.82. The disattenuated validity correlations ranged from 0.74 to 0.95. The observed estimate for the self-report data set was lower than the other estimates, but all of the predictive validity estimates were substantial. The lower reliability of the warmth/approachability measure in this condition is seen as the most likely reason for this deviation.

Discussion

The primary goal of this research was to develop a measure of nonverbal immediacy which could be used as a self-report or an observer report in a variety of communication contexts (instructional, organizational, interpersonal, etc.) with high reliability and validity. This goal was achieved.

A set of 26 items drawn from previous research was the basis for this new instrument. The scale items are balanced in terms of positively and negatively worded items. The factor analyses indicate that all of the items could be retained in the instrument for the self-report version and for the other-report across a variety to communication contexts.

It was determined that the reliability estimates for both versions of this instrument were 0.90 or above. This is substantially superior to previous nonverbal immediacy instruments used in communication research. The content validity of the instrument is very strong because it includes 13 different nonverbal components, with two items for each component. On its face, then, this instrument appears to represent the components of nonverbal immediacy considered by researchers and authors to be the essential components. The study also provided a preliminary indication of the predictive validity of both versions of the instrument. The validity estimates for the total sample, and for the four subsets of the data, ranged from moderate to very high. Use of the instrument in future research should provide additional indications of the instrument's validity. At this point, it appears that the scale is both reliable and valid.

REFERENCES

Andersen, J. F. (1978). *The relationship between teacher immediacy and teaching effectiveness.* Unpublished doctoral dissertation. Morgantown, WV: West Virginia University.

Andersen, J. F. (1979). Teacher immediacy as a mediator of teaching effectiveness. In D. Nimmo (Ed.), *Communication yearbook 3* (pp. 543–559). New Brunswick, NJ: Transaction Books.

Burgoon, J. K., Buller, D. B., Hale, J. L., & deTurck, M. A. (1984). Relational messages associated with nonverbal behaviors. *Human Communication Research, 10,* 351–378.

DeVellis, R. F. (1991) *Scale development: Theory and applications* (Applied Social Research Methods Series, volume 26). Newbury Park, CA: Sage.

Fowler, F. J., Jr. (1993). *Survey research methods* (2nd ed.) (Applied Social Research Methods Series, volume 1). Newbury Park, CA: Sage.

Gorham, J. S. (1988). The relationship between verbal teacher immediacy behaviors and student learning. *Communication Education, 37,* 40–53.

Hatcher, L. (1994). *A step-by-step approach to using the SAS system for factor analysis and structural equation modeling.* Cary, NC: SAS Institute.

Hess, J. A., Smythe, M. J., & Communication 451 (2001). Is teacher immediacy actually related to student cognitive learning? *Communication Studies, 52,* 197–219.

Levine, T. R., & McCroskey, J. C. (1990). Measuring trait communication apprehension: A test of rival measurement models of the PRCA-24. *Communication Monographs, 57,* 62–72.

McCroskey, J. C., & Richmond, V. P. (1992). Increasing teacher influence through immediacy. In V. P. Richmond & J. C. McCroskey (Eds.), *Power in the classroom: Communication, control, and concern* (pp. 101–119). Hillsdale, NJ: Lawrence Erlbaum.

McCroskey, J. C., & Richmond, V. P. (1996). *Fundamentals of human communication: An interpersonal perspective.* Prospect Heights, IL: Waveland.

McCroskey, J. C., Richmond, V. P., Sallinen, A., Fayer, J. M., & Barraclough, R. A. (1995). A cross-cultural and multi-behavioral analysis of the relationship between nonverbal immediacy and teacher evaluation. *Communication Education, 44,* 281–291.

Mehrabian, A. (1966). Immediacy: An indicator of attitudes in linguistic communication. *Journal of Personality, 34,* 26–34.

Mehrabian, A. (1971). *Silent messages.* Belmont, CA: Wadsworth.

Mehrabian, A. (1981). *Silent messages: Implicit communication of emotions and attitudes* (2nd. ed.). Belmont, CA: Wadsworth.

Richmond, V. P., Gorham, J. S., & McCroskey, J. C. (1987). The relationship between selected immediacy behaviors and cognitive learning. In M. A. McLaughlin (Ed.), *Communication yearbook 10* (pp. 574–590). Newbury Park, CA: Sage.

Richmond, V. P., & McCroskey, J. C. (2000a). *Nonverbal behavior in human relations* (4th ed.). Needham Heights, MA: Allyn & Bacon.

Richmond, V. P., & McCroskey, J. C. (2000b). The impact of supervisor and subordinate immediacy on relational and organizational outcomes. *Communication Monographs, 67,* 85–95.

Richmond, V. P., McCroskey, J. C., & Johnson, A. D. (2003). Development of the nonverbal immediacy scale (NIS): Measures of self- and other-perceived nonverbal immediacy. *Communication Quarterly, 51,* 504–517.

Robinson, R. Y., & Richmond, V. P. (1995). Validity of the verbal immediacy scale. *Communication Research Reports, 12,* 80–84.

Rocca, K. A., & McCroskey, J. C. (1999). The interrelationship of student ratings of instructors' immediacy, verbal aggressiveness, homophily, and interpersonal attractions. *Communication Education, 48,* 303–316.

GLOSSARY

Abstract: Accurate, self-contained, concise description of a research study.

Abstract Variables: Variables that change or differ over time or across situations or contexts.

Academic Division/Interest Group: Group of people who study a specific area of communication (e.g., organizational, instructional, intercultural, mass mediated, etc.).

Accelerated Longitudinal Design: Form of survey design where a research creates mini-age cohorts and studies them over a short period of time to ascertain how changes would occur across age groups over a longer period of time.

Acquiescence: When an individual fakes responses in order to cooperate with the investigator and give the researcher what he or she wants.

Alternate Forms Reliability: Reliability test where two measures of the same phenomena are used to measure the same group at two different times.

Alternative Hypothesis (H_1): Prediction that there is a relationship or a difference that has not occurred by chance or random error.

American Psychological Association (APA) Style: Components or features of a research manuscript that dictate how the manuscript should be presented beyond the scope of actual content as dictated by the American Psychological Association's style manual.

Analysis of Covariance (ANCOVA): Statistical test that allows a researcher to determine if a difference lies between groups on a dependent variable after the dependent variable has been mathematically adjusted for differences associated with one or more covariates.

Analytical Survey: Type of survey that explains people's attitudes and behaviors by identifying likely causal influences.

Anonymity: When a researcher does not know who participated in a study or which results belong to which participants in a study.

Antecedent: (1) The "if" statement within a logical proof. (2) What happened earlier in time.

Antecedent Variable: Variable that occurs prior to the experiment that could impact the way an independent variable or dependent variable functions.

Apparatus: Any appliance or device used in the conducting of a study.

Appeal to Authority: When people explain a phenomenon by believing that an authority has made it occur.

Appeal to General Empirical Rules: Explaining phenomena through proven scientific facts.

Argument: Set of propositions in which one follows logically as a conclusion from the others.

Assertiveness: Capacity to make requests, actively disagree, express positive or negative personal rights and feelings, initiate, maintain, or disengage from conversations, and stand up for oneself without attacking another.

Attitude: Predisposition to respond to people, ideas, or objects in an evaluative way.

Attributes: Specific values of a variable.

Attrition: Number of participants who left a study since it began.

Audience-Specific Behavior: Behavior exhibited in front of one audience that does not occur in front of other audiences.

Author Search: Database search for author's name in the author field.

Authorship Credit: Ethical principal that states that all researchers involved in a project should receive acknowledgment for their work on a research project.

Axiom: Generally accepted principle or rule.

Baseline: Initial score on some variable of interest.

Belief: Perception of reality about whether something is true or false.

Belmont Report: The 1979 report by the National Commission for the Protection of Human Subjects of Biomedical and Behavioral Research that established three basic guidelines for working with human participants: consent, beneficence, and justice.

Beta (β) Weights (regression coefficients): Value in a multiple linear regression that helps explain the degree to which a dependent variable takes varying values and can be interpreted as correlations.

Bimodal: When two values larger than the other values in a data set occur at equal frequency within the data set.

Boolean Logic: Form of symbolic logic created by George Boole that is the basis for electronic search engine technology.

Calculated Value: End result after completion of a mathematical formula related to a specific statistical test.

Call for Papers: Posting requesting scholars to send in manuscripts for possible consideration for a conference/convention or for journal publication.

Causation: Ability to determine that an act or agency truly produces an effect.

Central Limits Theorem: Theoretical idea that the mean of the scores obtained from the probability sample will be equal to the mean of the scores obtained from the population.

Channel: Method used to send a message (verbal, nonverbal, or mediated).

Chi (χ)-Square: Statistical test that evaluates whether the proportions of individuals who fall into categories of two or more nominal variables are equal to hypothesized values.

Chronological Order: Organizing a literature review by historical progression in terms of time.

Citation: When an author gives credit to another individual's thoughts

Cluster Sample: Sample created by identifying naturally occurring clusters of people with a target variable in a target population, randomly selected to participate in a research project.

Coder: Person actively involved in the coding process.

Coding: Process a researcher goes through to group one's variable of interest in a consistent way.

Codebook: Book researcher creates to explain the operationalization in a very clear and succinct way.

Coding Form: Form that contains all of the information in the codebook in a simple check-off sheet to make it easier for coders to code information quickly.

Cognitive Knowledge: Degree to which someone has actually learned a specific concept or skill.

Cohen's d: Effect size test utilized in an independent samples t-test.

Cohen's Kappa (κ): Statistic used to calculate intercoder reliability for two coders where none of the data are missing.

Communication: Process whereby one person stimulates meaning in the mind of another person (or persons) through verbal and nonverbal messages.

Communication Apprehension: Fear or anxiety associated with either real or anticipated communication with another person or persons.

Communication Trait: Hypothetical construct which accounts for certain kinds of communication behaviors.

Communications: Array of mass-mediated technologies people utilize to send messages.

Compare-and-Contrast Order: Organizing a literature review to show how research studies are similar to and different from each other.

Conceptual Equivalence: Issue involved in translating surveys from one language to another concerned with whether the basic concept a researcher is attempting to study in one culture even exists within another culture.

Conceptualization: Development and clarification of concepts or your germinal idea.

Concrete Variables: Variables that are stable or consistent.

Concurrent Validity: Form of validity concerned with whether scores taken at the same time are related to each other.

Confederate: Individual who, without the participants' knowledge, is actually part of the experiment being conducted.

Confidence Interval: The degree to which a researcher is certain he or she will accept a true null hypothesis.

Confidence Level: Level of confidence that the results found within a study are generalizable to the population and not due to chance.

Confidentiality: The treatment of information an individual has disclosed in a relationship of trust with the expectation that it will not, without permission, be divulged to others in ways inconsistent with the understanding of the original disclosure.

Confounding Variables: Variables that obscure the effects of your independent variable.

Consequent: The "then" statement within a logical proof.

Construct Validity: Degree to which the survey measures an intended nonobservable trait, which is used to explain observable behavior.

Constructive Replication: When a researcher duplicates a previous study but uses entirely new instrumentation, experimental procedures, and sample and data analysis techniques.

Content Analysis: Summarizing, quantitative analysis of messages.

Control: Process where an individual both prevents personal biases from interfering with the research study and makes sure there are no other explanations for what is seen in the study.

Control Group: Group that the researcher measures without attempting to manipulate in any way.

Convenience Sample: When participants are selected nonrandomly based on availability.

Correlation (r): Statistical test that determines whether two variables are positively, negatively, or not related to each other.

Cramér's Phi (Φ): Effect size test utilized in a chi-square.

Criterion Validity: Form of validity concerned with how accurately a new measure can predict a well-accepted criterion or previously validated concept.

Critical Value: (1) Value of the random variable at the boundary for accepting or reject the null hypothesis. (2) Value that a calculated value must be greater than in order to achieve statistical significance at a calculated confidence level.

Cronbach's Alpha (α): Scale reliability test that determines how well a set of items measures a unidimensional hypothetical construct.

Cross-Sectional Survey Design: Type of survey design where a researcher receives information from a group of participants at a given point in time.

Culture Shock: State of disorientation and anxiety that affects an individual who is exposed to a new culture or co-culture.

Curvilinear Relationship: Relationship between two variables plotted along a curve instead of a straight line.

Data: Collected measures of independent and dependent variables that can be used for statistical calculations.

Data Falsification: Any time you manipulate or alter the data to achieve the results wanted by a researcher.

Data Sharing: Ethical principle by which researchers share their data with other researchers to help further science.

Debriefing: Period following an experiment when a researcher corrects any deception, reaffirms the value of the experiment, and determines if the answers were changed based on what the participant assumed was occurring.

Decoding: Process a receiver goes through to assign meaning to a source's message.

Define Terms or Give Examples: Use of preexisting synonyms, definitions, or easily understood examples to provide an understanding of a phenomena.

Degrees of Freedom: Number of participant scores in a sample that can or are free to vary.

Degrees of Freedom Between: In a one-way ANOVA, number of participant scores in a sample that can or are free to vary between multiple groups.

Degrees of Freedom Within: In a one-way ANOVA, number of participant scores in a sample that can or are free to vary within a single group.

Deidentifying Data: Making sure the data cannot be linked back to the participants themselves.

Dependent Variable: Measured variable in a study whose changes are determined by changes in one or more independent variables.

Descriptive Statistics: Statistical tests used to describe the shape of a dataset.

Descriptive Survey: Type of survey designed to find out how common a phenomenon is within a given group of people.

Differences of Degree: When scores from two or more groups significantly differ from each other.

Differences in Kind: Differences that occur when two or more groups do different things associated with their groups.

Diminished Autonomy: When possible participants do not have the ability to intellectually discern for themselves whether participation in a research endeavor is ok.

Directional Research Question: When a researcher asks if there is either a positive or negative relationship or a specific significant difference between two or more variables.

Discussion Section: Section of a research manuscript that appears after the results section to provide an interpretation of the findings, acknowledge limitations, and propose future research.

Dunn-Sidak Test: Statistical test that readjusts the probability level to correct for possible compounded error due to multiple pairwise comparisons to help prevent Type I error.

Duplicate Data Publication: Publishing the same set of data in two different research publications.

Effect Size: Strength of a relationship or the magnitude of difference occurring between two variables or the degree to which a null hypothesis is false.

Electronic Database: Computerized system for searching and retrieving information.

Empathy: Capacity of an individual to put himself or herself into the shoes of another, to see things from the other person's vantage point.

Empiricism: Belief that science is only acceptable insofar as the phenomena in question can be "sensed" by average people.

Empirical Generalization: Attempt to describe a phenomenon based on what we know about it at this time.

Encoding: Process of creating messages we believe represent the meaning to be communicated and are likely to stimulate similar meaning in the mind of a receiver.

Ends: Outcomes that one desires to achieve.

Epistemology: Way of knowing.

Ethical Behavior: When a researcher uses positive means to achieve a positive end.

Ethics: Study of means and ends.

Ethnocentrism: View of one's culture as the center of the universe.

Evoke Empathy: Showing that a phenomenon had good, just, or moral reasons.

Experiment: When a researcher purposefully manipulates one or more variables (independent variables, or IVs) in the hope of seeing how this manipulation effects change or lack of change of other variables of interest (dependent variables, or DVs).

Experimental Group(s): Group(s) that a researcher attempts to manipulate in some clear way.

Experimenter Effects: Effects caused unknowingly by the experimenter on the participants.

Explanation: Attempt to satisfy one's curiosity about an observable event.

Eta-Square (η^2): Effect size test utilized in a one-way analysis of variance.

F-Test: Any statistical test that determines if two population variances area equal.

Face (Content) Validity: Form of validity where a researcher determines if the measure determines the appropriate construct by examining the specific questions.

Factor Analysis: A statistical device that enables researchers to determine if the responses on a set of scale items actually measure a single construct or multiple constructs.

Factorial Analysis of Variance: Statistical test where a researcher has multiple nominal independent variables and one interval/ratio dependent variable.

Factorial Experimental Design: Experimental design that utilizes two or more independent variables.

Faking Responses: Any circumstance in which a respondent to our instrument deliberately attempts to alter the results in some specific way.

Feedback: Response the receiver gives the source.

Fisher's Least Significant Difference (LSD): Post hoc test that is the equivalent of running a series of paired t-tests, but for which the alpha level is not controlled, so the chance of compounded error is great.

Future Directions: Subsection of the discussion section in which an author discusses where he or she thinks the research should continue.

General Linear Model (GLM): Linear model ($Y = mX + b$) where each object can have multiple measurements. The GLM underlies many different statistical tests, including one-way analysis of variance and regression.

General-to-Specific Order: Organizing a literature review to examine broad-based research first and then focus on specific studies that relate to the topic.

Generalizability: Notion that the results found from studying a sample can be assumed to be true of the entire population.

Germinal Idea: Spark that causes an individual to realize that something new can be researched or measured.

Hasty Generalization: Generalizing about something when not enough evidence is available to do so.

Hawthorne Effect: Effect caused when study participants know they are being observed.

Historical Flaw: Threat to a study's external validity that occurs because a historical event has caused a sample to change in a way that is not measurable.

Hoyt Analysis of Variance Reliability: Test statistic computed during a split-half reliability test.

Humanism: Belief in universal human qualities such as rationality, common history, experience, and belief.

Humor Assessment: Mental measure created by Wrench and Richmond (2004) to measure an individual's use of humor in interpersonal interactions.

Hypothesis: Tentative statement about the relationship between independent and dependent variables.

Hypothesis Testing: Process a researcher goes through using inferential statistics to determine whether or not we reject or accept the null hypothesis.

Illustration: Generalizable stories that can be applied to a variety of different contexts.

Independent Variable: (1) Variable whose numeric value determines the value of other variables. (2) Part of the research experiment that IS manipulated or changed.

Independent Variable Manipulation: When a researcher purposefully changes a variable to see how the effects of this change will affect other variables.

Inferential Statistics: Statistical tests that allow researchers to make inferences about some unknown aspect of a population from a sample.

Informed Consent: A person's voluntary agreement, based upon adequate knowledge and understanding of relevant information, to participate in research.

Institutional Review Board: Panel of people at institutions that receive federal funds established by Title 45, Code of Federal Regulations, Part 46 (45 CFR 46), which reviews all research proposals for possible risks to research participants and to make sure that all research participants are informed of their rights as research participants.

Instrumental Replication: When a researcher duplicates a previous study by measuring the dependent variable in the same way as the first study, but changes the independent variable to see if a different operationalization of the experimental procedures will give the same results.

Interaction Effect: Statistical difference test in a factorial ANOVA where differences on a dependent variable are examined by analyzing the combinations of the independent variables.

Intercoder Reliability: Test to determine if multiple coders are coding pieces of data in a stable, consistent fashion (most commonly reported as Cohen's kappa or Krippendorff's alpha).

Interval Variable: Variable where the values of the categories are classified in a logical order that represents equal distances between levels within each category.

Intervening Variable: Variable that intervenes between the independent variable and the dependent variable.

Interview Schedule: List of survey questions an interviewer asks an interviewee when conducting an oral survey.

Introduction: The first portion of a paper that contains an attention-getter, a link to the topic, the significance of the topic, an espousal of the credibility of the writer, a thesis statement, and a preview of the main points of the paper.

Isomorphism: Identity or similarity of form.

Known-to-Unknown Order: Organizing a literature review to examine current literature about the problem and then identify at the end what still is not known.

Kurtosis: The degree of peakedness of a distribution of scores.

Label the Phenomenon: Giving the phenomenon a name.

Language: A system of symbols or codes that represent certain ideas or meanings.

Latent/Hypothetical Variable: Variable that a researcher cannot directly observe, but can be inferred from other variables that are observable and measured directly.

Law of Parsimony: Law of science that states that scientists should look for the simplest assumption in the formulation of a theory and the simplest test to interpret data.

Likert Scale: Scale where participants are presented with a declarative statement and then asked to respond statements with a range of possible choices: strong disagree, disagree, neither agree or disagree, agree, or strong agree.

Limitations: Subsection in a manuscript's discussion section that highlights the weaknesses of the study including inappropriateness in the design, population, methods, or instrumentation.

Literal Replication: When a researcher duplicates a previous study keeping the instrumentation, experimental procedures, and sample as similar as possible.

Literature Reviews: Selection of available documents (published and unpublished) on a given topic that contain information, opinions, data, and evidence written from a particular point of that aid in a reader's understanding of pertinent literature prior to examining the results and discussion in a research study.

Longitudinal Survey Design: Type of survey design in which a researcher gathers information from a group of participants multiple times over a period of time.

Lurker Variable: Variable that explains both the independent variable and the dependent variable.

Machiavellian Ethic: When a researcher uses bad means to achieve a good end.

Main Effects: Statistical difference test in a factorial ANOVA where differences on a dependent variable are examined for each independent variable separately.

Major Premise: Premise of a syllogism that contains the major term (which is the predicate of the conclusion).

Manipulation Check: Procedure where a researcher inserts a quantitative measurement into a study to determine whether or not different conditions perceive the independent variable different.

Manipulation of an Independent Variable: Process a researcher goes through to purposefully alter or change an independent variable (IV) to see if this alteration in the IV has an effect on the dependent variable (DV) during an experiment.

Maturation: Threat to validity that occurs because it is possible that a portion of the estimated change is not as a result of IV manipulations, but as a result of the passage of time between the first measure of a DV to follow-up measures of the DV.

Mean: Sum of all of the scores in a sample divided by the number of scores in the sample.

Mean Squares Between: In a one-way ANOVA, the value calculated by dividing the between sum of squares by the between degrees of freedom.

Mean Squares Within: In a one-way ANOVA, the value calculated by dividing the within sum of squares by the within degrees of freedom.

Means: Tools or behaviors that one employs to achieve a desired outcome.

Measurement: Process of systematic observation and assignment of numbers to objects or events according to rules.

Measures of Central Tendency: Statistics that help describe the center of a distribution of data (e.g., mean, median, and mode).

Median: Middle value in a list of data.

Mental Measure: Any tool used for the measurement of mental functions like attitudes, beliefs, cognitive knowledge, perceived knowledge, and personality/behavioral traits.

Message: Information the source is stimulating in the mind of the receiver.

Method Section: Section of a research manuscript that discusses participants, apparatuses, procedures, and instrumentation.

Minor Premise: Premise of a syllogism that contains the minor term (the subject of the conclusion).

Mode: Number(s) that occur most frequently within a data set.

Modified Direct Translation: Form of translation where a translator performs a simple direct translation, after which the translation is given to a panel of experts to decide whether or not the survey translation is appropriate.

Mono-operation Bias: Validity flaw related to the single use of an independent variable, cause, program, or treatment in a study.

Multivariate Analysis of Variance: Difference test that can utilize one or more nominal, independent variables and two or more related interval/ratio-dependent variables.

Multivariate Tests: Statistical tests with two or more related dependent variables.

Negative Relationship: When a decrease in one variable corresponds to an increase in the other variable, or vice versa.

Network Sample: Participants are asked to refer researchers to other people who could serve as participants.

Neutral Relationship: When the change of one variable does not correspond with a change in another variable.

Nominal Variable: Qualitative variable where categories are mutually exclusive, equivalent, and exhaustive where the categories are not numerically oriented.

Nondirectional Research Question: When a researcher asks if there is a relationship between two or more variables or a significant difference occurs between two or more variables.

Nonparametric: Statistical tests that are associated with categories and ordering; these are tests observed at the nominal/ordinal levels.

Nonresponse: When a sampled unit does not respond to the request to be surveyed (unit nonresponse) or to particular survey questions (item nonresponse).

Nonresponse Bias: Systematic distortion of a statistic as a result of unit and item nonresponse.

Nonverbal Immediacy: The perceived physical and/or psychological closeness a receiver feels exists between her- or himself and a source that occurs as a result of nonverbal behavior.

Nonverbal Messages: Any communicated messages other than verbal messages.

Normative Equivalence: Issue involved in translating surveys from language to another language concerned with whether norms or social conventions will influence participants' responses during a survey.

Null Hypothesis (H_0): Hypothesis that predicts that groups will not vary on a dependent variable or that there is not a relationship between two variables.

Objective: The desire to create knowledge by examining facts through the scientific method without distorting one's findings through personal feelings, prejudices, and interpretations.

One-Tailed Hypothesis: Hypothesis that predicts the specific nature of the relationship or difference.

One-Way Analysis of Variance: Statistical test that evaluates whether there is a difference between two or more groups on a dependent variable.

Operationalization: Detailed description of the research operations or procedures necessary to assign units of analysis to the categories of a variable in order to represent conceptual properties.

Operational Replication: When a researcher duplicates a pervious study keeping the experimental procedures and sample as similar as possible, but changes the instrumentation.

Ordinal Variable: Qualitative variable where categories are mutually exclusive, equivalent, exhaustive where the categories represent clear numerical gradients, which allows for the rank ordering of the categories.

Outlier: A data point that is far away from the other data points.

Paper Presentation: Oral report about the research project typically followed by a response from a scholar who has conducted research in the area.

Pancultural: When something is the same across all cultures.

Panel Design: Type of longitudinal survey design used to examine participants who agree to be surveyed periodically over a given period of time.

Panel Discussion: Form of conference presentation where three or more individuals discuss a common topic in an informal format.

Parallel Blind Technique: Form of translation where two translators perform a simple direct translation on the same survey and then compare their translations.

Parameter: A value of a population.

Parametric: Statistical tests assume that the level of measurement that was employed in obtaining the data was at the interval/ratio level.

Paraphrasing: Including another author's ideas in your own words; involves summarizing or highlighting one or two important points.

Parenthetical Citation: Citation used within the text body of a manuscript that enables a reader to know where the information is being taken from—also referred to as internal citations.

Path Analysis: Extension of general linear model used to test the fit two or more causal models.

Peer Review: Process whereby an individual's scholarly work is critiqued by people who also conduct research in a specific area to make sure the new scholarly work is of a quality worthy of publication.

Perceived Knowledge: Degree to which someone believes that he or she has learned a specific concept or skill.

Personality: Total psychological makeup of an individual, which is a reflection of her or his experiences, motivations, attitudes, beliefs, values, and behaviors, derived from the interaction of these elements with the environment external to the individual.

Physical Sciences: Study of the objective aspects of nature.

Pilot Test: Small-scale study a researcher conducts to test the effectiveness of a survey or research procedures.

Plagiarism: Any time a writer does not properly cite or give credit to source wherefrom he or she is getting information.

Population: An entire set of objects, observations, or scores that have some characteristic in common.

Positive Relationship: When an increase in one variable corresponds to an increase in another variable, or a decrease in a variable corresponds to a decrease in another variable.

Poster Presentation: Visual report about the research project where people mingle around and ask questions about research projects that interest them.

Post Hoc Hypothesis Revision: The revision of hypotheses once an individual receives her or his results.

Power: Degree to which a researcher is certain he or she can reject a false null hypothesis.

Predictive (Prospective) Validity: Form of validity concerned with whether or not a person's score on a new measure can be used to predict future scores on another measure.

Prejudice: A priori judgments based on stereotypes.

Preview: Point in the introduction where a writer lists the specific sections that he or she is planning to cover in the main body of the literature review.

Primary Source: An original document that examines a phenomenon (e.g., poems, diaries, court records, and interviews to research results generated by experiments, surveys, ethnographies).

Principle of Beneficence: Researchers need to make sure that during the research process they maximize possible benefits and minimize possible harms to the research participants themselves.

Privacy: The individual control over the extent, timing, and circumstances of sharing oneself (physically, behaviorally, or intellectually) with others.

Probability: Relative frequency with which a phenomenon is likely to occur.

Probability Level: One minus the percentile confidence level.

Probability Sampling: Randomly selecting participants from a population of interest so all potential participants have an equal chance of being selected for the sample.

Probability Theory: The score that occurs most frequently in the sample will also be the score that should occur most frequently in the population.

Probability Value (p-value): Probability of obtaining a result at least as extreme as that calculated, which assumes that the null hypothesis is true (result occurred by chance).

Problem–Cause–Solution order: Organizing a literature review so that it moves from the problem to the solution.

Procedures: The sequence of actions or instructions a researcher follows while conducting a study.

Proposition: A statement that either confirms something or denies something.

Protected Health Information (PHI): Any individually identifiable health information (e.g., demographic data and biological specimens) transmitted or maintained by a covered entity.

Purposive Sample: Participants are nonrandomly picked to be in a study because of a specific characteristic the researcher is investigating.

Quasi-Experimental Design: Looks like an experimental design but likes randomization.

Questionnaire: A form containing a series of questions and mental measures given to a group of people in an attempt to gain statistical information about the group as part of a survey.

Quota Sample: Participants are separated into strata and then nonrandomly selected for participation in the study.

R-Squared (R^2): Indicates what proportion of the variability in a dependent variable can be predicted by its relationship with an independent variable(s).

Quotation: Exact use of another author's words in your writing.

Random Assignment: Procedures experimenters use for placing participants into a research condition that ensures that every participant in the sample has an equal chance of being in a research condition.

Random Probe Translation: Form of translation where a translator performs a simple direct translation and then the researcher pilot-tests the translation with a group of bilingual participants to determine if researcher's own understanding of the mental measure and that of the participants is the same.

Range: Distance between the largest value and the smallest value in the data set.

Rationale: Section of a research manuscript that explains the fundamental reasons for the hypotheses and research questions posed in the study.

Ratio Variable: Variable where the values of the categories are classified in a logical order that represents equal distances between levels within each category with the presence of an absolute zero point.

Receiver: Person who interprets a message (decoder).

Regression: Statistical test that examines whether an independent variable can linearly account for any of the variance in a dependent variable.

Regression to the Mean: The tendency for extreme scorers on one measurement to move (regress) closer to the mean on a later measurement causing a change that would normally not happen in the population.

Reinforcer Variables: Variables that enhance the effect of the independent variable on the dependent variable.

Relationship: Correspondence between two variables.

Reliability: Accuracy that a measure has, or producing stable, consistent measurements.

Repeated Measures ANOVA: Statistical test that allows a researcher to determine if differences in the same interval/ratio variable occur over three or more measurements of the variable.

Replication: Conducting more research on a specific topic to determine if original results occurred by error or remain consistent.

Research: Investigation or experimentation aimed at the discovery and interpretation of facts, revision of accepted theories or laws, and/or practical application of new or revised theories or laws.

Research Implications: Subsection in discussion section where an author indicates what her or his findings mean for the larger community of scholars' understanding of the topic.

Research Participant: A living individual about whom a researcher obtains either: (1) data through intervention or interaction with the individual; or (2) identifiable private information.

Research Question: Explicit question researchers ask about variables of interest.

Response Rate: Percentage of surveys returned compared to the percentage of surveys distributed.

Response Set: Any tendency that causes a person to give different responses to test items than hc or he would if the item were presented in a different form

Responsiveness: Capacity to be sensitive to the communication of others, to be a good listener, to make others comfortable in communicating, and to recognize the needs and desires of others.

Results Section: Section of a research manuscript where a researcher presents her or his empirical findings.

Retrospective Validity: Form of validity where a research attempts to relate a previously taken measure of a phenomenon with a newly designed measure of a phenomenon.

Rhetorical Question: Type of question that asks a listener to think about the question without audibly responding to it.

Sample: People or units that a researcher includes in the study.

Sampling: Selecting people or units for inclusion in a research study.

Sampling Bias: Systematic differences between the population and the sample that result from failing to draw representative cases.

Sampling Error: Degree to which a sample differs with respect to a specific variable from a population.

Sampling Frame: All members of the population accessible to the researcher.

Scalogram: Type of research scale that consists of a set of unidimensional items designed to measure an attitude or opinion where agreement with one item implies agreement with the preceding, less extreme items.

Scheffé: Post hoc test that assumes you wish to test all possible pairs and all possible combinations of means.

Science: The study of natural phenomena through quantitative observation, theoretical explanation, and experimentation.

Scientific Method: Empirical process where a researcher attempts to understand a phenomenon by using existing theories to make predictions, empirically observe the phenomenon based on the predictions, and lastly use the observations to make empirical generalizations that then help to refine the original theory.

Secondary Source: Restatements or analyses of primary sources.

Selection Threat: Threat to the validity of an experiment caused by whether or not the participants who have been selected to participate in an experiment have some characteristic that could slant the findings of the study.

Semantic Differential/Bipolar Adjective Scale: Type of research scale that asks respondents to rate their opinion on a linear scale that exists between two endpoints that have opposite meanings (e.g., Good/Bad, Dirty/Clean, Slow/Fast, Weak/Strong, Light/Heavy, Moral/Immoral, etc.).

Semantic Equivalence: Issue involved in translating surveys from one language to another concerned with whether scale items are translatable semantically from one language to the next

Significance Testing: The process to determine if chance causes a difference or relationship between two or more variables.

Simple Direct Translation: Form of survey translation where a researcher recruits a bilingual individual who takes the original survey and then translates this survey from the primary language to the secondary language.

Simple Random Sample: Sample created through some means of randomly deciding who in a target population will be asked to participate.

Situational (State) Behavior: Behavior that varies from one situation to another within the same context.

Skewness: Positive or negative direction an asymmetrical set of data points takes.

Specific-to-General Order: Organizing a literature review to try to make sense out of specific research studies so that conclusions can be drawn.

Split-Half Reliability: Scale reliability test where all of the items are randomly divided into two groups and then a correlation is calculated between the two sets of scores.

Sociocommunicative Orientation: An individual's trait assertive and responsive communicative behavior.

Sociocommunicative Style: An individual's assertive and responsive communicative behavior as perceived by another individual.

Social Desirability Bias: When a participant changes how he or she scores on a measure to be perceived in a "better light" than her or his actual scores would reveal.

Social Sciences: A group of fields that set out to study how humans live and interact.

Socially Desirable Responding: When an individual fakes responses to indicate beliefs that he or she thinks society accepts.

Source: Person who sends the message (encoder).

Standard Deviation: (1) Measure of the distribution of a set of data points around the mean. (2) Square root of the sum of squares divided by the number of data points minus one.

Statistic: The calculated numerical value that represents a sample or population.

Stereotype: A generalization about a group based on our perception that a group of people from a culture or co-culture as sharing one or several common characteristics.

Stratified Random Sample: Sample created by dividing a population into specific strata (group based on a characteristic important to the study) and then randomly selecting participants from each strata for inclusion.

Structural Equation Model: Powerful multivariate analysis that enables a variety of specialized versions of other statistical tests including regression models, causal modeling, confirmatory factor analysis, second order factor analysis, covariance structure models, and correlation structure models.

Student Newman-Keuls (SNK): Post hoc stepwise test for ordered means where the alpha level depends upon the number of "steps apart" each of the means are from each other.

Subjective: Creation of knowledge that arises out of the researcher's own opinions and perceptions.

Subjective Ethic: When a researcher uses good means, but achieves a bad end result.

Subject Search: Database search for key terms that the author has submitted to the subject field to describe the article or book.

Sum of Squares: Sum of all squared values for a set of data points minus the sum of data points squared divided by the number of data points.

Sum of Squares Between: Variation between groups in a study calculated by comparing the mean of each group with the mean of the overall sample.

Sum of Squares Within: Variation within groups in a study calculated by summing the squared deviations between scores on a dependent variable for each group and then summing the group values.

Suppressor Variables: Variables that suppress or reduce the effect of the independent variable on the dependent variable.

Survey: A social scientific method for gathering quantifiable information about a specific group of people by asking the group members questions about their individual attitudes, values, beliefs, behaviors, knowledge, and perceptions.

Syllogism: Form of logical argumentation where the logic deductively flows from a major premise, to a minor premise, to a conclusion.

Systematic Sample: Sample created by determining the sample size needed from a target population and then picking every nth person from the population for selection.

t-Test: Statistical test that evaluates whether there is a difference between two groups on a dependent variable.

Test–Retest Reliability: The same measure is administered to the same group on two separate occasions and the relationship between both measurements calculated.

Testing Flaw: Threat to a study's validity that occurs because the measurement of a DV at Time 1 affects the measurement of a DV at Time 2.

Theory: Proposed explanation for how a set of natural phenomena will occur, capable of making predictions about the phenomena for the future, and capable of being falsified through empirical observation.

Theory of Natural Selection: The process in nature where only the organisms best adapted to their environment tend to survive and transmit their genetic characteristics in increasing numbers to succeeding generations while those less adapted tend to be eliminated.

Theoretical Population: All of the members of a specific population, both accessible and not accessible to the researcher.

Thesis: Short declarative sentence that explains to a listener the purpose of a paper.

Threshold Effects: When changes in a specific dependent variable are only seen after an independent variable reaches a certain level.

Time Order: Idea that researchers can establish an exact order to when things occur—T_1 occurred and then T_2 occurred—through experimental procedures.

Title Search: Database search of the title field for words included in the title of an article or book.

Topical order: Organizing a literature review by main topics or issues and emphasizing the relationship of the issues to the main problem.

Trait Behavior: Behavior assumed to be consistent across contexts and specific situations within particular constructs.

Translation/Backtranslation: Form of translation where a translator performs a simple direct translation, after which another bilingual individual translates the work back to the first language.

Trend Design: Type of longitudinal survey design used to examine different samples of people at different points in time.

Truncation Symbols: Symbols used to ensure that your search looks for every possible version of a word.

Tukey's Honest Significant Difference Test (Tukey): Post hoc test for pairwise comparisons while controlling for Type I error and generating confidence intervals.

Two-Tailed Hypothesis: Hypothesis that predicts a significant relationship or difference, but does not indicate the specific nature of the relationship.

Type I (α) Error: When a researcher rejects a null hypothesis based on a sample when the null should be accepted.

Type II (β) Error: When a researcher accepts a null hypothesis based on a sample when the null hypothesis should be rejected.

Unethical Behavior: When a researcher uses bad means to achieve a bad end.

Unit of Analysis: Major phenomenon being analyzed within a study.

Univariate Test: Statistical test with one dependent variable.

Validity: Degree to which the measuring instrument measures what it is intended to measure.

Values: Numerical aspect directly associated with a specific attribute of a variable.

Variable: Any entity that can take on different values.

Variance: (1) Degree of variability around a mean. (2) Sum of squares divided by the number of data points minus one.

Verbal Immediacy: Use of language to foster an individual's perception of psychological and physical closeness.

Verbal Messages: Use of language to communicate a message.

Volunteer Sample: Participants who choose to be in a study; typically based on some form of reward.

Willingness to Communicate: A person's general level of desire to initiate communication with others.

INDEX